DODGE DURA 2001-03

MW00783393

CHILTON'S

Covers all models of Dodge Durango and Dakota Pick-ups

by Jay Storer

CHILTON *Automotive Books*

PUBLISHED BY **HAYNES NORTH AMERICA, Inc.**

Haynes ®

AUTOMOTIVE
PARTS &
ACCESSORIES
ASSOCIATION MEMBER

Manufactured in USA
©2005 Haynes North America, Inc.
ISBN 1 56392 570 2
Library of Congress Catalog Card No. 2005922574

Haynes Publishing Group
Sparkford Nr Yeovil
Somerset BA22 7JJ England

Haynes North America, Inc
861 Lawrence Drive
Newbury Park
California 91320 USA

ABCDE
FGHIJ
KLMNO
PQRS

7J1

Contents

1   TUNE-UP AND ROUTINE MAINTENANCE – 1-1

2   FOUR-CYLINDER ENGINE – 2A-1
V6 AND 5.2L/5.9L V8 ENGINES – 2B-1
4.7L OHC V8 ENGINE – 2C-1
GENERAL ENGINE OVERHAUL PROCEDURES – 2D-1

3   COOLING, HEATING AND AIR CONDITIONING SYSTEMS – 3-1

4   FUEL AND EXHAUST SYSTEMS – 4-1

5   ENGINE ELECTRICAL SYSTEMS – 5-1

6   EMISSIONS AND ENGINE CONTROL SYSTEMS – 6-1

Mechanic and photographer with a 2001 Dakota

ACKNOWLEDGEMENTS

Wiring diagrams and certain illustrations originated exclusively for Haynes North America, Inc. by Valley Forge Technical Information Services.

About this manual

ITS PURPOSE

The purpose of this manual is to help you get the best value from your vehicle. It can do so in several ways. It can help you decide what work must be done, even if you choose to have it done by a dealer service department or a repair shop; it provides information and procedures for routine maintenance and servicing; and it offers diagnostic and repair procedures to follow when trouble occurs.

We hope you use the manual to tackle the work yourself. For many simpler jobs, doing it yourself may be quicker than arranging an appointment to get the vehicle into a shop and making the trips to leave it and pick it up. More importantly, a lot of money can be saved by avoiding the expense the shop must pass on to you to cover its labor and overhead costs. An added benefit is the sense of satisfaction and accomplishment that you feel after doing the job yourself.

USING THE MANUAL

The manual is divided into Chapters. Each Chapter is divided into numbered Sections. Each Section consists of consecutively numbered paragraphs.

At the beginning of each numbered Section you will be referred to any illustrations which apply to the procedures in that Section. The reference numbers used in illustration captions pinpoint the pertinent Section and the Step within that Section. That is, illustration 3.2 means the illustration refers to Section 3 and Step (or paragraph) 2 within that Section.

Procedures, once described in the text, are not normally repeated. When it's necessary to refer to another Chapter, the reference will be given as Chapter and Section number. Cross references given without use of the word "Chapter" apply to Sections and/or paragraphs in the same Chapter. For example, "see Section 8" means in the same Chapter.

References to the left or right side of the vehicle assume you are sitting in the driver's seat, facing forward.

Even though we have prepared this manual with extreme care, neither the publisher nor the author can accept responsibility for any errors in, or omissions from, the information given.

→NOTE

A *Note* provides information necessary to properly complete a procedure or information which will make the procedure easier to understand.

⁂ CAUTION

A *Caution* provides a special procedure or special steps which must be taken while completing the procedure where the Caution is found. Not heeding a Caution can result in damage to the assembly being worked on.

⁂ WARNING

A *Warning* provides a special procedure or special steps which must be taken while completing the procedure where the Warning is found. Not heeding a Warning can result in personal injury.

Introduction to the Dodge Durango and Dodge Dakota pick-ups

Dodge Dakota pick-ups are available in standard, extended and Quad Cab body styles, in short-bed and long-bed models. The extended cab is a model of the Dakota with two smaller rear doors for access to the rear seat; the Quad Cab is a true four-door model. All cabs are single welded unit construction and bolted to the frame. All models are available in two-wheel drive (2WD) and four-wheel drive (4WD) versions. The Dodge Durango is a four-door sport-utility vehicle, based largely on the Dakota pickup.

Powertrain options include a 2.5L four-cylinder engine (2000 Dakota pickups only) and 3.9L V6 (Dakota only), 4.7L OHC V8, 5.2L V8 and 5.9L pushrod V8 engines. Transmissions used are either a five-speed manual, or automatic transmission in either four-speed or five-speed versions. The Durango is available only with a V8 engine and automatic transmission.

Chassis layout is conventional, with the engine mounted at the front and the power being transmitted through either the manual or automatic transmission to a driveshaft and solid rear axle. On 4WD models a transfer case also transmits power to the front axle by way of a driveshaft.

The front suspension on 2WD models features coil springs, upper and lower A-arm type front suspension with rack-and-pinion steering gear. Front suspension on 4WD models consists of torsion bars with upper and lower A-arms and a rack-and-pinion steering gear. All models have a solid axle and leaf springs at the rear. 4WD models use a solidly mounted aluminum differential housing with CV-jointed driveaxles at the front end.

All models are equipped with power assisted disc front brakes and either drum or disc rear brakes (rear disc brakes became available as an option in 2003). Rear Wheel Anti-Lock (RWAL) brakes are standard, while a four-wheel Anti-lock Braking System (ABS) is used on some models.

Vehicle Identification numbers

Modifications are a continuing and unpublicized process in vehicle manufacturing. Since spare parts manuals and lists are compiled on a numerical basis, the individual vehicle numbers are essential to correctly identify the component required.

VEHICLE IDENTIFICATION NUMBER (VIN)

This very important identification number is stamped on a plate attached to the left side of the dashboard just inside the windshield on the driver's side of the vehicle (see illustration). The VIN also appears on the Vehicle Certificate of Title and Registration. It contains information such as where and when the vehicle was manufactured, the model year and the body style.

VIN YEAR AND ENGINE CODES

Two particularly important pieces of information located in the VIN are the model year and engine codes. Counting from the left, the engine code is the eighth digit and the model year code is the 10th digit.

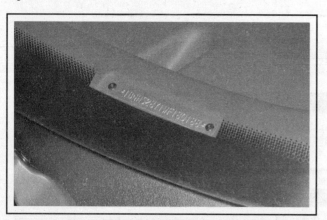

The VIN plate is visible from the outside of the vehicle, through the driver's side of the windshield

On the models covered by this manual the engine codes are:

Code	Engine
N	4.7L OHC V8
P	2.5L four-cylinder
X	3.9L V6
Y	5.2L V8
Z	5.9L V8

On the models covered by this manual the model year codes are:

Code	Year
Y	2000
1	2001
2	2002
3	2003

EQUIPMENT IDENTIFICATION PLATE

This plate is located on the left-front of the underside of the hood. It contains valuable information concerning the production of the vehicle as well as information on all production or optional equipment.

VEHICLE SAFETY CERTIFICATION LABEL

The Safety Certification label is affixed to the left front door pillar or the pillar-side of the door (see illustration). The plate contains the name of the manufacturer, the month and year of production, the Gross Vehicle Weight Rating (GVWR) and the safety certification statement. This label also contains the original tire sizes and recommended pressures, and the paint code. It is especially useful for matching the color and type of paint during repair work.

BODY CODE PLATE

All models have a Body Code plate, which contains information about the model, drivetrain, paint procedures, and other body information. There are seven lines of code, but you should be concerned with the lower three lines. If you need this information when purchasing

Typical Safety Certification label

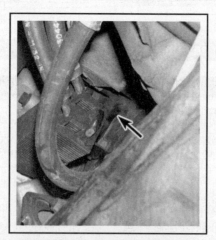

On V6 and 5.2L/5.9L V8 engines, the engine identification number is located on a machined pad at the left front of the engine (right front on 4.7L V8)

Automatic transmission identification number pad location

Typical transfer case identification tag location

Typical front axle (4WD) identification tag location

Rear axle gear ratios can be identified through the tag(s) (arrows) attached to the differential cover bolt(s) - some axles have only one tag

parts or having paint work done, write down the numbers from the bottom three lines and show it to your dealer for decoding. On Dakota models, the plate is attached to the cab on the passenger side, behind the rear trim panel. On Durango models, the plate is under the passenger seat, on the floorpan. To access the plate on Durango models, the seat must be removed, then remove the doorsill trim and pull the carpeting back to find the plate.

Most axles have more complete identification information on a decal glued to the axle tube (arrow)

ENGINE IDENTIFICATION NUMBER

The engine ID number on V6 and 5.2L/5.9L V8 engines is located at the left-front of the engine (see illustration). The identification number on 2.5L four-cylinder engines is on a machined pad on the block, between the third and fourth cylinders. On the 4.7L OHC V8 the number is located at the right front of the engine.

TRANSMISSION IDENTIFICATION NUMBER

The ID number on manual transmissions is located on the left side of the case. On automatic transmissions, the number is stamped on the left side of the transmission case above the oil pan flange (see illustration).

TRANSFER CASE IDENTIFICATION NUMBER

The transfer case identification plate is attached to the rear side of the case (see illustration).

AXLE IDENTIFICATION NUMBERS

On both front and rear axles the identification number is located on a tag attached to the differential cover (see illustrations).

Buying parts

Replacement parts are available from many sources, which generally fall into one of two categories - authorized dealer parts departments and independent retail auto parts stores. Our advice concerning these parts is as follows:

Retail auto parts stores: Good auto parts stores will stock frequently needed components which wear out relatively fast, such as clutch components, exhaust systems, brake parts, tune-up parts, etc. These stores often supply new or reconditioned parts on an exchange basis, which can save a considerable amount of money. Discount auto parts stores are often very good places to buy materials and parts needed for general vehicle maintenance such as oil, grease, filters, spark plugs, belts, touch-up paint, bulbs, etc. They also usually sell tools and general accessories, have convenient hours, charge lower prices and can often be found not far from home.

Authorized dealer parts department: This is the best source for parts which are unique to the vehicle and not generally available elsewhere (such as major engine parts, transmission parts, trim pieces, etc.).

Warranty information: If the vehicle is still covered under warranty, be sure that any replacement parts purchased - regardless of the source - do not invalidate the warranty!

To be sure of obtaining the correct parts, have engine and chassis numbers available and, if possible, take the old parts along for positive identification.

Maintenance techniques, tools and working facilities

MAINTENANCE TECHNIQUES

There are a number of techniques involved in maintenance and repair that will be referred to throughout this manual. Application of these techniques will enable the home mechanic to be more efficient, better organized and capable of performing the various tasks properly, which will ensure that the repair job is thorough and complete.

Fasteners

Fasteners are nuts, bolts, studs and screws used to hold two or more parts together. There are a few things to keep in mind when working with fasteners. Almost all of them use a locking device of some type, either a lockwasher, locknut, locking tab or thread adhesive. All threaded fasteners should be clean and straight, with undamaged threads and undamaged corners on the hex head where the wrench fits. Develop the habit of replacing all damaged nuts and bolts with new ones. Special locknuts with nylon or fiber inserts can only be used once. If they are removed, they lose their locking ability and must be replaced with new ones.

Rusted nuts and bolts should be treated with a penetrating fluid to ease removal and prevent breakage. Some mechanics use turpentine in a spout-type oil can, which works quite well. After applying the rust penetrant, let it work for a few minutes before trying to loosen the nut or bolt. Badly rusted fasteners may have to be chiseled or sawed off or removed with a special nut breaker, available at tool stores.

If a bolt or stud breaks off in an assembly, it can be drilled and removed with a special tool commonly available for this purpose. Most automotive machine shops can perform this task, as well as other repair procedures, such as the repair of threaded holes that have been stripped out.

Flat washers and lockwashers, when removed from an assembly, should always be replaced exactly as removed. Replace any damaged washers with new ones. Never use a lockwasher on any soft metal surface (such as aluminum), thin sheet metal or plastic.

Fastener sizes

For a number of reasons, automobile manufacturers are making wider and wider use of metric fasteners. Therefore, it is important to be able to tell the difference between standard (sometimes called U.S. or SAE) and metric hardware, since they cannot be interchanged.

All bolts, whether standard or metric, are sized according to diameter, thread pitch and length. For example, a standard 1/2 - 13 x 1 bolt is 1/2 inch in diameter, has 13 threads per inch and is 1 inch long. An M12 - 1.75 x 25 metric bolt is 12 mm in diameter, has a thread pitch of 1.75 mm (the distance between threads) and is 25 mm long. The two bolts are nearly identical, and easily confused, but they are not interchangeable.

In addition to the differences in diameter, thread pitch and length, metric and standard bolts can also be distinguished by examining the bolt heads. To begin with, the distance across the flats on a standard bolt head is measured in inches, while the same dimension on a metric bolt is sized in millimeters (the same is true for nuts). As a result, a standard wrench should not be used on a metric bolt and a metric wrench should not be used on a standard bolt. Also, most standard bolts have slashes radiating out from the center of the head to denote the grade or strength of the bolt, which is an indication of the amount of torque that can be applied to it. The greater the number of slashes, the greater the strength of the bolt. Grades 0 through 5 are commonly used on automobiles. Metric bolts have a property class (grade) number, rather than a slash, molded into their heads to indicate bolt strength. In this case, the higher the number, the stronger the bolt. Property class numbers 8.8, 9.8 and 10.9 are commonly used on automobiles.

Strength markings can also be used to distinguish standard hex nuts from metric hex nuts. Many standard nuts have dots stamped into one side, while metric nuts are marked with a number. The greater the number of dots, or the higher the number, the greater the strength of the nut.

Metric studs are also marked on their ends according to property class (grade). Larger studs are numbered (the same as metric bolts), while smaller studs carry a geometric code to denote grade.

It should be noted that many fasteners, especially Grades 0 through 2, have no distinguishing marks on them. When such is the case, the only way to determine whether it is standard or metric is to measure the thread pitch or compare it to a known fastener of the same size.

Standard fasteners are often referred to as SAE, as opposed to metric. However, it should be noted that SAE technically refers to a non-metric fine thread fastener only. Coarse thread non-metric fasteners are referred to as USS sizes.

Since fasteners of the same size (both standard and metric) may have different strength ratings, be sure to reinstall any bolts, studs or nuts removed from your vehicle in their original locations. Also, when replacing a fastener with a new one, make sure that the new one has a strength rating equal to or greater than the original.

Tightening sequences and procedures

Most threaded fasteners should be tightened to a specific torque value (torque is the twisting force applied to a threaded component such as a nut or bolt). Overtightening the fastener can weaken it and cause it to break, while undertightening can cause it to eventually come loose. Bolts, screws and studs, depending on the material they are made of and their thread diameters, have specific torque values, many of which are noted in the Specifications at the end of each Chapter. Be sure to follow the torque recommendations closely. For fasteners not assigned a specific torque, a general torque value chart is presented here as a guide. These torque values are for dry (unlubricated) fasteners threaded into steel or cast iron (not aluminum). As was previously mentioned, the size and grade of a fastener determine the amount of torque that can safely be applied to it. The figures listed here are approximate for Grade 2 and Grade 3 fasteners. Higher grades can tol-

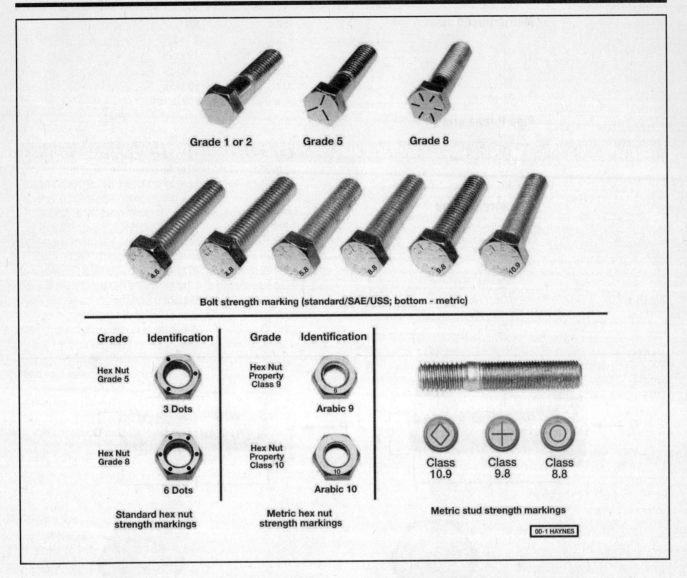

Grade 1 or 2   Grade 5   Grade 8

Bolt strength marking (standard/SAE/USS; bottom - metric)

Grade	Identification
Hex Nut Grade 5	3 Dots
Hex Nut Grade 8	6 Dots

Standard hex nut strength markings

Grade	Identification
Hex Nut Property Class 9	Arabic 9
Hex Nut Property Class 10	Arabic 10

Metric hex nut strength markings

Class 10.9   Class 9.8   Class 8.8

Metric stud strength markings

00-1 HAYNES

erate higher torque values.

Fasteners laid out in a pattern, such as cylinder head bolts, oil pan bolts, differential cover bolts, etc., must be loosened or tightened in sequence to avoid warping the component. This sequence will normally be shown in the appropriate Chapter. If a specific pattern is not given, the following procedures can be used to prevent warping.

Initially, the bolts or nuts should be assembled finger-tight only. Next, they should be tightened one full turn each, in a criss-cross or diagonal pattern. After each one has been tightened one full turn, return to the first one and tighten them all one-half turn, following the same pattern. Finally, tighten each of them one-quarter turn at a time until each fastener has been tightened to the proper torque. To loosen and remove the fasteners, the procedure would be reversed.

Component disassembly

Component disassembly should be done with care and purpose to help ensure that the parts go back together properly. Always keep track of the sequence in which parts are removed. Make note of special characteristics or marks on parts that can be installed more than one way, such as a grooved thrust washer on a shaft. It is a good idea to lay the disassembled parts out on a clean surface in the order that they were removed. It may also be helpful to make sketches or take instant photos of components before removal.

When removing fasteners from a component, keep track of their locations. Sometimes threading a bolt back in a part, or putting the washers and nut back on a stud, can prevent mix-ups later. If nuts and bolts cannot be returned to their original locations, they should be kept in a compartmented box or a series of small boxes. A cupcake or muffin tin is ideal for this purpose, since each cavity can hold the bolts and nuts from a particular area (i.e. oil pan bolts, valve cover bolts, engine mount bolts, etc.). A pan of this type is especially helpful when working on assemblies with very small parts, such as the carburetor, alternator, valve train or interior dash and trim pieces. The cavities can be marked with paint or tape to identify the contents.

Whenever wiring looms, harnesses or connectors are separated, it is a good idea to identify the two halves with numbered pieces of masking tape so they can be easily reconnected.

Gasket sealing surfaces

Throughout any vehicle, gaskets are used to seal the mating surfaces between two parts and keep lubricants, fluids, vacuum or pressure contained in an assembly.

Many times these gaskets are coated with a liquid or paste-type gasket sealing compound before assembly. Age, heat and pressure can sometimes cause the two parts to stick together so tightly that they are

Metric thread sizes

	Ft-lbs	Nm
M-6	6 to 9	9 to 12
M-8	14 to 21	19 to 28
M-10	28 to 40	38 to 54
M-12	50 to 71	68 to 96
M-14	80 to 140	109 to 154

Pipe thread sizes

	Ft-lbs	Nm
1/8	5 to 8	7 to 10
1/4	12 to 18	17 to 24
3/8	22 to 33	30 to 44
1/2	25 to 35	34 to 47

U.S. thread sizes

	Ft-lbs	Nm
1/4 - 20	6 to 9	9 to 12
5/16 - 18	12 to 18	17 to 24
5/16 - 24	14 to 20	19 to 27
3/8 - 16	22 to 32	30 to 43
3/8 - 24	27 to 38	37 to 51
7/16 - 14	40 to 55	55 to 74
7/16 - 20	40 to 60	55 to 81
1/2 - 13	55 to 80	75 to 108

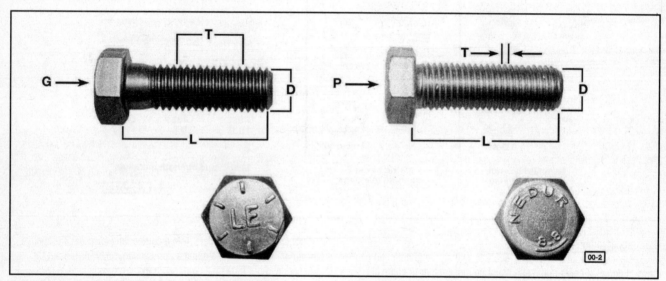

Standard (SAE and USS) bolt dimensions/grade marks

G   Grade marks (bolt strength)
L   Length (in inches)
T   Thread pitch (number of threads per inch)
D   Nominal diameter (in inches)

Metric bolt dimensions/grade marks

P   Property class (bolt strength)
L   Length (in millimeters)
T   Thread pitch (distance between threads in millimeters)
D   Diameter

very difficult to separate. Often, the assembly can be loosened by striking it with a soft-face hammer near the mating surfaces. A regular hammer can be used if a block of wood is placed between the hammer and the part. Do not hammer on cast parts or parts that could be easily damaged. With any particularly stubborn part, always recheck to make sure that every fastener has been removed.

Avoid using a screwdriver or bar to pry apart an assembly, as they can easily mar the gasket sealing surfaces of the parts, which must remain smooth. If prying is absolutely necessary, use an old broom handle, but keep in mind that extra clean up will be necessary if the wood splinters.

After the parts are separated, the old gasket must be carefully scraped off and the gasket surfaces cleaned. Stubborn gasket material can be soaked with rust penetrant or treated with a special chemical to soften it so it can be easily scraped off. A scraper can be fashioned from a piece of copper tubing by flattening and sharpening one end. Copper is recommended because it is usually softer than the surfaces to be scraped, which reduces the chance of gouging the part. Some gaskets can be removed with a wire brush, but regardless of the method used, the mating surfaces must be left clean and smooth. If for some reason the gasket surface is gouged, then a gasket sealer thick enough to fill scratches will have to be used during reassembly of the components. For most applications, a non-drying (or semi-drying) gasket sealer should be used.

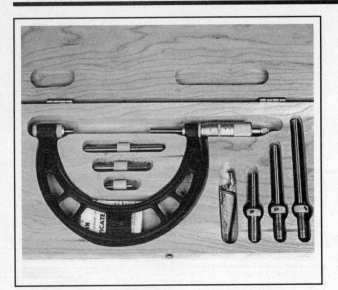

Micrometer set

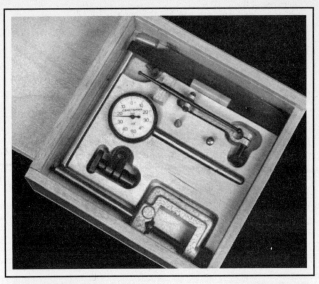

Dial indicator set

Hose removal tips

> ✳✳ **WARNING:**
>
> **If the vehicle is equipped with air conditioning, do not disconnect any of the A/C hoses without first having the system depressurized by a dealer service department or a service station.**

Hose removal precautions closely parallel gasket removal precautions. Avoid scratching or gouging the surface that the hose mates against or the connection may leak. This is especially true for radiator hoses. Because of various chemical reactions, the rubber in hoses can bond itself to the metal spigot that the hose fits over. To remove a hose, first loosen the hose clamps that secure it to the spigot. Then, with slip-joint pliers, grab the hose at the clamp and rotate it around the spigot. Work it back and forth until it is completely free, then pull it off. Silicone or other lubricants will ease removal if they can be applied between the hose and the outside of the spigot. Apply the same lubricant to the inside of the hose and the outside of the spigot to simplify installation.

As a last resort (and if the hose is to be replaced with a new one anyway), the rubber can be slit with a knife and the hose peeled from the spigot. If this must be done, be careful that the metal connection is not damaged.

If a hose clamp is broken or damaged, do not reuse it. Wire-type clamps usually weaken with age, so it is a good idea to replace them with screw-type clamps whenever a hose is removed.

TOOLS

A selection of good tools is a basic requirement for anyone who plans to maintain and repair his or her own vehicle. For the owner who has few tools, the initial investment might seem high, but when compared to the spiraling costs of professional auto maintenance and repair, it is a wise one.

To help the owner decide which tools are needed to perform the tasks detailed in this manual, the following tool lists are offered: *Maintenance and minor repair, Repair/overhaul* and *Special.*

The newcomer to practical mechanics should start off with the *maintenance and minor repair* tool kit, which is adequate for the simpler jobs performed on a vehicle. Then, as confidence and experience grow, the owner can tackle more difficult tasks, buying additional tools as they are needed. Eventually the basic kit will be expanded into the *repair and overhaul* tool set. Over a period of time, the experienced do-it-yourselfer will assemble a tool set complete enough for most repair and overhaul procedures and will add tools from the special category when it is felt that the expense is justified by the frequency of use.

Maintenance and minor repair tool kit

The tools in this list should be considered the minimum required for performance of routine maintenance, servicing and minor repair work. We recommend the purchase of combination wrenches (box-end and open-end combined in one wrench). While more expensive than open end wrenches, they offer the advantages of both types of wrench.

> *Combination wrench set (1/4-inch to 1 inch or 6 mm to 19 mm)*
> *Adjustable wrench, 8 inch*
> *Spark plug wrench with rubber insert*
> *Spark plug gap adjusting tool*
> *Feeler gauge set*
> *Brake bleeder wrench*
> *Standard screwdriver (5/16-inch x 6 inch)*
> *Phillips screwdriver (No. 2 x 6 inch)*
> *Combination pliers - 6 inch*
> *Hacksaw and assortment of blades*
> *Tire pressure gauge*
> *Grease gun*
> *Oil can*
> *Fine emery cloth*
> *Wire brush*
> *Battery post and cable cleaning tool*
> *Oil filter wrench*
> *Funnel (medium size)*
> *Safety goggles*
> *Jackstands (2)*
> *Drain pan*

➡**Note: If basic tune-ups are going to be part of routine maintenance, it will be necessary to purchase a good quality stroboscopic timing light and combination tachometer/dwell meter. Although they are included in the list of special tools, it is mentioned here because they are absolutely necessary for tuning most vehicles properly.**

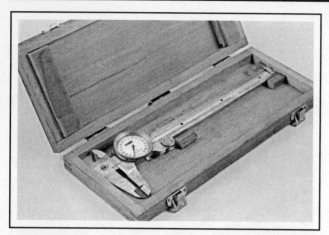

Dial caliper

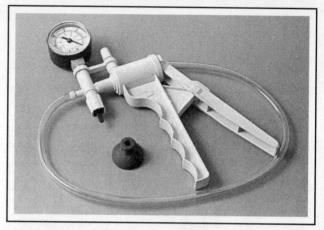

Hand-operated vacuum pump

Timing light

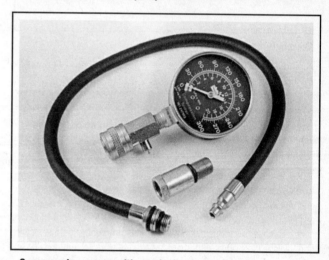

Compression gauge with spark plug hole adapter

Repair and overhaul tool set

These tools are essential for anyone who plans to perform major repairs and are in addition to those in the maintenance and minor repair tool kit. Included is a comprehensive set of sockets which, though expensive, are invaluable because of their versatility, especially when various extensions and drives are available. We recommend the 1/2-inch drive over the 3/8-inch drive. Although the larger drive is bulky and more expensive, it has the capacity of accepting a very wide range of large sockets. Ideally, however, the mechanic should have a 3/8-inch drive set and a 1/2-inch drive set.

> *Socket set(s)*
> *Reversible ratchet*
> *Extension - 10 inch*
> *Universal joint*
> *Torque wrench (same size drive as sockets)*
> *Ball peen hammer - 8 ounce*
> *Soft-face hammer (plastic/rubber)*
> *Standard screwdriver (1/4-inch x 6 inch)*
> *Standard screwdriver (stubby - 5/16-inch)*
> *Phillips screwdriver (No. 3 x 8 inch)*
> *Phillips screwdriver (stubby - No. 2)*
> *Pliers - vise grip*
> *Pliers - lineman's*
> *Pliers - needle nose*
> *Pliers - snap-ring (internal and external)*

> *Cold chisel - 1/2-inch*
> *Scribe*
> *Scraper (made from flattened copper tubing)*
> *Centerpunch*
> *Pin punches (1/16, 1/8, 3/16-inch)*
> *Steel rule/straightedge - 12 inch*
> *Allen wrench set (1/8 to 3/8-inch or 4 mm to 10 mm)*
> *A selection of files*
> *Wire brush (large)*
> *Jackstands (second set)*
> *Jack (scissor or hydraulic type)*

➡**Note: Another tool which is often useful is an electric drill with a chuck capacity of 3/8-inch and a set of good quality drill bits.**

Special tools

The tools in this list include those which are not used regularly, are expensive to buy, or which need to be used in accordance with their manufacturer's instructions. Unless these tools will be used frequently, it is not very economical to purchase many of them. A consideration would be to split the cost and use between yourself and a friend or friends. In addition, most of these tools can be obtained from a tool rental shop on a temporary basis.

This list primarily contains only those tools and instruments widely available to the public, and not those special tools produced by the vehicle manufacturer for distribution to dealer service departments. Occasionally, references to the manufacturer's special tools are

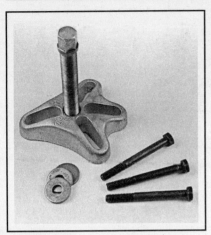

Damper/steering wheel puller

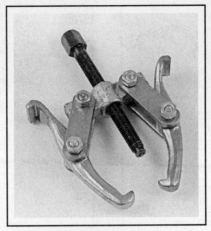

General purpose puller

Hydraulic lifter removal tool

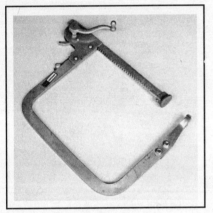

Valve spring compressor

Valve spring compressor

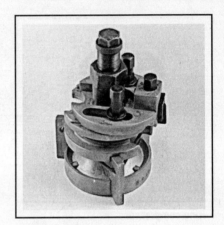

Ridge reamer

included in the text of this manual. Generally, an alternative method of doing the job without the special tool is offered. However, sometimes there is no alternative to their use. Where this is the case, and the tool cannot be purchased or borrowed, the work should be turned over to the dealer service department or an automotive repair shop.

Valve spring compressor
Piston ring groove cleaning tool
Piston ring compressor
Piston ring installation tool
Cylinder compression gauge
Cylinder ridge reamer
Cylinder surfacing hone
Cylinder bore gauge
Micrometers and/or dial calipers
Hydraulic lifter removal tool
Balljoint separator
Universal-type puller
Impact screwdriver
Dial indicator set
Stroboscopic timing light (inductive pick-up)
Hand operated vacuum/pressure pump
Tachometer/dwell meter
Universal electrical multimeter
Cable hoist
Brake spring removal and installation tools
Floor jack

Buying tools

For the do-it-yourselfer who is just starting to get involved in vehicle maintenance and repair, there are a number of options available when purchasing tools. If maintenance and minor repair is the extent of the work to be done, the purchase of individual tools is satisfactory. If, on the other hand, extensive work is planned, it would be a good idea to purchase a modest tool set from one of the large retail chain stores. A set can usually be bought at a substantial savings over the individual tool prices, and they often come with a tool box. As additional tools are needed, add-on sets, individual tools and a larger tool box can be purchased to expand the tool selection. Building a tool set gradually allows the cost of the tools to be spread over a longer period of time and gives the mechanic the freedom to choose only those tools that will actually be used.

Tool stores will often be the only source of some of the special tools that are needed, but regardless of where tools are bought, try to avoid cheap ones, especially when buying screwdrivers and sockets, because they won't last very long. The expense involved in replacing cheap tools will eventually be greater than the initial cost of quality tools.

Care and maintenance of tools

Good tools are expensive, so it makes sense to treat them with respect. Keep them clean and in usable condition and store them properly when not in use. Always wipe off any dirt, grease or metal chips before putting them away. Never leave tools lying around in the work

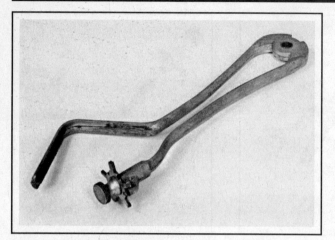

Piston ring groove cleaning tool

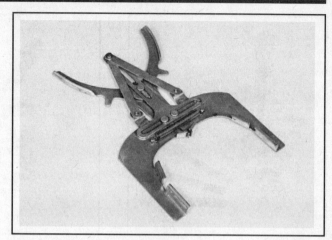

Ring removal/installation tool

Ring compressor

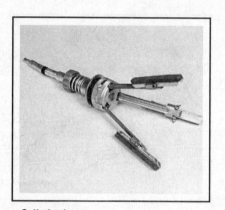

Cylinder hone

Brake hold-down spring tool

area. Upon completion of a job, always check closely under the hood for tools that may have been left there so they won't get lost during a test drive.

Some tools, such as screwdrivers, pliers, wrenches and sockets, can be hung on a panel mounted on the garage or workshop wall, while others should be kept in a tool box or tray. Measuring instruments, gauges, meters, etc. must be carefully stored where they cannot be damaged by weather or impact from other tools.

When tools are used with care and stored properly, they will last a very long time. Even with the best of care, though, tools will wear out if used frequently. When a tool is damaged or worn out, replace it. Subsequent jobs will be safer and more enjoyable if you do.

HOW TO REPAIR DAMAGED THREADS

Sometimes, the internal threads of a nut or bolt hole can become stripped, usually from overtightening. Stripping threads is an all-too-common occurrence, especially when working with aluminum parts, because aluminum is so soft that it easily strips out.

Usually, external or internal threads are only partially stripped. After they've been cleaned up with a tap or die, they'll still work. Sometimes, however, threads are badly damaged. When this happens, you've got three choices:

1) Drill and tap the hole to the next suitable oversize and install a larger diameter bolt, screw or stud.
2) Drill and tap the hole to accept a threaded plug, then drill and tap the plug to the original screw size. You can also buy a plug

already threaded to the original size. Then you simply drill a hole to the specified size, then run the threaded plug into the hole with a bolt and jam nut. Once the plug is fully seated, remove the jam nut and bolt.
3) The third method uses a patented thread repair kit like Heli-Coil or Slimsert. These easy-to-use kits are designed to repair damaged threads in straight-through holes and blind holes. Both are available as kits which can handle a variety of sizes and thread patterns. Drill the hole, then tap it with the special included tap. Install the Heli-Coil and the hole is back to its original diameter and thread pitch.

Regardless of which method you use, be sure to proceed calmly and carefully. A little impatience or carelessness during one of these relatively simple procedures can ruin your whole day's work and cost you a bundle if you wreck an expensive part.

WORKING FACILITIES

Not to be overlooked when discussing tools is the workshop. If anything more than routine maintenance is to be carried out, some sort of suitable work area is essential.

It is understood, and appreciated, that many home mechanics do not have a good workshop or garage available, and end up removing an engine or doing major repairs outside. It is recommended, however, that the overhaul or repair be completed under the cover of a roof.

A clean, flat workbench or table of comfortable working height is an absolute necessity. The workbench should be equipped with a vise that

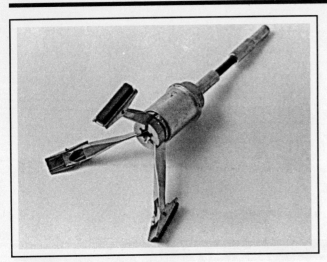

Brake cylinder hone

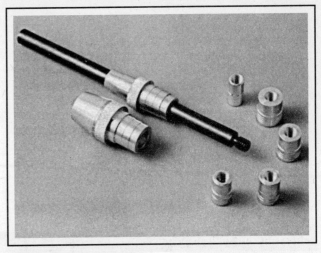

Clutch plate alignment tool

has a jaw opening of at least four inches.

As mentioned previously, some clean, dry storage space is also required for tools, as well as the lubricants, fluids, cleaning solvents, etc. which soon become necessary.

Sometimes waste oil and fluids, drained from the engine or cooling system during normal maintenance or repairs, present a disposal problem. To avoid pouring them on the ground or into a sewage system, pour the used fluids into large containers, seal them with caps and take them to an authorized disposal site or recycling center. Plastic jugs, such as old antifreeze containers, are ideal for this purpose.

Always keep a supply of old newspapers and clean rags available. Old towels are excellent for mopping up spills. Many mechanics use rolls of paper towels for most work because they are readily available and disposable. To help keep the area under the vehicle clean, a large cardboard box can be cut open and flattened to protect the garage or shop floor.

Whenever working over a painted surface, such as when leaning over a fender to service something under the hood, always cover it with an old blanket or bedspread to protect the finish. Vinyl covered pads, made especially for this purpose, are available at auto parts stores.

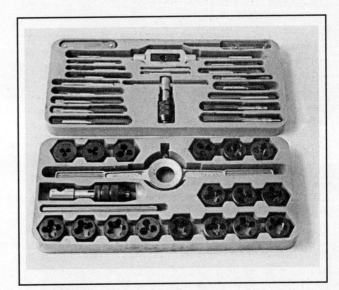

Tap and die set

Jacking and towing

JACKING

The jack supplied with the vehicle should only be used for raising the vehicle when changing a tire or placing jackstands under the frame. NEVER work under the vehicle or start the engine when the vehicle supported only by a jack.

The vehicle should be parked on level ground with the wheels blocked, the parking brake applied and the transmission in Park (automatic) or Reverse (manual). If the vehicle is parked alongside the roadway, or in any other hazardous situation, turn on the emergency hazard flashers. If a tire is to be changed, loosen the lug nuts one-half turn before raising off the ground.

Place the jack under the vehicle in the indicated positions (see illustrations). Operate the jack with a slow, smooth motion until the wheel is raised off the ground. Remove the lug nuts, pull off the wheel, install the spare and thread the lug nuts back on with the beveled side facing in. Tighten the lug nuts snugly, lower the vehicle until some weight is on the wheel, tighten them completely in a criss-cross pattern and remove the jack. Note that some spare tires are designed for temporary use only - don't exceed the recommended speed, mileage or other restriction instructions accompanying the spare.

TOWING

Equipment specifically designed for towing should be used and attached to the main structural members of the vehicle. Optional tow hooks may be attached to the frame at both ends of the vehicle; they are intended for emergency use only, for rescuing a stranded vehicle. Do not use the tow hooks for highway towing. Stand clear when using tow straps or chains, they may break causing serious injury.

Safety is a major consideration when towing and all applicable state and local laws must be obeyed. In addition to a tow bar, a safety chain must be used for all towing.

Two-wheel drive vehicles with automatic transmission may be towed with four wheels on the ground for a distance of 15 miles or less, as long as the speed doesn't exceed 30 mph. If the vehicle has to be towed more than 15 miles, place the rear wheels on a towing dolly.

Two-wheel drive vehicles with manual transmission can be towed without restrictions for a distance of 50 miles with the ignition lock in the Off position and the transmission in Neutral.

Four-wheel drive vehicles should be towed on a flatbed or with all four wheels off the ground to avoid damage to the transfer case.

If any vehicle is to be towed with the front wheels on the ground and the rear wheels raised, the ignition key must be turned to the OFF position to unlock the steering column and a steering wheel clamping device designed for towing must be used or damage to the steering column lock may occur.

Front jacking position with factory jack

Rear jacking position with factory jack

Booster battery (jump) starting

Observe the following precautions when using a booster battery to start a vehicle:

a) *Before connecting the booster battery, make sure the ignition switch is in the Off position.*
b) *Turn off the lights, heater and other electrical loads.*
c) *Your eyes should be shielded. Safety goggles are a good idea.*
d) *Make sure the booster battery is the same voltage as the dead one in the vehicle.*
e) *The two vehicles MUST NOT TOUCH each other.*
f) *Make sure the transmission is in Park.*
g) *If the booster battery is not a maintenance-free type, remove the vent caps and lay a cloth over the vent holes.*

Connect the red jumper cable to the positive (+) terminals of each battery.

Connect one end of the black cable to the negative (-) terminal of the booster battery. The other end of this cable should be connected to a good ground on the engine block (see illustration). Make sure the cable will not come into contact with the fan, drivebelts or other moving parts of the engine.

Start the engine using the booster battery, then, with the engine running at idle speed, disconnect the jumper cables in the reverse order of connection

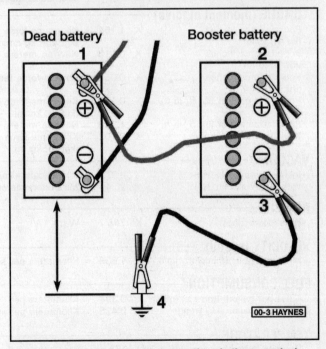

Make the booster battery cable connections in the numerical order shown (note that the negative cable of the booster battery is NOT attached to the negative terminal of the dead battery)

CONVERSION FACTORS

LENGTH (distance)
Inches (in)	X	25.4	= Millimeters (mm)	X 0.0394	= Inches (in)
Feet (ft)	X	0.305	= Meters (m)	X 3.281	= Feet (ft)
Miles	X	1.609	= Kilometers (km)	X 0.621	= Miles

VOLUME (capacity)
Cubic inches (cu in; in³)	X	16.387	= Cubic centimeters (cc; cm³)	X 0.061	= Cubic inches (cu in; in³)
Imperial pints (Imp pt)	X	0.568	= Liters (l)	X 1.76	= Imperial pints (Imp pt)
Imperial quarts (Imp qt)	X	1.137	= Liters (l)	X 0.88	= Imperial quarts (Imp qt)
Imperial quarts (Imp qt)	X	1.201	= US quarts (US qt)	X 0.833	= Imperial quarts (Imp qt)
US quarts (US qt)	X	0.946	= Liters (l)	X 1.057	= US quarts (US qt)
Imperial gallons (Imp gal)	X	4.546	= Liters (l)	X 0.22	= Imperial gallons (Imp gal)
Imperial gallons (Imp gal)	X	1.201	= US gallons (US gal)	X 0.833	= Imperial gallons (Imp gal)
US gallons (US gal)	X	3.785	= Liters (l)	X 0.264	= US gallons (US gal)

MASS (weight)
Ounces (oz)	X	28.35	= Grams (g)	X 0.035	= Ounces (oz)
Pounds (lb)	X	0.454	= Kilograms (kg)	X 2.205	= Pounds (lb)

FORCE
Ounces-force (ozf; oz)	X	0.278	= Newtons (N)	X 3.6	= Ounces-force (ozf; oz)
Pounds-force (lbf; lb)	X	4.448	= Newtons (N)	X 0.225	= Pounds-force (lbf; lb)
Newtons (N)	X	0.1	= Kilograms-force (kgf; kg)	X 9.81	= Newtons (N)

PRESSURE
Pounds-force per square inch (psi; lbf/in²; lb/in²)	X	0.070	= Kilograms-force per square centimeter (kgf/cm²; kg/cm²)	X 14.223	= Pounds-force per square inch (psi; lbf/in²; lb/in²)
Pounds-force per square inch (psi; lbf/in²; lb/in²)	X	0.068	= Atmospheres (atm)	X 14.696	= Pounds-force per square inch (psi; lbf/in²; lb/in²)
Pounds-force per square inch (psi; lbf/in²; lb/in²)	X	0.069	= Bars	X 14.5	= Pounds-force per square inch (psi; lbf/in²; lb/in²)
Pounds-force per square inch (psi; lbf/in²; lb/in²)	X	6.895	= Kilopascals (kPa)	X 0.145	= Pounds-force per square inch (psi; lbf/in²; lb/in²)
Kilopascals (kPa)	X	0.01	= Kilograms-force per square centimeter (kgf/cm²; kg/cm²)	X 98.1	= Kilopascals (kPa)

TORQUE (moment of force)
Pounds-force inches (lbf in; lb in)	X	1.152	= Kilograms-force centimeter (kgf cm; kg cm)	X 0.868	= Pounds-force inches (lbf in; lb in)
Pounds-force inches (lbf in; lb in)	X	0.113	= Newton meters (Nm)	X 8.85	= Pounds-force inches (lbf in; lb in)
Pounds-force inches (lbf in; lb in)	X	0.083	= Pounds-force feet (lbf ft; lb ft)	X 12	= Pounds-force inches (lbf in; lb in)
Pounds-force feet (lbf ft; lb ft)	X	0.138	= Kilograms-force meters (kgf m; kg m)	X 7.233	= Pounds-force feet (lbf ft; lb ft)
Pounds-force feet (lbf ft; lb ft)	X	1.356	= Newton meters (Nm)	X 0.738	= Pounds-force feet (lbf ft; lb ft)
Newton meters (Nm)	X	0.102	= Kilograms-force meters (kgf m; kg m)	X 9.804	= Newton meters (Nm)

VACUUM
Inches mercury (in. Hg)	X	3.377	= Kilopascals (kPa)	X 0.2961	= Inches mercury
Inches mercury (in. Hg)	X	25.4	= Millimeters mercury (mm Hg)	X 0.0394	= Inches mercury

POWER
Horsepower (hp)	X	745.7	= Watts (W)	X 0.0013	= Horsepower (hp)

VELOCITY (speed)
Miles per hour (miles/hr; mph)	X	1.609	= Kilometers per hour (km/hr; kph)	X 0.621	= Miles per hour (miles/hr; mph)

FUEL CONSUMPTION *
Miles per gallon, Imperial (mpg)	X	0.354	= Kilometers per liter (km/l)	X 2.825	= Miles per gallon, Imperial (mpg)
Miles per gallon, US (mpg)	X	0.425	= Kilometers per liter (km/l)	X 2.352	= Miles per gallon, US (mpg)

TEMPERATURE

Degrees Fahrenheit = (°C x 1.8) + 32   Degrees Celsius (Degrees Centigrade; °C) = (°F - 32) x 0.56

*It is common practice to convert from miles per gallon (mpg) to liters/100 kilometers (l/100km), where mpg (Imperial) x l/100 km = 282 and mpg (US) x l/100 km = 235

FRACTION/DECIMAL/MILLIMETER EQUIVALENTS

DECIMALS to MILLIMETERS

Decimal	mm	Decimal	mm
0.001	0.0254	0.500	12.7000
0.002	0.0508	0.510	12.9540
0.003	0.0762	0.520	13.2080
0.004	0.1016	0.530	13.4620
0.005	0.1270	0.540	13.7160
0.006	0.1524	0.550	13.9700
0.007	0.1778	0.560	14.2240
0.008	0.2032	0.570	14.4780
0.009	0.2286	0.580	14.7320
		0.590	14.9860
0.010	0.2540		
0.020	0.5080		
0.030	0.7620		
0.040	1.0160	0.600	15.2400
0.050	1.2700	0.610	15.4940
0.060	1.5240	0.620	15.7480
0.070	1.7780	0.630	16.0020
0.080	2.0320	0.640	16.2560
0.090	2.2860	0.650	16.5100
		0.660	16.7640
0.100	2.5400	0.670	17.0180
0.110	2.7940	0.680	17.2720
0.120	3.0480	0.690	17.5260
0.130	3.3020		
0.140	3.5560		
0.150	3.8100		
0.160	4.0640	0.700	17.7800
0.170	4.3180	0.710	18.0340
0.180	4.5720	0.720	18.2880
0.190	4.8260	0.730	18.5420
		0.740	18.7960
0.200	5.0800	0.750	19.0500
0.210	5.3340	0.760	19.3040
0.220	5.5880	0.770	19.5580
0.230	5.8420	0.780	19.8120
0.240	6.0960	0.790	20.0660
0.250	6.3500		
0.260	6.6040		
0.270	6.8580	0.800	20.3200
0.280	7.1120	0.810	20.5740
0.290	7.3660	0.820	21.8280
		0.830	21.0820
0.300	7.6200	0.840	21.3360
0.310	7.8740	0.850	21.5900
0.320	8.1280	0.860	21.8440
0.330	8.3820	0.870	22.0980
0.340	8.6360	0.880	22.3520
0.350	8.8900	0.890	22.6060
0.360	9.1440		
0.370	9.3980		
0.380	9.6520		
0.390	9.9060	0.900	22.8600
0.400	10.1600	0.910	23.1140
0.410	10.4140	0.920	23.3680
0.420	10.6680	0.930	23.6220
0.430	10.9220	0.940	23.8760
0.440	11.1760	0.950	24.1300
0.450	11.4300	0.960	24.3840
0.460	11.6840	0.970	24.6380
0.470	11.9380	0.980	24.8920
0.480	12.1920	0.990	25.1460
0.490	12.4460	1.000	25.4000

FRACTIONS to DECIMALS to MILLIMETERS

Fraction	Decimal	mm	Fraction	Decimal	mm
1/64	0.0156	0.3969	33/64	0.5156	13.0969
1/32	0.0312	0.7938	17/32	0.5312	13.4938
3/64	0.0469	1.1906	35/64	0.5469	13.8906
1/16	0.0625	1.5875	9/16	0.5625	14.2875
5/64	0.0781	1.9844	37/64	0.5781	14.6844
3/32	0.0938	2.3812	19/32	0.5938	15.0812
7/64	0.1094	2.7781	39/64	0.6094	15.4781
1/8	0.1250	3.1750	5/8	0.6250	15.8750
9/64	0.1406	3.5719	41/64	0.6406	16.2719
5/32	0.1562	3.9688	21/32	0.6562	16.6688
11/64	0.1719	4.3656	43/64	0.6719	17.0656
3/16	0.1875	4.7625	11/16	0.6875	17.4625
13/64	0.2031	5.1594	45/64	0.7031	17.8594
7/32	0.2188	5.5562	23/32	0.7188	18.2562
15/64	0.2344	5.9531	47/64	0.7344	18.6531
1/4	0.2500	6.3500	3/4	0.7500	19.0500
17/64	0.2656	6.7469	49/64	0.7656	19.4469
9/32	0.2812	7.1438	25/32	0.7812	19.8438
19/64	0.2969	7.5406	51/64	0.7969	20.2406
5/16	0.3125	7.9375	13/16	0.8125	20.6375
21/64	0.3281	8.3344	53/64	0.8281	21.0344
11/32	0.3438	8.7312	27/32	0.8438	21.4312
23/64	0.3594	9.1281	55/64	0.8594	21.8281
3/8	0.3750	9.5250	7/8	0.8750	22.2250
25/64	0.3906	9.9219	57/64	0.8906	22.6219
13/32	0.4062	10.3188	29/32	0.9062	23.0188
27/64	0.4219	10.7156	59/64	0.9219	23.4156
7/16	0.4375	11.1125	15/16	0.9375	23.8125
29/64	0.4531	11.5094	61/64	0.9531	24.2094
15/32	0.4688	11.9062	31/32	0.9688	24.6062
31/64	0.4844	12.3031	63/64	0.9844	25.0031
1/2	0.5000	12.7000	1	1.0000	25.4000

Automotive chemicals and lubricants

A number of automotive chemicals and lubricants are available for use during vehicle maintenance and repair. They include a wide variety of products ranging from cleaning solvents and degreasers to lubricants and protective sprays for rubber, plastic and vinyl.

CLEANERS

Carburetor cleaner and choke cleaner is a strong solvent for gum, varnish and carbon. Most carburetor cleaners leave a dry-type lubricant film which will not harden or gum up. Because of this film it is not recommended for use on electrical components.

Brake system cleaner is used to remove brake dust, grease and brake fluid from the brake system, where clean surfaces are absolutely necessary. It leaves no residue and often eliminates brake squeal caused by contaminants.

Electrical cleaner removes oxidation, corrosion and carbon deposits from electrical contacts, restoring full current flow. It can also be used to clean spark plugs, carburetor jets, voltage regulators and other parts where an oil-free surface is desired.

Demoisturants remove water and moisture from electrical components such as alternators, voltage regulators, electrical connectors and fuse blocks. They are non-conductive and non-corrosive.

Degreasers are heavy-duty solvents used to remove grease from the outside of the engine and from chassis components. They can be sprayed or brushed on and, depending on the type, are rinsed off either with water or solvent.

LUBRICANTS

Motor oil is the lubricant formulated for use in engines. It normally contains a wide variety of additives to prevent corrosion and reduce foaming and wear. Motor oil comes in various weights (viscosity ratings) from 0 to 50. The recommended weight of the oil depends on the season, temperature and the demands on the engine. Light oil is used in cold climates and under light load conditions. Heavy oil is used in hot climates and where high loads are encountered. Multi-viscosity oils are designed to have characteristics of both light and heavy oils and are available in a number of weights from 5W-20 to 20W-50.

Gear oil is designed to be used in differentials, manual transmissions and other areas where high-temperature lubrication is required.

Chassis and wheel bearing grease is a heavy grease used where increased loads and friction are encountered, such as for wheel bearings, balljoints, tie-rod ends and universal joints.

High-temperature wheel bearing grease is designed to withstand the extreme temperatures encountered by wheel bearings in disc brake equipped vehicles. It usually contains molybdenum disulfide (moly), which is a dry-type lubricant.

White grease is a heavy grease for metal-to-metal applications where water is a problem. White grease stays soft under both low and high temperatures (usually from -100 to +190-degrees F), and will not wash off or dilute in the presence of water.

Assembly lube is a special extreme pressure lubricant, usually containing moly, used to lubricate high-load parts (such as main and rod bearings and cam lobes) for initial start-up of a new engine. The assembly lube lubricates the parts without being squeezed out or washed away until the engine oiling system begins to function.

Silicone lubricants are used to protect rubber, plastic, vinyl and nylon parts.

Graphite lubricants are used where oils cannot be used due to contamination problems, such as in locks. The dry graphite will lubricate metal parts while remaining uncontaminated by dirt, water, oil or acids. It is electrically conductive and will not foul electrical contacts in locks such as the ignition switch.

Moly penetrants loosen and lubricate frozen, rusted and corroded fasteners and prevent future rusting or freezing.

Heat-sink grease is a special electrically non-conductive grease that is used for mounting electronic ignition modules where it is essential that heat is transferred away from the module.

SEALANTS

RTV sealant is one of the most widely used gasket compounds. Made from silicone, RTV is air curing, it seals, bonds, waterproofs, fills surface irregularities, remains flexible, doesn't shrink, is relatively easy to remove, and is used as a supplementary sealer with almost all low and medium temperature gaskets.

Anaerobic sealant is much like RTV in that it can be used either to seal gaskets or to form gaskets by itself. It remains flexible, is solvent resistant and fills surface imperfections. The difference between an anaerobic sealant and an RTV-type sealant is in the curing. RTV cures when exposed to air, while an anaerobic sealant cures only in the absence of air. This means that an anaerobic sealant cures only after the assembly of parts, sealing them together.

Thread and pipe sealant is used for sealing hydraulic and pneumatic fittings and vacuum lines. It is usually made from a Teflon compound, and comes in a spray, a paint-on liquid and as a wrap-around tape.

CHEMICALS

Anti-seize compound prevents seizing, galling, cold welding, rust and corrosion in fasteners. High-temperature anti-seize, usually made with copper and graphite lubricants, is used for exhaust system and exhaust manifold bolts.

Anaerobic locking compounds are used to keep fasteners from vibrating or working loose and cure only after installation, in the absence of air. Medium strength locking compound is used for small nuts, bolts and screws that may be removed later. High-strength locking compound is for large nuts, bolts and studs which aren't removed on a regular basis.

Oil additives range from viscosity index improvers to chemical treatments that claim to reduce internal engine friction. It should be noted that most oil manufacturers caution against using additives with their oils.

Gas additives perform several functions, depending on their chemical makeup. They usually contain solvents that help dissolve gum and varnish that build up on carburetor, fuel injection and intake parts. They also serve to break down carbon deposits that form on the inside surfaces of the combustion chambers. Some additives contain upper cylinder lubricants for valves and piston rings, and others contain chemicals to remove condensation from the gas tank.

MISCELLANEOUS

Brake fluid is specially formulated hydraulic fluid that can withstand the heat and pressure encountered in brake systems. Care must be taken so this fluid does not come in contact with painted surfaces or plastics. An opened container should always be resealed to prevent contamination by water or dirt.

Weatherstrip adhesive is used to bond weatherstripping around doors, windows and trunk lids. It is sometimes used to attach trim pieces.

Undercoating is a petroleum-based, tar-like substance that is designed to protect metal surfaces on the underside of the vehicle from corrosion. It also acts as a sound-deadening agent by insulating the bottom of the vehicle.

Waxes and polishes are used to help protect painted and plated surfaces from the weather. Different types of paint may require the use of different types of wax and polish. Some polishes utilize a chemical or abrasive cleaner to help remove the top layer of oxidized (dull) paint on older vehicles. In recent years many non-wax polishes that contain a wide variety of chemicals such as polymers and silicones have been introduced. These non-wax polishes are usually easier to apply and last longer than conventional waxes and polishes.

Safety first!

Regardless of how enthusiastic you may be about getting on with the job at hand, take the time to ensure that your safety is not jeopardized. A moment's lack of attention can result in an accident, as can failure to observe certain simple safety precautions. The possibility of an accident will always exist, and the following points should not be considered a comprehensive list of all dangers. Rather, they are intended to make you aware of the risks and to encourage a safety conscious approach to all work you carry out on your vehicle.

ESSENTIAL DOS AND DON'TS

DON'T rely on a jack when working under the vehicle. Always use approved jackstands to support the weight of the vehicle and place them under the recommended lift or support points.

DON'T attempt to loosen extremely tight fasteners (i.e. wheel lug nuts) while the vehicle is on a jack - it may fall.

DON'T start the engine without first making sure that the transmission is in Neutral (or Park where applicable) and the parking brake is set.

DON'T remove the radiator cap from a hot cooling system - let it cool or cover it with a cloth and release the pressure gradually.

DON'T attempt to drain the engine oil until you are sure it has cooled to the point that it will not burn you.

DON'T touch any part of the engine or exhaust system until it has cooled sufficiently to avoid burns.

DON'T siphon toxic liquids such as gasoline, antifreeze and brake fluid by mouth, or allow them to remain on your skin.

DON'T inhale brake lining dust - it is potentially hazardous (see *Asbestos* below).

DON'T allow spilled oil or grease to remain on the floor - wipe it up before someone slips on it.

DON'T use loose fitting wrenches or other tools which may slip and cause injury.

DON'T push on wrenches when loosening or tightening nuts or bolts. Always try to pull the wrench toward you. If the situation calls for pushing the wrench away, push with an open hand to avoid scraped knuckles if the wrench should slip.

DON'T attempt to lift a heavy component alone - get someone to help you.

DON'T rush or take unsafe shortcuts to finish a job.

DON'T allow children or animals in or around the vehicle while you are working on it.

DO wear eye protection when using power tools such as a drill, sander, bench grinder, etc. and when working under a vehicle.

DO keep loose clothing and long hair well out of the way of moving parts.

DO make sure that any hoist used has a safe working load rating adequate for the job.

DO get someone to check on you periodically when working alone on a vehicle.

DO carry out work in a logical sequence and make sure that everything is correctly assembled and tightened.

DO keep chemicals and fluids tightly capped and out of the reach of children and pets.

DO remember that your vehicle's safety affects that of yourself and others. If in doubt on any point, get professional advice.

ASBESTOS

Certain friction, insulating, sealing, and other products - such as brake linings, brake bands, clutch linings, torque converters, gaskets, etc. - may contain asbestos. Extreme care must be taken to avoid inhalation of dust from such products, since it is hazardous to health. If in doubt, assume that they do contain asbestos.

FIRE

Remember at all times that gasoline is highly flammable. Never smoke or have any kind of open flame around when working on a vehicle. But the risk does not end there. A spark caused by an electrical short circuit, by two metal surfaces contacting each other, or even by static electricity built up in your body under certain conditions, can ignite gasoline vapors, which in a confined space are highly explosive. Do not, under any circumstances, use gasoline for cleaning parts. Use an approved safety solvent.

Always disconnect the battery ground (-) cable at the battery before working on any part of the fuel system or electrical system. Never risk spilling fuel on a hot engine or exhaust component. It is strongly recommended that a fire extinguisher suitable for use on fuel and electrical fires be kept handy in the garage or workshop at all times. Never try to extinguish a fuel or electrical fire with water.

FUMES

Certain fumes are highly toxic and can quickly cause unconsciousness and even death if inhaled to any extent. Gasoline vapor falls into this category, as do the vapors from some cleaning solvents. Any draining or pouring of such volatile fluids should be done in a well ventilated area.

When using cleaning fluids and solvents, read the instructions on the container carefully. Never use materials from unmarked containers.

Never run the engine in an enclosed space, such as a garage. Exhaust fumes contain carbon monoxide, which is extremely poisonous. If you need to run the engine, always do so in the open air, or at least have the rear of the vehicle outside the work area.

If you are fortunate enough to have the use of an inspection pit, never drain or pour gasoline and never run the engine while the vehicle is over the pit. The fumes, being heavier than air, will concentrate in the pit with possibly lethal results.

THE BATTERY

Never create a spark or allow a bare light bulb near a battery. They normally give off a certain amount of hydrogen gas, which is highly explosive.

Always disconnect the battery ground (-) cable at the battery before working on the fuel or electrical systems.

If possible, loosen the filler caps or cover when charging the battery from an external source (this does not apply to sealed or maintenance-free batteries). Do not charge at an excessive rate or the battery may burst.

Take care when adding water to a non maintenance-free battery and when carrying a battery. The electrolyte, even when diluted, is very corrosive and should not be allowed to contact clothing or skin.

Always wear eye protection when cleaning the battery to prevent the caustic deposits from entering your eyes.

HOUSEHOLD CURRENT

When using an electric power tool, inspection light, etc., which operates on household current, always make sure that the tool is correctly connected to its plug and that, where necessary, it is properly grounded. Do not use such items in damp conditions and, again, do not create a spark or apply excessive heat in the vicinity of fuel or fuel vapor.

SECONDARY IGNITION SYSTEM VOLTAGE

A severe electric shock can result from touching certain parts of the ignition system (such as the spark plug wires) when the engine is running or being cranked, particularly if components are damp or the insulation is defective. In the case of an electronic ignition system, the secondary system voltage is much higher and could prove fatal.

Troubleshooting

CONTENTS

Section Symptom

Engine

1 Engine will not rotate when attempting to start
2 Engine rotates but will not start
3 Starter motor operates without rotating engine
4 Engine hard to start when cold
5 Engine hard to start when hot
6 Starter motor noisy or excessively rough in engagement
7 Engine starts but stops immediately
8 Engine lopes while idling or idles erratically
9 Engine misses at idle speed
10 Engine misses throughout driving speed range
11 Engine stalls
12 Engine lacks power
13 Engine backfires
14 Pinging or knocking engine sounds during acceleration or uphill
15 Engine diesels (continues to run) after switching off

Engine electrical system

16 Battery will not hold a charge
17 Alternator light fails to go out
18 Alternator light fails to come on when key is turned on

Fuel system

19 Excessive fuel consumption
20 Fuel leakage and/or fuel odor

Cooling system

21 Overheating
22 Overcooling
23 External coolant leakage
24 Internal coolant leakage
25 Coolant loss
26 Poor coolant circulation

Clutch

27 Fails to release (pedal pressed to the floor - shift lever does not move freely in and out of Reverse)
28 Clutch slips (engine speed increases with no increase in vehicle speed)
29 Grabbing (chattering) as clutch is engaged
30 Squeal or rumble with clutch fully engaged (pedal released)
31 Squeal or rumble with clutch fully disengaged (pedal depressed)
32 Clutch pedal stays on floor when disengaged

Manual transmission

33 Noisy in Neutral with engine running
34 Noisy in all gears
35 Noisy in one particular gear
36 Slips out of high gear
37 Difficulty in engaging gears
38 Oil leakage

Automatic transmission

39 General shift mechanism problems
40 Transmission will not downshift with accelerator pedal pressed to the floor
41 Transmission slips, shifts rough, is noisy or has no drive in forward or reverse gears
42 Fluid leakage

Transfer case

43 Transfer case is difficult to shift into the desired range
44 Transfer case noisy in all gears
45 Noisy or jumps out of four-wheel drive Low range
46 Lubricant leaks from the vent or output shaft seals

Driveshaft

47 Oil leak at front of driveshaft
48 Knock or clunk when the transmission is under initial load (just after transmission is put into gear)
49 Metallic grinding sound consistent with vehicle speed
50 Vibration

Axles

51 Noise
52 Vibration
53 Oil leakage

Driveaxles (4WD)

54 Clicking
55 Shudder on acceleration
56 Vibration on highway

Brakes

57 Vehicle pulls to one side during braking
58 Noise (high-pitched squeal with the brakes applied)
59 Excessive brake pedal travel
60 Brake pedal feels spongy when depressed
61 Excessive effort required to stop vehicle
62 Pedal travels to the floor with little resistance
63 Brake pedal pulsates during brake application

Suspension and steering systems

64 Vehicle pulls to one side
65 Shimmy, shake or vibration
66 Excessive pitching and/or rolling around corners or during braking
67 Excessively stiff steering
68 Excessive play in steering
69 Lack of power assistance
70 Excessive tire wear (not specific to one area)
71 Excessive tire wear on outside edge
72 Excessive tire wear on inside edge
73 Tire tread worn in one place

This section provides an easy reference guide to the more common problems that may occur during the operation of your vehicle. These problems and possible causes are grouped under various components or systems; i.e. Engine, Cooling System, etc., and also refer to the Chapter and/or Section that deals with the problem.

Remember that successful troubleshooting is not a mysterious black art practiced only by professional mechanics. It's simply the result of a bit of knowledge combined with an intelligent, systematic approach to the problem. Always work by a process of elimination, starting with the simplest solution and working through to the most complex - and never overlook the obvious. Anyone can forget to fill the gas tank or leave the lights on overnight, so don't assume that you are above such oversights.

Finally, always get clear in your mind why a problem has occurred and take steps to ensure that it doesn't happen again. If the electrical system fails because of a poor connection, check all other connections in the system to make sure that they don't fail as well. If a particular fuse continues to blow, find out why - don't just go on replacing fuses. Remember, failure of a small component can often be indicative of potential failure or incorrect functioning of a more important component or system.

ENGINE

1   Engine will not rotate when attempting to start

1   Battery terminal connections loose or corroded. Check the cable terminals at the battery. Tighten the cable or remove corrosion as necessary.
2   Battery discharged or faulty. If the cable connections are clean and tight on the battery posts, turn the key to the On position and switch on the headlights and/or windshield wipers. If they fail to function, the battery is discharged.
3   Automatic transmission not completely engaged in Park or Neutral or clutch pedal not completely depressed.
4   Broken, loose or disconnected wiring in the starting circuit. Inspect all wiring and connectors at the battery, starter solenoid and ignition switch.
5   Starter motor pinion jammed in flywheel ring gear. If manual transmission, place transmission in gear and rock the vehicle to manually turn the engine. Remove starter and inspect pinion and flywheel at earliest convenience (Chapter 5).
6   Starter solenoid faulty (Chapter 5).
7   Starter motor faulty (Chapter 5).
8   Ignition switch faulty (Chapter 12).

2   Engine rotates but will not start

1   Fuel tank empty, fuel filter plugged or fuel line restricted.
2   Fault in the fuel injection system (Chapter 4).
3   Battery discharged (engine rotates slowly). Check the operation of electrical components as described in the previous Section.
4   Battery terminal connections loose or corroded (see previous Section).
5   Fuel pump faulty (Chapter 4).
6   Excessive moisture on, or damage to, ignition components (see Chapter 5).
7   Worn, faulty or incorrectly gapped spark plugs (Chapter 1).
8   Broken, loose or disconnected wiring in the starting circuit (see previous Section).
9   Broken, loose or disconnected wires at the ignition coil (Chapter 5).

3   Starter motor operates without rotating engine

1   Starter pinion sticking. Remove the starter (Chapter 5) and inspect.
2   Starter pinion or flywheel teeth worn or broken. Remove the flywheel/driveplate access cover and inspect.

4   Engine hard to start when cold

1   Battery discharged or low. Check as described in Section 1.
2   Fault in the fuel or electrical systems (Chapters 4 and 5).
3   Injector(s) leaking (Chapter 4).
4   Distributor rotor carbon-tracked (Chapter 1).

5   Engine hard to start when hot

1   Air filter clogged (Chapter 1).
2   Fault in the fuel or electrical systems (Chapters 4 and 5).
3   Fuel not reaching the injectors (see Chapter 4).
4   Low cylinder compression (Chapter 2).
5   Malfunctioning EVAP system (Chapter 6).

6   Starter motor noisy or excessively rough in engagement

1   Pinion or flywheel gear teeth worn or broken. Remove the cover at the rear of the engine (if equipped) and inspect.
2   Starter motor mounting bolts loose or missing.

7   Engine starts but stops immediately

1   Loose or faulty electrical connections at distributor, coil or alternator.
2   Fault in the fuel or electrical systems (Chapters 4 and 5).
3   Vacuum leak at the gasket surfaces of the intake manifold or throttle body. Make sure all mounting bolts/nuts are tightened securely and all vacuum hoses connected to the manifold are positioned properly and in good condition.
4   Restricted intake or exhaust systems (Chapter 4)

8   Engine lopes while idling or idles erratically

1   Vacuum leakage. Check the mounting bolts/nuts at the throttle body and intake manifold for tightness. Make sure all vacuum hoses are connected and in good condition. Use a stethoscope or a length of fuel hose held against your ear to listen for vacuum leaks while the engine is running. A hissing sound will be heard. A soapy water solution will also detect leaks.
2   Fault in the fuel or electrical systems (Chapters 4 and 5).
3   Plugged PCV valve or hose (see Chapters 1 and 6).
4   Air filter clogged (Chapter 1).
5   Fuel pump not delivering sufficient fuel to the fuel injectors (see Chapter 4).
6   Leaking head gasket. Perform a compression check (Chapter 2).
7   Camshaft lobes worn (Chapter 2).

9   Engine misses at idle speed

1   Spark plugs worn, fouled or not gapped properly (Chapter 1).
2   Fault in the fuel or electrical systems (Chapters 4 and 5).
3   Faulty spark plug wires (Chapter 1).
4   Vacuum leaks at intake or hose connections. Check as described in Section 8.
5   Uneven or low cylinder compression. Check compression as described in Chapter 2.

10 Engine misses throughout driving speed range

1 Fuel filter clogged and/or impurities in the fuel system (Chapter 1).
2 Faulty or incorrectly gapped spark plugs (Chapter 1).
3 Fault in the fuel or electrical systems (Chapters 4 and 5).
4 Defective spark plug wires (Chapter 1).
5 Faulty emissions system components (Chapter 6).
6 Low or uneven cylinder compression pressures. Remove the spark plugs and test the compression with a gauge (Chapter 2).
7 Vacuum leaks at the throttle body, intake manifold or vacuum hoses (see Section 8).

11 Engine stalls

1 Idle speed incorrect. Refer to the VECI label.
2 Fuel filter clogged and/or water and impurities in the fuel system (Chapter 1).
3 Fault in the fuel system or sensors (Chapters 4 and 6).
4 Faulty emissions system components (Chapter 6).
5 Faulty or incorrectly gapped spark plugs (Chapter 1). Also check the spark plug wires (Chapter 1).
6 Vacuum leak at the throttle body, intake manifold or vacuum hoses. Check as described in Section 8.

12 Engine lacks power

1 Fault in the fuel or electrical systems (Chapters 4 and 5).
2 Faulty or incorrectly gapped spark plugs (Chapter 1).
3 Faulty coil (Chapter 5).
4 Brakes binding (Chapter 1).
5 Automatic transmission fluid level incorrect (Chapter 1).
6 Clutch slipping (Chapter 8).
7 Fuel filter clogged and/or impurities in the fuel system (Chapter 1).
8 Emissions control system not functioning properly (Chapter 6).
9 Use of substandard fuel. Fill the tank with the proper fuel.
10 Low or uneven cylinder compression pressures. Test with a compression tester, which will detect leaking valves and/or a blown head gasket (Chapter 2).
11 Restriction in the intake or exhaust system (Chapter 4).

13 Engine backfires

1 Emissions system not functioning properly (Chapter 6).
2 Fault in the fuel or electrical systems (Chapters 4 and 5).
3 Faulty secondary ignition system (cracked spark plug insulator or faulty plug wires) (Chapters 1 and 5).
4 Fuel injection system in need of adjustment or worn excessively (Chapter 4).
5 Vacuum leak at the throttle body, intake manifold or vacuum hoses. Check as described in Section 8.
6 Valves sticking (Chapter 2).
7 Crossed plug wires (Chapter 1).

14 Pinging or knocking engine sounds during acceleration or uphill

1 Incorrect grade of fuel. Fill the tank with fuel of the proper octane rating.
2 Fault in the fuel or electrical systems (Chapters 4 and 5).

3 Improper spark plugs. Check the plug type against the VECI label located in the engine compartment. Also check the plugs and wires for damage (Chapter 1).
4 Faulty emissions system (Chapter 6).
5 Vacuum leak. Check as described in Section 9.

15 Engine diesels (continues to run) after switching off

1 Idle speed too high. Refer to (Chapter 4).
2 Fault in the fuel or electrical systems (Chapters 4 and 5).
3 Excessive engine operating temperature. Probable causes of this are a low coolant level (see Chapter 1), malfunctioning thermostat, clogged radiator or faulty water pump (see Chapter 3).

ENGINE ELECTRICAL SYSTEM

16 Battery will not hold a charge

1 Alternator drivebelt defective or not adjusted properly (Chapter 1).
2 Electrolyte level low or battery discharged (Chapter 1).
3 Battery terminals loose or corroded (Chapter 1).
4 Alternator not charging properly (Chapter 5).
5 Loose, broken or faulty wiring in the charging circuit (Chapter 5).
6 Short in the vehicle wiring causing a continuous drain on the battery (refer to Chapter 12 and the Wiring Diagrams).
7 Battery defective internally.

17 Alternator light fails to go out

1 Fault in the alternator or charging circuit (Chapter 5).
2 Alternator drivebelt defective or not properly adjusted (Chapter 1).

18 Alternator light fails to come on when key is turned on

1 Instrument cluster warning light bulb defective (Chapter 12).
2 Alternator faulty (Chapter 5).
3 Fault in the instrument cluster printed circuit, dashboard wiring or bulb holder (Chapter 12).

FUEL SYSTEM

19 Excessive fuel consumption

1 Dirty or clogged air filter element (Chapter 1).
2 Emissions system not functioning properly (Chapter 6).
3 Fault in the fuel or electrical systems (Chapters 4 and 5).
4 Low tire pressure or incorrect tire size (Chapter 1).
5 Restricted exhaust system (Chapter 4).

20 Fuel leakage and/or fuel odor

1 Leak in a fuel feed or vent line (Chapter 4).
2 Tank overfilled. Fill only to automatic shut-off.
3 Evaporative emissions system canister clogged (Chapter 6).
4 Vapor leaks from system lines or injectors (Chapter 4).

COOLING SYSTEM

21   Overheating

1   Insufficient coolant in the system (Chapter 1).
2   Water pump drivebelt defective or not adjusted properly (Chapter 1).
3   Radiator core blocked or radiator grille dirty and restricted (see Chapter 3).
4   Thermostat faulty (Chapter 3).
5   Fan blades broken or cracked (Chapter 3).
6   Radiator cap not maintaining proper pressure. Have the cap pressure tested by a gas station or repair shop.
7   Fault in electrical circuit of 2.5L coolant fan (Chapter 3).

22   Overcooling

1   Thermostat faulty (Chapter 3).
2   Inaccurate temperature gauge (Chapter 12).
3   Fault in electrical circuit of 2.5L coolant fan (Chapter 3).

23   External coolant leakage

1   Deteriorated or damaged hoses or loose clamps. Replace hoses and/or tighten the clamps at the hose connections (Chapter 1).
2   Water pump seals defective. If this is the case, water will drip from the weep hole in the water pump body (Chapter 3).
3   Leakage from the radiator core or side tank(s). This will require the radiator to be professionally repaired (see Chapter 3 for removal procedures).
4   Engine drain plug(s) leaking (Chapter 1) or water jacket core plugs leaking (see Chapter 2).
5   Leakage at the heater core. Signs of leakage should show up on interior carpeting (Chapter 3).

24   Internal coolant leakage

➡**Note: Internal coolant leaks can usually be detected by examining the oil. Check the dipstick and inside of the valve cover for water deposits and an oil consistency like that of a milkshake.**

1   Leaking cylinder head gasket. Have the cooling system pressure tested.
2   Cracked cylinder bore or cylinder head. Remove the head(s) and inspect (Chapter 2).
3   Leaking intake manifold gasket.

25   Coolant loss

1   Too much coolant in the system (Chapter 1).
2   Coolant boiling away due to overheating (see Section 15).
3   External or internal leakage (see Sections 23 and 24).
4   Faulty radiator cap. Have the cap pressure tested.

26   Poor coolant circulation

1   Inoperative water pump. A quick test is to pinch the top radiator hose closed with your hand while the engine is idling, then let it loose. You should feel the surge of coolant if the pump is working properly (see Chapter 1).
2   Restriction in the cooling system. Drain, flush and refill the system (Chapter 1). If necessary, remove the radiator (Chapter 3) and have it reverse flushed.
3   Water pump drivebelt defective or not adjusted properly (Chapter 1).
4   Thermostat sticking (Chapter 3).
5   Drivebelt incorrectly routed, causing the pump to turn backward (Chapter 1).

CLUTCH

27   Fails to release (pedal pressed to the floor - shift lever does not move freely in and out of Reverse)

1   Leak in the clutch hydraulic system. Check the master cylinder, slave cylinder and lines (Chapters 1 and 8).
2   Clutch plate warped or damaged (Chapter 8).
3   Broken release bearing or fork (Chapter 8).

28   Clutch slips (engine speed increases with no increase in vehicle speed)

1   Clutch plate oil-soaked or lining worn. Remove clutch (Chapter 8) and inspect.
2   Clutch plate not seated. It may take 30 or 40 normal starts for a new one to seat.
3   Pressure plate worn (Chapter 8).

29   Grabbing (chattering) as clutch is engaged

1   Oil on clutch plate lining. Remove (Chapter 8) and inspect. Correct any leakage source.
2   Worn or loose engine or transmission mounts. These units move slightly when the clutch is released. Inspect the mounts and bolts (Chapter 2).
3   Worn splines on clutch plate hub. Remove the clutch components (Chapter 8) and inspect.
4   Warped pressure plate or flywheel. Remove the clutch components and inspect.

30   Squeal or rumble with clutch fully engaged (pedal released)

Release bearing binding on transmission bearing retainer. Remove clutch components (Chapter 8) and check bearing. Remove any burrs or nicks; clean and relubricate bearing retainer before installing.

31   Squeal or rumble with clutch fully disengaged (pedal depressed)

1   Worn, defective or broken release bearing (Chapter 8).
2   Worn or broken pressure plate springs (or diaphragm fingers) (Chapter 8).

32   Clutch pedal stays on floor when disengaged

1   Linkage or release bearing binding. Inspect the linkage or remove the clutch components as necessary.
2   Make sure proper pedal stop (bumper) is installed.

MANUAL TRANSMISSION

➡Note: All the following references are in Chapter 7A, unless noted.

33 Noisy in Neutral with engine running

1 Input shaft bearing worn.
2 Damaged main drive gear bearing.
3 Worn countershaft bearings.
4 Worn or damaged countershaft endplay shims.

34 Noisy in all gears

1 Any of the above causes, and/or:
2 Insufficient lubricant (see the checking procedures in Chapter 1).

35 Noisy in one particular gear

1 Worn, damaged or chipped gear teeth for that particular gear.
2 Worn or damaged synchronizer for that particular gear.

36 Slips out of high gear

1 Transmission loose on clutch housing.
2 Dirt between the transmission case and engine or misalignment of the transmission.

37 Difficulty in engaging gears

1 Clutch not releasing completely (see clutch adjustment in Chapter 1).
2 Loose or damaged shifter. Make a thorough inspection, replacing parts as necessary.

38 Oil leakage

1 Excessive amount of lubricant in the transmission (see Chapter 1 for correct checking procedures). Drain lubricant as required.
2 Transmission oil seal in need of replacement.

AUTOMATIC TRANSMISSION

➡Note: Due to the complexity of the automatic transmission, it's difficult for the home mechanic to properly diagnose and service this component. For problems other than the following, the vehicle should be taken to a dealer service department or a transmission shop.

39 General shift mechanism problems

1 Chapter 7B deals with checking and adjusting the shift cable on automatic transmissions. Common problems that may be attributed to poorly adjusted cable are:

   a) Engine starting in gears other than Park or Neutral.
   b) Indicator on shifter pointing to a gear other than the one actually being selected.
   c) Vehicle moves when in Park.

2 Refer to Chapter 7A to adjust the linkage.

40 Transmission will not downshift with accelerator pedal pressed to the floor

Throttle Valve (TV) cable misadjusted.

41 Transmission slips, shifts rough, is noisy or has no drive in forward or reverse gears

1 There are many probable causes for the above problems, but the home mechanic should be concerned with only one possibility - fluid level.
2 Before taking the vehicle to a repair shop, check the level and condition of the fluid as described in Chapter 1. Correct fluid level as necessary or change the fluid and filter if needed. If the problem persists, have a professional diagnose the probable cause.
3 If the transmission shifts late and the shifts are harsh, suspect a misadjusted TV cable.

42 Fluid leakage

1 Automatic transmission fluid is a deep red color. Fluid leaks should not be confused with engine oil, which can easily be blown by airflow to the transmission.
2 To pinpoint a leak, first remove all built-up dirt and grime from around the transmission. Degreasing agents and/or steam cleaning will achieve this. With the underside clean, drive the vehicle at low speeds so airflow will not blow the leak far from its source. Raise the vehicle and determine where the leak is coming from. Common areas of leakage are:

   a) **Pan:** Tighten the mounting bolts and/or replace the pan gasket as necessary (see Chapter 7B).
   b) **Filler pipe:** Replace the rubber seal where the pipe enters the transmission case.
   c) **Transmission oil lines:** Tighten the connectors where the lines enter the transmission case and/or replace the lines.
   d) **Vent pipe:** Transmission overfilled and/or water in fluid (see checking procedures, Chapter 1).
   e) **Speedometer connector:** Replace the O-ring where the speedometer sensor enters the transmission case (Chapter 7B).

TRANSFER CASE

43 Transfer case is difficult to shift into the desired range

1 Speed may be too great to permit engagement. Stop the vehicle and shift into the desired range.
2 Shift linkage loose, bent or binding. Check the linkage for damage or wear and replace or lubricate as necessary (Chapter 7C).
3 If the vehicle has been driven on a paved surface for some time, the driveline torque can make shifting difficult. Stop and shift into two-wheel drive on paved or hard surfaces.
4 Insufficient or incorrect grade of lubricant. Drain and refill the transfer case with the specified lubricant. (Chapter 1).
5 Worn or damaged internal components. Disassembly and overhaul of the transfer case, by a qualified shop, may be necessary.

44 Transfer case noisy in all gears

Insufficient or incorrect grade of lubricant. Drain and refill (Chapter 1).

45 Noisy or jumps out of four-wheel drive Low range

1 Transfer case not fully engaged. Stop the vehicle, shift into Neutral and then engage 4L.
2 Shift linkage loose, worn or binding. Tighten, repair or lubricate linkage as necessary.
3 Shift fork cracked, inserts worn or fork binding on the rail. Disassemble and repair as necessary (Chapter 7C).

46 Lubricant leaks from the vent or output shaft seals

1 Transfer case is overfilled. Drain to the proper level (Chapter 1).
2 Vent is clogged or jammed closed. Clear or replace the vent.
3 Output shaft seal incorrectly installed or damaged. Replace the seal and check contact surfaces for nicks and scoring.

DRIVESHAFT

47 Oil leak at seal end of driveshaft

Defective transmission or transfer case oil seal. See Chapter 7 for replacement procedures. While this is done, check the splined yoke for burrs or a rough condition that may be damaging the seal. Burrs can be removed with crocus cloth or a fine whetstone.

48 Knock or clunk when the transmission is under initial load (just after transmission is put into gear)

1 Loose or disconnected rear suspension components. Check all mounting bolts, nuts and bushings (see Chapter 10).
2 Loose driveshaft bolts. Inspect all bolts and nuts and tighten them to the specified torque.
3 Worn or damaged universal joint bearings. Check for wear (see Chapter 8).

49 Metallic grinding sound consistent with vehicle speed

Pronounced wear in the universal joint bearings. Check as described in Chapter 8.

50 Vibration

➡Note: Before assuming that the driveshaft is at fault, make sure the tires are perfectly balanced and perform the following test.

1 Install a tachometer inside the vehicle to monitor engine speed as the vehicle is driven. Drive the vehicle and note the engine speed at which the vibration (roughness) is most pronounced. Now shift the transmission to a different gear and bring the engine speed to the same point.
2 If the vibration occurs at the same engine speed (rpm) regardless of which gear the transmission is in, the driveshaft is NOT at fault since the driveshaft speed varies.
3 If the vibration decreases or is eliminated when the transmission is in a different gear at the same engine speed, refer to the following probable causes.
4 Bent or dented driveshaft. Inspect and replace as necessary (see Chapter 8).
5 Undercoating or built-up dirt, etc. on the driveshaft. Clean the shaft thoroughly and recheck.
6 Worn universal joint bearings. Remove and inspect (see Chapter 8).

7 Driveshaft and/or companion flange out of balance. Check for missing weights on the shaft. Remove the driveshaft (see Chapter 8) and reinstall 180-degrees from original position, then retest. Have the driveshaft professionally balanced if the problem persists.

AXLES

51 Noise

1 Road noise. No corrective procedures available.
2 Tire noise. Inspect tires and check tire pressures (Chapter 1).
3 Rear wheel bearings loose, worn or damaged (Chapter 8).

52 Vibration

See probable causes under *Driveshaft*. Proceed under the guidelines listed for the driveshaft. If the problem persists, check the rear wheel bearings by raising the rear of the vehicle and spinning the rear wheels by hand. Listen for evidence of rough (noisy) bearings. Remove and inspect (see Chapter 8).

53 Oil leakage

1 Pinion seal damaged (see Chapter 8).
2 Axleshaft oil seals damaged (see Chapter 8).
3 Differential inspection cover leaking. Tighten the bolts or replace the gasket as required (see Chapters 1 and 8).

DRIVEAXLES (4WD)

54 Clicking noise on turns

Worn or damaged outboard CV joints (Chapter 8).

55 Shudder or vibration during acceleration

1 Excessive toe-in. Have alignment checked.
2 Incorrect spring heights (Chapter 10).
3 Worn or damaged inboard or outboard CV joints (Chapter 8).
4 Sticking inboard CV joint assembly (Chapter 8).

56 Vibration at highway speeds

1 Out-of-balance front wheels and/or tires (Chapters 1 and 10).
2 Out-of-round front tires Chapters 1 and 10).
3 Worn CV joints (Chapter 8).

BRAKES

➡Note: Before assuming that a brake problem exists, make sure that the tires are in good condition and inflated properly (see Chapter 1), that the front-end alignment is correct and that the vehicle is not loaded with weight in an unequal manner.

57 Vehicle pulls to one side during braking

1 Defective, damaged or oil contaminated disc brake pads or shoes on one side. Inspect as described in Chapter 9.
2 Excessive wear of brake shoe or pad material or drum/disc on

one side. Inspect and correct as necessary.

   3 Loose or disconnected front suspension components. Inspect and tighten all bolts to the specified torque (Chapter 10).

   4 Defective drum brake or caliper assembly. Remove the drum or caliper and inspect for a stuck piston or other damage (Chapter 9).

   5 Inadequate lubrication of front brake caliper slide rails. Remove caliper and lubricate slide rails (Chapter 9).

58   Noise (high-pitched squeal with the brakes applied)

   1 Disc brake pads worn out. The noise comes from the wear sensor rubbing against the disc (does not apply to all vehicles) or the actual pad backing plate itself if the material is completely worn away. Replace the pads with new ones immediately (Chapter 9). If the pad material has worn completely away, the brake discs should be inspected for damage as described in Chapter 9.

   2 Missing or damaged brake pad insulators (disc brakes). Replace pad insulators (see Chapter 9).

   3 Linings contaminated with dirt or grease. Replace pads or shoes.

   4 Incorrect linings. Replace with correct linings.

59   Excessive brake pedal travel

   1 Partial brake system failure. Inspect the entire system (Chapter 9) and correct as required.

   2 Insufficient fluid in the master cylinder. Check (Chapter 1), add fluid and bleed the system if necessary (Chapter 9).

   3 Rear brakes not adjusting properly. Make a series of starts and stops while the vehicle is in Reverse. If this does not correct the situation, remove the drums and inspect the self-adjusters (Chapter 9).

60   Brake pedal feels spongy when depressed

   1 Air in the hydraulic lines. Bleed the brake system (Chapter 9).

   2 Faulty flexible hoses. Inspect all system hoses and lines. Replace parts as necessary.

   3 Master cylinder mounting bolts/nuts loose.

   4 Master cylinder defective (Chapter 9).

61   Excessive effort required to stop vehicle

   1 Power brake booster not operating properly (see check in Chapter 1, repairs in Chapter 9).

   2 Excessively worn linings or pads. Inspect and replace if necessary (Chapter 9).

   3 One or more caliper pistons or wheel cylinders seized or sticking. Inspect and rebuild as required (Chapter 9).

   4 Brake linings or pads contaminated with oil or grease. Inspect and replace as required (Chapter 9).

   5 New pads or shoes installed and not yet seated. It will take a while for the new material to seat against the drum (or disc).

62   Pedal travels to the floor with little resistance

   1 Little or no fluid in the master cylinder reservoir caused by leaking wheel cylinder(s), leaking caliper piston(s), loose, damaged or disconnected brake lines. Inspect the entire system and correct as necessary.

   2 Worn master cylinder seals (Chapter 9).

63   Brake pedal pulsates during brake application

   1 Caliper improperly installed. Remove and inspect (Chapter 9).

   2 Disc or drum defective. Remove (Chapter 9) and check for excessive lateral runout and parallelism. Have the disc or drum resurfaced or replace it with a new one.

SUSPENSION AND STEERING SYSTEMS

64   Vehicle pulls to one side

   1 Tire pressures uneven or tires mismatched (Chapter 1).

   2 Defective tire (Chapter 1).

   3 Excessive wear in suspension or steering components (Chapter 10).

   4 Front end in need of alignment.

   5 Front brakes dragging. Inspect the brakes as described in Chapter 9.

65   Shimmy, shake or vibration

   1 Tire or wheel out-of-balance or out-of-round. Have professionally balanced.

   2 Loose, worn or out-of-adjustment front wheel bearings (Chapter 1).

   3 Shock absorbers and/or suspension components worn or damaged (Chapter 10).

66   Excessive pitching and/or rolling around corners or during braking

   1 Defective shock absorbers. Replace as a set (Chapter 10).

   2 Broken or weak springs and/or suspension components. Inspect as described in Chapter 10.

67   Excessively stiff steering

   1 Lack of fluid in power steering fluid reservoir (Chapter 1).

   2 Incorrect tire pressures (Chapter 1).

   3 Lack of lubrication at steering joints (see Chapter 1).

   4 Front end out of alignment.

   5 Lack of power assistance (see Section 69).

68   Excessive play in steering

   1 Loose front wheel bearings (Chapters 1 and 10).

   2 Excessive wear in suspension or steering components (Chapter 10).

   3 Steering gearbox damaged or out of adjustment (Chapter 10).

69   Lack of power assistance

   1 Steering pump drivebelt faulty or not adjusted properly (Chapter 1).

   2 Fluid level low (Chapter 1).

   3 Hoses or lines restricted. Inspect and replace parts as necessary.

   4 Air in power steering system. Bleed the system (Chapter 10).

70   Excessive tire wear (not specific to one area)

   1 Incorrect tire pressures (Chapter 1).

   2 Tires out-of-balance. Have professionally balanced.

3   Wheels damaged. Inspect and replace as necessary.
4   Suspension or steering components excessively worn (Chapter 10).

71   Excessive tire wear on outside edge

1   Inflation pressures incorrect (Chapter 1).
2   Excessive speed in turns.
3   Front-end alignment incorrect. Have professionally aligned.
4   Suspension arm bent or twisted (Chapter 10).

72   Excessive tire wear on inside edge

1   Inflation pressures incorrect (Chapter 1).
2   Front-end alignment incorrect. Have professionally aligned.
3   Loose or damaged steering components (Chapter 10).

73   Tire tread worn in one place

1   Tires out-of-balance.
2   Damaged or buckled wheel. Inspect and replace if necessary.
3   Defective tire (Chapter 1).

Notes

1

TUNE-UP AND ROUTINE MAINTENANCE

1 Dodge Dakota and Durango Maintenance schedule

The following maintenance intervals are based on the assumption that the vehicle owner will be doing the maintenance or service work, as opposed to having a dealer service department do the work. These are the minimum maintenance intervals recommended by the factory for vehicles that are driven daily. If you wish to keep your vehicle in peak condition at all times, you may wish to perform some of these procedures even more often. Because frequent maintenance enhances the efficiency, performance and resale value of your car, we encourage you to do so. If you drive in dusty areas, tow a trailer, idle or drive at low speeds for extended periods or drive for short distances (less than four miles) in below freezing temperatures, shorter intervals are also recommended.

When the vehicle is new, follow the maintenance schedule to the letter, record the maintenance performed in your owners manual and keep all receipts to protect the new vehicle warranty. In many cases the initial maintenance check is done at no cost to the owner (check with your dealer service department for more information).

EVERY 250 MILES OR WEEKLY, WHICHEVER COMES FIRST

Check the engine oil level (Section 4)
Check the coolant level (Section 4)
Check the windshield washer fluid level (Section 4)
Check the brake and clutch fluid levels (Section 4)
Check the tires and tire pressures (Section 5)

EVERY 3000 MILES OR 3 MONTHS, WHICHEVER COMES FIRST

All items listed above, plus . . .

Check the power steering fluid level (Section 6)
Check the automatic transmission fluid level (Section 7)
Change the engine oil and filter (Section 8)

EVERY 6000 MILES OR 6 MONTHS, WHICHEVER COMES FIRST

All items listed above, plus . . .

Check the seat belts (Section 9)
Inspect the windshield wiper blades (Section 10)
Check and service the battery (Section 11)
Check the engine drivebelt (Section 12)
Inspect underhood hoses (Section 13)
Check the cooling system (Section 14)
Rotate the tires (Section 15)

EVERY 15,000 MILES OR 12 MONTHS, WHICHEVER COMES FIRST

All items listed above, plus . . .

Lubricate the steering linkage - 2WD (Section 16)
Check the fuel system (Section 17)
Check the brake system (Section 18) *
Check the exhaust system (Section 19)

Check the manual transmission lubricant level - 2.5L and 3.9L (Section 20)
Check the transfer case lubricant level - 4WD (Section 21)
Check the differential lubricant level (Section 22)

EVERY 22,500 MILES OR 18 MONTHS, WHICHEVER COMES FIRST

Check the steering, suspension and driveaxle boots (Section 23)
Lubricate the chassis components (Section 24) *
Check the front wheel bearings (2WD models) (Section 25)**

EVERY 30,000 MILES OR 30 MONTHS, WHICHEVER COMES FIRST

All items listed above, plus . . .

Change the brake fluid (Section 26)
Replace the air filter (Section 27)
Replace the spark plugs (Section 28)**

EVERY 37,500 MILES OR 30 MONTHS, WHICHEVER COMES FIRST

Change the automatic transmission fluid and filter (Section 29)**
Adjust the automatic transmission bands (Section 30)**
Change the manual transmission lubricant (Section 31)
Change the transfer case lubricant (Section 32)

EVERY 45,000 MILES OR 36 MONTHS, WHICHEVER COMES FIRST

Service the cooling system (drain, flush and refill) (Section 33)

EVERY 60,000 MILES OR 48 MONTHS, WHICHEVER COMES FIRST

Replace the Positive Crankcase Ventilation (PCV) valve (Section 34)
Inspect/replace the spark plug wires, distributor cap and rotor (Section 35)
Change the differential lubricant (Section 36)**

* This item is affected by "severe" operating conditions, as described below. If the vehicle is operated under severe conditions, perform all maintenance indicated with an asterisk (*) at 3000 mile/three-month intervals. Severe conditions exist if you mainly operate the vehicle . . .
in dusty areas
towing a trailer
idling for extended periods
driving at low speeds when outside temperatures remain below freezing and most trips are less than four miles long

** Perform this procedure every 15,000 miles if operated under one or more of the following conditions:
in heavy city traffic where the outside temperature regularly reaches 90-degrees F or higher
in hilly or mountainous terrain
frequent trailer towing
if the vehicle has been driven through deep water

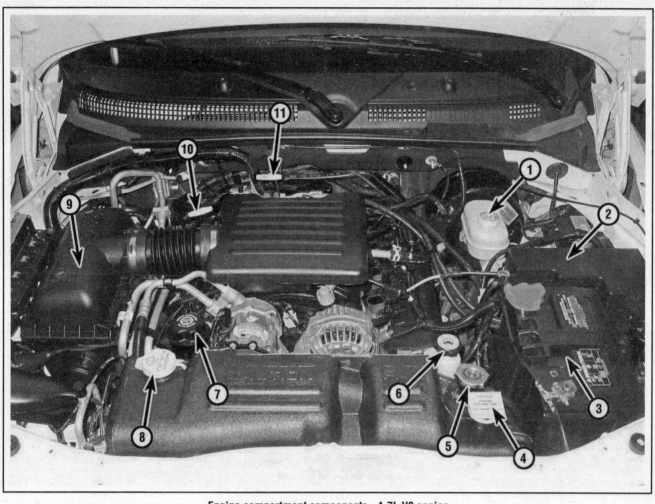

Engine compartment components - 4.7L V8 engine

1	Brake fluid reservoir	5	Cooling system pressure cap	9	Air filter housing
2	Fuse/relay block	6	Power steering fluid reservoir	10	Automatic transmission fluid dipstick
3	Battery	7	Engine oil filler cap	11	Engine oil dipstick
4	Coolant reservoir	8	Windshield washer fluid reservoir		

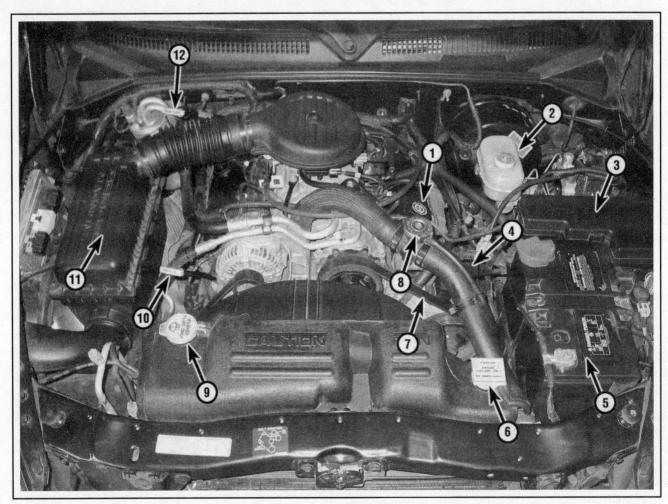

Engine compartment components - V6 engine (5.2L/5.9L engines similar)

1	Engine oil filler cap	5	Battery	9	Windshield washer fluid reservoir
2	Brake fluid reservoir	6	Coolant reservoir	10	Engine oil dipstick
3	Fuse/relay block	7	Drivebelt	11	Air filter housing
4	Power steering fluid reservoir	8	Cooling system pressure cap	12	Automatic transmission fluid dipstick

Typical engine compartment underside components

1	Engine oil filter	3	Engine oil drain plug	5	Balljoint
2	Tie-rod end	4	Automatic transmission fluid pan	6	Steering gear boot

Typical rear underside components

1	Rear shock absorber	4	Muffler	6	Fuel tank
2	Universal joint	5	Differential check/fill plug	7	Leaf spring
3	Exhaust pipe				

2   Introduction

This Chapter is designed to help the home mechanic maintain the Dodge Dakota pickup or Durango vehicle with the goals of maximum performance, economy, safety and reliability in mind.

Included is a master maintenance schedule, followed by procedures dealing specifically with each item on the schedule. Visual checks, adjustments, component replacement and other helpful items are included. Refer to the accompanying illustrations of the engine compartment and the underside of the vehicle for the locations of various components.

Servicing your vehicle in accordance with the mileage/time maintenance schedule and the step-by-step procedures will result in a planned maintenance program that should produce a long and reliable service life. Keep in mind that it's a comprehensive plan, so maintaining some items but not others at the specified intervals will not produce the same results.

As you service your vehicle, you will discover that many of the procedures can - and should - be grouped together because of the nature of the particular procedure you're performing or because of the close proximity of two otherwise unrelated components to one another.

For example, if the vehicle is raised for chassis lubrication, you should inspect the exhaust, suspension, steering and fuel systems while you're under the vehicle. When you're rotating the tires, it makes good sense to check the brakes since the wheels are already removed. Finally, let's suppose you have to borrow or rent a torque wrench. Even if you only need it to tighten the spark plugs, you might as well check the torque of as many critical fasteners as time allows.

The first step in this maintenance program is to prepare yourself before the actual work begins. Read through all the procedures you're planning to do, then gather up all the parts and tools needed. If it looks like you might run into problems during a particular job, seek advice from a mechanic or an experienced do-it-yourselfer.

OWNER'S MANUAL AND VECI LABEL INFORMATION

Your vehicle owner's manual was written for your year and model and contains very specific information on component locations, specifications, fuse ratings, part numbers, etc. The Owner's Manual is an important resource for the do-it-yourselfer to have; if one was not supplied with your vehicle, it can generally be ordered from a dealer parts department.

Among other important information, the Vehicle Emissions Control Information (VECI) label contains specifications and procedures for applicable tune-up adjustments and, in some instances, spark plugs (see Chapter 6 for more information on the VECI label). The information on this label is the exact maintenance data recommended by the manufacturer. This data often varies by intended operating altitude, local emissions regulations, month of manufacture, etc.

This Chapter contains procedural details, safety information and more ambitious maintenance intervals than you might find in manufacturer's literature. However, you may also find procedures or specifications in your Owner's Manual or VECI label that differ with what's printed here. In these cases, the Owner's Manual or VECI label can be considered correct, since it is specific to your particular vehicle.

3   Tune-up - general information

The term tune-up is used in this manual to represent a combination of individual operations rather than one specific procedure that will maintain a gasoline engine in proper tune.

If, from the time the vehicle is new, the routine maintenance schedule is followed closely and frequent checks are made of fluid levels and high wear items, as suggested throughout this manual, the engine will be kept in relatively good running condition and the need for additional work will be minimized.

More likely than not, however, there may be times when the engine is running poorly due to lack of regular maintenance. This is even more likely if a used vehicle, which has not received regular and frequent maintenance checks, is purchased. In such cases, an engine tune-up will be needed outside of the regular routine maintenance intervals.

The first step in any tune-up or diagnostic procedure to help correct a poor running engine is a cylinder compression check. A compression check (see Chapter 2D) will help determine the condition of internal engine components and should be used as a guide for tune-up and repair procedures. If, for instance, the compression check indicates serious internal engine wear, a conventional tune-up won't improve the performance of the engine and would be a waste of time and money. Because of its importance, the compression check should be done by someone with the right equipment and the knowledge to use it properly.

The following procedures are those most often needed to bring a generally poor running engine back into a proper state of tune.

MINOR TUNE-UP

Check all engine related fluids (Section 4)
Clean, inspect and test the battery (Section 11)
Check and adjust the drivebelt (Section 12)
Check all underhood hoses (Section 13)
Check the cooling system (Section 14)
Check the air filter (Section 27)
Replace the spark plugs (Section 28)
Inspect the spark plug and coil wires (Section 35)
Inspect the distributor cap and rotor (Section 35)

MAJOR TUNE-UP

All items listed under Minor tune-up, plus . . .

Replace the air filter (Section 27)
Replace the spark plug wires (Section 35)
Replace the distributor cap and rotor (Section 35)
Check the ignition system (Chapter 5)
Check the charging system (Chapter 5)

4   Fluid level checks (every 250 miles or weekly)

➡Note: The following are fluid level checks to be done on a 250 mile or weekly basis. Additional fluid level checks can be found in specific maintenance procedures that follow. Regardless of intervals, be alert to fluid leaks under the vehicle, which would indicate a fault to be corrected immediately.

4.2a The engine oil dipstick is clearly marked (5.2L/5.9L V8 shown, V6 similar)

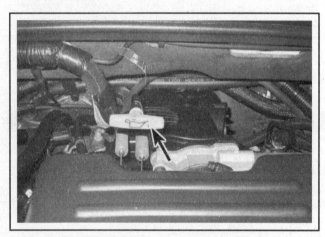

4.2b On the 4.7L V8 engine, the engine oil dipstick is located near the firewall

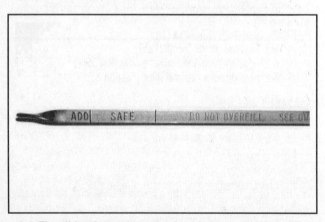

4.4 The oil level must be maintained between the marks at all times - it takes one quart of oil to raise the level from the ADD to SAFE mark

1   Fluids are an essential part of the lubrication, cooling, brake, clutch and windshield washer systems. Because the fluids gradually become depleted and/or contaminated during normal operation of the vehicle, they must be periodically replenished. See *Recommended lubricants* and fluids at the end of this Chapter before adding fluid to any of the following components.

➡Note: The vehicle must be on level ground when fluid levels are checked.

ENGINE OIL

◆ Refer to illustrations 4.2a, 4.2b, 4.4 and 4.6

2   The engine oil level is checked with a dipstick that extends through a tube and into the oil pan at the bottom of the engine (see illustration).

3   The oil level should be checked before the vehicle has been driven, or about 5 minutes after the engine has been shut off. If the oil is checked immediately after driving the vehicle, some of the oil will remain in the upper engine components, resulting in an inaccurate reading on the dipstick.

4   Pull the dipstick out of the tube and wipe all the oil from the end with a clean rag or paper towel. Insert the clean dipstick all the way back into the tube, then pull it out again. Note the oil at the end of the dipstick. Add oil as necessary to keep the level between the MIN and MAX marks or within the SAFE zone on the dipstick (see illustration).

5   Do not overfill the engine by adding too much oil since this may result in oil-fouled spark plugs, oil leaks or oil seal failures.

6   Oil is added to the engine after unscrewing a cap from the valve cover (see illustration). A funnel may help to reduce spills.

7   Checking the oil level is an important preventive maintenance step. A consistently low oil level indicates oil leakage through damaged seals, defective gaskets or past worn rings or valve guides. If the oil looks milky or has water droplets in it, the cylinder head gasket(s) may be blown or the head(s) or block may be cracked. The engine should be checked immediately. The condition of the oil should also be checked. Whenever you check the oil level, slide your thumb and index

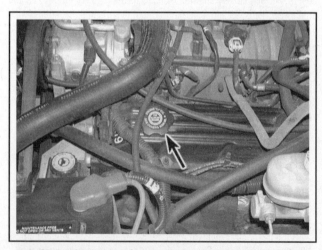

4.6 Oil is added to the engine after unscrewing the oil filler cap - always make sure the area around the opening is clean before removing the cap to prevent dirt from contaminating the engine (5.2L/5.9L V8 shown; on the 4.7L V8, the cap is on the right front of the engine)

finger up the dipstick before wiping off the oil. If you see small dirt or metal particles clinging to the dipstick, the oil should be changed (see Section 8).

ENGINE COOLANT

▶ **Refer to illustration 4.8**

> ❋❋ **WARNING:**
>
> **Do not allow antifreeze to come in contact with your skin or painted surfaces of the vehicle. Flush contaminated areas immediately with plenty of water. Antifreeze is highly toxic if ingested. Never leave antifreeze lying around in an open container or in puddles on the floor; children and pets are attracted by its sweet smell and may drink it. Check with local authorities on disposing of used anti-freeze. Many communities have collection centers that will see that antifreeze is disposed of safely.**

➡**Note: Non-toxic type antifreeze is now manufactured and available at local auto parts stores, but even this type should be disposed of properly.**

> ❋❋ **CAUTION:**
>
> **Never mix green-colored ethylene glycol antifreeze with silicate-free antifreeze that is red or orange.**

8   All vehicles covered by this manual are equipped with a pressurized coolant recovery system. A coolant reservoir located in the engine compartment is connected by a hose to the radiator filler neck (see illustration). If the engine overheats, coolant escapes through a valve in the radiator cap and travels through the hose into the reservoir. As the engine cools, the coolant is automatically drawn back into the cooling system to maintain the correct level.

> ❋❋ **WARNING:**
>
> **Do not remove the pressure cap to check the coolant level when the engine is warm.**

9   The coolant level in the reservoir should be checked regularly. The level in the reservoir varies with the temperature of the engine. When the engine is cold, the coolant level should be below the FULL mark on the dipstick. Once the engine has warmed up, the level should be at or near the FULL mark. If it isn't, allow the engine to cool, then remove the cap from the reservoir and add a 50/50 mixture of ethylene glycol-based antifreeze and water.

10   Drive the vehicle and recheck the coolant level. If only a small amount of coolant is required to bring the system up to the proper level, water can be used. However, repeated additions of water will dilute the antifreeze and water solution. In order to maintain the proper ratio of antifreeze and water, always top up the coolant level with the correct mixture. Do not use rust inhibitors or additives.

11   If the coolant level drops consistently, there may be a leak in the system. Inspect the radiator, hoses, filler cap, drain plugs and water pump (see Section 14). If no leaks are noted, have the cooling system pressure cap pressure-tested.

4.8 The coolant reservoir is located above the radiator - keep the level near the Full mark of the reservoir dipstick

12   If you have to remove the cooling system pressure cap, wait until the engine has cooled, then wrap a thick cloth around the cap and turn it to the first stop. If coolant or steam escapes, let the engine cool down longer, then remove the cap.

13   Check the condition of the coolant as well. It should be relatively clear. If it's brown or rust colored, the system should be drained, flushed and refilled. Even if the coolant appears to be normal, the corrosion inhibitors wear out, so it must be replaced at the specified intervals.

WINDSHIELD WASHER FLUID

14   Fluid for the windshield washer system is located in a plastic reservoir in the right side of engine compartment.

15   In milder climates, plain water can be used in the reservoir, but it should be kept no more than 2/3 full to allow for expansion if the water freezes. In colder climates, use windshield washer system antifreeze, available at any auto parts store, to lower the freezing point of the fluid. Mix the antifreeze with water in accordance with the manufacturer's directions on the container.

> ❋❋ **CAUTION:**
>
> **Don't use cooling system antifreeze - it will damage the vehicle's paint.**

16   To help prevent icing in cold weather, warm the windshield with the defroster before using the washer.

BATTERY ELECTROLYTE

17   These vehicles are equipped with a battery which is permanently sealed (except for vent holes) and has no filler caps. Water doesn't have to be added to these batteries at any time. If a maintenance-type battery is installed, the caps on the top of the battery should be removed periodically to check for a low electrolyte level. This check is most critical during the warm summer months. Add only distilled water to any battery.

4.19a Never let the brake fluid level drop below the MIN mark

4.19b The clutch fluid level should be kept at the top of the slotted window - never let it drop below the MIN mark, but do not overfill or siphon off fluid

BRAKE AND CLUTCH FLUID

♦ Refer to illustrations 4.19a and 4.19b

18 The brake master cylinder is mounted on the upper left of the engine compartment firewall. The clutch cylinder used on manual transmission models is mounted next to the master cylinder.

19 The translucent plastic reservoir allows the fluid inside to be checked without removing the cap (see illustrations). Note that the clutch system is a sealed unit and it shouldn't be necessary to add fluid under most conditions (see Chapter 8 for more information). Be sure to wipe the top of either reservoir cap with a clean rag to prevent contamination of the brake and/or clutch system before removing the cover.

➡Note: The clutch fluid level may actually rise in normal use as the clutch wears.

20 When adding fluid, pour it carefully into the reservoir to avoid spilling it on surrounding painted surfaces. Be sure the specified fluid is used, since mixing different types of brake fluid can cause damage to the system. See *Recommended lubricants and fluids* at the end of this Chapter or your owner's manual.

✷✷ WARNING:

Brake fluid can harm your eyes and damage painted surfaces, so use extreme caution when handling or pouring it. Do not use brake fluid that has been standing open or is more than one year old. Brake fluid absorbs moisture from the air. Moisture in the system can cause a dangerous loss of brake performance.

21 At this time, the fluid and master cylinder can be inspected for contamination. The system should be drained and refilled if deposits, dirt particles or water droplets are seen in the fluid.

22 After filling the reservoir to the proper level, make sure the cover or cap is on tight to prevent fluid leakage.

23 The brake fluid level in the master cylinder will drop slightly as the pads at the front wheels wear down during normal operation. If the master cylinder requires repeated additions to keep it at the proper level, it's an indication of leakage in the brake system, which should be corrected immediately. Check all brake lines and connections (see Section 19 for more information).

24 If, upon checking the master cylinder fluid level, you discover one or both reservoirs empty or nearly empty, the brake system should be bled and thoroughly inspected (see Chapter 9).

5 Tire and tire pressure checks (every 250 miles or weekly)

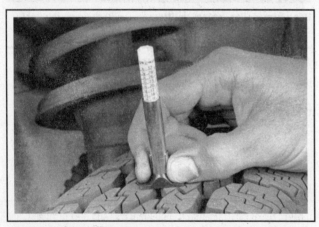

5.2 Use a tire tread depth indicator to monitor tire wear - they are available at auto parts stores and service stations and cost very little

♦ Refer to illustrations 5.2, 5.3, 5.4a, 5.4b and 5.8

1 Periodic inspection of the tires may spare you the inconvenience of being stranded with a flat tire. It can also provide you with vital information regarding possible problems in the steering and suspension systems before major damage occurs.

2 The original tires on this vehicle are equipped with 1/2-inch wide wear bands that will appear when tread depth reaches 1/16-inch, at which point the tires can be considered worn out. Tread wear can be monitored with a simple, inexpensive device known as a tread depth indicator (see illustration).

3 Note any abnormal tread wear (see illustration). Tread pattern

irregularities such as cupping, flat spots and more wear on one side than the other are indications of front end alignment and/or balance problems. If any of these conditions are noted, take the vehicle to a tire shop or service station to correct the problem.

4   Look closely for cuts, punctures and embedded nails or tacks. Sometimes a tire will hold air pressure for a short time or leak down very slowly after a nail has embedded itself in the tread. If a slow leak persists, check the valve stem core to make sure it's tight (see illustration). Examine the tread for an object that may have embedded itself in the tire or for a "plug" that may have begun to leak (radial tire punc-

tures are repaired with a plug that's installed in a puncture). If a puncture is suspected, it can be easily verified by spraying a solution of soapy water onto the puncture area (see illustration). The soapy solution will bubble if there's a leak. Unless the puncture is unusually large, a tire shop or service station can usually repair the tire.

5   Carefully inspect the inner sidewall of each tire for evidence of brake fluid leakage. If you see any, inspect the brakes immediately.

6   Correct air pressure adds miles to the lifespan of the tires, improves mileage and enhances overall ride quality. Tire pressure cannot be accurately estimated by looking at a tire, especially if it's a radial.

UNDERINFLATION

CUPPING

Cupping may be caused by:
- Underinflation and/or mechanical irregularities such as out-of-balance condition of wheel and/or tire, and bent or damaged wheel.
- Loose or worn steering tie-rod or steering idler arm.
- Loose, damaged or worn front suspension parts.

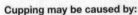
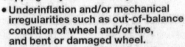

OVERINFLATION

INCORRECT TOE-IN OR EXTREME CAMBER

FEATHERING DUE TO MISALIGNMENT

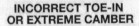

5.3 This chart will help you determine the condition of the tires and the probable cause(s) of abnormal wear

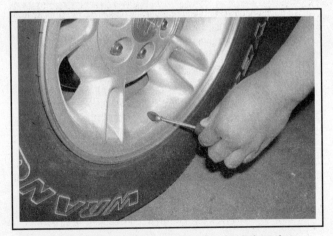

5.4a If a tire loses air on a steady basis, check the valve stem core first to make sure it's snug (special inexpensive wrenches are commonly available at auto parts stores)

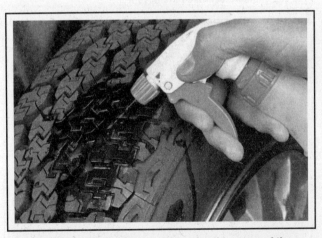

5.4b If the valve stem core is tight, raise the corner of the vehicle with the low tire and spray a soapy water solution onto the tread as the tire is turned slowly - leaks will cause small bubbles to appear

A tire pressure gauge is essential. Keep an accurate gauge in the vehicle. The pressure gauges attached to the nozzles of air hoses at gas stations are often inaccurate.

7   Always check tire pressure when the tires are cold. Cold, in this case, means the vehicle has not been driven over a mile in the three hours preceding a tire pressure check. A pressure rise of four to eight pounds is not uncommon once the tires are warm.

8   Unscrew the valve cap protruding from the wheel or hubcap and push the gauge firmly onto the valve stem (see illustration). Note the reading on the gauge and compare the figure to the recommended tire pressure shown on the placard on the driver's side door pillar. Be sure to reinstall the valve cap to keep dirt and moisture out of the valve stem mechanism. Check all four tires and, if necessary, add enough air to bring them up to the recommended pressure.

9   Don't forget to keep the spare tire inflated to the specified pressure (refer to your owner's manual or the tire sidewall).

5.8 To extend the life of the tires, check the air pressure at least once a week with an accurate gauge (don't forget the spare!)

6   Power steering fluid level check (every 3000 miles or 3 months)

6.2 The power steering fluid dipstick on V6 and V8 models (arrow) is located in the power steering pump reservoir - turn the cap counterclockwise to remove it

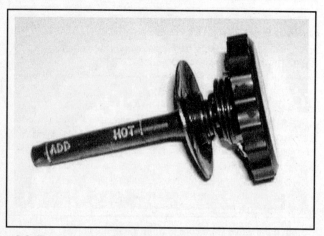

6.6 The power steering fluid dipstick has marks on it so the fluid can be checked hot or cold

▶ Refer to illustrations 6.2 and 6.6

1   Unlike manual steering, the power steering system relies on fluid which may, over a period of time, require replenishing.

2   On V6 and V8 models, the fluid reservoir for the power steering pump is located on the pump body at the front of the engine (see illustration). On four-cylinder models, the reservoir is mounted at the left (driver's) side of the radiator.

3   For the check, the front wheels should be pointed straight ahead and the engine should be off.

4   Use a clean rag to wipe off the reservoir cap and the area around the cap. This will help prevent any foreign matter from entering the reservoir during the check.

5   Twist off the cap and check the temperature of the fluid at the end of the dipstick with your finger.

6   Wipe off the fluid with a clean rag, reinsert the dipstick, then withdraw it and read the fluid level. The fluid should be at the proper level, depending on whether it was checked hot or cold (see illustration). Never allow the fluid level to drop below the lower mark on the dipstick.

7   If additional fluid is required, pour the specified type directly into the reservoir, using a funnel to prevent spills.

8   If the reservoir requires frequent fluid additions, all power steering hoses, hose connections, steering gear and the power steering pump should be carefully checked for leaks.

7 Automatic transmission fluid level check (every 3000 miles or 3 months)

▶ **Refer to illustrations 7.3 and 7.6**

1   The automatic transmission fluid level should be carefully maintained. Low fluid level can lead to slipping or loss of drive, while overfilling can cause foaming and loss of fluid.

2   With the parking brake set, start the engine, then move the shift lever through all the gear ranges, ending in Neutral. The fluid level must be checked with the vehicle level and the engine running at idle.

➡**Note: Incorrect fluid level readings will result if the vehicle has just been driven at high speeds for an extended period, in hot weather in city traffic, or if it has been pulling a trailer. If any of these conditions apply, wait until the fluid has cooled (about 30 minutes).**

3   With the transmission at normal operating temperature, remove the dipstick from the filler tube. The dipstick is located at the rear of the engine compartment on the passenger's side (see illustration).

➡**Note: Normal operating temperature is after a few minutes of engine operation, but on the 4.7L V8 models the transmission fluid should be checked after 15 miles of driving.**

4   Wipe the fluid from the dipstick with a clean rag and push it back into the filler tube until the cap seats.

5   Pull the dipstick out again and note the fluid level.

6   If the fluid is warm, the level should be between the two dimples (see illustration). If it's hot, the level should be in the crosshatched area, near the MAX line. If additional fluid is required, add it directly into the tube using a funnel. It takes about one pint to raise the level from the bottom of the crosshatched area to the MAX line with a hot transmission, so add the fluid a little at a time and keep checking the level until it's correct.

7   The condition of the fluid should also be checked along with the level. If the fluid at the end of the dipstick is a dark reddish-brown color, or if it smells burned, it should be changed. If you are in doubt about the condition of the fluid, purchase some new fluid and compare the two for color and smell.

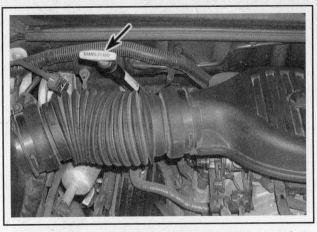

7.3 The automatic transmission dipstick (arrow) is located at the rear of the engine compartment, on the right (passenger's) side

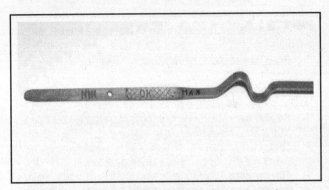

7.6 The automatic transmission fluid (when at operating temperature) must be kept in the crosshatched area (marked "OK") on the dipstick

8 Engine oil and filter change (every 3000 miles or 3 months)

▶ **Refer to illustrations 8.3, 8.9, 8.14 and 8.18**

1   Frequent oil changes are the most important preventive maintenance procedures that can be done by the home mechanic. As engine oil ages, it becomes diluted and contaminated, which leads to premature engine wear.

2   Although some sources recommend oil filter changes every other oil change, we feel that the minimal cost of an oil filter and the relative ease with which it is installed dictate that a new filter be installed every time the oil is changed.

3   Gather together all necessary tools and materials before beginning this procedure (see illustration on next page).

4   You should have plenty of clean rags and newspapers handy to mop up any spills. Access to the under side of the vehicle may be improved if the vehicle can be lifted on a hoist, driven onto ramps or supported by jackstands.

✳✳ **WARNING:**

Do not work under a vehicle which is supported only by a bumper, hydraulic or scissors-type jack.

5   If this is your first oil change, familiarize yourself with the locations of the oil drain plug and the oil filter.

6   Warm the engine to normal operating temperature. If the new oil or any tools are needed, use this warm-up time to gather everything necessary for the job. The correct type of oil for your application can be found in *Recommended lubricants and fluids* at the end of this Chapter.

7   With the engine oil warm (warm engine oil will drain better and more built-up sludge will be removed with it), raise and support the vehicle. Make sure it's safely supported!

8   Move all necessary tools, rags and newspapers under the vehicle. Set the drain pan under the drain plug. Keep in mind that the oil will initially flow from the pan with some force; position the pan accordingly.

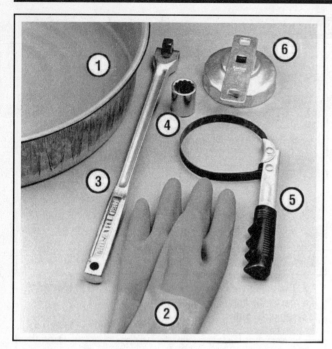

8.3 These tools are required when changing the engine oil and filter

1   *Drain pan* - It should be fairly shallow in depth, but wide to prevent spills
2   *Rubber gloves* - When removing the drain plug and filter, you will get oil on your hands (the gloves will prevent burns)
3   *Breaker bar* - Sometimes the oil drain plug is tight, and a long breaker bar is needed to loosen it
4   *Socket* - To be used with the breaker bar or a ratchet (must be the correct size to fit the drain plug - six-point preferred)
5   *Filter wrench* - This is a metal band-type wrench, which requires clearance around the filter to be effective
6   *Filter wrench* - This type fits on the bottom of the filter and can be turned with a ratchet or breaker bar (different-size wrenches are available for different types of filters)

9   Being careful not to touch any of the hot exhaust components, use a wrench to remove the drain plug near the bottom of the oil pan (see illustration). Depending on how hot the oil is, you may want to wear gloves while unscrewing the plug the final few turns.

10 Allow the oil to drain into the pan. It may be necessary to move the pan as the oil flow slows to a trickle.
11 After all the oil has drained, wipe off the drain plug with a clean rag. Small metal particles may cling to the plug and would immediately contaminate the new oil.
12 Clean the area around the drain plug opening and reinstall the plug. Tighten the plug securely with the wrench. If a torque wrench is available, use it to tighten the plug to the torque listed in this Chapter's Specifications.
13 Move the drain pan into position under the oil filter.
14 Use the oil filter wrench to loosen the oil filter (see illustration).
15 Completely unscrew the old filter. Be careful: it's full of oil. Empty the oil inside the filter into the drain pan, then lower the filter.
16 Compare the old filter with the new one to make sure they're the same type.
17 Use a clean rag to remove all oil, dirt and sludge from the area where the oil filter mounts to the engine. Check the old filter to make sure the rubber gasket isn't stuck to the engine. If the gasket is stuck to the engine (use a flashlight if necessary), remove it.
18 Apply a light coat of clean oil to the rubber gasket on the new oil filter (see illustration).
19 Attach the new filter to the engine, following the tightening directions printed on the filter canister or packing box. Most filter manufacturers recommend against using a filter wrench due to the possibility of overtightening and damage to the seal.
20 Remove all tools, rags, etc. from under the vehicle, being careful not to spill the oil in the drain pan, then lower the vehicle.
21 Move to the engine compartment and locate the oil filler cap.
22 Pour the fresh oil through the filler opening. A funnel may be helpful.
23 Refer to the engine oil capacity in this Chapter's Specifications and add the proper amount of fresh oil into the engine. Wait a few minutes to allow the oil to drain into the pan, then check the level on the oil dipstick (see Section 4 if necessary). If the oil level is above the hatched area, start the engine and allow the new oil to circulate.
24 Run the engine for only about a minute and then shut it off. Immediately look under the vehicle and check for leaks at the oil pan drain plug and around the oil filter.
25 With the new oil circulated and the filter now completely full, recheck the level on the dipstick and add more oil as necessary.
26 During the first few trips after an oil change, make it a point to check frequently for leaks and proper oil level.

8.9 Use a proper size box-end wrench or socket to remove the oil drain plug and avoid rounding it off

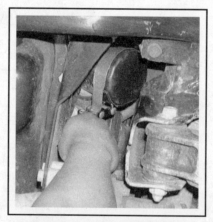

8.14 Since the oil filter is on very tight, you'll need a special wrench for removal - DO NOT use the wrench to tighten the new filter

8.18 Lubricate the oil filter gasket with clean engine oil before installing the filter on the engine

27 The old oil drained from the engine cannot be reused in its present state and should be disposed of. Check with your local auto parts store, disposal facility or environmental agency to see if they will accept the oil for recycling. After the oil has cooled it can be drained into a container (capped plastic jugs, topped bottles, milk cartons, etc.) for transport to one of these disposal sites. Don't dispose of the oil by pouring it on the ground or down a drain!

9 Seat belt check (every 6000 miles or 6 months)

1   Check seat belts, buckles, latch plates and guide loops for obvious damage and signs of wear.
2   Where the seat belt receptacle bolts to the floor of the vehicle, check that the bolts are secure.
3   See if the seat belt reminder light comes on when the key is turned to the Run or Start position. A chime should also sound.

10 Wiper blade inspection and replacement (every 6000 miles or 6 months)

⧫ Refer to illustration 10.3

➡Note: The left and right-hand wiper blades are not interchangeable. The driver's side insert has 8 pairs of claws securing the rubber element, while the right side has only six.

1   The windshield wiper blade elements should be checked periodically for cracks and deterioration. The wiper blade assemblies on these vehicles consists of a rubber blade element secured in a multi-jointed metal assembly.
2   Lift the wiper blade assembly away from the glass.
3   Press the release lever and slide the blade assembly out of the hook in the end of the wiper arm (see illustration).
4   The rubber blade element is not replaceable separately; the entire blade assembly must be replaced.
5   Installation is the reverse of removal.

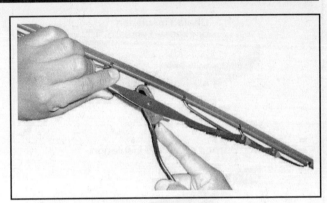

10.3 Depress the release lever (finger is on it here) and slide the wiper blade assembly down the wiper arm and out of the hook in the end of the arm

11 Battery check, maintenance and charging (every 6000 miles or 6 months)

⧫ Refer to illustrations 11.1, 11.5, 11.6a, 11.6b, 11.7a and 11.7b

❋❋ **WARNING:**

Certain precautions must be followed when checking and servicing the battery. Hydrogen gas, which is highly flammable, is always present in the battery cells, so keep lighted tobacco and all other open flames and sparks away from the battery. The electrolyte inside the battery is actually dilute sulfuric acid, which will cause injury if splashed on your skin or in your eyes. It will also ruin clothes and painted surfaces. When removing the battery cables, always detach the negative cable first and hook it up last!

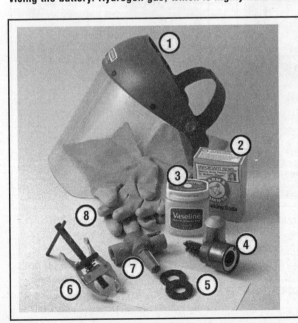

11.1 Tools and materials required for battery maintenance

1   *Face shield/safety goggles* - *When removing corrosion with a brush, the acidic particles can easily fly up into your eyes*
2   *Baking soda* - *A solution of baking soda and water can be used to neutralize corrosion*
3   *Petroleum jelly* - *A layer of this on the battery posts will help prevent corrosion*
4   *Battery post/cable cleaner* - *This wire brush cleaning tool will remove all traces of corrosion from the battery posts and cable clamps*
5   *Treated felt washers* - *Placing one of these on each post, directly under the cable clamps, will help prevent corrosion*
6   *Puller* - *Sometimes the cable clamps are very difficult to pull off the posts, even after the nut/bolt has been completely loosened. This tool pulls the clamp straight up and off the post without damage*
7   *Battery post/cable cleaner* - *Here is another cleaning tool that is a slightly different version of Number 4 above, but it does the same thing*
8   *Rubber gloves* - *Another safety item to consider when servicing the battery; remember that's acid inside the battery!*

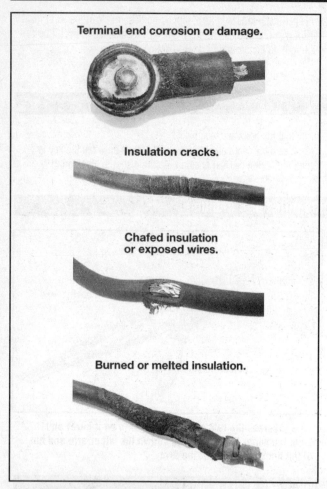

Terminal end corrosion or damage.

Insulation cracks.

Chafed insulation or exposed wires.

Burned or melted insulation.

11.5 Typical battery cable problems

1 A routine preventive maintenance program for the battery in your vehicle is the only way to ensure quick and reliable starts. But before performing any battery maintenance, make sure that you have the proper equipment necessary to work safely around the battery (see illustration).

2 There are also several precautions that should be taken whenever battery maintenance is performed. Before servicing the battery, always turn the engine and all accessories off and disconnect the cable from the negative terminal of the battery.

3 The battery produces hydrogen gas, which is both flammable and explosive. Never create a spark, smoke or light a match around the battery. Always charge the battery in a ventilated area.

4 Electrolyte contains poisonous and corrosive sulfuric acid. Do not allow it to get in your eyes, on your skin or on your clothes. Never ingest it. Wear protective safety glasses when working near the battery. Keep children away from the battery.

5 Note the external condition of the battery. If the positive terminal and cable clamp on your vehicle's battery is equipped with a rubber protector, make sure that it's not torn or damaged. It should completely cover the terminal. Look for any corroded or loose connections, cracks in the case or cover or loose hold-down clamps. Also check the entire length of each cable for cracks and frayed conductors (see illustration).

6 If corrosion, which looks like white, fluffy deposits is evident, particularly around the terminals, the battery should be removed for cleaning (see illustration). Loosen the cable clamp bolts with a wrench, being careful to remove the ground cable first, and slide them off the terminals (see illustration). Then disconnect the hold-down clamp bolt and nut, remove the clamp and lift the battery from the engine compartment.

7 Clean the cable clamps thoroughly with a battery brush or a terminal cleaner and a solution of warm water and baking soda (see illustration). Wash the terminals and the top of the battery case with the same solution but make sure that the solution doesn't get into the battery. When cleaning the cables, terminals and battery top, wear safety goggles and rubber gloves to prevent any solution from coming in contact with your eyes or hands. Wear old clothes too - even diluted, sulfuric acid splashed onto clothes will burn holes in them. If the terminals have been extensively corroded, clean them up with a terminal cleaner (see illustration). Thoroughly wash all cleaned areas with plain water.

8 Make sure that the battery tray is in good condition and the hold-down clamp bolts are tight. If the battery is removed from the tray, make

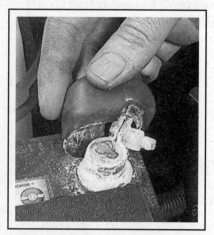

11.6a Battery terminal corrosion usually appears as light, fluffy powder

11.6b Removing the cable from a battery post with a wrench - sometimes special battery pliers are required for this procedure if corrosion has caused deterioration of the nut hex (always remove the ground cable first and hook it up last!)

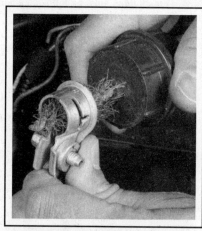

11.7a When cleaning the cable clamps, all corrosion must be removed (the inside of the clamp is tapered to match the taper on the post, so don't remove too much material)

11.7b Regardless of the type of tool used on the battery posts, a clean, shiny surface should be the result

sure no parts remain in the bottom of the tray when the battery is reinstalled. When reinstalling the hold-down clamp bolts, do not overtighten them.

9   Any metal parts of the vehicle damaged by corrosion should be covered with a zinc-based primer, then painted.

10 Information on removing and installing the battery can be found in Chapter 5. Information on jump starting can be found at the front of this manual.

CHARGING

⁂ **WARNING:**

When batteries are being charged, hydrogen gas, which is very explosive and flammable, is produced. Do not smoke or allow open flames near a charging or a recently charged battery. Wear eye protection when near the battery during charging. Also, make sure the charger is unplugged before connecting or disconnecting the battery from the charger.

➡Note: The manufacturer recommends the battery be removed from the vehicle for charging because the gas that escapes during this procedure can damage the paint. Fast charging with the battery cables connected can result in damage to the electrical system.

11 Slow-rate charging is the best way to restore a battery that's discharged to the point where it will not start the engine. It's also a good way to maintain the battery charge in a vehicle that's only driven a few miles between starts. Maintaining the battery charge is particularly important in the winter when the battery must work harder to start the engine and electrical accessories that drain the battery are in greater use.

12 It's best to use a one or two-amp battery charger (sometimes called a "trickle" charger). They are the safest and put the least strain on the battery. They are also the least expensive. For a faster charge, you can use a higher amperage charger, but don't use one rated more than 1/10th the amp/hour rating of the battery. Rapid boost charges that claim to restore the power of the battery in one to two hours are hardest on the battery and can damage batteries not in good condition. This type of charging should only be used in emergency situations.

13 The average time necessary to charge a battery should be listed in the instructions that come with the charger. As a general rule, a trickle charger will charge a battery in 12 to 16 hours.

14 Remove all the cell caps (if equipped) and cover the holes with a clean cloth to prevent spattering electrolyte. Disconnect the negative battery cable and hook the battery charger cable clamps up to the battery posts (positive to positive, negative to negative), then plug in the charger. Make sure it is set at 12-volts if it has a selector switch.

15 If you're using a charger with a rate higher than two amps, check the battery regularly during charging to make sure it doesn't overheat. If you're using a trickle charger, you can safely let the battery charge overnight after you've checked it regularly for the first couple of hours.

16 If the battery has removable cell caps, measure the specific gravity with a hydrometer every hour during the last few hours of the charging cycle. Hydrometers are available inexpensively from auto parts stores - follow the instructions that come with the hydrometer. Consider the battery charged when there's no change in the specific gravity reading for two hours and the electrolyte in the cells is gassing (bubbling) freely. The specific gravity reading from each cell should be very close to the others. If not, the battery probably has a bad cell(s).

17 Some batteries with sealed tops have built-in hydrometers on the top that indicate the state of charge by the color displayed in the hydrometer window. Normally, a bright-colored hydrometer indicates a full charge and a dark hydrometer indicates the battery still needs charging.

18 If the battery has a sealed top and no built-in hydrometer, you can hook up a digital voltmeter across the battery terminals to check the charge. A fully charged battery should read 12.6 volts or higher.

19 Further information on the battery and jump-starting can be found in Chapter 5 and at the front of this manual.

12 Drivebelt check, adjustment and replacement (every 6000 miles or 6 months)

▶ **Refer to illustrations 12.2, 12.4, 12.5, 12.6 and 12.8**

1   A single serpentine drivebelt is located at the front of the engine and plays an important role in the overall operation of the engine and its components. Due to its function and material make up, the belt is prone to wear and should be periodically inspected. The serpentine belt drives the alternator, power steering pump, water pump and air conditioning compressor.

2   With the engine off, open the hood and use your fingers (and a flashlight, if necessary), to move along the belt checking for cracks and separation of the belt plies. Also check for fraying and glazing, which gives the belt a shiny appearance (see illustration). Both sides of the belt should be inspected, which means you will have to twist the belt to check the underside.

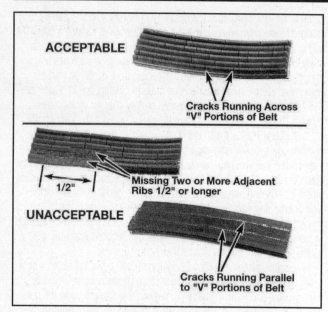

12.2 Check ribbed (serpentine) belts for signs of wear like these - if it looks worn, replace it

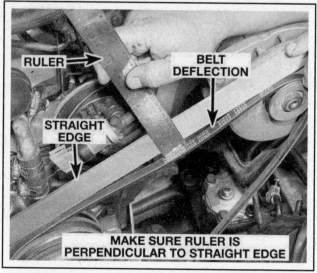

12.4 On four-cylinder engines, a ruler and straightedge can be used to determine the belt deflection (tension) between two pulleys

3 Check the ribs on the underside of the belt. They should all be the same depth, with none of the surface uneven.

4 On four-cylinder models, belt tension must be checked manually, by pushing on the belt at a distance halfway between two pulleys. Push firmly with your thumb and see how much the belt moves (deflects) (see illustration). As rule of thumb, if the distance from pulley center-to-pulley center is between 7 and 11 inches, the belt should deflect 1/4-inch. If the belt travels between pulleys spaced 12 to 16 inches apart, the belt should deflect 1/4 to 1/2-inch. Belt tension is adjusted by moving the belt idler pulley that is attached to the alternator mount (see illustration).

5 On V6 and V8 engines, the tension of the belt is maintained by a spring-loaded tensioner assembly and isn't adjustable. The belt should be replaced when the indexing line is lined up with the projection on the tensioner assembly (see illustration).

6 To replace the belt, rotate the tensioner (or loosen the idler pulley on 2.5L engines) to release belt tension (see illustration).

7 Remove the belt from the tensioner and auxiliary components and slowly release the tensioner.

8 Route the new belt over the various pulleys, again rotating the tensioner to allow the belt to be installed, then release the belt tensioner.

➡Note: A drivebelt routing decal is located on the radiator support to help during drivebelt installation (see illustration).

❊❊ WARNING:

On 2.5L and 4.7L V8 engines, the water pump operates in reverse rotation. If the belt routing diagram is not followed, the engine could overheat.

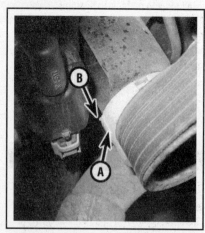

12.5 The serpentine drivebelt tensioner used on V6 and V8 models automatically applies the proper tension on the drivebelt, but it does have limits - the indexing line on the tensioner body (A) must not move beyond point B on the tensioner mount

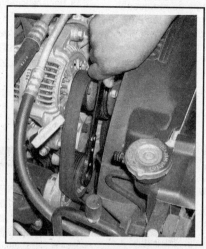

12.6 Rotate the automatic tensioner (V6 and V8) by turning its center bolt clockwise with a long wrench until the belt can be pulled off the pulley, then release the tensioner

12.8 The drivebelt routing diagram is found on the radiator support (V8 shown)

13 Underhood hose check and replacement (every 6000 miles or 6 months)

GENERAL

> ⚹⚹ **CAUTION:**
>
> Replacement of air conditioning hoses must be left to a dealer service department or air conditioning shop that has the equipment to depressurize the system safely and recover the refrigerant. Never remove air conditioning components or hoses until the system has been depressurized.

1 High temperatures in the engine compartment can cause the deterioration of the rubber and plastic hoses used for engine, accessory and emission systems operation. Periodic inspection should be made for cracks, loose clamps, material hardening and leaks. Information specific to the cooling system hoses can be found in Section 14.

2 Some, but not all, hoses are secured to their fittings with clamps. Where clamps are used, check to be sure they haven't lost their tension, allowing the hose to leak. If clamps aren't used, make sure the hose has not expanded and/or hardened where it slips over the fitting, allowing it to leak.

VACUUM HOSES

3 It's quite common for vacuum hoses, especially those in the emissions system, to be color-coded or identified by colored stripes molded into them. Various systems require hoses with different wall thickness, collapse resistance and temperature resistance. When replacing hoses, be sure the new ones are made of the same material.

4 Often the only effective way to check a hose is to remove it completely from the vehicle. If more than one hose is removed, be sure to label the hoses and fittings to ensure correct installation.

5 When checking vacuum hoses, be sure to include any plastic T-fittings in the check. Inspect the fittings for cracks and the hose where it fits over the fitting for distortion, which could cause leakage.

6 A small piece of vacuum hose (1/4-inch inside diameter) can be used as a stethoscope to detect vacuum leaks. Hold one end of the hose to your ear and probe around vacuum hoses and fittings, listening for the "hissing" sound characteristic of a vacuum leak.

> ⚹⚹ **WARNING:**
>
> When probing with the vacuum hose stethoscope, be very careful not to come into contact with moving engine components such as the drivebelt, cooling fan, etc.

FUEL HOSE

> ⚹⚹ **WARNING:**
>
> There are certain precautions that must be taken when inspecting or servicing fuel system components. Work in a well-ventilated area and do not allow open flames (cigarettes, appliances, etc.) or bare light bulbs near the work area. Mop up any spills immediately and do not store fuel soaked rags where they could ignite. The fuel system is under high pressure, so if any fuel lines are to be disconnected, the pressure in the system must be relieved first (see Chapter 4 for more information).

7 Check all rubber fuel lines for deterioration and chafing. Check especially for cracks in areas where the hose bends and just before fittings, such as where a hose attaches to the fuel filter.

8 High quality fuel line, made specifically for high-pressure fuel injection systems, must be used for fuel line replacement. Never, under any circumstances, use unreinforced vacuum line, clear plastic tubing or water hose for fuel lines.

9 Spring-type clamps are commonly used on fuel lines. These clamps often lose their tension over a period of time, and can be "sprung" during removal. Replace all spring-type clamps with screw clamps whenever a hose is replaced.

METAL LINES

10 Sections of metal line are routed along the frame, between the fuel tank and the engine. Check carefully to be sure the line has not been bent or crimped and that cracks have not started in the line.

11 If a section of metal fuel line must be replaced, only seamless steel tubing should be used, since copper and aluminum tubing don't have the strength necessary to withstand normal engine vibration.

12 Check the metal brake lines where they enter the master cylinder and brake proportioning unit for cracks in the lines or loose fittings. Any sign of brake fluid leakage calls for an immediate and thorough inspection of the brake system.

14 Cooling system check (every 6000 miles or 6 months)

▶ **Refer to illustration 14.4**

1 Many major engine failures can be attributed to a faulty cooling system. If the vehicle is equipped with an automatic transmission, the cooling system also cools the transmission fluid and thus plays an important role in prolonging transmission life.

2 The cooling system should be checked with the engine cold. Do this before the vehicle is driven for the day or after it has been shut off for at least three hours.

3 Remove the radiator cap by turning it to the left until it reaches a stop. If you hear a hissing sound (indicating there is still pressure in the system), wait until this stops. Now press down on the cap with the palm of your hand and continue turning to the left until the cap can be removed. Thoroughly clean the cap, inside and out, with clean water. Also clean the filler neck on the radiator. All traces of corrosion should be removed. The coolant inside the radiator should be relatively transparent. If it is rust-colored, the system should be drained, flushed and

Check for a chafed area that could fail prematurely.

Check for a soft area indicating the hose has deteriorated inside.

Overtightening the clamp on a hardened hose will damage the hose and cause a leak.

Check each hose for swelling and oil-soaked ends. Cracks and breaks can be located by squeezing the hose.

14.4 Hoses, like drivebelts, have a habit of failing at the worst possible time - to prevent the inconvenience of a blown radiator or heater hose, inspect them carefully as shown here

refilled (see Section 33). If the coolant level is not up to the top, add additional antifreeze/coolant mixture (see Section 4).

4   Carefully check the large upper and lower radiator hoses along with the smaller diameter heater hoses that run from the engine to the firewall. Inspect each hose along its entire length, replacing any hose that is cracked, swollen or shows signs of deterioration. Cracks may become more apparent if the hose is squeezed (see illustration). Regardless of condition, it's a good idea to replace hoses with new ones every two years.

5   Make sure all hose connections are tight. A leak in the cooling system will usually show up as white or rust-colored deposits on the areas adjoining the leak. If wire-type clamps are used at the ends of the hoses, it may be a good idea to replace them with more secure screw-type clamps.

6   Use compressed air or a soft brush to remove bugs, leaves, etc. from the front of the radiator or air conditioning condenser. Be careful not to damage the delicate cooling fins or cut yourself on them.

7   Every other inspection, or at the first indication of cooling system problems, have the cap and system pressure tested. If you don't have a pressure tester, most repair shops will do this for a minimal charge.

15   Tire rotation (every 6000 miles or 6 months)

♦ **Refer to illustrations 15.2a and 15.2b**

1   The tires should be rotated at the specified intervals and whenever uneven wear is noticed.

2   Tires must be rotated in the recommended pattern (see illustrations).

➡**Note: Some radial tires are "directional," and will have a small arrow molded into the sidewall.**

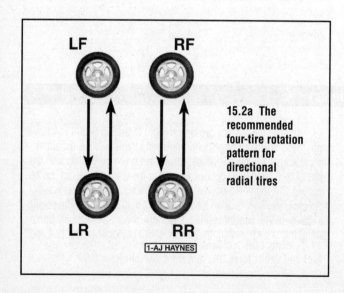

15.2a The recommended four-tire rotation pattern for directional radial tires

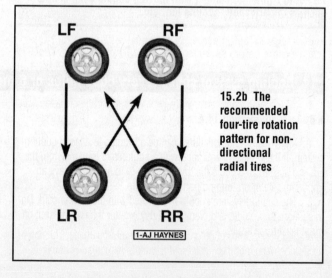

15.2b The recommended four-tire rotation pattern for non-directional radial tires

3   Refer to the information in *Jacking and towing* at the front of this manual for the proper procedures to follow when raising the vehicle and changing a tire. If the brakes are to be checked, don't apply the parking brake as stated. Make sure the tires are blocked to prevent the vehicle from rolling as it's raised.

4   Preferably, the entire vehicle should be raised at the same time.

This can be done on a hoist or by jacking up each corner and then lowering the vehicle onto jackstands placed under the frame rails. Always use four jackstands and make sure the vehicle is safely supported.

5   After rotation, check and adjust the tire pressures as necessary. Tighten the lug nuts to the torque listed in this Chapter's Specifications.

16 Steering linkage lubrication (2WD models) (every 15,000 miles or 12 months)

1   The tie-rod ends on models equipped with lubrication fittings have a more frequent lubrication schedule than the rest of the suspension components.

2   The tie-rod ends on models equipped with lubrication fittings can be lubricated with a standard grease gun through the fitting at the bottom of the tie-rod end. Refer to Section 24 for the basic procedure.

17 Fuel system check (every 15,000 miles or 12 months)

▶ **Refer to illustration 17.7**

❊❊ WARNING:

Gasoline is extremely flammable, so take extra precautions when you work on any part of the fuel system. Don't smoke or allow open flames or bare light bulbs near the work area, and don't work in a garage where a gas-type appliance (such as a water heater or clothes dryer) is present. Since gasoline is carcinogenic, wear latex gloves when there's a possibility of being exposed to fuel, and, if you spill any fuel on your skin, rinse it off immediately with soap and water. Mop up any spills immediately and do not store fuel-soaked rags where they could ignite. When you perform any kind of work on the fuel system, wear safety glasses and have a Class B type fire extinguisher on hand. The fuel system is under constant pressure, so, before any lines are disconnected, the fuel system pressure must be relieved (see Chapter 4).

1   If you smell gasoline while driving or after the vehicle has been sitting in the sun, inspect the fuel system immediately.

2   Remove the gas filler cap and inspect if for damage and corrosion. The gasket should have an unbroken sealing imprint. If the gasket is damaged or corroded, install a new cap.

3   Inspect the fuel feed and return lines for cracks. Make sure that the connections between the fuel lines and the fuel injection system are tight.

❊❊ WARNING:

Your vehicle is fuel injected, so you must relieve the fuel system pressure before servicing fuel system components. The fuel system pressure-relief procedure is outlined in Chapter 4.

4   If the fuel injectors are visible, look for signs of fuel leakage (wet spots) around any of the injectors, they may need new O-rings (see Chapter 4).

5   Since some components of the fuel system - the fuel tank and part of the fuel feed and return lines, for example - are underneath the vehicle, they can be inspected more easily with the vehicle raised on a hoist. If that's not possible, raise the vehicle and support it on jackstands.

6   With the vehicle raised and safely supported, inspect the gas tank and filler neck for punctures, cracks and other damage. The connection between the filler neck and the tank is particularly critical.

Sometimes a rubber filler neck will leak because of loose clamps or deteriorated rubber. Inspect all fuel tank mounting brackets and straps to be sure that the tank is securely attached to the vehicle.

❊❊ WARNING:

Do not, under any circumstances, try to repair a fuel tank (except rubber components). A welding torch or any open flame can easily cause fuel vapors inside the tank to explode.

7   Carefully check all rubber hoses and metal lines leading away from the fuel tank (see illustration). Check for loose connections, deteriorated hoses, crimped lines and other damage. Repair or replace damaged sections as necessary (see Chapter 4).

8   The evaporative emissions control system can also be a source of fuel odors. The function of the system is to store fuel vapors from the fuel tank in a charcoal canister until they can be routed to the intake manifold where they mix with incoming air before being burned in the combustion chambers.

9   The most common symptom of a faulty evaporative emissions system is a strong odor of fuel in the engine compartment. If a fuel odor has been detected, and you have already checked the areas described above, check the charcoal canister, located under the rear of the vehicle, and the hoses connected to it (see illustration 17.7).

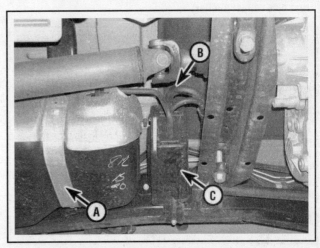

17.7 Inspect the fuel tank mounting straps (A), the various fuel and vapor lines (B), and the EVAP canister (C)

18 Brake system check (every 15,000 miles or 12 months)

☀ WARNING :

The dust created by the brake system is harmful to your health. Never blow it out with compressed air and don't inhale any of it. An approved filtering mask should be worn when working on the brakes. Do not, under any circumstances, use petroleum-based solvents to clean brake parts. Use brake system cleaner only! Try to use non-asbestos replacement parts whenever possible.

➡Note: For detailed photographs of the brake system, refer to Chapter 9.

1   In addition to the specified intervals, the brakes should be inspected every time the wheels are removed or whenever a defect is suspected.

2   Any of the following symptoms could indicate a potential brake system defect: The vehicle pulls to one side when the brake pedal is depressed; the brakes make squealing or dragging noises when applied; brake pedal travel is excessive; the pedal pulsates; or brake fluid leaks, usually onto the inside of the tire or wheel.

18.7a With the wheel off, check the thickness of the inner pad through the inspection hole (front disc shown, optional rear disc caliper similar)

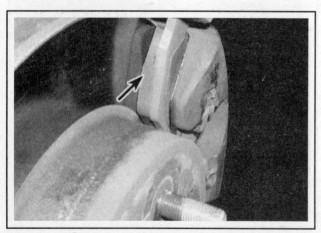

18.7b The outer pad (arrow) is more easily checked at the edge of the caliper

3   Loosen the wheel lug nuts.
4   Raise the vehicle and place it securely on jackstands.
5   Remove the wheels (see *Jacking and towing* at the front of this book, or your owner's manual, if necessary).

DISC BRAKES

◆ Refer to illustrations 18.7a, 18.7b, 18.9 and 18.11

6   There are two pads (an outer and an inner) in each caliper. The pads are visible with the wheels removed.

7   Check the pad thickness by looking at each end of the caliper and through the inspection window in the caliper body (see illustrations). If the lining material is less than the thickness listed in this Chapter's Specifications, replace the pads.

➡Note: Keep in mind that the lining material is riveted or bonded to a metal backing plate and the metal portion is not included in this measurement.

8   If it is difficult to determine the exact thickness of the remaining pad material by the above method, or if you are at all concerned about the condition of the pads, remove the caliper(s), then remove the pads from the calipers for further inspection (refer to Chapter 9).

9   Once the pads are removed from the calipers, clean them with brake cleaner and re-measure them with a ruler or a vernier caliper (see illustration).

10   Measure the disc thickness with a micrometer to make sure that it still has service life remaining. If any disc is thinner than the specified minimum thickness, replace it (refer to Chapter 9). Even if the disc has service life remaining, check its condition. Look for scoring, gouging and burned spots. If these conditions exist, remove the disc and have it resurfaced (see Chapter 9).

11   Before installing the wheels, check all brake lines and hoses for damage, wear, deformation, cracks, corrosion, leakage, bends and twists, particularly in the vicinity of the rubber hoses at the calipers (see illustration). Check the clamps for tightness and the connections for leakage. Make sure that all hoses and lines are clear of sharp edges, moving parts and the exhaust system. If any of the above conditions are noted, repair, reroute or replace the lines and/or fittings as necessary (see Chapter 9).

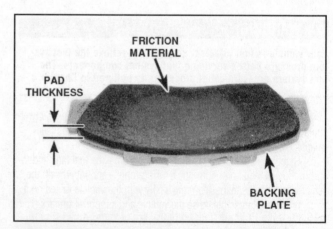

18.9 If a more precise measurement of pad thickness is necessary, remove the pads and measure the remaining friction material

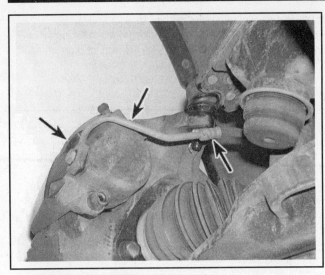

18.11 Check along the brake hoses and at each fitting (arrows) for deterioration and cracks

DRUM BRAKES

▶ **Refer to illustrations 18.15, 18.17, 18.18 and 18.19**

12 Make sure the parking brake is off, then tap on the outside of the drum with a rubber mallet to loosen it.

13 Remove the brake drums.

➡**Note: If the drum won't come off, it may be rusted to the axle at the center hole. Apply a little penetrating oil, allow it to soak in, and try again.**

14 If the drum still cannot be pulled off, the parking brake lever will have to be lifted slightly off its stop. This is done by first removing the small plug from the backing plate.

15 With the plug removed, insert a thin screwdriver and lift the adjusting lever off the star wheel, then use an adjusting tool or screwdriver to back off the star wheel several turns (see illustration). This will move the brake shoes away from the drum. If the drum still won't pull off, tap around its inner circumference with a soft-face hammer.

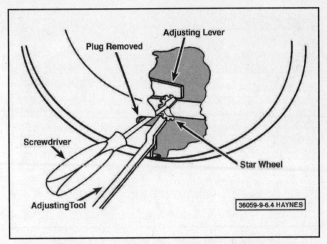

18.15 Use a thin screwdriver to push the lever away, then use an adjusting tool or another screwdriver to back off the star wheel

16 With the drums removed, carefully clean the brake assembly with brake system cleaner.

✳✳ WARNING:

Don't blow the dust out with compressed air and don't inhale any of it (it is harmful to your health).

17 Note the thickness of the lining material on both brake shoes. If the material has worn away to within 1/32-inch of the recessed rivets or 1/16-inch of the metal backing on bonded type shoes, the shoes should be replaced (see illustration). The shoes should also be replaced if they're cracked, glazed (shiny areas), or covered with brake fluid.

18 Make sure all the brake assembly springs are connected and in good condition (see illustration).

19 Check the brake components for signs of fluid leakage. With your finger or a small screwdriver, carefully pry back the rubber cups on the

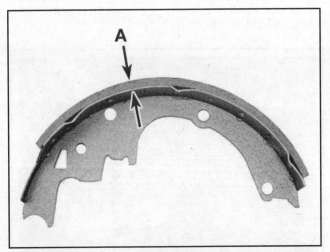

18.17 If the lining is bonded to the brake shoe, measure the lining thickness from the outer surface to the metal shoe, as shown here; if the lining is riveted to the shoe, measure from the lining outer surface to the rivet head

18.18 Typical assembled view of a rear drum brake

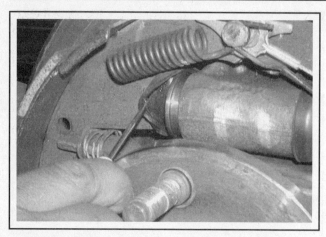

18.19 To check for wheel cylinder leakage, use a small screwdriver to pry the boot away from the cylinder

wheel cylinder located at the top of the brake shoes (see illustration). Any leakage here is an indication that the wheel cylinders should be replaced immediately (see Chapter 9). Also, check all hoses and connections for signs of leakage.

20 Clean the inside of the drum with brake system cleaner. Again, be careful not to breathe the dust.

21 Check the inside of the drum for cracks, score marks, deep scratches and "hard spots" which will appear as small discolored areas. If imperfections cannot be removed with fine emery cloth, the drum

must be taken to an automotive machine shop for resurfacing.

22 Repeat the procedure for the remaining wheel. If the inspection reveals that all parts are in good condition, reinstall the brake drums, install the wheels and lower the vehicle to the ground.

BRAKE BOOSTER CHECK

23 Sit in the driver's seat and perform the following sequence of tests.

24 With the brake fully depressed, start the engine - the pedal should move down a little when the engine starts.

25 With the engine running, depress the brake pedal several times - the travel distance should not change.

26 Depress the brake, stop the engine and hold the pedal in for about 30 seconds - the pedal should neither sink nor rise.

27 Restart the engine, run it for about a minute and turn it off. Then firmly depress the brake several times - the pedal travel should decrease with each application.

28 If your brakes do not operate as described, the brake booster has failed. Refer to Chapter 9 for the replacement procedure.

PARKING BRAKE

29 One method of checking the parking brake is to park the vehicle on a steep hill with the parking brake set and the transmission in Neutral. If the parking brake cannot prevent the vehicle from rolling, it's in need of adjustment (see Chapter 9).

19 Exhaust system check (every 15,000 miles or 12 months)

▶ **Refer to illustrations 19.2a and 19.2b**

1   With the engine cold (at least three hours after the vehicle has been driven), check the complete exhaust system from the manifold to the end of the tailpipe. Be careful around the catalytic converter, which may be hot even after three hours. The inspection should be done with the vehicle on a hoist to permit unrestricted access. If a hoist isn't available, raise the vehicle and support it securely on jackstands.

2   Check the exhaust pipes and connections for signs of leakage and/or corrosion indicating a potential failure. Make sure that all brack-

ets and hangers are in good condition and tight (see illustrations).

3   Inspect the underside of the body for holes, corrosion, open seams, etc. which may allow exhaust gasses to enter the passenger compartment. Seal all body openings with silicone sealant or body putty.

4   Rattles and other noises can often be traced to the exhaust system, especially the hangers, mounts and heat shields. Try to move the pipes, mufflers and catalytic converter. If the components can come in contact with the body or suspension parts, secure the exhaust system with new brackets and hangers.

19.2a Inspect the muffler (B) for signs of deterioration, and all hangers (A)

19.2b Inspect all flanged joints (arrow indicates pipe-to-manifold joint) for signs of exhaust gas leakage

20 Manual transmission lubricant level check (every 15,000 miles or 12 months)

1 The manual transmission has a filler plug which must be removed to check the lubricant level. If the vehicle is raised to gain access to the plug, be sure to support it safely on jackstands - DO NOT crawl under a vehicle that is supported only by a jack! Be sure the vehicle is level or the check may be inaccurate.

2 Using the appropriate wrench, unscrew the plug from the transmission; some models require an Allen wrench. The drain plug will be found on the bottom of the case, while the fill plug is up a few inches

from there on the right-hand side of the case.

3 Use your little finger to reach inside the housing to feel the lubricant level. The level should be at or near the bottom of the plug hole. If it isn't, add the recommended lubricant through the plug hole with a syringe or squeeze bottle.

4 Install and tighten the plug. Check for leaks after the first few miles of driving.

21 Transfer case lubricant level check (4WD models) (every 15,000 miles or 12 months)

◆ **Refer to illustration 21.1**

1 The transfer case lubricant level is checked by removing the upper plug located at the rear of the case (see illustration).

2 After removing the plug, reach inside the hole. The lubricant level should be just at the bottom of the hole. If not, add the appropriate lubricant through the opening.

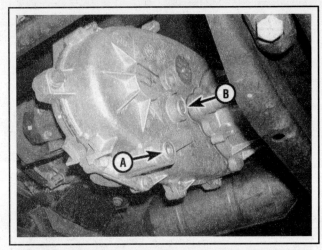

21.1 The drain plug (A) and fill plug (B) are on the rear cover of the transfer case

22 Differential lubricant level check (every 15,000 miles or 12 months)

◆ **Refer to illustration 22.2**

➡**Note: 4WD vehicles have two differentials - one in the center of each axle. 2WD vehicles have one differential - in the center of the rear axle. On 4WD vehicles, be sure to check the lubricant level in both differentials.**

1 The filler plug on all front and most rear differentials is a threaded metal type while the rear differential on some models may have a rubber press-in filler plug which must be removed to check the lubricant level. If the vehicle is raised to gain access to the plug, be sure to support it safely on jackstands - DO NOT crawl under the vehicle when it's supported only by the jack. Be sure the vehicle is level or the check may not be accurate.

2 Remove the plug from the filler hole in the differential housing or cover (see illustration).

3 The lubricant level should be at the bottom of the filler hole. If not, use a pump or squeeze bottle to add the recommended lubricant until it just starts to run out of the opening. On some models a tag is located in the area of the plug which gives information regarding lubricant type.

4 Install the plug securely into the filler hole.

22.2 Remove the rear axle filler plug (arrow) to check the differential lubricant level (rear axle shown, front 4WD axle similar)

23 Suspension, steering and driveaxle boot check (every 22,500 miles or 18 months)

➡Note: The steering linkage and suspension components should be checked periodically. Worn or damaged suspension and steering linkage components can result in excessive and abnormal tire wear, poor ride quality and vehicle handling and reduced fuel economy. For detailed illustrations of the steering and suspension components, refer to Chapter 10.

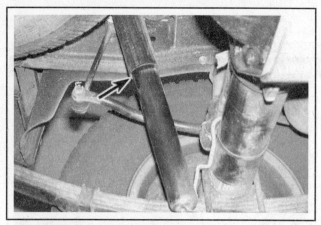

23.6 Check for signs of fluid leakage at this point on shock absorbers (rear shock shown)

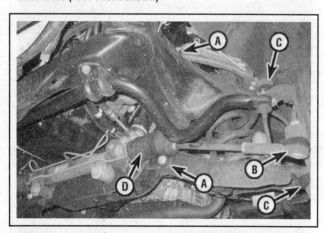

23.9a Examine the mounting points for the upper and lower control arms on the front suspension (A), the tie-rod ends (B), the balljoints (C), and the steering gear boots (D)

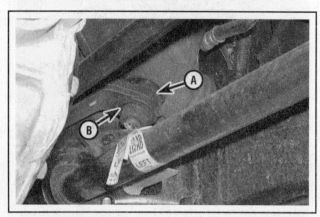

23.9b Inspect the steering gear for signs of lubricant leakage (A) and make sure the Pitman arm nut (B) is tight

SHOCK ABSORBER CHECK

▸ **Refer to illustration 23.6**

1   Park the vehicle on level ground, turn the engine off and set the parking brake. Check the tire pressures.

2   Push down at one corner of the vehicle, then release it while noting the movement of the body. It should stop moving and come to rest in a level position within one or two bounces.

3   If the vehicle continues to move up-and-down or if it fails to return to its original position, a worn or weak shock absorber is probably the reason.

4   Repeat the above check at each of the three remaining corners of the vehicle.

5   Raise the vehicle and support it securely on jackstands.

6   Check the shock absorbers for evidence of fluid leakage (see illustration). A light film of fluid is no cause for concern. Make sure that any fluid noted is from the shocks and not from some other source. If leakage is noted, replace the shocks as a set.

7   Check the shocks to be sure that they are securely mounted and undamaged. Check the upper mounts for damage and wear. If damage or wear is noted, replace the shocks as a set (front or rear).

8   If the shocks must be replaced, refer to Chapter 10 for the procedure.

STEERING AND SUSPENSION CHECK

▸ **Refer to illustrations 23.9a, 23.9b and 23.11**

9   Visually inspect the steering and suspension components (front and rear) for damage and distortion. Look for damaged seals, boots and bushings and leaks of any kind. Examine the bushings where the control arms meet the chassis (see illustrations).

10 Clean the lower end of the steering knuckle. Have an assistant grasp the lower edge of the tire and move the wheel in-and-out while you look for movement at the steering knuckle-to-control arm balljoint. If there is any movement the suspension balljoint(s) must be replaced.

11 Grasp each front tire at the front and rear edges, push in at the front, pull out at the rear and feel for play in the steering system com-

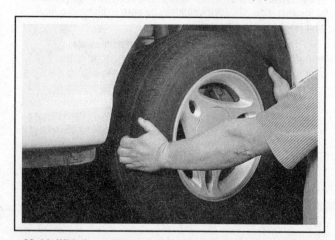

23.11 With the steering wheel in the locked position and the vehicle raised, grasp the front tire as shown and try to move it back-and-forth - if any play is noted, check the steering gear mounts and tie-rod ends for looseness

ponents. If any freeplay is noted, check the idler arm and the tie-rod ends for looseness (see illustration).

12 Additional steering and suspension system information and illustrations can be found in Chapter 10.

DRIVEAXLE BOOT CHECK (4WD MODELS)

13 The driveaxle boots are very important because they prevent dirt, water and foreign material from entering and damaging the constant velocity (CV) joints. Oil and grease can cause the boot material to deteriorate prematurely, so it's a good idea to wash the boots with soap and water. Because it constantly pivots back and forth following the steering action of the front hub, the outer CV boot wears out sooner and should be inspected regularly.

14 Inspect the boots for tears and cracks as well as loose clamps. If there is any evidence of cracks or leaking lubricant, they must be replaced as described in Chapter 8.

24 Chassis lubrication (every 22,500 miles or 18 months)

▶ **Refer to illustration 24.1 and 24.2**

1   Refer to *Recommended lubricants and fluids* at the end of this Chapter to obtain the necessary grease, etc. You'll also need a grease gun (see illustration). If a suspension component has no grease fitting in place, this indicates the part is sealed and doesn't require periodic lubrication. Some components on 4WD models have fittings that aren't on 2WD versions, and vice-versa.

2   Look under the vehicle and locate the grease fittings (see illustration).

3   For easier access under the vehicle, raise it with a jack and place jackstands under the frame. Make sure it's safely supported by the stands. If the wheels are to be removed at this interval for tire rotation or brake inspection, loosen the lug nuts slightly while the vehicle is still on the ground.

4   Before beginning, force a little grease out of the nozzle to remove any dirt from the end of the gun. Wipe the nozzle clean with a rag.

5   With the grease gun and plenty of clean rags, crawl under the vehicle and begin lubricating the components.

6   Wipe one of the grease fitting nipples clean and push the nozzle firmly over it. Pump the gun until the component is completely lubricated. On balljoints, stop pumping when the rubber seal is firm to the touch. Do not pump too much grease into the fitting as it could rupture the seal. For all other suspension and steering components, continue pumping grease into the fitting until it oozes out of the joint between the two components. If it escapes around the grease gun nozzle, the nipple is clogged or the nozzle is not completely seated on the fitting. Resecure the gun nozzle to the fitting and try again. If necessary, replace the fitting with a new one.

7   Wipe the excess grease from the components and the grease fitting. Repeat the procedure for the remaining fittings.

8   Clean the fitting and pump grease into the driveline universal joints until the grease can be seen coming out of the contact points. There is a grease fitting on the front U-joint of the driveshaft on some models, and on the sliding joint of the front driveshaft on 4WD models. The other U-joints are sealed and do not require lubrication.

➡**Note: Most replacement driveshaft U-joints aren't permanently sealed, and are sold with grease fittings. If your U-joints have been replaced, make sure you include them in your routine chassis lubrication.**

9   Also clean and lubricate the parking brake cable, along with the cable guides and levers. This can be done by smearing some of the chassis grease onto the cable and its related parts with your fingers.

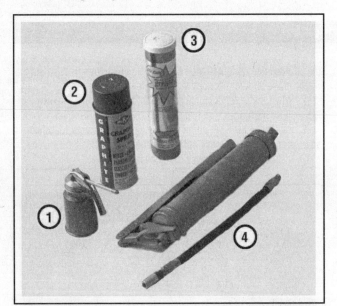

24.1 Materials required for chassis and body lubrication

1 *Engine oil - Light engine oil in a can like this can be used for door and hood hinges*
2 *Graphite spray - Used to lubricate lock cylinders*
3 *Grease - Grease, in a variety of types and weights, is available for use in a grease gun. Check the Specifications for your requirements*
4 *Grease gun - A common grease gun, shown here with a detachable hose and nozzle, is needed for chassis lubrication. After use, clean it thoroughly!*

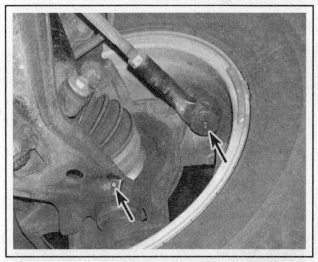

24.2 Wipe the dirt from the grease fittings before pushing the grease gun nozzle onto the fitting - arrows indicate two of the fittings; the upper is the tie-rod end, the lower one is for the lower balljoint

25 Front wheel bearing check (2WD models) (every 22,500 miles or 18 months)

1 Front wheel bearings are incorporated into the front hub on 2WD models, and are serviced as a unit.

2 Because the hub/bearing assembly is "lifetime-lubricated," there is no need for periodic lubrication. They should, however, be checked at regular intervals for wear.

3 Raise the vehicle and suitably support the front end with jackstands. Grasp the tire/wheel at the top and bottom and rock them to check for noticeable play.

4 If any amount of play is felt, refer to Chapter 9 and remove the wheel, brake caliper and brake disc.

5 Rock just the hub itself on the spindle. If any play is felt, the hub/bearing assembly should be replaced. Refer to Chapter 10 for hub/bearing replacement.

26 Brake fluid change (every 30,000 miles or 24 months)

✻✻ WARNING:

Brake fluid can harm your eyes and damage painted surfaces, so use extreme caution when handling or pouring it. Do not use brake fluid that has been standing open or is more than one year old. Brake fluid absorbs moisture from the air. Excess moisture can cause a dangerous loss of braking effectiveness.

1 At the specified intervals, the brake fluid should be drained and replaced. Since the brake fluid may drip or splash when pouring it, place plenty of rags around the master cylinder to protect any surrounding painted surfaces.

2 Before beginning work, purchase the specified brake fluid (see *Recommended lubricants and fluids* at the end of this Chapter).

3 Remove the cap from the master cylinder reservoir.

4 Using a hand suction pump or similar device, withdraw the fluid from the master cylinder reservoir.

5 Add new fluid to the master cylinder until it rises to the base of the filler neck.

6 Bleed the brake system as described in Chapter 9 at all four brakes until new and uncontaminated fluid is expelled from the bleeder screw. Be sure to maintain the fluid level in the master cylinder as you perform the bleeding process. If you allow the master cylinder to run dry, air will enter the system.

7 Refill the master cylinder with fluid and check the operation of the brakes. The pedal should feel solid when depressed, with no sponginess.

✻✻ WARNING:

Do not operate the vehicle if you are in doubt about the effectiveness of the brake system.

27 Air filter replacement (every 30,000 miles or 24 months)

▶ **Refer to illustrations 27.3a and 27.3b**

1 At the specified intervals, the air filter element should be replaced with a new one.

2 On all models, the air filter is housed in a black plastic box mounted on the inner fenderwell on the right side of the engine compartment.

3 Detach the spring clips and pull the housing cover up, then lift the air filter element out of the housing (see illustrations). Wipe out the inside of the air filter housing with a clean rag.

4 While the cover is off, be careful not to drop anything down into the air filter housing.

5 Place the new filter element in the air filter housing. Make sure it seats properly in the groove of the housing.

6 Installation is the reverse of removal.

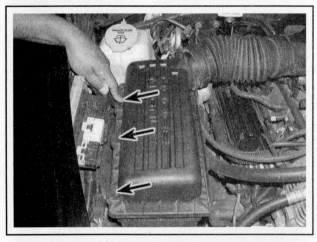

27.3a Release the three spring clips (arrows) and lift the air filter housing cover

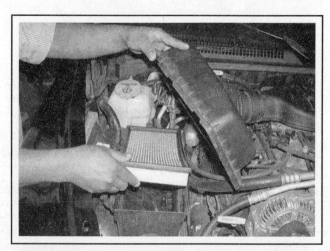

27.3b The cover slips out of slots on the housing to allow room for replacement of the filter

28 Spark plug replacement (every 30,000 miles or 24 months)

♦ Refer to illustrations 28.2, 28.5a, 28.5b, 28.6a, 28.6b, 28.8, 28.9, 28.10 and 28.11

➡ Note: There are no spark plug wires on the 4.7L V8 engine. Instead the plugs are fired by individual coils, one mounted directly over each plug.

1   The spark plugs are threaded into the sides of the cylinder heads, adjacent to the exhaust ports.

2   In most cases, the tools necessary for spark plug replacement include a spark plug socket which fits onto a ratchet (spark plug sockets are padded inside to prevent damage to the porcelain insulators on the new plugs), various extensions and a gap gauge to check and adjust the gaps on the new plugs (see illustration). A special plug wire removal tool is available for separating the wire boots from the spark plugs, but it isn't absolutely necessary. A torque wrench should be used to tighten the new plugs.

3   The best approach when replacing the spark plugs is to purchase the new ones in advance, adjust them to the proper gap and replace them one at a time. When buying the new spark plugs, be sure to obtain the correct plug type for your particular engine. This information can be found on the *Emission Control Information* label located under the hood, in the factory owner's manual and the Specifications at the end of this Chapter. If differences exist between the plug specified on the emissions label and in the owner's manual, assume that the emissions label is correct.

4   Allow the engine to cool completely before attempting to remove any of the plugs. While you're waiting for the engine to cool, check the new plugs for defects and adjust the gaps.

5   The gap is checked by inserting the proper-thickness gauge between the electrodes at the tip of the plug (see illustration). The gap between the electrodes should be the same as the one specified on the *Emissions Control Information* label or in this Chapter's Specifications. The wire should just slide between the electrodes with a slight amount of drag. If the gap is incorrect, use the adjuster on the gauge body to bend the curved side electrode slightly until the proper gap is obtained

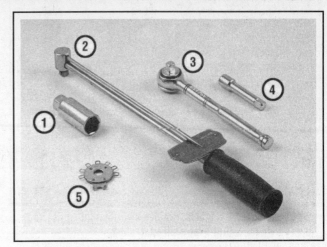

28.2 Tools required for changing spark plugs

1   **Spark plug socket** - *This will have special padding inside to protect the spark plug's porcelain insulator*
2   **Torque wrench** - *Although not mandatory, using this tool is the best way to ensure the plugs are tightened properly*
3   **Ratchet** - *Standard hand tool to fit the spark plug socket*
4   **Extension** - *Depending on model and accessories, you may need special extensions and universal joints to reach one or more of the plugs*
5   **Spark plug gap gauge** - *This gauge for checking the gap comes in a variety of styles. Make sure the gap for your engine is included*

(see illustration). If the side electrode is not exactly over the center electrode, bend it with the adjuster until it is. Check for cracks in the porcelain insulator (if any are found, the plug should not be used).

6   With the engine cool, remove the spark plug wire from one spark plug. Pull only on the boot at the end of the wire - do not pull on the wire. A plug wire removal tool should be used if available (see illustra-

28.5a Spark plug manufacturers recommend using a wire-type gauge when checking the gap - if the wire does not slide between the electrodes with a slight drag, adjustment is required

28.5b To change the gap, bend the side electrode only, as indicated by the arrows, and be very careful not to crack or chip the porcelain insulator surrounding the center electrode

28.6a A tool like this one makes the job of removing the spark plug boot easier - twist it back-and-forth and pull only on the boot

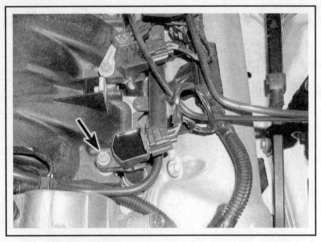

28.6b On 4.7L V8 engines, remove the mounting nut(s) and the individual coil(s) over each spark plug

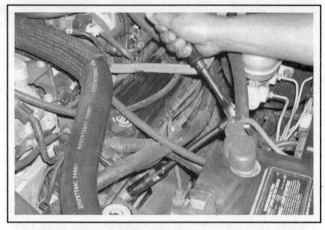

28.8 Use a socket and extension to unscrew the spark plugs - various length extensions and perhaps a flex-joint may be required to reach some plugs

A normally worn spark plug should have light tan or gray deposits on the firing tip.

A carbon fouled plug, identified by soft, sooty, black deposits, may indicate an improperly tuned vehicle. Check the air cleaner, ignition components and engine control system.

An oil fouled spark plug indicates an engine with worn piston rings and/or bad valve seals allowing excessive oil to enter the chamber.

This spark plug has been left in the engine too long, as evidenced by the extreme gap- Plugs with such an extreme gap can cause misfiring and stumbling accompanied by a noticeable lack of power.

A physically damaged spark plug may be evidence of severe detonation in that cylinder. Watch that cylinder carefully between services, as a continued detonation will not only damage the plug, but could also damage the engine.

A bridged or almost bridged spark plug, identified by a build-up between the electrodes caused by excessive carbon or oil build-up on the plug.

28.9 Inspect the spark plug to determine engine running conditions

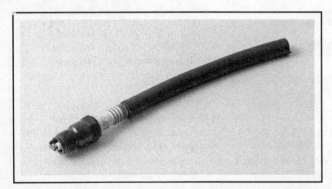

28.10 A length of snug-fitting rubber hose will save time and prevent damaged threads when installing the spark plugs

tion). On 4.7L V8 engines, remove the individual coil mounted over each spark plug (see illustration).

7   If compressed air is available, use it to blow any dirt or foreign material away from the spark plug hole. The idea here is to eliminate the possibility of debris falling into the cylinder as the spark plug is removed.

8   Place the spark plug socket over the plug and remove it from the engine by turning it in a counterclockwise direction (see illustration).

9   Compare the spark plug with this chart to get an indication of the general running condition of the engine.

10 Thread one of the new plugs into the hole until you can no longer turn it with your fingers, then tighten it with a torque wrench (if available) or the ratchet. It might be a good idea to slip a short length of

rubber hose over the end of the plug to use as a tool to thread it into place (see illustration). The hose will grip the plug well enough to turn it, but will start to slip if the plug begins to cross-thread in the hole - this will prevent damaged threads and the accompanying repair costs.

11 Attach the plug wire to the new spark plug, again using a twisting motion on the boot until it's seated on the spark plug. On V6 and 5.2L/5.9L V8 engines, make sure there is an air gap between the lip of the boot and the top of the metal spark plug heat shields (see illustration).

12 Repeat the procedure for the remaining spark plugs, replacing them one at a time to prevent mixing up the spark plug wires.

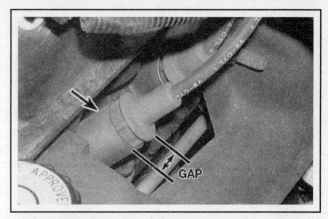

28.11 Make sure there is an air gap between the lip of the boot and the top of the metal spark plug heat shield (A) used on V6 and 5.2L/5.9L V8 engines

29 Automatic transmission fluid and filter change (every 37,500 miles or 30 months)

▶ Refer to illustrations 29.6, 29.11a and 29.11b

1 At the specified intervals, the transmission fluid should be drained and replaced. Since the fluid will remain hot long after driving, perform this procedure only after the engine has cooled down completely. The manufacturer also recommends adjusting the transmission bands at this time, since this procedure requires removing the fluid pan (see Section 30).

2 Before beginning work, purchase the specified transmission fluid (see *Recommended lubricants and fluids* at the end of this Chapter) and a new filter.

3 Other tools necessary for this job include a floor jack, jackstands to support the vehicle in a raised position, a drain pan capable of holding at least four quarts, newspapers and clean rags.

4 Raise the vehicle and support it securely on jackstands.

5 Place the drain pan underneath the transmission pan. Remove the rear and side pan mounting bolts, but only loosen the front pan bolts approximately four turns.

6 Carefully pry the transmission pan loose with a screwdriver, allowing the fluid to drain (see illustration).

7 Remove the remaining bolts, pan and gasket. Carefully clean the gasket surface of the transmission to remove all traces of the old gasket and sealant.

8 Drain the fluid from the transmission pan, clean the pan with solvent and dry it with compressed air, if available.

➡Note: Some models are equipped with magnets in the transmission pan to catch metal debris. Clean the magnet thoroughly. A small amount of metal material is normal at the magnet. If there is considerable debris, consult a dealer or transmission specialist.

9 Remove the filter from the valve body inside the transmission. Use a gasket scraper to remove any traces of old gasket material that remain on the valve body.

➡Note: Be very careful not to gouge the delicate aluminum gasket surface on the valve body.

10 Install a new gasket and filter. On many replacement filters, the gasket is attached to the filter to simplify installation.

⁂ CAUTION:

On most models, the seal can be installed on the filter first, then the seal/filter can be pushed in place and secured. On models with 45RE and 545RFE transmissions, install the filter seal into the valve body first, then install the filter.

11 Make sure the gasket surface on the transmission pan is clean,

29.6 With the front bolts in place but loose, pull the rear of the pan down to drain the fluid

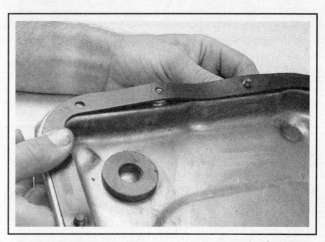

29.11a Place a new gasket in position on the pan and install the bolts to hold it in place

29.11b Hold the pan in place and install all of the bolts snugly before tightening them fully

then install a new gasket on the pan (see illustration). Put the pan in place against the transmission and, working around the pan, tighten each bolt a little at a time to the torque listed in this Chapter's Specifications (see illustration).

➡**Note: On 2002 and later models, the gasket on 42RE and 46RE transmissions is reusable if in good condition. On models with 45RFE or 545RFE transmissions, RTV sealant is used instead of a gasket. Clean the pan and transmission surfaces thoroughly with lacquer thinner and apply a continuous bead of RTV sealant to the pan, then bolt it in place and tighten to Specifications within five minutes.**

12 Lower the vehicle and add approximately 4 quarts of the specified type of automatic transmission fluid through the filler tube (see Section 7).

13 With the transmission in Park and the parking brake set, run the engine at a fast idle, but don't race it.

14 Move the gear selector through each range and back to Park. Check the fluid level. It will probably be low. Add enough fluid to bring the level between the two dimples on the dipstick.

15 Check under the vehicle for leaks during the first few trips. Check the fluid level again when the transmission is hot (see Section 7).

---

30 Automatic transmission band adjustment (42RE and 46RE transmissions) (every 37,500 miles or 30 months)

▶ **Refer to illustration 30.7**

1   The transmission bands should be adjusted at the specified interval when the transmission fluid and filter are being replaced (see Section 29).

FRONT (KICKDOWN) BAND

2   The front band adjusting screw is located on the left side (outside) of the transmission case, between the throttle lever and the fitting where the fluid cooling line connects from the fluid cooler.

3   Raise the front of the vehicle and support it securely on jackstands.

4   Loosen the adjusting screw locknut approximately five turns, then loosen the adjusting screw a few turns. Make sure the adjusting screw turns freely, with no binding; lubricate it with penetrating oil if necessary.

5   Tighten the adjusting screw to 72 in-lbs of torque, then back it off the number of turns listed in this Chapter's Specifications. Hold the adjusting screw from turning, then tighten the locknut to the torque listed in this Chapter's Specifications.

REAR (LOW-REVERSE) BAND

6   To gain access to the rear band, the fluid pan must be removed (see Section 29).

7   Loosen the adjusting screw locknut and back it off five to six

turns (see illustration). Make sure the screw turns freely in the lever.

8   Tighten the adjusting screw to 72 in-lbs of torque, then back it off the number of turns listed in this Chapter's Specifications. Hold the screw from turning, then tighten the locknut to the torque listed in this Chapter's Specifications.

9   Install the transmission fluid pan and refill the transmission (see Section 29).

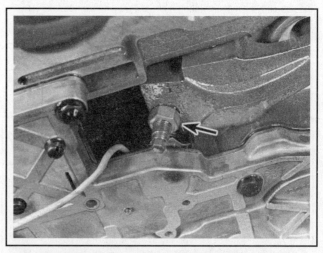

30.7 Loosen the rear band locknut so the adjusting screw can be turned

31 Manual transmission lubricant change (every 37,500 miles or 30 months)

1   This procedure should be performed after the vehicle has been driven so the lubricant will be warm and therefore will flow out of the transmission more easily. Raise the vehicle and support it securely on jackstands.

2   Move a drain pan, rags, newspapers and wrenches under the transmission. Remove the fill plug from the side of the transmission case.

3   Remove the transmission drain plug at the bottom of the case and allow the lubricant to drain into the pan.

4   After the lubricant has drained completely, reinstall the plug and tighten it securely.

5   Using a hand pump, syringe or squeeze bottle, fill the transmission with the specified lubricant until it begins to leak out through the hole. Reinstall the fill plug and tighten it securely.

6   Lower the vehicle.

7   Drive the vehicle for a short distance, then check the drain and fill plugs for leakage.

32 Transfer case lubricant change (4WD models) (every 37,500 miles or 30 months)

1   This procedure should be performed after the vehicle has been driven so the lubricant will be warm and therefore will flow out of the transfer case more easily.

2   Raise the vehicle and support it securely on jackstands.

3   Remove the filler plug from the case (see illustration 21.1).

4   Remove the drain plug from the lower part of the case and allow the lubricant to drain completely.

5   After the case is completely drained, carefully clean and install

the drain plug. Tighten the plug securely.

6   Fill the case with the specified lubricant until it is level with the lower edge of the filler hole.

7   Install the filler plug and tighten it securely.

8   Drive the vehicle for a short distance and recheck the lubricant level. In some instances a small amount of additional lubricant will have to be added.

33 Cooling system servicing (draining, flushing and refilling) (every 45,000 miles or 36 months)

✳✳ WARNING:

Do not allow antifreeze to come in contact with your skin or painted surfaces of the vehicle. Flush contacted areas immediately with plenty of water. Do not store new coolant or leave old coolant lying around where it is easily accessible to children and pets, because they are attracted by its sweet smell. Ingestion of even a small amount can be fatal. Wipe up the garage floor and drip pan coolant spills immediately. Keep antifreeze containers covered and repair leaks in your cooling system immediately. Antifreeze is flammable - be sure to read the precautions on the container.

➡**Note: Non-toxic coolant is available at local auto parts stores. Although the coolant is non-toxic when fresh, proper disposal is still required.**

DRAINING

▶ **Refer to illustrations 33.3 and 33.4**

1   Periodically, the cooling system should be drained, flushed and refilled to replenish the antifreeze mixture and prevent formation of rust and corrosion, which can impair the performance of the cooling system and cause engine damage. When the cooling system is serviced, all hoses and the pressure cap should be checked and replaced if necessary.

2   Apply the parking brake and block the wheels.

✳✳ WARNING:

If the vehicle has just been driven, wait several hours to allow the engine to cool down before beginning this procedure.

3   Move a large container under the radiator drain to catch the coolant. The drain plug is located on the lower left side of the radiator (see illustration). Attach a 3/8-inch diameter hose to the drain fitting (if possible) to direct the coolant into the container, then open the drain fitting (a pair of pliers may be required to turn it). Remove the pressure cap.

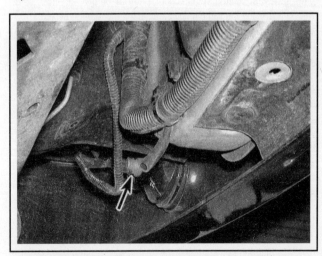

33.3 The radiator drain (arrow) is located at the corner of the radiator

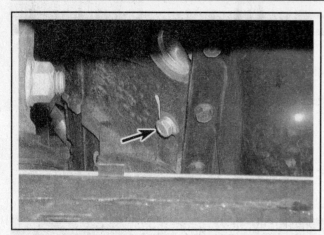

33.4 Cylinder block drain (arrow) - there is one on each side of the block

4   After coolant stops flowing out of the radiator, move the container under the engine block drain plugs - there's one on each side of the block (see illustration). Remove the plugs and allow the coolant in the block to drain.

➡Note: Frequently, the coolant will not drain from the block after the plug is removed. This is due to a rust layer that has built up behind the plug. Insert a Phillips screwdriver into the hole to break the rust barrier.

5   While the coolant is draining, check the condition of the radiator hoses, heater hoses and clamps (refer to Section 13 if necessary).

6   Replace any damaged clamps or hoses. Reinstall the drain plugs and tighten them securely.

FLUSHING

▶ **Refer to illustration 33.9**

7   Once the system is completely drained, remove the thermostat from the engine (see Chapter 3). Then reinstall the thermostat housing without the thermostat. This will allow the system to be thoroughly flushed.

8   Reinstall the lower radiator hose and tighten the radiator drain plug. Turn your heating system controls to Hot, so that the heater core will be flushed at the same time as the rest of the cooling system.

9   Disconnect the upper radiator hose, then place a garden hose in the upper radiator inlet and flush the system until the water runs clear at the upper radiator hose (see illustration).

10   In severe cases of contamination or clogging of the radiator, remove the radiator (see Chapter 3) and have a radiator repair facility clean and repair it if necessary.

11   Many deposits can be removed by the chemical action of a cleaner available at auto parts stores. Follow the procedure outlined in the manufacturer's instructions.

➡Note: When the coolant is regularly drained and the system refilled with the correct antifreeze/water mixture, there should be no need to use chemical cleaners or descalers.

REFILLING

12   To refill the system, install the thermostat, reconnect any radiator

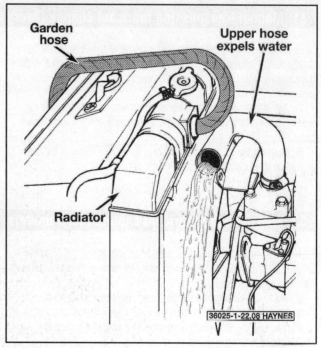

33.9 With the thermostat removed, disconnect the upper radiator hose and flush the radiator and engine block with a garden hose

hoses and install the reservoir and the overflow hose.

13   Place the heater temperature control in the maximum heat position.

14   Make sure to use the proper coolant listed in this Chapter's Specifications. Slowly fill the cooling system with the recommended mixture of antifreeze and water to the base of the filler neck. Then add coolant to the reservoir until it reaches the FULL mark. Wait five minutes and recheck the coolant level in the radiator, adding if necessary.

All except 4.7L V8 engine

15   Place the heater temperature control and the blower motor speed control to their maximum setting.

16   Leave the pressure cap off and run the engine in a well-ventilated area until the thermostat opens (coolant will begin flowing through the radiator and the upper radiator hose will become hot).

17   Turn the engine off and let it cool. Add more coolant mixture to bring the level back up to the base of the filler neck.

18   Squeeze the upper radiator hose to expel air, then add more coolant mixture if necessary. Replace the radiator cap.

4.7L V8 engine

19   Install the pressure cap and the reservoir cap. Start the engine and raise the engine speed to 3,000 rpm, holding it there for 10 seconds.

20   Stop the engine, remove the pressure cap and add coolant up to the FULL level. Reinstall the pressure cap. Add coolant to the reservoir, as necessary, to bring it up to the FULL mark.

All models

21   Start the engine, allow it to reach normal operating temperature and check for leaks.

34   Positive Crankcase Ventilation (PCV) valve replacement (every 60,000 miles or 48 months)

▶ **Refer to illustrations 34.2a and 34.2b**

1   The PCV valve is located in the valve cover on V6 and 5.2L/5.9L V8 engines. On 4.7L V8 engines, the PCV is located in the neck of the oil filler tube, at the front of the right cylinder head.

➡**Note: The four-cylinder Dakota engine does not have a PCV valve.**

2   With the engine idling at normal operating temperature, pull the valve (with hose attached) from the rubber grommet in the cover (see illustrations).

3   Place your finger over the valve opening. If there's no vacuum at the valve, check for a plugged hose, manifold port, or the valve itself.

Replace any plugged or deteriorated hoses.

4   Turn off the engine and shake the PCV valve, listening for a rattle. If the valve doesn't rattle, replace it with a new one.

5   To replace the valve, pull it from the end of the hose, noting its installed position.

6   When purchasing a replacement PCV valve, make sure it's for your particular vehicle and engine size. Compare the old valve with the new one to make sure they're the same.

7   Push the valve into the end of the hose until it's seated.

8   Inspect the rubber grommet for damage and hardening. Replace it with a new one if necessary.

9   Push the PCV valve and hose securely into position.

34.2a The PCV valve (arrow) on V6 and 5.2L/5.7L V8 engines is located in the right valve cover - pull it out and check for vacuum with your finger

34.2b On 4.7L V8 engines, rotate the PCV valve 90-degrees counterclockwise and pull straight out to remove it

35   Spark plug wires and distributor cap and rotor - check and replacement (every 60,000 miles or 48 months)

▶ **Refer to illustrations 35.10 and 35.13**

➡**Note: The 4.7L V8 does not have a distributor or spark plug wires. Individual coils are mounted directly over each spark plug and controlled by the PCM.**

1   The spark plug wires should be checked at the recommended intervals and whenever new spark plugs are installed in the engine.

2   Begin this procedure by making a visual check of the spark plug wires while the engine is running. In a darkened garage (make sure there is adequate ventilation) start the engine and observe each plug wire. Be careful not to come into contact with any moving engine parts. If there is a break in the wire, you will see arcing or a small spark at the damaged area. If arcing is noticed, make a note to obtain new wires, then allow the engine to cool and check the distributor cap and rotor.

3   Disconnect the plug wire from one spark plug. To do this, grab the rubber boot, twist slightly and pull the wire free. Do not pull on the wire itself, only on the rubber boot.

4   Check inside the boot for corrosion, which will look like a white crusty powder. Push the wire and boot back onto the end of the spark plug. It should be a tight fit on the plug. If it isn't, remove the wire and use a pair of pliers to carefully crimp the metal connector inside the

boot until it fits securely on the end of the spark plug.

5   Using a clean rag, wipe the entire length of the wire to remove any built-up dirt and grease. Once the wire is clean, check for holes, burned areas, cracks and other damage. Don't bend the wire excessively or the conductor inside might break.

6   Disconnect the wire from the distributor cap. Pull the wire straight out of the cap. Pull only on the rubber boot during removal. Check for corrosion and a tight fit in the same manner as the spark plug end. Reattach the wire to the distributor cap.

7   Check the remaining spark plug wires one at a time, making sure they are securely fastened at the distributor and the spark plug when the check is complete.

8   If new spark plug wires are required, purchase a new set for your specific engine model. Wire sets are available pre-cut, with the rubber boots already installed. Remove and replace the wires one at a time to avoid mix-ups in the firing order. The wire routing is extremely important, so be sure to note exactly how each wire is situated before removing it.

9   Remove the distributor cap screws. Pull up on the cap, with the wires attached, to separate it from the distributor, then position it to one side.

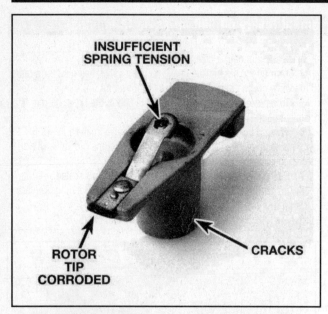

35.10 The ignition rotor should be checked for wear and corrosion as indicated here (if in doubt about its condition, buy a new one)

10 The rotor is now visible on the end of the distributor shaft. Check it carefully for cracks and carbon tracks. Make sure the center terminal spring tension is adequate and look for corrosion and wear on the rotor tip (see illustration). If in doubt about its condition, replace it with a new one.

11 If replacement is required, detach the rotor from the shaft and install a new one. The rotor is a press fit on the shaft and can be pried or pulled off.

12 The rotor is indexed to the shaft so it can only be installed one way. It has an internal key that must line up with a slot in the end of the shaft (or vice versa).

13 Check the distributor cap for carbon tracks, cracks and other damage. Closely examine the terminals on the inside of the cap for excessive corrosion and damage (see illustration). Slight deposits are normal. Again, if in doubt about the condition of the cap, replace it with a new one. Be sure to apply a small dab of silicone dielectric grease to each terminal before installing the cap. Also, make sure the carbon brush (center terminal) is correctly installed in the cap - a wide gap between the brush and rotor will result in rotor burn-through and/or damage to the distributor cap.

14 To replace the cap, simply separate it from the distributor and transfer the spark plug wires, one at a time, to the new cap. Be very careful not to mix up the wires!

15 Reattach the cap to the distributor, then install the screws to hold it in place.

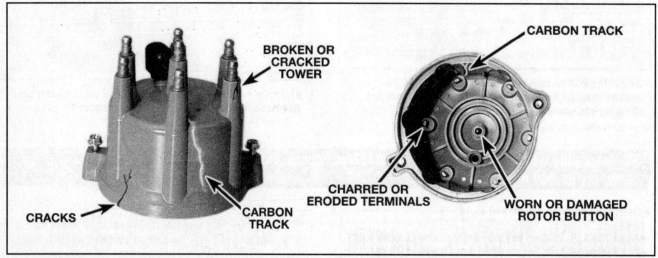

35.13 Shown here are some of the common defects to look for when inspecting the distributor cap (if in doubt about its condition, install a new one)

36 Differential lubricant change (every 60,000 miles or 48 months)

▶ **Refer to illustration 36.3, 36.4a, 36.4b, 36.4c and 36.6**

1 This procedure should be performed after the vehicle has been driven so the lubricant will be warm and therefore will flow out of the differential more easily.

2 Raise the vehicle and support it securely on jackstands. If the differential has a bolt-on cover at the rear, it is usually easiest to remove the cover to drain the lubricant (which will also allow you to inspect the differential). If there's no bolt-on cover, look for a drain plug at the bottom of the differential housing. If there's not a drain plug and

no cover, you'll have to remove the lubricant through the filler plug hole with a suction pump. If you'll be draining the lubricant by removing the cover or a drain plug, move a drain pan, rags, newspapers and wrenches under the vehicle.

3 Remove the filler plug from the differential. If a suction pump is being used, insert the flexible hose. Work the hose down to the bottom of the differential housing and pump the lubricant out (see illustration). If you'll be draining the lubricant through a drain plug, remove the plug and allow the lubricant to drain into the pan, then reinstall the drain plug.

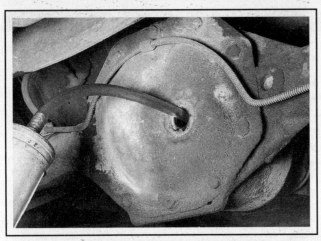

36.3 This is the easiest way to remove the lubricant: Remove the differential filler plug, then work the end of the hose to the bottom of the differential housing and draw out the old lubricant with a hand pump

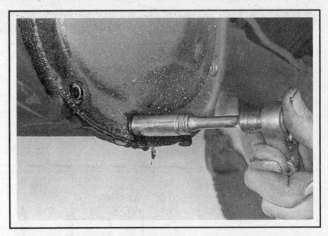

36.4a Remove the bolts from the lower edge of the cover . . .

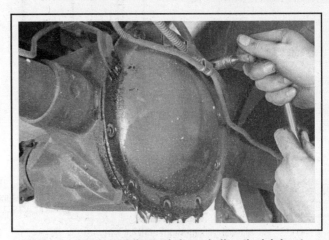

36.4b . . . then loosen the top bolts and allow the lubricant to drain out

4   If the differential is being drained by removing the cover plate, remove the bolts on the lower half of the plate. Loosen the bolts on the upper half and use them to keep the cover loosely attached. Allow the oil to drain into the pan, then completely remove the cover (see illustrations).

5   Using a lint-free rag, clean the inside of the cover and the accessible areas of the differential housing. As this is done, check for chipped gears and metal particles in the lubricant, indicating that the differential should be more thoroughly inspected and/or repaired.

6   Thoroughly clean the gasket mating surfaces of the differential housing and the cover plate. Use a gasket scraper or putty knife to remove all traces of the old gasket (see illustration).

7   Apply a thin layer of RTV sealant to the cover flange, then press a new gasket into position on the cover. Make sure the bolt holes align properly.

8   Place the cover on the differential housing and install the bolts. Tighten the bolts securely.

9   Use a hand pump, syringe or squeeze bottle to fill the differential housing with the specified lubricant until it's level with the bottom of the plug hole.

10 Install the filler plug and make sure it is secure.

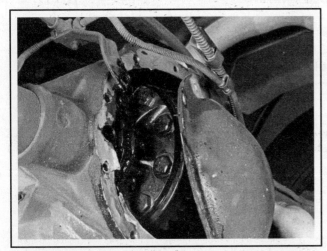

36.4c After the lubricant has drained, remove the remaining bolts and the cover

36.6 Carefully scrape the old gasket material off to ensure a leak-free seal

Recommended lubricants and fluids

➡Note: Listed here are manufacturer recommendations at the time this manual was written. Manufacturers occasionally upgrade their fluid and lubricant specifications, so check with your local auto parts store for current recommendations.

Engine oil type	API grade "certified for gasoline engines"
Engine oil viscosity	See accompanying chart

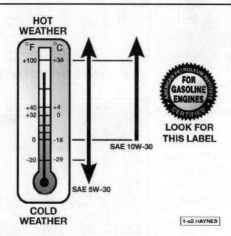

Engine oil viscosity chart - for best fuel economy and cold starting, select the lowest SAE viscosity grade for the expected temperature range

Automatic transmission fluid type	
2000 models	Mopar 7176 ATF Plus 3 or DEXRON III
2001 and later models	Mopar 9602 ATF Plus 4
Manual transmission lubricant type,	
NV1500 or NV3500	Mopar manual transmission lubricant part no. 4874464
Transfer case lubricant type	DEXRON III automatic transmission fluid
Differential lubricant type	SAE 75W-90, GL-5 gear lubricant or Mopar ATF+4
Limited slip differential	Add Mopar hypoid gear oil additive friction modifier, or equivalent, to the specified lubricant
Brake fluid type	DOT 3 brake fluid
Power steering fluid	Mopar power steering fluid or Mopar ATF+4
Chassis grease type	NLGI LB chassis grease
Front wheel bearing grease	NLGI GC high-temperature wheel bearing grease
Wheel bearings and chassis	NLGI GC-LB chassis grease

Capacities*

Cooling system	
Four-cylinder engine	9.8 qts
V6 engine	14.3 qts
5.2L/5.9L V8 engine	14.3 qts
4.7L V8 engine	17.0 qts
Engine oil (with filter change)	
Four-cylinder engine	4.5 qts
V6 engine	
2000 models	4.5 qts
2001 and later models	4.0 qts
5.2L/5.9L V8 engine	5.0 qts
4.7L V8 engine	6.0 qts

Automatic transmission
  Drain and refill
    42RE, 46RE   4.0 qts
    45RFE, 545RFE   5.0 qts
  Dry fill   9.0 to 14 qts (depending on model and options)
Manual transmission
  4WD   4.2 pts
  2WD   4.8 pts
Transfer case
  NP231 and NP231-HD   2.5 pts
  NP242 (Dakota)   2.5 pts
  NP242 (Durango)   3.0 pts
Front axle (4WD)
  2000   3.0 pts
  2001 through 2003   3.5 pts
Rear axle**
  8-1/4 inch
    2000   4.4 pts
    2001 through 2003   4.7 pts
  9-1/4 inch   4.9 pts

All capacities approximate. Add as necessary to bring up to the appropriate level.
**Add four ounces of friction modifier if equipped with a limited slip differential.*

Ignition system

Spark plug type
  Four-cylinder engine   Champion RC12ECC or equivalent
  V6 and 5.2L/5.9L V8 engines   Champion RC12LC4 or equivalent
  4.7L V8 engine   Champion RC12MCC4
Spark plug gap
  Four-cylinder engine   0.035 inch
  V6 and V8 engines   0.040 inch
Firing order
  Four-cylinder engine   1-3-4-2
  V6 engine   1-6-5-4-3-2
  V8 engine   1-8-4-3-6-5-7-2

4-cylinder engine

Four-cylinder engine cylinder location
and distributor rotation diagram

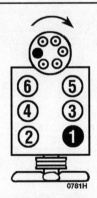

V6 engine

V6 engine cylinder location and
distributor rotation diagram

0782H

5.2L/5.9L V8 engines

V8 (5.2L/5.9L) engine cylinder
location and distributor rotation
diagram - 4.7L V8 engines use
an individual coil for each spark
plug instead of a distributor

The blackened terminal shown on the distributor cap indicates the Number One spark plug wire position

Brakes

Disc brake pad lining thickness (minimum)	1/8 inch
Drum brake shoe lining thickness (minimum)	
Riveted shoes (thickness above rivets)	1/32 inch
Bonded shoes	1/16 inch

Automatic transmission band adjustment

Front band	
42RE transmission (four-cylinder engine)	Tighten to 72 in-lbs, back off 3 turns
46RE transmission	Tighten to 72 in-lbs, back off 2-7/8 turns
45RFE transmission	NA
Rear band	
42RE transmission (four-cylinder engine)	Tighten to 72 in-lbs, back off 4 turns
46RE transmission	Tighten to 72 in-lbs, back off 2 turns
45RFE transmission	NA

Torque specifications   Ft-lbs (unless otherwise indicated)

Automatic transmission band adjusting screw locknut	
Front band	25
Rear band	30
Automatic transmission pan bolts	156 in-lbs
Differential cover bolts	30
Transfer case drain/fill plug	15 to 25
Manual transmission drain/fill plug	
NV1500	25
NV3500	14 to 20
Spark plugs	
All except 4.7L V8 engine	30
4.7L V8 engine	20
Engine oil drain plug	25
Oxygen sensor	22
Wheel lug nuts	85 to 115

Section

Reference to other Chapters

2A

FOUR-
CYLINDER
ENGINE

1 General information

This Part of Chapter 2 is devoted to in-vehicle repair procedures for the 2.5 liter inline four-cylinder engine. Information concerning engine removal and installation, as well as engine block and cylinder head overhaul, is in Part D of this Chapter.

The following repair procedures are based on the assumption that the engine is installed in the vehicle. If the engine has been removed from the vehicle and mounted on a stand, many of the steps included in this Part of Chapter 2 will not apply.

The Specifications included in this Part of Chapter 2 apply only to the engine and procedures in this Part. The Specifications necessary for rebuilding the block and cylinder head are found in Part D.

2 Repair operations possible with the engine in the vehicle

Many major repair operations can be accomplished without removing the engine from the vehicle.

Clean the engine compartment and the exterior of the engine with some type of pressure washer before any work is done. A clean engine will make the job easier and will help keep dirt out of the internal areas of the engine.

If vacuum, exhaust, oil or coolant leaks develop, indicating a need for gasket or seal replacement, the repairs can generally be made with the engine in the vehicle. The intake and exhaust manifold gaskets, oil pan gasket and cylinder head gasket are all accessible with the engine in place.

Exterior engine components such as the intake and exhaust mani-folds, the oil pan (and the oil pump), the water pump, the starter motor, the alternator, the distributor and the fuel injection components can be removed for repair with the engine in place.

Since the cylinder head can be removed without pulling the engine, valve component servicing can also be accomplished with the engine in the vehicle.

In extreme cases caused by a lack of necessary equipment, repair or replacement of piston rings, pistons, connecting rods and rod bearings is possible with the engine in the vehicle. However, this practice is not recommended because of the cleaning and preparation work that must be done to the components involved.

3 Top Dead Center (TDC) for number one piston - locating

⯈ **Refer to illustrations 3.5 and 3.9**

➥**Note: The following procedure is based on the assumption that the distributor is correctly installed. If you are trying to locate TDC to install the distributor correctly, piston position must be determined by feeling for compression at the number one spark plug hole, then aligning the ignition timing marks as described in Step 8.**

1   Top Dead Center (TDC) is the highest point in the cylinder that each piston reaches as it travels up-and-down when the crankshaft turns. Each piston reaches TDC on the compression stroke and again on the exhaust stroke, but TDC generally refers to piston position on the compression stroke.

2   Positioning the piston(s) at TDC is an essential part of many procedures such as rocker arm removal, camshaft and timing chain/sprocket removal and distributor removal.

3   Before beginning this procedure, be sure to place the transmission in Neutral and apply the parking brake or block the rear wheels. Also, remove the spark plugs (see Chapter 1) and disable the ignition system. Detach the coil wire from the center terminal of the distributor cap and ground it on the block with a jumper wire.

4   In order to bring any piston to TDC, the crankshaft must be turned using one of the methods outlined below. When looking at the front of the engine, normal crankshaft rotation is clockwise.

   a) *The preferred method is to turn the crankshaft with a socket and ratchet attached to the bolt threaded into the front of the crankshaft.*

   b) *A remote starter switch, which may save some time, can also be used. Follow the instructions included with the switch. Once the piston is close to TDC, use a socket and ratchet, as described in the previous paragraph.*

   c) *If an assistant is available to turn the ignition switch to the Start position in short bursts, you can get the piston close to TDC without a remote starter switch. Make sure your assistant is out of the vehicle, away from the ignition switch, then use a socket and ratchet (as described in Paragraph a) to complete the procedure.*

5   Note the position of the terminal for the number one spark plug wire on the distributor cap (see illustration). If the terminal isn't marked, follow the plug wire from the number one cylinder spark plug to the cap.

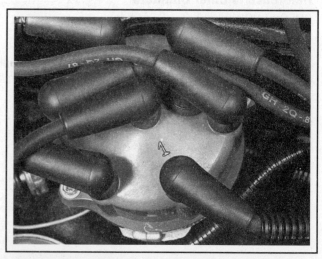

3.5 Locate the number one spark plug terminal on the distributor cap, then make a mark on the distributor housing directly under the number one plug terminal

6   Use a felt-tip pen or chalk to make a mark on the distributor body directly under the terminal.

7   Detach the cap from the distributor and set it aside (see Chapter 1 if necessary).

8   Turn the crankshaft (see Step 4) until the notch in the crankshaft pulley is aligned with the 0 on the timing plate (located at the front of the engine).

9   Look at the distributor rotor - it should be pointing directly at the mark you made on the distributor body (see illustration). If it is, proceed to Step 12.

10   If the rotor is 180-degrees off, the number one piston is at TDC on the exhaust stroke.

11   To get the piston to TDC on the compression stroke, turn the crankshaft one complete turn (360-degrees) clockwise. The rotor should now be pointing at the mark on the distributor. When the rotor is pointing at the number one spark plug wire terminal in the distributor cap and the ignition timing marks are aligned, the number one piston is at TDC on the compression stroke.

12   After the number one piston has been positioned at TDC on the compression stroke, TDC for any of the remaining pistons can be located by turning the crankshaft and following the firing order. Mark the remaining spark plug wire terminal locations on the distributor body just like you did for the number one terminal, then number the

3.9 Remove the distributor cap and verify that the rotor is pointing at the mark (arrow)

marks to correspond with the cylinder numbers. As you turn the crankshaft, the rotor will also turn. When it's pointing directly at one of the marks on the distributor, the piston for that particular cylinder is at TDC on the compression stroke.

4   Valve cover - removal and installation

▶ **Refer to illustration 4.4**

❊❊ **CAUTION:**

The valve cover gasket on these engines is an integral part of the valve cover. DO NOT scrape, peel or nick the sealing surface on the valve cover. If damaged is noted, replacement of the entire valve cover will be necessary.

1   Disconnect the negative cable from the battery.

2   Remove the fresh air inlet tube and the CCV hose from the valve cover.

3   Label and disconnect any remaining hoses, wires and cables as necessary to provide clearance for valve cover removal.

4   Remove the valve cover retaining bolts and lift off the cover.

➡**Note: If the cover is stuck to the head, bump the cover with a block of wood and a hammer to release it (see illustration). If it still will not come loose, try to slip a flexible putty knife between the head and cover to break the seal. Don't pry at the cover-to-head joint, as damage to the sealing surface and cover flange will result and oil leaks will develop.**

5   Prior to installation, remove all traces of dirt, oil and old gasket material from the cylinder head with a scraper. Clean the mating surfaces with lacquer thinner or acetone and a clean rag.

6   Inspect the mating surface on the cover for damage and warpage. Correct or replace as necessary.

7   The original dark gray gasket material on the cover should not be

4.4 Use a soft face hammer to break the cover loose - DO NOT pry between the cover and the cylinder head

removed. If sections of the gasket material are missing or are compressed, replace the cover. However, small sections with minor damage such as small cracks, cuts or chips may be repaired with a sealant. The new sealant material must be smoothed over to maintain gasket height. Allow the gasket material to cure prior to installing the cover.

8   The remainder of the installation is the reverse of removal.

9   Start the engine and check for oil leaks.

5 Rocker arms and pushrods - removal, inspection and installation

REMOVAL

▶ **Refer to illustration 5.4**

1 Detach the valve cover from the cylinder head (see Section 4).

2 Beginning at the front of the cylinder head, loosen the rocker arm cap screws, one turn at a time to avoid damage.

3 Remove the capscrews, bridges, pivots and rocker arms. Store them in marked containers (they must be reinstalled in their original locations).

4 Remove the pushrods and store them separately to make sure they don't get mixed up during installation (see illustration).

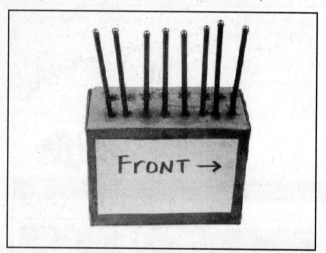

5.4 If more than one pushrod is being removed, store them in a perforated cardboard box to prevent mix-ups during installation - note the label indicating the front of the engine

INSPECTION

5 Check each rocker arm for wear, cracks and other damage, especially where the pushrods and valve stems contact the rocker arm faces.

6 Make sure the hole at the pushrod end of each rocker arm is open.

7 Check each rocker arm pivot area for wear, cracks and galling. If the rocker arms are worn or damaged, replace them with new ones and use new pivots as well.

8 Inspect the pushrods for cracks and excessive wear at the ends. Roll each pushrod across a piece of plate glass to see if it's bent (if it wobbles, it's bent).

INSTALLATION

9 Lubricate the lower ends of the pushrods with clean engine oil or moly-base grease and install them in their original locations. Make sure each pushrod seats completely in the lifter socket.

10 Apply moly-base grease to the ends of the valve stems and the upper ends of the pushrods before positioning the rocker arms and installing the capscrews.

11 Set the rocker arms in place, then install the pivots, bridges and capscrews. Apply moly-base grease to the pivots to prevent damage to the mating surfaces before engine oil pressure builds up. Tighten the bolts one turn at a time to the torque listed in this Chapter's Specifications.

12 Reinstall the valve cover and run the engine. Check for oil leaks and unusual valve train noises.

6 Valve springs, retainers and seals - replacement

▶ **Refer to illustrations 6.4, 6.8, 6.10 and 6.17**

➡**Note: Broken valve springs and defective valve stem seals can be replaced without removing the cylinder heads. Two special tools and a compressed air source are normally required to perform this operation, so read through this Section carefully and rent or buy the tools before beginning the job.**

1 Remove the valve cover referring to Section 4.

2 Remove the spark plug from the cylinder which has the defective component. If all of the valve stem seals are being replaced, all of the spark plugs should be removed.

3 Turn the crankshaft until the piston in the affected cylinder is at top dead center (TDC) on the compression stroke (see Section 3 for instructions). If you're replacing all of the valve stem seals, begin with cylinder number one and work on the valves for one cylinder at a time. Move from cylinder-to-cylinder following the firing order sequence (see the Specifications listed at the end of this Chapter).

4 Thread an adapter into the spark plug hole (see illustration) and connect an air hose from a compressed air source to it. Most auto parts stores can supply the air hose adapter.

➡**Note: Many cylinder compression gauges utilize a screw-in fitting that may work with your air hose quick-disconnect fitting.**

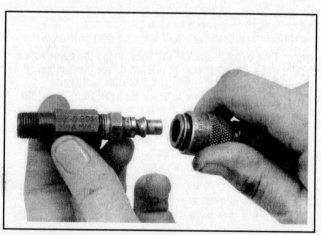

6.4 This is what the air hose adapter that threads into the spark plug hole looks like - they're commonly available at most auto parts stores

6.8 Once the spring is depressed, the keepers can be removed with a small magnet or needle-nose pliers (a magnet is preferred to prevent dropping the keepers)

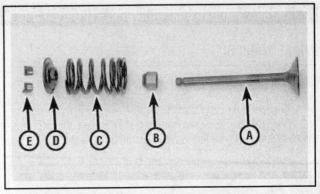

6.10 Valve and related components

A	Valve	D	Retainer
B	Valve stem seal	E	Keepers
C	Valve spring		

5   Remove the rocker arm and pivot for the valve with the defective part and pull out the pushrod. If all of the valve stem seals are being replaced, all of the rocker arms and pushrods should be removed (see Section 5).

6   Apply compressed air to the cylinder. The valves should be held in place by the air pressure.

❋❋ WARNING:

If the cylinder isn't exactly at TDC, air pressure may force the piston down, causing the engine to quickly rotate. DO NOT leave a wrench on the vibration damper bolt or you may be injured by the tool.

7   Stuff shop rags into the cylinder head holes around the valves to prevent parts and tools from falling into the engine.

8   Using a socket and a hammer gently tap on the top of the each valve spring retainer several times (this will break the bond between the valve keeper and the spring retainer and allow the keeper to separate from the valve spring retainer as the valve spring is compressed), then use a valve-spring compressor to compress the spring. Remove the keepers with small needle-nose pliers or a magnet (see illustration).

➡Note: Several different types of tools are available for compressing the valve springs with the head in place. One type grips the lower spring coils and presses on the retainer as the knob is turned, while the lever-type utilizes the rocker arm bolt for leverage. Both types work very well, although the lever type is usually less expensive.

9   Remove the valve spring and retainer.

➡Note: If air pressure fails to retain the valve in the closed position during this operation, the valve face or seat may be damaged. If so, the cylinder head will have to be removed for repair.

10 Remove the old valve stem seals, noting differences between the intake and exhaust seals (see illustration).

11 Wrap a rubber band or tape around the top of the valve stem so the valve won't fall into the combustion chamber, then release the air pressure.

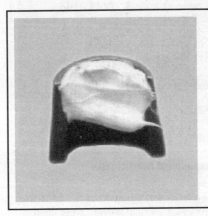

6.17 Apply a small dab of grease to the keepers before installation - it will hold them in place on the valve stem as the spring is released

12 Inspect the valve stem for damage. Rotate the valve in the guide and check the end for eccentric movement, which would indicate that the valve is bent.

13 Move the valve up-and-down in the guide and make sure it doesn't bind. If the valve stem binds, either the valve is bent or the guide is damaged. In either case, the head will have to be removed for repair.

14 Reapply air pressure to the cylinder to retain the valve in the closed position, then remove the tape or rubber band from the valve stem. If a rope was used instead of air pressure, rotate the crankshaft in the normal direction of rotation until slight resistance is felt.

15 Lubricate the valve stem with engine oil and install a new seal on the valve guide. Intake seals are marked "INT" and are black in color, while exhaust seals are brown and marked "EXH."

16 Install the spring in position over the valve.

17 Install the valve spring retainer. Compress the valve spring and carefully position the keepers in the groove. Apply a small dab of grease to the inside of each keeper to hold it in place (see illustration).

18 Remove the pressure from the spring tool and make sure the keepers are seated.

19 Disconnect the air hose and remove the adapter from the spark plug hole.

20 Refer to Section 5 and install the rocker arm(s) and pushrod(s).

21 Install the spark plug(s) and hook up the wire(s).

22 Refer to Section 4 and install the valve cover.

23 Start and run the engine, then check for oil leaks and unusual sounds coming from the valve cover area.

7   Intake and exhaust manifolds - removal and installation

INTAKE MANIFOLD

▶ **Refer to illustrations 7.7 and 7.9**

1   Disconnect the cable from the negative terminal of the battery.

2   Drain the cooling system (see Chapter 1). Remove the air cleaner assembly and relieve the fuel system pressure (see Chapter 4).

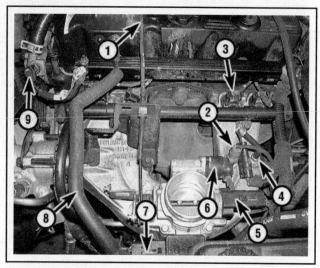

7.7 Typical engine compartment components

1   *Accelerator cable*
2   *Intake Air Temperature (IAT) sensor*
3   *Fuel injector(s)*
4   *Vacuum port*
5   *Throttle Position Sensor (TPS)*
6   *Idle Air Control (IAC) motor*
7   *Manifold Absolute Pressure (MAP) sensor*
8   *Crankcase Ventilation (CCV) hose*
9   *Electronic Coolant Temperature (ECT) sensor*

3   Remove the drivebelt (see Chapter 1).

4   Unbolt the power steering pump and brackets (if equipped) from the intake manifold and water pump, and set aside without disconnect-

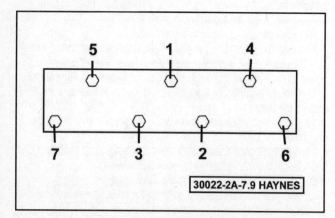

7.9 Intake and exhaust manifold tightening sequence

ing the hoses (see Chapter 10).

5   Disconnect the accelerator linkage (see Chapter 4) and, if equipped, the cruise control linkage. On models equipped with an automatic transmission, disconnect the kickdown cable at the throttle body.

6   Disconnect any vacuum hoses attached to the intake manifold or throttle body such as the power brake booster, the crankcase ventilation (CCV) and molded vacuum harness.

7   Disconnect the electrical connectors from the IAC valve, IAT, TPS, MAP and the coolant temperature sensors (see illustration). Disconnect the O2 sensor and the crankshaft position sensor electrical connectors from the bracket at the rear of the manifold. Disconnect the connectors from the fuel injectors and pull the electrical harness away from the manifold.

8   Remove the fuel rail and fuel injectors as an assembly (see Chapter 4).

9   Remove bolts number two through five, then loosen (but DO NOT remove) bolts number one and nuts number six and seven (see illustration).

10 Remove the intake manifold and gaskets from the cylinder head and locating dowels. If the manifold sticks to the cylinder head after all bolts have been removed, tap it with a soft-faced mallet or a block of wood and hammer while supporting the manifold.

11 Thoroughly clean the mating surfaces, removing all traces of gasket material.

12 If the manifold is replaced, transfer all fittings to the new one.

13 Position the new manifold gaskets on the cylinder head and install the intake manifold.

14 Tighten the intake manifold bolts (along with the exhaust manifold bolts and nuts) in several stages in the sequence shown to the torque listed in this Chapter's Specifications (see illustration 7.9).

15 Install the remaining parts in the reverse order of removal.

16 Run the engine and check for vacuum leaks and proper operation.

EXHAUST MANIFOLD

✳ WARNING:

Allow the engine to cool to room temperature before performing this procedure.

17 Raise the vehicle and place it securely on jackstands.

18 Remove the two nuts securing the exhaust pipe to the exhaust manifold. It may be necessary to apply penetrating oil to the threads.

19 Lower the vehicle.

20 Remove the intake manifold (see Steps 1 through 10).

21 Remove bolt number one and nuts number six and seven and spacers (see illustration 7.9).

22 Remove the exhaust manifold and gaskets from the cylinder head. If the manifold sticks to the cylinder head after all bolts have been removed, tap it with a soft-faced mallet or a block of wood and hammer while supporting the manifold.

23 Thoroughly clean the mating surfaces, removing all traces of gasket material.

24 Position the new manifold gaskets on the cylinder head locating dowels, then install the exhaust manifold and spacers.

➡**Note: The exhaust manifold must be centered over the end studs and spacers prior to installing the nuts. Finger tighten the nuts on the end studs.**

25 Install the intake manifold (see Steps 11 through 16). Tighten the bolts and nuts in several stages in the sequence shown to the torque listed in this Chapter's Specifications (see illustration 7.9).

26 Install the remaining parts in the reverse order of removal.

27 Run the engine and check for exhaust leaks.

8   Cylinder head - removal and installation

▸ **Refer to illustrations 8.9, 8.12 and 8.13**

❊❊ WARNING:

Allow the engine to cool to room temperature before following this procedure.

1 Remove the valve cover, rocker arms and pushrods (see Sections 4 and 5).

2 Remove the drivebelt as described in Chapter 1.

3 Unbolt the power steering pump (if equipped) and set it aside without disconnecting the hoses.

4 Remove the intake and exhaust manifolds (see Section 7).

5 On air-conditioned models, remove the bolts that secure the air conditioning compressor bracket to the engine, then remove the through bolt that secures the alternator to the air conditioning compressor bracket. Set the compressor aside without disconnecting the hoses.

6 Label, then disconnect the wire from the coolant temperature sending unit on the cylinder head (if not already done).

7 Label the spark plug wires and remove the spark plugs.

8 Remove the ignition coil and bracket from the cylinder head.

9 Remove the cylinder head retaining bolts and lift the head off the engine (see illustration). If the head is stuck to the engine block, it may be necessary to tap it with a soft-face hammer or a block of wood and a hammer to break the seal.

❊❊ CAUTION:

The manufacturer recommends replacing the cylinder head bolts any time the cylinder head is removed.

10 Stuff clean shop towels into the cylinders to keep debris from falling into the engine Thoroughly clean the gasket surfaces, removing all traces of gasket material. Run an appropriate sized tap into the cylinder head bolt holes of the engine block. Ensure all bolt holes are clean and dry.

11 Inspect the cylinder head for cracks and check it for warpage. Refer to Chapter 2, Part C, for cylinder head servicing procedures.

12 Install the new gasket with the word TOP (see illustration) on the cylinder head side. Place the cylinder head on the engine.

13 Install new cylinder head bolts and coat the threads of the No. 7 bolt (in tightening sequence) with Loctite Pipe Sealant with Teflon no. 592 (or equivalent). Tighten the bolts in steps to the sequence shown (see illustration) and to the torque listed in this Chapter's Specifications.

❊❊ CAUTION 1:

During the final tightening step, bolt No. 7 is tightened to a lower torque than the other bolts. DO Not overtighten bolt No. 7.

8.9 If necessary, use a prybar to separate the cylinder head from the block. Be sure not to damage any gasket surfaces while applying pressure on the tool

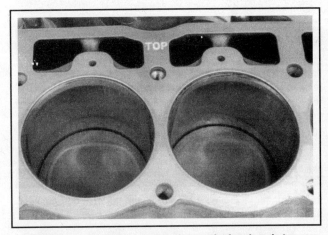

8.12 Be sure the "TOP" designation on the head gasket faces up

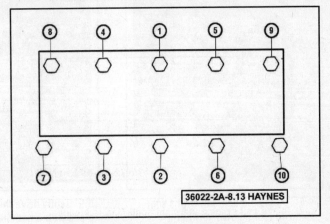

36022-2A-8.13 HAYNES

8.13 Cylinder head bolt tightening sequence

The manufacturer recommends replacing the cylinder head bolts any time the cylinder head is removed.

14   Install the remaining components in the reverse order of removal.
15   Change the oil and filter (see Chapter 1).
16   Refill the cooling system and run the engine, checking for leaks and proper operation.

9   Crankshaft front oil seal - replacement

▶ Refer to illustrations 9.5, 9.7, 9.9 and 9.10

➡Note: The crankshaft front oil seal can be replaced with the timing chain cover in place. However, due to the limited amount of room available, you may conclude that the procedure would be easier if the cover were removed from the engine first. If so, refer to Section 10 for the cover removal and installation procedure.

1   Disconnect the cable from the negative terminal of the battery.
2   Remove the drivebelt (see Chapter 1). Unscrew the fan shroud mounting bolts and position the shroud out of the way.
3   Raise the vehicle and place it securely on jackstands.
4   Remove the large vibration damper-to-crankshaft bolt. To keep the crankshaft from turning, remove the starter (see Chapter 5) or the transmission inspection cover and have an assistant wedge a large screwdriver against the ring gear teeth.
5   Using the proper puller (commonly available from auto parts stores), detach the vibration damper from the crankshaft (see illustration).

⁂ **CAUTION:**

Do not use a puller with jaws that grip the outer edge of the damper. The puller must be the type that utilizes bolts to apply force to the center of the damper hub only.

6   If the seal is being replaced with the timing chain cover removed, support the cover on top of two blocks of wood and drive the seal out from the backside with a hammer and punch.

⁂ **CAUTION:**

Be careful not to scratch, gouge or distort the area that the seal fits into or a leak will develop.

9.5 Use a vibration damper removal tool such as this one - do not use a gear puller with jaws; it will damage the damper

7   If the seal is being removed while the cover is still attached to the engine block, carefully pry the seal out of the cover with a seal removal tool or a large screwdriver (see illustration).

⁂ **CAUTION:**

Be careful not to scratch, gouge or distort the area that the seal fits into or an oil leak will develop.

8   Clean the bore to remove any old seal material and corrosion. Position the new seal in the bore with the seal lip (the side with the spring) facing IN (toward the engine). A small amount of oil applied to the outer edge of the new seal will make installation easier.
9   Place the seal in the cover with the lip (open end) facing in, then

9.7 Pry the old seal out with a seal removal tool (shown here) or a screwdriver

9.9 Gently drive the new seal into place with a hammer and large socket

9.10 If the sealing surface of the damper hub has a wear groove from contact with the seal, repair sleeves are available at most auto parts stores

drive the seal into the bore with a large socket and hammer until it's completely seated (see illustration). Select a socket that's the same outside diameter as the seal and make sure the new seal is pressed into place until it bottoms against the cover flange.

10 Check the surface of the damper that the oil seal rides on. If the surface has been grooved from long-time contact with the seal, a press-on sleeve may be available to renew the sealing surface (see illustration). This sleeve is pressed into place with a hammer and a

block of wood and is commonly available from auto parts stores.

11 Secure the Woodruff key in its groove in the crankshaft using RTV sealant. Lubricate the seal lips with engine oil and reinstall the vibration damper.

12 Install the vibration damper-to-crank-shaft bolt and tighten it to the torque listed in this Chapter's Specifications.

13 The remainder of installation is the reverse of the removal.

10 Timing chain cover - removal and installation

▶ **Refer to illustration 10.10**

1 Remove the vibration damper (see Section 9, Steps 1 through 5).

2 Remove the fan and the water pump pulley (see Chapter 3).

3 Remove the air conditioning compressor (if equipped). Set the compressor aside without disconnecting the hoses. Remove the air conditioning/alternator bracket from the cylinder head. Remove the accessory drive bracket, if equipped.

4 Remove the oil pan-to-timing chain cover bolts and the timing chain cover-to-block bolts and stud nuts.

5 Separate the timing chain cover from the engine. Avoid damaging the sealing surfaces; do not force tools between the cover and block.

6 Thoroughly clean the cover and all sealing surfaces, removing any traces of gasket material. Drive the old oil seal out from the rear of the timing chain cover and replace it with a new one (see Section 9).

7 Trim the end tabs off the new oil pan gaskets to correspond with those cut off the original gasket. Attach the new end tabs to the oil pan with cement.

8 Coat the timing chain cover-to-oil pan end seal tab recesses generously with RTV sealant and position the seal onto the oil pan.

9 Position the timing chain cover on the engine block.

10 Partially install the vibration damper to center the timing chain cover (see illustration). Install several cover-to-engine block bolts and tighten them finger tight (just enough to hold the cover in place).

11 Remove the vibration damper and install the remaining cover-to-

block bolts and the oil pan-to-cover bolts and tighten them to the torque listed in this Chapter's Specifications.

12 Reinstall the remaining parts in the reverse order of removal.

13 Run the engine and check for oil leaks.

10.10 Partially install the vibration damper to center the timing chain cover, install the upper mounting bolts to hold the cover in place, then remove the damper and install the remaining bolts

11 Timing chain and sprockets - removal, inspection and installation

▶ **Refer to illustrations 11.4, 11.5, 11.6a and 11.6b**

1 Set the number one piston at Top Dead Center (TDC) (see Section 3).

2 Remove the timing chain cover (see Section 10) slightly loosen the camshaft sprocket retaining bolt.

3 Slide the oil slinger off the crankshaft.

4 Reinstall the vibration damper bolt and rotate the crankshaft until the zero timing mark on the crankshaft sprocket is lined up with the timing mark on the camshaft sprocket (see illustration).

11.4 The timing marks on the sprockets (arrows) should be lined up as shown

11.5 While compressing the tensioner with one screwdriver, lock the mechanism with the other screwdriver

11.6a Remove the thrust pin and spring (arrow), then remove the bolt in the center of the camshaft sprocket

5   Turn the tensioner lever to the unlock position. Pull the tensioner block toward the tensioner lever to compress the spring. Hold the block and turn the tensioner lever to the lock position (see illustration).

6   Remove the camshaft thrust pin and spring and the sprocket-retaining bolt and washer (see illustration). Slip both sprockets and the chain off as an assembly (see illustration).

7   Clean the components and inspect for wear and damage. Excessive chain slack and teeth that are deformed, chipped, pitted or discolored call for replacement. Always replace the sprockets and chain as a set. Inspect the tensioner for excessive wear and replace it, if necessary.

➡ **Note 1: If tensioner replacement is necessary it will require removal of the oil pan (see Section 13). Inspect the camshaft pin for damage and replace it, if necessary.**

➡ **Note 2: Broken spring loaded type camshaft pins can be removed by tightening a self-tapping screw into the end of the pin and pulling the pin out. Broken dowel type camshaft pins will require removal of the camshaft (see Section 12) because of inadequate space in the engine compartment. Once the camshaft is removed the dowel pin can be drilled out using a 5/32-inch drill bit.**

8   Install the crankshaft/camshaft sprockets and timing chain. Ensure the marks on the sprockets are still properly aligned (see illustration 11.4).

9   Install the camshaft sprocket retaining bolt and washer and tighten to the torque listed in this Chapter's Specifications.

10 To verify correct installation of the timing chain, turn the crank-

11.6b The timing chain and sprockets are removed and installed as an assembly

shaft to place the camshaft sprocket timing mark at approximately the two o'clock position. This positions the crankshaft timing mark where the adjacent tooth meshes with the chain at the five thirty o'clock position. Count the number of chain pins between the timing marks of both sprockets. There must be 20 pins.

11 Release the tensioner by turning the lever to the unlock position. Be sure the tensioner is released before installing the timing cover.

12 Install the oil slinger and the remaining parts in the reverse order of removal. Refer to the appropriate sections for instructions.

12   Camshaft and lifters - removal and installation

➡ **Note: To determine the extent of cam lobe wear, the lobe lift should be checked prior to camshaft removal. Camshaft and lifter inspection procedures can be found in Chapter 2D.**

REMOVAL

▸ **Refer to illustrations 12.5, 12.6 and 12.7**

1   Disconnect the cable from the negative terminal of the battery.

2   Remove the radiator and air conditioning condenser if equipped (see Chapter 3).

3   Remove the distributor (see Chapter 5).

4   Refer to the appropriate Sections and remove the valve cover, rocker arms, pushrods and the timing chain and sprockets.

5   There are several ways to extract the lifters from the bores. A special tool designed to grip and remove lifters is manufactured by many tool companies and is widely available, but it may not be required in every case (see illustration). On newer engines without a lot

12.5 Removing lifters with special tool

12.6 If you're removing more than one lifter, keep them in order in a clearly labeled box

12.7 Support the camshaft near the block

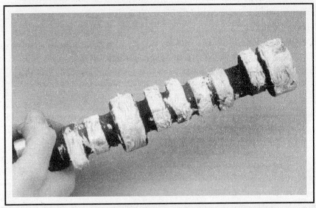

12.8 Be sure to apply camshaft installation lube to the cam lobes and bearing journals before installing the camshaft

of varnish buildup, the lifters can often be removed with a small magnet or even with your fingers. A machinist's scribe with a bent end can be used to pull the lifters out by positioning the point under the retainer ring inside the top of each lifter.

✳✳ CAUTION:

Do not use pliers to remove the lifters unless you intend to replace them with new ones.

6 Remove the lifters from the engine block. Store the lifters in a clearly labeled box to ensure that they are reinstalled in their original locations (see illustration).

7 Install a bolt in the end of the camshaft to use as a handle. Carefully slide the camshaft out of the block.

✳✳ CAUTION:

To avoid damage to the camshaft bearings as the lobes pass over them, support the camshaft near the block as it is withdrawn (see illustration).

➡Note: If the camshaft appears to have been rubbing against the timing chain cover, examine the oil pressure relief holes in the rear cam journal and ensure they are free of debris.

INSTALLATION

▶ Refer to illustration 12.8

8 Lubricate the camshaft bearing journals and lobes with camshaft installation lube (see illustration).

9 Slide the camshaft into the engine. Support the cam near the block and be careful not to scrape or nick the bearings.

10 Temporarily place the camshaft sprocket onto the camshaft and turn the camshaft until the timing mark is aligned with the centerline of the crankshaft (see Section 11). Remove the sprocket.

11 Install the lifters, timing chain and sprockets and the remaining components in the reverse order of removal. Refer to the appropriate Sections for installation instructions.

➡Note: If the original cam and lifters are being reinstalled, be sure to install the lifters in their original locations. If a new camshaft was installed, be sure to install new lifters.

12 Add coolant and change the oil and filter (see Chapter 1).

13 Start the engine and check for leaks and unusual noises.

13 Oil pan - removal and installation

▶ **Refer to illustration 13.8**

1 Disconnect the cable from the negative terminal of the battery.

2 Raise the vehicle and support it securely on jackstands.

3 Drain the engine oil and remove the oil filter (see Chapter 1).

4 Disconnect the exhaust pipe at the catalytic converter and lower pipe (see Chapter 4) and hangers and tie the system aside.

5 Remove the starter (see Chapter 5) and the bellhousing inspection cover.

6 Support the engine from above with an engine hoist, take the weight off the engine mounts with the hoist and remove the engine mount through-bolts (see Section 17).

7 Raise the engine sufficiently to allow access for oil pan removal.

8 Where the transmission cooler lines are mounted along the oil pan rail, disconnect them from the oil pan studs and set them aside. Remove the bolts (see illustration) and detach the oil pan. Don't pry between the block and pan or damage to the sealing surfaces may result and oil leaks could develop. If the pan is stuck, dislodge it with a soft-face hammer or a block of wood and a hammer.

9 Use a scraper to remove all traces of sealant from the pan and block, then clean the mating surfaces with lacquer thinner or acetone.

10 Install the new gasket onto the cylinder block and timing chain cover. At the four corners where the gaskets meet the front cover and rear main cap, apply a small bead of RTV sealant.

11 Install the oil pan and tighten the mounting bolts to the torque listed in this Chapter's Specifications. Note that the 1/4-inch diameter

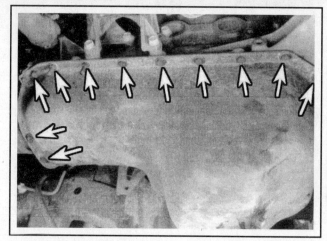

13.8 Remove the bolts from the perimeter of the oil pan

and 5/16-inch diameter bolts have different torques. Start at the center of the pan and work out toward the ends in a spiral pattern.

12 Install the bellhousing dust cover and the starter, then reconnect the exhaust pipe to the manifold and hanger brackets.

13 Lower the vehicle.

14 Install a new filter and add oil to the engine.

15 Reconnect the negative battery cable.

16 Start the engine and check for leaks.

14 Oil pump - removal and installation

1 Remove the oil pan (see Section 13).

2 Remove the two oil pump attaching bolts from the engine block.

3 Detach the oil pump and strainer assembly from the block.

✳✳ CAUTION:

DO NOT disturb the position of the oil pump pick-up tube. If the tube is moved for any reason, the manufacturer recommends replacing it with a new one to assure an air tight seal between the pump body and the pick-up tube.

4 If the pump is defective, replace it with a new one. If the engine is being completely overhauled, install a new oil pump - don't reuse the original or attempt to rebuild it.

5 To install the pump, turn the shaft so the gear tang mates with the slot on the lower end of the distributor drive. The oil pump should slide easily into place. If it doesn't, pull it off and turn the tang until it's aligned with the distributor drive.

6 Install a new gasket and the pump attaching bolts. Tighten them to the torque listed in this Chapter's Specifications.

7 Reinstall the oil pan (see Section 13).

8 Add oil, run the engine and check for leaks.

15 Rear main oil seal - replacement

▶ **Refer to illustration 15.8**

1 The rear main bearing oil seal can be replaced without removing the oil pan or crankshaft.

2 Remove the transmission (see Chapter 7).

3 If equipped with a manual transmission, remove the pressure plate and clutch disc (see Chapter 8).

4 Remove the flywheel or driveplate (see Section 16).

5 Using a seal removal tool or a large screwdriver, carefully pry the seal out of the block. Don't scratch or nick the crankshaft in the process.

6 Clean the bore in the block and the seal contact surface on the crankshaft. Check the crankshaft surface for scratches and nicks that could damage the new seal lip and cause oil leaks. If the crankshaft is damaged, the only alternative is a new or different crankshaft.

7 Apply a light coat of engine oil or multi-purpose grease to the

seal lip and to the outer edge of the new seal.

8   Carefully work the seal lip over the end of the crankshaft, then tap the new seal into place with a hammer and a large socket (if available) or a punch (see illustration). The seal lip must face toward the front of the engine and the outer (felt) lip must not protrude past the flywheel mounting surface.

9   Install the flywheel or driveplate, using new bolts (see Section 16).

10   If equipped with a manual transmission, reinstall the clutch disc and pressure plate.

11   Reinstall the transmission as described in Chapter 7.

15.8 If a socket isn't available, tap around the outer edge of the new seal with a hammer and punch to seat it squarely in the bore (typical installation shown)

16 Flywheel/driveplate - removal and installation

▶ **Refer to illustrations 16.3 and 16.4**

1   Raise the vehicle and support it securely on jackstands, then refer to Chapter 7 and remove the transmission.

2   Remove the pressure plate and clutch disc (see Chapter 8) (manual transmission equipped vehicles). Now is a good time to check/replace the clutch components and pilot bearing.

3   Use paint or a center-punch to make alignment marks on the flywheel/driveplate and crankshaft to ensure correct alignment during reinstallation (see illustration).

4   Remove the bolts that secure the flywheel/driveplate to the crankshaft (see illustration). Discard the bolts, as they cannot be reused. If the crankshaft turns, hold the flywheel with a pry bar or wedge a screwdriver into the ring gear teeth to jam the flywheel.

5   Remove the flywheel/driveplate from the crankshaft. Since the flywheel is fairly heavy, be sure to support it while removing the last bolt.

6   Clean the flywheel to remove grease and oil. Inspect the surface for cracks, rivet grooves, burned areas and score marks. Light scoring can be removed with emery cloth. Check for cracked and broken ring

gear teeth or a loose ring gear. Lay the flywheel on a flat surface and use a straightedge to check for warpage.

7   Clean and inspect the mating surfaces of the flywheel/driveplate and the crankshaft. If the crankshaft rear seal is leaking, replace it before reinstalling the flywheel/driveplate.

8   Position the flywheel/driveplate against the crankshaft. Be sure to align the marks made during removal. Note that some engines have an alignment dowel or staggered bolt holes to ensure correct installation. Before installing the new bolts, apply thread locking compound to the threads.

✳✳ CAUTION:

The flywheel mounting bolts should only be used once. Replace the bolts if they were used before.

9   Wedge a screwdriver into the ring gear teeth to keep the flywheel/driveplate from turning as you tighten the bolts to the torque listed in this Chapter's Specifications.

10   The remainder of installation is the reverse of the removal.

16.3 Before removing the flywheel, index it to the crankshaft (arrow)

16.4 To prevent the flywheel from turning, hold a pry bar against two bolts or wedge a large screwdriver into the flywheel ring gear

17 Engine mounts - check and replacement

1 Engine mounts seldom require attention, but broken or deteriorated mounts should be replaced immediately or the added strain placed on the driveline components may cause damage or wear.

CHECK

2 During the check, the engine must be raised slightly to remove the weight from the mounts.

3 Raise the vehicle and support it securely on jackstands, then position a jack under the engine oil pan. Place a large block of wood between the jack head and the oil pan, then carefully raise the engine just enough to take the weight off the mounts.

✳✳ WARNING:

DO NOT place any part of your body under the engine when it's supported only by a jack!

4 Check for relative movement between the mount plates and the engine or frame (use a large screwdriver or prybar to attempt to move the mounts). If movement is noted, lower the engine and tighten the mount fasteners.

5 Check the mounts to see if the rubber is cracked, hardened or separated from the metal plates which would indicate a need for replacement.

6 Rubber preservative should be applied to the mounts to slow deterioration.

REPLACEMENT

7 Disconnect the cable from the negative terminal of the battery, then raise the vehicle and support it securely on jackstands (if not already done).

8 Raise the engine slightly with a jack or hoist (make sure the fan doesn't hit the radiator or shroud). Remove the bolt and nut that secure the mount to the frame bracket.

9 Remove the nuts and bolts securing the mount to engine block and detach the mount.

10 Installation is the reverse of removal. Use thread locking compound on the mount bolts and be sure to tighten them securely.

Specifications

General

Displacement	150 cubic inches (2.5 liters)
Bore and stroke	3.88 x 3.19 inches
Cylinder numbers (front-to-rear)	1-2-3-4
Firing order	1-3-4-2
Distributor rotation (viewed from above)	Clockwise
Cylinder compression pressure	
Normal operating range	120 to 150 psi
Minimum	100 psi
Maximum variation between cylinders	30 psi

4-cylinder engine

Cylinder location and distributor rotation

The blackened terminal shown on the distributor cap indicates the Number One spark plug wire position

Camshaft

Journal diameter	
No. 1	2.029 to 2.030 inch
No. 2	2.019 to 2.020 inch
No. 3	2.009 to 2.010 inch
No. 4	1.999 to 2.000 inch
Endplay	None
Lobe lift	
Intake	0.254 inch
Exhaust	0.259 inch
Valve lift	
Intake	0.4145 inch
Exhaust	0.4075 inch

Oil pump

Minimum pressure at curb idle	13 psi
Operating pressure	37 to 75 psi at 1600 rpm or above

Torque specifications — Ft-lbs (unless otherwise indicated)

Camshaft sprocket bolt	80
Cylinder head bolts (in sequence - see illustration 8.13)	
Bolts 1 through 6 and 8, 9, 10	110
Bolt 7	100
Flywheel-to-crankshaft bolts	
Step 1	50
Step 2	Turn an additional 60-degrees
Intake and exhaust manifold bolts	
Bolt 1	30
Bolts 2 through 5	23
Nuts 6 and 7	126 in-lbs
Oil pan mounting bolts	
1/4 x 20	84 in-lbs
5/16 x 18	132 in-lbs

Torque specifications	Ft-lbs (unless otherwise indicated)
Oil pump bolts	17
Rocker arm capscrews	21
Valve cover-to-cylinder head bolts	115 in-lbs
Timing chain tensioner-to-block bolt	168 in-lbs
Timing chain cover-to-block bolts	
1/4 inch	60 in-lbs
5/16 inch	192 in-lbs
Vibration damper bolt	80

2B

V6 AND
5.2L/5.9L
V8 ENGINES

Section

Reference to other Chapters

1   General information

This part of Chapter 2 is devoted to in-vehicle repair procedures for V6 and V8 engines. All information concerning engine removal and installation and engine block and cylinder head overhaul can be found in Part D of this Chapter.

Since the repair procedures included in this Part are based on the assumption that the engine is still installed in the vehicle, if they are being used during a complete engine overhaul (with the engine already out of the vehicle and on a stand) many of the steps included here will not apply.

The specifications included in this Part of Chapter 2 apply only to the procedures found here. The specifications necessary for rebuilding the block and cylinder heads are included in Part D.

Though the engines covered vary greatly in displacement, they all share the same basic design. The 5.2L and 5.9L V8's have been in the corporate line for decades, and the V6 is basically the same design without two of the cylinders.

2   Repair operations possible with the engine in the vehicle

Many major repair operations can be accomplished without removing the engine from the vehicle.

Clean the engine compartment and the exterior of the engine with some type of pressure washer before any work is done. A clean engine will make the job easier and will help keep dirt out of the internal areas of the engine.

Depending on the components involved, it may be a good idea to remove the hood to improve access to the engine as repairs are performed (refer to Chapter 11 if necessary).

If oil or coolant leaks develop, indicating a need for gasket or seal replacement, the repairs can generally be made with the engine in the vehicle. The oil pan gasket, the cylinder head gaskets, intake and exhaust manifold gaskets, timing chain cover gaskets and the crankshaft oil seals are all accessible with the engine in place.

Exterior engine components, such as the water pump, the starter motor, the alternator, the distributor and the fuel injection components, as well as the intake and exhaust manifolds, can be removed for repair with the engine in place.

Since the cylinder heads can be removed without removing the engine, valve component servicing can also be accomplished with the engine in the vehicle.

Inspection or replacement of the timing chain and sprockets and the oil pump is possible with the engine in place.

In extreme cases caused by a lack of necessary equipment, repair or replacement of piston rings, pistons, connecting rods and rod bearings is possible with the engine in the vehicle. However, this practice is not recommended because of the cleaning and preparation work that must be done to the components involved.

3   Top Dead Center (TDC) for number one piston - locating

▶ **Refer to illustrations 3.4, 3.6 and 3.7**

1   Top Dead Center (TDC) is the highest point in the cylinder that each piston reaches as it travels up-and-down when the crankshaft turns. Each piston reaches TDC on the compression stroke and again on the exhaust stroke, but TDC generally refers to piston position on the compression stroke. The timing marks at the front of the engine are referenced to the number one piston at TDC on the compression stroke.

2   Positioning the pistons at TDC is an essential part of many procedures such as camshaft removal, timing chain replacement and distributor removal.

3   In order to bring any piston to TDC, the crankshaft must be turned using one of the methods outlined below. When looking at the front of the engine, normal crankshaft rotation is clockwise.

❊❊ **WARNING:**

Before beginning this procedure, be sure to place the transmission in Neutral (manual) or Park (automatic), apply the parking brake and block the wheels. Disable the ignition system by disconnecting the coil wire from the distributor cap and grounding it on the engine block.

4   Scribe or paint a small mark on the distributor body directly

below the number one spark plug wire terminal in the distributor cap (see illustration).

5   Remove the distributor cap as described in Chapter 1 and position it aside with the spark plug wires attached.

3.4 Mark the base of the distributor below the number one spark plug terminal (arrows)

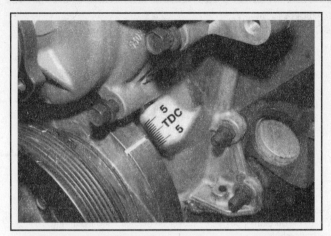

3.6 Align the full-width groove on the damper with the "0" or "TDC" marks on the timing cover

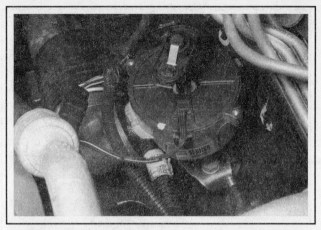

3.7 When the rotor is pointing at the number one spark plug wire terminal in the distributor cap (which is indicated by the mark on the distributor body) and the timing marks are aligned, the number one piston is at TDC on the compression stroke

6   Turn the crankshaft with a large socket and breaker bar attached to the large bolt that is threaded into the damper until the line on the vibration damper is aligned with the zero or "TDC" mark on the timing indicator (see illustration).

7   The rotor should now be pointing directly at the mark on the distributor body (see illustration).

8   If the rotor is 180-degrees off, the piston is at TDC on the exhaust stroke, turn the crankshaft one complete turn (360-degrees) clockwise to position it at TDC on the compression stroke. The rotor should now be pointing at the mark. When the rotor is pointing at the number one spark plug wire terminal in the distributor cap (which is indicated by the mark on the distributor body) and the timing marks are aligned, the number one piston is at TDC on the compression stroke.

9   After the number one piston has been positioned at TDC on the compression stroke, TDC for any of the remaining cylinders can be located by rotating the crankshaft, in the normal direction of rotation,

until the distributor rotor is pointing to the distributor cap spark plug wire terminal and following the firing order.

➡Note: You can also mark the vibration damper every 120-degrees (V6) or 90-degrees (V8) from TDC. After TDC for number 1 is found, rotate the crankshaft to the first mark to locate TDC for the next cylinder in the firing order, etc.

10   An alternative method to locating TDC can be performed as follows: Remove the number 1 spark plug. Disable the ignition as described in Step 3. Place a finger over the number 1 spark plug hole and rotate the crankshaft with a breaker bar until compression pressure is felt being expelled from the spark plug hole. Continue rotating the crankshaft until the TDC mark lines up. This will be TDC for number 1 piston.

---

4   Valve covers - removal and installation

REMOVAL

▶ Refer to illustrations 4.6 and 4.7

1   Disconnect the cable from the negative terminal of the battery.

2   If you're removing the right (passenger's side) valve cover, remove the air cleaner duct.

3   Remove the spark plug wires from the spark plugs, labeling them if necessary for correct installation (see Chapter 1).

4   Remove the breather tube or PCV valve and hose from the valve cover. Remove or position aside any remaining hoses such as the power brake booster vacuum hose, the heater hoses and the evaporative emission hoses that would interfere with the removal of the valve cover(s).

5   Remove the plastic spark plug wire holders from the valve cover studs and position the holders/wires out of the way.

✳✳ CAUTION:

Pull straight up on the plastic holders - they can easily break if pulled at an angle.

6   Remove the valve cover mounting bolts.

➡Note: Some of the fasteners have studs - mark the valve covers at each stud so they can be installed in the proper location (see illustration).

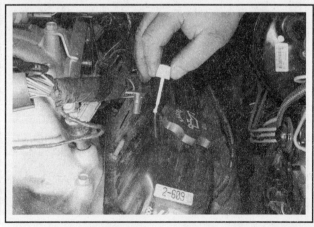

4.6 Remove the valve cover mounting bolts - some fasteners have studs, so mark their locations before removal

4.7 After striking the valve cover with a rubber mallet to break it loose, pull it straight up

7   Remove the valve cover (see illustration).

➡**Note: If the cover is stuck to the head, bump the cover with a block of wood and a hammer to release it. If it still will not come loose, try to slip a flexible putty knife between the head and cover to break the seal. Don't pry at the cover-to-head joint, as damage to the sealing surface and cover flange will result and oil leaks will develop.**

INSTALLATION

8   The mating surfaces of each cylinder head and valve cover must be perfectly clean when the covers are installed. Use a gasket scraper to remove all traces of sealant or old gasket, then wipe the mating surfaces with a cloth saturated with lacquer thinner or acetone. If there is sealant or oil on the mating surfaces when the cover is installed, oil leaks may develop.

➡**Note: The steel-backed silicone gaskets can be reused if they haven't been damaged.**

9   Make sure all threaded holes are clean. Run a tap into them to remove corrosion and restore damaged threads.

10 Mate the gaskets to the heads before installing the covers.

11 Carefully position the cover on the head and install the bolts/studs.

12 Tighten the bolts/studs in three steps to the torque listed in this Chapter's Specifications.

✳✳ CAUTION:

DON'T over-tighten the valve cover bolts.

13 The remaining installation steps are the reverse of removal.

14 Start the engine and check carefully for oil leaks as the engine warms up.

5   Rocker arms and pushrods - removal, inspection and installation

REMOVAL

▶ **Refer to illustrations 5.2 and 5.3**

1   Label and remove each spark plug wire from the spark plugs (see Chapter 1 if necessary). Refer to Section 4 and detach the valve covers from the cylinder heads.

2   Loosen the rocker arm pivot bolts one at a time and detach the rocker arms, bolts, pivots and retainer/guide plate (see illustration). Keep track of the rocker arm positions, since they must be returned to the same locations. Store each set of rocker components separately in a marked plastic bag to ensure that they're reinstalled in their original locations.

3   Remove the pushrods and store them separately to make sure they don't get mixed up during installation (see illustration).
Inspection

4   Check each rocker arm for wear, cracks and other damage, especially where the pushrods and valve stems contact the rocker arm.

5   Check the pivot seat in each rocker arm and the pivot faces. Look for galling, stress cracks and unusual wear patterns. If the rocker

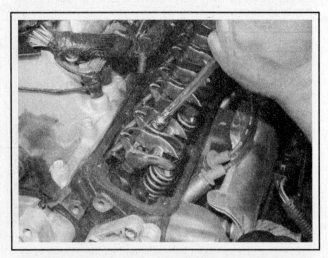

5.2 Remove the mounting bolts, pivots and rocker arms

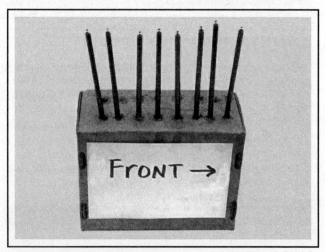

5.3 A perforated cardboard box can be used to store the pushrods to ensure they are reinstalled in their original locations - note the arrow indicating the front of the engine

5.9 Lubricate the pushrod ends and the valve stems with engine assembly lube before installing the rocker arms

5.10 Align the "V6" or "V8" neutral mark before installing and tightening rocker arms

arms are worn or damaged, replace them with new ones and install new pivots or shafts as well.

➡**Note: Keep in mind that there is no valve adjustment on these engines, so excessive wear or damage in the valve train can easily result in excessive valve clearance, which in turn will cause valve noise when the engine is running.**

6   Make sure the hole at the pushrod end of each rocker arm is open.

7   Inspect the pushrods for cracks and excessive wear at the ends, also check that the oil hole running through each pushrod is not clogged. Roll each pushrod across a piece of plate glass to see if it's bent (if it wobbles, it's bent).

INSTALLATION

♦ **Refer to illustrations 5.9 and 5.10**

8   Lubricate the lower end of each pushrod with clean engine oil or engine assembly lube and install them in their original locations. Make sure each pushrod seats completely in the lifter socket.

9   Apply engine assembly lube to the ends of the valve stems, the

upper ends of the pushrods and to the pivot faces to prevent damage to the mating surfaces on initial start-up (see illustration).

10   Rotate the crankshaft damper until the "V6" or the "V8" mark on the damper lines up with the TDC or Zero mark on the timing cover (see illustration). This represents a neutral point in the engine's directional rotation and the point at which the rocker arms can be tightened.

❋❋ CAUTION:

Do not rotate the engine at all after matching these marks. Once the rockers are all bolted down, allow at least five minutes for the hydraulic lifters to "bleed down" before turning or starting the engine.

11   Install the rocker arms, pivots, retainers and bolts. Tighten the rocker arm bolts to the torque listed in this Chapter's Specifications. As the bolts are tightened, make sure the pushrods seat properly in the rocker arms.

12   Refer to Section 4 and install the valve covers. Start the engine, listen for unusual valve train noses and check for oil leaks at the valve cover gaskets.

6   Valve springs, retainers and seals - replacement

♦ **Refer to illustrations 6.5, 6.8, 6.15 and 6.19**

➡**Note: Broken valve springs and defective valve stem seals can be replaced without removing the cylinder head. Two special tools and a compressed air source are normally required to perform this operation, so read through this Section carefully and rent or buy the tools before beginning the job.**

1   Remove the spark plugs (see Chapter 1).

2   Remove the valve covers (see Section 4).

3   Rotate the crankshaft until the number one piston is at Top Dead Center on the compression stroke (see Section 3).

4   Remove the rocker arms for the number 1 piston.

5   Thread an adapter into the spark plug hole and connect an air hose from a compressed air source to it (see illustration). Most auto parts stores can supply the air hose adapter.

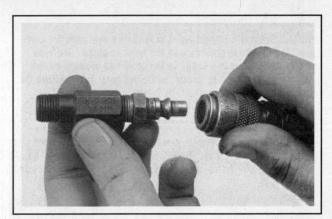

6.5 This is what the air hose adapter that fits into the spark plug hole looks like - they're commonly available from auto parts stores

6.8 Once the spring is compressed, the keepers can be removed with a small magnet or needle-nose pliers (a magnet is preferred to prevent dropping the keepers)

6.15 Be sure to install the seals on the correct valve stems

1   Exhaust valve seal
2   Intake valve seal

6.19 Apply small dab of grease to each keeper as shown here before installation - it'll hold them in place on the valve stem as the spring is released

➡**Note: Many cylinder compression gauges utilize a screw-in fitting that may work with your air hose quick-disconnect fitting. If a cylinder compression gauge fitting is used it will be necessary to remove the schrader valve from the end of the fitting before using it in this procedure.**

6   Apply compressed air to the cylinder. The valves should be held in place by the air pressure.

❊❊ **WARNING:**

If the cylinder isn't exactly at TDC, air pressure may force the piston down, causing the engine to quickly rotate. DO NOT leave a wrench on the vibration damper bolt or you may be injured by the tool.

---

7   Stuff shop rags into the cylinder head holes around the valves to prevent parts and tools from falling into the engine.

8   Using a socket and a hammer gently tap on the top of the each valve spring retainer several times (this will break the bond between the valve keeper and the spring retainer and allow the keeper to separate from the valve spring retainer as the valve spring is compressed), then use a valve-spring compressor to compress the spring. Remove the keepers with small needle-nose pliers or a magnet (see illustration).

➡**Note: Several different types of tools are available for compressing the valve springs with the head in place. One type, shown here, grips the lower spring coils and presses on the retainer as the knob is turned, while the lever-type utilizes the rocker arm bolt for leverage. Both types work very well, although the lever type is usually less expensive.**

9   Remove the valve spring and retainer.

➡**Note: If air pressure fails to retain the valve in the closed position during this operation, the valve face or seat may be damaged. If so, the cylinder head will have to be removed for repair.**

10   Remove the old valve stem seals, noting differences between the intake and exhaust seals.

11   Wrap a rubber band or tape around the top of the valve stem so the valve won't fall into the combustion chamber, then release the air pressure.

12   Inspect the valve stem for damage. Rotate the valve in the guide and check the end for eccentric movement, which would indicate that the valve is bent.

13   Move the valve up-and-down in the guide and make sure it does not bind. If the valve stem binds, either the valve is bent or the guide is damaged. In either case, the head will have to be removed for repair.

14   Reapply air pressure to the cylinder to retain the valve in the closed position, then remove the tape or rubber band from the valve stem.

15   If you're working on an exhaust valve, install the new exhaust valve seal on the valve stem and push it down to the top of the valve guide (see illustration).

16   If you're working on an intake valve, install a new intake valve stem seal over the valve stem and press it down over the valve guide. Don't force the intake valve seal against the top of the guide.

❊❊ **CAUTION:**

Do not install an exhaust valve seal on an intake valve, as high oil consumption will result.

---

17   Install the spring and retainer in position over the valve.

18   Compress the valve spring assembly only enough to install the keepers in the valve stem.

19   Position the keepers in the valve stem groove. Apply a small dab of grease to the inside of each keeper to hold it in place if necessary (see illustration). Remove the pressure from the spring tool and make sure the keepers are seated.

20   Disconnect the air hose and remove the adapter from the spark plug hole.

21   Repeat the above procedure on the remaining cylinders, following the firing order sequence (see this Chapter's Specifications). Bring each piston to Top Dead Center on the compression stroke before applying air pressure (see Section 3).

22   Reinstall the rocker arm assemblies and the valve covers (see Sections 4 and 5).

23   Allow the engine to sit for five minutes before starting to allow the lifters to "bleed down." Start the engine, then check for oil leaks and unusual sounds coming from the valve cover area. Allow the engine to idle for at least five minutes before revving the engine.

7 Intake manifold - removal and installation

REMOVAL

◆ **Refer to illustrations 7.7a, 7.7b, 7.10, 7.11, 7.15 and 7.16**

1 Disconnect the cable from the negative terminal of the battery.
2 Drain the cooling system (see Chapter 1).
3 Remove the air cleaner assembly and relieve the fuel system pressure (see Chapter 4).
4 Rotate the accessory belt tensioner over enough to slip the serpentine belt off the idler pulley and remove the belt (see Chapter 1).
5 Remove the alternator (see Chapter 5).
6 On air-conditioned models, remove the air-conditioning compressor and set it aside (see Chapter 3).

✷✷ CAUTION:

Do not disconnect the refrigerant lines.

7 Remove the idler pulley and the alternator/air conditioning compressor bracket from the front of the engine (see illustrations).
8 Disconnect the accelerator linkage (see Chapter 4) and, if equipped, the cruise control linkage. On models equipped with an automatic transmission, disconnect the kickdown cable at the throttle body.
9 Disconnect any vacuum hoses attached to the intake manifold or throttle body such as the power brake booster, the PCV, EVAP control and the cruise control vacuum supply hose.
10 Remove the upper radiator hose from the engine, then disconnect the heater hose and water pump bypass hose from the intake manifold (see illustration).
11 Label and then disconnect the electrical connectors to the fuel injectors, the MAP sensor, the TPS, the IAC valve and the coolant temperature sensors (see illustration).
12 Disconnect any remaining electrical connectors connected to the intake manifold or throttle body and pull the whole engine wiring harness up and over the intake manifold to the rear of the engine.
13 Remove the fuel rails and injectors as an assembly (see Chapter 4). The two fuel rails can be pulled straight up with the injectors still attached, but it will take some force to dislodge the injectors from the

7.7a Remove the idler pulley . . .

7.7b . . . and the A/C compressor alternator bracket

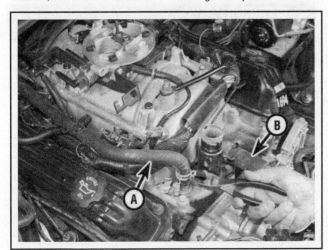

7.10 Disconnect the heater hose from the manifold (A), and the water-pump bypass hose (B)

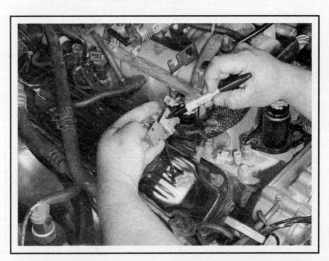

7.11 Disconnect the electrical connectors from the throttle body, fuel injectors and the intake manifold - label each connector clearly to aid in the reassembly process

7.15 Pry the intake manifold upward by a casting protrusion only, not between the gasket surfaces

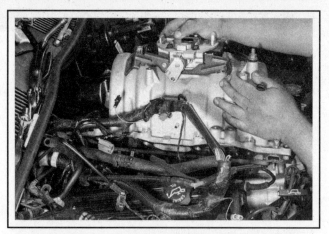

7.16 The intake manifold is somewhat heavy and bulky so get a good grip before lifting it up - watch for wires or hoses hanging up as you remove the manifold

intake manifold.

14 Label and remove each spark plug wire from the spark plugs (see Chapter 1 if necessary). Unlatch the two distributor cap retaining screws using a 1/4-inch-drive socket and proper-length extension. Feed the distributor cap and spark plug wires from behind the intake manifold and out of the engine compartment.

15 Loosen the intake manifold mounting bolts in 1/4-turn increments in the reverse order of the tightening sequence until they can be removed by hand (see illustration 7.24). The manifold will probably be stuck to the cylinder heads and force may be required to break the gasket seal. A pry bar can be positioned to pry up a casting projection at the front of the manifold to break the bond made by the gasket (see illustration).

❊❊ CAUTION:

Do not pry between the block and manifold or the heads and manifold or damage to the gasket sealing surfaces may result and vacuum leaks could develop.

16 Remove the intake manifold (see illustration). As the manifold is lifted from the engine, be sure to check for and disconnect anything still attached to the manifold.

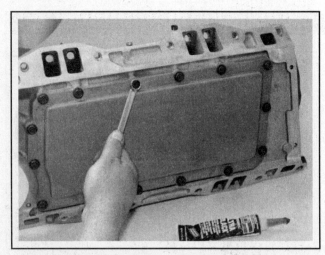

7.19 Remove the plenum pan from under the intake manifold, clean the gasket surfaces and replace the gasket with a new one

INSTALLATION

▶ **Refer to illustrations 7.19, 7.21, 7.22 and 7.24**

➡**Note: The mating surfaces of the cylinder heads, block and manifold must be perfectly clean when the manifold is installed. Gasket removal solvents in aerosol cans are available at most auto parts stores and may be helpful when removing old gasket material that is stuck to the heads and manifold. Be sure to follow the directions printed on the container.**

17 Remove carbon deposits from the exhaust crossover passages (if equipped). Use a gasket scraper to remove all traces of sealant and old gasket material, then wipe the mating surfaces with a cloth saturated with lacquer thinner or acetone. If there is old sealant or oil on the mating surfaces when the manifold is installed, oil or vacuum leaks may develop. Cover the lifter valley with shop rags to keep debris out of the engine. Use a vacuum cleaner to remove any gasket material that falls into the intake ports in the heads.

18 Use a tap of the correct size to chase the threads in the bolt holes, then use compressed air (if available) to remove the debris from the holes.

❊❊ WARNING:

Wear safety glasses or a face shield to protect your eyes when using compressed air.

19 The intake manifold has a stamped, sheetmetal pan on the bottom, called the plenum pan (see illustration). If you have the intake manifold off for any reason, it's a good idea to replace the gasket under this pan. Use a small layer of RTV sealant on the gasket and tighten the bolts in a criss-cross pattern to the torque listed in this Chapter's Specifications starting in the center of the manifold and working out towards the ends, in three steps.

20 Apply a thin coat of RTV sealant to the cylinder head around water jackets.

21 Position the side gaskets on the cylinder heads. Note that the gaskets are marked LT for left or RT for right (see illustration) or the words "Manifold Side" may appear, If so, this will ensure proper installation. Make sure they are installed on the correct side and all intake port openings, coolant passage holes and bolt holes are aligned correctly.

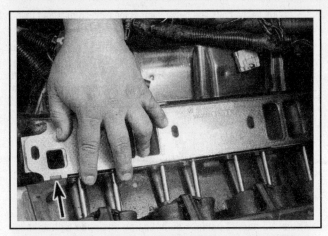

7.21 The gaskets must be installed on the proper side; some may be marked left or right or "manifold side" - line up the ports and make sure the side gasket's cutouts clear the tabs on the head gasket (arrow) front and rear

22 Apply a thin, uniform coating of quick-dry gasket cement to the intake manifold end seals and the cylinder block contact surfaces. Install the front and rear end seals on the block over the dowels (if equipped) and the end tangs. Refer to the instructions with the gasket set for further information. Apply RTV sealant at the four corners where the gaskets meet (see illustration).

23 Carefully set the manifold in place.

✳✳ CAUTION:

Do not disturb the gaskets and DO NOT move the manifold fore-and-aft after it contacts the front and rear seals or the gaskets will be pushed out of place.

24 Install the intake manifold bolts and tighten the bolts following the recommended sequence (see illustration) to the torque listed in this Chapter's Specifications. Do not overtighten the bolts or gasket leaks may develop.

25 The remaining installation steps are the reverse of removal. Add

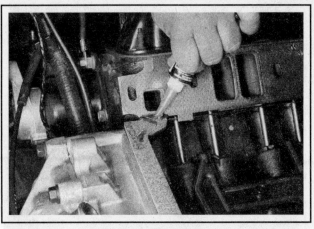

7.22 Apply a bead of RTV sealant to the four corners, where the end gaskets meet the side gaskets - the bead should be slightly higher than the end rail gaskets

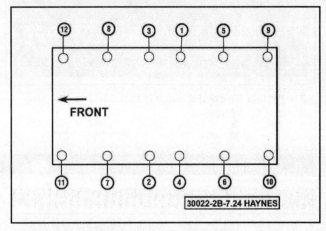

30022-2B-7.24 HAYNES

7.24 Intake manifold bolt-tightening sequence - V6 and V8 engines

coolant, start the engine and check carefully for oil, vacuum and coolant leaks at the intake manifold joints.

8   Exhaust manifolds - removal and installation

REMOVAL

♦ **Refer to illustrations 8.2 and 8.3**

✳✳ WARNING:

Allow the engine to cool completely before performing this procedure.

1 Disconnect the cable from the negative terminal of the battery.

2 Raise the vehicle and support it securely on jackstands. Disconnect the exhaust pipe-to-manifold connections (see illustration). Its a good idea to apply penetrating oil on the studs/bolts and let it soak 10 minutes before attempting to remove them.

8.2 Remove the exhaust pipe-to-manifold nuts

3   Lower the vehicle and remove the heat shield from the exhaust manifold(s) (see illustration).

➡**Note: If your working on the passenger side exhaust manifold it will be necessary to remove the air cleaner cover and housing (see Chapter 4) to allow access to the manifold bolts.**

4   Using a wrench remove the heat shield support extensions and washers from the exhaust manifold studs.

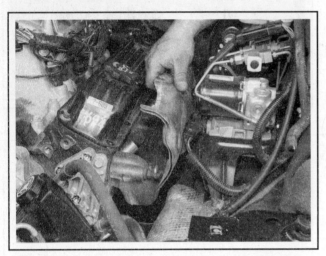

8.3 Remove the exhaust manifold heat shield and the heat shield support extensions

5   Remove the bolts and nuts retaining the exhaust manifold to the cylinder head.

➡**Note: If any of the studs come out of the head while removing the manifolds, use new studs on reassembly. The coarse-threaded ends of the studs should be coated with a non-hardening sealant such as Permatex No. 2 to prevent the possibility of water leaks from the cylinder head.**

6   Remove the manifold(s).

INSTALLATION

7   Installation is the reverse of removal. Clean the manifold gasket surface and check for cracks and flatness, also clean the exhaust port gasket surface on the cylinder head.

➡**Note: V6 and V8 engines do not come equipped with exhaust manifold gaskets from the manufacturer although many aftermarket gasket manufacturers do provide exhaust manifold gaskets for V6 and V8 engines. If an exhaust leak at the manifold is noticeable, it would be wise to have the manifold surfaced at an automotive machine shop and to use a replacement exhaust manifold gasket when installing the manifold.**

8   Install the manifold(s) and fasteners. Tighten the bolts/nuts to the torque listed in this Chapter's Specifications. Work from the center to the ends and approach the final torque in three steps. Install the heat shields extensions and washers, then install the heat shields.

9   Apply anti-seize compound to the exhaust manifold-to-exhaust pipe bolts and tighten them securely.

9   Cylinder heads - removal and installation

REMOVAL

▶ **Refer to illustrations 9.6, 9.7a and 9.7b**

1   Disconnect the cable from the negative terminal of the battery and drain the cooling system (see Chapter 1).

2   Remove the valve covers (see Section 4).

3   Remove the intake manifold (see Section 7).

4   Detach both exhaust manifolds from the cylinder heads (see Section 8). Remove the ignition coil (see Chapter 5) and the drivebelt

tensioner from the right cylinder head.

5   Remove the rocker arms and pushrods (see Section 5).

✳✳ CAUTION:

Again, as mentioned in Section 5, keep all the parts in order so they are reinstalled in the same location.

6   Loosen the head bolts in 1/4-turn increments in the reverse order of the tightening sequence (see illustration 9.16a and 9.16b) until they can be removed by hand.

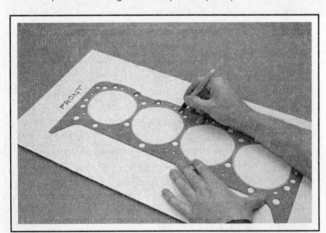

9.6 To avoid mixing up the head bolts, use a new gasket to transfer the bolt pattern to a piece of cardboard, then punch holes to accept the bolts

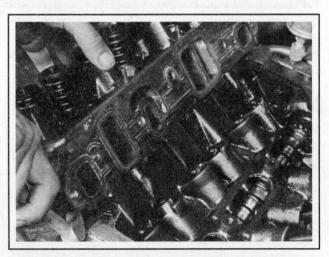

9.7a Pry on a casting protrusion to break the head loose

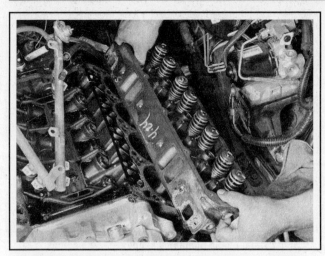

9.7b Once loose, get a good hold on the cylinder head and remove it from the engine block

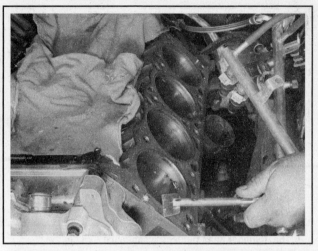

9.10 Keep the intake valley covered with shop rags while removing all traces of old gasket material

➡ Note: There will be different-length head bolts for different locations, so store the bolts in a cardboard holder or some type of container as they are removed (see illustration). This will ensure that the bolts are reinstalled in their original holes.

7   Lift the heads off the engine. If resistance is felt, do not pry between the head and block as damage to the mating surfaces will result. To dislodge the head, place a block of wood against the end of it and strike the wood block with a hammer, or lift on a casting protrusion (see illustrations). Store the heads on blocks of wood to prevent damage to the gasket sealing surfaces.

8   Cylinder head disassembly and inspection procedures are covered in detail in Chapter 2, Part D.

INSTALLATION

▶ Refer to illustrations 9.10, 9.12, 9.13, 9.16a and 9.16b

9   The mating surfaces of the cylinder heads and block must be perfectly clean when the heads are installed. Gasket removal solvents are available at auto parts stores and may prove helpful.

10   Use a gasket scraper to remove all traces of carbon and old gasket material (see illustration), then wipe the mating surfaces with a cloth saturated with lacquer thinner or acetone. If there is oil on the mating surfaces when the heads are installed, the gaskets may not seal correctly and leaks may develop. When working on the block, cover the lifter valley with shop rags to keep debris out of the engine. Use a vacuum cleaner to remove any debris that falls into the cylinders.

11   Check the block and head mating surfaces for nicks, deep scratches and other damage. If damage is slight, it can be removed with emery cloth. If it is excessive, machining may be the only alternative.

12   Use a tap of the correct size to chase the threads in the head bolt holes in the block. Mount each bolt in a vise and run a die down the threads to remove corrosion and restore the threads (see illustration). Dirt, corrosion, sealant and damaged threads will affect torque readings.

13   Position the new gaskets over the dowels in the block (see illustration).

14   Carefully position the heads on the block without disturbing the gaskets.

15   Before installing the head bolts, coat the threads with a non-hardening sealant such as Permatex No. 2.

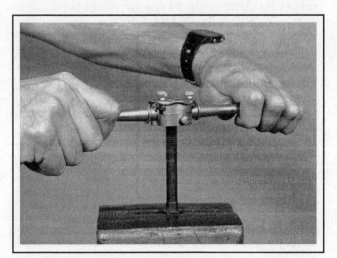

9.12 A die should be used to remove sealant and corrosion from the bolt threads prior to installation

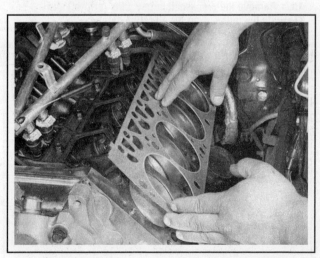

9.13 Install the new head gasket over the dowels at each end of the cylinder head

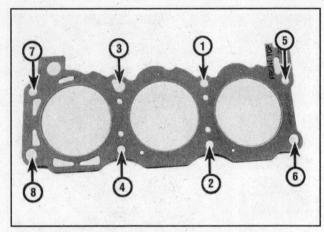

9.16a Cylinder head tightening sequence - V6 engine

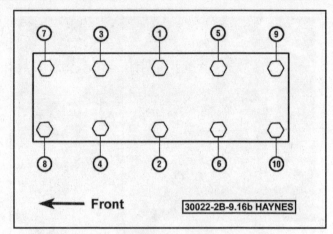

9.16b Cylinder head tightening sequence - V8 engines

16 Install the bolts in their original locations and tighten them finger tight. Following the recommended sequence (see illustrations), tighten the bolts in several steps to the torque listed in this Chapter's Specifications.

17 The remaining installation steps are the reverse of removal.
18 Add coolant and change the oil and filter (see Chapter 1). Start the engine and check for proper operation and coolant or oil leaks.

10 Crankshaft front oil seal - replacement

10.3 Remove the crankshaft pulley bolts (arrows) and separate the pulley from the vibration damper

10.5 Use a bolt-on puller to remove the vibration damper

▶ **Refer to illustrations 10.3, 10.5, 10.7, 10.9 and 10.10**

1 Disconnect the cable from the negative terminal of the battery.
2 Refer to Chapter 3 and remove the engine cooling fan, then refer to Chapter 1 and remove the engine drivebelt.
3 Remove the bolts and separate the crankshaft pulley from the vibration damper (see illustration).
4 Remove the large vibration damper-to-crankshaft bolt. To keep the crankshaft from turning, remove the starter (see Chapter 5) and have an assistant wedge a large screwdriver against the ring gear teeth.
5 Using the proper puller (commonly available from auto parts stores), detach the vibration damper from the crankshaft (see illustration).

✳✳ CAUTION:

Do not use a puller with jaws that grip the outer edge of the damper. The puller must be the type that utilizes bolts to apply force to the center of the damper hub only.

6 If the seal is being replaced with the timing chain cover removed, support the cover on top of two blocks of wood and drive the seal out from the backside with a hammer and punch.

✳✳ CAUTION:

Be careful not to scratch, gouge or distort the area that the seal fits into or a leak will develop.

7 If the seal is being removed while the cover is still attached to the engine block, carefully pry the seal out of the cover with a seal removal tool or a large screwdriver (see illustration).

✳✳ CAUTION:

Be careful not to scratch, gouge or distort the area that the seal fits into or an oil leak will develop.

10.7 If you're replacing the seal with the timing chain cover installed, pry it out with a seal removal tool

10.9 Use a seal driver or large-diameter pipe to drive the new seal into the cover

10.10 If the sealing surface of the damper hub has a wear groove from contact with the seal, repair sleeves are available at most auto parts stores

8   Clean the bore to remove any old seal material and corrosion. Position the new seal in the bore with the seal lip (usually the side with the spring) facing IN (toward the engine). A small amount of oil applied to the outer edge of the new seal will make installation easier.

9   Drive the seal into the bore with a large socket and hammer until it's completely seated (see illustration). Select a socket that's the same outside diameter as the seal and make sure the new seal is pressed into place until it bottoms against the cover flange.

10 Check the surface of the damper that the oil seal rides on. If the surface has been grooved from long-time contact with the seal, a press-on sleeve may be available to renew the sealing surface (see illustra-

tion). This sleeve is pressed into place with a hammer and a block of wood and is commonly available from auto parts stores.

11 Lubricate the seal lips with engine oil and reinstall the vibration damper. Use a vibration damper installation tool to press the damper onto the crankshaft.

12 Install the vibration damper-to-crankshaft bolt and tighten it to the torque listed in this Chapter's Specifications. Install the crankshaft pulley and tighten the bolts to the torque listed in this Chapter's Specifications.

13 The remainder of installation is the reverse of the removal.

11 Timing chain - removal, inspection and installation

REMOVAL AND INSPECTION

▶ **Refer to illustrations 11.9a, 11.9b, 11.11, 11.14, 11.15a and 11.15b**

1   Remove the fan assembly (see Chapter 3) and the crankshaft pulley and damper (see Section 10).

2   Refer to Chapter 1 and drain the cooling system.

3   Remove the alternator (see Chapter 5).

4   On air-conditioned models, remove the air conditioning compressor and set it aside (see Chapter 3).

✳✳ CAUTION:

Do not disconnect the refrigerant lines.

5   Remove the idler pulley and the alternator/air conditioning compressor bracket from the front of the engine (see illustrations 7.7a and 7.7b).

6   Remove the water pump (see Chapter 3).

7   Remove and set aside the power steering pump with the lines still connected (see Chapter 10).

➡ **Note: On some models it may only be necessary to remove the bolt securing the power steering oil cooler to help facilitate removal of the timing cover.**

8   Loosen the oil pan bolts and remove the front two oil pan bolts,

that thread into the timing chain cover - they're most easily accessed from below.

➡ **Note: Even though this procedure can be done without the removal of the oil pan, it is difficult on some models and oil pan removal may actually simplify the job (see Section 13).**

9   Remove the remaining timing chain cover mounting bolts and separate the timing chain cover from the block and oil pan (see illustrations). The cover may be stuck; if so, use a putty knife to break the gasket seal. The cover is easily damaged, so DO NOT attempt to pry it off.

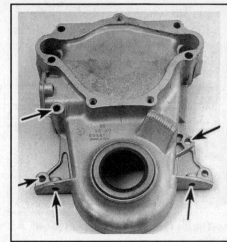

11.9a Timing chain cover lower bolt hole locations (arrows) - upper through-bolts secure the water pump and the timing chain cover to the block and are detached when the water pump is removed

11.9b Remove the timing chain cover from the engine - being careful not damage the oil pan gasket

11.14 Loosen the camshaft sprocket bolt (A), then rotate the engine clockwise by the crankshaft bolt until the timing marks (B) align

❄ CAUTION:

Remove the cover as carefully as possible, so as not to tear the one-piece oil pan gasket. If the gasket becomes torn, the oil pan will have to be removed and a new gasket installed.

10 Inspect the timing chain stretch. Attach a socket and torque wrench to the camshaft sprocket bolt and apply force in the normal direction of crankshaft rotation (30 ft-lbs if the cylinder heads are still in position complete with rocker arms, or 15 ft-lbs if the cylinder heads have been removed). Don't allow the crankshaft to rotate. If necessary, wedge a screwdriver into the flywheel ring gear teeth (with the starter removed) so that it can't move.

➡ Note: On V6 engines It will be necessary to compress the timing chain tensioner shoe before inspecting the timing chain stretch (see step 17).

11 Place a ruler on top of the chain above the camshaft gear. Line up a mark on the ruler with the edge of a chain link. Apply the same amount of force used in Step 10 in the opposite direction of rotation and note the amount of movement of the chain. If it exceeds 1/8-inch, a new timing chain set will be required.

➡: Always replace the timing chain, camshaft and crankshaft sprockets as set.

12 Inspect the camshaft sprocket for damage or wear. The camshaft sprocket on some models is steel, but most original-equipment cam sprockets will be an aluminum sprocket with a nylon coating on the teeth. This nylon coating may be cracked or breaking off in small pieces. These pieces tend to end up in the oil pan and may eventually plug the oil pump pickup screen. If the pieces have come off the camshaft sprocket, the oil pan should be removed to properly clean or replace the oil pump pickup screen.

13 Inspect the crankshaft sprocket for damage or wear. The crankshaft sprocket is a steel sprocket, but the teeth can be grooved or worn enough to cause a poor meshing of the sprocket and the chain.

14 After inspection has been completed, loosen the camshaft sprocket bolt, then rotate the engine in the normal direction of rotation (clockwise) until the timing marks are aligned (see illustration). Remove the bolt from the camshaft sprocket.

15 The sprockets on the camshaft and crankshaft can be removed with a two or three-jaw puller or by using two screwdrivers (see illustrations), but be careful not to damage the threads in the end of the crankshaft.

➡ Note: If the timing chain cover oil seal has been leaking, refer to Section 10 and install a new one.

11.15a The sprocket on the camshaft can be removed with a two or three-jaw puller . . .

11.15b . . . or with two screwdrivers

INSTALLATION

▶ **Refer to illustration 11.19**

➡**Note: Timing chains must be replaced as a set with the camshaft and crankshaft sprockets. Never put a new chain on old sprockets.**

16 Use a gasket scraper to remove all traces of old gasket material and sealant from the cover and engine block. Stuff a shop rag into the opening at the front of the oil pan to keep debris out of the engine. Wipe the cover and block sealing surfaces with a cloth saturated with lacquer thinner or acetone.

17 On V6 engines, lock the timing chain tensioner into the compressed position as follows: Install the crankshaft sprocket onto the crankshaft. Carefully place a large flat-blade screwdriver between the crankshaft sprocket and the tensioner shoe. Compress the tensioner shoe until the shoe hole aligns with the bracket hole, then insert a suitable size pin through both holes to keep the shoe locked. Remove the screwdriver and the crankshaft sprocket. Inspect the timing chain tensioner for wear and damage, replace if necessary.

➡**Note: The tensioner must be placed in the compressed or locked position before the timing chain can be installed.**

18 Align the crankshaft sprocket with the Woodruff key and press the sprocket onto the crankshaft with the vibration damper bolt, a large socket and some washers or tap it gently into place until it is completely seated.

❋❋ CAUTION:

If resistance is encountered, do not hammer the sprocket onto the crankshaft. It may eventually move onto the shaft, but it may be cracked in the process and fail later, causing extensive engine damage.

19 Loop the new chain over the camshaft sprocket, then turn the sprocket until the timing mark is at the bottom (see illustration). Mesh the chain with the crankshaft sprocket and position the camshaft sprocket on the end of the camshaft. If necessary, turn the camshaft so the key fits into the sprocket keyway with the timing mark in the 6 o'clock position (see illustration 11.14). When the chain is installed, the timing marks MUST align as shown.

20 Apply a thread locking compound to the camshaft sprocket bolt threads and tighten the bolt to the torque listed in this Chapter's Specifications.

21 Lubricate the chain with clean engine oil.

22 On 1998 and later V6 engines, remove the pin from the tensioner

11.19 Slip the chain and camshaft sprocket in place over the crankshaft sprocket with the camshaft sprocket timing mark (arrow) at the bottom

shoe and bracket. Make sure the tensioner shoe has released and is pressing against the timing chain. Verify that the timing marks are still aligned properly (see illustration 11.14) and readjust if necessary.

23 Check for cracks and deformation of the oil pan gasket before installing the timing cover. If the gasket has deteriorated or is damaged, it must be replaced before reinstalling the timing chain cover.

24 Apply a thin layer of RTV sealant to both sides of the new cover gasket and the corners of the pan and block, then position the new cover gasket on the engine. The sealant will hold it in place.

25 Install the timing chain cover on the block and tighten the bolts, a little at a time, until you reach the torque listed in this Chapter's Specifications.

26 Install the two oil pan bolts, bringing the oil pan up against the timing chain cover, and tighten the rest of the pan bolts, if they were previously loosened.

27 Lubricate the oil seal contact surface of the vibration damper hub with clean engine oil, then install the damper on the end of the crankshaft. The keyway in the damper must be aligned with the Woodruff key in the crankshaft nose. If the damper cannot be seated by hand, slip the large washer over the bolt, install the bolt and tighten it to pull the damper into place. Tighten the bolt to the torque listed in this Chapter's Specifications.

28 The remaining installation steps are the reverse of removal.

29 Add coolant and check the oil level (see Chapter 1). Run the engine and check for oil and coolant leaks.

12 Camshaft and lifters - removal and installation

REMOVAL

▶ **Refer to illustrations 12.3, 12.4, 12.7, 12.8 and 12.10**

1 Refer to the appropriate Sections and remove the intake manifold, valve covers, rocker arms, pushrods and the timing chain.

2 Remove the radiator and air conditioning condenser (see Chapter 3).

3 Remove the distributor (see Chapter 5) and the distributor drive gear (see illustration on next page).

12.3 Pull up on the distributor drive gear to remove it, rotating it clockwise until it can be removed through the distributor hole in the block - upon installation be sure the slot is aligned so that a line drawn through the slot crosses the front intake bolt hole in the left head, when the No. 1 piston is at TDC

12.7 Arrange a method of storing the lifters in order before removing them - a divided cardboard box handy for storage of the lifters

12.8 Remove the camshaft thrust plate and oil tab

1	Thrust plate	3	Oil tab
2	Thrust plate bolts		

12.4 Before removing the lifters note the paint marks (arrows) that indicate which side of the roller lifters face the valley - apply marks if none are visible

4   Before removing the lifters and yokes note the marks showing which side of the lifter faces the lifter "valley." If they aren't marked, apply some paint dabs before removing the yokes (see illustration).

⁕⁕ **CAUTION:**

The lifters must be installed the same way to aim the oil feed holes properly.

5   Remove the lifter yoke retainer.
6   There are several ways to extract the lifters from the bores. A special tool designed to grip and remove lifters is manufactured by many tool companies and is widely available, but it may not be required in every case. On newer engines without a lot of varnish buildup, the lifters can often be removed with a small magnet or even with your fingers. A machinist's scribe with a bent end can be used to pull the lifters out by positioning the point under the retainer ring inside the top of each lifter.

⁕⁕ **CAUTION:**

Do not use pliers to remove the lifters unless you intend to replace them with new ones. The pliers will damage the precision machined and hardened lifters, rendering them useless.

7   Remove the lifter guides (aligning yokes) and lifters. Store the lifters in a clearly labeled box to ensure that they are reinstalled in their original locations (see illustration).
8   Unbolt and remove the camshaft thrust plate and oil tab (see illustration). Note how the oil tab is installed so you can return it to its original location on reassembly.
9   Thread a long bolt into the camshaft sprocket bolt hole to use as a handle when removing the camshaft from the block.
10 Carefully pull the camshaft out. Support the cam near the block so the lobes do not nick or gouge the bearings as it is withdrawn (see illustration). Inspect the camshaft, bearings and lifters as described in Chapter 2D.

INSTALLATION

◆ **Refer to illustration 12.11**

11 Lubricate the camshaft bearing journals and cam lobes with

12.10 Thread a long bolt into the camshaft sprocket bolt hole to use as a handle - as the camshaft is being removed, support it near the block so the lobes do not nick the bearings

12.11 Be sure to apply camshaft installation lube to the cam lobes and bearing journals before installing the camshaft

camshaft installation lube (see illustration).

12 Slide the camshaft slowly and gently into the engine. Support the cam near the block and be careful not to scrape or nick the bearings. Only install the camshaft far enough to allow the installation of the camshaft thrust plate. Pushing it in too far could dislodge the camshaft plug at the rear of the engine, causing an oil leak.

13 Install with the camshaft thrust plate or timing chain tensioner (1998 and later V6 engines) as it was originally (see illustration 12.8).

14 Align the timing marks on the crankshaft and camshaft sprockets, install the timing chain and sprockets (see Section 11), then check the camshaft endplay as described in Chapter 2D.

15 With the timing chain marks aligned, rotate the engine 360 degrees to bring the No.1 piston to TDC on the compression stroke. Install the distributor drive gear as shown in illustration 12.3.

➥Note: Removing the spark plugs will allow the engine to rotated easier.

16 Lubricate the lifters with clean engine oil and install them in the block. If the original lifters are being reinstalled, be sure to return them to their original locations, and with the paint marks facing the valley and the oil-feed holes on the side of the lifter body facing UP, away from the crankshaft. Install the lifter yokes and the lifter yoke retainer.

➥Note: The lifter yokes must be installed with their arrows pointing toward the camshaft.

17 Refer to the appropriate Sections and install the timing chain cover, vibration damper, pushrods and rocker arms.

18 The remaining installation steps are the reverse of removal.

19 Change the oil and install a new oil filter (see Chapter 1).

20 Start the engine, check for oil pressure and leaks.

✳✳ CAUTION:

Do not run the engine above a fast idle until all the hydraulic lifters have filled with oil and become quiet again.

21 If a new camshaft and lifters have been installed, the engine should be brought to operating temperature and run at a fast idle for 15 to 20 minutes to "break in" the new components. Change the oil and filter again after 500 miles of operation.

13 Oil pan - removal and installation

REMOVAL

➧ **Refer to illustration 13.7**

1 Disconnect the cable from the negative terminal of the battery. Raise the vehicle and support it securely on jackstands (see Chapter 1).

2 Drain the engine oil (see Chapter 1). Remove the engine oil dip-stick.

3 Remove the flywheel inspection cover.

4 Disconnect and lower the exhaust Y pipe from the engine (see illustration 8.2).

5 Support the engine from above with an engine hoist, take the weight off the engine mounts with the hoist, being careful not to let the distributor cap come in contact with the firewall. Remove the distributor cap if necessary. On 4WD vehicles remove the front axle assembly (see Chapter 8).

6 Remove the engine mounts and on 4WD vehicles the engine mount support brackets (see Section 17).

7 Remove all the oil pan bolts (see illustration), then lower the pan

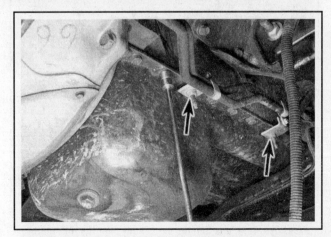

13.7 Remove the bolts around the perimeter of the oil pan - if the vehicle is equipped with an automatic transmission remove and note the location of the transmission cooler line retainers (arrows)

from the engine. The pan will probably stick to the engine, so strike the pan with a rubber mallet until it breaks the gasket seal.

> ✳✳ **CAUTION:**

Before using force on the oil pan, be sure all the bolts have been removed. Carefully slide the oil pan out, to the rear.

INSTALLATION

8   Wash out the oil pan with solvent.

9   Thoroughly clean the mounting surfaces of the oil pan and engine block of old gasket material and sealer. If the oil pan is distorted at the bolt-hole areas, straighten the flange by supporting it from below on a 1x4 wood block and tapping the bolt holes with the rounded end of a ball-peen hammer. Wipe the gasket surfaces clean with a rag soaked in lacquer thinner or acetone.

10   Apply some RTV sealant to the corners where the front cover meets the block and at the rear where the rear main cap meets the block. Then attach the one-piece oil pan gasket to the engine block with contact cement-type gasket adhesive.

11   Prepare four pan alignment dowels from 5/16-inch bolts 1.5-inches long. Cut off the bolt heads and slot the ends with a hacksaw.

12   Install the four alignment dowels into the frontmost and rearmost pairs of pan bolt holes in the block.

13   Lift the pan into position, slipping it over the alignment dowels and being careful not to disturb the gasket, install several bolts finger tight.

14   Check that the gasket isn't sticking out anywhere around the block's perimeter. When all the bolts are in place, replace the alignment dowels with four pan bolts.

15   Starting at the ends and alternating from side-to-side towards the center, tighten the bolts to the torque listed in this Chapter's Specifications.

16   The remainder of installation is the reverse of removal.

17   Add the proper type and quantity of oil (see Chapter 1), start the engine and check for leaks before placing the vehicle back in service.

14 Oil pump - removal, inspection and installation

14.2 Remove the bolts (arrows) and lower the oil pump

14.10 Inspect the end of the oil pump driveshaft (arrow) for excessive wear, position the pump body over the rear main cap, then slowly rotate the oil pump until it aligns with the driveshaft, install the mounting bolts and tighten them to the correct specification

REMOVAL

▶ **Refer to illustration 14.2**

1   Remove the oil pan (see Section 13).

2   While supporting the oil pump, remove the oil pump mounting bolts (see illustration).

3   Lower the pump and pickup screen assembly from the vehicle.

INSPECTION

4   Remove the oil pump cover and withdraw the rotors from the pump body. Clean the components with solvent, dry them thoroughly and inspect for any obvious damage.

5   Place a straightedge across the inner surface of the oil pump cover and try to insert a .0015-inch feeler gauge under it. If the gauge fits, the oil pump assembly should be replaced.

6   Measure the thickness of the inner and outer rotor with a micrometer. If either is less than the minimum thickness listed in this Chapter's Specifications, the pump assembly should be replaced.

7   Install the rotors into the pump body and measure the clearance between the outer rotor and the body, between the inner and outer rotors, and the clearance over the rotors. Compare these measurements to this Chapter's Specifications. If any components are scored, scratched or worn beyond the Specifications, replace the oil pump assembly. If the parts are serviceable, replace the cover and tighten the bolts to the torque listed in this Chapter's Specifications.

INSTALLATION

▶ **Refer to illustration 14.10**

8   If removed, thread the oil pickup tube and screen into the oil pump and tighten it.

※※ CAUTION:

Be absolutely certain that the pickup screen is properly tightened so that no air can be sucked into the oiling system at this connection.

9   Prime the pump by pouring clean motor oil into the pickup tube, while turning the pump by hand.

10 Position the pump on the engine with a new gasket, if required. Make sure the pump driveshaft is aligned with the oil pump.

11 Install the mounting bolts and tighten them to the torque listed in this Chapter's Specifications.

12 Install the oil pan and add oil.

13 Run the engine and check for oil pressure and leaks.

15 Rear main oil seal - replacement

♦ Refer to illustration 15.4

➡Note: If you're installing a new seal during a complete engine overhaul, ignore the steps in this procedure that concern removal of external parts. Also, since the crankshaft is already removed, it's not necessary to use any special tools to remove the upper seal half; remove and install the upper seal half the same way as the lower seal half.

1   Remove the oil pan (see Section 13).

2   Remove the oil pump (see Section 14).

3   The rear main seal can be replaced with the engine in the vehicle. The rear main seal is a two-piece design, made from Viton rubber.

4   Remove the bolts and detach the rear main bearing cap from the engine (see illustration).

5   Remove the lower half of the oil seal from the bearing cap and the upper half from the block.

➡Note: It may be easier to remove the upper rear seal when the two main bearing caps ahead of the rear cap are loosened slightly. ALL the main bearing caps should be retightened to Specifications after the new seal and rear cap are installed.

6   Clean the bearing cap and engine block surfaces carefully to degrease them and remove any sealant.

7   Lightly oil the lips of the new crankshaft seals.

※※ CAUTION:

Always wipe the crankshaft surface clean, then oil it lightly before installing a new seal.

8   Rotate a new seal half into cylinder block with the paint stripe (yellow on some models, white on others) toward the rear of the engine.

※※ CAUTION:

Hold your thumb firmly against the outside diameter of the seal as you're rotating it into place. This will prevent the seal outside diameter from being shaved from contact with the sharp edge of the engine block. If the seal gets damaged, oil leaks may occur.

9   Place the other seal half in the bearing cap with the paint stripe toward the rear.

10 Apply a drop of Loctite 515 or equivalent on either side of the cap (on the surface that mates with the block), and a small amount of RTV sealant in the slots on either side of the cap. Install the cap quickly after applying the Loctite and sealant. Tighten the rear main bearing cap (and ALL the other bearing caps if you loosened any of the others) to the torque listed in the Chapter 2D Specifications.

11 Install the oil pump and oil pan.

12 The remainder of installation is the reverse of removal. Fill the pan with oil, run the engine and check for leaks.

15.4 Remove the bolts (arrows) and detach the rear main bearing cap from the engine

16 Flywheel/driveplate - removal and installation

♦ **Refer to illustration 16.2**

1   Remove the transmission (see Chapter 7). If your vehicle has a manual transmission, the pressure plate and clutch will also have to be removed (see Chapter 8).

2   Wedge a large screwdriver in the starter ring gear teeth or driveplate hole to keep the crankshaft from turning, then remove the mounting bolts. Mark the flywheel relationship to the crankshaft for later alignment (see illustration). Since it's fairly heavy, support the flywheel as the last bolt is removed.

❋❋ WARNING:

The ring gear teeth may be sharp, wear gloves to protect your hands.

16.2 Before removing the flywheel or driveplate, mark its relationship to the crankshaft

3   Pull straight back on the flywheel/driveplate to detach it from the crankshaft. On some models there may be a thin spacer installed between the driveplate and crankshaft. Automatic transmission equipped models may have a retainer ring between the bolts and the driveplate.

4   On manual transmission equipped models, check the pilot bushing and replace it if necessary (see Chapter 8). Clean the flywheel with lacquer thinner, especially around the mounting area, and clean the rear

flange of the crankshaft.

5   Installation is the reverse of removal. Be sure to align the marks made during removal. Use a non-hardening thread locking compound on the bolt threads and tighten them to the torque listed in this Chapter's Specifications in a criss-cross pattern.

17 Engine mounts - check and replacement

1   Engine mounts seldom require attention, but broken or deteriorated mounts should be replaced immediately or the added strain placed on the driveline components may cause damage or wear.

CHECK

2   During the check, the engine must be raised slightly to remove the weight from the mounts.

3   Raise the vehicle and support it securely on jackstands, then position a jack under the engine oil pan. Place a large wood block between the jack head and the oil pan, then carefully raise the engine just enough to take the weight off the mounts.

❋❋ WARNING:

DO NOT place any part of your body under the engine when it's supported only by a jack!

4   Check for relative movement between the mount plates and the engine or frame (use a large screwdriver or prybar to attempt to move the mounts). If movement is noted, lower the engine and tighten the mount fasteners.

5   Check the mounts to see if the rubber is cracked, hardened or separated from the metal plates which would indicate a need for replacement.

6   Rubber preservative should be applied to the mounts to slow deterioration.

REPLACEMENT

♦ **Refer to illustrations 17.11a and 17.11b**

7   Disconnect the cable from the negative terminal of the battery.

8   Raise the front of the vehicle and support it securely on jackstands.

9   Support the engine with a lifting device from above.

❋❋ CAUTION:

Do not connect the lifting device to the intake manifold.

Raise the engine just enough to take the weight off the engine mounts.

2WD models

10 Remove the engine mount-to-frame support bracket through-bolt.

11 Remove the mount-to-engine block bolts, then remove the mount and the heat shield (if equipped) (see illustrations).

12 Place the heat shield and the new mount in position, install the mount-to-engine block bolts and tighten the bolts to the torque listed in this Chapter's Specifications.

4WD models

13 Remove the front axle assembly (see Chapter 8). If removing the driver's side engine mount remove the starter (see Chapter 5)

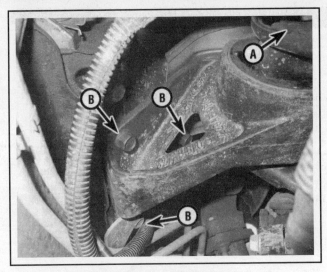

17.11a Driver's side engine mount details

   A   *Through-bolt*
   B   *Mount-to-engine block bolts*

14 Remove the engine mount to frame support bracket through-bolt.
15 Remove the engine mount to engine support bracket bolt and nuts.
16 Raising the engine more, if necessary, remove the engine mount(s).
17 To remove the engine support brackets simply remove the bolts from the engine block and transmission housing.
18 If removed, place the engine support bracket(s) in position and install the engine support bracket to engine block and transmission housing, Tighten the bolts to the torque listed in this Chapter's Specifications.

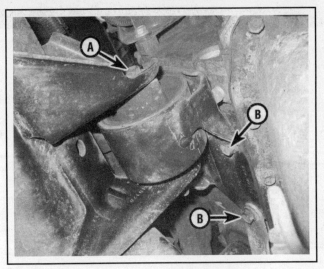

17.11b Passenger's side engine mount details

   A   *Through-bolt*
   B   *Mount-to-engine block bolts (not all are visible in this photo)*

19 Install the engine mount onto the engine support bracket and tighten the bolts to the torque listed in this Chapter's Specifications.

All models

20 After the engine mounts have been installed onto the engine, lower the engine while guiding the engine mount and through-bolt into the frame support bracket. Install the through-bolt nut and tighten it to the torque listed in this Chapter's Specifications.
21 The remainder of the installation is the reverse of removal. Remove the engine hoist and the jackstands and lower the vehicle.

Specifications

General

Displacement
    3.9L V6   238 cubic inches
    5.2L V8   318 cubic inches
    5.9L V8   360 cubic inches
Bore and stroke
    3.9L V6   3.91 x 3.31 inches
    5.2L V8   3.91 x 3.31 inches
    5.9L V8   4.00 x 3.58 inches
Cylinder numbers (front-to-rear)
    V6
        Left (driver's) side   1-3-5
        Right side   2-4-6
        Firing order   1-6-5-4-3-2
    V8
        Left (driver's) side   1-3-5-7
        Right side   2-4-6-8
        Firing order   1-8-4-3-6-5-7-2
Distributor rotation (viewed from above)   Clockwise
Cylinder compression pressure
    Minimum   100 psi
    Maximum variation between cylinders   40 psi

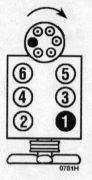

Cylinder location and distributor rotation - V6 engine

V6 engine

Cylinder location and distributor rotation - V8 engines

5.2L/5.9L V8 engines

The blackened terminal shown on the distributor cap indicates the Number One spark plug wire position

Camshaft

Journal diameters
    V6
        No. 1   1.998 to 1.999 inches
        No. 2   1.982 to 1.983 inches
        No. 3   1.951 to 1.952 inches
        No. 4   1.5605 to 1.5615 inches
    5.2L V8
        No. 1   1.998 to 1.999 inches
        No. 2   1.982 to 1.983 inches
        No. 3   1.967 to 1.968 inches
        No. 4   1.951 to 1.952 inches
        No. 5   1.5605 to 1.5615 inches
    5.9L V8
        No. 1   2.000 to 2.001 inches
        No. 2   1.984 to 1.985 inches
        No. 3   1.969 to 1.970 inches
        No. 4   1.950 to 1.952 inches
        No. 5   1.559 to 1.562 inches

Endplay
    V6 and V8   0.002 to 0.010 inch
Valve lift
    V6 and 5.2L V8
        Intake   0.432 inch
        Exhaust   0.432 inch
    5.9L V8
        Intake   0.410 inch
        Exhaust   0.417 inch

Oil pump

Minimum pressure at curb idle	6 psi
Operating pressure	30 to 80 psi at 3000 rpm
Outer rotor thickness limit	0.825 inch minimum
Outer rotor diameter limit	2.469 inches minimum
Inner rotor thickness limit	0.825 inch minimum
Clearance over rotors	0.004 inch maximum
Outer rotor clearance limit	0.014 inch maximum
Rotor tip clearance limit	0.008 inch maximum

Torque specifications — Ft-lbs (unless otherwise indicated)

Camshaft sprocket bolt	50
Camshaft thrust plate/timing chain tensioner bolts (V6)	210 in-lbs
Camshaft thrust plate bolts (V8)	210 in-lbs
Crankshaft pulley bolts	210 in-lbs
Cylinder head bolts (in sequence - see illustrations 9.16a and 9.16b)	
First step	50
Second step	105
Engine support bracket-to-block bolts	30
Engine support bracket-to-transmission housing (4WD models)	65
Engine mount-to-engine support bracket nut	30
Engine mount-to-engine support bracket through bolt (4WD models)	75
Engine mount-to-frame rail through bolt/nuts	75
Exhaust manifold bolts/nuts	25
Exhaust pipe flange nuts	20 to 25
Flywheel/driveplate bolts	55
Intake manifold bolts	
V6	
Step 1	Tighten bolts 1 and 2 in increments of 12 in-lbs, to 72 in-lbs
Step 2	Tighten bolts 3 through 12 in sequence, to 72 in-lbs
Step 3	Check to make sure that all bolts are tightened to 72 in-lbs
Step 4	Tighten all bolts, in sequence, to 144 in-lbs
Step 5	Check to make sure all bolts are tightened to 144 in-lbs
V8	
Step 1	Tighten bolts 1 through 4 in increments of 12 in-lbs, to 72 in-lbs
Step 2	Tighten bolts 5 through 12 in sequence, to 72 in-lbs
Step 3	Check to make sure that all bolts are tightened to 72 in-lbs
Step 4	Tighten all bolts, in sequence, to 144 in-lbs
Step 5	Check to make sure all bolts are tightened to 144 in-lbs

Torque specifications   Ft-lbs (unless otherwise indicated)

Intake plenum pan bolts	
V6 and 5.9L V8	
Step 1	48 in-lbs
Step 2	84 in-lbs
Step 3	84 in-lbs
5.2L V8	
Step 1	24 in-lbs
Step 2	84 in-lbs
Step 3	84 in-lbs
Oil pan bolts/studs	215 in-lbs
Oil pump cover bolts	95 in-lbs
Oil pump mounting bolts	30
Rocker arm bolts	21
Timing chain cover bolts	30
Valve cover nuts/studs	95 in-lbs
Vibration damper-to-crankshaft bolt	
V6 and 5.2L V8	135
5.9L V8	180
Water pump-to-cover bolts	30

➡ **Note: Refer to Part D for additional specifications.**

2C

4.7L V8 ENGINE

Section

Reference to other Chapters

1 General information

This Part of Chapter 2 is devoted to in-vehicle repair procedures for the 4.7L V8 engine. These engines utilize a cast iron engine block with eight cylinders arranged in a "V" shape at a 90-degree angle between the two banks. The overhead camshaft aluminum cylinder heads are equipped with replaceable valve guides and seats. Stamped steel rocker arms with an integral roller bearing actuate the valves.

All information concerning engine removal and installation and engine block and cylinder head overhaul can be found in Part D of this Chapter.

The following repair procedures are based on the assumption that the engine is installed in the vehicle. If the engine has been removed from the vehicle and mounted on a stand, many of the steps outlined in this Part of Chapter 2 will not apply.

The Specifications included in this Part of Chapter 2 apply only to the procedures contained in this Part. Part D of Chapter 2 contains the Specifications necessary for cylinder head and engine block rebuilding.

2 Repair operations possible with the engine in the vehicle

Many major repair operations can be accomplished without removing the engine from the vehicle.

Clean the engine compartment and the exterior of the engine with some type of degreaser before any work is done. It will make the job easier and help keep dirt out of the internal areas of the engine.

Depending on the components involved, it may be helpful to remove the hood to improve access to the engine as repairs are performed (refer to Chapter 11, if necessary). Cover the fenders to prevent damage to the paint. Special pads are available, but an old bedspread or blanket will also work.

If vacuum, exhaust, oil or coolant leaks develop, indicating a need for gasket or seal replacement, the repairs can generally be made with the engine in the vehicle. The intake and exhaust manifold gaskets, oil pan gasket, crankshaft oil seals and cylinder head gaskets are all accessible with the engine in place.

Exterior engine components, such as the intake and exhaust manifolds, the oil pan, the oil pump, the water pump (see Chapter 3), the starter motor, the alternator and the fuel system components (see Chapter 4) can be removed for repair with the engine in place.

Since the cylinder heads can be removed without pulling the engine, valve component servicing can also be accomplished with the engine in the vehicle. Replacement of the camshafts, timing chains and sprockets are also possible with the engine in the vehicle.

In extreme cases caused by a lack of necessary equipment, repair or replacement of piston rings, pistons, connecting rods and rod bearings is possible with the engine in the vehicle. However, this practice is not recommended because of the cleaning and preparation work that must be done to the components involved.

3 Top Dead Center (TDC) for number one piston - locating

▶ **Refer to illustrations 3.5 and 3.8**

1   Top Dead Center (TDC) is the highest point in the cylinder that each piston reaches as it travels up the cylinder bore. Each piston reaches TDC on the compression stroke and again on the exhaust stroke, but TDC generally refers to piston position on the compression stroke.

2   Positioning the piston(s) at TDC is an essential part of many procedures such as valve timing, camshaft and timing chain/sprocket removal.

3   Before beginning this procedure, be sure to place the transmission in Neutral and apply the parking brake or block the rear wheels. Also, disable the ignition system by disconnecting the primary electrical connectors at the ignition coil packs and remove the spark plugs (see Chapter 1).

4   In order to bring any piston to TDC, the crankshaft must be turned using one of the methods outlined below. When looking at the front of the engine, normal crankshaft rotation is clockwise.

  a) *The preferred method is to turn the crankshaft with a socket and ratchet attached to the bolt threaded into the front of the crankshaft. Apply pressure on the bolt in a clockwise direction only. Never turn the bolt counterclockwise.*

  b) *A remote starter switch, which may save some time, can also be used. Follow the instructions included with the switch. Once the piston is close to TDC, use a socket and ratchet as described in the previous paragraph.*

  c) *If an assistant is available to turn the ignition switch to the Start position in short bursts, you can get the piston close to TDC without a remote starter switch. Make sure your assistant is out of the vehicle, away from the ignition switch, then use a socket and ratchet as described in Paragraph (a) to complete the procedure.*

5   Install a compression pressure gauge in the number one spark plug hole (refer to Chapter 2D). It should be a gauge with a screw-in fitting and a hose at least six inches long (see illustration).

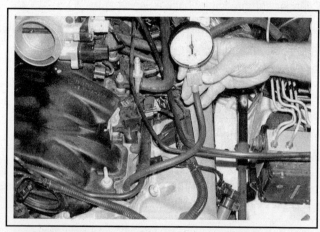

3.5 A compression gauge can be used in the number one plug hole to assist in finding TDC

6   Rotate the crankshaft using one of the methods described above while observing for pressure on the compression gauge. The moment the gauge shows pressure indicates that the number one cylinder has begun the compression stroke.

7   Once the compression stroke has begun, TDC for the compression stroke is reached by bringing the piston to the top of the cylinder.

8   Continue turning the crankshaft until the notch in the crankshaft damper is aligned with the TDC mark on the timing chain cover (see illustration). At this point, the number one cylinder is at TDC on the compression stroke. If the marks are aligned but there was no compression, the piston was on the exhaust stroke. Continue rotating the crankshaft 360-degrees (1-turn).

➡ **Note: If a compression gauge is not available, you can simply place a blunt object over the spark plug hole and listen for compression as the engine is rotated. Once compression at the No.1 spark plug hole is noted the remainder of the Step is the same.**

9   After the number one piston has been positioned at TDC on the compression stroke, TDC for any of the remaining cylinders can be located by turning the crankshaft 90-degrees and following the firing

3.8 Align the groove in the damper with the TDC mark on the timing chain cover

order (refer to the Specifications). Rotating the engine 90-degrees past TDC #1 will put the engine at TDC compression for cylinder #8.

4   Valve cover - removal and installation

▶ **Refer to illustrations 4.4, 4.5, 4.9, 4.11 and 4.12**

REMOVAL

1   Disconnect the cable from the negative terminal of the battery.

2   Remove the air intake duct and the throttle body resonator (see Chapter 4).

3   Detach the electrical connector(s) from the ignition coils and the fuel injectors on the side from which the valve cover is to be removed. If both valve covers are to be removed, disconnect all of the connectors from the ignition coils and the fuel injectors.

Left valve cover

4   Unclip the fuel injector wiring harness from the studs on the valve cover and position it aside (see illustration).

5   Remove the valve cover studs and bolts (see illustration). Make a note of the stud locations before removal to ensure correct positioning during installation.

6   Detach the valve cover.

➡ **Note: If the cover sticks to the cylinder head, use a block of wood and a hammer to dislodge it. If the cover still won't come loose, pry on it carefully, but don't distort the sealing flange.**

Right valve cover

7   Remove the air cleaner assembly (see Chapter 4).

8   Partially drain the cooling system until the level is below heater hoses (see Chapter 1 if necessary), then remove the heater hoses from the engine and the retaining clips and position them aside.

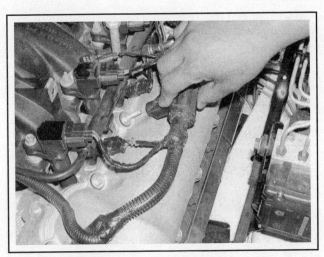

4.4 Detach the wiring harness from the valve cover studs and position it aside

4.5 Left valve cover mounting details - arrows indicate stud locations

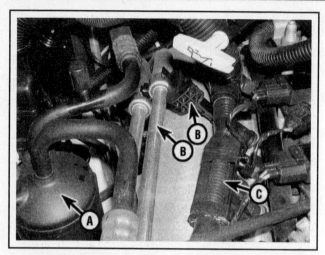

4.9 When working on the right valve cover, it will be necessary to position aside the accumulator (A), the heater hoses and bracket (B) and the fuel injection wiring harness (C)

9 Remove the engine drivebelt (see Chapter 1), then unbolt the air conditioning compressor from the engine and position it aside without disconnecting the refrigerant lines. Also loosen the air conditioning accumulator bracket (see illustration).

10 Detach the breather hose and filter assembly from the rear of the right cylinder head.

11 Remove the PCV hose from the oil fill tube, then remove the oil fill tube (with the PCV valve attached) from the cylinder head (see illustration).

12 Remove the valve cover studs/nuts and bolts (see illustration). Make a note of the stud locations before removal to ensure correct

4.12 Right valve cover mounting details - arrows indicate stud locations

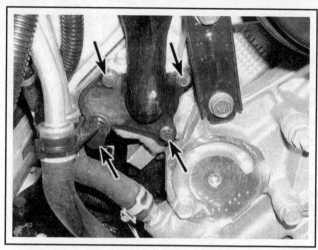

4.11 Oil filler tube mounting bolts/nut (arrows) - detach the heater hose bracket from the stud to access the nut

positioning during installation.

13 Detach the valve cover.

➡**Note: If the cover sticks to the cylinder head, use a block of wood and a hammer to dislodge it. If the cover still won't come loose, pry on it carefully, but don't distort the sealing flange.**

INSTALLATION

14 The mating surfaces of each cylinder head and valve cover must be perfectly clean when the covers are installed. Use a gasket scraper to remove all traces of sealant or old gasket material, then clean the mating surfaces with lacquer thinner or acetone (if there's sealant or oil on the mating surfaces when the cover is installed, oil leaks may develop). Be extra careful not to nick or gouge the mating surfaces with the scraper.

※※ **CAUTION:**

Do not use harsh cleaners when cleaning the valve covers or damage to the covers may occur.

15 Clean the mounting bolt or stud threads with a wire brush if necessary to remove any corrosion and restore damaged threads. Use a tap to clean the threaded holes in the heads.

16 Place the valve cover and new gasket in position, then install the stud/nuts and bolts in the correct location from which they where removed. Tighten the bolts in several steps to the torque listed in this Chapter's Specifications.

17 Complete the installation by reversing the removal procedure. Start the engine and check carefully for oil leaks.

5   Rocker arms and hydraulic lash adjusters - removal, inspection and installation

♦ Refer to illustrations 5.5, 5.7 and 5.8

➡ Note 1: A special valve spring compressor available from most aftermarket specialty tool manufacturers will be required for this procedure. The only other alternative to accomplishing this task without the use of this special tool is to remove the timing chains and the camshafts, which requires major disassembly of the engine and surrounding components.

➡ Note 2: This engine is a non-freewheeling engine and the pistons must be down in the cylinder bore before the valve and spring assembly can be compressed to allow rocker arm removal.

1   Before beginning this procedure, be sure to place the transmission in Park and apply the parking brake or block the rear wheels. Also, disable the ignition system by disconnecting the primary electrical connectors at the ignition coils and remove the spark plugs (see Chapter 1).

2   Remove the valve cover(s) (see Section 4).

3   Before the rocker arms and lash adjusters are removed, arrange to label and store them, so they can be kept separate and reinstalled on the same valve they were removed from.

4   Rotate the engine with a socket and ratchet in a clockwise direction only by the crankshaft pulley/vibration damper bolt until the piston(s) are positioned correctly to remove the rocker arms from the corresponding cylinders as follows:

  a) *Remove the rocker arms from cylinders No. 2 and 8 with the No.1 piston at TDC on the compression stroke (see Section 3).*

  b) *Remove the rocker arms from cylinders No. 3 and 5 with the No. 1 piston at TDC on the exhaust stroke. Rotate the crankshaft exactly 360-degrees (1-turn) from TDC on the compression stroke to bring the No.1 piston to TDC on the exhaust stroke. This is also verified by observing that the "V8" marks on the camshaft sprocket are pointing straight upward.*

  c) *Remove the rocker arms from cylinders No. 4 and 6 with the No. 3 piston at TDC on the compression stroke.*

  d) *Remove the rocker arms from cylinders No. 1 and 7 with the No. 2 piston at TDC on the compression stroke.*

5   Hook the valve spring compressor around the base of the camshaft. Depress the valve spring just enough to release tension on the rocker arm to be removed. Once tension on the rocker arm is

5.5 Using a special type valve spring compressor, depress the valve spring just enough to remove the rocker arm

relieved, the rocker arm can be removed by simply pulling it out (see illustration).

6   If you're removing or replacing only a few of the rockers arms or lash adjusters, locate the cylinder number of the rocker arm or lash adjuster you wish to remove in Step 4, then rotate the crankshaft to the corresponding position. Remember to keep the rocker arm and lash adjuster for each valve together so they can be reinstalled in the same locations. Refer to Section 3 as necessary to help position the designated cylinder at TDC.

7   Once the rocker arms are removed, the lash adjusters can be pulled out of the cylinder head and stored with the corresponding rocker arm (see illustration).

8   Inspect each rocker arm for wear, cracks and other damage. Make sure the rollers turn freely and show no signs of wear, also check the pivot area for wear, cracks and galling (see illustration).

9   Inspect the lash adjuster contact surfaces wear or damage. Make sure the lash adjusters move up and down freely in their bores on the cylinder head without excessive side to side play.

10   Installation is the reverse of removal with the following exceptions: Always install the lash adjuster first and make sure they're at least partially full of oil before installation. This is indicated by little or no lash adjuster plunger travel.

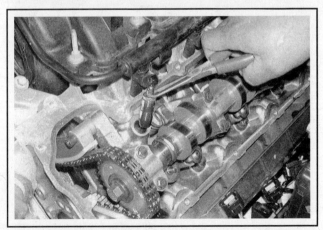

5.7 Pull the lash adjuster up and out of its bore to remove it from the cylinder head

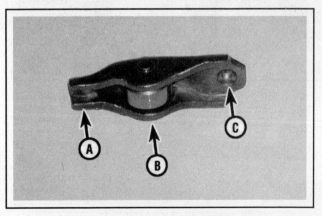

5.8 Inspect the rocker arms at the following locations

A Valve stem seat	C Lash adjuster pocket
B Roller	

6 Valve springs, retainers and seals - replacement

♦ Refer to illustrations 6.5, 6.7a, 6.7b, 6.8, 6.13 and 6.15

➡ Note: Broken valve springs and defective valve stem seals can be replaced without removing the cylinder heads. Two special tools and a compressed air source are normally required to perform this operation, so read through this Section carefully. The special-type of valve spring compressor required for rocker arm and valve spring removal may not be available at all tool rental yards, so check on the availability before beginning the job.

1 Remove the valve cover(s) (see Section 4).

2 Refer to Section 5 and remove the rocker arms from the affected cylinder head.

3 Remove the spark plug (see Chapter 1) from the cylinder that has the defective component. If all of the valve stem seals are being replaced, all of the spark plugs and rockers arms should be removed.

4 Turn the crankshaft until the piston in the affected cylinder is at Top Dead Center on the compression stroke (refer to Section 3). If you're replacing all of the valve stem seals, begin with cylinder number one and work on the valves for one cylinder at a time. Move from cylinder-to-cylinder following the firing order sequence (see this Chapter's Specifications).

5 Thread a long adapter into the spark plug hole and connect an air hose from a compressed air source to it (see illustration). Most auto parts stores can supply the air hose adapter.

➡ Note: Because of the length of the spark plug wells, it will be necessary to use a long spark plug adapter with a length of hose attached (as used on many cylinder compression gauges) utilizing a quick-disconnect fitting to hook to your air source.

6 Apply 90 to 100 psi of compressed air to the cylinder.

✷✷ WARNING:

The piston may be forced down by the compressed air, causing the crankshaft to turn suddenly. If the wrench used when positioning the number one piston at TDC is still attached to the bolt in the crankshaft nose, it could cause damage or injury when the crankshaft moves.

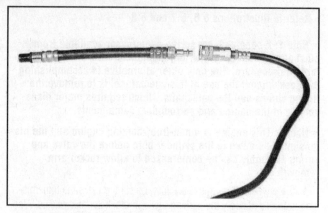

6.5 You'll need an air hose adapter this long to reach down into the spark plug tubes - they're commonly available from auto parts stores

7 Stuff shop rags into the cylinder head holes around the valves to prevent parts and tools from falling into the engine, then use a valve spring compressor to compress the spring. Remove the valve stem locks with small needle-nose pliers or a magnet (see illustrations).

➡ Note: The valves should be held in place by the air pressure. If the valve faces or seats are in poor condition, leaks may prevent air pressure from retaining the valves. If the valves cannot hold air, the cylinder head should be removed and taken to a machine shop for a valve job.

8 Remove the spring retainer and valve spring, then remove the valve stem seal (see illustration).

9 Wrap a rubber band or tape around the top of the valve stem so the valve won't fall into the combustion chamber, then release the air pressure.

10 Inspect the valve stem for damage. Rotate the valve in the guide and check the end for eccentric movement, which would indicate that the valve is bent.

11 Move the valve up-and-down in the guide and make sure it doesn't bind. If the valve stem binds, either the valve is bent or the guide is

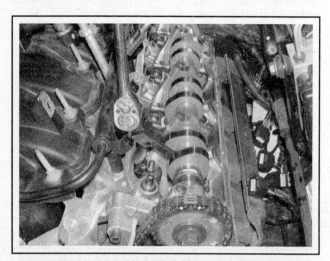

6.7a Compress the valve spring enough to release the valve stem locks . . .

6.7b . . . and lift them out with a magnet or needle-nose pliers

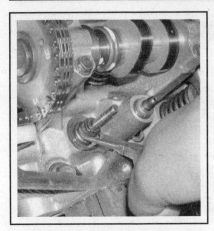

6.8 A pair of pliers will be required to remove the valve stem seal from the valve guide

6.13 Using a deep socket and hammer, gently tap the new seals onto the valve guide only until seated

6.15 Apply a small dab of grease to each valve stem lock as shown here before installation - it will hold them in place on the valve stem as the spring is released

damaged. In either case, the head will have to be removed for repair.

12 Reapply air pressure to the cylinder to retain the valve in the closed position, then remove the tape or rubber band from the valve stem.

13 Lubricate the valve stems with engine oil and install the valve spring seat/valve seal assembly over the top of the valves stems. Using the stem of the valves as a guide, slide the seals down to the top of each valve guide. Using a hammer and a deep socket or seal installation tool, gently tap each seal into place until it's completely seated on the guide (see illustration). Don't twist or cock the seals during installation or they won't seal properly on the valve stems. Make sure the garter spring (if equipped) is still in place around the top of the seal.

14 Install the spring and retainer in position over the valve with the colored mark (if equipped) on the spring facing UP. Compress the valve spring assembly only enough to install the keepers in the valve stem.

15 Position the keepers in the valve stem groove. Apply a small dab of grease to the inside of each keeper to hold it in place if necessary (see illustration). Remove the pressure from the spring tool and make sure the keepers are seated.

16 Disconnect the air hose and remove the adapter from the spark plug hole.

17 Repeat the above procedure on the remaining cylinders, following the firing order sequence (see the Specifications). Bring each piston to top dead center on the compression stroke before applying air pressure.

18 Refer to Section 5 and install the rocker arms.

19 Refer to Section 4 and install the valve covers.

20 Install the spark plug(s) and the ignition coils referring to the appropriate sections as necessary.

21 Start and run the engine, then check for oil leaks and unusual sounds coming from the valve cover area.

7 Timing chain and sprockets - removal, inspection and installation

➡Note 1: **Special tools are necessary to complete this procedure. Read through the entire procedure and obtain the special tools before beginning work.**

➡Note 2: **The 4.7L engine utilizes three timing chains to produce proper valve timing. The primary timing chain runs around the crankshaft sprocket and the idler gear sprocket. This chain synchronizes the crankshaft and pistons with the idler gear, while two secondary timing chains run around the rear of the idler gear and up to the camshaft sprockets to synchronize the valve timing with the crankshaft.**

REMOVAL

▶ **Refer to illustrations 7.7, 7.11, 7.13, 7.14, 7.15, 7.16a, 7.16b, 7.17 and 7.18**

1 Disconnect the cable from the negative terminal of the battery.

2 Drain the cooling system (see Chapter 1).

3 Refer to Chapter 3 and remove the cooling fan, the accessory drivebelt and the fan shroud from the engine compartment.

4 Detach the heater hoses and the lower radiator hose from the timing chain cover and position them aside.

5 Unbolt the power steering pump and set it aside without disconnecting the fluid lines (see Chapter 10).

6 Remove the alternator (see Chapter 5). Also unbolt the air conditioning compressor (if equipped) and position it aside without disconnecting the refrigerant lines.

7 Remove the accessory drivebelt tensioner from the timing chain cover (see illustration).

7.7 Drivebelt tensioner retaining bolt (arrow)

7.11 When the engine is at TDC on the exhaust stroke, the crankshaft pulley/vibration damper is aligned with the mark on the timing chain cover and the "V8" marks on the camshaft sprockets should be pointing to the 12 o'clock position

7.13 Timing chain cover retaining bolts

8 Remove the valve covers (see Section 4) and the spark plugs (see Chapter 1).

9 Remove all of the rocker arms following the procedure outlined in Section 5.

➡Note: This step is not absolutely necessary, but it will help make alignment of the camshaft sprockets easier upon installation and also eliminate any possibility of the pistons contacting the valves during this procedure, since the 4.7L V8 is an interference engine.

10 Remove the camshaft position sensor from the right cylinder head (see Chapter 6).

11 Position the number one piston at TDC on the exhaust stroke (see Section 3). Visually confirm the engine is at TDC on the exhaust stroke, by verifying that the timing mark on the crankshaft pulley/vibration damper is aligned with the mark on the timing chain cover and the "V8" marks on the camshaft sprockets are pointing straight up in the 12 o'clock position (see illustration 3.8 and the accompanying illustration).

12 Remove the crankshaft pulley (see Section 12).

13 Remove the timing chain cover and the water pump as an assembly (see illustration). Note that various types and sizes of bolts are used. They must be reinstalled in their original locations. Mark each bolt or make a sketch to help remember where they go.

14 Cover the oil pan opening with shop rags to prevent any components from falling into the engine. Collapse the primary timing chain tensioner with a pair of locking pliers and install a locking pin into the holes in the tensioner body to keep it in the retracted position (see illustration).

15 Remove the secondary timing chain tensioners (see illustration).

7.14 Locking the primary timing chain tensioner in the retracted position

7.15 Secondary timing chain tensioner mounting bolts (arrows)

7.16a Removing the left camshaft sprocket bolt while holding the sprocket with a pin spanner wrench - note the chain guide access plug

16 Remove the camshaft sprocket retaining bolts (see illustrations). Pull the camshaft sprockets off the camshaft hubs one at a time. Lower the sprocket(s) into the cylinder head opening until the chain can be displaced from around the sprocket, then remove the camshaft sprockets from the engine and let the secondary chains fall down between the timing chain guides.

✳✳ WARNING 1:

If the rocker arms were not removed as suggested in Step 9, it will be necessary to hold the camshafts from rotating with a set of locking pliers while the sprocket is being removed. Work on one camshaft and sprocket at a time starting with the left sprocket and proceeding to the right sprocket. After the sprocket is removed from the camshaft(s), let the camshaft slowly rotate to its neutral position. This is typically 15-degrees clockwise on the left camshaft sprocket and 45-degrees counterclockwise on the right camshaft. Pressure from the valve springs will make the camshafts rotate as the sprockets are removed. Sudden movement of the camshafts may allow the valves to strike the pistons.

✳✳ WARNING 2:

Never install the locking pliers on a camshaft lobe as damage to the camshaft will occur. When using locking pliers, always rotate the camshaft with locking pliers by the base shaft.

✳✳ WARNING 3:

Do not rotate the crankshaft or camshafts separately after the secondary timing chains are loosened or removed with the rocker arms installed in the engine as piston or valve damage may occur. The only exception to this rule is when the camshafts must be rotated slightly, to realign the camshaft sprockets with the camshafts during installation.

✳✳ CAUTION:

The right camshaft sprocket is identified by the camshaft position sensor ring which is fastened to the rear of the sprocket. Be extremely careful not to damage or place a magnetic object of any kind near the camshaft position sensor ring or a no start condition may occur after installation.

17 Remove the idler sprocket bolt, then detach the idler sprocket,

7.16b The right camshaft sprocket is identified by the camshaft position sensor ring (arrow) which is fastened to the rear of the sprocket - be extremely careful not to damage or place a magnetic object of any kind near the camshaft position sensor ring or a no start condition may occur after installation

7.17 Remove the primary timing chain and the secondary chains as an assembly from the engine

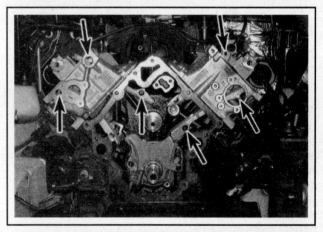

7.18 Timing chain guide and tensioner arm pivot bolts (arrows)

the crankshaft sprocket, the primary timing chain and the secondary timing chains as an assembly (see illustration).

18 Remove the cylinder head access plugs (see illustrations 7.16a and 7.16b). Also remove the oil fill tube (if not already removed) from the front of the right cylinder head. Detach the timing chain guides and tensioner arms (see illustration).

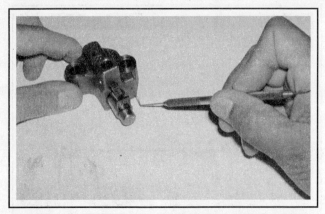

7.19 If excessive wear on the chain guides is evident, check the oil jet on the side of each secondary tensioner for a clogging

7.21 Primary timing chain tensioner/oil pump mounting bolts

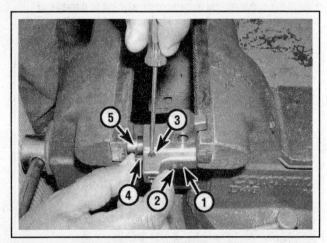

7.22 Locking the secondary tensioner(s) in the retracted position - note the "identification" mark on the side of the tensioner, as they are not interchangeable

1	Insert locking pin	4	Ratchet
2	Identification mark	5	Tensioner piston
3	Ratchet pawl		

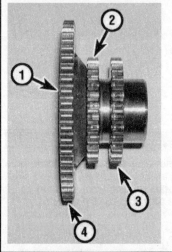

7.25 Side view of the idler gear

1   Idler sprocket assembly
2   Left camshaft (secondary) chain teeth
3   Right camshaft (secondary) chain teeth
4   Primary timing chain teeth

INSPECTION

▶ **Refer to illustration 7.19**

19 Inspect the camshaft and crankshaft sprockets for wear on the teeth and keyways. Inspect the chains for cracks or excessive wear of the rollers. Inspect the facing of the chain guides and tensioner arm for excessive wear. If any of the components show signs of excessive wear or the chain guides are grooved in excess of 0.039 inch deep they must be replaced. If any of the timing chain guides are excessively grooved or melted, the tensioner lube jet may be clogged. Be sure to remove the jet and blow compressed air through it to remove any debris or foreign material (see illustration). Also inspect the idler sprocket bushing and spline joint for wear (see Chapter 2D).

➡ **Note: Secondary timing chain stretch can be checked by removing the timing chain cover and the water pump assembly, then rotate the engine clockwise until the pistons in the secondary tensioners reach their maximum travel or extension. Using a machinist's ruler or a dial caliper, measure the piston protrusion or extension from the stepped ledge on the piston to the tensioner housing on each tensioner. If the maximum exten-**

sion of either tensioner piston exceeds 0.590 inch, the secondary timing chains are worn beyond their limits and should be replaced.

INSTALLATION

▶ **Refer to illustrations 7.21, 7.22, 7.25, 7.26, 7.28, 7.33, 7.41a and 7.41b**

20 If removed, install the timing chain guides and tensioner pivot arms back onto the engine and tighten the bolts to the torque listed in this Chapter's Specifications. Apply several drops of medium strength thread-locking compound to the tensioner pivot arm bolts before installing them. Note that the silver bolts retain the guides to the cylinder head and the black colored bolts retain the guides to the engine block.

21 If the primary timing chain tensioner was removed or replaced install it back onto the engine in the locked position and tighten the bolts to the torque listed in this Chapter's Specifications (see illustration).

22 Working on one secondary timing chain tensioner at a time, compress the tensioner piston in a vise until the stepped edge is flush with the tensioner body (see illustration). Insert a small scribe or other suitable tool into the side of the tensioner body and push the spring loaded ratchet pawl away from the ratchet mechanism, then push the ratchet down into the tensioner body until it's approximately 0.080 inch

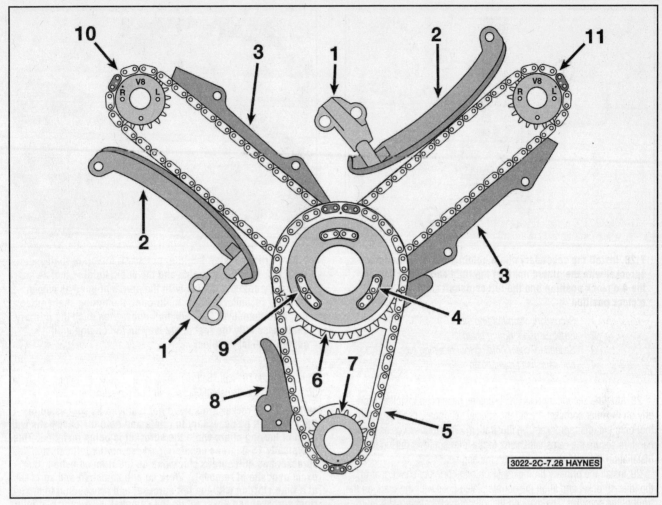

7.26 Timing chain installation details

1 Secondary timing chain tensioner	7 Crankshaft sprocket
2 Secondary tensioner arm	8 Primary chain tensioner
3 Chain guide	9 Two plated links on left camshaft chain
4 Two plated links on right camshaft chain	10 Right camshaft sprocket and secondary chain
5 Primary chain	11 Left camshaft sprocket and secondary chain
6 Idler sprocket	

away from the tensioner body. Insert the end of a paper clip into the hole on the front of the tensioner to lock the tensioner in place.

23 After the two secondary tensioners have been compressed and locked into place, install them on the engine and tighten the bolts to the torque listed in this Chapter's Specifications. Make sure the tensioner with the "R" mark is installed on the right (passenger side) secondary chain and the tensioner with "L" mark is installed on the left (driver's side) secondary chain. The secondary chain tensioners cannot be switched with one another. Also make sure the plate behind the left secondary chain tensioner is installed correctly.

24 If you purchased a new timing chain verify that you have the correct timing chain for your vehicle by counting the number of links the chain has and comparing the new chain with the old chain. Also compare the position of the colored links in the new chain with the position of the colored links in the old chain.

25 Note that the idler sprocket has three drive gears incorporated into it. The front or forward facing gear (the largest of the three) is for the primary timing chain, the second or middle gear is for the left secondary chain and the third or rear gear is for the right secondary sprocket (see illustration). The next 5 Steps will involve assembling the timing chains onto the idler sprocket on a workbench.

26 Place the idler sprocket on a workbench with the mark on the front in the 12 o'clock position. Loop the right camshaft chain over the rear gear (farthest away from the primary chain gear) on the idler sprocket and position it so that the two plated links on the chain are visible through the lower (4 o'clock) window in the idler sprocket (see illustration).

27 Loop the left camshaft chain over the front of the idler sprocket and position it over the middle gear so that the two plated links on the chain are visible through the lower (8 o'clock) window in the idler sprocket.

➡**Note: After the left chain is in position, the two plated links on the right chain will no longer be visible through the 4 o'clock window in the idler sprocket, so be sure that the right camshaft chain is installed correctly before installing the left camshaft chain.**

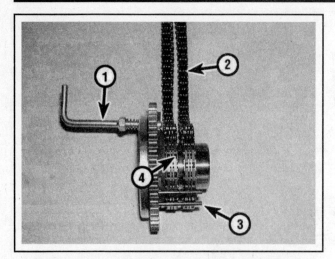

7.28 Install the secondary chain holding tool onto the idler sprocket with the plated links on the right camshaft chain in the 4 o'clock position and the left camshaft chain in the 8 o'clock position

1   *Secondary chain holding tool*
2   *Right camshaft timing chain*
3   *Secondary chain holding tool retaining pins*
4   *Left camshaft timing chain*

28 After the secondary (camshaft) chains have been installed properly on the idler sprocket, install the special secondary chain holding tool onto the idler sprocket (see illustration). This tool serves as a third hand, to secure the camshaft chains to the idler sprocket during the installation of the idler sprocket onto the engine.

29 Install the primary timing chain onto the primary chain gear of the idler sprocket and align the double plated links with the mark on the front of the sprocket. The mark on the idler sprocket should still be in the 12 o'clock position.

30 Insert the teeth of the crankshaft sprocket into the primary timing chain with the mark on the crankshaft sprocket pointing down in the 6 o'clock position and aligned with the single plated link on the chain.

31 Lubricate the idler shaft and bushing with clean engine oil.

32 Install the idler sprocket, the crankshaft sprocket and the timing chains with the chain holding tool as an assembly onto the engine. Slide the crankshaft sprocket over the keyway on the crankshaft and position the idler sprocket partially over the idler shaft (just enough to hold the primary chain in place). Then feed the secondary chains up through the chain guides and the cylinder head.

➡**Note: It may be easier to bend a hook in the end of a coat hanger to help pull the secondary chains up through the timing chain guides and the cylinder head opening.**

33 Loop the secondary chains over the camshaft hubs and secure them with rubber bands to remove the slack from the chains, then push the idler gear, primary timing chain and the crankshaft sprocket assembly back on to the engine until they're fully seated against the block (see illustration).

34 Align the "L" mark on the left camshaft sprocket with the plated link on the left camshaft chain and position the camshaft sprocket over the camshaft hub (see illustration 7.26). The camshaft may have to be rotated slightly to align the dowel pin on the camshaft with the slot on the sprocket.

35 Align the "R" mark on right camshaft sprocket with the plated link on the right camshaft chain and position the camshaft sprocket over the

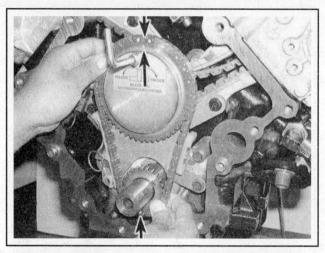

7.33 Partially install the idler sprocket, the crankshaft sprocket, the timing chains and the chain holding tool as an assembly onto the engine with the marks aligned as shown - feed the secondary chains up through the timing chain guides and loop them over the camshaft hubs, then push the primary chain assembly the rest of the way on the engine until it's seated against the block

camshaft hub. The camshaft may have to be rotated slightly to align the dowel pin on the camshaft with the slot on the sprocket.

➡**Note: If the rocker arms *were not* removed as suggested in Step 9, it will be necessary to rotate and hold the camshafts with a set of locking pliers while the sprocket is being installed. This is typically 15-degrees counterclockwise on the left camshaft sprocket and 45-degrees clockwise on the right camshaft (the exact opposite of removal). Work on one camshaft and sprocket at a time starting with the left sprocket and proceeding to the right sprocket and never rotate the camshaft by a camshaft lobe or damage to the camshaft will occur.**

36 Thoroughly clean the camshaft and idler sprocket bolts. Make sure all oil is removed from the bolt threads before installation, as over-tightening of bolts may occur if oil is not removed, then lubricate the bolt washers with small amount of clean engine oil making sure not to get oil on the threads.

37 Install the camshaft sprocket bolts finger tight. Remove the secondary timing chain holding tool from the idler sprocket, then install the idler sprocket retaining bolt and tighten it to the torque listed in this Chapter's Specifications.

38 Verify that all the plated timing chain links are aligned as shown in illustration 7.26.

39 Remove the locking pins from the primary timing chain tensioner and the secondary timing chain tensioners.

✵✵ CAUTION:

Do not manually extend the tensioners by hand; doing so will only over extend the tensioners and lead to premature timing chain wear.

40 Rotate the engine two complete revolutions and reverify the position of the timing marks again. The idler sprocket mark should be located in the 12 o'clock position and the crankshaft sprocket mark should be located in the 6 o'clock position with the "V8" marks on the camshaft sprockets located in the 12 o'clock position.

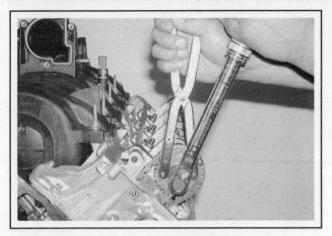

7.41a Tightening the left camshaft sprocket bolt

7.41b Tightening the right camshaft sprocket bolt

41 Using a spanner wrench to hold the sprockets from turning, tighten the camshaft sprocket bolts to the torque listed in this Chapter's Specifications (see illustrations).

42 Remove all traces of old sealant or gasket material from the timing chain cover and the engine block.

43 Place the timing cover and gasket in position on the engine and install the bolts in their original locations and tighten the bolts to the torque listed in this Chapter's Specifications.

44 The remainder of the installation is the reverse of removal. Be sure to use pipe sealant on the cylinder head plugs to prevent oil leaks.

8   Camshafts - removal, inspection and installation

➡ Note 1: Special tools are necessary to complete this procedure. Read through the entire procedure and obtain the special tools before beginning work.

➡ Note 2: The camshafts should always be thoroughly inspected before installation and camshaft endplay should always be checked prior to camshaft removal.

REMOVAL

▶ Refer to illustrations 8.7 and 8.9

1 Disconnect the cable from the negative terminal of the battery.

2 Remove the valve covers (see Section 4).

3 Remove the rocker arms (see Section 5).

4 Rotate the engine with a socket and ratchet (in a clockwise direction only) by the crankshaft pulley/vibration damper bolt until the "V8" marks on the camshaft sprockets are located in the 12 o'clock position (see illustration 7.11).

5 Using a permanent marker, apply alignment marks to the secondary timing chain links on either side of the "V8" marks on both camshaft sprockets to help aid the installation process (4 marks total).

6 Using a spanner wrench to hold the camshaft sprockets from turning, loosen the camshaft sprocket bolts several turns, then retighten the bolts by hand until they're snug up against the sprocket. If the camshaft sprockets have rotated during the bolt loosening process, rotate the engine clockwise until the "V8" marks on the cam sprockets are realigned in the 12 o'clock position.

7 Install a timing chain tensioner wedge through the opening in the top of the cylinder head and force the wedge down between the narrowest section of the secondary chain (see illustration). If both camshafts are to be removed, two timing chain wedges will be necessary (one for the left camshaft chain and one for the right camshaft chain). The wedge is used to secure the chain and the secondary tensioner in place while the camshaft is removed.

⁂ CAUTION 1:

Failure to use a timing chain wedge will allow the secondary tensioner to over-extend and require removal of the timing chain cover to reset the tensioners.

⁂ CAUTION 2:

Never force the wedge past the narrowest section of the secondary timing chain as damage to the tensioner will occur.

If a timing chain wedge is not available, they may be fabricated using a block of wood that is 3/8 to 1/2-inch thick and a piece of wire to pull the wedge out of the cylinder head after installation.

8.7 The wedge is pushed down between the chain strands to secure the secondary chain and the tensioner in place while the camshaft is removed - this wedge is fabricated from a block of wood and a piece of wire

8.9 Verify that the camshaft bearing caps are marked to ensure correct reinstallation - do not mix-up the caps from the left cylinder head with the caps from the right cylinder head

8 Remove the camshaft sprocket retaining bolt(s) and detach the camshaft sprocket(s) from the camshaft hub(s). Disengage the camshaft chain(s) from the sprocket(s) and remove the camshaft sprocket(s) from the engine.

9 Verify the markings on the camshaft bearing caps. The caps should be marked from 1 to 5 with arrow marks on the caps indicating the front of the engine (see illustration). If both camshafts are being removed, use a permanent marker to mark each bearing cap on the right cylinder head with an "R" and each bearing cap on the left cylinder head with an "L" to indicate from which cylinder head they came from. Loosen the camshaft bearing caps in two or three steps, in the reverse order of the tightening sequence (see illustration 8.19).

✳✳ CAUTION:

Keep the caps in order. They must go back in the same location they were removed from.

10 Detach the bearing caps, then remove the camshaft(s) from the cylinder head. Mark the camshaft(s) "Left" or "Right" to indicate which cylinder head it came from.

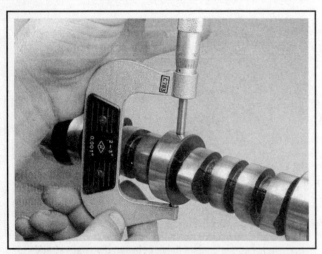

8.13 Measure the outside diameter of each camshaft journal and the inside diameter of each bearing to determine the oil clearance measurement

8.12 Inspect the cam bearing surfaces in each cylinder head for pits, score marks and abnormal wear - if wear or damage is noted, the cylinder head must be replaced

11 Inspect the camshafts as described in Steps 12 through 16. Also inspect the camshaft secondary sprockets for wear on the teeth. Inspect the chains for cracks or excessive wear of the rollers. If any of the components show signs of excessive wear they must be replaced.

INSPECTION

▶ **Refer to illustrations 8.12, 8.13 and 8.16**

12 Visually check the camshaft bearing surfaces for pitting, score marks, galling and abnormal wear. If the bearing surfaces are damaged, the cylinder head may have to be replaced (see illustration).

13 Measure the outside diameter of each camshaft bearing journal and record your measurements (see illustration). Compare them to the journal outside diameter specified in this Chapter, then measure the inside diameter of each corresponding camshaft bearing (with the caps torqued in place) and record the measurements. Subtract each cam journal outside diameter from its respective cam bearing bore inside diameter to determine the oil clearance for each bearing. Compare the results to the specified journal-to-bearing clearance. If any of the measurements fall outside the standard specified wear limits in this Chapter, either the camshaft or the cylinder head, or both, must be replaced.

14 Check camshaft runout by placing the camshaft back into the cylinder head and set up a dial indicator on the center journal. Zero the dial indicator. Turn the camshaft slowly and note the dial indicator readings. Runout should not exceed .0010 inch. If the measured runout exceeds the specified runout, replace the camshaft.

15 Check the camshaft endplay by placing a dial indicator with the stem in line with the camshaft and touching the snout. Push the camshaft all the way to the rear and zero the dial indicator. Next, pry the camshaft to the front as far as possible and check the reading on the dial indicator. The distance it moves is the endplay. If it's greater than the Specifications listed in this Chapter, check the bearing caps for wear. If the bearing caps are worn, the cylinder head must be replaced.

16 Compare the camshaft lobe height by measuring each lobe with a micrometer (see illustration). Measure each of the intake lobes and write the measurements and relative positions down on a piece of paper. Then measure each of the exhaust lobes and record the measurements and relative positions also. This will let you compare all of the intake lobes to one another and all of the exhaust lobes to one another. If the difference between the lobes exceeds 0.005 inch the camshaft

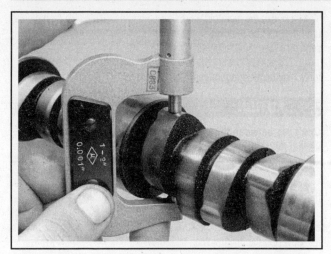

8.16 Measuring cam lobe height with a micrometer, make sure you move the micrometer to get the highest reading (top of cam lobe)

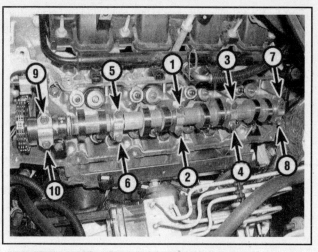

8.19 Camshaft bearing cap TIGHTENING sequence

should be replaced. Do not compare intake lobe heights to exhaust lobe heights, as lobe lift may be different. Only compare intake lobes to intake lobes and exhaust lobes to exhaust lobes for this comparison.

INSTALLATION

▶ **Refer to illustration 8.19**

17 Apply moly-based engine assembly lubricant to the camshaft lobes and journals and install the camshaft(s) into the cylinder head. The dowel pin on the left camshaft should be at the 1 o'clock position, and the pin on the right camshaft in the 10 o'clock position. If the old camshafts are being used, make sure they're installed in the exact location from which they came.

18 Install the bearing caps and bolts and tighten them hand tight.

19 Tighten the bearing cap bolts in several steps, to the torque listed

in this Chapter's Specifications, using the proper tightening sequence (see illustration).

20 Engage the camshaft sprocket teeth with the camshaft drive chain links so that the "V8" mark on the sprocket(s) is between the two marks made in Step 5 during removal, then position the sprocket over the dowel on the camshaft hub. At this point the chain marks and the "V8" marks on the sprocket should be pointing up in the 12 o'clock position.

21 Thoroughly clean the camshaft sprocket bolts. Make sure all oil is removed from the bolt threads before installation, as over-tightening of bolts may occur if oil is not removed, then lubricate the bolt washers with a small amount of clean engine oil making sure not to get oil on the threads.

22 Install the camshaft sprocket bolts and tighten them to the torque listed in this Chapter's Specifications (see illustration 7.41a and 7.41b).

23 Remove the timing chain wedge(s).

24 Install the rocker arms (see Section 5).

25 The remainder of installation is the reverse of removal.

9 Intake manifold - removal and installation

※ WARNING:

The engine must be completely cool before beginning this procedure.

REMOVAL

▶ **Refer to illustration 9.4**

1 Relieve the fuel pressure (see Chapter 4).

2 Disconnect the cable from the negative terminal of the battery.

3 Refer to Chapter 4 and remove the air intake duct from the throttle body.

4 Label and disconnect the vacuum hoses, the electrical connectors and the ground straps attached to the intake manifold and the throttle body (see illustration). Also remove the engine oil dipstick, the hood-to-cowl seal and the right engine lifting stud. When removing the oil dipstick, detach the nut from the stud on the intake manifold, then

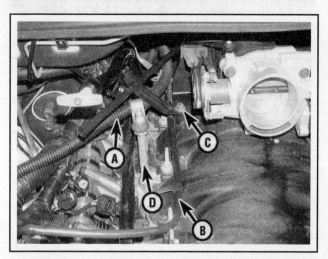

9.4 Label and disconnect the wiring harnesses (A), the vacuum hoses (B), the oil dipstick tube (C) and the hood-to-cowl seal (D)

follow the dipstick tube to the rear of the engine block and remove the bolt securing the tube at the back of the block. Pull the dipstick tube up and out of the engine block to remove it.

5 Detach the throttle cable and the cruise control cable from the throttle body and the throttle cable bracket (see Chapter 4).

6 Remove the accessory drivebelt (see Chapter 1).

7 Remove the alternator and the ignition coils (see Chapter 5).

8 Unbolt the air conditioning compressor and position it aside without disconnecting the refrigerant lines (see Chapter 3).

9 Remove the fuel rails and injectors, then remove the throttle body (see Chapter 4).

10 Refer to Chapter 1 and partially drain the cooling system, then refer to Chapter 6 and remove the coolant temperature sensor. This step is necessary to allow clearance for the intake manifold as it is removed. Also remove the heater hoses.

9.17 Intake manifold TIGHTENING sequence

11 Loosen the manifold mounting bolts/nuts in 1/4-turn increments until they can be removed by hand in the reverse order of the tightening sequence (see illustration 9.17).

12 The manifold will probably be stuck to the cylinder heads and force may be required to break the gasket seal.

✳✳ CAUTION:

Don't pry between the manifold and the heads or damage to the gasket sealing surfaces may occur, leading to vacuum leaks.

13 Label and detach any remaining hoses which would interfere with the removal of the intake manifold.

14 Lift the manifold up level with the vehicle and remove it from the engine. Interference with the cowl will be apparent, but with careful maneuvering the manifold can be removed.

INSTALLATION

▶ **Refer to illustration 9.17**

➡**Note: There are individual press-in-place gaskets for each intake port.**

15 Clean and inspect the intake manifold-to-cylinder head sealing surfaces. Inspect the gaskets on the manifold for tears or cracks replacing them if necessary. The gaskets can be reused if not damaged.

16 Position the manifold on the engine making sure the gaskets and manifold are aligned correctly over the cylinder heads, then install the intake manifold bolts hand tight.

17 Following the recommended tightening sequence, tighten the bolts, in several steps, to the torque listed in this Chapter's Specifications (see illustration).

18 The remainder of the installation is the reverse of the removal procedure. Fill the cooling system, run the engine and check for fuel, vacuum and coolant leaks.

10 Exhaust manifold - removal and installation

✳✳ WARNING:

The engine must be completely cool before beginning this procedure.

REMOVAL

1 Disconnect the cable from the negative terminal of the battery.

2 Block the rear wheels, set the parking brake, raise the front of the vehicle and support it securely on jackstands. Working below the vehicle, disconnect the electrical connectors from the oxygen sensors. Unbolt the front Y-pipe from both manifolds, then detach the Y-pipe from the exhaust system (see Chapter 4).

➡**Note: It will be necessary to detach the center exhaust system mount from the transmission and loosen the exhaust pipe clamp to accomplish this task.**

Left manifold

3 With the vehicle still in the raised position, remove the mounting bolts at the heat shield and the lower exhaust manifold bolts.

4 Lower the vehicle. Working in the engine compartment, remove the air intake duct and the throttle body resonator (see Chapter 4).

5 Remove the mounting bolts at the front of the heat shield and detach the heat shield from the manifold.

6 Remove the upper exhaust manifold bolts.

7 Working below the vehicle again, remove the lower manifold bolts and lower the manifold from the vehicle.

Right manifold

8 Remove the starter (see Chapter 5).

9 Working in the engine compartment, remove the air cleaner housing, resonator and inlet hose (see Chapter 4).

10 Partially drain the cooling system until the level is below heater hoses (see Chapter 1 if necessary), then remove the heater hoses from the engine and the retaining clips and position them aside.

11 Remove the engine drivebelt (see Chapter 1), then unbolt the air conditioning compressor from the engine and position it aside without disconnecting the refrigerant lines. Also loosen the air conditioning accumulator bracket (see illustration 4.9).

12 Remove the exhaust manifold heat shield mounting bolts and lift the heat shields from the engine compartment.

13 Remove the upper manifold mounting bolts.
14 Working below the vehicle, detach the lower manifold mounting bolts and lower manifold from the vehicle.

INSTALLATION

15 Clean the mating surfaces to remove all traces of old gasket material, then inspect the manifold for distortion and cracks. Warpage can be checked with a precision straightedge held against the mating flange. If a feeler gauge thicker than 0.030-inch can be inserted between the straightedge and flange surface, take the manifold to an automotive machine shop for resurfacing.
16 Place the exhaust manifold in position with a new gasket and install the mounting bolts finger tight.
17 Starting in the middle and working out toward the ends, tighten the mounting bolts in several increments, to the torque listed in this Chapter's Specifications.
18 Install the remaining components in the reverse order of removal.

✳ CAUTION:

Do not overtighten the exhaust manifold heat shields as distortion and cracks may occur.

19 Start the engine and check for exhaust leaks between the manifold and cylinder head and between the manifold and exhaust pipe.

11 Cylinder head - removal and installation

✳ WARNING:

The engine must be completely cool before beginning this procedure.

➡Note: The following procedure describes how to remove the cylinder heads with the camshaft(s) and the exhaust manifold(s) still attached to the cylinder head.

REMOVAL

1 Refer to Section 7 and remove the timing chains, sprockets and the timing chain guides.
2 Remove the intake manifold (see Section 9).
3 Raise the front of the vehicle and support it securely on jackstands.
4 Working below the vehicle, disconnect the electrical connector(s) from the oxygen sensor(s). Unbolt the front Y-pipe(s) from the exhaust manifolds.
5 Label and remove any remaining items attached to the cylinder head, such as coolant fittings, ground straps, cables, hoses, wires or brackets.
6 Using a breaker bar and the appropriate sized socket, loosen the cylinder head bolts in 1/4-turn increments until they can be removed by hand. Loosen the bolts in the reverse order of the tightening sequence (see illustration 11.19a) to avoid warping or cracking the head.

✳ CAUTION:

Do not attempt to remove the head until you have removed all 14 bolts.

7 Lift the cylinder head off the engine block with the camshaft in place and the exhaust manifold attached. If it's stuck, very carefully pry up at the front end of the cylinder head, beyond the gasket surface, at a casting protrusion.
8 Remove all external components from the head to allow for thorough cleaning and inspection.
➡Note: See Chapter 2, Part D, for cylinder head inspection and servicing procedures.

INSTALLATION

▶ **Refer to illustrations 11.19a and 11.19b**

9 The mating surfaces of the cylinder head and block must be perfectly clean when the head is installed.

✳ CAUTION:

While the head is off the engine, do not set the gasket-surface-side down on the bench or floor, or the gasket surface could be damaged.

10 Use a gasket scraper to remove all traces of carbon and old gasket material from the cylinder head and engine block being careful not to gouge the aluminum, then clean the mating surfaces with lacquer thinner or acetone. If there's oil on the mating surfaces when the head is installed, the gasket may not seal correctly and leaks could develop. When working on the block, stuff the cylinders with clean shop rags to keep out debris. Use a vacuum cleaner to remove material that falls into the cylinders.
11 Check the block and head mating surfaces for nicks, deep scratches and other damage. If damage is slight, it can be removed with a fine file; if it's excessive, machining may be the only alternative.
12 Use a tap of the correct size to chase the threads in the head bolt holes, then clean the holes with compressed air - make sure that nothing remains in the holes.

✳ WARNING:

Wear eye protection when using compressed air!

13 Check each cylinder head bolt for stretching. If the diameter of the bolt threads has necked down anywhere in the threaded area, the bolts have exceeded the maximum amount of stretch and will need to be replaced.
14 Check the cylinder head for warpage (see Chapter 2D). Check the head gasket, intake and exhaust manifold surfaces.
15 Install any components that were removed from the head such as the lash adjusters, the exhaust manifold and the camshaft back onto the cylinder head.
16 Position the new cylinder head gasket over the dowel pins on the

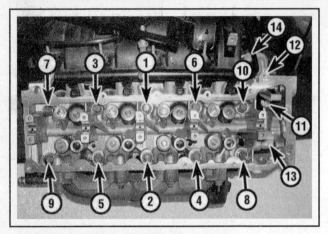

11.19a Cylinder head TIGHTENING sequence

11.19b Using an angle measurement gauge during the final stages of tightening

block noting which side of the gasket faces up.

17 Carefully set the head over the dowels on the block without disturbing the gasket.

18 Before installing the 11 mm head bolts (bolts 1 through 10), apply a small amount of clean engine oil to the threads and hardened washers (if equipped). The chamfered side of the washers must face the bolt heads. Before installing the 8 mm head bolts (bolts 11 through 14), apply a small amount of thread sealant to the bolt threads.

19 Install the bolts in their original locations and tighten them finger tight. Then tighten all the bolts in five steps, following the proper sequence to the torque and angle of rotation listed in this Chapter's Specifications (see illustrations).

20 Install the timing chain guides, the timing chains and the timing chain sprockets as described in Section 7. The remaining installation steps are the reverse of removal.

21 Refill the cooling system and change the engine oil and filter (see Chapter 1).

22 Start the engine and check for oil and coolant leaks.

12 Crankshaft pulley/vibration damper - removal and installation

▶ **Refer to illustrations 12.4, 12.5 and 12.6**

※ WARNING:

Wait until the engine is completely cool before beginning this procedure.

1 Disconnect the cable from the negative terminal of the battery.

2 Refer to Chapter 3 and remove the cooling fans and shroud assembly. Also drain the cooling system and remove the upper radiator hose.

3 Remove the drivebelts (see Chapter 1) and position the belt tensioner away from the crankshaft pulley.

4 Use a strap wrench around the crankshaft pulley to hold it while using a breaker bar and socket to remove the crankshaft pulley center bolt (see illustration).

5 Pull the damper off the crankshaft with a puller (see illustration).

12.4 Use a strap wrench to hold the crankshaft pulley while removing the center bolt (a chain-type wrench may be used if you wrap a section of old drivebelt or a rag around the crankshaft pulley first)

12.5 The use of a three jaw puller will be necessary to remove the crankshaft pulley - always place the puller jaws around the pulley hub, not the outer ring

⁜ CAUTION:

The jaws of the puller must only contact the hub of the pulley - not the outer ring.

➡Note: A long Allen-head bolt should be inserted into the crankshaft nose for the puller's tapered tip to push against to prevent damage to the crankshaft threads.

6   Check the surface on the pulley hub that the oil seal rides on. If the surface has been grooved from long-time contact with the seal, a press-on sleeve may be available to renew the sealing surface (see illustration). This sleeve is pressed into place with a hammer and a block of wood and is commonly available at auto parts stores for various applications.

7   Lubricate the pulley hub with clean engine oil. Align the slot in the pulley with the key on the crankshaft and push the crankshaft pulley on the crankshaft as far as it will go. Use a vibration damper installation tool to press the pulley the rest of the way onto the crankshaft.

8   Install the crankshaft pulley retaining bolt and tighten it to the torque listed in this Chapter's Specifications.

9   The remainder of installation is the reverse of the removal.

12.6 If the sealing surface of the pulley hub has a wear groove from contact with the seal, repair sleeves are available at most auto parts stores

13 Crankshaft front oil seal - replacement

◆ **Refer to illustrations 13.2 and 13.4**

1   Remove the crankshaft pulley from the engine (see Section 12).

2   Carefully pry the seal out of the cover with a seal removal tool or a large screwdriver (see illustration).

⁜ CAUTION:

Be careful not to scratch, gouge or distort the area that the seal fits into or an oil leak will develop.

3   Clean the bore to remove any old seal material and corrosion.

Position the new seal in the bore with the seal lip (usually the side with the spring) facing IN (toward the engine). A small amount of oil applied to the outer edge of the new seal will make installation easier - but don't overdo it!

4   Drive the seal into the bore with a seal driver or a large socket and hammer until it's completely seated (see illustration). Select a socket that's the same outside diameter as the seal and make sure the new seal is pressed into place until it bottoms against the cover flange.

5   Lubricate the seal lips with engine oil and reinstall the crankshaft pulley.

6   The remainder of installation is the reverse of the removal. Run the engine and check for oil leaks.

13.2 Pry the seal out very carefully with a seal removal tool or screwdriver, being careful not to nick or gouge the seal bore or the crankshaft

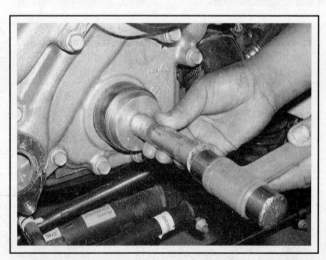

13.4 Use a seal driver or large-diameter socket to drive the new seal into the cover

14 Oil pan - removal and installation

REMOVAL

▶ **Refer to illustrations 14.5 and 14.7**

1 Disconnect the cable from the negative terminal of the battery.

2 Apply the parking brake and block the rear wheels. Raise the front of the vehicle and place it securely on jackstands. Drain the engine oil (see Chapter 1).

3 Disconnect the electrical connectors from the oxygen sensors. Unbolt the front Y-pipe from both manifolds, then detach the Y-pipe from the exhaust system (see Chapter 4).

➡**Note: It will be necessary to detach the center exhaust system mount from the transmission and loosen the exhaust pipe clamp to accomplish this task.**

4 Remove the transmission oil cooler lines from the right side of the oil pan.

5 Remove the transmission-to-oil pan support brace at the rear of the pan (see illustration).

6 Remove the starter (see Chapter 5). Also detach any clips securing the transmission oil cooler lines that would interfere with removal of the oil pan. On 2WD models, remove the intake manifold (see Section 9) and raise the engine with a crane from above to allow enough clearance for the oil pan to be removed from below. On 4WD models, remove the front axle assembly (see Chapter 8).

7 Remove the bolts and nuts, noting the stud locations, then carefully separate the oil pan from the block. Don't pry between the block and the pan or damage to the sealing surfaces and gasket could occur and oil leaks may develop. Instead, tap on the side of the oil pan with a rubber mallet if necessary to break the gasket seal (see illustration).

8 Remove the oil pump pick-up tube (see illustrations 15.3a and 15.3b) and detach the oil pan gasket/windage tray from the engine block.

INSTALLATION

▶ **Refer to illustration 14.13**

9 Clean the oil pan with solvent and remove any gasket material from the block and the pan mating surfaces. Clean the mating surfaces with lacquer thinner or acetone and make sure the bolt holes in the block are clear. Check the oil pan flange for distortion, particularly around the bolt holes.

10 Inspect the oil pan gasket for cuts and tears, replacing it if necessary. If the gasket is in good condition it can be reused.

➡**Note: The oil pan gasket and the windage tray are a one piece design, therefore must be replaced together.**

11 Position the oil pan gasket in place on the block and install the oil pump pick-up tube. (see Section 15). Always use a new O-ring on the pick-up tube and tighten the pick-up tube-to-oil pump bolt first, when installing it.

12 Place the oil pan in position on the block and install the nuts/bolts.

13 After the fasteners are installed, tighten all the bolts in several steps, following the proper sequence to the torque listed in this Chapter's Specifications (see illustration).

14 Place the transmission-to-oil pan support brace in position and install the vertically mounted bolts. Torque the vertical mounted bolts to 10 in-lbs, then install the horizontally mounted bolts. Torque the horizontal mounted bolts to 40 ft-lbs, then retorque the vertical mounted bolts to 40 ft-lbs (see illustration 14.5).

15 The remaining steps are the reverse of the removal procedure.

16 Refill the engine with oil (see Chapter 1), replace the filter, run it until normal operating temperature is reached and check for leaks.

14.5 Remove the exhaust Y-pipe (A) and the transmission-to-oil pan support brace (B), then position the transmission cooler lines (C) aside

14.7 If the oil pan is stuck to the gasket, gently tap on the side of the oil pan to break the gasket seal

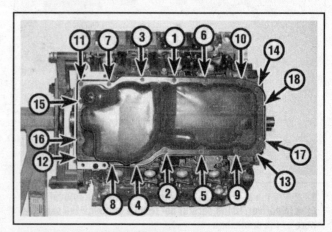

14.13 Oil pan TIGHTENING sequence

15 Oil pump - removal, inspection and installation

REMOVAL

► **Refer to illustrations 15.3a, 15.3b and 15.4**

1 Refer to Section 7 and remove the timing chains and sprockets.
2 Remove the oil pan (see Section 14).

15.3a Remove the bolt (arrow) securing the oil pump pick-up tube to the oil pump - when installing the pick up tube always tighten this bolt first

15.3b Remove the nuts (arrows) securing the oil pump pick-up to the main caps and remove the pick-up tube

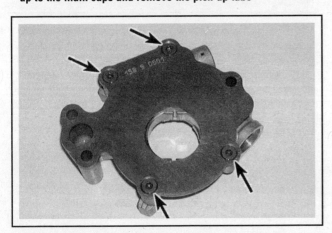

15.6 Remove the screws (arrows) and lift the cover off

3 Remove the oil pump pick-up tube (see illustrations).
4 Remove the bolts and detach the primary timing chain tensioner the front of the oil pump (see illustration).
5 Gently pry the oil pump housing outward enough to clear the flats on the crankshaft and remove it from the engine.

INSPECTION

► **Refer to illustrations 15.6, 15.8a 15.8b, 15.8c, 15.8d, 15.8e and 15.8f**

6 Remove the screws holding the front cover on the oil pump housing (see illustration).
7 Clean all components with solvent, then inspect them for wear and damage.

❊❊ CAUTION:

The oil pressure relief valve and spring are an integral part of the oil pump housing. Removal of the relief valve and spring from the oil pump housing will damage the oil pump and require replacement of the entire oil pump assembly.

8 Check the clearance of the following oil pump components with a

15.4 Oil pump housing/primary timing chain tensioner retaining bolts (arrows)

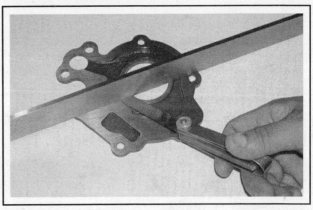

15.8a Place a straightedge across the oil pump cover and check it for warpage with a feeler gauge

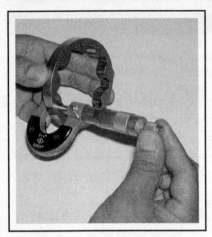

15.8b Use a micrometer or dial caliper to check the thickness and the diameter of the outer rotor

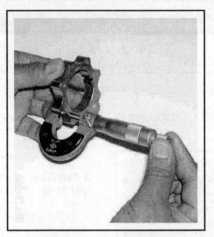

15.8c Use a micrometer or dial caliper to check the thickness of the inner rotor

15.8d Check the outer rotor-to-housing clearance

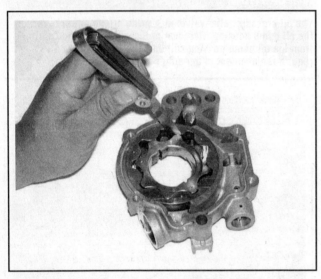

15.8e Check the clearance between the tips of the inner and outer rotors

15.8f Using a straightedge and feeler gauge, check the side clearance between the surface of the oil pump and the inner and outer rotors

feeler gauge and a micrometer or dial caliper (see illustrations) and compare the measurements to the clearance listed in this Chapter's Specifications:

   a) *Cover flatness*
   b) *Outer rotor diameter and thickness*
   c) *Inner rotor thickness*
   d) *Outer rotor-to-body clearance*
   e) *Inner rotor-to-outer rotor tip clearance*
   f) *Cover-to-inner rotor side clearance*
   g) *Cover-to-outer rotor side clearance*

If any clearance is excessive, replace the entire oil pump assembly.

➡**Note: Pack the pump with petroleum jelly to prime it.**

9 Assemble the oil pump and tighten all fasteners to the torque listed in this Chapter's Specifications. Install the oil pressure regulator valve, spring and washer, then tighten the oil pressure regulator valve cap.

INSTALLATION

10 To install the pump, turn the flats in the rotor so they align with the flats on the crankshaft and push the oil pump back into position against the block.

11 Position the primary timing chain tensioner over the oil pump and install the pump-to-block bolts. Tighten the oil pump/primary timing chain tensioner bolts to the torque listed in this Chapter's Specifications.

12 The remainder of installation is the reverse of removal.

16 Driveplate - removal and installation

1 Raise the vehicle and support it securely on jackstands, then refer to Chapter 7B and remove the transmission.

⁂ WARNING:

The engine must be supported from above with an engine hoist or three-bar support fixture before working underneath the vehicle with the transmission removed.

2 Now would be a good time to check and replace the transmission front pump seal.

3 Use paint or a center-punch to make alignment marks on the driveplate and crankshaft to ensure correct alignment during reinstallation.

4 Remove the bolts that secure the driveplate to the crankshaft. If the crankshaft turns, jam a large screwdriver or prybar through the driveplate to keep the crankshaft from turning, then remove the mounting bolts.

5 Pull straight back on the driveplate to detach it from the crankshaft.

6 Installation is the reverse of removal. Be sure to align the matching paint marks. Use thread locking compound on the bolt threads and tighten them in several steps, in a criss-cross pattern, to the torque listed in this Chapter's Specifications.

17 Rear main oil seal - replacement

➧ Refer to illustrations 17.2 and 17.5

1 These models use a one-piece rear main seal that is sandwiched between the engine block and the lower main bearing cap assembly, or "bed plate" as it's often referred to. Replacing this seal requires removal of the transmission, torque converter and driveplate. Refer to Chapter 7 for the transmission removal procedures.

2 The seal can be removed by prying it out of the engine block with a screwdriver, being careful not to nick the crankshaft surface (see illustration). Wrap the screwdriver tip with tape to avoid damage. Be sure to note how far it's recessed into the housing bore before removal so the new seal can be installed to the same depth.

3 Thoroughly clean the seal bore in the block with a shop towel. Remove all traces of oil and dirt.

4 Lubricate the outside diameter of the seal and the seal lip with clean engine oil and install the seal over the end of the crankshaft. Make sure the lip of the seal points toward the engine.

5 Preferably, a seal installation tool (available at most auto parts store) should be used to press the new seal back into place. If the proper seal installation tool is unavailable, use a large socket, section of pipe or a blunt tool and carefully drive the new seal squarely into the seal bore and flush with the rear of the engine block (see illustration).

6 The remainder of installation is the reverse of the removal procedure.

17.2 Pry the seal out very carefully with a seal removal tool or screwdriver - if the crankshaft is damaged, the new seal will leak!

17.5 The rear oil seal can be pressed into place with a seal installation tool, a section of pipe or a blunt object shown here - in any case be sure the seal is installed squarely into the seal bore and flush with the rear of the engine block

18 Engine mounts - check and replacement

▶ **Refer to illustrations 18.12a and 18.12b**

1   There are three powertrain mounts on the vehicles covered by this manual; left and right engine mounts attached to the engine block and to the frame and a rear mount attached to the transmission and the frame. The rear transmission mount is covered in Chapter 7B. Engine mounts seldom require attention, but broken or deteriorated mounts should be replaced immediately or the added strain placed on the driveline components may cause damage or wear.

CHECK

2   During the check, the engine must be raised slightly to remove the weight from the mounts.

3   Raise the vehicle and support it securely on jackstands, then position a jack under the engine oil pan. Place a large wood block between the jack head and the oil pan, then carefully raise the engine just enough to take the weight off the mounts.

✳ WARNING:

DO NOT place any part of your body under the engine when it's supported only by a jack!

4   Check for relative movement between the inner and outer portions of the mount (use a large screwdriver or prybar to attempt to move the mounts). If movement is noted, lower the engine and tighten the mount fasteners.

5   Check the mounts to see if the rubber is cracked, hardened or separated from the metal casing which would indicate a need for replacement.

6   Rubber preservative should be applied to the mounts to slow deterioration.

REPLACEMENT

7   Disconnect the cable from the negative terminal of the battery.
8   Remove the engine cooling fan and shroud (see Chapter 3).
9   Raise the front of the vehicle and support it securely on jack-stands.
10 Support the engine with a lifting device from above.

✳ CAUTION:

Do not connect the lifting device to the intake manifold.

Raise the engine just enough to take the weight off the engine mounts. If you're removing the driver's side engine mount, removal of the oil filter will be necessary.

11 Working below the vehicle, remove the engine mount-to-frame support bracket through-bolt.

12 Remove the mount-to-engine block bolts, then raise the engine until the mounts can be maneuvered past the frame bracket and removed from the vehicle (see illustrations).

13 To remove the engine mount support brackets, simply remove the bolts from the frame and remove the brackets from the engine compartment.

14 After the engine mounts have been installed onto the engine, lower the engine while guiding the engine mount and through-bolt into the frame support bracket. Install the through-bolt nut and tighten it to the torque listed in this Chapter's Specifications.

15 The remainder of installation is the reverse of removal. Remove the engine hoist and the jackstands and lower the vehicle.

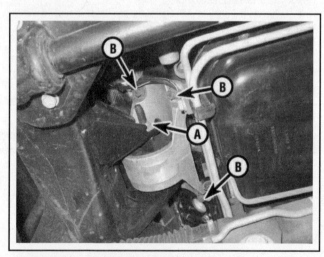

18.12b Passenger's side engine mount details

A   Through-bolt/nut   B   Mount-to-engine block bolts

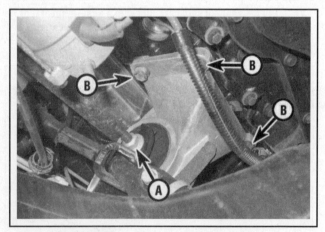

18.12a Driver's side engine mount details

A   Through-bolt/nut   B   Mount-to-engine block bolts

Specifications

General

Displacement	287 cubic inches
Bore and stroke	3.66 x 3.40 inches
Cylinder numbers (front to rear)	
Left bank	1-3-5-7
Right bank	2-4-6-8
Firing order	1-8-4-3-6-5-7-2

4.7L V8 engine

Cylinder identification diagram

Camshaft

Endplay	0.003 to 0.0079 inch
Valve lift	
Intake	0.443 inch
Exhaust	0.4292 inch
Camshaft bearing oil clearance	
Standard	0.001 to 0.0026 inch
Service limit	0.0026 inch
Camshaft journal diameter	1.0227 to 1.0235 inch
Camshaft bore diameter	1.0245 to 1.0252 inch

Timing chain

Idler gear endplay	0.004 to 0.010 inch

Oil pump

Cover warpage limit	0.001 inch
Inner and outer rotor thickness	0.4756 inch
Outer rotor diameter (minimum)	3.3843 inches
Outer rotor-to-housing clearance (maximum)	
2000	0.0186 inch
2001 and later models	0.0093 inch
Inner rotor-to-outer rotor lobe clearance	0.006 inch
Oil pump housing-to-rotor side clearance	0.0014 to 0.0038 inch

Torque specifications

	Ft-lbs (unless otherwise indicated)
Camshaft sprocket bolts (non-oiled)	90
Camshaft bearing cap bolts	100 in-lbs
Crankshaft pulley/vibration damper bolt	130
Cylinder head bolts	
Step one	
11 mm bolts (1 through 10)	15
Step two	
11 mm bolts (1 through 10)	35
Step three	
8 mm bolts (11 through 14)	18
Step four	
11 mm bolts (1 through 10)	Turn an additional 90-degrees
Step five	
8 mm bolts (11 through 14)	22

Torque specifications — Ft-lbs (unless otherwise indicated)

Driveplate bolts	45
Engine mount bracket-to-block bolts	45
Engine mount through bolt/nut	45
Exhaust manifold bolts	18
Exhaust manifold heat shield nuts	
Step 1	72 in-lbs
Step 2	Loosen an additional 45-degrees
Intake manifold bolts	105 in-lbs
Oil pan bolts	132 in-lbs
Oil pan drain plug	25
Oil pick-up tube mounting bolt/nut	21
Oil pump mounting bolts	21
Oil pump cover screws	105 in-lbs
Timing chain cover bolts	40
Timing chain guide bolts	21
Timing chain guide access plugs	15
Timing chain idler sprocket bolt	25
Timing chain tensioner arm pivot bolt	150 in-lbs
Timing chain tensioner (secondary)	21
Timing chain tensioner (primary)	21
Transmission-to-oil pan support brace	40
Valve cover bolts	105 in-lbs
Water outlet housing	105 in-lbs

Section

Reference to other Chapters

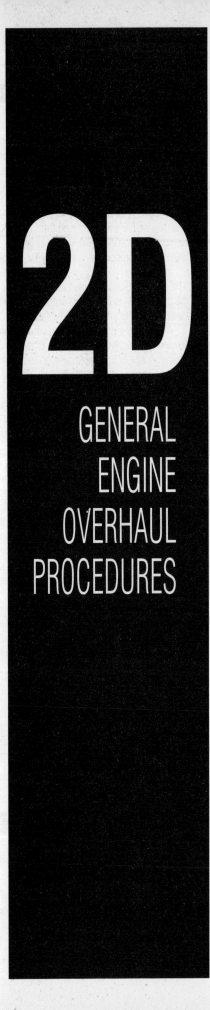

2D

GENERAL
ENGINE
OVERHAUL
PROCEDURES

1 General information - engine overhaul

Included in this portion of Chapter 2 are the general overhaul procedures for the cylinder head(s) and internal engine components.

The information ranges from advice concerning preparation for an overhaul and the purchase of replacement parts to detailed, step-by-step procedures covering removal and installation of internal engine components and the inspection of parts.

The following Sections have been written based on the assumption that the engine has been removed from the vehicle. For information concerning in-vehicle engine repair, as well as removal and installation of the external components necessary for the overhaul, see Sections 5 and 7, and Chapters 2A, 2B and 2C.

The Specifications included in this Part are only those necessary for the inspection and overhaul procedures which follow. Refer to Parts, A, B or C for additional Specifications.

It's not always easy to determine when, or if, an engine should be completely overhauled, as a number of factors must be considered.

High mileage is not necessarily an indication that an overhaul is needed, while low mileage doesn't preclude the need for an overhaul. Frequency of servicing is probably the most important consideration. An engine that's had regular and frequent oil and filter changes, as well as other required maintenance, will most likely give many thousands of miles of reliable service. Conversely, a neglected engine may require an overhaul very early in its life.

Excessive oil consumption is an indication that piston rings, valve seals and/or valve guides are in need of attention. Make sure that oil leaks aren't responsible before deciding that the rings and/or guides are bad. Perform a cylinder compression check to determine the extent of the work required (see Section 3).

Check the oil pressure with a gauge installed in place of the oil pressure sending unit (see Section 2) and compare it to the Specifications. If it's extremely low, the bearings and/or oil pump are probably worn out. Also check the vacuum readings under various conditions (see Section 4).

Loss of power, rough running, knocking or metallic engine noises, excessive valve train noise and high fuel consumption rates may also point to the need for an overhaul, especially if they're all present at the same time. If a complete tune-up doesn't remedy the situation, major mechanical work is the only solution.

An engine overhaul involves restoring the internal parts to the specifications of a new engine. During an overhaul, the piston rings are replaced and the cylinder walls are reconditioned (rebored and/or honed). If a rebore is done by an automotive machine shop, new over-size pistons will also be installed. The main bearings, connecting rod bearings and camshaft bearings are generally replaced with new ones

and, if necessary, the crankshaft may be reground to restore the journals. Generally, the valves are serviced as well, since they're usually in less-than-perfect condition at this point.

While the engine is being overhauled, other components, such as the distributor, starter and alternator, can be rebuilt as well. The end result should be a like new engine that will give many thousands of trouble free miles.

→Note: Critical cooling system components such as the hoses, drivebelts, thermostat and water pump MUST be replaced with new parts when an engine is overhauled.

There are engine rebuilders who will not guarantee their work if the radiator hasn't been professionally cleaned at the time of rebuilt-engine installation. The radiator should be checked carefully to ensure that it isn't clogged or leaking (see Chapter 3). Also, we don't recommend overhauling the oil pump - always install a new one when an engine is rebuilt.

Before beginning the engine overhaul, read through the entire procedure to familiarize yourself with the scope and requirements of the job. Overhauling an engine isn't difficult if you have the right equipment and follow the instructions carefully, but it is time-consuming. Plan on the vehicle being tied up for a minimum of two weeks, especially if parts must be taken to an automotive machine shop for repair or reconditioning. Check on availability of parts and make sure that any necessary special tools and equipment are obtained in advance.

Most work can be done with typical hand tools, although a number of precision measuring tools are required for inspecting parts to determine if they must be replaced. Often an automotive machine shop will handle the inspection of parts and offer advice concerning reconditioning and replacement.

→Note: Always wait until the engine has been completely disassembled and all components, especially the engine block, have been inspected before deciding what service and repair operations must be performed by an automotive machine shop.

Since the block's condition will be the major factor to consider when determining whether to overhaul the original engine or buy a rebuilt one, never purchase parts or have machine work done on other components until the block has been thoroughly inspected. As a general rule, time is the primary cost of an overhaul, so it doesn't pay to install worn or substandard parts.

As a final note, to ensure maximum life and minimum trouble from a rebuilt engine, everything must be assembled with care in a spotlessly-clean environment.

2 Oil pressure check

▶ **Refer to illustrations 2.2a, 2.2b, 2.2c and 2.5**

1 Low engine oil pressure can be a sign of an engine in need of rebuilding. A "low oil pressure" indicator (often called an "idiot light") is not a test of the oiling system. Such indicators only come on when the oil pressure is dangerously low. Even an original pressure gauge in

the instrument panel is only a relative indication, although it's much better for driver information than a warning light. An accurate test can only be performed with a mechanical (not electrical) oil pressure gauge. When used in conjunction with an accurate tachometer, the engine's oil pressure performance can be compared to the manufacturer's Specifications for that year and model.

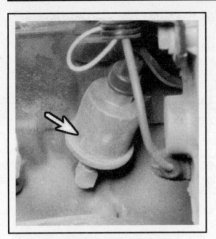

2.2a Oil pressure sending unit location - four cylinder engine

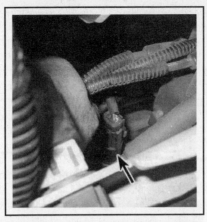

2.2b Oil pressure sending unit location (to the right of the distributor) - V6 and 5.2L/5.9L V8 engines

2.2c Oil pressure sending unit location - 4.7L V8 engine

2   Locate the oil pressure indicator sending unit (see illustrations).

3   Remove the oil pressure sending unit and install a fitting which will allow you to directly connect your hand-held, mechanical oil pressure gauge. Use Teflon tape or sealant on the threads of the adapter and the fitting on the end of your gauge's hose.

4   Connect an accurate tachometer to the engine, according to the tachometer manufacturer's instructions.

5   Check the oil pressure with the engine running (full operating temperature) at the specified engine speed, and compare it to this Chapter's Specifications (see illustration). If it's extremely low, the bearings and/or oil pump are probably worn out.

2.5 Check the oil pressure with the engine running (full operating temperature) at the specified engine speed and compare it to this Chapter's Specifications

3   Compression check

▶ **Refer to illustration 3.6**

1   A compression check will tell you what mechanical condition the upper end (pistons, rings, valves, head gaskets) of your engine is in. Specifically, it can tell you if the compression is down due to leakage caused by worn piston rings, defective valves and seats or a blown head gasket.

➡**Note: The engine must be at normal operating temperature and the battery must be fully charged for this check.**

2   Begin by cleaning the area around the spark plugs before you remove them (compressed air should be used, if available). The idea is to prevent dirt from getting into the cylinders as the compression check is being done.

3   Remove all of the spark plugs from the engine (see Chapter 1).

4   Block the throttle wide open.

5   Detach the coil wire from the center of the distributor cap and ground it on the engine block. If you're working on a 4.7L V8 engine, detach the electrical connectors from all of the ignition coils. Use a jumper wire with alligator clips on each end to ensure a good ground. The fuel pump circuit should also be disabled (see Chapter 4).

6   Install the compression gauge in the number one spark plug

hole (see illustration).

7   Crank the engine over at least seven compression strokes and

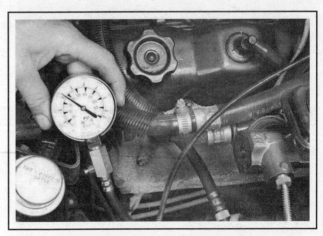

3.6 A compression gauge with a threaded fitting for the spark plug hole is preferred over the type that requires hand pressure to maintain the seal

watch the gauge. The compression should build up quickly in a healthy engine. Low compression on the first stroke, followed by gradually increasing pressure on successive strokes, indicates worn piston rings. A low compression reading on the first stroke, which doesn't build up during successive strokes, indicates leaking valves or a blown head gasket (a cracked head could also be the cause). Deposits on the undersides of the valve heads can also cause low compression. Record the highest gauge reading obtained.

8   Repeat the procedure for the remaining cylinders and compare the results to this Chapter's Specifications.

9   Add some engine oil (about three squirts from a plunger-type oil can) to each cylinder, through the spark plug hole, and repeat the test.

10   If the compression increases after the oil is added, the piston rings are definitely worn. If the compression doesn't increase significantly, the leakage is occurring at the valves or head gasket. Leakage

past the valves may be caused by burned valve seats and/or faces or warped, cracked or bent valves.

11   If two adjacent cylinders have equally-low compression, there's a strong possibility that the head gasket between them is blown. The appearance of coolant in the combustion chambers or the crankcase would verify this condition.

12   If one cylinder is slightly lower than the others, and the engine has a rough idle, a worn lobe on the camshaft could be the cause.

13   If the compression is unusually high, the combustion chambers are probably coated with carbon deposits. If that's the case, the cylinder head(s) should be removed and decarbonized.

14   If compression is way down or varies greatly between cylinders, it would be a good idea to have a leak-down test performed by an automotive repair shop. This test will pinpoint exactly where the leakage is occurring and how severe it is.

4   Vacuum gauge diagnostic checks

♦ **Refer to illustrations 4.4 and 4.6**

1   A vacuum gauge provides valuable information about the condition of internal engine components. You can check for worn rings or cylinder walls, leaking head or intake manifold gaskets, restricted exhaust, stuck or burned valves, weak valve springs, improper ignition or valve timing and ignition problems.

2   Unfortunately, vacuum gauge readings are easy to misinterpret, so they should be used in conjunction with other tests to confirm the diagnosis.

3   Both the absolute readings and the rate of needle movement are important for accurate interpretation. Most gauges measure vacuum in inches of mercury (in-Hg). The following references to vacuum assume the diagnosis is being performed at sea level. As elevation increases (or atmospheric pressure decreases), the reading will decrease. For every 1,000 foot increase in elevation above approximately 2000 feet, the gauge readings will decrease about one inch of mercury.

4   Connect the vacuum gauge directly to intake manifold vacuum, not to ported (throttle body) vacuum (see illustration). Be sure no hoses are left disconnected during the test or false readings will result.

5   Before you begin the test, allow the engine to warm up com-

pletely. Block the wheels and set the parking brake. With the transmission in Park or Neutral, start the engine and allow it to run at normal idle speed.

⁂ WARNING:

Always keep your hands, loose clothing and tools clear of the fan and do not stand in front of the vehicle or in line with the fan when the engine is running.

6   Read the vacuum gauge; an average, healthy engine should normally produce about 17 to 22 inches of vacuum with a fairly steady needle (see illustration). Refer to the following vacuum gauge readings and what they indicate about the engine's condition:

a)   *A low steady reading usually indicates a leaking gasket between the intake manifold and throttle body, a leaky vacuum hose, late ignition timing or incorrect camshaft timing. Check ignition timing with a timing light and eliminate all other possible causes, utilizing the tests provided in this Chapter before you remove the timing chain cover to check the timing marks.*

b)   *If the reading is three to eight inches below normal and it fluctuates at that low reading, suspect an intake manifold gasket leak at an intake port or a faulty fuel injector.*

c)   *If the needle has regular drops of about two-to-four inches at a steady rate, the valves are probably leaking. Perform a compression check or leak-down test to confirm this.*

d)   *An irregular drop or down-flick of the needle can be caused by a sticking valve or an ignition misfire. Perform a compression check or leak-down test and read the spark plugs.*

e)   *A rapid vibration of about four inches Hg vibration at idle combined with exhaust smoke indicates worn valve guides. Perform a leak-down test to confirm this. If the rapid vibration occurs with an increase in engine speed, check for a leaking intake manifold gasket or head gasket, weak valve springs, burned valves or ignition misfire.*

f)   *A slight fluctuation, say one inch up and down, may mean ignition problems. Check all the usual tune-up items and, if necessary, run the engine on an ignition analyzer.*

g)   *If there is a large fluctuation, perform a compression or leak-down test to look for a weak or dead cylinder or a blown head gasket.*

h)   *If the needle moves slowly through a wide range, check for a*

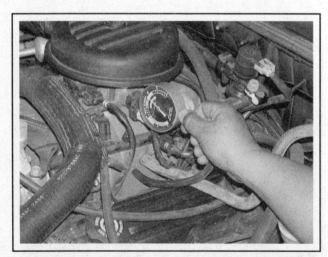

4.4   An inexpensive vacuum gauge can tell you a lot about an engine's condition

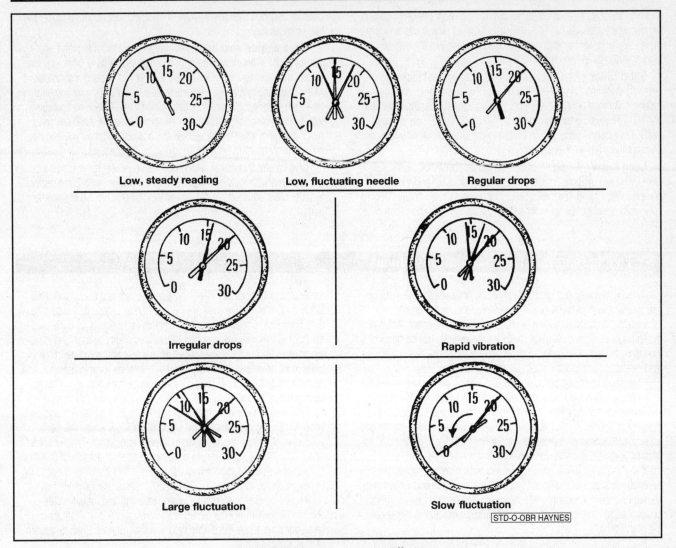

Low, steady reading   Low, fluctuating needle   Regular drops

Irregular drops   Rapid vibration

Large fluctuation   Slow fluctuation

STD-O-OBR HAYNES

4.6 Typical vacuum gauge readings

clogged PCV system, incorrect idle fuel mixture, carburetor/throttle body or intake manifold gasket leaks.

i) Check for a slow return after revving the engine by quickly snapping the throttle open until the engine reaches about 2,500 rpm and let it shut. Normally the reading should drop to near zero, rise above normal idle reading (about 5 in. Hg over) and then return to the previous idle reading. If the vacuum returns slowly and doesn't peak when the throttle is snapped shut, the rings may be worn. If there is a long delay, look for a restricted exhaust system (often the muffler or catalytic converter). An easy way to check this is to temporarily disconnect the exhaust ahead of the suspected part and re-test.

5   Engine rebuilding alternatives

The do-it-yourselfer is faced with a number of options when performing an engine overhaul. The decision to replace the engine block, piston/connecting rod assemblies and crankshaft depends on a number of factors, with the number one consideration being the condition of the block. Other considerations are cost, access to machine shop facilities, parts availability, time required to complete the project and the extent of prior mechanical experience on the part of the do-it-yourselfer.

Some of the rebuilding alternatives include:

Individual parts - If the inspection procedures reveal that the engine block and most engine components are in reusable condition, purchasing individual parts may be the most economical alternative. The block, crankshaft and piston/connecting rod assemblies should all be inspected carefully. Even if the block shows little wear, the cylinder bores should be surface-honed.

Crankshaft kit - This rebuild package consists of a reground crankshaft and a matched set of pistons and connecting rods. The pistons will already be installed on the connecting rods. Piston rings and the necessary bearings will be included in the kit. These kits are commonly available for standard cylinder bores, as well as for engine blocks which have been bored to a regular oversize.

Short block - A short block consists of an engine block with renewed crankshaft and piston/connecting rod assemblies already installed. All new bearings are incorporated and all clearances will be correct. The existing cylinder head(s), camshaft, valve train components and external parts can be bolted to the short block with little or no machine shop work necessary.

Long block - A long block consists of a short block plus an oil pump, oil pan, cylinder heads, valve covers, camshaft and valve train components, timing sprockets, timing chain and timing cover. All components are installed with new bearings, seals and gaskets incorpo-

rated throughout. The installation of manifolds and external parts is all that is necessary.

Used engine assembly - While overhaul provides the best assurance of a like-new engine, used engines available from wrecking yards and importers are often a very simple and economical solution. Many used engines come with warranties, but always give any engine a thorough diagnostic check-out before purchase. Check compression, vacuum and also for signs of oil leakage. If possible, have the seller run the engine, ether in the vehicle or on a test stand so you can be sure it runs smoothly with no knocking or other noises.

Give careful thought to which alternative is best for you and discuss the situation with local automotive machine shops, auto parts dealers or parts store countermen before ordering or purchasing replacement parts.

6 Engine removal - methods and precautions

If you've decided that an engine must be removed for overhaul or major repair work, several preliminary steps should be taken.

Locating a suitable place to work is extremely important. Adequate work space, along with storage space for the vehicle, will be needed. If a shop or garage isn't available, at the very least a flat, level, clean work surface made of concrete or asphalt is required.

Cleaning the engine compartment and engine before beginning the removal procedure will help keep your tools and your hands clean.

An engine hoist or A-frame will also be necessary. Make sure the equipment is rated in excess of the combined weight of the engine and accessories. Safety is of primary importance, considering the potential hazards involved in lifting the engine out of the vehicle.

If the engine is being removed by a novice, a helper should be available. Advice and aid from someone more experienced would also be helpful. There are many instances when one person cannot simultaneously perform all of the operations required when lifting the engine out of the vehicle.

Plan the operation ahead of time. Arrange for or obtain all of the tools and equipment you'll need prior to beginning the job. Some of

the equipment necessary to perform engine removal and installation safely and with relative ease are (in addition to an engine hoist) a heavy duty floor jack, complete sets of wrenches and sockets as described in the front of this manual, wooden blocks and plenty of rags and cleaning solvent for mopping up spilled oil, coolant and gasoline. If the hoist must be rented, make sure that you arrange for it in advance and perform all of the operations possible without it beforehand. This will save you money and time.

Plan for the vehicle to be out of use for quite a while. A machine shop will be required to perform some of the work which the do-it-yourselfer can't accomplish without special equipment. These shops often have a busy schedule, so it would be a good idea to consult them before removing the engine in order to accurately estimate the amount of time required to rebuild or repair components that may need work.

Always be extremely careful when removing and installing the engine. Serious injury can result from careless actions. Plan ahead, take your time and a job of this nature, although major, can be accomplished successfully.

7 Engine - removal and installation

✳✳ WARNING 1:

The air conditioning system is under high pressure. Do not loosen any hose fittings or remove any components until after the system has been discharged. Air conditioning refrigerant should be properly discharged into an EPA-approved recovery/recycling unit at a dealer service department or an automotive air conditioning repair facility. Always wear eye protection when disconnecting air conditioning system fittings.

✳✳ WARNING 2:

Gasoline is extremely flammable, so take extra precautions when you work on any part of the fuel system. Don't smoke or allow open flames or bare light bulbs near the work area, and don't work in a garage where a gas-type appliance (such as a water heater or a clothes dryer) is present. Since gasoline is carcinogenic, wear latex gloves when there's a possibility of

being exposed to fuel, and, if you spill any fuel on your skin, rinse it off immediately with soap and water. Mop up any spills immediately and do not store fuel-soaked rags where they could ignite. The fuel system is under constant pressure, so, if any fuel lines are to be disconnected, the fuel pressure in the system must be relieved first (see Chapter 4 for more information). When you perform any kind of work on the fuel system, wear safety glasses and have a Class B type fire extinguisher on hand.

✳✳ WARNING 3:

The models covered by this manual are equipped with Supplemental Restraint systems (SRS), more commonly known as airbags. Always disable the airbag system before working in the vicinity of the impact sensors, steering column or instrument panel to avoid the possibility of accidental deployment of the airbag, which could cause personal injury (see Chapter 12).

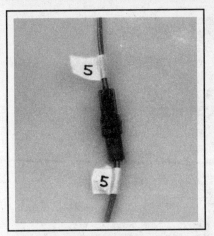

7.5 Label both ends of each wire before unplugging the connector

7.11 Set the power steering pump aside with the lines still connected - be sure it's upright so fluid won't spill

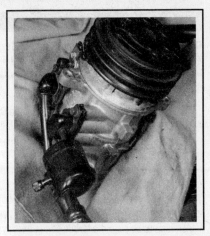

7.12 Unbolt the air conditioning compressor and set it out of the way

REMOVAL

▶ **Refer to illustrations 7.5, 7.11, 7.12, 7.19 and 7.24**

1 Refer to Chapter 4 and relieve the fuel system pressure, then disconnect the cable from the negative terminal of the battery.

2 Cover the fenders and cowl and remove the hood (see Chapter 11). Special pads are available to protect the fenders, but an old bedspread or blanket will also work.

3 Remove the air cleaner assembly (see Chapter 4).

4 Drain the cooling system (see Chapter 1).

5 Label the vacuum lines, emissions system hoses, wiring connectors, ground strap and fuel lines, to ensure correct reinstallation (see illustration), then detach them. If there's any possibility of confusion, make a sketch of the engine compartment and clearly label the lines, hoses and wires.

6 Label and detach all coolant hoses from the engine. Remove the battery, and on 4.7L models remove the battery tray as well (see Chapter 5).

7 Remove the cooling fan, shroud and radiator (see Chapter 3).

8 Remove the drivebelt(s) (see Chapter 1). On V6 and 5.2L/5.9L V8 engines, remove the distributor cap and spark plug wires to avoid contact with the firewall as the engine is lifted from the vehicle.

9 Disconnect the fuel lines running from the engine to the chassis (see Chapter 4). Plug or cap all open fittings/lines.

10 Disconnect the throttle linkage (and TV linkage/cruise control cable, if equipped) from the throttle body (see Chapter 4).

11 On power steering equipped vehicles, unbolt the power steering pump (see Chapter 10). Leave the lines/hoses attached (see illustration) and make sure the pump is kept in an upright position in the engine compartment (use wire or rope to restrain it out of the way).

12 On air conditioned vehicles, unbolt the compressor (see Chapter 3) and set it aside. Do not disconnect the hoses (see illustration).

13 Remove the alternator (see Chapter 5).

14 Working under the vehicle, drain the engine oil (see Chapter 1).

15 Unbolt the exhaust system from the engine (see Chapter 4)

16 Remove the starter motor (see Chapter 5).

17 Remove the transmission inspection cover from the lower half of the transmission bellhousing (see Chapter 7B). If you're working on a vehicle with an automatic transmission, refer to Chapter 7B and remove

7.19 On some 4.7L V8 engines there are lifting studs that protrude from the cylinder heads and the front of the water pump

the torque converter-to-driveplate fasteners.

18 Support the transmission with a jack. Position a block of wood between the jack and transmission to prevent damage to the transmission. Special transmission jacks with safety chains are available - use one if possible.

19 Attach an engine sling or a length of chain to the lifting brackets on the engine (see illustration).

➡ **Note: Some 4.7L V8 engines may not be equipped with lifting studs or brackets; instead, threaded holes are provided for stud or bolt installation.**

✳✳ CAUTION:

DO NOT lift the engine by the intake manifold. Lift the engine by the block or the cylinder head(s) only.

20 Roll the hoist into position and connect the sling to it. Take up the slack in the sling or chain, but don't lift the engine.

✳✳ WARNING:

DO NOT place any part of your body under the engine when it's supported only by a hoist or other lifting device.

21 Remove the transmission-to-engine block bolts.

22 Remove the engine mount-to-frame bolts on 2WD vehicles. On 4WD vehicles remove the engine mounts and the engine mount support brackets (see Chapter 2A, 2B or 2C for engine mount and bracket removal procedures).

23 Recheck to be sure nothing is still connecting the engine to the transmission or vehicle. Disconnect anything still remaining.

24 Raise the engine slightly. Carefully work it forward to separate it from the transmission. If you're working on a vehicle with an automatic transmission, be sure the torque converter stays in the transmission (clamp a pair of vise-grips to the housing to keep the converter from sliding out). If you're working on a vehicle with a manual transmission, the input shaft must be completely disengaged from the clutch. Slowly raise the engine out of the engine compartment (see illustration). Check carefully to make sure nothing is hanging up.

25 Remove the flywheel/driveplate and mount the engine on an engine stand.

INSTALLATION

26 Install the flywheel/driveplate on the engine (see Chapter 2A or 2B). Check the engine and transmission mounts. If they're worn or damaged, replace them.

27 If you're working on a vehicle with a manual transmission, install the clutch and pressure plate onto the flywheel (see Chapter 7A). Now is a good time to install a new clutch.

28 Carefully lower the engine into the engine compartment - make sure the engine mounts line up.

29 If you're working on a vehicle with an automatic transmission, guide the torque converter into the crankshaft following the procedure outlined in Chapter 7B.

30 If you're working on a vehicle with a manual transmission, apply a dab of high-temperature grease to the input shaft and guide it into the crankshaft pilot bearing until the bellhousing is flush with the engine block.

7.24 Pull the engine forward as far as possible to clear the transmission, then lift the engine high enough to clear the body

➡**Note: It may be necessary to place the transmission into first gear, then turn the output shaft on the transmission until the teeth on the input shaft align with the teeth on the clutch disc.**

31 Install the transmission-to-engine bolts and tighten them securely.

✳✳ CAUTION:

DO NOT use the bolts to force the transmission and engine together!

32 Reinstall the remaining components in the reverse order of removal.

33 Add coolant, oil, power steering and transmission fluid as needed. If you're working on a 4.7L V8, be sure to properly bleed the cooling system of air.

34 Run the engine and check for leaks and proper operation of all accessories, then install the hood and test drive the vehicle.

35 Have the air conditioning system recharged and leak tested.

8 Engine overhaul - disassembly sequence

1 It's much easier to disassemble and work on the engine if it's mounted on a portable engine stand. A stand can often be rented quite cheaply from an equipment rental yard. Before the engine is mounted on a stand, the flywheel/driveplate should be removed from the engine.

2 If a stand isn't available, it's possible to disassemble the engine with it blocked up on the floor. Be extra careful not to tip or drop the engine when working without a stand.

3 If you're going to obtain a rebuilt engine, all external components must come off first to be transferred to the replacement engine, just as they will if you're doing a complete engine overhaul yourself. These include:

Alternator and brackets
Emissions control components
Distributor, spark plug wires and spark plugs
Thermostat and housing cover
Water pump
Fuel injection components
Intake/exhaust manifold(s)
Oil filter
Engine mounts
Clutch and flywheel/driveplate

➡**Note: When removing the external components from the engine, pay close attention to details that may be helpful or important during installation. Note the installed position of gaskets, seals, spacers, pins, brackets, washers, bolts and other small items.**

4 If you're obtaining a short block, which consists of the engine block, crankshaft, pistons and connecting rods all assembled, then the cylinder head(s), oil pan and oil pump will have to be removed as well. See *Engine rebuilding alternatives* for additional information regarding the different possibilities to be considered.

5 If you're planning a complete overhaul, the engine must be dis-

assembled and the internal components removed in the following order:

> Valve cover(s)
> Intake and exhaust manifolds
> Rocker arms and pushrods (lash adjusters on 4.7L V8)
> Cylinder head(s)
> Valve lifters (all but 4.7L V8)
> Oil pan
> Timing cover
> Timing chain(s) and sprockets
> Camshaft(s)
> Oil pump
> Piston/connecting rod assemblies
> Bedplate assembly (4.7L V8)
> Crankshaft and main bearings

6   Before beginning the disassembly and overhaul procedures, make sure the following items are available. Also, refer to Section 22 for a list of tools and materials needed for engine reassembly.

> Common hand tools
> Small cardboard boxes or plastic bags for storing parts
> Gasket scraper
> Ridge reamer
> Vibration damper puller
> Micrometers
> Telescoping gauges
> Dial-indicator set
> Valve spring compressor
> Cylinder surfacing hone
> Piston ring groove-cleaning tool
> Electric drill motor
> Tap and die set
> Wire brushes
> Oil gallery brushes
> Cleaning solvent

9   Cylinder head - disassembly

▶ **Refer to illustrations 9.2, 9.3 and 9.4**

➡**Note: New and rebuilt cylinder heads are commonly available for most engines at dealerships and auto parts stores. Due to the fact that some specialized tools are necessary for the disassembly and inspection procedures, and some parts may not be readily available, it may be more practical and economical for the home mechanic to purchase replacement head(s) rather than taking the time to disassemble, inspect and recondition the original(s).**

1   Cylinder head disassembly involves removal of the intake and exhaust valves and related components. If they're still in place, remove the rocker arm bolts, pivots and rocker arms from the cylinder head studs. Label the parts or store them separately so they can be reinstalled in their original locations.

2   Before the valves are removed, arrange to label and store them, along with their related components, so they can be kept separate and reinstalled in the same valve guides they were removed from (see illustration).

3   Compress the springs on the first valve with a spring compressor and remove the keepers (see illustration). Carefully release the valve spring compressor and remove the retainer, the spring and the spring seat (if used).

9.2 A small plastic bag, with an appropriate label, can be used to store the valve train components so they can be kept together and reinstalled in the correct guide

➡**Note: A special type of valve spring compressor is required on 4.7L V8's (see Chapter 2C).**

4   Pull the valve out of the head, then remove the oil seal from the guide. If the valve binds in the guide (won't pull through), push it back

9.3 Use a valve spring compressor to compress the spring, then remove the keepers with a magnet or needle-nose pliers

9.4 If the valve won't pull through the guide, deburr the edge of the stem and the area around the top of the keeper groove with a file

into the head and deburr the area around the keeper groove with a fine file or whetstone (see illustration).

5   Repeat the procedure for the remaining valves. Remember to keep all the parts for each valve together so they can be reinstalled in the same locations.

10 Cylinder head - cleaning and inspection

CLEANING

▶ **Refer to illustrations 10.12, 10.14, 10.15, 10.16, 10.17 and 10.18**

1   Thorough cleaning of the cylinder head(s) and related valve train components, followed by a detailed inspection, will enable you to decide how much valve service work must be done during the engine overhaul.

➥**Note: If the engine was severely overheated, the cylinder head is probably warped (see Step 12).**

2   Scrape all traces of old gasket material and sealing compound off the head gasket, intake manifold and exhaust manifold sealing surfaces. Be very careful not to gouge the cylinder head. Special gasket removal solvents that soften gaskets and make removal much easier are available at auto parts stores.

3   Remove all built up scale from the coolant passages.

4   Run a stiff wire brush through the various holes to remove deposits that may have formed in them.

5   Run an appropriate size tap into each of the threaded holes to remove corrosion and thread sealant that may be present. If compressed air is available, use it to clear the holes of debris produced by this operation.

✳ WARNING:

Wear eye protection when using compressed air!

6   Clean the rocker arm pivot bolt threads with a wire brush.

7   Clean the cylinder head with solvent and dry it thoroughly. Compressed air will speed the drying process and ensure that all holes and recessed areas are clean.

6   Once the valves and related components have been removed and stored in an organized manner, the head should be thoroughly cleaned and inspected. If a complete engine overhaul is being done, finish the engine disassembly procedures before beginning the cylinder head cleaning and inspection process.

➥**Note: Decarbonizing chemicals are available and may prove very useful when cleaning cylinder heads and valve train components. They are very caustic and should be used with caution. Be sure to follow the instructions on the container.**

8   Clean the rocker arms, pivot balls or fulcrums, nuts or bolts and pushrods with solvent and dry them thoroughly (don't mix them up during the cleaning process). Compressed air will speed the drying process and can be used to clean out the oil passages.

9   Clean all the valve springs, spring seats, keepers and retainers (or rotators) with solvent and dry them thoroughly. Do the components from one valve at a time to avoid mixing up the parts.

10   Scrape off any heavy deposits that may have formed on the valves, then use a motorized wire brush to remove deposits from the valve heads and stems. Again, make sure the valves don't get mixed up.

INSPECTION

➥**Note: Be sure to perform all of the following inspection procedures before concluding that machine shop work is required. Make a list of the items that need attention.**

Cylinder head

11   Inspect the head very carefully for cracks, evidence of coolant leakage and other damage. If cracks are found, check with an automotive machine shop concerning repair. If repair isn't possible, a new cylinder head must be obtained.

12   Using a straightedge and feeler gauge, check the head gasket mating surface for warpage (see illustration). If the warpage exceeds the specified limit, it can be resurfaced at an automotive machine shop.

➥**Note 1: If the V6 or V8 engine heads are resurfaced, the intake manifold flanges may also require machining.**

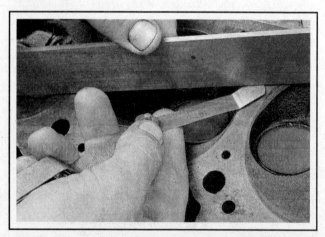

10.12 Check the cylinder head surface for warpage by trying to slip a feeler gauge under the straightedge - see the Specifications for the maximum warpage and use a feeler gauge of that size

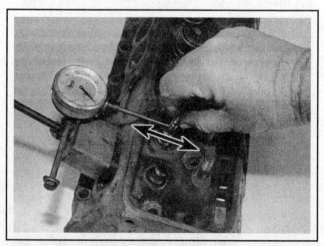

10.14 A dial indicator can be used to determine the valve stem-to-guide clearance - move the stem as indicated by the arrows

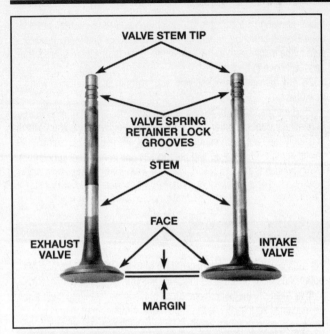

10.15 Check for valve wear at the points shown here

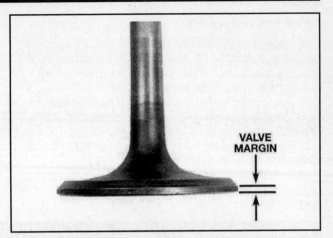

10.16 Valve margin width must be as specified - if no margin exists, the valve cannot be reused

➡Note 2: The manufacturer recommends replacing the cylinder heads on 4.7L V8's if the warpage exceeds the specified amount. Be sure to consult with your local automotive machine shop for alternate solutions before replacing the cylinder heads.

13 Examine the valve seats in each of the combustion chambers. If they're pitted, cracked or burned, the head will require valve service that's beyond the scope of the home mechanic.

14 Check the valve stem-to-guide clearance by measuring the lateral movement of the valve stem with a dial indicator attached securely to the head (see illustration). The valve must be in the guide and approximately 1/16-inch off the seat. The total valve stem movement indicated by the gauge needle must be divided by two to obtain the actual clearance. After this is done, if there's still some doubt regarding the condition of the valve guides, they should be checked by an automotive machine shop (the cost should be minimal). if the clearance is excessive, the machine shop will have to install new valve guides in the head(s).

Valves

15 Carefully inspect each valve for uneven wear, deformation, cracks, pits and burned areas (see illustration). Check the valve stem for scuffing and galling and the neck for cracks. Rotate the valve and check for any obvious indication that it's bent. Look for pits and excessive wear on the end of the stem. The presence of any of these conditions indicates the need for valve service by an automotive machine shop.

16 Measure the margin width on each valve (see illustration). Any valve with a margin narrower than that listed in this Chapter's Specifications will have to be replaced with a new one.

Valve components

17 Check each valve spring for wear (on the ends) and pits. Measure the free length and compare it to this Chapter's Specifications (see illustration). Any springs that are shorter than specified have sagged and should not be reused. The tension of all springs should be checked with a special fixture before deciding that they're suitable for use in a rebuilt engine (take the springs to an automotive machine shop for this check).

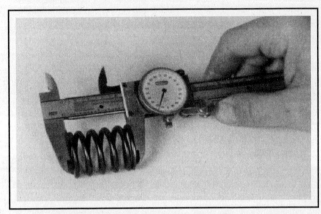

10.17 Measure the length of each valve spring with a dial or vernier caliper

18 Stand each spring on a flat surface and check it for squareness (see illustration). If any of the springs are distorted or sagged, replace all of them with new parts. Springs that aren't square can cause accelerated guide wear.

19 Check the spring retainers (or rotators) and keepers for obvious wear and cracks. Any questionable parts should be replaced with new ones, as extensive damage will occur if they fail during engine operation.

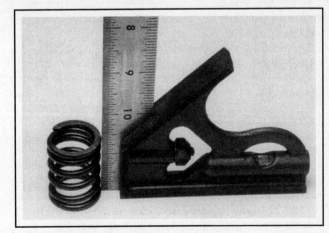

10.18 Check each spring for squareness

Rocker arm components

20 Check the rocker arm faces (the areas that contact the pushrod ends and valve stems) for pits, wear, galling, score marks and rough spots. Check the rocker arm pivot contact areas and pivots as well. Look for cracks in each rocker arm and nut or bolt.

21 Inspect the pushrod ends for scuffing and excessive wear. Roll each pushrod on a flat surface, like a piece of plate glass, to determine if it's bent.

22 Check the rocker arm bolt holes in the cylinder heads for damaged threads and secure installation.

23 On 4.7L V8 engines, refer to Chapter 2, Part C for the camshaft, rocker arm and lash adjuster inspection procedures. Be sure to check the camshaft bearing journals in the cylinder heads before the head is sent to the machine shop for a valve job. If the journals are scored, the head will have to be replaced.

24 Any damaged or excessively worn parts must be replaced with new ones.

25 If the inspection process indicates that the valve components are in generally poor condition and worn beyond the limits specified, which is usually the case in an engine that's being overhauled, reassemble the valves in the cylinder head and refer to Section 11 for valve servicing recommendations.

11 Valves - servicing

1 Because of the complex nature of the job and the special tools and equipment needed, servicing of the valves, the valve seats and the valve guides, commonly known as a valve job, should be done by a professional.

2 The home mechanic can remove and disassemble the head(s), do the initial cleaning and inspection, then reassemble and deliver it (or them) to a dealer service department or an automotive machine shop for the actual service work. Doing the inspection will enable you to see what condition the head and valvetrain components are in and will ensure that you know what work and new parts are required when dealing with an automotive machine shop.

3 The dealer service department, or automotive machine shop, will remove the valves and springs, recondition or replace the valves and valve seats, recondition the valve guides, check and replace the valve springs, spring retainers or rotators and keepers (as necessary), replace the valve seals with new ones, reassemble the valve components and make sure the installed spring height is correct. The cylinder head gasket surface will also be resurfaced if it's warped. On V6 and V8 engines, both heads must be surfaced the same amount, and if more than .020-inch is taken off, the bottom and sides of the intake manifold must also be machined so that all passage and holes still line up properly.

⁂ CAUTION:

Check with your automotive machine shop before surfacing 4.7L V8 cylinder heads. The manufacturer does not recommend surfacing these heads.

4 After the valve job has been performed by a professional, the head will be in like-new condition. When the head is returned, be sure to clean it again before installation on the engine to remove any metal particles and abrasive grit that may still be present from the valve service or head resurfacing operations. Use compressed air, if available, to blow out all the oil holes, bolt holes and coolant passages.

12 Cylinder head - reassembly

▶ **Refer to illustrations 12.6, 12.9 and 12.10**

1 Regardless of whether or not a head was sent to an automotive repair shop for valve servicing, make sure it's clean before beginning reassembly.

2 If a head was sent out for valve servicing, the valves and related components will already be in place. Begin the reassembly procedure with Step 8.

3 Beginning at one end of the head, lubricate and install the first valve. Apply moly-base grease or clean engine oil to the valve stem.

4 Repeat the procedure for the remaining valves. Be sure to return the components to their original locations - don't mix them up!

5 Valve stem seals are manufactured in several different varieties. The first type of seal is called a Positive type seal. This type of seal stays in its installed position while the valve moves up and down so it can meter a precise amount of oil to the valve guide. Positive type seals use a small press fit between the seal and the valve guide to hold the seal in place. Always apply a small amount of oil to the top of the valve guide and valve stem when installing positive type seals, this will help ease the installation process and possible misalignment of the seal. The second type of seal is called an Umbrella seal. This type of seal is simply placed over the valve stem and pushed down to the top of the valve guide, when the valve opens for first time the seal is pushed up on the valve stem (the distance of the valve lift) where it stays for the remainder of its service life. Umbrella seals will then move up and down with the valve as it opens and closes, shrouding oil that is supplied to the rocker arms from going directly down into the valve guide. Most valve seal kits come equipped with a plastic installation tool which must be inserted over the end of valve stem during installation of the seal. Once the seal installation tool is inserted over the valve stem, the valve seal can easily slide past the valve keeper grooves preventing premature damage to the seal.

6 Intake and exhaust valves on these models require different seals, DO NOT mix them up! Four cylinder engines are equipped with positive type seals and are identified on the top of each seal by the initials "INT" for the intake valve which is typically black in color and by "EXH" for the exhaust valve which is typically brown in color. V6 and V8 engines are equipped with a positive type seal on the intake valve and an umbrella seal on the exhaust valve (see illustration).

➡**Note: The seals on 4.7L V8 engines are the same for intake and exhaust (they are interchangeable).**

7 Install new valve seals on each of the intake and exhaust valves. Gently push each seal into place until it's completely seated on the

12.6 Valve seal installation details - V6 and 5.2L/5.9L V8 engines

1   *Exhaust valve seal (umbrella type)*
2   *Intake valve seal (positive type)*

12.9 Apply a small dab of grease to each keeper as shown here before installation - it will hold them in place on the valve stem as the spring is released

12.10 Be sure to check the valve spring installed height (the distance from the top of the seat/shims to the top of the shield or the bottom of the retainer)

guide. Don't twist or cock the seals during installation or they won't seal properly on the valve stems.

➡**Note: Some positive type seals may require the use a small mallet and a seal installer or deep socket to gently tap the seal onto the boss on the head.**

8   Place the valve springs and retainers in place on the head and apply pressure with the spring compressor.

9   Position the keepers in the upper groove, then slowly release the compressor and make sure the keepers seat properly. Apply a small dab of grease to each keeper to hold it in place if necessary (see illustration).

10 Check the installed valve spring height with a ruler graduated in 1/32-inch increments or a dial caliper. If the head was sent out for service work, the installed height should be correct (but don't automatically assume that it is). The measurement is taken from the top of each spring seat or shim(s) to the bottom of the retainer (see illustration). If

the height is greater than specified, shims can be added under the springs to correct it.

❋❋ **CAUTION:**

Don't, under any circumstances, shim the springs to the point where the installed height is less than specified.

11 Apply moly-base grease to the rocker arm faces and the pivots, then install the rocker arms and pivots on the cylinder head, returning them to their original locations.

➡**Note: On 4.7L V8 engines, it's best to install the rocker arms only after the cylinder heads/camshafts and the timing chains have been installed on the engine, then follow the rocker arm procedure in Chapter 2, Part C.**

13 Pistons/connecting rods - removal

◗ **Refer to illustrations 13.1, 13.3, 13.4 and 13.6**

➡**Note: Prior to removing the piston/connecting rod assemblies, remove the cylinder head(s), the oil pan and the oil pump by referring to the appropriate Sections in Chapter 2A or 2B.**

1   Use your fingernail to feel if a ridge has formed at the upper limit of ring travel (about 1/4-inch down from the top of each cylinder). If carbon deposits or cylinder wear have produced ridges, they must be completely removed with a special tool (see illustration). Follow the manufacturer's instructions provided with the tool. Failure to remove the ridges before attempting to remove the piston/connecting rod assemblies may result in piston breakage.

2   After the cylinder ridges have been removed, turn the engine upside-down so the crankshaft is facing up.

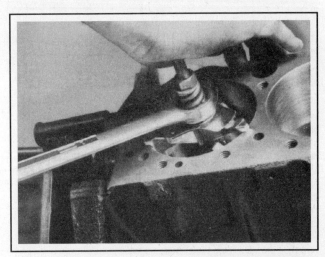

13.1 A ridge reamer is required to remove the ridge from the top of each cylinder - do this before removing the pistons!

13.3 Check the connecting rod side clearance (endplay) with a feeler gauge as shown here between the rod and the crankshaft journal

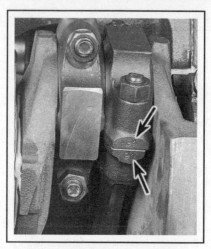

13.4 The connecting rods should be marked with the corresponding cylinder number at the parting line of each rod and cap

13.6a To prevent damage to the crankshaft journals and cylinder walls, slip sections of rubber hose over the rod bolts before removing the piston/rod assemblies

3   Before the connecting rods are removed, check the endplay with feeler gauges. Slide them between the first connecting rod and the crankshaft throw until the play is removed (see illustration). The endplay is equal to the thickness of the feeler gauge(s). If the endplay exceeds the service limit, new connecting rods will be required. If new rods (or a new crankshaft) are installed, the endplay may fall under the specified minimum (if it does, the rods will have to be machined to restore it - consult an automotive machine shop for advice if necessary). Repeat the procedure for the remaining connecting rods.

4   Check the connecting rods and caps for identification marks (see illustration). If they aren't plainly marked, use a small center punch to make the appropriate number of indentations on each rod and cap (1, 2, 3, etc., depending on the engine type and cylinder they're associated with).

※ CAUTION:

Do not use a punch to mark the caps on 4.7L engines, as damage to the rod cap will occur. Use a marking pen only to identify the rod caps.

5   Loosen each of the connecting rod cap nuts 1/2-turn at a time until they can be removed by hand. Remove the number one connecting rod cap and bearing insert. Don't drop the bearing insert out of the cap.

6   Slip a short length of plastic or rubber hose over each connecting rod cap bolt to protect the crankshaft journal and cylinder wall as the piston is removed (see illustration).

→Note: On 4.7L V8 engines, the rod bolts are removed with the caps, so it may be helpful to make a pair of connecting rod guide tools. Take two of the old rod bolts (the engine must be reassembled with new bolts only), cut the heads off and slip a short length of tight-fitting rubber hose over the cut ends of each bolt. Screw the guides into the connecting rod when installing a piston/rod assembly to keep from scoring the cylinder wall (see illustration).

13.6b On 4.7L engines, it will be necessary to make connecting rod guide tools to remove/install the piston and connecting rod assemblies

7   Remove the bearing insert and push the connecting rod/piston assembly out through the top of the engine. Use a wooden hammer handle to push on the upper bearing surface in the connecting rod (DO NOT tap on the connecting rod bolt). If resistance is felt, double-check to make sure that all of the ridge was removed from the cylinder.

8   Repeat the procedure for the remaining cylinders.

9   After removal, reassemble the connecting rod caps and bearing inserts in their respective connecting rods and install the cap nuts finger tight. Leaving the old bearing inserts in place until reassembly will help prevent the connecting rod bearing surfaces from being accidentally nicked or gouged.

10 Don't separate the pistons from the connecting rods (see Section 18 for additional information).

14 Crankshaft - removal

♦ Refer to illustrations 14.1, 14.3, 14.4a, 14.4b and 14.5

➡Note: The crankshaft can be removed only after the engine
has been removed from the vehicle. It's assumed that the flywheel or driveplate, vibration damper, timing chain, oil pan, oil
pump and piston/connecting rod assemblies have already been
removed.

1   Before the crankshaft is removed, check the endplay Mount a
dial indicator with the stem in line with the crankshaft and just touching
one of the crank throws or the nose of the crank (see illustration).

2   Push the crankshaft all the way to the rear and zero the dial indicator. Next, pry the crankshaft to the front as far as possible and check
the reading on the dial indicator. The distance that it moves is the endplay. If it's greater than specified, check the crankshaft thrust surfaces
for wear. If no wear is evident, new main bearings should correct the
endplay.

3   If a dial-indicator isn't available, feeler gauges can be used. Gently pry or push the crankshaft all the way to the front of the engine. Slip
feeler gauges between the crankshaft and the front face of the thrust
main bearing to determine the clearance (see illustration).

4   Check the main bearing caps to see if they're marked to indicate
their locations. They should be numbered consecutively from the front of
the engine to the rear (see illustration). If they aren't, mark them with
number-stamping dies or a center punch (see illustration). Main bearing
caps often have a cast-in arrow, which points to the front of the engine. If
not, mark a paint arrow before removing the main caps. Loosen the main
bearing cap bolts 1/4-turn at a time each, until they can be removed by
hand. Note if any stud bolts are used and make sure they're returned to
their original locations when the crankshaft is reinstalled.

5   Gently tap the caps with a soft-face hammer, then separate them
from the engine block. If necessary, use the bolts as levers to remove
the caps. Try not to drop the bearing inserts if they come out with the
caps.

➡Note: On 4.7L V8 engines, it will be necessary to pry the bedplate off the engine block (see illustration).

6   Carefully lift the crankshaft out of the engine. It may be a good
idea to have an assistant available, since the crankshaft is quite heavy.

14.1 Checking the crankshaft endplay with a dial indicator

14.3 Checking crankshaft endplay with a feeler gauge

With the upper bearing inserts in place in the engine block and the
lower bearing inserts in place in the main bearing caps, return the caps
to their respective locations on the engine block and tighten the bolts
finger tight.

**14.4a Main bearing caps are
typically marked to indicate their
locations (arrows) - they should be
numbered consecutively from the
front of the engine to the rear**

**14.4b If the main cap numbers
aren't marked or they're not visible,
mark the caps with a number stamp
or a center punch**

**14.5 On 4.7L V8 engines, pry the
bedplate off the engine block at the
casting protrusion only, then remove
the bedplate to access the crankshaft -
be careful not to drop the lower bearing
inserts when removing the bedplate**

15 Engine block - cleaning

▶ **Refer to illustrations 15.1a, 15.1b, 15.4, 15.6a, 15.6b, 15.9 and 15.11**

1 Most engine core plugs are corroded firmly in place on an engine that has been in service for years. Use a small punch at the edge of the plug and carefully drive that edge in with a hammer (see illustration). Drive one edge in only far enough for the opposite side to protrude far enough to grab it with locking pliers and pull out (see illustration).

✳✳ CAUTION:

The core plugs (also known as freeze or soft plugs) may be difficult or impossible to retrieve if they're driven completely into the block coolant passages.

2 Using a gasket scraper, remove all traces of gasket material from the engine block. Be very careful not to nick or gouge the gasket sealing surfaces.

3 Remove the main bearing caps and separate the bearing inserts from the caps and the engine block. Tag the bearings, indicating which cylinder they were removed from and whether they were in the cap or the block, then set them aside.

4 Remove all of the threaded oil-gallery plugs from the block (see illustration). The plugs are usually very tight - they may have to be drilled out and the holes retapped. Use new plugs when the engine is reassembled.

5 The engine should be taken to an automotive machine shop to be steam cleaned or hot tanked, although with patience it can be cleaned at home.

6 On 4.7L V8's, inspect the idler shaft at the front of the engine block for damage. Even if damage to the shaft isn't evident, its a good idea to remove the idler shaft from the engine before the block is hot-tanked, since oil is fed from the main oil gallery through the idler shaft to oil the idler gear (see illustrations).

7 After the block is returned, clean all oil holes and oil galleries one more time. Brushes specifically designed for this purpose are available at most auto parts stores. Flush the passages with warm water until the water runs clear, dry the block thoroughly and wipe all machined surfaces with a light, rust preventive oil. If you have access

15.1a The core plugs should be removed carefully by tapping in one side . . .

15.1b . . . then pulling out the opposite side with locking pliers

15.4 Removal of all the oil gallery plugs (arrows) will allow a more thorough cleaning of debris from the internal oil passages of the engine block

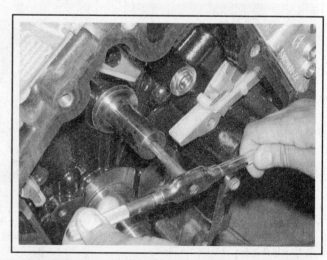

15.6a Tap the end of the idler shaft to accept a slide hammer tool - the factory has predrilled the end of the shaft to accept a 12mm x 1.75 tap

15.6b Use a slide hammer to pull the idler shaft from the block - when installing the idler shaft use the idler gear retaining bolt and washer to pull the shaft back into the block

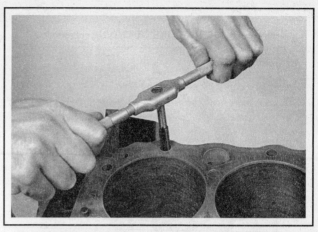

15.9 All bolts in the block, particularly the main bearing cap and head bolt holes, should be cleaned with the proper-sized tap

to compressed air, use it to speed the drying process and to blow out all the oil holes and galleries.

> ⁂ **WARNING:**
>
> **Wear eye protection when using compressed air!**

8   If the block isn't extremely dirty or sludged up, you can do an adequate cleaning job with hot soapy water and a stiff brush. Take plenty of time and do a thorough job. Regardless of the cleaning method used, be sure to clean all oil holes and galleries very thoroughly, dry the block completely and coat all machined surfaces with light oil.

9   The threaded holes in the block must be clean to ensure accurate torque readings during reassembly. Run the proper size tap into each of the holes to remove rust, corrosion, thread sealant or sludge and restore damaged threads (see illustration). If possible, use compressed air to clear the holes of debris produced by this operation.

> ⁂ **WARNING:**
>
> **Wear eye protection when using compressed air! Now is a good time to clean the threads on the head bolts and the main bearing cap bolts as well.**

10   Reinstall the main bearing caps and tighten the bolts finger tight.

11   After coating the sealing surfaces of the new core plugs with core plug sealant, install them in the engine block (see illustration). Make

15.11 A large socket on an extension can be used to drive the new core plugs into the block - go slowly and stop when the plug is evenly flush with the block

sure they're driven in straight and seated properly or leakage could result. Special tools are available for this purpose, but a large socket, with an outside diameter that will just slip into the core plug, a 1/2-inch drive extension and a hammer will work just as well.

12   Apply non-hardening sealant (such as Permatex no. 2 or Teflon pipe sealant) to the new oil gallery plugs and thread them into the holes in the block. Make sure they're tightened securely.

13   If the engine isn't going to be reassembled right away, cover it with a large plastic trash bag to keep it clean.

16   Engine block - inspection

♦ **Refer to illustrations 16.4a, 16.4b and 16.4c**

1   Before the block is inspected, it should be cleaned as described in Section 15.

2   Visually check the block for cracks, rust and corrosion. Look for

stripped threads in the threaded holes. It's also a good idea to have the block checked for hidden cracks by an automotive machine shop that has the special equipment to do this type of work. If defects are found, have the block repaired, if possible, or replaced.

3   Check the cylinder bores for scuffing and scoring.

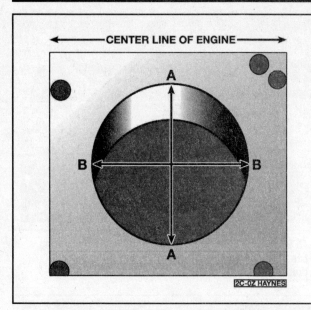

16.4a Measure the diameter of each cylinder at point A and at point B in three places, just under the wear ridge, at the center of the bore and at the bottom of the bore - out of round is the difference in diameter between point A and B at any place in the cylinder - taper is the difference in diameter between the top and the bottom of the cylinder

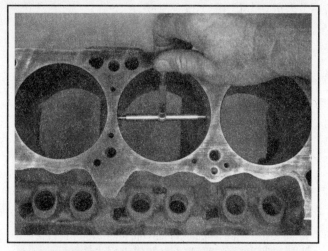

16.4b The ability to "feel" when the telescoping gauge is at the correct point will be developed over time, so work slowly and repeat the check until you're satisfied the bore measurement is accurate

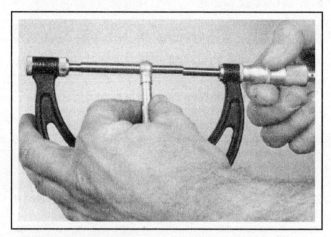

16.4c The gauge is then measured with a micrometer to determine the bore size

4   Measure the diameter of each cylinder at the top (just under the ridge area), center and bottom of the cylinder bore, parallel to the crankshaft axis (see illustrations).

5   Next, measure each cylinder's diameter at the same three locations across the crankshaft axis. Compare the results to this Chapter's Specifications.

6   If the required precision measuring tools aren't available, the piston-to-cylinder clearances can be obtained, though not quite as accurately, using feeler-gauge stock. Feeler gauge stock comes in 12-inch lengths and various thicknesses and is generally available at auto parts stores.

7   To check the clearance, select a feeler gauge and slip it into the cylinder along with the matching piston. The piston must be positioned exactly as it normally would be. The feeler gauge must be between the piston and cylinder on one of the thrust faces (90-degrees to the piston-pin bore).

8   The piston should slip through the cylinder (with the feeler gauge in place) with moderate pressure.

9   If it falls through or slides through easily, the clearance is excessive and a new piston will be required. If the piston binds at the lower end of the cylinder and is loose toward the top, the cylinder is tapered. If tight spots are encountered as the piston/feeler gauge is rotated in the cylinder, the cylinder is out-of-round.

10 Repeat the procedure for the remaining pistons and cylinders.

11 If the cylinder walls are badly scuffed or scored, or if they're out-of-round or tapered beyond the limits given in the specifications, have the engine block rebored and honed at an automotive machine shop. If a rebore is done, oversize pistons and rings will be required.

➡ **Note: On the 4.7L V8 engine, the factory recommends replacing the engine block if the cylinder bore is out of specifications; however, check with your local machine shop for alternative possibilities.**

12 If the cylinders are in reasonably-good condition and not worn to the outside of the limits, and if the piston-to-cylinder clearances can be maintained properly, then they don't have to be rebored. Honing is all that's necessary (see Section 17).

13 Using a precision straightedge and feeler gauge, check the block deck (the surface that mates with the cylinder head) for distortion and compare the results to this Chapter's Specifications.

17 Cylinder honing

▶ **Refer to illustrations 17.3a and 17.3b**

  1   Prior to engine reassembly, the cylinder bores must be honed so the new piston rings will seat correctly and provide the best possible combustion-chamber seal.

➡**Note: If you don't have the tools or don't want to tackle the honing operation, most automotive machine shops will do it for a reasonable fee.**

  2   Before honing the cylinders, install the main bearing caps and tighten the bolts to the torque listed in this Chapter's Specifications.

  3   Two types of cylinder hones are commonly available - the flex hone or "bottle brush" type and the more traditional surfacing hone with spring-loaded stones. Both will do the job, but for the less experienced mechanic the "bottle brush" hone will probably be easier to use. You'll also need some kerosene or honing oil, rags and an electric drill motor. Proceed as follows:

    a) *Mount the hone in the drill motor, compress the stones (if applicable) and slip it into the first cylinder* (see illustration). *Be sure to wear safety goggles or a face shield!*

    b) *Lubricate the cylinder with plenty of honing oil or kerosene, turn on the drill and move the hone up-and-down in the cylinder at a pace that will produce a fine crosshatch pattern on the cylinder walls. Ideally, the crosshatch lines should intersect at approximately a 60-degree angle* (see illustration). *Be sure to use plenty of lubricant and don't take off any more material than is absolutely necessary to produce the desired finish.*

➡**Note: Piston ring manufacturers may specify a smaller crosshatch angle than the traditional 60-degrees - read and follow any instructions included with the new rings.**

    c) *Don't withdraw the hone from the cylinder while it's running. Instead, shut off the drill and continue moving the hone up-and-down in the cylinder until it comes to a complete stop, then compress the stones and withdraw the hone. If you're using a "bottle brush" type hone, stop the drill motor, then turn the chuck in the normal direction of rotation while withdrawing the hone from the cylinder.*

    d) *Wipe the oil out of the cylinder and repeat the procedure for the remaining cylinders.*

  4   After the honing job is complete, chamfer the top edges of the cylinder bores with a small file so the rings won't catch when the pistons are installed. Be very careful not to nick the cylinder walls with the end of the file.

  5   The entire engine block must be washed again very thoroughly with warm, soapy water to remove all traces of the abrasive grit produced during the honing operation.

➡**Note: The bores can be considered clean when a lint-free white cloth - dampened with clean engine oil - used to wipe them out doesn't pick up any more honing residue, which will show up as gray areas on the cloth. Be sure to run a brush**

17.3a A "bottle brush" hone is the easiest type of hone to use

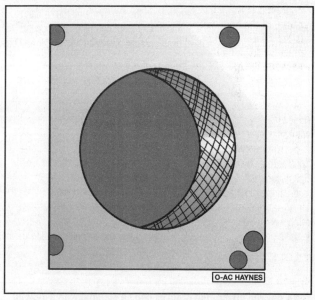

17.3b The cylinder hone should leave a smooth, crosshatch pattern with the lines intersecting at approximately a 60-degree angle

through all oil holes and galleries and flush them with running water.

  6   After rinsing, dry the block and apply a coat of light rust preventive oil to all machined surfaces. Wrap the block in a plastic trash bag to keep it clean and set it aside until reassembly.

18 Pistons/connecting rods - inspection

▶ **Refer to illustrations 18.4a, 18.4b, 18.10 and 18.11**

➡**Note: Most engines in the years covered by this manual use pistons that are Moly-Coated after the final machining process. Never replace the Moly-Coated pistons with tin-coated pistons. Do not use a micrometer to measure the outside diameter of a coated piston, as the results will be misleading. To establish the piston-to-bore clearance in these engines, a dial bore gauge capable of reading down to 0.0001 inch must be used. If you plan on using factory replacement pistons always consult your dealer service department for the proper piston selection process after measuring the cylinder bore.**

1   Before the inspection process can be carried out, the piston/connecting rod assemblies must be cleaned and the original piston rings removed from the pistons.

➡**Note: Always use new piston rings when the engine is reassembled.**

2   Using a piston-ring installation tool, carefully remove the rings from the pistons. Be careful not to nick or gouge the pistons in the process.

3   Scrape all traces of carbon from the top of the piston. A hand-held wire brush or a piece of fine emery cloth can be used once the majority of the deposits have been scraped away. Do not, under any cir-

cumstances, use a wire brush mounted in a drill motor to remove deposits from the pistons. The piston material is soft and may be eroded away by the wire brush.

4   Use a piston-ring groove cleaning tool to remove carbon deposits from the ring grooves. If a tool isn't available, a piece broken off the old ring will do the job. Be very careful to remove only the carbon deposits - don't remove any metal and do not nick or scratch the sides of the ring grooves (see illustrations).

5   Once the deposits have been removed, clean the piston/rod assemblies with solvent and dry them with compressed air (if available). Make sure the oil return holes in the back sides of the ring grooves are clear.

6   If the pistons and cylinder walls aren't damaged or worn excessively, and if the engine block is not rebored, new pistons won't be necessary. Normal piston wear appears as even vertical wear on the piston thrust surfaces and slight looseness of the top ring in its groove. New piston rings, however, should always be used when an engine is rebuilt.

7   Carefully inspect each piston for cracks around the skirt, at the pin bosses and at the ring lands.

8   Look for scoring and scuffing on the thrust faces of the skirt, holes in the piston crown and burned areas at the edge of the crown. If the skirt is scored or scuffed, the engine may have been suffering from overheating and/or abnormal combustion, which caused excessively high operating temperatures. Such pistons should be replaced. The cooling and lubrication systems should be checked thoroughly. A hole in the piston crown is an indication that abnormal combustion (preignition) was occurring. Burned areas at the edge of the piston crown are usually evidence of spark knock (detonation). If any of the above problems exist, the causes must be corrected or the damage will occur again. The causes may include intake air leaks, incorrect fuel/air mixture and incorrect ignition timing.

9   Corrosion of the piston, in the form of small pits, indicates that coolant is leaking into the combustion chamber and/or the crankcase. Again, the cause must be corrected or the problem may persist in the rebuilt engine.

10 Measure the piston ring side clearance by laying a new piston ring in each ring groove and slipping a feeler gauge in beside it (see illustration). Check the clearance at three or four locations around each groove. Be sure to use the correct ring for each groove - they are different. If the side clearance is greater than specified, new pistons will have to be used.

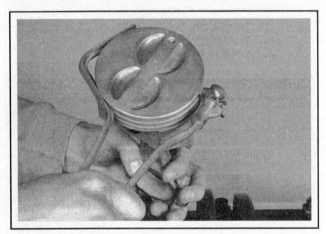

18.4a The piston ring grooves can be cleaned with a special tool, as shown here . . .

18.4b . . . or a section of a broken ring

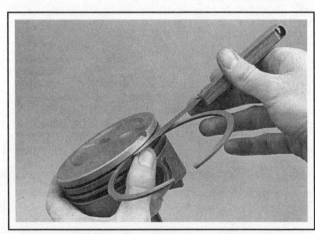

18.10 Check the ring side clearance with a feeler gauge at several points around the groove

11 Check the piston-to-bore clearance by measuring the bore (see Section 16) and the piston diameter. Make sure the pistons and bores are correctly matched. Measure the piston across the skirt, at a 90-degree angle to and in line with the bottom of the piston pin boss (see illustration). Subtract the piston diameter from the bore diameter to obtain the clearance. If it's greater than specified, the block will have to be rebored and new pistons and rings installed.

12 Check the piston-to-rod clearance by twisting the piston and rod in opposite directions. Any noticeable play indicates excessive wear, which must be corrected. The piston/connecting rod assemblies should be taken to an automotive machine shop to have the pistons and rods resized and new pins installed.

13 If the pistons must be removed from the connecting rods for any reason, they should be taken to an automotive machine shop. While they are there, have the connecting rods checked for bend and twist, since automotive machine shops have special equipment for this purpose.

➡Note: Unless new pistons and/or connecting rods must be installed, do not disassemble the pistons and connecting rods.

14 Check the connecting rods for cracks and other damage. Temporarily remove the rod caps, lift out the old bearing inserts, wipe the rod and cap bearing surfaces clean and inspect them for nicks, gouges and scratches. After checking the rods, replace the old bearings, slip the caps into place and tighten the nuts finger tight.

18.11 On engines without moly-coated pistons, measure the piston diameter at a 90-degree angle to the piston pin and in line with the bottom of the piston pin boss

➡Note: If the engine is being rebuilt because of a connecting rod knock, be sure to install new or reconditioned connecting rods.

19 Crankshaft - inspection

♦ Refer to illustrations 19.3, 19.4, 19.6 and 19.8

1 Check the main and connecting rod bearing journals for uneven wear, scoring, pits and cracks.

2 Rub a penny across each journal several times. If a journal picks up copper from the penny, it's too rough and must be reground.

3 Remove all burrs from the crankshaft oil holes with a stone, file or scraper (see illustration).

4 Clean the crankshaft with solvent and dry it with compressed air (if available). Be sure to clean the oil holes with a stiff brush and flush them with solvent (see illustration).

5 Check the rest of the crankshaft for cracks and other damage. It should be magnafluxed to reveal hidden cracks - an automotive machine shop will handle the procedure.

6 Using a micrometer, measure the diameter of the main and connecting rod journals and compare the results to the specifications (see illustration). By measuring the diameter at a number of points around

19.3 The oil holes should be chamfered so sharp edges don't gouge or scratch the new bearings

19.4 Use a wire or stiff plastic bristle brush to clean the oil passages in the crankshaft

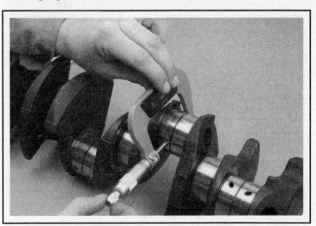

19.6 Measure the diameter of each crankshaft journal at several points to detect taper and out-of-round conditions

19.8 If the rear seal has worn a groove in the crankshaft journal, or if the seal contact surfaces are nicked or scratched, the new seal will leak

each journal's circumference, you'll be able to determine whether or not the journal is out-of-round. Take the measurement at each end of the journal, near the crank throws, to determine if the journal is tapered.

7 If the crankshaft journals are damaged, tapered, out-of-round or worn beyond the limits given in the specifications, have the crankshaft reground by an automotive machine shop. Be sure to use the correct-size bearing inserts if the crankshaft is reconditioned.

8 Check the oil seal journal at rear of the crankshaft for wear and damage (see illustration). If the seal has worn a groove in the journal, or if it's nicked or scratched, the new seal may leak when the engine is reassembled. In some cases, an automotive machine shop may be able to repair the journal by pressing on a thin sleeve. If repair isn't feasible, a new or different crankshaft should be installed.

9 On 4.7L V8 engines, inspect the reluctor ring at the rear of the crankshaft for damage, replacing it if necessary. Damage to this component can cause severe driveability problems.

10 Refer to Section 20 and examine the main and rod bearing inserts.

20 Main and connecting rod bearings - inspection

▶ **Refer to illustration 20.1**

1 Even though the main and connecting rod bearings should be replaced with new ones during the engine overhaul, the old bearings should be retained for close examination, as they may reveal valuable information about the condition of the engine (see illustration).

2 Bearing failure occurs because of lack of lubrication, the presence of dirt or other foreign particles, overloading the engine and corrosion. Regardless of the cause of bearing failure, it must be corrected before the engine is reassembled to prevent it from happening again.

3 When examining the bearings, remove them from the engine block, the main bearing caps, the connecting rods and the rod caps and lay them out on a clean surface in the same general position as their location in the engine. This will enable you to match any bearing problems with the corresponding crankshaft journal.

4 Dirt and other foreign particles get into the engine in a variety of ways. It may be left in the engine during assembly, or it may pass through filters or the PCV system. It may get into the oil, and from there into the bearings. Metal chips from machining operations and normal engine wear are often present. Abrasives are sometimes left in engine components after reconditioning, especially when parts are not thoroughly cleaned using the proper cleaning methods. Whatever the source, these foreign objects often end up embedded in the soft bearing material and are easily recognized. Large particles will not embed in the bearing and will score or gouge the bearing and journal. The best prevention for this cause of bearing failure is to clean all parts thoroughly and keep everything spotlessly clean during engine assembly. Frequent and regular engine oil and filter changes are also recommended.

5 Lack of lubrication (or lubrication breakdown) has a number of interrelated causes. Excessive heat (which thins the oil), overloading (which squeezes the oil from the bearing face) and oil leakage or throw off (from excessive bearing clearances, worn oil pump or high engine speeds) all contribute to lubrication breakdown. Blocked oil passages, which usually are the result of misaligned oil holes in a bearing shell, will also oil starve a bearing and destroy it. When lack of lubrication is the cause of bearing failure, the bearing material is wiped or extruded from the steel backing of the bearing. Temperatures may increase to the point where the steel backing turns blue from overheating.

6 Driving habits can have a definite effect on bearing life. Low speed operation in too high a gear (lugging the engine) puts very high loads on bearings, which tends to squeeze out the oil film. These loads cause the bearings to flex, which produces fine cracks in the bearing face (fatigue failure). Eventually the bearing material will loosen in pieces and tear away from the steel backing. Short-trip driving leads to corrosion of bearings because insufficient engine heat is produced to drive off the condensed water and corrosive gases. These products collect in the engine oil, forming acid and sludge. As the oil is carried to the engine bearings, the acid attacks and corrodes the bearing material.

7 Incorrect bearing installation during engine assembly will lead to bearing failure as well. Tight-fitting bearings leave insufficient bearing oil clearance and will result in oil starvation. Dirt or foreign particles trapped behind a bearing insert result in high spots on the bearing which lead to failure.

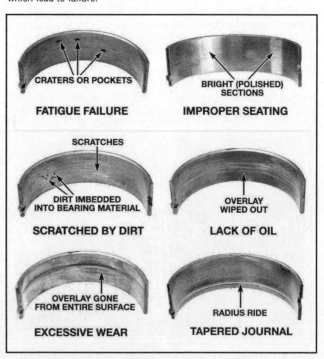

20.1 Typical bearing failures

21 Camshaft, lifters and bearings - inspection

CAMSHAFT

Lobe lift check

▶ Refer to illustrations 21.2, 21.8a and 21.8b

1   The first and easiest method to check camshaft lobe lift is through the use of a dial indicator with the camshaft installed in the engine block and the rocker arms and spark plugs removed.

➡ **Note: The following method can also be used if the cylinder heads and or pushrods have been removed by simply mounting the dial indicator on the deck surface of the engine block and placing the plunger against the top surface of the lifter on the cylinder you're checking.**

2   Beginning with the number one cylinder, mount a dial indicator on the engine and position the plunger against the top surface of the pushrod or lifter. Position the number one cylinder at TDC on the compression stroke (see Section 3). The plunger should be directly above and in line with the pushrod (see illustration).

3   Zero the dial indicator, then very slowly turn the crankshaft in the normal direction of rotation (clockwise) until the indicator needle stops and begins to move in the opposite direction. The point at which it stops indicates maximum cam lobe lift.

4   Record this figure for future reference, then reposition the piston at TDC on the compression stroke again.

5   Move the dial indicator to the other number one cylinder pushrod or lifter and repeat the check. Be sure to record the results for each valve.

6   Repeat the check for the remaining valves. Since each piston must be at TDC on the compression stroke for this procedure, work from cylinder-to-cylinder following the firing order sequence.

7   The second method for measuring camshaft lobe lift is obtained through the use of a micrometer with the camshaft removed from the engine block.

8   Using this method, measure the camshaft lobe height and the base circle (see illustrations). The difference between the two measurements is the lobe lift (lobe height minus base circle = lobe lift). Record this figure for future reference and repeat the check on the remaining camshaft lobes.

9   After the lobe lift check is complete, multiply all the recorded figures by the rocker arm ratio (1.5:1 V6 and V8 engines or 1.6:1 for four-

21.2 Checking camshaft lobe lift with the camshaft installed in the engine - always make sure the dial indicator plunger is directly in-line with the pushrod or lifter

cylinder engines) to obtain the total valve lift for each valve. Compare the results to the specifications in this Chapter. If the valve lift is 0.003 inch less than specified, cam lobe wear has occurred and a new camshaft should be installed.

Bearing journals, lobes and bearings

▶ Refer to illustration 21.11

10 After the camshaft has been removed from the engine, cleaned with solvent and dried, inspect the bearing journals for uneven wear, pitting and evidence of seizure. If the journals are damaged, the bearing inserts in the block are probably damaged as well. Both the camshaft and bearings will have to be replaced.

➡ **Note: Camshaft bearing replacement requires special tools and expertise that place it beyond the scope of the average home mechanic. The tools for bearing removal and installation are available at stores that carry automotive tools, possibly even found at a tool rental business. It is advisable though, if bearings are bad and the procedure is beyond your ability, remove the engine block and take it to an automotive machine shop to ensure that the job is done correctly.**

21.8a If the camshaft is removed from the engine, lobe lift can be obtained by measuring camshaft lobe height . . .

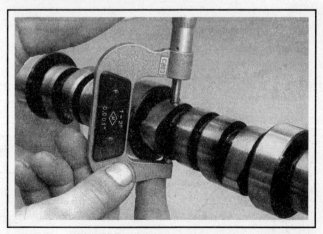

21.8b . . . and by measuring the camshaft base circle - the difference between the two measurements equals lobe lift

ENGINE BEARING ANALYSIS

Debris

Babbitt bearing embedded with debris from machinings

Microscopic detail of debris

Microscopic detail of gouges

Overplated copper alloy bearing gouged by cast iron debris

Aluminum bearing embedded with glass beads

Microscopic detail of glass beads

Damaged lining caused by dirt left on the bearing back

Misassembly

Result of a lower half assembled as an upper - blocking the oil flow

Excessive oil clearance is indicated by a short contact arc

Polished and oil-stained backs are a result of a poor fit in the housing bore

Result of a wrong, reversed, or shifted cap

Overloading

Damage from excessive idling which resulted in an oil film unable to support the load imposed

Damaged upper connecting rod bearings caused by engine lugging; the lower main bearings (not shown) were similarly affected

The damage shown in these upper and lower connecting rod bearings was caused by engine operation at a higher-than-rated speed under load

Misalignment

A warped crankshaft caused this pattern of severe wear in the center, diminishing toward the ends

A poorly finished crankshaft caused the equally spaced scoring shown

A tapered housing bore caused the damage along one edge of this pair

A bent connecting rod led to the damage in the "V" pattern

Lubrication

Result of dry start: The bearings on the left, farthest from the oil pump, show more damage

Result of a low oil supply or oil starvation

Severe wear as a result of inadequate oil clearance

Corrosion

Microscopic detail of corrosion

Corrosion is an acid attack on the bearing lining generally caused by inadequate maintenance, extremely hot or cold operation, or interior oils or fuels

Microscopic detail of cavitation

Example of cavitation - a surface erosion caused by pressure changes in the oil film

Damage from excessive thrust or insufficient axial clearance

Bearing affected by oil dilution caused by excessive blow-by or a rich mixture

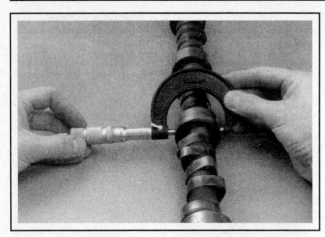

21.11 Check the diameter of each camshaft bearing journal to pinpoint excessive wear and out-of-round conditions

11 Measure the bearing journals with a micrometer to determine if they are excessively worn or out-of-round (see illustration).

12 Check the camshaft lobes for heat discoloration, score marks, chipped areas, pitting and uneven wear. If the lobes are in good condition and if the valve lift measurements recorded earlier are as specified, the camshaft can be reused.

LIFTERS

♦ **Refer to illustrations 21.13, 21.14a, 21.14b and 21.16**

13 Clean the lifters with solvent and dry them thoroughly without mixing them up. Check each lifter wall and pushrod seat and for score marks and uneven wear (see illustration). If the lifter walls are damaged or worn (which is not very likely), inspect the lifter bores in the engine block as well. If the pushrod seats are worn, check the pushrod ends.

Conventional hydraulic lifters (four cylinder engines)

14 Check each lifter foot for scuffing, score marks and uneven wear (see illustrations).

15 If new lifters are being installed, a new camshaft must also be installed. If a new camshaft is installed, then use new lifters as well.

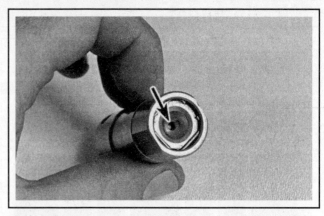

21.13 Check the pushrod seat (arrow) in the top of each lifter for wear

Never install used lifters unless the original camshaft is used and the lifters can be installed in their original locations.

Hydraulic roller lifters (V6 and 5.2L/5.9L V8 engines)

16 Check the rollers carefully for wear and damage and make sure they turn freely without excessive play (see illustration).

17 Used roller lifters can be reinstalled with a new camshaft and the original camshaft can be used if new lifters are installed.

✳✳ CAUTION:

When replacing any of the valvetrain components on V6 engines, make sure the replacement parts are for the exact year of your engine. Match the design of the replacement part to your old part when making any replacement, or serious oiling problems could develop.

Hydraulic lash adjusters (4.7L V8 engines)

18 The 4.7L engine is an overhead cam design that does not use pushrod, and the roller rocker arms act directly on the valves. Hydraulic lash adjusters at the opposite ends of the rocker arms keep the valvetrain quiet.

19 See Chapter 2C, Section 5 for removal, inspection and installation information.

21.14a On conventional hydraulic type lifters, check the foot of each lifter for pitting and galling . . .

21.14b . . . then use another lifter to check that the foot of each lifter is slightly convex - if the foot is concave it should be replaced

21.16 The roller on hydraulic roller lifters must turn freely - check for wear and excessive play as well

22 Engine overhaul - reassembly sequence

1   Before beginning engine reassembly, make sure you have all the necessary new parts, gaskets and seals as well as the following items on hand:

> Common hand tools
> 3/8-inch and 1/2-inch-drive torque wrenches
> Piston ring installation tool
> Piston ring compressor
> Vibration damper installation tool
> Short lengths of rubber or plastic hose to fit over connecting rod bolts
> Plastigage
> Feeler gauges
> A fine-tooth file
> New engine oil
> Engine assembly lube or moly-base grease
> Gasket sealant
> Thread locking compound

2   In order to save time and avoid problems, engine reassembly must be done in the following general order:

> New camshaft bearings (must be done by automotive machine shop)
> Piston rings
> Crankshaft and main bearings
> Piston/connecting rod assemblies
> Camshaft and lifters
> Timing chain and sprockets
> Cylinder head(s), pushrods and rocker arms
> Oil pump
> Timing cover
> Oil pan
> Intake and exhaust manifolds
> Rocker arm cover(s)
> Flywheel/driveplate

23 Piston rings - installation

▶ **Refer to illustrations 23.3, 23.4, 23.5, 23.9a, 23.9b and 23.12**

1   Before installing the new piston rings, the ring end gaps must be checked. It's assumed that the piston ring side clearance has been checked and verified correct (see Section 18).

2   Lay out the piston/connecting rod assemblies and the new ring sets so the ring sets will be matched with the same piston and cylinder during the end gap measurement and engine assembly.

3   Insert the top (number one) ring into the first cylinder and square it up with the cylinder walls by pushing it in with the top of the piston (see illustration). The ring should be near the bottom of the cylinder, at the lower limit of ring travel.

4   To measure the end gap, slip feeler gauges between the ends of the ring until a gauge equal to the gap width is found (see illustration). The feeler gauge should slide between the ring ends with a slight amount of drag. Compare the measurement to the Specifications. If the gap is larger or smaller than specified, double-check to make sure you have the correct rings before proceeding.

5   If the gap is too small, it must be enlarged or the ring ends may

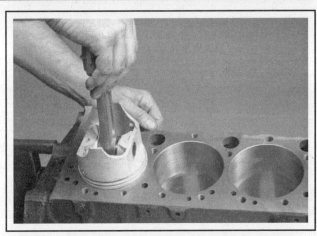

23.3 When checking piston ring end gap, the ring must be square in the cylinder bore - use a piston to push it down approximately two inches from the bottom of the bore

23.4 With the ring square in the cylinder, measure the end gap with feeler gauges

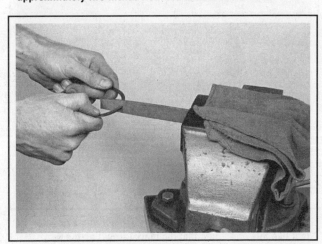

23.5 If the end gap is too small, clamp a fine file in a vise and file the ring ends a little at a time and re-measure in the bore - file from the outside of the ring inward only

23.9a Installing the spacer/expander in the oil control ring groove

23.9b Slip the oil ring side rails in by hand - do not use a ring expander

come in contact with each other during engine operation, which can cause serious damage to the engine. The end gap can be increased by filing the ring ends very carefully with a fine file. Mount the file in a vise equipped with soft jaws, slip the ring over the file with the ends contacting the file face and slowly move the ring to remove material from the ends. When performing this operation, file only from the outside in (see illustration). The ring ends must be filed squarely, and any tiny burrs on the end should be removed before final ring installation.

6   Excess end gap isn't critical unless it's greater than 0.040-inch. Again, double-check to make sure you have the correct rings for your engine.

7   Repeat the procedure for each ring that will be installed in the first cylinder and for each ring in the remaining cylinders. Remember to keep rings, pistons and cylinders matched up.

8   Once the ring end gaps have been checked/corrected, the rings can be installed on the pistons.

9   The oil control ring (lowest one on the piston) is usually installed first. It's normally composed of three separate components. Slip the spacer/expander into the groove (see illustration). If an anti-rotation

tang is used, make sure it's inserted into the drilled hole in the ring groove. Next, install the lower side rail. Don't use a piston ring installation tool on the oil ring side rails, as they may be damaged. Instead, place one end of the side rail into the groove between the spacer/expander and the ring land, hold it firmly in place and slide a finger around the piston while pushing the rail into the groove (see illustration). Next, install the upper side rail in the same manner.

10   After the three oil ring components have been installed, check to make sure that both the upper and lower side rails can be turned smoothly in the ring groove and that the expander ends are butted together.

11   The number two (middle) ring is installed next. It's usually stamped with a mark which must face up, toward the top of the piston. The chamfer on the number two ring must face down on all engines, with one dot facing up on the four-cylinder engines and with two dots facing up and on V6 and V8's, the ID mark is a drill point, a stamped letter O, an oval depression or the word TOP.

❋ CAUTION:

Always follow the instructions printed on the ring package or box - different manufacturers may require different approaches. Do not mix up the top and middle rings, as they have different cross sections.

12   Use a piston ring installation tool and make sure the identification mark is facing the top of the piston, then slip the ring into the middle groove on the piston (see illustration). Don't expand the ring any more than necessary to slide it over the piston.

13   Install the number one (top) ring in the same manner. Making sure that the dot or mark (if equipped) is facing up. On four cylinder engines the top ring has no mark or chamfer so it can be installed in either direction. On V6 and V8 engines the number one (top) ring must be installed with its chamfer UP while the second ring must have the chamfer DOWN. Be careful not to confuse the number one and number two rings. Typically, the second ring on V6 and V8 engines has two dots on the UP side, and the top ring has one dot on the UP side. The second ring on four cylinder engines has one dot on the UP side and no markings on the top ring. Always check the instructions with the ring set your are using.

14   Repeat the procedure for the remaining pistons and rings.

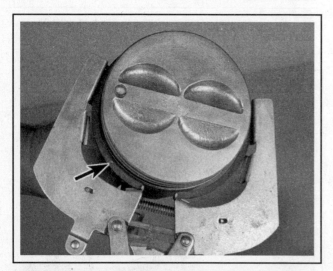

23.12 Install the compression rings using a ring-expander tool like this one - note that the mark (arrow) on the ring should face UP

24 Crankshaft - installation and main bearing oil clearance check

1   Crankshaft installation is the first major step in engine reassembly. It's assumed at this point that the engine block and crankshaft have been cleaned, inspected and repaired or reconditioned.

2   Position the engine with the bottom facing up.

3   Remove the main bearing cap bolts and lift out the caps. Lay the caps out in the proper order to ensure correct installation.

4   If they're still in place, remove the old bearing inserts from the block and the main bearing caps. Wipe the main bearing surfaces of the block and caps with a clean, lint free cloth. They must be kept spotlessly clean!

MAIN BEARING OIL CLEARANCE CHECK

▶ **Refer to illustrations 24.7a, 24.7b, 24.9, 24.10a, 24.10b, and 24.13**

5   Clean the back sides of the new main bearing inserts and lay the bearing half with the oil groove in each main bearing saddle in the block. Lay the other bearing half from each bearing set in the corresponding main bearing cap or the corresponding saddle in the bedplate on 4.7L engines. Make sure the tab on each bearing insert fits into the recess in the block or cap. Also, the oil holes in the block must line up with the oil holes in the bearing insert.

✳✳ CAUTION:

Do not hammer the bearings into place and don't nick or gouge the bearing faces. No lubrication should be used at this time.

6   Clean the faces of the bearings in the block and the crankshaft main bearing journals with a clean, lint-free cloth. Check or clean the oil holes in the crankshaft, as any dirt here can go only one way - straight through the new bearings.

7   Once you're certain the crankshaft is clean, carefully lay it in position in the main bearings. On 4.7L engines, install the thrust bearings, which are a two-piece design (see illustrations). There are front and rear thrust bearings - do not mix them up! Pry the crankshaft forward and install the rear thrust bearing, then pry rearward and install the front thrust bearing.

➡**Note: The oil grooves must face toward the crankshaft.**

8   Before the crankshaft can be permanently installed, the main bearing oil clearance must be checked.

24.9 Lay the Plastigage strips (arrow) on the main bearing journals, parallel to the crankshaft centerline

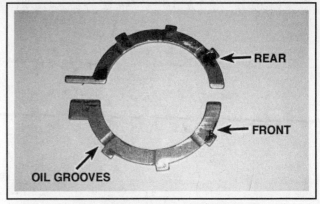

24.7a Thrust bearing identification - 4.7L V8 engine

24.7b Insert the thrust bearing into the machined surface between the crankshaft and the upper bearing saddle, then rotate it down into the block until it is flush with the parting line of the main bearing saddle - make sure the oil grooves on the thrust bearings face the crankshaft

9   Trim several pieces of the appropriate-size Plastigage (they must be slightly shorter than the width of the main bearings) and place one piece on each crankshaft main bearing journal, parallel with the journal axis (see illustration).

10 Clean the faces of the bearings in the caps or bedplate on 4.7L engines and install the caps in their respective positions (don't mix them up) with the arrows pointing toward the front of the engine (see

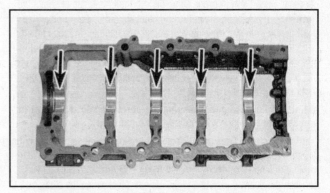

24.10a On the 4.7L engine, the bearings are laid into the corresponding saddles in the bedplate . . .

24.10b . . . then the bedplate is set over the crankshaft onto the dowels on the engine block

24.13 Compare the width of the crushed Plastigage to the scale on the envelope, taking the measurement at the widest point of the Plastigage

24.18a Install the new neoprene upper seal half in the engine block . . .

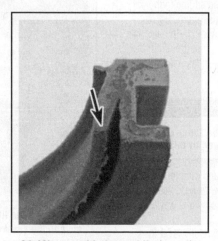

24.18b . . . with the seal lip (arrow) facing the front of the engine

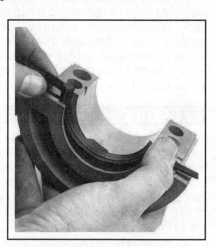

24.19 Install the new neoprene lower seal half in the rear main cap

illustrations). Don't disturb the Plastigage. Apply a light coat of oil to the bolt threads and the under sides of the bolt heads, then install them.

11 Tighten the main bearing cap bolts or bedplate bolts on 4.7L engines, starting in the center and working towards the ends, in three steps, to the torque listed in this Chapter's Specifications. Don't rotate the crankshaft at any time during this operation!

12 Remove the bolts and carefully lift off the main bearing caps or bedplate. Keep them in order. Don't disturb the Plastigage or rotate the crankshaft. If any of the main bearing caps are difficult to remove, tap them gently from side-to-side with a soft-face hammer to loosen them.

13 Compare the width of the crushed Plastigage on each journal to the scale printed on the Plastigage envelope to obtain the main bearing oil clearance (see illustration). Check the Specifications to make sure it's correct.

➡Note: **Make sure you are using the correct scale, both metric and standard ones are included in the package.**

14 If the clearance is not as specified, the bearing inserts may be the wrong size (which means different ones will be required). Before deciding that different inserts are needed, make sure that no dirt or oil was between the bearing inserts and the caps or block when the clearance was measured. If the Plastigage is noticeably wider at one end than the

other, the journal may be tapered.

15 Carefully scrape all traces of the Plastigage material off the main bearing journals and/or the bearing faces. Don't nick or scratch the bearing faces (a plastic credit card edge does the job).

FINAL CRANKSHAFT INSTALLATION

▶ **Refer to illustrations 24.18a, 24.18b, 24.19, 24.20 and 24.22**

16 Carefully lift the crankshaft out of the engine. Clean the bearing faces in the block, then apply a thin, uniform layer of engine assembly lube to each of the bearing surfaces.

17 Lubricate the crankshaft surfaces that contact the oil seals with clean engine oil.

18 On V6 and 5.2L/5.9L V8 engines install the upper half of the rear main seal into the block (see illustrations) with the paint facing the rear of the engine and the seal lip facing towards the front of the engine.

19 Install a new rear main oil seal lower half in the rear main cap (see illustration)

20 Make sure the crankshaft journals are clean, then lay the crankshaft back in place in the block. Clean the faces of the bearings in the

24.20 Cylinder block-to-bedplate sealant application - 4.7L V8 engine

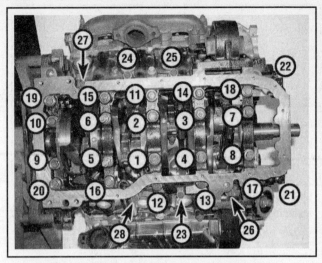

24.22 Bedplate TIGHTENING sequence - 4.7L V8 engine

caps or bedplate, then apply lubricant to them. On 4.7L engines, make sure the thrust bearings are installed as described in Step 7, then apply a 1/8-inch bead of RTV sealant to the engine block (see illustration) and install the bedplate over the dowels on the block. On V6 and 5.2L/5.9L engines, install all the caps in their respective positions, except the rear main cap, with the arrows pointing toward the front of the engine.

21 Apply a light coat of oil to the bolt threads and the under sides of the bolt heads, then install them. Apply a dab of Loctite 515 or RTV sealant to each side of the rear main cap and install the rear main cap (see Chapter 2B, Section 15).

22 On V6 and 5.2L /5.9L V8 engines, tighten all main bearing cap bolts, except the number three thrust bearing cap, to the torque listed in this Chapter's Specifications. Pry the crankshaft slightly back and forth in the block to seat the thrust bearings, then tighten the number 3 main

cap to Specifications. On 4.7L V8 engines, tighten the bedplate bolts in four steps in the sequence listed in the Specifications (see illustration).

➡**Note: Since RTV sealant is the only gasket material between the bedplate and the block, it is critical to adhere to the sealant manufacturers instructions for application and drying times.**

23 Check the crankshaft endplay with a feeler gauge or a dial indicator as described in Section 14. The endplay should be correct if the crankshaft thrust faces aren't worn or damaged and new bearings have been installed.

24 On four cylinder engines install the rear main seal as described in Chapter 2A. On manual transmission-equipped models, install a new pilot bearing in the end of the crankshaft (see Chapter 8).

25 Rotate the crankshaft a number of times by hand to check for any obvious binding.

25 Pistons/connecting rods - installation and rod bearing oil clearance check

▶ Refer to illustrations 25.3, 25.5, 25.9, 25.11, 25.13 and 25.17

❊❊ CAUTION:

The rod bolts on 4.7L V8 engines are a torque-to-yield design and must be replaced whenever they are loosened or removed.

1 Before installing the piston/connecting rod assemblies, the cylinder walls must be perfectly clean, the top edge of each cylinder must be chamfered, and the crankshaft must be in place.

2 Remove the cap from the end of the number one connecting rod (refer to the marks made during removal). Remove the original bearing inserts and wipe the bearing surfaces of the connecting rod and cap with a clean, lint-free cloth. They must be kept spotlessly clean.

CONNECTING ROD BEARING OIL CLEARANCE CHECK

3 Clean the back side of the new upper bearing insert, then lay it in place in the connecting rod. Make sure the tab on the bearing fits into the recess in the rod (see illustration). Don't hammer the bearing insert

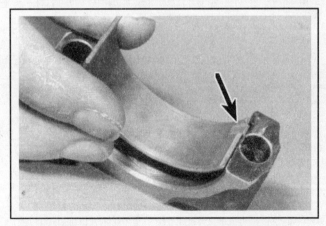

25.3 Make sure the bearing tang fits securely into the notch on the rod cap

into place and be very careful not to nick or gouge the bearing face. Don't lubricate the bearing at this time.

4 Clean the back side of the other bearing insert and install it in the rod cap. Again, make sure the tab on the bearing fits into the recess

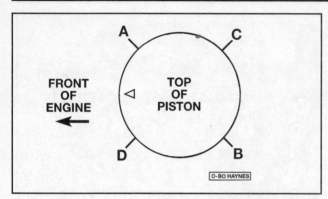

25.5 Position the piston ring gaps as shown here before installing the piston/connecting rod assembly into the engine

A   Oil ring expander
B   Oil ring lower rail
C   Top ring gap and upper oil ring rail
D   Second ring gap

25.9 The notch (arrow) on the pistons must face forward

in the cap, and don't apply any lubricant. It's critically important that the mating surfaces of the bearing and connecting rod are perfectly clean and oil free when they're assembled.

5   Position the piston ring gaps at intervals around the piston (see illustration).

6   Slip a section of plastic or rubber hose over each connecting rod cap bolt. On 4.7L V8 engines, use the connecting rod guide tools made during removal of the connecting rods/pistons.

7   Lubricate the piston and rings with clean engine oil and attach a piston-ring compressor to the piston. Leave the skirt protruding about 1/4-inch to guide the piston into the cylinder. The rings must be compressed until they're flush with the piston.

8   Rotate the crankshaft until the number one connecting rod journal is at BDC (bottom dead center) and apply a coat of engine oil to the cylinder walls.

9   With the arrow or notch on top of the piston (see illustration) facing the front of the engine, gently insert the piston/connecting rod assembly into the number one cylinder bore and rest the bottom edge of the ring compressor on the engine block.

10   Tap the top edge of the ring compressor to make sure it's contacting the block around its entire circumference.

11   Gently tap on the top of the piston with the end of a wooden hammer handle (see illustration) while guiding the end of the connecting rod into place on the crankshaft journal. The piston rings may try to pop out of the ring compressor just before entering the cylinder bore, so keep some downward pressure on the ring compressor. Work slowly, and if any resistance is felt as the piston enters the cylinder, stop immediately. Find out what's hanging up and fix it before proceeding. Do not, for any reason, force the piston into the cylinder - you might break a ring and/or the piston.

12   Once the piston/connecting rod assembly is installed, the connecting rod bearing oil clearance must be checked before the rod cap is permanently bolted in place.

13   Cut a piece of the appropriate size Plastigage slightly shorter than the width of the connecting rod bearing and lay it in place on the number one connecting rod journal, parallel with the journal axis (see illustration).

14   Clean the connecting rod cap bearing face, remove the protective hoses from the connecting rod bolts and install the rod cap. Make sure the mating mark on the cap is on the same side as the mark on the connecting rod.

15   Install the nuts (or bolts on 4.7L V8 engines) and tighten them to

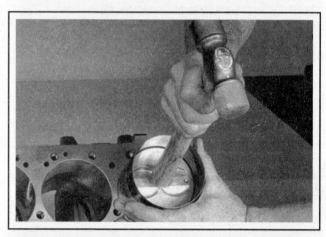

25.11 Drive the piston in gently with the end of a wooden hammer handle - go evenly and stop if you feel an obstruction

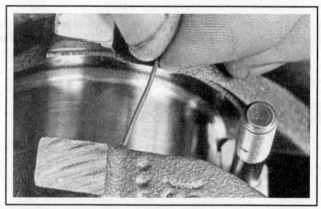

25.13 Lay the Plastigage strips on each rod bearing journal, parallel to the crankshaft centerline

the torque listed in this Chapter's Specifications, working up to it in three steps. If you're working on a 4.7L V8, use a pair of old rod bolts for checking the oil clearance - save the new bolts for the final installation.

➡**Note:** Use a thin-wall socket to avoid erroneous torque readings that can result if the socket is wedged between the rod cap and nut. If the socket tends to wedge itself between the nut and the cap, lift up on it slightly until it no longer contacts the cap. Do not rotate the crankshaft at any time during this operation.

16 Remove the nuts and detach the rod cap, being very careful not to disturb the Plastigage.

17 Compare the width of the crushed Plastigage to the scale printed on the Plastigage envelope to obtain the oil clearance (see illustration). Compare it to the Specifications to make sure the clearance is correct.

18 If the clearance is not as specified, the bearing inserts may be the wrong size (which means different ones will be required). Before deciding that different inserts are needed, make sure that no dirt or oil was between the bearing inserts and the connecting rod or cap when the clearance was measured. Also, recheck the journal diameter. If the Plastigage was wider at one end than the other, the journal may be tapered, in which case the crankshaft needs to be machined.

FINAL CONNECTING ROD INSTALLATION

19 Carefully scrape all traces of the Plastigage material off the rod journal and/or bearing face. Be very careful not to scratch the bearing - use your fingernail or the edge of a credit card.

20 Make sure the bearing faces are perfectly clean, then apply a uniform layer of clean moly-base grease or engine assembly lube to both of them. You'll have to push the piston into the cylinder to expose the face of the bearing insert in the connecting rod - be sure to slip the protective hoses over the rod bolts first.

21 Slide the connecting rod back into place on the journal, remove the protective hoses from the rod cap bolts, install the rod cap and tighten the nuts to the torque listed in this Chapter's Specifications. Again, work up to the torque in three steps.

22 Repeat the entire procedure for the remaining pistons/connecting rods.

23 The important points to remember are:

a) *Keep the back sides of the bearing inserts and the insides of the connecting rods and caps perfectly clean when assembling them.*

b) *Make sure you have the correct piston/rod assembly for each cylinder.*

c) *The notch or mark on the piston must face the front of the engine.*

d) *Stagger the ring end gaps (see illustration 25.5).*

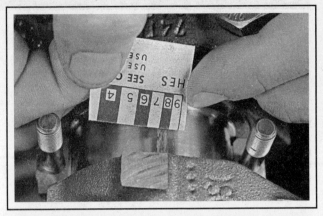

25.17 Measure the width of the crushed Plastigage to determine the rod bearing oil clearance and compare it to the Specifications

e) *Lubricate the cylinder walls with clean oil.*

f) *Lubricate the bearing faces when installing the rod caps after the oil clearance has been checked.*

24 After all the piston/connecting rod assemblies have been properly installed, rotate the crankshaft a number of times by hand to check for any obvious binding.

25 As a final step, the connecting rod side clearance must be checked. Refer to Section 13 for this procedure.

26 Compare the measured side clearance to the Specifications to make sure it's correct. If it was correct before disassembly and the original crankshaft and rods were reinstalled, it should still be right. If new rods or a new crankshaft were installed, the side clearance may be inadequate. If so, the rods will have to be removed and taken to an automotive machine shop for resizing.

27 The remainder of the engine assembly work is in attaching the cylinder heads, valvetrain, front cover, water pump, flywheel, intake and exhaust manifolds and accessories, all of which are covered in Chapter 2A, 2B or 2C.

26 Initial start-up and break-in after overhaul

❉❉ WARNING:

Have a fire extinguisher handy when starting the engine for the first time.

1 Once the engine has been installed in the vehicle, double-check the engine oil and coolant levels.

2 With the spark plugs out of the engine and the ignition system disabled (see Section 3), crank the engine until oil pressure registers on the gauge or the light goes out.

3 Install the spark plugs, connect the plug wires and restore the ignition system functions (see Section 3).

4 Start the engine. It may take a few moments for the fuel system to build up pressure, but the engine should start without a great deal of effort.

➡**Note: If backfiring occurs through the throttle body, recheck the valve timing and ignition timing.**

5 After the engine starts, it should be allowed to warm up to normal operating temperature. Do not allow the engine to exceed a fast idle until the hydraulic lifters pump up and become quiet again (usu-

ally about five minutes).

6 While the engine is warming up, make a thorough check for fuel, oil and coolant leaks. If a new camshaft and lifters have been installed during the overhaul, the engine should run at a fast idle for 15 minutes after the lifters pump up and become quiet (keep an eye on the temperature gauge and don't allow the engine to overheat) to "break in" the cam and lifters.

7 Shut the engine off and recheck the engine oil and coolant levels.

8 Drive the vehicle to an area with minimum traffic, accelerate from 30 to 50 mph, then allow the vehicle to slow to 30 mph with the throttle closed. Repeat the procedure 10 or 12 times. This will load the piston rings and cause them to seat properly against the cylinder walls. Check again for oil and coolant leaks.

9 Drive the vehicle gently for the first 500 miles (no sustained high speeds) and keep a constant check on the oil level. It is not unusual for an engine to use oil during the break-in period.

10 At approximately 500 to 600 miles, change the oil and filter.

11 For the next few hundred miles, drive the vehicle normally. Do not pamper it or abuse it.

12 After 2000 miles, change the oil and filter again and consider the engine broken in.

GLOSSARY

B

Backlash - The amount of play between two parts. Usually refers to how much one gear can be moved back and forth without moving gear with which it's meshed.

Bearing Caps - The caps held in place by nuts or bolts which, in turn, hold the bearing surface. This space is for lubricating oil to enter.

Bearing clearance - The amount of space left between shaft and bearing surface. This space is for lubricating oil to enter.

Bearing crush - The additional height which is purposely manufactured into each bearing half to ensure complete contact of the bearing back with the housing bore when the engine is assembled.

Bearing knock - The noise created by movement of a part in a loose or worn bearing.

Blueprinting - Dismantling an engine and reassembling it to EXACT specifications.

Bore - An engine cylinder, or any cylindrical hole; also used to describe the process of enlarging or accurately refinishing a hole with a cutting tool, as to bore an engine cylinder. The bore size is the diameter of the hole.

Boring - Renewing the cylinders by cutting them out to a specified size. A boring bar is used to make the cut.

Bottom end - A term which refers collectively to the engine block, crankshaft, main bearings and the big ends of the connecting rods.

Break-in - The period of operation between installation of new or rebuilt parts and time in which parts are worn to the correct fit. Driving at reduced and varying speed for a specified mileage to permit parts to wear to the correct fit.

Bushing - A one-piece sleeve placed in a bore to serve as a bearing surface for shaft, piston pin, etc. Usually replaceable.

C

Camshaft - The shaft in the engine, on which a series of lobes are located for operating the valve mechanisms. The camshaft is driven by gears or sprockets and a timing chain. Usually referred to simply as the cam.

Carbon - Hard, or soft, black deposits found in combustion chamber, on plugs, under rings, on and under valve heads.

Cast iron - An alloy of iron and more than two percent carbon, used for engine blocks and heads because it's relatively inexpensive and easy to mold into complex shapes.

Chamfer - To bevel across (or a bevel on) the sharp edge of an object.

Chase - To repair damaged threads with a tap or die.

Combustion chamber - The space between the piston and the cylinder head, with the piston at top dead center, in which air-fuel mixture is burned.

Compression ratio - The relationship between cylinder volume (clearance volume) when the piston is at top dead center and cylinder volume when the piston is at bottom dead center.

Connecting rod - The rod that connects the crank on the crankshaft with the piston. Sometimes called a con rod.

Connecting rod cap - The part of the connecting rod assembly that attaches the rod to the crankpin.

Core plug - Soft metal plug used to plug the casting holes for the coolant passages in the block.

Crankcase - The lower part of the engine in which the crankshaft rotates; includes the lower section of the cylinder block and the oil pan.

Crank kit - A reground or reconditioned crankshaft and new main and connecting rod bearings.

Crankpin - The part of a crankshaft to which a connecting rod is attached.

Crankshaft - The main rotating member, or shaft, running the length of the crankcase, with offset throws to which the connecting rods are attached; changes the reciprocating motion of the pistons into rotating motion.

Cylinder sleeve - A replaceable sleeve, or liner, pressed into the cylinder block to form the cylinder bore.

D

Deburring - Removing the burrs (rough edges or areas) from a bearing.

Deglazer - A tool, rotated by an electric motor, used to remove glaze from cylinder walls so a new set of rings will seat.

E

Endplay - The amount of lengthwise movement between two parts. As applied to a crankshaft, the distance that the crankshaft can move forward and back in the cylinder block.

F

Face - A machinist's term that refers to removing metal from the end of a shaft or the face of a larger part, such as a flywheel.

Fatigue - A breakdown of material through a large number of loading and unloading cycles. The first signs are cracks followed shortly by breaks.

Feeler gauge - A thin strip of hardened steel, ground to an exact thickness, used to check clearances between parts.

Free height - The unloaded length or height of a spring.

Freeplay - The looseness in a linkage, or an assembly of parts, between the initial application of force and actual movement. Usually perceived as slop or slight delay.

Freeze plug - See Core plug.

G

Gallery - A large passage in the block that forms a reservoir for engine oil pressure.

Glaze - The very smooth, glassy finish that develops on cylinder walls while an engine is in service.

H

Heli-Coil - A rethreading device used when threads are worn or damaged. The device is installed in a retapped hole to reduce the thread size to the original size.

I

Installed height - The spring's measured length or height, as installed on the cylinder head. Installed height is measured from the spring seat to the underside of the spring retainer.

J

Journal - The surface of a rotating shaft which turns in a bearing.

K

Keeper - The split lock that holds the valve spring retainer in position on the valve stem.

Key - A small piece of metal inserted into matching grooves machined into two parts fitted together - such as a gear pressed onto a shaft - which prevents slippage between the two parts.

Knock - The heavy metallic engine sound, produced in the combustion chamber as a result of abnormal combustion - usually detonation. Knock is usually caused by a loose or worn bearing. Also referred to as detonation, pinging and spark knock. Connecting rod or main bearing knocks are created by too much oil clearance or insufficient lubrication.

L

Lands - The portions of metal between the piston ring grooves.

Lapping the valves - Grinding a valve face and its seat together with lapping compound.

Lash - The amount of free motion in a gear train, between gears, or in a mechanical assembly, that occurs before movement can begin. Usually refers to the lash in a valve train.

Lifter - The part that rides against the cam to transfer motion to the rest of the valve train.

M

Machining - The process of using a machine to remove metal from a metal part.

Main bearings - The plain, or babbitt, bearings that support the crankshaft.

Main bearing caps - The cast iron caps, bolted to the bottom of the block, that support the main bearings.

O

O.D. - Outside diameter.

Oil gallery - A pipe or drilled passageway in the engine used to carry engine oil from one area to another.

Oil ring - The lower ring, or rings, of a piston; designed to prevent excessive amounts of oil from working up the cylinder walls and into the combustion chamber. Also called an oil-control ring.

Oil seal - A seal which keeps oil from leaking out of a compartment. Usually refers to a dynamic seal around a rotating shaft or other moving part.

O-ring - A type of sealing ring made of a special rubberlike material; in use, the O-ring is compressed into a groove to provide the sealing action.

Overhaul - To completely disassemble a unit, clean and inspect all parts, reassemble it with the original or new parts and make all adjustments necessary for proper operation.

P

Pilot bearing - A small bearing installed in the center of the flywheel (or the rear end of the crankshaft) to support the front end of the input shaft of the transmission.

Pip mark - A little dot or indentation which indicates the top side of a compression ring.

Piston - The cylindrical part, attached to the connecting rod, that moves up and down in the cylinder as the crankshaft rotates. When the fuel charge is fired, the piston transfers the force of the explosion to the connecting rod, then to the crankshaft.

Piston pin (or wrist pin) - The cylindrical and usually hollow steel pin that passes through the piston. The piston pin fastens the piston to the upper end of the connecting rod.

Piston ring - The split ring fitted to the groove in a piston. The ring contacts the sides of the ring groove and also rubs against the cylinder wall, thus sealing space between piston and wall. There are two types of rings: Compression rings seal the compression pressure in the combustion chamber; oil rings scrape excessive oil off the cylinder wall.

Piston ring groove - The slots or grooves cut in piston heads to hold piston rings in position.

Piston skirt - The portion of the piston below the rings and the piston pin hole.

Plastigage - A thin strip of plastic thread, available in different sizes, used for measuring clearances. For example, a strip of plastigage is laid across a bearing journal and mashed as parts are assembled. Then parts are disassembled and the width of the strip is measured to determine clearance between journal and bearing. Commonly used to measure crankshaft main-bearing and connecting rod bearing clearances.

Press-fit - A tight fit between two parts that requires pressure to force the parts together. Also referred to as drive, or force, fit.

Prussian blue - A blue pigment; in solution, useful in determining the area of contact between two surfaces. Prussian blue is commonly used to determine the width and location of the contact area between the valve face and the valve seat.

R

Race (bearing) - The inner or outer ring that provides a contact surface for balls or rollers in bearing.

Ream - To size, enlarge or smooth a hole by using a round cutting tool with fluted edges.

Ring job - The process of reconditioning the cylinders and installing new rings.

Runout - Wobble. The amount a shaft rotates out-of-true.

S

Saddle - The upper main bearing seat.

Scored - Scratched or grooved, as a cylinder wall may be scored by abrasive particles moved up and down by the piston rings.

Scuffing - A type of wear in which there's a transfer of material between parts moving against each other; shows up as pits or grooves in the mating surfaces.

Seat - The surface upon which another part rests or seats. For example, the valve seat is the matched surface upon which the valve face rests. Also used to refer to wearing into a good fit; for example, piston rings seat after a few miles of driving.

Short block - An engine block complete with crankshaft and piston and, usually, camshaft assemblies.

Static balance - The balance of an object while it's stationary.

Step - The wear on the lower portion of a ring land caused by excessive side and back-clearance. The height of the step indicates the ring's extra side clearance and the length of the step projecting from the back wall of the groove represents the ring's back clearance.

Stroke - The distance the piston moves when traveling from top dead center to bottom dead center, or from bottom dead center to top dead center.

Stud - A metal rod with threads on both ends.

T

Tang - A lip on the end of a plain bearing used to align the bearing during assembly.

Tap - To cut threads in a hole. Also refers to the fluted tool used to cut threads.

Taper - A gradual reduction in the width of a shaft or hole; in an engine cylinder, taper usually takes the form of uneven wear, more pronounced at the top than at the bottom.

Throws - The offset portions of the crankshaft to which the connecting rods are affixed.

Thrust bearing - The main bearing that has thrust faces to prevent excessive end-play, or forward and backward movement of the crankshaft.

Thrust washer - A bronze or hardened steel washer placed between two moving parts. The washer prevents longitudinal movement and provides a bearing surface for thrust surfaces of parts.

Tolerance - The amount of variation permitted from an exact size of measurement. Actual amount from smallest acceptable dimension to largest acceptable dimension.

U

Umbrella - An oil deflector placed near the valve tip to throw oil from the valve stem area.

Undercut - A machined groove below the normal surface.

Undersize bearings - Smaller diameter bearings used with re-ground crankshaft journals.

V

Valve grinding - Refacing a valve in a valve-refacing machine.

Valve train - The valve-operating mechanism of an engine; includes all components from the camshaft to the valve.

Vibration damper - A cylindrical weight attached to the front of the crankshaft to minimize torsional vibration (the twist-untwist actions of the crankshaft caused by the cylinder firing impulses). Also called a harmonic balancer.

W

Water jacket - The spaces around the cylinders, between the inner and outer shells of the cylinder block or head, through which coolant circulates.

Web - A supporting structure across a cavity.

Woodruff key - A key with a radiused backside (viewed from the side).

Specifications

Inline four-cylinder engine

General

Displacement	150 cubic inches (2.5 liters)
Cylinder compression pressure	120 to 150 psi
Maximum variation between cylinders	30 psi
Oil pump	
Minimum pressure at curb idle (600 rpm)	13 psi
Operating pressure	37 to 75 psi at 1600 rpm or above

Engine block

Bore diameter	3.875 to 3.8775 inches
Taper	0.001 inch
Out-of-round	0.001 inch
Deck (head gasket surface) warpage limit	0.002 inch per 6 inches
Lifter bore diameter	0.9055 to 0.9065 inch

Cylinder head and valves

Head warpage limit	0.002 inch per 6 inches
Valve margin (minimum)	0.031 inch
Valve length	
Intake	4.899 to 4.924 inches
Exhaust	4.927 to 4.952 inches
Valve face angle, intake and exhaust	45-degrees
Valve seat angle, intake and exhaust	44.5-degrees
Valve stem diameter	0.0311 to 0.312 inch
Valve stem-to-guide clearance	0.001 to 0.003 inch
Valve spring free length	1.876 inches
Valve spring installed height	1.64 inches

Crankshaft and connecting rods

Rod journal diameter	2.0934 to 2.0955 inches
Rod bearing oil clearance	
Desired	0.0015 to 0.002 inch
Allowable	0.001 to 0.003 inch
Connecting rod side clearance (endplay)	0.010 to 0.019 inch
Main bearing journal diameter	2.4996 to 2.5001 inches
Main bearing oil clearance	
Desired	0.002 inch
Allowable	0.001 to 0.0025 inch
Crankshaft endplay (at thrust bearing)	0.0015 to 0.0065 inch
Maximum taper and out-of-round (all journals)	0.0005 inch

Pistons and rings

Piston-to-bore clearance	0.0008 to 0.0015 inch
Piston ring end gap	
Compression rings	
Top compression ring	0.0090 to 0.0240 inch
Second compression ring	0.0190 to 0.0380 inch
Oil control ring (steel rails)	0.010 to 0.060 inch

Inline four-cylinder engine (continued)

Pistons and rings

Piston ring groove clearance
  Compression rings .... 0.0017 to 0.0033 inch
  Oil control ring .... 0.0024 to 0.0083 inch

Torque specifications *   Ft-lbs (unless otherwise indicated)

Main bearing cap bolts 80
Connecting rod cap nuts 33

* Note: Refer to Part A for additional torque specifications.

V6 and 5.2L/5.9L V8 engines

General

Displacement
  3.9 liter V6 .... 238 cubic inches
  5.2 liter V8 .... 318 cubic inches
  5.9 liter V8 .... 360 cubic inches
Cylinder compression pressure
  Minimum .... 100 psi
  Maximum variation between cylinders .... 40 psi
Oil pump
  Minimum pressure at curb idle (600 rpm) .... 6 psi
  Operating pressure .... 30 to 80 psi at 3000 rpm

Engine block

Bore diameter
  3.9L and 5.2L .... 3.910 to 3.912 inches
  5.9L .... 4.000 to 4.002 inches
Taper (maximum) .... 0.010 inch
Out-of-round (maximum) .... 0.005 inch
Deck (head gasket surface) warpage limit .... 0.002 inch per 6 inches
Lifter bore diameter .... 0.9051 to 0.9059 inch

Cylinder head and valves

Head warpage limit .... 0.002 inch per 6 inches
Valve margin (minimum) .... 0.047 inch
Valve length
  3.9L and 5.2L
    Intake .... 4.893 to 4.918 inches
    Exhaust .... 4.907 to 4.932 inches
  5.9L
    Intake .... 4.969 to 4.994 inches
    Exhaust .... 4.978 to 5.012 inches

V6 and 5.2L/5.9L V8 engines (continued)

Cylinder head and valves (continued)

Valve face angle, intake and exhaust	43.25 to 43.75-degrees
Valve seat angle, intake and exhaust	44.25 to 44.75-degrees
Valve seat width	
Intake	0.040 to 0.060 inch
Exhaust	0.060 to 0.080 inch
Valve stem diameter	
3.9L and 5.2L (intake and exhaust)	0.311 to 0.312 inch
5.9L	
Intake	0.372 to 0.373 inch
Exhaust	0.371 to 0.372 inch
Valve stem-to-guide clearance	0.001 to 0.003 inch
Valve spring free length	1.967 inches
Valve spring installed height	1.64 inches

Crankshaft and connecting rods

Rod journal diameter	2.124 to 2.125 inches
Rod bearing oil clearance	
Desired	0.0005 to 0.0022 inch
Allowable	0.003 inch
Connecting rod side clearance (endplay)	0.006 to 0.014 inch
Main bearing journal diameter	
3.9L and 5.2L	2.4995 to 2.5005 inches
5.9L	2.8095 to 2.8105 inches
Main bearing oil clearance	
Journal 1	0.005 to 0.0015 inch
Journals 2, 3 and 4	
Desired	0.005 to 0.0020 inch
Allowable	0.0025 inch
Journal 5 (V8 only)	
Desired	0.005 to 0.0020 inch
Allowable	0.0025 inch
Crankshaft endplay	0.002 to 0.007 inch
Maximum taper and out-of-round (all journals)	0.001 inch

Pistons and rings

Piston-to-bore clearance	0.0005 to 0.0015 inch
Piston ring end gap	
3.9L and 5.2L	
Compression rings	0.010 to 0.020 inch
Oil control ring (steel rails)	0.010 to 0.050 inch
5.9L	
Compression rings	
Top ring	0.012 to 0.022 inch
Second ring	0.022 to 0.031 inch
Oil control ring (steel rails)	0.015 to 0.055 inch
Piston ring groove clearance	
3.9L and 5.2L	
Compression rings	0.0015 to 0.0030 inch
Oil control ring (steel rails)	0.002 to 0.008 inch

Piston ring groove clearance
    5.9L

Compression rings	0.0016 to 0.0033 inch
Oil control ring (steel rails)	0.002 to 0.008 inch maximum

Torque specifications*   Ft-lbs (unless otherwise indicated)

Main bearing cap bolts	85
Connecting rod cap bolts	45

* Note: Refer to Part B for additional torque specifications.

4.7L OHC V8 engines

General

Displacement	287 cubic inches
Cylinder compression pressure	140 to 180 psi
Maximum variation between cylinders	30 psi (from the highest reading)
Oil pressure	
Minimum pressure at curb idle (600 rpm)	4 psi
Operating pressure (3000 rpm)	25 to 80 psi

Engine block

Bore diameter	3.6616 to 3.6622 inches
Taper (maximum)	0.002 inch
Out-of-round (maximum)	0.003 inch
Deck (head gasket surface) warpage limit	0.002 inch per 6 inches

Cylinder head and valves

Head warpage limit	0.002 inch per 6 inches
Valve margin (minimum)	0.047 inch
Valve length	
Intake	4.4666 to 4.4965 inches
Exhaust	4.5244 to 5.5543 inches
Valve face angle, intake and exhaust	45-degrees
Valve seat angle, intake and exhaust	44.5-degrees
Valve seat width, intake and exhaust	0.070 to 0.090 inch
Valve stem diameter	
Intake	0.2729 to 0.2739 inch
Exhaust	0.2717 to 0.2718 inch
Valve stem-to-guide clearance	
Intake	0.0008 to 0.0028 inch
Exhaust	0.0019 to 0.0039 inch
Valve spring free length	
2000 to 2002 models	1.9134 inches
2003 and later models	1.9291 inches
Valve spring installed height	
2000 to 2002 models	
Intake	1.613 inches
Exhaust	1.606 inches
2003 and later models, intake and exhaust	1.580 inches

4.7L OHC V8 engines (continued)

Crankshaft and connecting rods

Rod journal diameter	2.0076 to 2.0082 inches
Rod bearing oil clearance**	0.0006 to 0.0022 inch
Connecting rod side clearance (endplay)	0.004 to 0.0138 inch
Main bearing journal diameter	2.4996 to 2.5005 inches
Main bearing oil clearance	0.0008 to 0.0021 inch
Crankshaft endplay	0.0021 to 0.0112 inch
Maximum taper (all journals)	0.004 inch
Maximum out-of-round (all journals)	0.002 inch

Pistons and rings

Piston-to-bore clearance	See Sections 16 and 17
Piston ring end gap	
Compression rings	0.015 to 0.025 inch
Oil control ring (steel rails)	0.010 to 0.030 inch
Piston ring groove clearance	
Top ring	0.002 to 0.0037 inch
Second ring	0.0016 to 0.0031 inch
Oil control ring (steel rails)	0.007 to 0.0091 inch

Torque specifications*   Ft-lbs (unless otherwise indicated)

Bedplate bolts	
Step 1	
Tighten bolts 11 through 22	40
Step 2	
Tighten bolts 1 through 10	25 in-lbs
Step 3	
Tighten bolts 1 through 10	Turn an additional 90 degrees
Step 4	
Tighten bolts 23 through 28	20
Connecting rod cap bolts	
Step 1	20
Step 2	Turn an additional 90 degrees

* Note: Refer to Part C for additional torque specifications.

** Note: These are the manufacturer's specifications for new engines at the time this manual was written. Typically during a rebuild, a suitable tolerance for main and rod bearing oil clearances is 0.001 to 0.002 inch.

Section

Reference to other Chapters

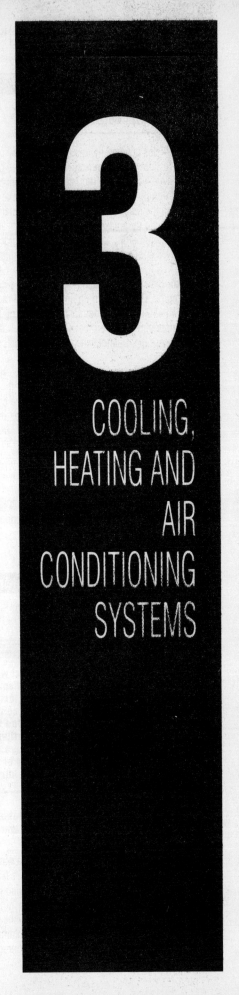

3

COOLING,
HEATING AND
AIR
CONDITIONING
SYSTEMS

1 General information

ENGINE COOLING SYSTEM

All vehicles covered by this manual employ a pressurized engine cooling system with thermostatically controlled coolant circulation. An impeller-type water pump mounted on the front of the block pumps coolant through the engine. The coolant flows around each cylinder and toward the rear of the engine. Cast-in coolant passages direct coolant around the intake and exhaust ports, near the spark plug areas and in close proximity to the exhaust valve guides. The four-cylinder and 4.7L V8 cooling system uses a "reverse-rotation" design water pump.

A wax-pellet type thermostat is located in a housing near the front of the engine. During warm up, the closed thermostat prevents coolant from circulating through the radiator. As the engine nears normal operating temperature, the thermostat opens and allows hot coolant to travel through the radiator, where it's cooled before returning to the engine.

The cooling system is sealed by a pressure-type cap, which raises the boiling point of the coolant and increases the cooling efficiency of the radiator. If the system pressure exceeds the cap pressure-relief value, the excess pressure in the system forces the spring-loaded valve inside the cap off its seat. This allows excess pressure to escape to the overflow tube into a coolant recovery reservoir.

The coolant reservoir serves as both the point at which fresh coolant is added to the cooling system to maintain the proper fluid level and as a holding tank for overheated coolant.

In-line four-cylinder engines use an electric fan to draw air through the radiator while V6 and V8 engines are equipped with a typical viscous type clutch fan.

HEATING SYSTEM

The heating system consists of a blower fan and heater core located in the heater box, the hoses connecting the heater core to the engine cooling system and the heater/air conditioning control head on the instrument panel. Hot engine coolant is circulated through the heater core. When the heater mode is activated, a flap door opens to expose the heater box to the passenger compartment. A fan switch on the control head activates the blower motor, which forces air through the core, heating the air.

AIR CONDITIONING SYSTEM

The air conditioning system consists of a condenser mounted in front of the radiator, an evaporator mounted adjacent to the heater core, a compressor mounted on the engine, an accumulator which stores liquid refrigerant and removes excess moisture, and the plumbing connecting all of the above components.

A blower fan forces the warmer air of the passenger compartment through the evaporator core (sort of a radiator-in-reverse), transferring the heat from the air to the refrigerant. The liquid refrigerant boils off into low pressure vapor, taking the heat with it when it leaves the evaporator.

A rear air conditioning system is optional equipment on Durango models. This unit includes a separate roof-mounted evaporator core, blower motor and overhead controls. The rear air conditioning controls will only operate when the A/C mode is selected from the front A/C controls. Although the rear blower motor will operate independently to help circulate passenger compartment air.

2 Antifreeze/coolant - general information

▶ **Refer to illustration 2.4**

※ WARNING:

Do not allow antifreeze to come in contact with your skin or painted surfaces of the vehicle. Rinse off spills immediately with plenty of water. Antifreeze is highly toxic if ingested. Never leave antifreeze lying around in an open container or in puddles on the floor; children and pets are attracted by it's sweet smell and may drink it. Check with local authorities about disposing of used antifreeze. Many communities have collection centers which will see that antifreeze is disposed of safely. Never dump used anti-freeze on the ground or pour it into drains.

➡ Note: Non-toxic antifreeze is now available at local auto parts stores, Although the coolant is non-toxic when fresh, proper disposal is still required.

The cooling system should be filled with a water/ethylene-glycol based antifreeze solution, which will prevent freezing down to at least -20°F, or lower if local climate requires it. It also provides protection against corrosion and increases the coolant boiling point.

The cooling system should be drained, flushed and refilled at the specified intervals (see Chapter 1). Old or contaminated antifreeze solutions are likely to cause damage and encourage the formation of rust and scale in the system. Always keep antifreeze containers covered and repair leaks in your cooling system as soon as they are noticed.

Before adding antifreeze, check all hose connections, because antifreeze tends to leak through very minute openings. Engines don't normally consume coolant, so if the level goes down, find the cause

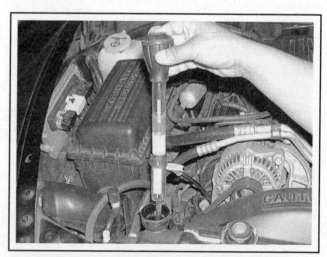

2.4 An inexpensive hydrometer can be used to test the condition of your coolant

and correct it.

The exact mixture of antifreeze-to-water which you should use depends on the relative weather conditions. The mixture should contain at least 50-percent antifreeze, but should never contain more than 70- percent antifreeze. Consult the mixture ratio chart on the antifreeze container before adding coolant. Hydrometers are available at most auto parts stores to test the coolant (see illustration). Use antifreeze which meets the vehicle manufacturer's specifications.

3 Thermostat - check and replacement

✳ WARNING:

Do not remove the radiator cap, drain the coolant or replace the thermostat until the engine has cooled completely.

CHECK

1   Before assuming the thermostat is to blame for a cooling system problem, check the coolant level, drivebelt tension (see Chapter 1) and temperature gauge (or light) operation.

2   If the engine seems to be taking a long time to warm up (based on heater output or temperature gauge operation), the thermostat is probably stuck open. Replace the thermostat with a new one.

3   If the engine runs hot, use your hand to check the temperature of the upper radiator hose. If the hose isn't hot, but the engine is, the thermostat is probably stuck closed, preventing the coolant inside the engine from escaping to the radiator. Replace the thermostat.

✳ CAUTION:

Don't drive the vehicle without a thermostat. The computer may stay in open loop and emissions and fuel economy will suffer.

4   If the upper radiator hose is hot, it means that the coolant is flowing and the thermostat is open. Consult the *Troubleshooting* Section at the front of this manual for cooling system diagnosis.

REPLACEMENT

▶ **Refer to illustrations 3.8, 3.10a, 3.10b, 3.13, 3.14a, 3.14b and 3.15**

5   Disconnect the cable from the negative terminal of the battery.

6   Drain the cooling system (see Chapter 1). If the coolant is rela-

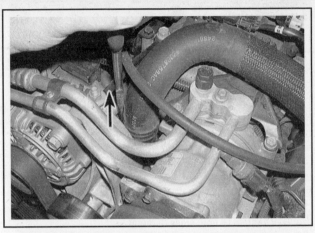

3.8 Remove the upper radiator hose and the alternator support bracket (arrow) on 5.2L/5.9L V6 and V8 engines

tively new or in good condition (see Chapter 1), save it and reuse it.

7   On V6 and 5.2L/5.9L V8 engines, follow the upper radiator hose to the engine to locate the thermostat housing. On 4.7L engines, follow the lower radiator hose to the thermostat housing.

8   Loosen the hose clamp(s), then detach the hose(s) from the thermostat housing (see illustration). If a hose is stuck, twist it to break the seal, then pull it off. If a hose is old or deteriorated, cut it off and install a new one.

9   If the outer surface of the hose fitting(s) on the thermostat housing is deteriorated (corroded, pitted, etc.) it may be damaged further by hose removal. If it is, the thermostat housing will have to be replaced.

10 Remove the bolts and detach the thermostat housing (see illustrations). If the cover is stuck, tap it with a soft-face hammer to jar it loose. Be prepared for some coolant to spill as the gasket seal is broken. On four cylinder engines disconnect the coolant temperature sensor.

3.10a Thermostat housing mounting bolts (arrows) - V6 and V8 engines

3.10b Thermostat housing location - 4.7L V8 engine - view here is from below, at the front of the engine

11 Note how it's installed (which end is facing out), then remove the thermostat.

12 On V6 and 5.2L/5.9L V8 engines, stuff a rag into the engine opening, then remove all traces of old gasket material and sealant from the housing and cover with a gasket scraper. Remove the rag from the

3.13 Before installing the gasket, apply a thin, uniform layer of RTV sealant to both sides of the gasket

opening and clean the gasket mating surfaces with lacquer thinner or acetone. On 4.7L engines, simply remove the rubber O-ring from around the thermostat.

13 On V6 and 5.2L/5.9L V8 engines, install the new thermostat in the machined groove in the housing. Make sure the correct end faces out - the spring end is normally directed into the engine. Apply a thin, uniform layer of RTV sealant to both sides of the new gasket (see illustration) and position it on the housing.

14 On 4.7L V8 engines, install a new O-ring around the thermostat. Be sure to align the rubber tab on the inside of the O-ring groove with the notch on the thermostat (see illustration). Then align the rubber tab on the outside of the O-ring with the notch on the thermostat housing and insert the thermostat and O-ring into the thermostat housing (see illustration).

15 Install the thermostat housing and bolts (see illustration). Tighten the bolts to the torque listed in this Chapter's Specifications.

16 Reattach the hose(s) to the fitting(s) and tighten the hose clamp(s) securely. On four-cylinder engines reconnect the wiring for the coolant temperature sensor.

17 Refill the cooling system (see Chapter 1).

18 Start the engine and allow it to reach normal operating temperature, then check for leaks and proper thermostat operation (as described in Steps 2 through 4).

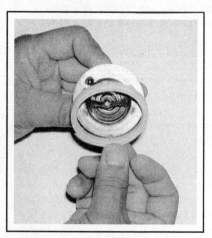

3.14a On 4.7L V8 engines, align the notch on the thermostat with the rubber tab on the inner O-ring groove . . .

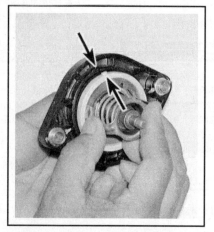

3.14b . . . then align the tab (lower arrow) on the outer diameter of the O-ring with the notch in the thermostat housing (upper arrow) and insert the thermostat into the thermostat housing

3.15 When installing the thermostat housing on V6 and 5.2L/5.9L V8 engines make sure the "FRONT" mark on the housing (arrow) points towards the front of the vehicle

4   Engine cooling fan - check and component replacement

✳ WARNING:

To avoid possible injury or damage, DO NOT operate the engine with a damaged fan. Do not attempt to repair fan blades. Always replace a damaged fan with a new one.

CHECK

Electric fan

1   To test a fan motor, disconnect the electrical connector at the motor and use fused jumper wires to connect the fan directly to the battery. If the fan still doesn't work, replace the motor.

2   If the motor tests OK, check the 10 amp fuse in the interior compartment fuse box and the 40 amp fuse located in the engine compartment power distribution center (see Chapter 12). In either fuse box, look for the "radiator fan" designation in the fuse legend.

3   If the fuses are OK, remove the cooling fan relay from the power distribution center in the engine compartment. Test the relay as described in Chapter 12, replacing it if necessary.

4   If the relay is OK, refer to the wiring diagrams at the end of Chapter 12 and check for battery voltage at terminal 30 of the relay connector with the ignition key Off and for battery voltage at terminal 86 with the ignition key On. There should be battery voltage.

5   If voltage does exist at the relay connector check the circuits between the PCM and relay and the fan motor and relay.

6   If voltage does not exist at the relay connector repair the circuits between the power distribution center and relay or the interior fuse box and relay. Also test the coolant temperature sensor and circuit for proper operation (see Chapter 6).

Mechanical fan

7   Disconnect the cable from the negative terminal of the battery and rock the fan back and forth by hand to check for excessive bearing play.

8   With the engine cold (and not running), turn the fan blades by hand. The fan should turn freely.

9   Visually inspect for substantial fluid leakage from the clutch assembly. If problems are noted, replace the clutch assembly.

10 With the engine completely warmed up, turn off the ignition switch and disconnect the negative battery cable from the battery. Turn the fan by hand. Some drag should be evident. If the fan turns easily, replace the fan clutch.

REPLACEMENT

Electric fan

11 Disconnect the cable from the negative terminal of the battery.

12 Disconnect the electrical connector at the motor.

13 Remove the retaining clips securing the top of the fan shroud to the radiator.

14 Tilt the fan and shroud assembly towards the engine and lift it out of the engine compartment.

15 Installation is the reverse of removal.

Mechanical fan

▶ Refer to illustrations 4.17, 4.18a. 4.18b and 4.21

16 Disconnect the cable from the negative terminal of the battery.

17 Loosen the fan retaining nut but DO NOT remove it.

➡**Note: A special tool, obtainable at most auto parts stores, is required to loosen the fan on V6 and V8 models. The fan attaches to the water pump with a large central nut that is part of the fan drive (see illustration). The tool holds the four bolts of the water pump pulley while a large wrench is used to loosen**

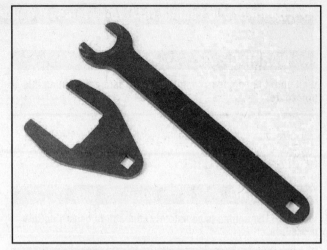

4.17 Typical fan wrench set (available at most auto parts stores)

the large drive nut. Sometimes it is possible to hold the water pump pulley by applying considerable hand pressure to the serpentine belt while the large nut is turned counterclockwise (right-hand threads), but it may require the tool if the fan has been installed for years.

18 Disconnect the hoses from the coolant bottle and windshield washer tank. Remove the two bolts securing the upper portion of the fan shroud/coolant/windshield washer reservoir to the radiator, and remove the shroud/reservoir assembly (see illustrations).

19 Unbolt and lift out the fan/clutch assembly.

20 Carefully inspect the fan blades for damage and defects. Replace it if necessary.

21 At this point, the fan may be unbolted from the clutch, if necessary (see illustration). If the fan clutch is stored, position it with the radiator side facing down.

22 Installation is the reverse of removal. Be sure to tighten the fan and clutch mounting nuts evenly and securely.

4.18a Remove the bolt from the left side of the fan shroud/coolant reservoir . . .

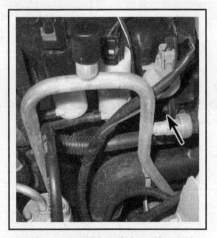

4.18b . . . and this bolt from the right side of the fan shroud/windshield washer reservoir, then lift the assembly from the radiator

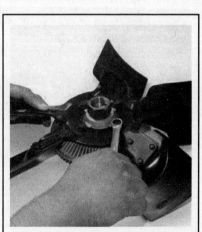

4.21 Remove the four bolts retaining the fan to the fan clutch - when the fan clutch is stored off the engine, place it with the radiator side DOWN

5 Radiator and coolant reservoir - removal and installation

✳✳ WARNING:

Wait until the engine is completely cool before beginning this procedure.

1 Disconnect the cable from the negative terminal of the battery.

COOLANT RESERVOIR

✳✳ WARNING:

Wait until the engine is completely cool before beginning this procedure.

2 Pinch off the reservoir overflow tube and remove the tube from the radiator filler neck.

3 Remove the upper fan shroud (see illustrations 4.18a and 4.18b).

4 The coolant reservoir is part of the upper fan shroud. These must be replaced as a unit.

5 Installation is the reverse of removal.

RADIATOR

▶ **Refer to illustrations 5.7 and 5.11**

6 Drain the cooling system (see Chapter 1). If the coolant is relatively new or in good condition, save it and reuse it.

7 Loosen the hose clamps, then detach the radiator hoses from the fittings on the radiator (see illustration). If they're stuck, grasp each hose near the end and twist it to break the seal, then pull it off - be careful not to distort the radiator fittings! If the hoses are old or deteriorated, cut them off and install new ones.

8 Disconnect the coolant reservoir hose from the radiator filler neck.

9 If the vehicle is equipped with an automatic transmission, disconnect the cooler lines from the rear of the radiator. Use a drip pan to catch spilled fluid. Plug the lines and fittings after they've been disconnected.

10 Disconnect the electric fan connector.

11 Remove the two upper radiator mounting bolts and carefully lift out the radiator (see illustration). Don't spill coolant on the vehicle or scratch the paint.

12 With the radiator removed, the electric fan assembly (if equipped) can be removed from the radiator (two bolts).

13 With the radiator removed, it can be inspected for leaks and damage. If it needs repair, have a radiator shop or dealer service department perform the work as special techniques are required.

14 Whenever the radiator is removed from the vehicle, make note of the location of the various rubber seals (top, bottom and sides) and their location. They should be put back exactly as originally installed to ensure proper cooling.

15 Bugs and dirt can be removed from the front of the radiator with a garden hose, followed by compressed air and a soft brush. Don't bend the cooling fins as this is done. When blowing out the core, direct the hose or air line only from the engine side out.

16 Check the radiator mounts for deterioration and make sure there's nothing in them when the radiator is installed.

17 Installation is the reverse of removal. Fill the cooling system with the proper mixture of antifreeze and water. Refer to Chapter 1 if necessary.

18 Start the engine and check for leaks. Allow the engine to reach normal operating temperature, indicated by the upper radiator hose becoming hot. Recheck the coolant level and add more if required.

19 If you're working on an automatic transmission-equipped vehicle, check and add fluid as needed.

5.7 Detach the clamps (arrow) and remove the upper and lower hose from radiator

5.11 Remove the two radiator mounting bolts

6 Water pump - check and replacement

CHECK

▶ **Refer to illustrations 6.3 and 6.4**

1   A failure in the water pump can cause serious engine damage due to overheating.

2   There are several ways to check the operation of the water pump while it's installed on the engine. If the pump is defective, it should be replaced with a new or rebuilt unit.

3   Water pumps are equipped with weep or vent holes. If a failure occurs in the pump seal, coolant will leak from the hole. In most cases you'll need a flashlight to find the hole on the water pump from underneath to check for leaks (see illustration).

4   If the water pump shaft bearings fail there may be a howling sound at the front of the engine while it's running. Shaft wear can be felt if the water pump pulley is rocked up and down (see illustration). Don't mistake drivebelt slippage, which causes a squealing sound, for water pump bearing failure.

5   It is possible for a water pump to be bad, even if it doesn't howl or leak water. Sometimes the fins on the back of the impeller can corrode away until the pump is no longer effective. The only way to check for this is to remove the pump for examination.

REPLACEMENT

▶ **Refer to illustrations 6.12a, 6.12b and 6.12c**

❋❋ WARNING:

Wait until the engine is completely cool before beginning this procedure.

6   Disconnect the cable from the negative terminal of the battery.

7   Drain the cooling system (see Chapter 1). If the coolant is relatively new or in good condition, save it and reuse it.

8   Remove the cooling fan and shroud (see Section 4).

6.3 The water pump weep hole (arrow) will drip coolant when the seal on the pump shaft fails

9   Remove the drivebelts (see Chapter 1) and the water pump pulley.

10 Loosen the clamps and detach the hoses from the water pump. If they're stuck, grasp each hose near the end and twist it to break the seal, then pull it off. If the hoses are deteriorated, cut them off and install new ones.

11 On four-cylinder models, remove the power steering pump and the power steering pump bracket (see Chapter 10). Don't disconnect the hoses and keep it upright to avoid spilling fluid. On V6 and V8 remove the water pump coolant return tube mounting bolt.

12 Remove the bolts and detach the water pump from the engine. Note the locations of the various lengths and different types of bolts as they're removed to ensure correct installation (see illustrations). On 5.2L/5.9L V8 models, reach above the water pump with pliers to release the hose clamp on the bypass hose (see illustration).

6.4 Grasp the water pump flange and try to rock the shaft back and forth to check for play

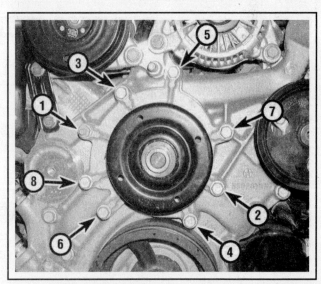

6.12a Water pump mounting bolts - 4.7L V8 engine (during installation, tighten the bolts in the sequence shown)

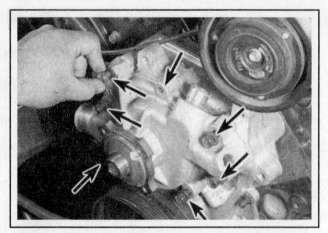

6.12b Water pump bolt locations - V6 and 5.2L/5.9L V8 engines (not all bolts are visible in this photo)

6.12c Reach behind the water pump with pliers to detach the bypass hose - V6 and 5.2L/5.9L V8 engines

13 Clean the bolt threads and the threaded holes in the engine to remove corrosion and sealant.

14 Compare the new pump to the old one to make sure they're identical. On four-cylinder models, remove the heater hose fitting from the old pump and transfer it to the new pump, using sealant on the threads. If the old pump is being reused, check the impeller blades on the backside for corrosion. If any fins are missing or badly corroded, replace the pump with a new one.

✳✳ CAUTION:

Water pumps on four-cylinder and 4.7L V8 engines are of "reverse-rotation" design. Four-cylinder pumps are marked on the impeller with an "R;" If you install a replacement pump, be sure it is marked this way, or overheating will result. 4.7L V8 pumps are not marked.

15 Remove all traces of old gasket material from the engine with a gasket scraper.

16 Clean the engine and new water pump mating surfaces with lacquer thinner or acetone.

17 Apply a thin coat of RTV sealant to the engine side of the new gasket.

18 Apply a thin layer of RTV sealant to the gasket mating surface of the new pump, then carefully mate the gasket and the pump. Slip a couple of bolts through the pump mounting holes to hold the gasket in place (see illustration).

19 Carefully attach the pump and gasket to the engine and thread the bolts into the holes finger tight.

20 Install the remaining bolts (if they also hold an accessory bracket in place, be sure to reposition the bracket at this time). Tighten them to the torque listed in this Chapter's Specifications in 1/4-turn increments.

21 Reinstall all parts removed for access to the pump. Make sure the serpentine drivebelt is installed as originally routed (see Chapter 1) or overheating could result.

22 Refill the cooling system and check the drivebelt tension (see Chapter 1). Run the engine and check for leaks.

7 Coolant temperature sending unit - check and replacement

1   The coolant temperature indicator system is composed of a temperature gauge or warning light mounted in the dash and a coolant temperature sensor mounted on the engine. This coolant temperature sensor doubles as an information sensor for the fuel and emissions systems (see Chapter 6) and as a sending unit for the temperature gauge.

2   If an overheating indication occurs, check the coolant level in the system and then make sure the wiring to the instrument cluster is secure and all fuses are intact.

3   Check the operation of the coolant temperature sensor (see Chapter 6). If the sensor is defective, replace it by following the procedure in that Chapter.

4   If the coolant temperature sensor is good, have the temperature gauge checked by a dealer service department or other properly equipped repair shop. This test will require a scan tool to access the information as it is processed by the Powertrain Control Module (PCM).

8 Blower motor circuit - check

▶ **Refer to illustrations 8.4, 8.6 and 8.8**

1   Check the fuse and all connections in the circuit for looseness and corrosion. Make sure the battery is fully charged.

2   With the transmission in Park, the parking brake securely

applied, turn the ignition switch to the On position (engine not running).

3   The blower motor is located under the glove compartment area of the dash, near the firewall. Bend back the clip on one of the blower

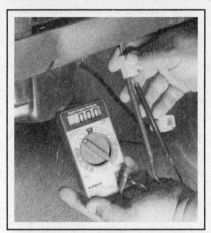

8.4 Disconnect the electrical connector to the blower motor and attach a voltmeter to the harness side of the connector

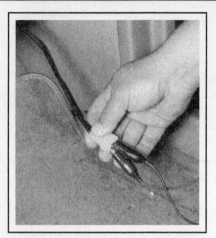

8.6 Supply a ground connection and fused battery voltage directly to the blower side of the connector to see if the blower operates

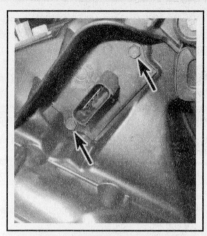

8.8 Under the instrument panel on the right side, remove the two screws to take out the blower motor resistor

motor mounting screws and release the wiring harness, pulling it down for easier disconnection of the connector.

4   Connect a voltmeter to the blower motor connector (see illustration).

5   Move the blower switch through each of its positions with the ignition key On and note the voltage readings. Changes in voltage indicates that the motor speeds will also vary as the switch is moved to the different positions. Slower speeds will deliver less voltage to the blower, and the HIGH position will bypass the resistor to supply a full 12 volts.

6   If there is voltage, but the blower motor does not operate, connect a jumper wire between the motor ground terminal and a good chassis ground. Connect a fused jumper wire between the battery positive terminal and the positive terminal on the motor side of the connector (see illustration). If the motor now works, remove the jumper wire, and if the motor stops working when the ground wire is removed, check for bad ground and re-test. If the motor still doesn't work, the blower motor is probably faulty.

7   If there's no voltage at the motor, refer to Chapter 12 and check the fuse in the interior compartment fuse box and the fuse located in the engine compartment power distribution center. Check the HVAC

relay located in the power distribution center in the engine compartment. If the relay is OK, check for power to the relay connector with the ignition On and Off. There should be battery voltage at two terminals with the ignition key ON.

➡Note: On Dakota models, a relay is used only on 2000 models. On Durango models, a relay is used only for the rear heating/air conditioning circuit.

8   If there's voltage at the relay connector remove the blower resistor block connector and check it for voltage (see illustration). If there's voltage at any of the connector terminals, check the resistor block for continuity and the wiring between the resistor block and the motor for an open or short.

9   If there's no voltage to the resistor, remove the heater control panel (see Section 10) and, with the ignition ON, check for voltage at the connector for the blower motor switch.

10   If there's no voltage, check the wiring between the fuse panel and the switch for an open or a short.

11   If there's voltage, connect one end of a jumper wire to the terminal of the switch connector with voltage. Connect the other end of the jumper to each of the terminals that supply voltage to the resistor block. If the motor now operates normally, replace the switch.

9   Blower motor - removal and installation

✳✳ WARNING:

The models covered by this manual are equipped with Supplemental Restraint systems (SRS), more commonly known as airbags. Always disable the airbag system before working in the vicinity of the impact sensors, steering column or instrument panel to avoid the possibility of accidental deployment of the airbag, which could cause personal injury (see Chapter 12).

1   Disconnect the cable from the negative terminal of the battery.

FRONT BLOWER MOTOR

▸ Refer to illustration 9.4

✳✳ WARNING:

If you're working on a 2000 Durango or a 2001 or earlier Dakota model, have the air conditioning system discharged by a licensed air conditioning technician.

2   On 2000 Durango and 2000/2001 Dakota models, remove the instrument panel (see Chapter 11). On later models, remove only the passenger-side kick panel.

3   On 2000 Durango and 2000/2001 Dakota models, disconnect the vacuum hoses, actuating cables, electrical wiring and if equipped the air conditioning refrigerant lines and remove the heater and air conditioning housing from the vehicle (see Section 11). On later models, disconnect the electrical connector from the blower motor.

4   Remove the blower motor mounting screws and remove the motor (see illustration).

5   Detach the fan retainer clip from the motor shaft (see illustration).

6   Slip the fan off the old motor shaft, mount it on the new motor and install the retainer clip.

7   Place the blower motor in position, making sure the seal is in place and install the mounting screws.

8   The remainder of the installation is the reverse of removal.

REAR BLOWER MOTOR (DURANGO MODELS)

9   Remove the right rear interior trim panel from the vehicle (see Chapter 11).

10 Disconnect the blower motor electrical connector at the rear blower.

11 Remove the blower motor retaining screws. Lower the blower

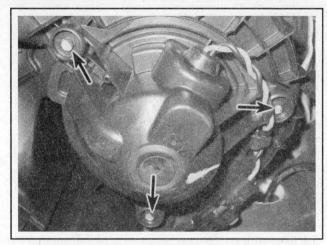

9.4 The front blower motor is mounted to the heater and air conditioning housing by three screws

motor housing enough to disconnect the air conditioning unit wire harness connector and remove the rear blower motor and housing from the vehicle.

12 Installation is the reverse of removal.

10 Heater and air conditioning control assembly - removal and installation

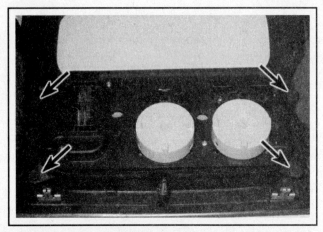

10.4 Remove the retaining screws (arrows) securing the air conditioning and heater control panel

▶ Refer to illustration 10.4

❋ WARNING:

The models covered by this manual are equipped with Supplemental Restraint systems (SRS), more commonly known as airbags. Always disable the airbag system before working in the vicinity of the impact sensors, steering column or instrument panel to avoid the possibility of accidental deployment of the airbag, which could cause personal injury (see Chapter 12).

1   Disconnect the cable from the negative terminal of the battery.

2   Remove the instrument cluster bezel (see Chapter 11).

3   Pull the air conditioning and heater control panel forward and disconnect the electrical connectors, temperature control cable and vacuum plug.

4   Remove the four mounting screws from the heater and air conditioning control panel (see illustration).

5   To install the control, reverse the removal procedure.

11 Heater core - removal and installation

▶ Refer to illustration 11.3

❋ WARNING 1:

The models covered by this manual are equipped with Supplemental Restraint systems (SRS), more commonly known as airbags. Always disable the airbag system before working in the vicinity of the impact sensors, steering column or instrument panel to avoid the possibility of accidental deployment of the airbag, which could cause personal injury (see Chapter 12).

❋ WARNING 2:

The air conditioning system is under high pressure. Do not loosen any hose fittings or remove any components until after the system has been discharged. Air conditioning refrigerant should be properly discharged into an EPA-approved recovery/recycling unit at a dealer service department or an automotive air conditioning repair facility. Always wear eye protection when disconnecting air conditioning system fittings.

→Note: Heater core removal on these models is a difficult task for the home mechanic. It can be done with slow, careful attention to detail, but many fasteners and wiring connectors are difficult to get at behind the instrument panel. The entire instrument panel must be removed to allow the heater/air conditioning unit to be removed from the car.

1   On air-conditioned models, have the system discharged (see **Warning 2** above).
2   Disconnect the cable from the negative terminal of the battery.
3   Drain the cooling system (see Chapter 1) and disconnect the heater hoses at the heater core inlet and outlet. On air-conditioned models, disconnect the air conditioning lines from the evaporator at the firewall (see illustration). Special tools are required to disconnect the fittings on some models.
4   Remove the console, lower the steering column and remove the instrument panel assembly (see Chapter 11).
5   Label and disconnect the electrical connectors, vacuum supply hoses and temperature control cables from the heater/air conditioning unit and the blower motor resistor. Disconnect the vacuum hoses at each of the vacuum actuators labeling them to assure correct installation.
6   Remove the evaporator drain tube.
7   Remove the defrost duct (above the heater/air conditioning unit).
8   Remove the nuts from the studs securing the heater/air condi-

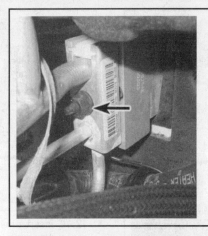

11.3 Detach the refrigerant lines from the firewall - on some models a spring-lock coupling tool may be necessary to disconnect the air conditioning lines

tioning housing to the firewall and pull the heater/air conditioning unit from the vehicle.
9   Remove the housing cover and remove the heater core by pulling it straight up and out of the housing.
10   Installation is the reverse of removal. Refill the cooling system (see Chapter 1). Have the air conditioning system (if equipped) evacuated, recharged and leak-tested.
11   Start the engine and check for proper operation.

12   Air conditioning and heating system - check and maintenance

▶ **Refer to illustration 12.5**

1   The following maintenance checks should be performed on a regular basis to ensure that the air conditioning continues to operate at peak efficiency:

   a) *Check the compressor drivebelt. If it's worn or deteriorated, replace it* (see Chapter 1).
   b) *Check the drivebelt tension and, if necessary, adjust it* (see Chapter 1).
   c) *Check the system hoses. Look for cracks, bubbles, hard spots and deterioration. Inspect the hoses and all fittings for oil bubbles and seepage. If there's any evidence of wear, damage or leaks, replace the hose(s).*
   d) *Inspect the condenser fins for leaves, bugs and other debris. Use a "fin comb" or compressed air to clean the condenser.*
   e) *Make sure the system has the correct refrigerant charge.*

2   It's a good idea to operate the system for about 10 minutes at least once a month, particularly during the winter. Long-term non-use can cause hardening, and subsequent failure, of the seals.
3   Leaks in the air conditioning system are best spotted when the system is brought up to temperature and pressure, by running the engine with the air conditioning ON for five minutes. Shut the engine off and inspect the air conditioning hoses and connections. Traces of oil usually indicate refrigerant leaks.
4   Because of the complexity of the air conditioning system and the special equipment necessary to service it, in-depth troubleshooting and repairs are not included in this manual. However, simple checks and component replacement procedures are provided in this Chapter.
5   If the air conditioning system doesn't operate at all, check the fuse panel and the air conditioning relay, located in the relay box in the engine compartment (see illustration).

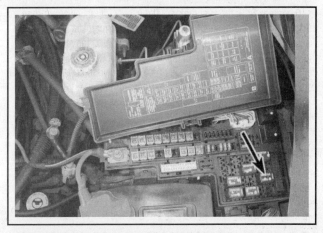

12.5 Air conditioning relay location (arrow)

6   The most common cause of poor cooling is simply a low system refrigerant charge. If a noticeable drop in cool air output occurs, the following quick check will help you determine if the refrigerant level is low.

CHECKING THE REFRIGERANT CHARGE

▶ **Refer to illustrations 12.9 and 12.10**

7   Warm the engine up to normal operating temperature.
8   Place the air conditioning temperature selector at the coldest setting and put the blower at the highest setting. Open the doors (to make sure the air conditioning system doesn't cycle off as soon as it cools the passenger compartment).

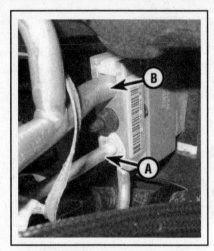

12.9 Evaporator core inlet line (A) and outlet line (B)

12.10 Insert a thermometer in the center duct while operating the air conditioning system - the output air should be 35 to 40 degrees F less than the ambient temperature, depending on humidity (but not lower than 40-degrees F)

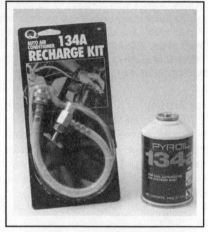

12.12 A basic charging kit for 134a systems is available at most auto parts stores - it must say 134a (not R-12) and so should the 12-ounce can of refrigerant

9 With the compressor engaged - the clutch will make an audible click and the center of the clutch will rotate - feel the evaporator inlet pipe with one hand while placing your other hand on the evaporator outlet pipe (see illustration).

10 The pipe (thinner tubing) leading from the condenser outlet to the evaporator should be cold, and the evaporator outlet line (the thicker tubing that leads back to the compressor) should be slightly colder (3 to 10 degrees F). If the evaporator outlet is considerably warmer than the inlet, the system needs a charge. Insert a thermometer in the center air distribution duct (see illustration) while operating the air conditioning system - the temperature of the output air should be 35 to 40 degrees F below the ambient air temperature (down to approximately 40 degrees F). If the ambient (outside) air temperature is very high, say 110-degrees F, the duct air temperature may be as high as 60 degrees F, but generally the air conditioning is 35 to 40-degrees F cooler than the ambient air. Further inspection or testing of the system requires special tools and techniques and is beyond the scope of this manual.

11 If the inlet pipe has frost accumulation or feels cooler than the accumulator surface, the refrigerant charge is low.

ADDING REFRIGERANT

▶ Refer to illustrations 12.12, 12.15 and 12.16

12 Buy an R-134A automotive charging kit at an auto parts store. A charging kit includes a 12-ounce can of refrigerant, a tap valve and a short section of hose that can be attached between the tap valve and the system low side service valve (see illustration). Because one can of refrigerant may not be sufficient to bring the system charge up to the proper level, it's a good idea to buy a couple of additional cans. Make sure that one of the cans contains red refrigerant dye. If the system is leaking, the red dye will leak out with the refrigerant and help you pinpoint the location of the leak.

✳✳ WARNING:

Never add more than two cans of refrigerant to the system.

13 Hook up the charging kit by following the manufacturer's instructions.

✳✳ WARNING:

DO NOT hook the charging kit hose to the system high side! The fittings on the charging kit are designed to fit only on the low side of the system.

14 Back off the valve handle on the charging kit and screw the kit onto the refrigerant can, making sure first that the O-ring or rubber seal inside the threaded portion of the kit is in place.

✳✳ WARNING:

Wear protective eyewear when dealing with pressurized refrigerant cans.

15 Remove the dust cap from the low-side charging port (just above the coolant recovery tank) and attach the quick-connect fitting on the kit hose (see illustration).

16 Warm up the engine and turn on the air conditioner. Keep the charging kit hose away from the fan and other moving parts. The charging process requires the compressor to be running. If the clutch cycles off, remove the loss of charge switch connector (see illustration) and attach a jumper wire. This will keep the compressor engaged.

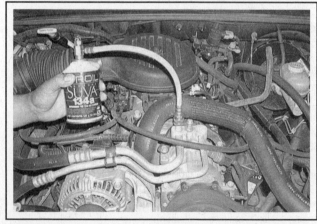

12.15 Add refrigerant to the system at the low-pressure port

17 Turn the valve handle on the kit until the stem pierces the can, then back the handle out to release the refrigerant. You should be able to hear the rush of gas. Add refrigerant to the low side of the system until both the accumulator surface and the evaporator inlet pipe feel about the same temperature . Allow stabilization time between each addition.

18 If you have an accurate thermometer, you can place it in the center air conditioning duct inside the vehicle and keep track of the outlet air temperature. A charged system that is working properly should cool to 40 degrees F. If the ambient (outside) air temperature is very high, say 110-degrees F, the duct air temperature may be as high as 60-degrees F, but generally the air conditioning is 30 to 50-degrees F cooler than the ambient air.

19 When the can is empty, turn the valve handle to the closed position and release the connection from the low-side port. Replace the dust cap.

20 Remove the charging kit from the can and store the kit for future

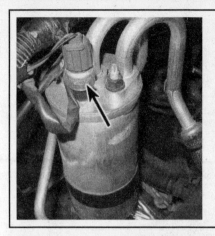

12.16 The loss of charge switch is mounted on the accumulator on Dakota models (shown), and on the suction line to the evaporator at the firewall on Durango models

use with the piercing valve in the UP position, to prevent inadvertently piercing the can on the next use.

13 Air conditioning compressor clutch circuit - check

1 Proper operation of the compressor clutch is essential to the function of the air conditioning system. If your system doesn't seem to get cold, first check the clutch operation.

2 With the engine warmed up, set the air conditioning temperature selector on the coldest setting and the fan on high. Open the doors (to make sure the air conditioning system doesn't cycle off as soon as it cools the passenger compartment down).

3 Have an assistant push the A/C button while you observe the front of the compressor. The clutch will make an audible click and the center of the clutch should rotate. If it doesn't, shut the engine off and disconnect the air conditioning system pressure switch (see illustrations 12.16). Insert a paper clip as a jumper and try the air conditioning again as in Steps 1 and 2. If it works now, the system pressure is too high or too low. Have your system tested by a dealer service department or air conditioning shop.

4 If the clutch still didn't operate, check the appropriate fuses. Inspect the fuse in the interior fuse panel under the cover at the left end of the dash on the driver's side, then the larger fuse in the engine compartment power distribution center (see Chapter 12).

5 While at the Power Distribution Center, remove the compressor clutch relay and test it (see Chapter 12). With the relay out and the ignition Off, check for battery power at terminal 30 of the relay connector. There should be battery power. With the key On, there should be battery power at terminal 86 of the relay connector. Refer to the wiring diagrams at the end of Chapter 12 if necessary.

6 With the engine running and the air conditioning on, connect sockets 30 and 87 for the compressor clutch relay with a jumper wire and listen for the clutch to click as you make the connection.

7 If the clutch still doesn't operate, turn off the engine, disconnect the clutch connector at the compressor and attach a jumper wire long enough to allow use of an ohmmeter to check for continuity between the number 87 terminal of the clutch relay socket and the socket in the compressor clutch connector. If there is no continuity, check for a open in the circuit between the relay box and the compressor clutch connector.

8 If the compressor clutch operates when terminals 30 and 87 are connected with a jumper wire and the above check are OK, check for an open in the circuit from the PCM to the relay box.

14 Air conditioning receiver-drier/accumulator - removal and installation

▶ **Refer to illustrations 14.4a and 14.4b**

✳✳ WARNING:

The air conditioning system is under high pressure. Do not loosen any hose fittings or remove any components until after the system has been discharged. Air conditioning refrigerant should be properly discharged into an EPA-approved recovery/recycling unit at a dealer service department or an automotive air conditioning repair facility. Always wear eye protection when disconnecting air conditioning system fittings.

1 Have the air conditioning system discharged (see **Warning** above).

2 Disconnect the cable from the negative terminal of the battery.

3 On Dakota models, disconnect the electrical connector from the pressure switch near the top of the accumulator.

4 Disconnect the refrigerant lines (see illustrations) from the receiver-drier (Durango models) or the accumulator (Dakota models).

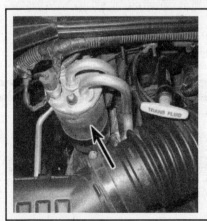

14.4a Accumulator location - Dakota models

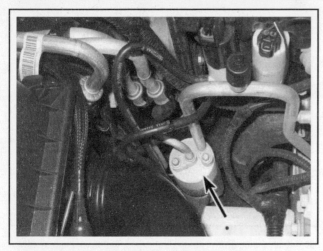

14.4b Receiver-drier location - Durango models

5   Plug the open fittings to prevent entry of dirt and moisture.

6   On Dakota models loosen the clamp bolt on the mounting bracket and lift the accumulator out engine compartment. On 2000 and 2001 Durango models, remove the screws that secure the receiver-drier mounting bracket to the fenderwell at the right-front of the engine compartment and remove it. On later Durango models, the filter/drier is located on the right rear of the firewall as on the pickup models.

7   If a new receiver-drier or accumulator is being installed, add fresh refrigerant oil (a type designated as compatible with refrigerant R-134a) to the new component. The manufacturer recommends adding 4 fluid ounces to the accumulator on Dakota models and 1 fluid ounce of refrigerant oil to the receiver-drier on Durango models, but always check the instructions which come with the new component first.

8   Installation is the reverse of removal.

→Note: New R-134a compatible O-rings should be used in each spring-lock coupling during reassembly.

9   Take the vehicle back to the shop that discharged it. Have the air conditioning system evacuated, charged and leak tested.

15 Air conditioning compressor - removal and installation

▶ Refer to illustration 15.5

✳✳ WARNING:

The air conditioning system is under high pressure. Do not loosen any hose fittings or remove any components until after the system has been discharged. Air conditioning refrigerant should be properly discharged into an EPA-approved recovery/recycling unit at a dealer service department or an automotive air conditioning repair facility. Always wear eye protection when disconnecting air conditioning system fittings.

→Note: The accumulator and fixed orifice tube (Dakota models, see Sections 14 and 17) or the receiver-drier (Durango models, see Section 14) should be replaced whenever the compressor is replaced.

1   Have the air conditioning system discharged (see **Warning** above).

2   Disconnect the cable from the negative terminal of the battery.

3   Disconnect the compressor clutch electrical connector.

4   Remove the drivebelt (see Chapter 1).

5   Disconnect the refrigerant lines from the compressor (see illustration). Plug the open fittings to prevent entry of dirt and moisture.

6   Unbolt the compressor from the mounting brackets and lift it out of the vehicle. On V6 and 5.2L/5.9L V8 engines, you'll have to detach the upper radiator hose from its support bracket and reposition it to get the compressor out.

7   If a new compressor is being installed, follow the directions with the compressor regarding the draining of excess oil prior to installation.

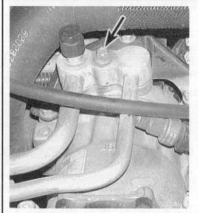

15.5 The refrigerant lines on the compressor are retained by a bolt (arrow), use a wrench to remove the lines, then plug the openings on the compressor and the lines

→Note: Any replacement compressor used must be designated as compatible with refrigerant R-134a.

8   The clutch may have to be transferred from the original to the new compressor.

9   Installation is the reverse of removal. On 4.7L V8 models, install and tighten the bolt for the single-ear mounting first, then install and tighten the rear bolt. Replace all O-rings with new ones specifically made for air conditioning system use (and compatible with refrigerant R-134a) and lubricate them with refrigerant oil. Any refrigerant oil added must also be compatible with refrigerant R-134a.

10   Have the system evacuated, recharged and leak tested by the shop that discharged it.

16 Air conditioning condenser - removal and installation

▶ Refer to illustrations 16.4 and 16.5

✳✳ WARNING 1:

The models covered by this manual are equipped with Supplemental Restraint systems (SRS), more commonly known as airbags. Always disable the airbag system before working in the vicinity of the impact sensors, steering column or instrument panel to avoid the possibility of accidental deployment of the airbag, which could cause personal injury (see Chapter 12).

The air conditioning system is under high pressure. Do not loosen any hose fittings or remove any components until after the system has been discharged. Air conditioning refrigerant should be properly discharged into an EPA-approved recovery/ recycling unit at a dealer service department or an automotive air conditioning repair facility. Always wear eye protection when disconnecting air conditioning system fittings.

1   Have the air conditioning system discharged (see **Warning** above).

2   Disconnect the cable from the negative terminal of the battery.

3   On 2000 V8 models, remove the radiator (see Section 5).

4   Disconnect the refrigerant lines from the condenser by first removing the nuts at the pipe connections (see illustration). Wiggle and twist the pipes on either side of the connection and pull them apart.

16.4 The air conditioning line connections at the condenser are secured by nuts - no special tools are needed to disconnect them

5   Remove the mounting bolts from the condenser brackets (see illustration).

6   Lift the condenser out of the vehicle and plug the lines to keep dirt and moisture out.

7   If the original condenser will be reinstalled, store it with the line fittings on top to prevent oil from draining out.

8   If a new condenser is being installed, pour one ounce of refrigerant oil into it prior to installation (an oil designated as compatible with refrigerant R-134a).

➡Note: New R-134a compatible O-rings should be used in each spring-lock coupling during reassembly.

9   Reinstall the components in the reverse order of removal. Be sure to install the sealing strips (if equipped) around the condenser and radiator.

10 Have the system evacuated, recharged and leak tested by the shop that discharged it.

16.5 Remove the mounting bolts from each lower corner, pull the condenser up and detach it from the front of the radiator

17 Air conditioning fixed orifice tube (Dakota models) - general information and replacement

GENERAL INFORMATION

The fixed orifice tube assembly is the restriction between the high-pressure and low-pressure liquid refrigerant. It meters the flow of liquid refrigerant into the evaporator core.

Evaporator temperature is controlled by sensing the pressure inside the evaporator core with a pressure-operated electric switch. The switch controls compressor operation to keep the evaporator within the required pressure limits.

If, when the system is checked with the appropriate gauges, the high-pressure reads extremely high and low-pressure reads almost a vacuum, the fixed orifice tube is plugged and must be replaced.

REPLACEMENT

The air conditioning system is under high pressure. Do not loosen any hose fittings or remove any components until after the system has been discharged. Air conditioning refrigerant must be properly discharged into an EPA-approved/recovery/ recycling unit at a dealer service department or an automotive air conditioning repair facility. Always wear eye protection when disconnecting air conditioning system fittings.

▶ **Refer to illustration 17.6**

1   Have the system discharged and the refrigerant recovered at an air-conditioning shop.

2   Disconnect the cable from the negative terminal of the battery.

3   Disconnect the liquid line (it's the smaller diameter one) from the condenser outlet line.

4   Using two wrenches, disconnect the two halves of the liquid line.

➡Note: Sometimes this connection is located under a length of foam insulation.

5   Cap or plug the line to the condenser to prevent the entry of dirt or moisture.

6   Using needle-nose pliers, pull the orifice tube out of the line leading to the evaporator (see illustration).

➡**Note: If the orifice tube breaks off inside the refrigerant line, a special extractor tool is available at most auto parts stores to pull it out.**

7   Installation is the reverse of removal. Have the system evacuated, recharged and leak-tested by a dealer service department or an air conditioning repair facility.

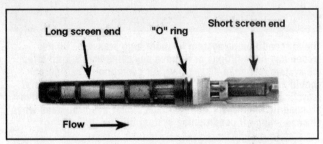

17.6 The orifice tube is equipped with a tapered mesh screen that must be clean and must not have any holes or damage

18 Air conditioning expansion valve (Durango models) - removal and installation

✴ WARNING:

The air conditioning system is under high pressure. Do not loosen any hose fittings or remove any components until after the system has been discharged. Air conditioning refrigerant should be properly discharged into an EPA-approved recovery/ recycling unit at a dealer service department or an automotive air conditioning repair facility. Always wear eye protection when disconnecting air conditioning system fittings.

1   Have the air conditioning system discharged (see **Warning** above).
2   Disconnect the cable from the negative terminal of the battery.

FRONT EXPANSION VALVE

3   Disconnect the refrigerant lines at the firewall from the evaporator core (see illustration 11.3).
4   Remove thve expansion valve mounting screws and detach the expansion valve from the evaporator core mounting flange. Cap or plug the refrigerant openings immediately to prevent any dirt or excessive moisture from entering the system.
5   Installation is the reverse of removal. Have the system evacuated, recharged and leak-tested by a dealer service department or an air conditioning repair facility.

REAR EXPANSION VALVE

6   Disconnect the underbody refrigerant lines at the front expansion valve and at the body pillar.
7   On 2000 models only, remove the underbody refrigerant line retaining clamps and remove the underbody lines from the vehicle. Cap or plug the refrigerant openings immediately to prevent any dirt or excessive moisture from entering the system.
8   On 2001 and later models, remove the right rear interior trim panel for access.
9   Remove the screw securing the front half of the refrigerant lines to the expansion valve and detach the front lines from the expansion valve.
10 Remove the screws securing the expansion valve to the rear half of refrigerant lines and detach the expansion valve from the rear lines. Cap or plug all remaining refrigerant openings immediately to prevent any dirt or excessive moisture from entering the system.
11 Installation is the reverse of removal. Have the system evacuated, recharged and leak-tested by a dealer service department or an air conditioning repair facility.v

Specifications

General

Coolant capacity	See Chapter 1
Radiator cap pressure rating	14 to 18 psi
Thermostat opening temperature	195° F

Torque specifications

	Ft-lbs (unless otherwise indicated)
Fan blade-to-fan clutch bolts	20
Thermostat housing bolts	
Four-cylinder engine	15
V6 and 5.2L/5.9L V8 engines	200 in-lbs
4.7L V8 engine	112 in-lbs
Water pump attaching bolts	
Four-cylinder engine	23
V6 engine and 5.2L/5.9L V8 engines	30
4.7L V8 engine	40
Water pump pulley-to-hub bolts	
(V6 and 5.2L/5.9L V8 engines)	20

Section

Reference to other Chapters

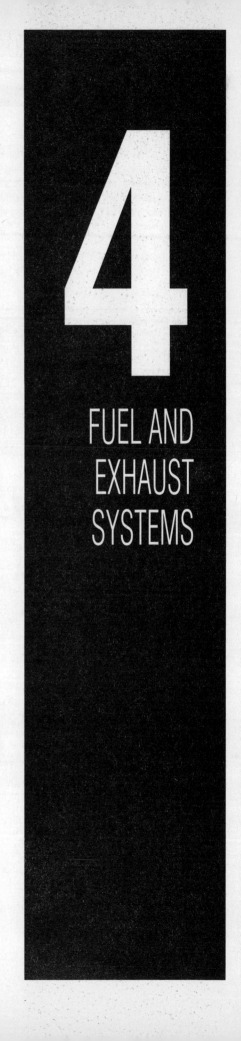

4

FUEL AND EXHAUST SYSTEMS

1 General information

▶ **Refer to illustration 1.1**

All models covered by this manual are equipped with a sequential Multi Port Fuel Injection (MPFI) system (see illustration). This system uses timed impulses to sequentially inject the fuel directly into the intake ports of each cylinder. The injectors are controlled by the Powertrain Control Module (PCM). The PCM monitors various engine parameters and delivers the exact amount of fuel, in the correct sequence, into the intake ports.

All models are equipped with an electric fuel pump, mounted in the fuel tank. It is necessary to remove the fuel tank for access to the fuel pump. The fuel level sending unit is an integral component of the fuel pump and it must be removed from the fuel tank in the same manner. These vehicles are equipped with a "returnless" fuel system. The fuel pressure regulator is mounted on top of the fuel pump/fuel level sending unit module. Regulated fuel is sent to the fuel rail and excess fuel is bled off into the tank.

The exhaust system consists of exhaust manifolds, a catalytic converter, an exhaust pipe and a muffler. Each of these components is replaceable. For further information regarding the catalytic converter, refer to Chapter 6.

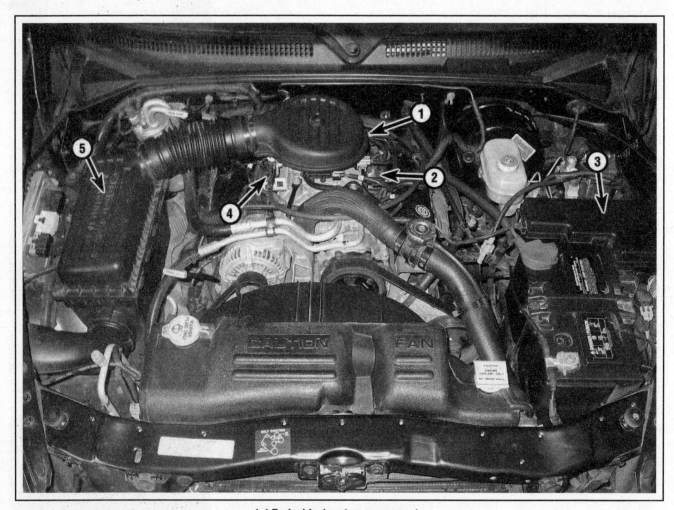

1.1 Typical fuel system components

1	Throttle body	3	Fuel pump relay	5	Air filter
2	Fuel rail and injectors	4	Accelerator cable		

2 Fuel pressure relief procedure

1   Remove the fuel filler cap (this will relieve any pressure that has built-up in the tank).

2   Remove the fuel pump relay from the Power Distribution Center in the engine compartment (you can identify the relays by looking at the underside of the Power Distribution Center cover).

➡Note: This procedure may set a fuel pump relay trouble code. A scan tool will be needed to erase this code after you have finished the fuel system work.

3   Start the engine and let it run until it dies. Crank the engine for several seconds.

4   Turn the ignition key to the Off position. Reinstall the fuel pump relay.

5   Disconnect the cable from the negative terminal of the battery before beginning work on the fuel system.

3 Fuel pump/fuel pressure - check

➡Note: On all models, the fuel pump is located inside the fuel tank (see Section 7).

PRELIMINARY CHECK

1   If you suspect insufficient fuel delivery, first inspect all fuel lines to ensure that the problem is not simply a leak in a line.

2   Set the parking brake and have an assistant turn the ignition switch to the ON position while you listen to the fuel pump (inside the fuel tank). You should hear a "whirring" sound, lasting for a couple of seconds indicating the fuel pump is operating. If the fuel pump is operating, proceed to the pressure check.

3   If there is no sound, check the fuel pump circuit, referring to Chapter 12 and the wiring diagrams. Check the related fuses, the fuel pump relay and the related wiring to ensure power is reaching the fuel pump connector. Check the ground circuit for continuity.

4   If the power and ground circuits are good and the fuel pump does not operate, replace the fuel pump (see Section 7).

PRESSURE CHECK

◆ Refer to illustrations 3.6a, 3.6b and 3.6c

➡Note: In order to perform the fuel pressure test, you will need a fuel pressure gauge capable of measuring high fuel pressure. The fuel gauge must be equipped with the proper fittings or adapters required to attach it to the fuel rail.

5   Relieve the fuel pressure (see Section 2).

6   Remove the cap from the fuel pressure test port (if equipped) on the fuel rail and attach a fuel pressure gauge (see illustrations). If the fuel rail is not equipped with a test port, disconnect the fuel line from the fuel rail and connect a fuel pressure gauge using a special adapter (see illustration).

3.6a The fuel pressure test port is located on the fuel rail

3.6b Connect the fuel pressure gauge to the test port and observe the fuel pressure with the engine idling

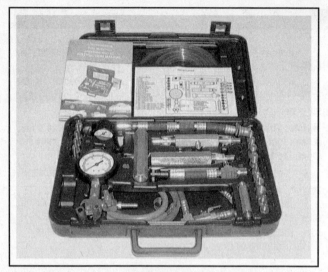

3.6c This fuel pressure testing kit contains all the necessary fittings and adapters, along with the fuel pressure gauge, to test most automotive fuel systems

7 Start the engine and check the pressure on the gauge, comparing your reading with the pressure listed in this Chapter's Specifications.

8 If the fuel pressure is lower than specified, check the fuel lines and the fuel filter for restrictions. If no restriction is found, replace the fuel pump (see Section 7).

9 If fuel pressure is higher than specified, replace the fuel pressure regulator/fuel filter (see Section 14).

10 If the fuel pressure is within specifications, turn the engine off and monitor the fuel pressure for five minutes. The fuel pressure should not drop below 30 psi within five minutes. If it does, there is a leak in the fuel line, a fuel injector is leaking or the fuel pump module check valve is defective. To determine the problem area, perform the following:

→**Note: A special fuel gauge adapter hose, with a T-fitting, is required for the following tests.**

11 Install the adapter hose, then turn on the ignition key to power-up the fuel system. Clamp off the adapter hose between the T-fitting and the line to the fuel pump, the turn the ignition key off. If the pressure drops below 30 psi within five minutes, a fuel injector (or injectors) is leaking (or the fuel rail may be leaking, but such a leak would be very apparent).

12 With the adapter hose installed, clamp off the adapter hose between the T-fitting and the fuel rail. Turn the ignition key on to energize the fuel pump, then turn the key off. If the pressure drops below 30 psi within five minutes, the fuel line is leaking, the check valve in the fuel pressure regulator is defective or the fuel pump is defective.

a) *Check the entire length of the fuel line for leaks.*
b) *If no leaks are found in the fuel line and the pressure dropped quickly, replace the fuel pressure regulator/fuel filter.*
c) *If no leaks are found in the fuel line and the pressure dropped slowly, replace the fuel pump.*

4 Fuel lines and fittings - repair and replacement

❋❋ WARNING:

Gasoline is extremely flammable, so take extra precautions when you work on the fuel system. See the *Warning* in Section 2.

1 Always relieve the fuel pressure before servicing fuel lines or fittings (see Section 2).

2 The fuel feed and vapor lines extend from the fuel tank to the engine compartment. The lines are secured to the underbody with clip and screw assemblies. These lines must be occasionally inspected for leaks, kinks and dents.

3 If evidence of dirt is found in the system or fuel filter during disassembly, the line should be disconnected and blown out. Check the fuel strainer on the fuel pump module for damage and deterioration.

STEEL TUBING

4 If replacement of a fuel line or emission line is called for, use tubes/hoses meeting the manufacturers specification.

5 Don't use copper or aluminum tubing to replace steel tubing. These materials cannot withstand normal vehicle vibration.

6 Because fuel lines used on fuel-injected vehicles are under high pressure, they require special consideration.

7 Some fuel lines have threaded fittings with O-rings. Any time the fittings are loosened to service or replace components:

a) *Use a backup wrench while loosening and tightening the fittings.*
b) *Check all O-rings for cuts, cracks and deterioration. Replace any that appear hardened, worn or damaged.*
c) *If the lines are replaced, always use original equipment parts, or parts that meet the original equipment standards.*

FLEXIBLE HOSE

♦ **Refer to illustrations 4.11a, 4.11b, 4.11c, 4.11d, 4.11e and 4.11f**

8 In the event of any fuel line damage (metal or flexible lines) it is necessary to replace the damaged lines with factory replacement parts. Others may fail from the high pressures of this system.

9 Relieve the fuel pressure before disconnecting the fitting (see Section 2).

10 Remove all fasteners attaching the lines to the vehicle body.

11 There are various methods of disconnecting the fittings, depending upon the type of quick-connect fitting installed on the fuel line (see

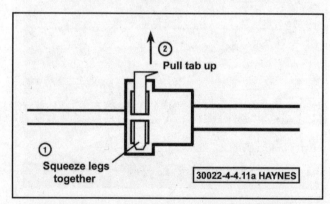

4.11a To disconnect a single-tab type fitting, squeeze the tab legs together, pull up on the tab and pull the lines apart - discard the tab and obtain a new one for reassembly

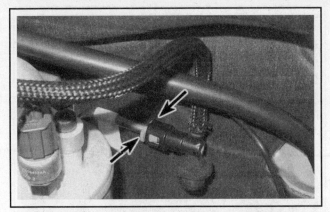

4.11b To disconnect a two-tab type fitting, squeeze the two plastic retaining tabs together . . .

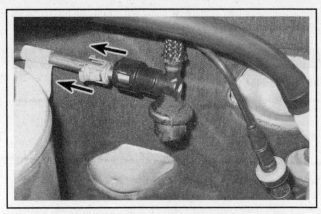

4.11c . . . and pull the metal line out of the quick-connect fitting - for installation they snap together

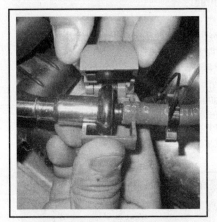

4.11d To disconnect a spring-lock coupling, install the special tool (available at most auto parts stores) onto the line . . .

4.11e . . . close the clamshell halves of the tool around the coupling . . .

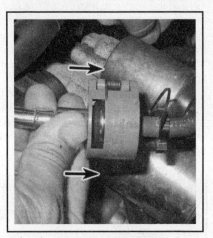

4.11f . . . push the tool into the coupling to disengage the garter spring, then pull the lines apart

illustrations). Clean any debris from around the fitting. Disconnect the fitting and carefully remove the fuel line from the vehicle.

> ❊❊ **CAUTION:**
>
> **The quick-connect fittings are not serviced separately. Do not attempt to repair these types of fuel lines in the event the fitting or line becomes damaged. Replace the entire fuel line as an assembly.**

12 Don't route fuel hose within four inches of any part of the exhaust system or within ten inches of the catalytic converter. Metal lines and rubber hoses must never be allowed to chafe against the frame. A minimum of 1/4-inch clearance must be maintained around a line or hose to prevent contact with the frame.

13 Installation is the reverse of removal with the following additions:

a) *Clean the quick-connect fittings with a lint-free cloth and apply clean engine oil to the fittings.*
b) *After connecting a quick-connect fitting, check the integrity of the connection by attempting to pull the lines apart.*
c) *Use new O-rings at the threaded fittings (if equipped).*
d) *Cycle the ignition key On and Off several times and check for leaks at the fitting, before starting the engine.*

5   Fuel tank - removal and installation

▶ Refer to illustrations 5.5, 5.8 and 5.9

> ❊❊ **WARNING:**
>
> **Gasoline is extremely flammable, so take extra precautions when you work on the fuel system. See the *Warning* in Section 2.**

1 Relieve the fuel system pressure (see Section 2).
2 Remove the fuel tank filler cap to relieve fuel tank pressure.
3 Disconnect the cable from the negative battery terminal.
4 Siphon the fuel into an approved gasoline container, using a siphoning kit (available at most auto parts stores). An alternative method is to disconnect the fuel line at the fuel rail and attach a fuel line adapter (available from tool companies). Connect the adapter with

a hose to an approved gasoline container and operate the fuel pump to empty the tank.

⁕⁕ WARNING:

NEVER start the siphoning action with your mouth!

5   On Dakota models, open the fuel fill door and remove the fill tube bezel screws (see illustration).

6   Raise the vehicle and support it securely on jackstands.

7   Remove the fuel tank skid plate, if equipped. On models with a two-piece driveshaft, unbolt the driveshaft center bearing bracket and support the driveshaft. Center-punch and drill out (3/8-inch drill) the rivets securing the crossmember (which is below the fuel tank) and remove the crossmember.

8   On Durango models, loosen the hose clamps and disconnect the fuel inlet and vent hoses from the fuel tank (see illustration).

9   Position a transmission jack under the fuel tank. Remove the fuel tank strap nuts and position the straps aside (see illustration). Lower the tank just enough to access the top of the tank.

10 Disconnect the fuel line from the fuel pump module (see Section 4).

11 Disconnect the electrical connector from the fuel pump module.

12 Disconnect the EVAP hose from the rollover valve.

13 Lower the jack and remove the tank from the vehicle.

14 On Dakota models, if necessary, disconnect the fuel fill and vent tubes as follows (see illustration):

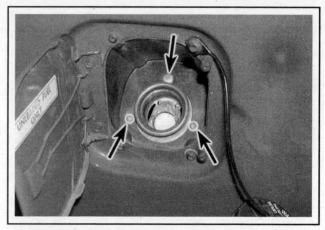

5.5 On Dakota models, remove the fill tube bezel screws (three or four as required)

a) *Push the tube onto the tank fitting as far as possible.*
b) *Push the sleeve into the fitting.*
c) *While holding the sleeve in the fitting, pull the tube off the tank.*

15 Drain the remaining fuel into an approved gasoline container through the vent tube fitting.

16 Installation is the reverse of removal. On models with a two-piece driveshaft, reinstall the support bearing crossmember after the tank is installed, then secure it with new bolts/nuts instead of rivets.

5.8 On Durango models, loosen the hose clamps (arrows) and disconnect the fuel inlet and vent hoses from the tank

5.9 Remove the fuel tank strap nuts (arrows) and position the straps aside

6   Fuel tank cleaning and repair - general information

1   The fuel tanks installed in the vehicles covered by this manual are made of plastic and are not repairable.

2   If the fuel tank is removed from the vehicle, it should not be placed in an area where sparks or open flames could ignite the fumes coming out of the tank. Be especially careful inside a garage where a gas-type appliance is located, because it could cause an explosion.

7   Fuel pump - removal and installation

▶ Refer to illustrations 7.5 and 7.6

✸✸ WARNING:

Gasoline is extremely flammable, so take extra precautions when you work on the fuel system. See the *Warning* in Section 2.

1   Relieve the fuel system pressure (see Section 2).

2   Disconnect the cable from the negative battery terminal.

3   Remove the fuel tank from the vehicle (see Section 5). Clean the top of the tank in the area of the fuel pump module to prevent debris entering the tank while the module is removed.

4   Note the position of the fuel pressure regulator/fuel filter, rollover valve and fuel pump electrical connector. The fuel pump module must be installed in the original position or the fuel level float may contact the side of the tank. Apply an alignment mark if necessary.

5   On Dakota models, turn the locknut counterclockwise to remove it (see illustration). If the locknut is difficult to turn, use a large pair of adjustable pliers or a strap wrench to loosen it. On Durango models, use a brass drift and hammer to rotate the lockring counterclockwise while prying back on the lock tab.

6   Remove the fuel pump module unit from the tank (see illustration). Angle the assembly slightly to avoid damaging the fuel level sending unit float.

7   The electric fuel pump is not serviced separately. In the event of failure, the complete assembly must be replaced.

8   Installation is the reverse of removal.

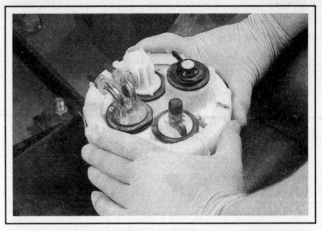

7.5 On Dakota models, loosen the fuel pump module locknut by turning it counterclockwise

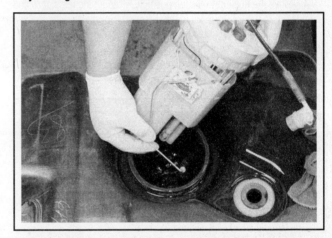

7.6 Carefully remove the fuel pump module from the tank

8   Fuel level sending unit - check and replacement

✸✸ WARNING:

Gasoline is extremely flammable, so take extra precautions when you work on the fuel system. See the *Warning* in Section 2.

CHECK

▶ Refer to illustrations 8.2 and 8.3

1   Remove the fuel tank and the fuel pump module (see Sections 5 and 7).

2   Connect the probes of an ohmmeter to the two center terminals of the fuel pump module electrical connector (see illustration).

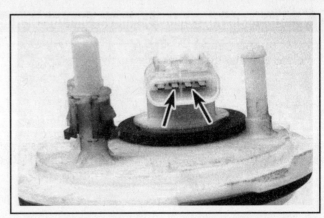

8.2 Connect an ohmmeter to the two center terminals of the fuel pump module connector

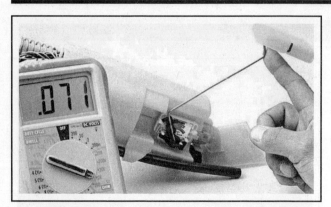

8.3 Measure the resistance of the fuel level sending unit with the float lowered (empty tank) and then with the float raised (full tank)

3   Position the float in the down (empty) position (see illustration). Measure the resistance and compare it to the values listed in this Chapter's Specifications.

4   Move the float up to the full position. Measure the resistance and compare it to the values listed in this Chapter's Specifications.

5   If the fuel level sending unit resistance is incorrect or if the resistance does not change smoothly as the float travels from empty to full, replace the fuel level sending unit assembly.

REPLACEMENT

▶ **Refer to illustrations 8.8a and 8.8b**

6   Remove the fuel tank and the fuel pump module (see Sections 5 and 7).

7   Disconnect the electrical connector inside the module.

8   Separate the fuel level sending unit wire terminals from the module connector as follows (see illustrations):

  a) *Remove the locking collar from inside the connector.*
  b) *Using a small pick, depress the locking finger on the terminal and push the terminal in.*
  c) *Pull the wire and terminal out of the connector from the backside.*

9   Using a small screwdriver or pick, pry the lock tab out of the notch and slide the fuel level sending unit down the tracks. Note the routing of the wiring for installation.

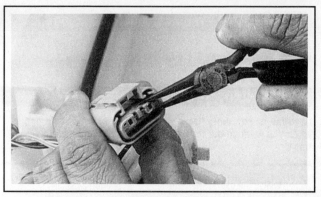

8.8a Carefully remove the locking collar from the connector

10   Slide the level sending unit onto the tracks and engage the lock tab with the notch. Route the wiring as originally installed.

11   Insert the wire terminals into the connector and install the locking collar. Make sure the wire terminals are locked in place by attempting to pull them out from the backside. If necessary carefully bend the locking fingers out before inserting them into the connector.

12   Connect the electrical connector to the fuel pump module and install the module in the fuel tank (see Section 7).

13   The remainder of installation is the reverse of removal.

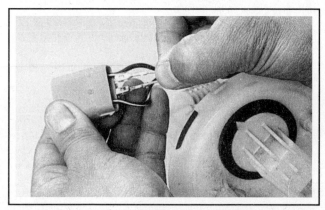

8.8b Using a small pick, depress the terminal locking finger and push the terminal into the connector, then pull the two fuel level sending unit wires and terminals out of the connector

9   Air cleaner assembly - removal and installation

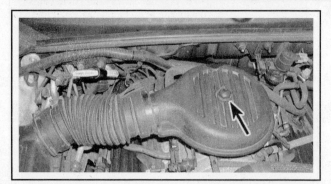

9.2 Loosen the nut at the throttle body (arrow), detach the latches from the air cleaner cover and remove the air intake duct and air cleaner cover assembly (V6 and 5.2L/5.9L V8 engine shown)

▶ **Refer to illustrations 9.2 and 9.3**

1   Detach the cable from the negative battery terminal.

2   Loosen the air intake duct nut (V6 and 5.2L/5.9L V8) or clamp (four-cylinder) at the throttle body and detach the latches from the air cleaner cover (see illustration). Remove the air intake duct and air cleaner cover as an assembly.

3   Remove the air cleaner housing mounting screws (see illustration).

4   Lift the housing up, detach the fresh air intake duct from the inner fender and remove the assembly from the engine compartment.

5   If necessary, loosen the hose clamps and separate the air intake duct from the air cleaner cover.

6   Installation is the reverse of removal.

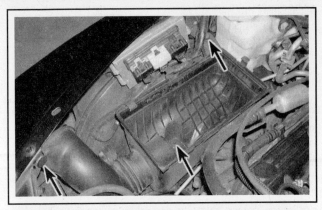

9.3 Remove the air cleaner housing mounting screws and detach the fresh air intake duct fastener at the inner fender (arrows)

10 Accelerator cable - replacement

▶ **Refer to illustrations 10.2, 10.3 and 10.5**

1   Disconnect the cable from the negative battery terminal. Remove the air intake duct from the throttle body.

2   Rotate the throttle lever and separate the cable end from the throttle lever stud (see illustration).

3   On V6 and 5.2L/5.9L V8 models, push in on the tab to release the accelerator cable retainer from the bracket and lift the cable straight up and out of the bracket (see illustration).

4   On four-cylinder models, squeeze the tabs on the cable housing together and push the cable through the bracket. On 4.7L V8 models, disconnect the cable at the accelerator pedal, then pull out some slack at the throttle body end. Push the cable end forward off the pin on the throttle body arm.

5   Working under the dash, remove the heater duct and detach the cable from the accelerator pedal (see illustration).

6   Press in on the tabs of the cable retainer and push the cable through the firewall and into the engine compartment. Remove the cable.

7   Installation is the reverse of removal.

10.2 Rotate the throttle lever and detach the cable from the stud

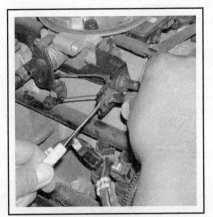

10.3 On V6 and 5.2L/5.9L V8 models, use a flat bladed screwdriver to depress the locking tab and remove the cable from the bracket

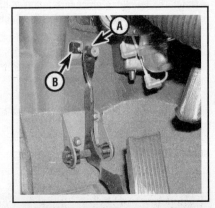

10.5 Pull the accelerator cable out of the grommet and slide the cable through the slot in the end of the pedal assembly (A), then squeeze the housing retaining tabs (B) together and push the cable into the engine compartment

11 Fuel injection system - general information

The sequential Multi Port Fuel Injection (MPFI) system consists of three sub-systems: air intake, emissions and engine control and fuel delivery. The system uses a Powertrain Control Module (PCM) along with the sensors (coolant temperature sensor, Throttle Position Sensor (TPS), Manifold Absolute Pressure (MAP) sensor, oxygen sensor, etc.) to determine the proper air/fuel ratio under all operating conditions.

The fuel injection system and the emissions and engine control system are closely linked in function and design. For additional information, refer to Chapter 6.

AIR INTAKE SYSTEM

The air intake system consists of the air cleaner, the air intake ducts, the throttle body, the idle control system, the air intake plenum and the intake manifold.

When the engine is idling, the air/fuel ratio is controlled by the idle air control system, which consists of the Powertrain Control Module (PCM) and the idle air control valve. The idle air control valve is controlled by the PCM and is opened and closed depending upon the running conditions of the engine (air conditioning system, power steering, cold and warm running etc.). This idle air control regulates the amount of airflow past the throttle plate and into the intake manifold, thus increasing or decreasing the engine idle speed. The PCM receives information from the sensors (vehicle speed, coolant temperature, air conditioning, power steering mode etc.) and adjusts the idle according to the demands of the engine and driver. Refer to Chapter 6 for information on the idle air control valve.

EMISSIONS AND ENGINE CONTROL SYSTEM

The emissions and engine control system is described in detail in Chapter 6.

FUEL DELIVERY SYSTEM

The fuel delivery system consists of these components: The fuel pump, the fuel pressure regulator/fuel filter, the fuel rail and the fuel injectors.

The fuel pump is an in-line, direct drive type. Fuel is drawn through a filter into the pump, flows past the armature through the one-way valve, passes through another filter and is delivered to the injectors. A relief valve prevents excessive pressure build-up by opening in the event of a blockage in the discharge side and allowing fuel to flow from the high to the low pressure side.

The pressure regulator maintains a constant fuel pressure to the injectors. Excess fuel is routed back to the fuel tank through the fuel pressure regulator.

→**Note: The fuel pressure regulator is mounted on top of the fuel pump module.**

The injectors are solenoid-actuated pintle types consisting of a solenoid, plunger, needle valve and housing. When current is applied to the solenoid coil, the needle valve raises and pressurized fuel squirts out the nozzle. The injection quantity is determined by the length of time the valve is open (the length of time during which current is supplied to the solenoid coils).

The Automatic Shutdown (ASD) relay and the fuel pump relay are contained within the Power Distribution Center, which is located in the left side of the engine compartment. The ASD relay connects battery voltage to the fuel injectors and the ignition coil while the fuel pump relay connects battery voltage only to the fuel pump. If the PCM senses there is NO signal from the camshaft or crankshaft sensors (as with the engine running or cranking), the PCM will de-energize both relays.

12 Fuel injection system - check

▶ **Refer to illustrations 12.7, 12.8 and 12.10**

→**Note: The following procedure is based on the assumption that the fuel pressure is adequate (see Section 3).**

1 Check all electrical connectors that are related to the system. Check the ground wire connections on the intake manifold for tightness. Loose connectors and poor grounds can cause many problems that resemble more serious malfunctions.

2 Check to see that the battery is fully charged, as the control unit and sensors depend on an accurate supply voltage in order to properly meter the fuel.

3 Check the air filter element - a dirty or partially blocked filter will severely impede performance and economy (see Chapter 1).

4 Check the related fuses. If a blown fuse is found, replace it and see if it blows again. If it does, search for a grounded wire in the harness.

5 Check the air intake duct to the intake manifold for leaks, which will result in an excessively lean mixture. Also check the condition of all vacuum hoses connected to the intake manifold.

6 Remove the air intake duct from the throttle body and check for dirt, carbon or other residue build-up. If it's dirty, clean it with carburetor cleaner spray and a toothbrush.

7 With the engine running, place an automotive stethoscope against each injector, one at a time, and listen for a clicking sound, indicating operation (see illustration). If you don't have a stethoscope, place the tip of a screwdriver against the injector and listen through

12.7 Use a stethoscope to determine if the injectors are working properly - they should make a steady clicking sound that rises and falls with engine speed changes

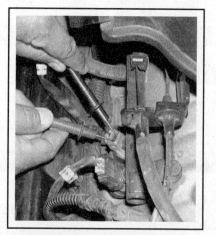

12.8 Measure the resistance of each injector across the two terminals of the injector

12.10 Install the "noid" light (available at most auto parts stores) into each injector electrical connector and confirm that it blinks when the engine is cranking

the handle.

8   Disconnect the injector electrical connectors and measure the resistance of each injector (see illustration). Compare the measurements with the resistance values listed in this Chapter's Specifications.

9   Turn the ignition key On and check for battery voltage at the dark green/orange wire terminal of one of the injector harness connectors. If battery voltage is not present, check the ASD relay and related wiring (see Chapter 12).

10   Install an injector test light ("noid" light) into each injector electrical connector, one at a time (see illustration). Crank the engine over. Confirm that the light flashes evenly on each connector. This tests the PCM control of the injectors. If the light does not flash, have the PCM checked at a dealer service department or other properly equipped repair facility.

11   The remainder of the engine control system checks can be found in Chapter 6.

13   Throttle body - removal and installation

▶ Refer to illustrations 13.6a and 13.6b

> **⁂ WARNING:**
>
> **Wait until the engine is completely cool before beginning this procedure.**

1   Disconnect the cable from the negative battery terminal.
2   Remove the air intake duct.
3   Disconnect the TPS, IAC and MAP sensor connectors from the throttle body.
4   Label and detach all vacuum hoses from the throttle body.
5   Detach the accelerator cable (see Section 10) and, if equipped, the transmission throttle valve cable and cruise control cable.
6   Remove the mounting bolts/nuts and remove the throttle body and gasket (see illustrations).
7   Remove all traces of old gasket material from the throttle body and intake manifold and install a new gasket.
8   Install the throttle body and tighten the bolts to the torque listed in this Chapter's Specifications.
9   The remainder of installation is the reverse of removal.

13.6a Remove the four nuts and separate the throttle body from the intake manifold (5.2L/5.9L V8 engine shown, V6 engine similar)

13.6b Throttle body mounting bolts - 4.7L V8 engine

14   Fuel pressure regulator/fuel filter - replacement

> **⁂ WARNING:**
>
> **Gasoline is extremely flammable, so take extra precautions when you work on the fuel system. See the *Warning* in Section 2.**

> **⁂ CAUTION:**
>
> **Do not pull the fuel pressure regulator/fuel filter unit out more than three inches or damage to the fuel tube may result.**

➡ Note: The fuel filter requires service only when a fuel contamination problem is suspected.

1   Relieve the fuel system pressure (see Section 2).
2   Disconnect the cable from the negative battery terminal.
3   Remove the fuel tank (see Section 5).
4   Note the installed direction of the fuel line fitting. Remove the fuel pressure regulator/fuel filter by gently twisting and pulling the unit from the rubber grommet.

5   Cut the hose clamp that retains the fuel tube to the regulator/filter.
6   Carefully pull the tube off fuel pressure regulator/fuel filter and remove the assembly.
7   Install the tube, with a new clamp, onto the fuel pressure regulator/fuel filter assembly. Tighten the clamp using the appropriate hose clamp pliers.
8   Press the fuel pressure regulator/fuel filter assembly into the grommet with the fuel line fitting pointing the same direction as originally installed.
9   The remainder of installation is the reverse of removal.

15 Fuel rail and injectors - removal and installation

✳✳ WARNING:

Gasoline is extremely flammable, so take extra precautions when you work on the fuel system. See the *Warning* in Section 2.

15.7 Disconnect the electrical connectors from the injectors - note the numbered tags on the wiring harness

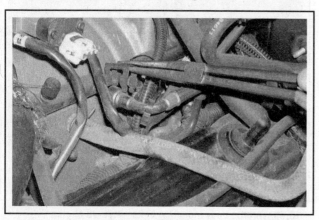

15.8a To disconnect the fuel line from the fuel rail, remove the safety clip from the quick-connect fitting . . .

REMOVAL

▶ Refer to illustrations 15.7, 15.8a, 15.8b, 15.9a, 15.9b and 15.10

1 Relieve the fuel pressure (see Section 2).
2 Disconnect the cable from the negative battery terminal.
3 Remove the air intake duct.
4 On four-cylinder models, perform the following:

a) *Disconnect the accelerator control cable, the transmission throttle valve cable and the cruise control cable (if equipped) from the throttle body.*

b) *Remove the cable bracket mounting bolts and position the cables and bracket aside.*

c) *Disconnect the vent hose from the fuel damper (if equipped).*

5 On V6 and V8 models, perform the following:

a) *On all models except 4.7L V8, remove the throttle body (see Section 13). Position the control cables and brackets aside.*

b) *Remove the air conditioning compressor-to-intake manifold bracket, if equipped.*

c) *On V6 and 5.2L/5.9L V8 models, disconnect the electrical connector from the intake air temperature sensor.*

d) *On V6 and 5.2L/5.9L V8 models, remove the canister purge solenoid from the intake manifold. On 4.7L V8 models, disconnect the electrical connectors from the rear of the alternator.*

e) *On 4.7L V8 models, refer to Chapter 5 and remove the first three ignition coils on each side of the engine.*

6 Clearly label and remove any vacuum hoses or electrical wiring that will interfere with the fuel rail removal. Detach any wiring harness retainers from the fuel rail.

7 Disconnect the fuel injector electrical connectors and position the harness aside (see illustration). To disconnect the electrical connectors, push the sliding portion (red plastic) away from the injector, depressing the spring tab to release the slider all the way.

➡**Note: Each connector should be numbered with the corresponding cylinder number. If the number tag is obscured or missing, renumber the connectors.**

8 Detach the fuel line from the fuel rail (see illustrations).
9 Clean any debris from around the injectors. Remove the fuel rail

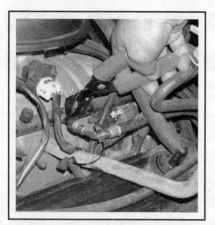

15.8b . . . insert the fuel line disconnect tool into the fitting and disconnect the fuel line from the fuel rail (V8 engine shown)

15.9a On V6 and 5.2L/5.9L V8 models, remove the bolts that secure the fuel rail to the intake manifold (right side shown, left side similar)

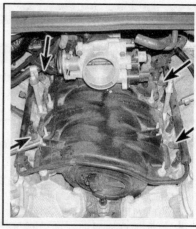

15.9b Fuel rail mounting bolts - 4.7L V8

mounting nuts/bolts (see illustrations). Gently rock the fuel rail and injectors to loosen the injectors and remove the fuel rail and fuel injectors as an assembly.

✳✳ CAUTION:

Do not attempt to separate the left and right fuel rails on a V6 or V8 model. Both sides are serviced together as an assembly.

10 Remove the injector(s) from the fuel rail assembly remove and discard the O-rings (see illustration).

➡**Note: Whether you're replacing an injector or a leaking O-ring, it's a good idea to remove all the injectors from the fuel rail and replace all the O-rings.**

INSTALLATION

11 Coat the new seal rings with clean engine oil and slide them onto the injectors.

12 Coat the new O-rings with clean engine oil and install them on the injector(s), then insert each injector into its corresponding bore in the fuel rail. Install the injector retaining clip.

13 Install the injector and fuel rail assembly on the intake manifold. Make sure the injectors are fully seated, then tighten the fuel rail mounting nuts to the torque listed in this Chapter's Specifications.

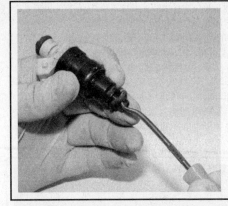

15.10 Carefully remove the O-rings from the injector

14 Connect the fuel line and make sure its securely installed. If equipped with a latch-clip type fitting, make sure the latch-clip is properly seated.

15 Connect the electrical connectors to each injector, referring to the numbered tags.

16 The remainder of installation is the reverse of removal.

17 After the injector/fuel rail assembly installation is complete, turn the ignition switch to On, but don't operate the starter (this activates the fuel pump for about two seconds, which builds up fuel pressure in the fuel lines and the fuel rail). Repeat this about two or three times, then check the fuel lines, fuel rail and injectors for fuel leakage.

16 Exhaust system servicing - general information

✳✳ WARNING:

Inspection and repair of exhaust system components should be done only after enough time has elapsed after driving the vehicle to allow the system components to cool completely. Also, when working under the vehicle, make sure it is securely supported on jackstands.

1 The exhaust system consists of the exhaust manifold(s), the catalytic converter, the muffler, the tailpipe and all connecting pipes, brackets, hangers and clamps. The exhaust system is attached to the body with mounting brackets and rubber hangers. If any of the parts are improperly installed, excessive noise and vibration will be transmitted to the body.

MUFFLER AND PIPES

▶ **Refer to illustrations 16.2 and 16.4**

2 Conduct regular inspections of the exhaust system to keep it safe and quiet (see illustration). Look for any damaged or bent parts, open seams, holes, loose connections, excessive corrosion or other defects which could allow exhaust fumes to enter the vehicle. Also check the catalytic converter when you inspect the exhaust system (see below). Deteriorated exhaust system components should not be repaired; they should be replaced with new parts.

3 If the exhaust system components are extremely corroded or rusted together, welding equipment will probably be required to remove

16.2 Inspect the exhaust system rubber hangers for damage

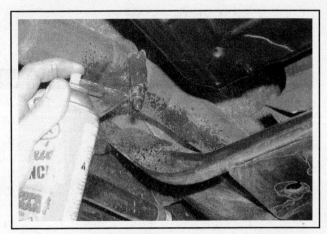

16.4 Spray penetrating oil onto the U-bolt clamp nuts before attempting to remove them

them. The convenient way to accomplish this is to have a muffler repair shop remove the corroded sections with a cutting torch. If, however, you want to save money by doing it yourself (and you don't have a welding outfit with a cutting torch), simply cut off the old components with a hacksaw. If you have compressed air, special pneumatic cutting chisels can also be used. If you do decide to tackle the job at home, be sure to wear safety goggles to protect your eyes from metal chips and work gloves to protect your hands.

4   Here are some simple guidelines to follow when repairing the exhaust system:

16.6 Inspect the catalytic converter and heat shield for damage

a) *Work from the back to the front when removing exhaust system components.*

b) *Apply penetrating oil to the exhaust system component fasteners to make them easier to remove (see illustration).*

c) *Use new gaskets, hangers and clamps when installing exhaust systems components.*

d) *Apply anti-seize compound to the threads of all exhaust system fasteners during reassembly.*

e) *Be sure to allow sufficient clearance between newly installed parts and all points on the underbody to avoid overheating the floor pan and possibly damaging the interior carpet and insulation. Pay particularly close attention to the catalytic converter and heat shield.*

CATALYTIC CONVERTER

▶ **Refer to illustration 16.6**

✸✸ WARNING:

The converter gets very hot during operation. Make sure it has cooled down before you touch it.

➥**Note: See Chapter 6 for additional information on the catalytic converter.**

5   Periodically inspect the heat shield for cracks, dents and loose or missing fasteners.

6   Inspect the converter for cracks or other damage (see illustration).

7   The converter is welded to the exhaust pipe, if the converter must be replaced, take the vehicle to a muffler shop.

Specifications

General

Fuel pressure

    2000 models   44.2 to 54.2 psi

    2001 and later models   47.2 to 51.2 psi

Fuel injector resistance   10.8 to 13.2 ohms @ 68-degrees F

Fuel level sending unit resistance

    Empty   214 to 226 ohms

    Full   14 to 26 ohms

Torque specifications Ft-lbs (unless otherwise indicated)   Nm

Throttle body mounting nuts

    Four-cylinder engine and 4.7L V8   100 in-lbs

    V6 and V8 engines   200 in-lbs

Fuel rail mounting bolts

    Four-cylinder engine   100 in-lbs

    V6 and 5.2L/5.9L V8 engines   200 in-lbs

    4.7L V8 engine   20

Fuel tank mounting nuts   30 ft-lbs

Section

Reference to other Chapters

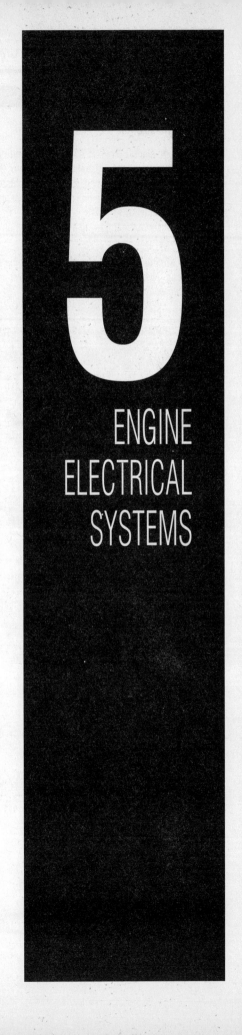

5

ENGINE ELECTRICAL SYSTEMS

1 General information

▶ **Refer to illustration 1.1**

The engine electrical systems include all ignition, charging and starting components (see illustration). Because of their engine-related functions, these components are discussed separately from chassis electrical devices such as the lights, the instruments, etc. (which are included in Chapter 12).

Always observe the following precautions when working on the electrical systems:

a) *Be extremely careful, when servicing engine electrical components. They are easily damaged if checked, connected or handled improperly.*

b) *Never leave the ignition switch on for long periods of time with the engine off.*

c) *Don't disconnect the battery cables while the engine is running.*

d) *Maintain correct polarity when connecting a battery cable from another vehicle during jump starting.*

e) *Always disconnect the negative cable first and hook it up last or the battery may be shorted by the tool being used to loosen the cable clamps.*

It's also a good idea to review the safety-related information regarding the engine electrical systems located in the *Safety First* section near the front of this manual before beginning any operation included in this Chapter.

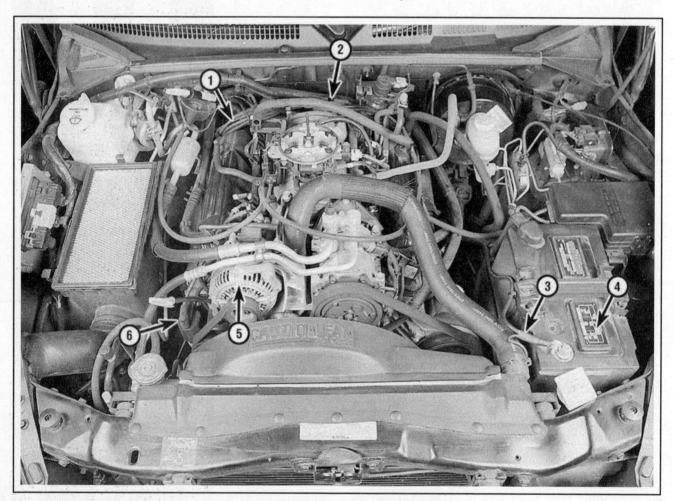

1.1 Typical engine electrical system components

1	Spark plug wires	3	Battery cable (negative)	5	Alternator
2	Distributor	4	Battery	6	Ignition coil

2 Battery - emergency jump starting

Refer to the *Booster battery (jump) starting* procedure at the front of this manual.

3 Battery - check and replacement

※※ WARNING:

Hydrogen gas is produced by the battery, so keep open flames and lighted cigarettes away from it at all times. Always wear eye protection when working around a battery. Rinse off spilled electrolyte immediately with large amounts of water.

※※ CAUTION:

Always disconnect the negative cable first and hook it up last or the battery may be shorted by the tool being used to loosen the cable clamps.

CHECK

◗ Refer to illustrations 3.2 and 3.3

1 Disconnect the negative battery cable, then the positive cable from the battery.

2 Check the battery state of charge. Visually inspect the indicator eye on the top of the battery, if the indicator eye is clear, charge the battery as described in Chapter 1. Next perform an open voltage circuit test using a digital voltmeter (see illustration).

➡Note: The battery's surface charge must be removed before accurate voltage measurements can be made. Turn On the high beams for ten seconds, then turn them Off, let the vehicle stand for two minutes.

With the engine and all accessories Off, touch the negative probe of the voltmeter to the negative terminal of the battery and the positive probe to the positive terminal of the battery. The battery voltage should be 12.4 volts or more. If the battery is less than the specified voltage, charge the battery before proceeding to the next test. Do not proceed with the battery load test unless the battery charge is correct.

3 Perform a battery load test. An accurate check of the battery condition can only be performed with a load tester (available at most auto parts stores). This test evaluates the ability of the battery to operate the starter and other accessories during periods of heavy amperage draw (load). Install a special battery load testing tool onto the terminals (see illustration). Load test the battery according to the tool manufacturer's

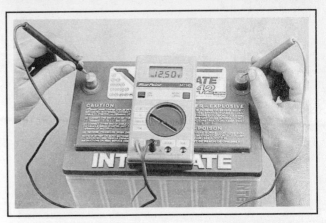

3.2 To test the open circuit voltage of the battery, connect a voltmeter to the battery - a fully charged battery should measure at least 12.4 volts (depending on outside air temperature)

instructions. This tool utilizes a carbon pile to increase the load demand (amperage draw) on the battery. Maintain the load on the battery for 15 seconds or less and observe that the battery voltage does not drop below 9.6 volts. If the battery condition is weak or defective, the tool will indicate this condition immediately.

➡Note: Cold temperatures will cause the minimum voltage requirements to drop slightly. Follow the chart given in the tool manufacturer's instructions to compensate for cold climates. Minimum load voltage for freezing temperatures (32 degrees F) should be approximately 9.1 volts.

REPLACEMENT

◗ Refer to illustrations 3.5 and 3.8

4 Disconnect the negative battery cable, then the positive cable from the battery.

5 Remove the battery hold-down clamp and thermo-guard if equipped (see illustration).

6 Lift out the battery. Be careful - it's heavy.

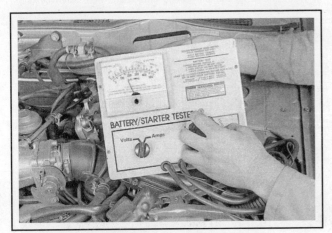

3.3 Connect a battery load tester to the battery and check the battery condition under load following the tool manufacturer's instructions

3.5 Remove the bolts (arrows) and detach the hold-down clamp from the battery tray

3.8 If necessary, remove the battery tray mounting bolts (arrows) and remove the battery tray

➡Note: Battery straps and handlers are available at most auto parts stores for a reasonable price. They make it easier to remove and carry the battery.

7 While the battery is out, inspect the area underneath the tray for corrosion.

8 If corrosion has leaked down past the battery tray, remove the bolts, unsnap the power distribution center from the tray and lift the tray out (see illustration). Disconnect the electrical connector for the battery temperature sensor. If equipped with an EVAP system leak detection pump, disconnect the electrical connector and hoses from the pump, it may remain attached to the battery tray if desired.

9 Use baking soda to clean the deposits from the metal to prevent further oxidation, then spray the area under the tray with a rust-inhibiting paint.

10 If you are replacing the battery, make sure you get one that's identical, with the same dimensions, amperage rating, cold cranking rating, etc.

11 Installation is the reverse of removal.

4 Battery cables - check and replacement

4.4a Always disconnect the negative battery cable first, then the positive cable

▶ Refer to illustrations 4.4a, 4.4b, 4.4c, 4.4d and 4.4e

1 Periodically inspect the entire length of each battery cable for damage, cracked or burned insulation and corrosion. Poor battery cable connections can cause starting problems and decreased engine performance.

2 Check the cable-to-terminal connections at the ends of the cables for cracks, loose wire strands and corrosion. The presence of white, fluffy deposits under the insulation at the cable terminal connection is a sign that the cable is corroded and should be replaced. Check the terminals for distortion, missing mounting bolts and corrosion.

3 When removing the cables, always disconnect the negative cable first and hook it up last or the battery may be shorted by the tool used to loosen the cable clamps. Even if only the positive cable is being replaced, be sure to disconnect the negative cable from the battery first (see Chapter 1 for further information regarding battery cable removal).

4 Disconnect the old cables from the battery, then trace each of them to their opposite ends and detach them from the starter solenoid, power distribution center and ground terminals, as necessary (see illus-

4.4b Detach any retaining clips (arrow) along the entire length of the cable

4.4c The negative cable is attached to the radiator support (arrow) . . .

4.4d . . . and the engine block

trations). Note the routing of each cable to ensure correct installation.

5   If you are replacing either or both of the battery cables, take them with you when buying new cables. It is vitally important that you replace the cables with identical parts. Cables have characteristics that make them easy to identify: positive cables are usually red and larger in cross-section; ground cables are usually black and smaller in cross-section.

6   Clean the threads of the solenoid or ground connection with a wire brush to remove rust and corrosion. Apply a light coat of battery terminal corrosion inhibitor or petroleum jelly to the threads to prevent future corrosion.

7   Attach the cable to the solenoid or ground connection and tighten the mounting nut/bolt securely.

8   Before connecting a new cable to the battery, make sure that it reaches the battery post without having to be stretched.

9   Connect the positive cable first, followed by the negative cable.

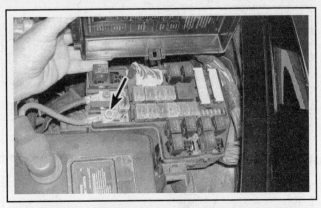

4.4e Remove the nut (arrow) and detach one branch of the positive cable from the power distribution center - disconnect the other branch from the starter motor

5   Ignition system - general information

All models are equipped with a computer controlled electronic ignition system. The ignition system consists of the spark plugs, spark plug wires, distributor, ignition coil, camshaft position sensor, crankshaft position sensor and the Powertrain Control Module (PCM). The PCM controls the ignition timing, spark and advance characteristics for the engine. The ignition timing is not adjustable, therefore, changing the position of the distributor will not affect the timing in any way.

The 4.7L engine does not have a distributor or spark plug wires. There are eight individual ignition coils, one mounted directly over each spark plug. The PCM controls the operation of the coils, firing each coil in sequence.

The distributor, on models so equipped, is gear-driven from the camshaft. The distributor contains the rotor, camshaft position sensor and pulse ring. The distributor is not equipped with centrifugal or vacuum advance mechanisms. The camshaft position sensor is a hall-effect device triggered by the pulse ring connected to the distributor shaft. The signal generated by camshaft position sensor is used by the computer for cylinder identification and fuel synchronization. The camshaft position sensor may be removed from the distributor while in the vehicle. Refer to Chapter 6 for additional information on the camshaft position sensor.

➡**Note: The camshaft position sensor may be referred to as a sync signal generator or a switch plate assembly by dealership or parts store personnel.**

The PCM controls the ignition system by opening and closing the ignition coil ground circuit. The computerized ignition system provides complete control of the ignition timing by determining the optimum timing in response to engine speed, coolant temperature, throttle position and vacuum in the intake manifold. These parameters are relayed to the PCM by the camshaft position sensor, crankshaft position sensor, throttle position sensor (TPS), coolant temperature sensor and MAP Sensor. Refer to Chapter 6 for additional information on the various sensors.

6   Ignition system - check

✳✳ WARNING:

Because of the very high voltage generated by the ignition system, extreme care should be taken whenever an operation is performed involving ignition components. This not only includes the ignition coil, distributor and spark plug wires, but related items connected to the system as well, such as any test equipment.

1   Check the battery state of charge (see Section 3).
2   Check all ignition wiring connections for tightness, cuts, corrosion or any other signs of a bad connection.

ENGINE STARTS, BUT MISFIRES

▸ **Refer to illustrations 6.3a and 6.3b**

3   Use a calibrated ignition tester to verify adequate secondary voltage at each of the spark plug wires (see illustrations). If bright blue well defined sparks occur at each spark plug wire the ignition system is

6.3a To use a calibrated ignition tester, simply disconnect a spark plug wire, connect it to the tester, clip the tester to a convenient ground and crank the engine over - if there's enough power to fire the plug, bright blue sparks will be visible between the electrode tip and the tester body (weak sparks or intermittent sparks are the same as no sparks)

6.3b To use a calibrated tester on 4.7L V8 models, remove an ignition coil and connect the tester to the spark plug boot, clip the tester to a convenient ground and crank the engine over - the sparks must be bright blue

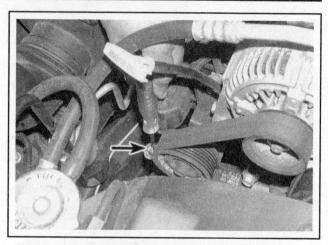

6.7 Disconnect the ignition coil electrical connector and check for battery voltage at the dark green/orange wire terminal with the ignition On

operating properly; check the spark plugs (see Chapter 1), check the engine for a mechanical problem (see Chapter 2) and/or check the fuel injection system (see Chapter 4).

4　If any of the wires fail the spark test, use an ohmmeter to check the resistance of the spark plug wire. Compare your measurement with the resistance listed in this Chapter's Specifications. Replace any defective spark plug wire. A faulty or poor connection at that plug could also result in a misfire. Also, check for carbon deposits inside the spark plug boot. If the spark plug wires are good, check the spark plugs, distributor cap and rotor (see Chapter 1).

ENGINE WILL NOT START

▶ **Refer to illustrations 6.7 and 6.9**

5　Disconnect the ignition coil wire from the center of the distributor cap, connect a calibrated ignition tester to the coil wire, crank the engine and check for spark (see illustration 6.3). If adequate sparks occur at the coil wire, perform Steps 3 and 4.

6　If no sparks occur at the coil wire, use an ohmmeter to check the resistance of the coil wire. Compare your measurement with the resistance listed in this Chapter's Specifications. Replace the coil wire if defective.

7　Check for battery voltage to the ignition coil (see illustration). If battery voltage is not available at the ignition coil check the operation of the Automatic Shutdown (ASD) relay (see Chapter 12).

8　Using an ohmmeter, check the primary and secondary resistance of the ignition coil (see Section 7).

9　If all the checks are correct, check the trigger signal from the PCM. Using an LED-type test light, backprobe the coil driver terminal (black/gray wire) and check for a flashing light as an assistant cranks over the engine (see illustration).

6.9 Backprobe the coil driver terminal with a suitable probe, connect the negative lead of a test light to an engine ground point and touch the tip of the test light to the probe - the test light should flash as the engine is cranked

✳ WARNING:

Keep all loose clothing, hair, etc. away from the drivebelt and engine cooling fan as the engine is operated or seriously injury may result.

10　If the test light does not flash, check the operation of the camshaft position sensor and the crankshaft position sensor (see Chapter 6). If the sensors are good, have the PCM diagnosed by a dealer service department or other qualified automotive repair shop.

7 Ignition coil - check and replacement

CHECK

▶ **Refer to illustrations 7.4a, 7.4b, 7.5a and 7.5b**

1　Remove the ignition coil from the coil bracket (see Steps 8 and 9).

2　Clean the outer case and check it for cracks and other damage.

3　Clean the coil primary terminals and check the coil tower terminal for corrosion. Clean it with a wire brush if any corrosion is found.

4　Check the coil primary resistance by attaching the leads of an ohmmeter to the positive and negative terminals of the connector (see illustrations). Compare the measured resistance to the value listed in

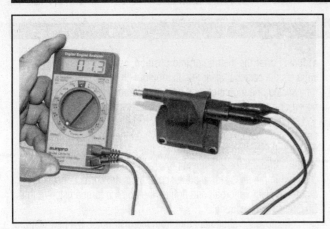

7.4a Connect an ohmmeter to the two primary wiring connector terminals and check the coil primary resistance (all except 4.7L V8)

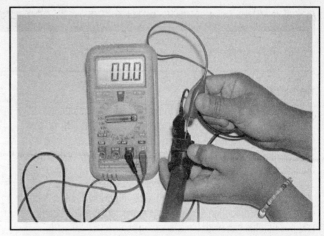

7.4b To test primary resistance on 4.7L V8 individual coils, measure the resistance across the two terminals of the coil connector

this Chapter's Specifications.

5   Check the coil secondary resistance by connecting one of the ohmmeter leads to the positive terminal of the connector and the other ohmmeter lead to the high-tension terminal (see illustrations). Compare the measured resistance to the value listed in this Chapter's Specifications.

6   If the measured resistances are not as specified, the coil is defective and should be replaced with a new one.

7   It is essential for proper operation of the ignition system that all coil terminals and wires be kept clean and dry.

REPLACEMENT

▶ Refer to illustrations 7.9a and 7.9b

➡Note: The ignition coil is mounted on a bracket at the front of the right cylinder head on V6 and 5.2L/5.9L V8 models. On four-cylinder models, it's mounted on a bracket attached to the engine block, behind the distributor. On 4.7L V8's, the coils are mounted over each spark plug.

8   Disconnect the primary wiring electrical connector and remove the high-tension lead from the coil.

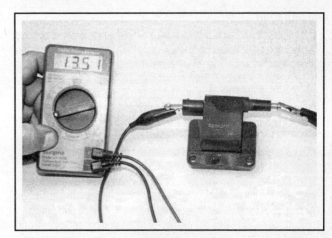

7.5a Connect an ohmmeter to the positive primary wiring connector terminal and the high-tension terminal and check the coil secondary resistance (all except 4.7L V8)

9   Remove the ignition coil mounting bolts and detach it from the coil bracket (see illustrations).

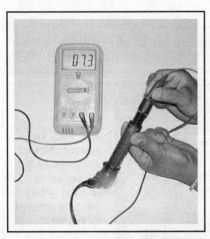

7.5b To measure secondary resistance on 4.7L V8 coils, connect an ohmmeter between the spark plug terminal and one of the primary terminals

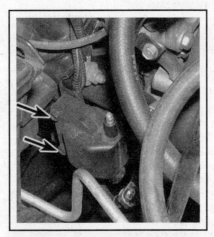

7.9a Remove the ignition coil mounting bolts and detach the coil from the bracket (V6 and 5.2L/5.9L V8 models)

7.9b Remove the one bolt on each coil on 4.7L V8 engines, then disconnect the electrical connector

8   Distributor - removal and installation

FOUR-CYLINDER ENGINE

Removal

1   Disconnect the cable from the negative battery terminal.

2   Position the engine with number one cylinder at TDC on the compression stroke (see Chapter 2).

3   Remove the air intake duct from the throttle body and air cleaner housing.

4   Disconnect the electrical connector from the distributor.

5   Disconnect the coil wire from the distributor cap. Loosen the distributor cap mounting screws, remove the cap from the distributor and position the cap (with the spark plug wires attached) aside.

6   Remove the distributor hold-down bolt and clamp. Pull the distributor straight up and out of the engine block. Remove and discard the gasket.

Installation

7   If the crankshaft has been moved while the distributor is out, the number one piston must be repositioned at TDC. This can be done by feeling for compression pressure at the number one spark plug hole as the crankshaft is rotated. Once compression is felt, continue rotating the crankshaft until the mark on the crankshaft damper is aligned with the zero or TDC mark on the timing indicator.

8   Check the position of the slot in the oil pump drive gear. The slot should be pointing at approximately the 10 o'clock position. If it isn't, insert a large flat-blade screwdriver into the slot and rotate it to the proper position.

9   Remove the camshaft position sensor and rotate the distributor shaft until the alignment hole in the plastic ring aligns with the hole in the bottom of the distributor housing. Insert a 3/16-inch drift punch through the holes to lock the distributor in the number one cylinder firing position.

➡**Note: Several alignment holes are provided in the plastic ring for different applications. Make sure the hole for the four-cylinder engine (as shown in the illustration) is the one you're using. On new replacement distributors, a plastic pin installed by the manufacturer should be in place.**

10   Clean the distributor mounting surface on the engine block and install a new gasket.

11   Install the rotor on the distributor shaft. Insert the distributor into the engine block with the slot in the distributor base positioned at one

o'clock. Lower the distributor into position, as the distributor gear engages the camshaft gear the distributor will rotate clockwise. When fully seated, the mounting bolt hole should be centered in the slot. If necessary, rotate the distributor slightly to engage the oil pump.

12   When the distributor is correctly installed; the engine is positioned with number one cylinder at TDC on the compression stroke, the rotor is pointing at approximately three o'clock, the alignment pin is installed through the alignment holes and the mounting bolt hole is centered in the base slot. If all the conditions are correct, install the mounting clamp and bolt and tighten the bolt the torque listed in this Chapter's Specifications.

13   Remove the alignment tool from the distributor. If a new distributor was installed, pull the plastic pin from the bottom of the housing. Install the camshaft position sensor and the rotor.

14   The remainder of installation is the reverse of removal.

V6 AND 5.2L/5.9L V8 ENGINES

Removal

▶ **Refer to illustrations 8.19 and 8.20**

15   Disconnect the cable from the negative battery terminal. Remove the air cleaner assembly.

16   Position the engine with number one cylinder at TDC on the compression stroke (see Chapter 2).

17   Disconnect the electrical connector from the distributor.

18   Disconnect the coil wire from the distributor cap. Loosen the distributor cap mounting screws, remove the cap from the distributor and position the cap (with the spark plug wires attached) aside.

19   The distributor rotor should be pointing at the camshaft position sensor alignment mark, if necessary apply a paint mark on the edge of the distributor body directly below the rotor tip and in line with it (see illustration).

20   Mark the position of the distributor base to the engine to ensure the distributor can be re-installed in exactly the same position as originally installed (see illustration).

21   Remove the distributor hold-down bolt and pull out the distributor. Remove and discard the O-ring.

Installation

22   If the crankshaft has been moved while the distributor is out, the number one piston must be repositioned at TDC. This can be done by

8.19 With number one cylinder at TDC on the compression stroke, the rotor should be pointing at the camshaft position sensor alignment mark - apply a dab of white paint on the mark for better visibility

8.20 Mark the position of the distributor body to the engine (arrows) (intake manifold removed for clarity)

feeling for compression pressure at the number one spark plug hole as the crankshaft is rotated. Once compression is felt, continue rotating the crankshaft until the mark on the crankshaft damper is aligned with the zero or TDC mark on the timing indicator.

23 Install a new O-ring on the distributor housing.

24 Turn the rotor until it aligns with the camshaft position sensor alignment mark.

→Note: If the engine is being reassembled (as in an engine overhaul), make sure the distributor drive gear is properly installed (see Chapter 2A).

25 Insert the distributor into the engine block and align the marks

made in Step 20. The distributor must be installed the same position it was in before removal. Make sure the rotor remains aligned with the camshaft position sensor alignment mark.

→Note: If the alignment marks are lost or driveability symptoms appear after installing the distributor, take the vehicle to a dealer service department or other properly equipped repair facility and have the fuel synchronization reset with special equipment.

26 Install the distributor hold-down clamp and tighten the bolt to the torque listed in this Chapter's Specifications.

27 The remainder of installation is the reverse of removal.

9 Charging system - general information and precautions

The charging system includes the alternator, a charge indicator light, the battery, the Powertrain Control Module (PCM), a fusible link and the wiring between all the components. The charging system supplies electrical power for the ignition system, the lights, the radio, etc. The alternator is driven by a serpentine drivebelt at the front of the engine.

The alternator control system within the PCM regulates the DC current output of the alternator in accordance with driving conditions. Depending upon electric load, vehicle speed, battery temperature and accessories (air conditioning system, radio, cruise control etc.), the system will adjust the amount of DC current generated, creating less load on the engine.

The purpose of the voltage regulator is to limit the alternator voltage output to a preset value. This prevents power surges, circuit overloads, etc., during peak voltage output. The voltage regulator is contained within the PCM and in the event of failure, the PCM must be replaced as a single unit.

The charging system doesn't ordinarily require periodic maintenance. However, the drivebelt, battery, harness wires and connections should be inspected at the intervals outlined in Chapter 1.

The dashboard warning light should come ON when the ignition key is turned to ON, but it should go off immediately after the engine is

started. If it remains on, there is a malfunction in the charging system. Some vehicles are also equipped with a voltmeter. If the voltmeter indicates abnormally high or low voltage, check the charging system (see Section 10).

Be very careful when making electrical circuit connections to a vehicle equipped with an alternator and note the following:

a) *When reconnecting wires to the alternator from the battery, be sure to note the polarity.*

b) *Before using arc welding equipment to repair any part of the vehicle, disconnect the wires from the alternator and the battery terminals.*

c) *Never start the engine with a battery charger connected.*

d) *Always disconnect both battery cables before using a battery charger.*

e) *The alternator is turned by an engine drivebelt which could cause serious injury if your hands, hair or clothes become entangled in it with the engine running.*

f) *Because the alternator is connected directly to the battery, it could arc or cause a fire if overloaded or shorted out.*

g) *Wrap a plastic bag over the alternator and secure it with rubber bands before steam-cleaning the engine.*

10 Charging system - check

▶ **Refer to illustration 10.3**

→Note: These vehicles are equipped with an On-Board Diagnostic (OBD) system that is useful for detecting charging system problems. Refer to Chapter 6 for the list of diagnostic codes and procedures for obtaining the codes.

1 If a malfunction occurs in the charging circuit, do not immediately assume that the alternator is causing the problem. First check the following items:

a) *The battery cables where they connect to the battery. Make sure the connections are clean and tight.*

b) *The battery electrolyte specific gravity (by observing the charge indicator on the battery). If it is low, charge the battery.*

c) *Check the external alternator wiring and connections.*

d) *Check the drivebelt condition and tension (see Chapter 1).*

e) *Check the alternator mounting bolts for tightness.*

f) *Run the engine and check the alternator for abnormal noise.*

2 Using a voltmeter, check the battery voltage with the engine off. It should be approximately 12.4 to 12.6 volts with a fully charged battery.

3 Start the engine and check the battery voltage again. It should now be greater than the voltage recorded in Step 2, but not more

10.3 To measure battery voltage, attach the voltmeter leads to the battery terminals (engine OFF) - to measure charging voltage, start the engine

than 15 volts (see illustration).

4   If the indicated voltage reading is less or more than the specified charging voltage, have the charging system checked at a dealer service department or other properly equipped repair facility. The voltage regulator on these models is contained within the PCM and it cannot be adjusted, removed or tampered with in any way.

11 Alternator - removal and installation

♦ **Refer to illustrations 11.2, 11.4a and 11.4b**

1   Disconnect the cable from the negative battery terminal.

2   Disconnect the output wire and the field terminals from the alternator (see illustration).

3   Loosen the tensioner pulley, then detach the serpentine drivebelt (see Chapter 1).

4   Remove the mounting nuts/bolts and separate the alternator from the engine (see illustrations).

5   If you are replacing the alternator, take the old one with you when purchasing a replacement unit. Make sure the new/rebuilt unit looks identical to the old alternator. Look at the terminals - they should be the same in number, size and location as the terminals on the old alternator. Finally, look at the identification numbers - they will be stamped into the housing or printed on a tag attached to the housing. Make sure the numbers are the same on both alternators.

6   Many new/rebuilt alternators do not have a pulley installed, so you may have to switch the pulley from the old unit to the new/rebuilt one. When buying an alternator, find out the shop's policy regarding pulleys; some shops will perform this service free of charge.

7   Installation is the reverse of removal. Tighten the mounting bolts to the torque listed in this Chapter's Specifications.

8   Install the drivebelt (see Chapter 1).

9   Check the charging voltage to verify proper operation of the alternator (see Section 10).

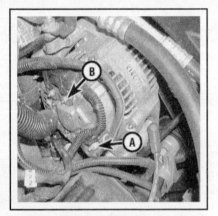

11.2 Disconnect the alternator electrical connections

  A   *B+ terminal (output)*
  B   *Field terminals*

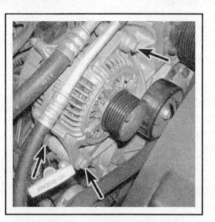

11.4a Remove the alternator mounting nut/bolts (arrows) and remove the alternator from the bracket (V6 and 5.2L/5.9L V8 models)

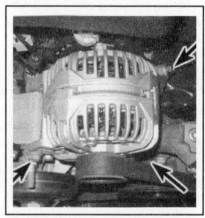

11.4b Alternator mounting bolts - 4.7L V8 models

12 Starting system - general information and precautions

The starter motor assembly installed on these engines uses a planetary gear reduction drive. This type starter motor assembly is serviced as a complete unit. If any component of the starter motor fails, including the solenoid, the entire assembly must be replaced.

The starting system consists of the battery, starter relay, starter motor assembly and the wiring connecting the components.

The starter motor assembly is installed on the lower part of the engine, next to the transmission bellhousing.

When the ignition key is turned to the START position, the starter solenoid is actuated through the starter control circuit which includes a starter relay located in the Power Distribution Center. The starter solenoid then connects the battery to the starter motor. The battery supplies the electrical energy to the starter motor, which does the actual work of cranking the engine.

Always observe the following precautions when working on the starting system:

  a) *Excessive cranking of the starter motor can overheat it and cause serious damage. Never operate the starter motor for more than 15 seconds at a time without pausing to allow it to cool for at least two minutes.*

  b) *The starter is connected directly to the battery and could arc or cause a fire if mishandled, overloaded or shorted.*

  c) *Always detach the cable from the negative terminal of the battery before working on the starting system.*

13 Starter motor and circuit check

♦ **Refer to illustration 13.4**

1   If a malfunction occurs in the starting circuit, do not immediately assume that the starter is causing the problem. First, check the following items:

  a) *Make sure the battery cable clamps, where they connect to the battery, are clean and tight.*

b) Check the condition of the battery cables (see Section 4). *Replace any defective battery cables with new parts.*

c) Test the condition of the battery (see Section 3). *If it does not pass all the tests, replace it with a new battery.*

d) Check the starter motor wiring and connections.

e) Check the starter motor mounting bolts for tightness.

f) Check the related fuses in the engine compartment fuse box (see Chapter 12). *If they're blown, determine the cause and repair the circuit.*

g) Check the ignition switch circuit for correct operation (see Chapter 12).

h) Check the starter relay (see Chapter 12).

i) Check the operation of the clutch safety switch (see Chapter 8) *or* the Park/Neutral position switch (see Chapter 7). *These systems must operate correctly to provide battery voltage to the starter solenoid.*

2   If the starter does not activate when the ignition switch is turned to the start position, check for battery voltage to the starter solenoid. This will determine if the solenoid is receiving the correct voltage from the ignition switch. Install a 12-volt test light or a voltmeter to the starter solenoid positive terminal. While an assistant turns the ignition switch to the start position, observe the test light or voltmeter. The test light should shine brightly or battery voltage should be indicated on the voltmeter. If voltage is not available to the starter solenoid, refer to the wiring diagrams in Chapter 12 and check the fuses and starter relay in series with the starting system. If voltage is available but there is no movement from the starter motor, remove the starter from the engine (see Section 14) and bench test the starter (see Step 4).

3   If the starter turns over slowly, check the starter cranking voltage and the current draw from the battery. This test must be performed with the starter assembly on the engine. Crank the engine over (for 10 seconds or less) and observe the battery voltage. It should not drop below 8.5 volts. Also, observe the current draw using an amp meter. Typically a starter should not exceed 300 amps (slightly less for the four-cylinder engine). If the starter motor amperage draw is excessive, have it tested by a dealer service department or other qualified repair shop. There are several conditions that may affect the starter cranking potential. The battery must be in good condition and the battery cold-cranking rating must not be under-rated for the particular application. Be sure to check the battery specifications carefully. The battery terminals

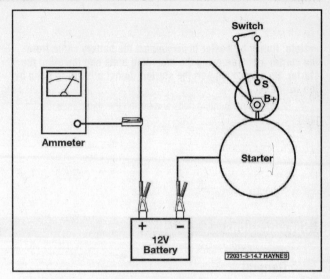

13.4 Starter motor bench testing details

and cables must be clean and not corroded. Also, in cases of extreme cold temperatures, make sure the battery and/or engine block is warmed before performing the tests.

4   If the starter is receiving voltage but does not activate, remove and check the starter motor assembly on the bench. Most likely the solenoid is defective. In some rare cases, the engine may be seized so be sure to try and rotate the crankshaft pulley (see Chapter 2A, 2B or 2C) before proceeding. With the starter assembly mounted in a vise on the bench, install one jumper cable from the positive terminal of a test battery to the B+ terminal on the starter. Install another jumper cable from the negative terminal of the battery to the body of the starter (see illustration). Install a starter switch and apply battery voltage to the solenoid S terminal (for 10 seconds or less) and observe the solenoid plunger, shift lever and overrunning clutch extend and rotate the pinion drive. If the pinion drive extends but does not rotate, the solenoid is operating but the starter motor is defective. If there is no movement but the solenoid clicks, the solenoid and/or the starter motor is defective. If the solenoid plunger extends and rotates the pinion drive, the starter assembly is operating properly.

14 Starter motor - removal and installation

▶ **Refer to illustrations 14.3 and 14.4**

➡ **Note: The starter is located on the left side of the bellhousing on all models except the 2.5L four-cylinder.**

1   Detach the cable from the negative terminal of the battery.

2   On 4WD models, remove the front axle skid plate (if equipped).

3   Disconnect the wires from the terminals on the starter motor solenoid (see illustration). Disconnect any clips securing the wiring to the starter.

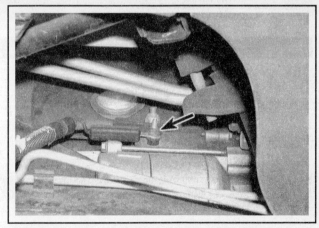

14.3 Remove the nut and disconnect the wiring from the starter motor

➡Note: It may be easier to disconnect the battery cable from the starter after removing the mounting bolts and lowering the starter. Be sure to support the starter, do not allow it to hang by the wiring.

4   Remove the mounting bolts and detach the starter (see illustration).

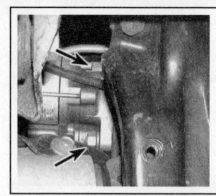

14.4 Remove the starter mounting nut and bolt - V6/V8 models

Specifications

General

Battery voltage	
Engine off	12.0 to 12.6 volts
Engine running	13.5 to 15 volts
Firing order	
Four-cylinder	1-3-4-2
V6	1-6-5-4-3-2
V8	1-8-4-3-6-5-7-2

Ignition system

Ignition coil resistance (at 70 to 80 degrees F)	
4.7L V8	
Primary resistance	0.6 to 0.9 ohms
Secondary resistance	6000 to 9000 ohms
All other models	
Diamond	
Primary resistance	0.96 to 1.18 ohms
Secondary resistance	11,300 to 15,300 ohms
Toyodenso	
Primary resistance	0.95 to 1.20 ohms
Secondary resistance	11,300 to 13,300 ohms
Spark plug/coil wire resistance	
Minimum	3,000 ohms per foot
Maximum	12,000 ohms per foot

Torque specifications

	Ft-lbs
Distributor hold-down bolt	17
Alternator mounting bolts	
Four-cylinder	41
V6 and 5.2L/5.9L V8	30
4.7L V8	
Short bolt	55
Long bolt	40
Vertical bolt	40
Starter mounting bolt/nut	
Four-cylinder	40
V6 and V8	50

Section

6

EMISSIONS AND ENGINE CONTROL SYSTEMS

1 General information

▶ **Refer to illustrations 1.1a, 1.1b and 1.7**

To prevent pollution of the atmosphere from incompletely burned and evaporating gases, and to maintain good driveability and fuel economy, a number of emission control systems are incorporated (see illustrations). They include the:

Electronic engine control system
Evaporative emissions control system
Crankcase ventilation system
Catalytic converter

All of these systems are linked, directly or indirectly, to the emission control system.

The Sections in this Chapter include general descriptions, checking procedures within the scope of the home mechanic and component replacement procedures (when possible) for each of the systems listed above.

Before assuming that an emissions control system is malfunction-ing, check the fuel and ignition systems carefully. The diagnosis of some emission control devices requires specialized tools, equipment and training. If checking and servicing become too difficult or if a procedure is beyond your ability, consult a dealer service department. Remember, the most frequent cause of emissions problems is simply a loose or broken vacuum hose or wire, so always check the hose and wiring connections first.

This doesn't mean, however, that emission control systems are particularly difficult to maintain and repair. You can quickly and easily perform many checks and do most of the regular maintenance at home with common tune-up and hand tools.

➡**Note: Because of a Federally mandated warranty which covers the emission control system components, check with your dealer about warranty coverage before working on any emissions-related systems. Once the warranty has expired, you may wish to perform some of the component checks and/or replacement procedures in this Chapter to save money.**

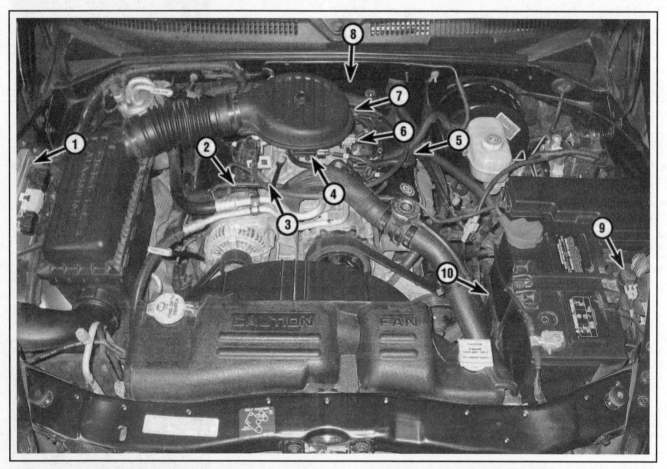

1.1a Typical emissions and engine control system components - V6 and 5.2L/5.9L V8 models

1	Powertrain Control Module	6	Throttle position sensor
2	Engine coolant temperature sensor (located behind alternator)	7	Idle air control valve (at rear of throttle body)
3	Intake air temperature sensor	8	Camshaft position sensor (located inside distributor)
4	Manifold absolute pressure sensor	9	EVAP purge solenoid
5	PCV valve	10	Battery temperature sensor (located under battery)

1.1b Typical emission and engine control system components - 4.7L V8 models

1.   Powertrain Control Module
2.   Throttle position sensor
3.   Idle air control valve
4.   Intake air temperature sensor
5.   Battery temperature sensor (located under battery)

6.   Engine coolant temperature sensor (located in front of intake manifold)
7.   Manifold absolute pressure sensor
8.   PCV valve

Pay close attention to any special precautions outlined in this Chapter. It should be noted that the illustrations of the various systems may not exactly match the system installed on the vehicle you're working on because of changes made by the manufacturer during production or from year-to-year.

A Vehicle Emissions Control Information (VECI) label is located in the engine compartment (see illustration). This label contains important emissions specifications and adjustment information, as well as a vacuum hose schematic with emissions components identified. When servicing the engine or emissions systems, the VECI label in your particular vehicle should always be checked for up-to-date information.

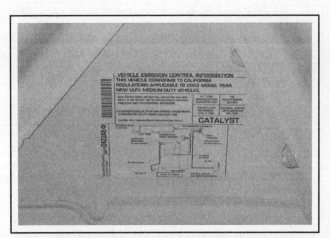

1.7 The Vehicle Emission Control Information (VECI) label is located in the engine compartment (on the bottom of the hood) and contains information on the emission devices on your vehicle, vacuum line routing, etc.

2 On Board Diagnosis system and trouble codes

DIAGNOSTIC TOOL INFORMATION

♦ **Refer to illustrations 2.1, 2.2 and 2.4**

1   A digital multimeter is necessary for checking fuel injection and emission related components (see illustration). A digital volt-ohmmeter is preferred over the older style analog multimeter for several reasons. The analog multimeter cannot display the volts-ohms or amps measurement in hundredths and thousandths increments. When working with electronic circuits which are often very low voltage, this accurate reading is most important. Another good reason for the digital multimeter is the high impedance circuit. The digital multimeter is equipped with a high resistance internal circuitry (10 million ohms). Because a voltmeter is hooked up in parallel with the circuit when testing, it is vital that none of the voltage being measured should be allowed to travel the parallel path set up by the meter itself. This dilemma does not show itself when measuring larger amounts of voltage (9 to 12 volt circuits) but if you are measuring a low voltage circuit such as the oxygen sensor signal voltage, a fraction of a volt may be a significant amount when diagnosing a problem. However, there are several exceptions where using an analog voltmeter may be necessary to test certain sensors.

2   Hand-held scanners are the most powerful and versatile tools for analyzing engine management systems used on later model vehicles (see illustration). Each brand scan tool must be examined carefully to match the year, make and model of the vehicle you are working on.

3   With the arrival of the Federally mandated emission control system (OBD-II), a specially designed scanner has been developed. Several tool manufacturers have released OBD-II scan tools for the home mechanic. Ask the parts salesman at a local auto parts store for additional information concerning dates and costs.

4   Another type of code reader may be available for some models at parts stores (see illustration). These tools simplify the procedure for extracting codes from the engine management computer by simply "plugging in" to the diagnostic connector on the vehicle wiring harness.

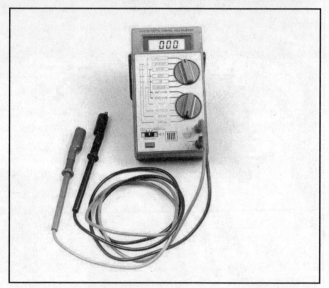

2.1 Digital multimeters can be used for testing all types of circuits; because of their high impedance, they are much more accurate than analog meters for measuring low-voltage computer circuits

ON BOARD DIAGNOSTIC SYSTEM GENERAL DESCRIPTION

5   All models described in this manual are equipped with the second generation On Board Diagnostic (OBD-II) system. The systems consist of an on-board computer, known as the Powertrain Control Module (PCM), and information sensors, which monitor various functions of the engine and send data to the PCM. On models with electronic automatic transmissions, there is also a transmission control computer. On 2003 and later models with a 4.7L V8 and automatic transmission, the two computers have been combined into one, which is called the Next Generation Controller, or NGC1.

6   Based on the data and the information programmed into the computer's memory, the PCM generates output signals to control various engine functions via control relays, solenoids and other output actuators. The PCM is specifically calibrated to optimize the emissions, fuel economy and driveability of the vehicle.

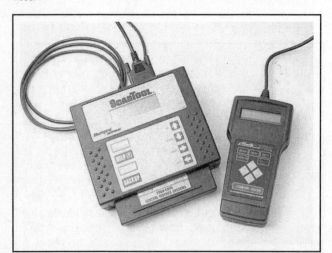

2.2 Scanners like the Actron Scantool and the AutoXray XP240 are powerful diagnostic aids - programmed with comprehensive diagnostic information, they can tell you just about anything you want to know about your engine management system

2.4 Trouble code tools simplify the task of extracting the trouble codes

7 Because of a Federally mandated warranty which covers the emissions system components and because any owner-induced damage to the PCM, the sensors and/or the control devices may void the warranty, it isn't a good idea to attempt diagnosis or replacement of the PCM at home while the vehicle is under warranty. Take the vehicle to a dealer service department if the PCM or a system component malfunctions.

Information sensors

8 **Battery temperature sensor** - The battery temperature sensor senses the temperature of the battery. The PCM uses this information in controlling the voltage output of the alternator.

9 **Camshaft position sensor** - The camshaft position sensor provides information on camshaft position. The PCM uses this information, along with the crankshaft position sensor information, to control fuel injection synchronization.

10 **Crankshaft position sensor** - The crankshaft position sensor senses crankshaft position (TDC) during each engine revolution. The PCM uses this information to control ignition timing and fuel injection synchronization.

11 **Engine coolant temperature sensor** - The engine coolant temperature sensor senses engine coolant temperature. The PCM uses this information to control the fuel mixture and ignition timing.

12 **Intake air temperature sensor** - The intake air temperature senses the temperature of the air entering the intake manifold. The PCM uses this information to control the fuel mixture.

13 **Manifold absolute pressure sensor** - The manifold absolute pressure monitors intake manifold pressure and ambient barometric pressure. The PCM uses this input signal to determine engine load and adjust the fuel mixture accordingly.

14 **Oxygen sensor** - The oxygen sensors generate a voltage signal that varies with the difference between the oxygen content of the exhaust and the oxygen in the surrounding air. The PCM uses this information to determine if the fuel system is running rich or lean.

15 **Power steering pressure switch** - The power steering pressure switch is used on four-cylinder and 4.7L V8 models to detect high line pressure in the power steering system. The PCM uses this input signal to adjust the idle speed under increased engine loads during low-speed vehicle maneuvers.

16 **Throttle position sensor** - The throttle position sensor senses throttle movement and position. This signal enables the PCM to determine when the throttle is closed, in a cruise position, or wide open. The PCM uses this information to control fuel delivery and ignition timing.

17 **Transmission pressure and temperature sensors** - The transmission pressure and temperature sensor signals are used by the PCM to control shift operation (four-speed electronic automatic transmission only).

18 **Rear wheel speed sensor** - The PCM receives vehicle speed information from the antilock brake system rear wheel speed sensor.

19 **Miscellaneous PCM inputs** - In addition to the various sensors, the PCM monitors various switches and circuits to determine vehicle operating conditions. The switches and circuits include:

   a) *Air conditioning system*
   b) *Auto shutdown relay*
   c) *Battery voltage*
   d) *Brake On/Off switch*
   e) *Cruise control system*
   f) *Engine oil pressure*
   g) *EVAP leak detection pump operation*
   h) *Fuel level*
   i) *Ignition switch*
   j) *Overdrive switch*
   k) *Park/neutral position switch*
   l) *Sensor signal and ground circuits*

Output actuators

20 **Air conditioning clutch relay** - The PCM controls the operation of the air conditioning compressor clutch with the air conditioning clutch relay.

21 **Automatic shutdown relay** - The automatic shut down relay supplies battery power to the fuel injectors, ignition coil and oxygen sensor heaters. The PCM controls the operation of the automatic shutdown relay.

22 **Check Engine light** - The PCM will illuminate the Check Engine light if a malfunction in the electronic engine control system occurs.

23 **Cruise control vacuum and vent solenoids** - The cruise control system operation is controlled by the PCM.

24 **Engine cooling fan relay (four-cylinder only)** - The engine cooling fan, on four-cylinder models, is controlled by the PCM according to information received from the engine coolant temperature sensor.

25 **EVAP canister purge solenoid** - The evaporative emission canister purge solenoid is a solenoid valve, operated by the PCM to purge the fuel vapor canister and route fuel vapor to the intake manifold for combustion.

26 **EVAP leak detection pump** - Some models are equipped with a self-diagnostic EVAP leak detection system. The system checks the integrity of the EVAP system when the engine is started cold. The PCM controls the operation of the EVAP leak detection pump.

27 **Fuel injectors** - The PCM opens the fuel injectors individually in firing order sequence. The PCM also controls the time the injector is held open (pulse width). The pulse width of the injector (measured in milliseconds) determines the amount of fuel delivered. For more information on the fuel delivery system and the fuel injectors, including injector replacement, refer to Chapter 4.

28 **Fuel pump relay** - The fuel pump relay is activated by the PCM with the ignition switch in the Start or Run position. When the ignition switch is turned on, the relay is activated to supply initial line pressure to the system. Refer to Chapter 12 or your owner's manual for more information on relay location. For more information on fuel pump check and replacement, refer to Chapter 4.

29 **Idle air control valve** - The idle air control valve controls the amount of air allowed to bypass the throttle plate when the throttle valve is closed or at idle position. The more air allowed to bypass the throttle plate, the higher the idle speed. The idle air control valve opening and the resulting idle speed is controlled by the PCM.

30 **Ignition coil** - The PCM controls the ignition coil by grounding the primary circuit to the ignition coil which generates high voltage in the secondary circuit, thus sending spark from the ignition coil to the distributor. The PCM controls ignition timing depending on engine operation conditions. Refer to Chapter 5 for more information on the ignition coil.

31 **Tachometer** - The PCM operates the tachometer from the information received from the crankshaft position sensor.

32 **Transmission shift control solenoids** - The PCM receives input signals from various sensors and switches such as the vehicle speed sensor, transmission temperature sensor, throttle position sensor and manifold absolute pressure sensor to determine shifting points, required line pressure and torque converter lock-up operations of the transmission (four-speed electronic automatic transmission only).

33 **Voltage regulator** - The PCM controls the charging system voltage by grounding the alternator field driver circuit depending on electrical load requirements. The voltage regulator circuitry is fully contained within the PCM. Any failure in the voltage regulator circuitry requires replacement of the PCM.

OBTAINING DIAGNOSTIC TROUBLE CODES

▶ **Refer to illustration 2.36**

➡**Note: The diagnostic trouble codes on all models can be extracted from the Powertrain Control Module (PCM) only by using a specialized scan tool. Have the vehicle diagnosed by a dealer service department or other qualified automotive repair facility if the proper scan tool is not available.**

34 The PCM will illuminate the Malfunction Indicator Lamp on the dash if it recognizes a fault in the system. The light will remain illuminated until the problem is repaired and the code is cleared or the PCM does not detect any malfunction for several consecutive drive cycles.

35 The diagnostic codes for the On Board Diagnostic (OBD) system can only be extracted from the PCM using a scan tool on all models.

36 The preferred code extraction method requires a special scan tool that is programmed to interface with the OBD system by plugging into the diagnostic connector (see illustration). When used, the scan tool has the ability to diagnose in-depth driveability problems and it allows freeze frame data to be retrieved from the PCM stored memory. Freeze frame data is an OBD II PCM feature that records all related sensor and actuator activity on the PCM data stream whenever an engine control or emissions fault is detected and a trouble code is set. This ability to look at the circuit conditions and values when the malfunction occurs provides a valuable tool when trying to diagnose intermittent driveability problems. If the tool is not available and intermittent driveability problems exist, have the vehicle checked at a dealer service department or other qualified repair shop.

2.36 The diagnostic connector is typically located under the instrument panel

CLEARING DIAGNOSTIC TROUBLE CODES

37 After the system has been repaired, the codes must be cleared from the PCM memory using a scan tool.

✳✳ CAUTION:

Do not disconnect the battery from the vehicle in an attempt to clear the codes. If necessary, have the codes cleared by a dealer service department or other qualified repair facility.

38 Always clear the codes from the PCM before starting the engine after a new electronic emission control component is installed onto the engine. The PCM stores the operating parameters of each sensor. The PCM may set a trouble code if a new sensor is allowed to operate before the parameters from the old sensor have been erased.

DIAGNOSTIC TROUBLE CODE IDENTIFICATION

39 The accompanying list of diagnostic trouble codes is a compilation of the codes that may be encountered. Not all codes pertain to all models and not all codes will illuminate the Malfunction Indicator Light (MIL) when set.

OBD-II TROUBLE CODES

➡**Note: Not all trouble codes apply to all models.**

Code	Probable cause
P0031	Upstream oxygen sensor heater circuit low (left cylinder bank)
P0032	Upstream oxygen sensor heater circuit high (left cylinder bank)
P0037	Downstream oxygen sensor heater circuit low (left cylinder bank)
P0038	Downstream oxygen sensor heater circuit high (left cylinder bank)
P0051	Upstream oxygen sensor heater circuit low (right cylinder bank)
P0052	Upstream oxygen sensor heater circuit high (right cylinder bank)
P0071	Ambient/battery temperature sensor/circuit problem

Code	Probable cause
P0040	Upstream oxygen sensors swapped (crossed wiring harnesses)
P0041	Downstream oxygen sensors swapped (crossed wiring harnesses)
P0068	Throttle Position (TP) sensor inconsistent with Mass Air Flow sensor
P0102	Mass Air Flow (MAF) sensor circuit, low input
P0103	Mass Air Flow (MAF) sensor circuit, high input
P0106	Barometric pressure out of range, Manifold Absolute Pressure sensor/circuit problem
P0107	MAP sensor circuit, low voltage
P0108	MAP sensor circuit, high voltage
P0109	MAP sensor circuit intermittent
P0111	Intake Air Temperature (IAT) sensor circuit, performance problem
P0112	Intake Air Temperature (IAT) sensor circuit, low input
P0113	Intake Air Temperature (IAT) sensor circuit, high input
P0116	Engine Coolant Temperature (ECT) circuit range/performance problem
P0117	Engine Coolant Temperature (ECT) sensor circuit, low input
P0118	Engine Coolant Temperature (ECT) sensor circuit, high input
P0121	Throttle Position (TP) circuit out of range or performance problem
P0122	Throttle Position (TP) sensor circuit, low input
P0123	Throttle Position (TP) sensor circuit, high input
P0125	Insufficient coolant temperature for closed loop fuel control
P0128	Coolant temperature below thermostat regulated temperature
P0131	Upstream oxygen sensor circuit problem (left cylinder bank)
P0132	Upstream oxygen sensor circuit, high voltage (left cylinder bank)
P0133	Upstream oxygen sensor circuit, slow response (left cylinder bank)
P0135	Upstream oxygen sensor heater circuit problem (left cylinder bank)
P0136	Downstream oxygen sensor circuit problem (left cylinder bank)
P0137	Downstream oxygen sensor circuit, low voltage (left cylinder bank)
P0138	Downstream oxygen sensor circuit, high voltage (left cylinder bank)
P0139	Downstream oxygen sensor circuit, slow response (left cylinder bank)
P0141	Downstream oxygen sensor heater circuit problem (left cylinder bank)
P0148	Fuel delivery error
P0151	Upstream oxygen sensor circuit, low voltage (right cylinder bank)
P0152	Upstream oxygen sensor circuit, high voltage (right cylinder bank)
P0153	Upstream oxygen sensor circuit, slow response (right cylinder bank)
P0155	Upstream oxygen sensor heater circuit problem (right cylinder bank)

OBD-II TROUBLE CODES (continued)

Code	Probable cause
P0156	Downstream oxygen sensor circuit problem (right cylinder bank)
P0157	Downstream oxygen sensor circuit, low voltage (right cylinder bank)
P0158	Downstream oxygen sensor circuit, high voltage (right cylinder bank)
P0159	Downstream oxygen sensor circuit, slow response (right cylinder bank)
P0161	Downstream oxygen sensor heater circuit problem (right cylinder bank)
P0171	System too lean (left cylinder bank)
P0172	System too rich (left cylinder bank)
P0174	System too lean (right cylinder bank)
P0175	System too rich (right cylinder bank)
Code	Probable cause
P0176	Flexible Fuel (FF) sensor circuit malfunction
P0180	Engine Fuel Temperature (EFT) sensor A circuit, low input
P0181	Engine Fuel Temperature (EFT) sensor A circuit, range/performance
P0183	Engine Fuel Temperature (EFT) sensor circuit, high input
P0190	Fuel Rail Pressure (FRP) sensor circuit malfunction
P0191	Fuel Rail Pressure (FRP) sensor circuit performance
P0192	Fuel Rail Pressure (FRP) sensor circuit, low input
P0193	Fuel Rail Pressure (FRP) sensor circuit, high input
P0196	Engine Oil Temperature sensor circuit range/performance problem
P0197	Engine Oil Temperature sensor circuit, low input
P0198	Engine Oil Temperature sensor circuit, high input
P0201	Injector no. 1 circuit malfunction
P0202	Injector no. 2 circuit malfunction
P0203	Injector no. 3 circuit malfunction
P0204	Injector no. 4 circuit malfunction
P0205	Injector no. 5 circuit malfunction
P0206	Injector no. 6 circuit malfunction
P0207	Injector no. 7 circuit malfunction
P0208	Injector no. 8 circuit malfunction
P0219	Engine overspeed condition
P0221	Throttle Position (TP) sensor B circuit range/performance problem
P0222	Throttle Position (TP) sensor B circuit, low input

Code	Probable cause
P0223	Throttle Position (TP) sensor B circuit, high input
P0230	Fuel pump primary circuit malfunction
P0231	Fuel pump secondary circuit low
P0232	Fuel pump secondary circuit high
P0297	Vehicle over speed condition
P0298	Engine oil over temperature condition
P0300	Random misfire detected
P0301	Cylinder no. 1 misfire detected
P0302	Cylinder no. 2 misfire detected
P0303	Cylinder no. 3 misfire detected
P0304	Cylinder no. 4 misfire detected
P0305	Cylinder no. 5 misfire detected
P0306	Cylinder no. 6 misfire detected
P0307	Cylinder no. 7 misfire detected
P0308	Cylinder no. 8 misfire detected
P0315	PCM unable to learn crankshaft pulse wheel tooth spacing
P0316	Misfire occurred during first 1000 engine revolutions
P0320	No crank reference signal detected by PCM
P0325	Knock sensor 1 circuit malfunction (left cylinder bank)
P0326	Knock sensor 1 circuit range/performance (left cylinder bank)
P0330	Knock sensor 2 circuit malfunction (right cylinder bank)
P0331	Knock sensor 2 circuit range/performance (right cylinder bank)
P0340	Camshaft Position (CMP) sensor circuit malfunction
P0345	Camshaft Position (CMP) sensor circuit malfunction
P0351	Ignition coil 1 primary circuit malfunction
P0352	Ignition coil 2 primary circuit malfunction
P0353	Ignition coil 3 primary circuit malfunction
P0354	Ignition coil 4 primary circuit malfunction
P0355	Ignition coil 5 primary circuit malfunction
P0356	Ignition coil 6 primary circuit malfunction
Code	Probable cause
P0357	Ignition coil 7 primary circuit malfunction
P0358	Ignition coil 8 primary circuit malfunction
P0400	EGR flow failure (outside the minimum or maximum limits)

OBD-II TROUBLE CODES (continued)

Code	Probable cause
P0401	Exhaust Gas Recirculation (EGR) valve, insufficient flow detected
P0402	Exhaust Gas Recirculation (EGR) valve, excessive flow detected
P0403	EGR solenoid circuit shorted or open
P0404	EGR position sensor/circuit problem
P0405	EGR position sensor circuit, low voltage detected
P0406	EGR position sensor circuit, high voltage detected
P0411	Secondary Air Injection (AIR) system, upstream flow
P0412	Secondary Air Injection (AIR) system, circuit malfunction
P0420	Catalyst system efficiency below threshold (left cylinder bank)
P0421	Warm-up catalyst efficiency below threshold (left cylinder bank)
P0431	Warm-up catalyst efficiency below threshold (right cylinder bank)
P0432	Catalyst system efficiency below threshold (right cylinder bank)
P0441	EVAP purge flow monitor problem
P0442	EVAP control system, small leak detected
P0443	EVAP control system, canister purge valve circuit malfunction
P0446	EVAP control system canister vent solenoid circuit malfunction
P0451	Fuel tank pressure sensor circuit out of range or performance problem
P0452	Fuel tank pressure sensor circuit, low input
P0453	Fuel tank pressure sensor circuit, high input
P0455	EVAP control system, big leak detected
P0456	EVAP control system, very small leak detected
P0457	EVAP control system, leak detected (fuel filler neck cap loose or off)
P0460	Fuel level sensor circuit malfunction
P0461	Fuel level sensor circuit malfunction
P0462	Fuel level sensor circuit, low input
P0463	Fuel level sensor circuit, high input
P0480	Low speed fan control relay circuit malfunction
P0481	High speed fan control primary circuit failure
P0500	Vehicle Speed Sensor (VSS) malfunction
P0501	Vehicle Speed Sensor (VSS) range/performance problem
P0503	Vehicle Speed Sensor (VSS), intermittent malfunction
P0505	Idle Air Control (IAC) system malfunction

Code	Probable cause
P0506	Idle Air Control (IAC) rpm lower than expected
P0507	Idle Air Control (IAC) rpm higher than expected
P0508	Idle Air Control (IAC) valve signal circuit low
P0509	Idle Air Control (IAC) valve signal circuit high
P0511	Idle Air Control (IAC) circuit malfunction
P0513	Invalid SKIM key
P0516	Battery temperature sensor low
P0517	Battery temperature sensor high
P0519	Idle speed performance problem
P0522	Oil pressure sensor circuit, voltage too low
P0523	Oil pressure sensor circuit, voltage too high
P0532	Air conditioning pressure sensor low
P0533	Air conditioning pressure sensor high
P0534	Low air conditioning cycling period
P0537	Air conditioning evaporator temperature circuit, low input
P0538	Air conditioning evaporator temperature circuit, high input
P0551	Power Steering Pressure (PSP) sensor circuit malfunction
Code	Probable cause
P0552	Power Steering Pressure (PSP) sensor circuit malfunction
P0553	Power Steering Pressure (PSP) sensor circuit malfunction
P0562	Battery voltage low
P0563	Battery voltage high
P0600	PCM serial communication failure
P0601	PCM internal controller failure
P0602	PCM programming error
P0603	Powertrain Control Module (PCM) Keep-Alive-Memory (KAM) test error
P0605	Powertrain Control Module (PCM) Read-Only-Memory (ROM) error
P0606	Powertrain Control Module (PCM) internal communication error
P0622	Alternator field circuit open or shorted
P0627	Fuel pump relay circuit problem
P0703	Brake switch circuit input malfunction
P0704	Clutch pedal position switch malfunction
P0720	Insufficient input from Output Shaft Speed (OSS) sensor
P0721	Noise interference on Output Shaft Speed (OSS) sensor signal

OBD-II TROUBLE CODES (continued)

Code	Probable cause
P0722	No signal from Output Shaft Speed (OSS) sensor
P0723	Output Shaft Speed (OSS) sensor circuit, intermittent failure
P0812	Reverse Switch (RS) input circuit malfunction
P0850	Park/Neutral Position switch performance problem

3 Powertrain Control Module - removal and installation

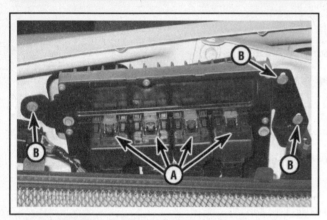

3.2 The PCM is mounted to the right side of the engine compartment

A   Electrical connectors   B   Mounting bolts

▶ **Refer to illustration 3.2**

➡ **Note: Avoid static electricity damage to the Powertrain Control Module (PCM) by grounding yourself to the body of the vehicle before touching the PCM and using a special anti-static pad to store the PCM on, once it is removed.**

1   Disconnect the cable from the negative battery terminal.
2   Remove the cover (if equipped) and disconnect the electrical connectors from the PCM (see illustration).
3   Remove the bolts that retain the PCM to the mounting bracket and remove the unit from the engine compartment.
4   Installation is the reverse of removal.

4 Throttle position sensor - check and replacement

4.2 Throttle body and related components - four-cylinder engine

1   Throttle body
2   Idle air control valve
3   Throttle position sensor

4   Manifold absolute pressure sensor

1   The Throttle Position Sensor (TPS) is located on the end of the throttle shaft on the throttle body. By monitoring the output voltage from the TPS, the PCM can determine fuel delivery based on throttle valve angle (driver demand). A broken or loose TPS can cause intermittent bursts of fuel from the injectors and an unstable idle because the PCM thinks the throttle is moving.

CHECK

▶ **Refer to illustrations 4.2, 4.3a, 4.3b and 4.4**

➡ **Note: Performing the following test will set a diagnostic trouble code and illuminate the Check Engine light. Be prepared to clear the diagnostic trouble code after performing the tests and making the necessary repairs (see Section 2).**

2   Locate the Throttle Position Sensor (TPS) on the throttle body (see illustration).

4.3a TPS location (V6 and 5.2L/5.9L V8 models) and connector terminal identification

4.3b Throttle position sensor location - 4.7L V8 models

3   Before checking the throttle position sensor, check the voltage supply and ground circuits from the PCM. Disconnect the electrical connector from the throttle position sensor (see illustrations). Connect the leads of a voltmeter to terminals 1 and 3 of the connector (the two outer terminals). Turn the ignition key On - the voltage should read approximately 5.0 volts. If the voltage is incorrect, check the wiring from the throttle position sensor to the PCM. If the circuits are good, have the PCM checked at a dealer service department or other properly equipped repair facility.

4   To check the TPS operation, reconnect the connector to the TPS and using a suitable probe, backprobe the center wire terminal of the TPS connector (see illustration). Connect the positive lead of a voltmeter to the probe and the negative lead to a good engine ground point. Turn the ignition key On - with the throttle fully closed the voltage

should read between 0.35 and 0.90 volts. Gradually open the throttle - the voltage should increase smoothly to approximately 4.5 volts at wide-open throttle. If the test results are incorrect, replace the TPS.

REPLACEMENT

▶ **Refer to illustration 4.6**

5   Disconnect the electrical connector from the TPS.
6   Remove the TPS mounting screws and remove the TPS from the throttle body (see illustration).
7   When installing the TPS, be sure to align the socket locating tangs on the TPS with the throttle shaft in the throttle body.
8   Installation is the reverse of removal.

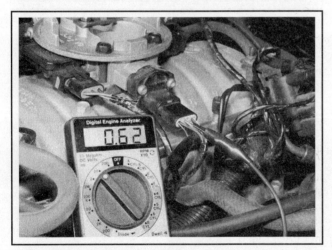

4.4 To check the TPS, backprobe the center wire terminal of the TPS connector with a voltmeter

4.6 Remove the TPS mounting screws

5   Manifold absolute pressure sensor - check and replacement

1   The Manifold Absolute Pressure (MAP) sensor monitors the intake manifold pressure changes resulting from changes in engine load and speed and converts the information into a voltage output. The PCM uses the MAP sensor to control fuel delivery and ignition timing.

The PCM will receive information as a voltage signal that will vary from 1.0 to 1.5 volts at closed throttle (high vacuum) and 4.0 to 4.5 volts at wide open throttle (low vacuum). The MAP sensor is located on the throttle body.

5.3a MAP sensor location (V6 and 5.2L/5.9L V8 models) and connector terminal identification

5.3b Manifold absolute pressure sensor location - 4.7L V8 models

5.4 To check the MAP sensor, backprobe the center wire terminal of the MAP sensor connector with a voltmeter

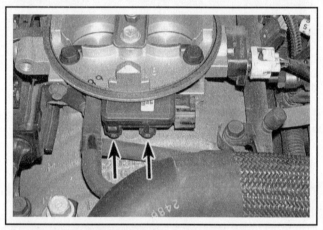

5.6 Remove the MAP sensor mounting screws (V6 and 5.2L/5.9L engine shown)

CHECK

▶ Refer to illustrations 5.3a, 5.3b and 5.4

➡Note: Performing the following test will set a diagnostic trouble code and illuminate the Check Engine light. Be prepared to clear the diagnostic trouble code after performing the tests and making the necessary repairs (see Section 2).

2   Check the small rubber hose connecting the MAP sensor to the throttle body for damage and a snug fit. Check the terminals in the connector and the wires leading to the sensor for looseness and breaks. Repair as required.

3   Before checking the manifold absolute pressure sensor, check the voltage supply and ground circuits from the PCM. Disconnect the electrical connector from the manifold absolute pressure sensor (see illustrations).

➡Note: If you're working on a four-cylinder engine, see illustration 4.2.

Connect the leads of a voltmeter to terminals 1 and 3 of the harness connector (the two outer terminals). Turn the ignition key On - the voltage should read approximately 5.0 volts. If the voltage is incorrect, check the wiring from the manifold absolute pressure sensor to the

PCM. If the circuits are good, have the PCM checked at a dealer service department or other properly equipped repair facility.

4   To check the MAP sensor operation, reconnect the connector to the MAP sensor and using a suitable probe, backprobe the center wire terminal of the MAP sensor connector (see illustration). Connect the positive lead of a voltmeter to the probe and the negative lead to a good engine ground point. Turn the ignition key On - with the engine not running the voltage should read 4.0 to 5.0 volts. Start the engine and allow it to idle - the voltage should decrease to approximately 1.5 to 2.0 volts. If the test results are incorrect, replace the MAP sensor.

REPLACEMENT

▶ Refer to illustration 5.6

5   Disconnect the electrical connector from the MAP sensor.

6   Remove the screws that retain the MAP sensor to the throttle body (see illustration). Remove the MAP sensor and disconnect the hose from the throttle body.

7   Installation is the reverse of removal. On 4.7L V8 models, check the condition of the O-ring and replace if necessary before installing the map sensor.

6 Intake air temperature sensor - check and replacement

1   The intake air temperature sensor is located in the intake manifold. The sensor is a thermistor (a resistor which varies the value of its resistance in accordance with temperature changes). The change in the resistance values will directly affect the voltage signal from the sensor to the PCM. As the sensor temperature INCREASES, the resistance values will DECREASE. As the sensor temperature DECREASES, the resistance values will INCREASE.

CHECK

▶ Refer to illustrations 6.2a, 6.2b, 6.2c and 6.3

➡Note: Performing the following test will set a diagnostic trouble code and illuminate the Check Engine light. Be prepared to clear the diagnostic trouble code after performing the tests and making the necessary repairs (see Section 2).

2   Before checking the intake air temperature sensor, check the voltage supply and ground circuits from the PCM. Disconnect the electrical connector from the intake air temperature sensor and connect a voltmeter to the two terminals of the harness connector (see illustrations). Turn the ignition key On - the voltage should read approximately 5.0 volts. If the voltage is incorrect, check the wiring from the intake air temperature sensor to the PCM. If the circuits are good, have the PCM checked at a dealer service department or other properly equipped repair facility.

3   With the ignition switch OFF, disconnect the electrical connector from the intake air temperature sensor. Using an ohmmeter, measure the resistance between the two terminals on the sensor while it is completely cold (50 to 80-degrees F). Reconnect the electrical connector to the sensor, start the engine and warm it up until it reaches operating temperature (180 to 200-degrees F), disconnect the connector and check the resistance again. Compare your measurements to the resistance chart (see illustration). If the sensor resistance test results are incorrect, replace the intake air temperature sensor.

REPLACEMENT

4   Disconnect the electrical connector from the intake air temperature sensor.

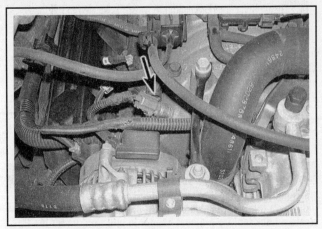

6.2a Intake air temperature sensor location - V6 and V8 models

6.2b Intake air temperature sensor location - four-cylinder models

5   Unscrew the sensor from the intake manifold and remove the intake air temperature sensor.
6   Installation is the reverse of removal.

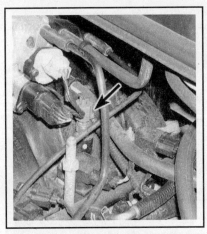

6.2c Intake air temperature sensor location - 4.7L V8 models

Temperature (F)	Minimum resistance	Maximum resistance
50	17,990 ohms	21,810 ohms
77	9,120 ohms	10,880 ohms
104	4,900 ohms	5,750 ohms
140	2,310 ohms	2,670 ohms
176	1,170 ohms	1,340 ohms
212	640 ohms	720 ohms
248	370 ohms	410 ohms

6.3 Intake air temperature sensor and engine coolant temperature sensor approximate temperature vs. resistance values

7   Engine coolant temperature sensor - check and replacement

1   The engine coolant temperature sensor is located in the intake manifold, behind the alternator on V6 and 5.2L/5.9L V8 models and in the thermostat housing on four-cylinder models. On 4.7L V8 models, the sensor is located at the front center of the intake manifold. The sensor is a thermistor (a resistor which varies the value of its resistance in accordance with temperature changes). The change in the resistance values will directly affect the voltage signal from the sensor to the PCM. As the sensor temperature INCREASES, the resistance values will DECREASE. As the sensor temperature DECREASES, the resistance values will INCREASE.

✳ CAUTION:

On some models the connector is hard to reach. Instead of pulling on the harness, which might damage the connector, fabricate a hook tool from a coat hanger to pull from under the lip of the connector.

CHECK

▸ Refer to illustrations 7.2a, 7.2b and 7.2c

➡Note: Performing the following test will set a diagnostic trouble code and illuminate the Malfunction Indicator Light. Be prepared to clear the diagnostic trouble code after performing the tests and making the necessary repairs (see Section 2).

2   Before checking the engine coolant temperature sensor, check the voltage supply and ground circuits from the PCM. Disconnect the electrical connector from the engine coolant temperature sensor and connect a voltmeter to the two terminals of the harness connector (see illustrations). Turn the ignition key On - the voltage should read approximately 5.0 volts. If the voltage is incorrect, check the wiring from the engine coolant temperature sensor to the PCM. If the circuits are good, have the PCM checked at a dealer service department or other properly equipped repair facility.

3   With the ignition switch OFF, disconnect the electrical connector from the engine coolant temperature sensor. Using an ohmmeter, measure the resistance between the two terminals on the sensor while it is completely cold (50 to 80-degrees F). Reconnect the electrical connector to the sensor, start the engine and warm it up until it reaches operating temperature (180 to 200-degrees F), disconnect the connector and check the resistance again. Compare your measurements to the resistance chart (see illustration 6.3). If the sensor resistance test results are incorrect, replace the engine coolant temperature sensor.

REPLACEMENT

✳ WARNING:

Wait until the engine is completely cool before beginning this procedure.

4   Partially drain the cooling system (see Chapter 1).
5   Disconnect the electrical connector from the sensor and carefully unscrew the sensor.

✳ CAUTION:

Handle the coolant sensor with care. Damage to this sensor will affect the operation of the entire fuel injection system.

6   Before installing the new sensor, wrap the threads with Teflon sealing tape to prevent leakage and thread corrosion.
7   Installation is the reverse of removal.

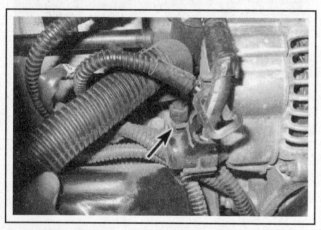

7.2a On V6 and 5.2L/5.9L V8 models, the engine coolant temperature sensor is located on the intake manifold, right behind the alternator

7.2b Engine coolant temperature sensor location - four-cylinder models

7.2c Engine coolant temperature sensor location - 4.7L V8 models

8 Crankshaft position sensor - check and replacement

1 The crankshaft position sensor determines the timing for the fuel injection and ignition on each cylinder. It also detects engine RPM. The crankshaft position sensor is a Hall-Effect device triggered by notches in the flywheel/driveplate. On four-cylinder models, the sensor is mounted on the transmission bellhousing at the left rear of the engine. On V6 and V8 models, the crankshaft sensor is mounted on the engine block behind the right cylinder head. The engine will not operate if the PCM does not receive a crankshaft position sensor input.

CHECK

▶ **Refer to illustration 8.2**

➡ **Note 1: Performing the following test will set a diagnostic trouble code and illuminate the Malfunction Indicator Light. Be prepared to clear the diagnostic trouble code after performing the tests and making the necessary repairs (see Section 2).**

➡ **Note 2: An analog (non-digital) voltmeter is required to check the crankshaft position sensor operation.**

2 Before checking the crankshaft position sensor, check the voltage supply and ground circuits from the PCM. Follow the wiring harness up from the crankshaft position sensor to locate the harness connector. Disconnect the electrical connector and connect the positive lead of a voltmeter to terminal number three and the negative lead to terminal number two of the harness connector (see illustration).

➡ **Note: On V6 and 5.2L/5.9L V8 engines, the electrical connector for the crankshaft position sensor is near the distributor (see illustration 9.4 for location).**

Turn the ignition key On - the voltage should read approximately 5.0 volts. If the voltage is incorrect, check the wiring from the crankshaft position sensor to the PCM. If the circuits are good, have the PCM checked at a dealer service department or other properly equipped repair facility.

3 To check the crankshaft position sensor operation, reconnect the connector to the crankshaft position sensor and using a suitable probe, backprobe terminal number one of the crankshaft position sensor connector. Connect the positive lead of an analog voltmeter to the probe and the negative lead to a good engine ground point. Turn the ignition key On. Rotate the engine slowly with a breaker bar and socket attached to the crankshaft pulley center bolt while watching the meter. The voltage should fluctuate between 0.0 and 5.0 volts as the notches in the flywheel/driveplate pass the sensor. If the test results are incorrect, replace the crankshaft position sensor.

➡ **Note: Rotate the engine slowly through at least one complete revolution. Removing the spark plugs from the engine will make the crankshaft much easier to turn.**

REPLACEMENT

Four-cylinder models

4 Remove the air intake duct.

5 Disconnect the crankshaft sensor wiring harness connector, remove the mounting bolts and remove the sensor from the bellhousing.

6 Installation is the reverse of removal. Use only the original bolts

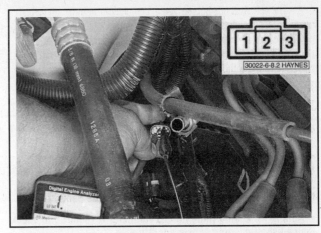

8.2 Disconnect the electrical connector from the crankshaft position sensor and check the power and ground circuits on the harness side

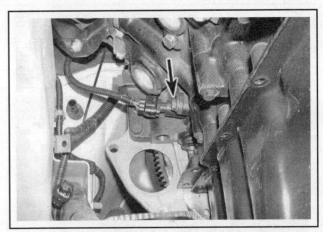

8.10 On 4.7L V8 models, remove the bolt and withdraw the crankshaft position sensor from the engine block

to mount the sensor; they are machined to correctly space the sensor to the flywheel/driveplate. Tighten the bolts to 108 in-lbs.

V6 and V8 models

▶ **Refer to illustration 8.10**

7 Loosen the right front wheel lug nuts. Apply the parking brake and block the rear wheels. Raise the front vehicle and support it securely on jackstands.

8 Remove the right front wheel and the inner fender splash shield.

9 Disconnect the crankshaft sensor wiring harness connector.

10 Remove the crankshaft sensor mounting bolts. The sensor on 5.2L/5.9L V8 models is at the bellhousing, just behind the exhaust manifold, while on 4.7L V8's it is on the block (see illustration).

11 Installation is the reverse of removal. Use only the original bolts to mount the sensor, they are machined to correctly space the sensor to the flywheel/driveplate. Tighten the bolts to 70 in-lbs on V6 and 5.2L/5.9L V8 engines, and 21 ft-lbs on 4.7L V8 engines. On 4.7L V8 applications, apply engine oil lightly to the O-ring on the sensor before installation.

9 Camshaft position sensor - check and replacement

1   The camshaft position sensor, in conjunction with the crankshaft position sensor, determines the timing for the fuel injection on each cylinder. The camshaft position sensor is a Hall-Effect device triggered by a pulse ring in the distributor. The sensor is mounted in the distributor and can be removed without removing the distributor from the engine.

CHECK

▶ **Refer to illustration 9.4**

➡ **Note 1: Performing the following test will set a diagnostic trouble code and illuminate the Malfunction Indicator light. Be prepared to clear the diagnostic trouble code after performing the tests and making the necessary repairs (see Section 2).**

➡ **Note 2: An analog (non-digital) voltmeter is required to check the camshaft position sensor operation.**

2   Remove the air intake duct.
3   Remove the ignition coil wire from the distributor cap. Using a

heavy gauge jumper wire, ground the ignition coil wire terminal to the engine block. Remove the fuel pump fuse from the power distribution center.

❊❊ WARNING:

Failure to disable the fuel and ignition system before performing this procedure could result in vehicle damage or person injury.

4   Before checking the camshaft position sensor, check the voltage supply and ground circuits from the PCM. Disconnect the electrical connector from the camshaft position sensor and connect the positive lead of a voltmeter to terminal number three and the negative lead to terminal number two of the harness connector (see illustration). Turn the ignition key On - the voltage should read approximately 5.0 volts. If the voltage is incorrect, check the wiring from the camshaft position sensor to the PCM. If the circuits are good, have the PCM checked at a dealer service department or other properly equipped repair facility.

5   To check the camshaft position sensor operation, reconnect the connector to the camshaft position sensor and using a suitable probe, backprobe terminal number one of the camshaft position sensor connector. Connect the positive lead of an analog voltmeter to the probe and the negative lead to a good engine ground point. Turn the ignition key to Start - with the engine cranking, the voltage should fluctuate between 0.0 and 5.0 volts. If the test results are incorrect, replace the camshaft position sensor.

❊❊ WARNING:

Make sure that the meter leads, loose clothing, long hair, etc. are away from the moving parts of the engine (drivebelt, cooling fan, etc.) before cranking the engine over.

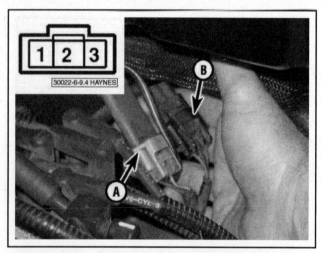

9.4 Camshaft position sensor electrical connector location (A), between the distributor and the firewall (V6 and 5.2L/5.9L V8 models) and terminal identification. B is the electrical connector for the crankshaft position sensor

REPLACEMENT

▶ **Refer to illustrations 9.9a and 9.9b**

6   Remove the air intake duct.
7   Remove the distributor cap and rotor from the distributor (see

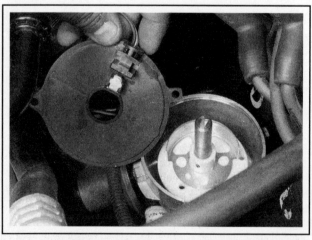

9.9a Carefully remove the camshaft position sensor from the distributor (V6 and 5.2L/5.9L V8 engine shown)

9.9b On 4.7L V8 models, remove the bolt and withdraw the camshaft position sensor from the right cylinder head (see here from below)

Chapter 1).

8   Disconnect the electrical connector from the camshaft position sensor.

9   Remove the camshaft position sensor from the distributor (see illustration). On 4.7L V8 engines, the sensor is located in the right cylinder head (see illustration).

10 Installation is the reverse of removal. Align the tab on the camshaft position sensor with the notch in the distributor housing.

10 Power steering pressure switch (four-cylinder and 4.7L V8 models only) - check and replacement

1   The power steering pressure switch is a normally closed switch, mounted in the pressure line between the steering gear and the power steering pump. When steering system pressure reaches a high-pressure set point, the switch opens and sends a signal to the PCM. The PCM uses the signal to maintain engine idle speed during parking maneuvers.

2   Check the operation of the power steering pressure switch if the engine stalls during parking or if the engine idles continuously at high rpm.

CHECK

▶ **Refer to illustration 10.3**

3   Disconnect the power steering pressure switch connector and connect an ohmmeter to the terminals on the switch body (see illustration).

4   Start the engine and allow it to idle.

> ✳✳✳ **WARNING:**
>
> **Make sure that the meter leads, loose clothing, long hair, etc. are away from the moving parts of the engine (drivebelt, cooling fan, etc.) before starting the engine.**

5   Turn the steering wheel to point the front wheels straight ahead and read the ohmmeter. It should indicate continuity (zero resistance).

6   Turn the steering wheel to either side and watch the ohmmeter. The power steering pressure switch should open as the wheel nears the steering stop on either side, and the meter should indicate no continu-

10.3 The power steering pressure switch is located in the high pressure line

ity (infinite resistance).

7   If the switch fails either test, replace it.

REPLACEMENT

8   Disconnect the electrical connector from the switch. Place a suitable drain pan under the power steering high pressure line.

9   Unscrew the switch from the high pressure line. Use a back-up wrench of the line block to prevent twisting the line.

10 Install and connect the new switch. Refer to Chapter 10 and bleed air from the power steering system. Add fluid as required (see Chapter 1).

11 Oxygen sensor - general information and replacement

▶ **Refer to illustration 11.1**

1   The oxygen in the exhaust reacts with the elements inside the oxygen sensor to produce a voltage output that varies from 0.1 volt (high oxygen, lean mixture) to 0.9 volt (low oxygen, rich mixture). The upstream oxygen sensor (mounted in the exhaust system before the catalytic converter) (see illustration) provides a feedback signal to the PCM that indicates the amount of leftover oxygen in the exhaust. The PCM monitors this variable voltage continuously to determine the required fuel injector pulse width and to control the engine air/fuel ratio. A mixture ratio of 14.7 parts air to 1 part fuel is the ideal ratio for minimum exhaust emissions, as well as the best combination of fuel economy and engine performance. Based on oxygen sensor signals, the PCM tries to maintain this air/fuel ratio of 14.7:1 at all times.

2   The downstream oxygen sensor (mounted in the exhaust system after the catalytic converter) has no effect on PCM control of the air/fuel ratio. However, the downstream sensor is identical to the

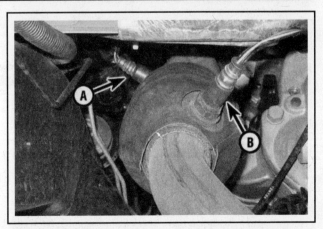

11.1 The upstream oxygen sensor (A) is located before the catalytic converter; the downstream oxygen sensor (B) is located after, or at the bottom of the catalytic converter (4.7L V8 model shown. This is the left bank converter, seen from below)

11.9 A special slotted socket, allowing clearance for the wiring harness, may be required for oxygen sensor removal (the tool is available at most auto parts stores)

upstream sensor and operates in the same way. The PCM uses the downstream signal to monitor the efficiency of the catalytic converter. A downstream oxygen sensor will produce a slower fluctuating voltage signal that reflects the lower oxygen content in the post-catalyst exhaust.

3   An oxygen sensor produces no voltage when it is below its normal operating temperature of about 600-degrees F. During this warm-up period, the PCM operates in an open-loop fuel control mode. It does not use the oxygen sensor signal as a feedback indication of residual oxygen in the exhaust. Instead, the PCM controls fuel metering based on the inputs of other sensors and its own programs.

4   Proper operation of an oxygen sensor depends on four conditions:

   a) **Electrical** - The low voltages generated by the sensor require good, clean connections which should be checked whenever a sensor problem is suspected or indicated.

   b) **Outside air supply** - The sensor needs air circulation to the internal portion of the sensor. Whenever the sensor is installed, make sure the air passages are not restricted.

   c) **Proper operating temperature** - The PCM will not react to the sensor signal until the sensor reaches approximately 600-degrees F. This factor must be considered when evaluating the performance of the sensor.

   d) **Unleaded fuel** - Unleaded fuel is essential for proper operation of the sensor.

5   The PCM can detect several different oxygen sensor problems and set diagnostic trouble codes to indicate the specific fault (see Section 2). When an oxygen sensor fault occurs, the PCM will disregard the oxygen sensor signal voltage and revert to open-loop fuel control as described previously.

REPLACEMENT

▶ **Refer to illustration 11.9**

6   The exhaust pipe contracts when cool, and the oxygen sensor may be hard to loosen when the engine is cold. To make sensor removal easier, start and run the engine for a minute or two; then shut it off. Be careful not to burn yourself during the following procedure. Also observe these guidelines when replacing an oxygen sensor.

   a) The sensor has a permanently attached pigtail and electrical connector, which should not be removed from the sensor. Damage or removal of the pigtail or electrical connector can harm operation of the sensor.

   b) Keep grease, dirt and other contaminants away from the electrical connector and the louvered end of the sensor.

   c) Do not use cleaning solvents of any kind on the oxygen sensor.

   d) Do not drop or roughly handle the sensor.

7   Raise the vehicle and place it securely on jackstands.

8   Disconnect the electrical connector from the sensor.

9   Using a suitable wrench or specialized oxygen sensor socket, unscrew the sensor from the exhaust manifold (see illustration).

10   Anti-seize compound must be used on the threads of the sensor to aid future removal. The threads of most new sensors will be coated with this compound. If not, be sure to apply anti-seize compound before installing the sensor.

✴✴ CAUTION:

Do not get anti-seize on the probe portion of the sensor, or the tip will be contaminated and the sensor will have to be replaced.

11   Install the sensor and tighten it securely.

12   Reconnect the electrical connector to the sensor and lower the vehicle.

12 Battery temperature sensor - check and replacement

1   The battery temperature sensor provides the PCM with information on battery temperature. The PCM uses this information to regulate the charging system voltage. The PCM increases the charging system voltage at colder temperatures and decreases the charging system voltage at warmer temperatures.

CHECK

2   Locate the sensor harness from under the battery and follow the lead to the electrical connector. Disconnect the connector.

3   Using an ohmmeter, measure the resistance of the sensor across the two terminals of the sensor connector. At 75 to 80-degrees F the sensor resistance should be 9,000 to 11,000 ohms.

4   If the resistance is not as specified, replace the sensor.

REPLACEMENT

5   Remove the battery (see Chapter 5).

6   Disconnect the electrical connector from the sensor harness.

7   Pry the sensor from the battery tray and pull the harness and connector through the hole.

8   Installation is the reverse of removal.

13 Idle air control valve - check and replacement

1   The idle speed is controlled by the Idle Air Control (IAC) valve, located on the throttle body. The IAC valve regulates the air bypassing the throttle plate by moving the pintle in or out of the air passage. The IAC valve is controlled by the PCM, adjusting the idle speed depending upon the running conditions of the engine (air conditioning system, power steering, cold and warm running etc.).

CHECK

▶ **Refer to illustrations 13.3a and 13.3b**

➡**Note: Performing the following test will set a diagnostic trouble code and illuminate the Malfunction Indicator light. Be prepared to clear the diagnostic trouble code after performing the tests and making the necessary repairs (see Section 2).**

2   A scan tool is required for complete testing of the IAC valve and circuits. However, there are several tests the home mechanic can perform on the IAC system to verify operation but they are limited and are useful only in the case of definite IAC valve failure.

3   When the engine is started cold, the IAC valve should vary the idle as the engine begins to warm-up. Allow the engine to warm-up, then disconnect the electrical connector from the IAC valve and listen carefully for a change in the idle (see the accompanying illustrations and illustration 4.2). Connect the IAC valve electrical connector and place a load on the engine by placing the transmission in gear (automatic), turning the air conditioning on and/or operating the power steering. The idle should remain steady or increase slightly. If the engine stumbles or stalls, or if there are obvious signs that the IAC valve is not working, stop the engine and continue testing.

4   Disconnect the electrical connector from the IAC valve. Using an ohmmeter, measure the resistance across the two outside terminals of the IAC valve, then measure the resistance across the two inside terminals - the resistance should be about the same on both sets. If one or

13.3a The IAC valve is located at the rear of the throttle body on V6 and 5.2L/5.9L V8 models

both checks indicate an open circuit, replace the IAC valve.

5   If the IAC valve is good, have the PCM diagnosed by a dealer service department or other qualified repair shop.

REPLACEMENT

▶ **Refer to illustration 13.7**

6   Disconnect the electrical connector from the IAC valve.

7   Remove the two mounting screws from the valve and withdraw it from the throttle body (see illustration).

8   Installation is the reverse of removal. Be sure to install a new O-ring.

13.3b Idle air control valve location - 4.7L V8 models

13.7 Remove the idle air control valve mounting screws and remove it from the throttle body

14 Crankcase ventilation system

◆ Refer to illustrations 14.2, 14.3a and 14.3b

1   The crankcase ventilation system reduces hydrocarbon emissions by scavenging crankcase vapors. It does this by circulating fresh air from the air cleaner through the crankcase, where it mixes with blow-by gases. The gases are drawn by intake manifold vacuum into the intake manifold, where they mix with the incoming air/fuel mixture and are consumed during normal combustion.

2   The four-cylinder engine is equipped with a fixed orifice crankcase ventilation system. This system operates the same as the conventional PCV system but it does not use the vacuum control valve. Instead, a molded vacuum tube connects manifold vacuum to the valve cover. The vacuum tube contains a fixed orifice of a calibrated size (see illustration). It meters the amount of crankcase vapors drawn out of the engine. A fresh air supply hose from the air intake duct is connected to the rear of the valve cover. When the engine is running, fresh air enters the engine and mixes with the crankcase vapors. Manifold vacuum draws the vapor/air mixture through the fixed orifice and into the intake manifold.

3   V6 and V8 models are equipped with a Positive Crankcase Ventilation (PCV) system. The main component of this system is the PCV valve. Crankcase vapors are drawn from the crankcase by the PCV valve. On V6 and 5.2L/5.9L V8 models the valve is mounted in the left valve cover (see illustration). On 4.7L V8 models, the PCV valve is mounted on the engine oil filler tube (see illustration). To maintain idle quality and good driveability, the PCV valve restricts the flow when the intake manifold vacuum is high. When intake manifold vacuum is lower, maximum vapor flow is allowed through the valve.

4   Checking and replacement of the PCV valve is covered in Chapter 1.

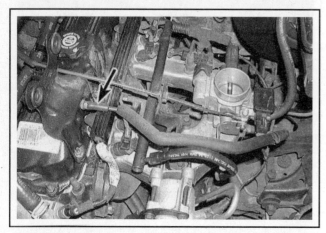

14.2 Four-cylinder models are equipped with a fixed orifice fitting connected to the valve cover

14.3a On V6 and 5.2L/5.9L V8 models, the PCV valve is located in the left valve cover

14.3b On 4.7L V8 models, the PCV valve is located in the oil filler tube

15 Evaporative emissions control system

1   The fuel evaporative emissions control (EVAP) system absorbs fuel vapors from the fuel tank and, during engine operation, releases them into the engine intake system where they mix with the incoming air/fuel mixture.

2   The evaporative system employs a canister filled with activated charcoal to absorb fuel vapors.

3   The fuel tank filler cap is fitted with a two-way valve as a safety device. The valve vents fuel vapors to the atmosphere if the evaporative control system fails.

4   Another fuel cut-off valve (fuel tank rollover valve), mounted on the fuel tank, regulates fuel vapor flow from the fuel tank to the char-coal canister, based on the pressure or vacuum caused by temperature changes. The fuel tank rollover valve prevents fuel flow to the canister in the event the vehicle rolls over in an accident.

5   After passing through the two-way valve, fuel vapor is carried by vent hoses to the charcoal canister. The activated charcoal in the canister absorbs and stores these vapors.

6   When the engine is running and warmed to a pre-set temperature, a purge control solenoid allows a purge control diaphragm valve in the charcoal canister to be opened by intake manifold vacuum. Fuel vapors from the canister are then drawn through the purge control diaphragm valve by intake manifold vacuum. The duty cycle of the

EVAP purge control solenoid regulates the rate of flow of the fuel vapors from the canister to the throttle body. The PCM controls the purge control solenoid. During cold running conditions and hot start time delay, the PCM does not energize the solenoid. After the engine has warmed up to the correct operating temperatures, the PCM purges the vapors into the throttle body according to the running conditions of the engine. The PCM will cycle (ON then OFF) the purge control solenoid about 5 to 10 times per second. The flow rate will be controlled by the pulse width or length of time the solenoid is allowed to be energized.

7   Some models are equipped with a leak detection monitor system. The system is a self-diagnostic system designed to detect a leak in the EVAP system. Each time the engine is started cold, the PCM energizes the leak detection pump. The pump pressurizes the EVAP system then shuts off. The PCM is able to detect a leak if the pump continues to run, unable to pressurize the system. If a leak is detected, the PCM will trigger a diagnostic trouble code (see Section 2).

CHECK

➡**Note: The evaporative emissions control system, like all emissions control systems, is protected by a Federally-mandated warranty (5 years or 50,000 miles at the time this manual was written). The EVAP system probably won't fail during the service life of the vehicle; however, if it does, the hoses or charcoal canister are usually to blame.**

8   Always check the hoses first. A disconnected, damaged or missing hose is the most likely cause of a malfunctioning EVAP system. Refer to the Vacuum Hose Routing Diagram (on the underside of the hood) to determine whether the hoses are correctly routed and attached. Repair any damaged hoses or replace any missing hoses as necessary.

9   Check the related fuses and wiring to the purge control solenoid. Refer to the wiring diagrams at the end of Chapter 12, if necessary. The purge control solenoid valve is normally closed - no vapors will pass through the ports. When the PCM energizes the solenoid (by completing the circuit to ground), the valve opens and vapors flow through.

10 A scan tool is required to thoroughly check the system. If the above checks fail to identify the problem area, have the system diagnosed by a dealer service department or other qualified repair shop.

COMPONENT REPLACEMENT

▶ **Refer to illustrations 15.11 and 15.15**

EVAP canister

11 The EVAP canister is located under the vehicle, mounted to the left frame rail, ahead of the fuel tank (see illustration).

12 Raise the vehicle and support it securely on jackstands.

13 Label and remove the hoses from the canister. Remove the mounting nut and remove the canister.

14 Installation is the reverse of removal.

Purge control solenoid

15 The purge control solenoid is mounted at the right rear of the engine compartment on four-cylinder models, and along the left side of the engine compartment on all other models (see illustration).

16 Disconnect the electrical connector. Label and remove the hoses from the purge control solenoid.

17 Remove the mounting bolts and remove the purge control solenoid from the bracket.

18 Installation is the reverse of removal.

Leak detection pump

19 The leak detection pump (if equipped) is located under the battery tray.

20 Remove the battery and the battery tray (see Chapter 5).

21 Remove the power distribution center mounting bolts and position the power distribution center aside.

22 Disconnect the electrical connector and remove the hoses from the leak detection pump.

23 Remove the mounting bolts and remove the leak detection pump.

24 Installation is the reverse of removal.

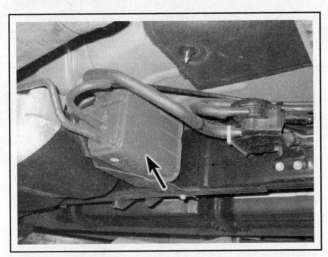

15.11 The EVAP canister is mounted on the left frame rail

15.15 On most models, the purge control solenoid is mounted on the left side of the engine compartment

16 Catalytic converter

➡ **Note: Because of a Federally mandated extended warranty which covers emissions-related components such as the catalytic converter, check with a dealer service department before replacing the converter at your own expense.**

1 A catalytic converter is an emission control device added to the exhaust system to reduce pollutants from the exhaust gas stream. A single-bed converter design is used in combination with a three-way (reduction) catalyst. The catalytic coating on the three-way catalyst contains platinum and rhodium, which lowers the levels of oxides of nitrogen (NOx) as well as hydrocarbons (HC) and carbon monoxide (CO).

2 The test equipment for a catalytic converter is expensive and highly sophisticated. If you suspect that the converter on your vehicle is malfunctioning, take it to a dealer or authorized emissions inspection facility for diagnosis and repair.

3 Whenever the vehicle is raised for servicing of underbody components, check the converters for leaks, corrosion, dents and other damage. Check the welds/flange bolts that attach the front and rear ends of the converter to the exhaust system. If damage is discovered, the converter should be replaced.

4 Although catalytic converters don't break too often, they can become plugged. The easiest way to check for a restricted converter is to use a vacuum gauge to diagnose the effect of a blocked exhaust on intake vacuum.

   a) *Connect a vacuum gauge to an intake manifold vacuum source.*
   b) *Warm the engine to operating temperature, place the transmission in park (automatic) or neutral (manual) and apply the parking brake.*
   c) *Note and record the vacuum reading at idle.*
   d) *Open the throttle until the engine speed is about 2000 rpm.*
   e) *Release the throttle quickly and record the vacuum reading.*
   f) *Perform the test three more times, recording the reading after each test.*
   g) *If the reading after the fourth test is more than one in-Hg lower than the reading recorded at idle, the catalytic converter, muffler or exhaust pipes may be plugged or restricted.*

Section

Reference to other Chapters

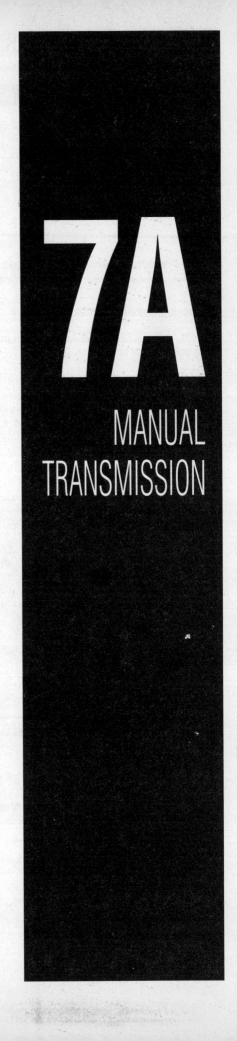

7A

MANUAL
TRANSMISSION

1 General information

The vehicles covered by this manual are equipped with a manual or an automatic transmission. Information on the manual transmission is included in this Part of Chapter 7. Information on the automatic transmission can be found in Part B of this Chapter.

Vehicles equipped with a manual transmission use either an NV1500 or an NV3500. Both units are five-speeds with internal shift mechanisms.

Depending on the cost of having a transmission overhauled, it might be a better idea to replace it with a used or rebuilt unit. Your local dealer or transmission shop should be able to supply information concerning cost, availability and exchange policy. Regardless of how you decide to remedy a transmission problem, you can still save a lot of money by removing and installing the unit yourself.

2 Extension housing oil seal - replacement

▶ **Refer to illustrations 2.4 and 2.6**

➡**Note: This procedure also applies to the transfer case extension housing seal on 4WD models.**

1 Oil leaks frequently occur due to wear of the extension housing oil seal. Replacement of this seal is relatively easy, since it can be performed without removing the transmission from the vehicle.

2 The extension housing oil seal is located at the extreme rear of the transmission, where the driveshaft is attached. If leakage at the seal is suspected, raise the vehicle and support it securely on jackstands. If the seal is leaking, transmission lubricant will be built up on the front of the driveshaft and may be dripping from the rear of the transmission.

3 Remove the driveshaft (see Chapter 8).

4 Using a chisel and hammer, carefully pry the oil seal out of the rear of the transmission (see illustration). Do not damage the splines on the transmission output shaft.

5 If the oil seal cannot be removed with a chisel, a special oil seal removal tool (available at most auto parts stores) will be required.

6 Using a large section of pipe or a very large deep socket as a drift, install the new oil seal (see illustration). Drive it into the bore squarely and make sure it's completely seated.

7 Lubricate the splines of the transmission output shaft and the outside of the driveshaft yoke with lightweight grease, then install the driveshaft (see Chapter 8). Be careful not to damage the lip of the new seal.

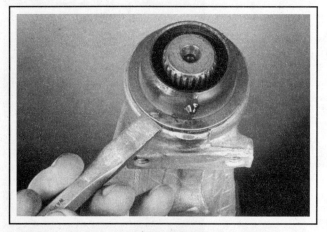

2.4 Use a hammer and chisel to dislodge the rear seal

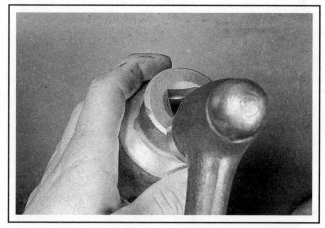

2.6 A large socket can be used to drive the new seal into the bore

3 Shift lever - removal and installation

1 If equipped, remove the center console (see Chapter 11). With the parking brake on and the wheels blocked, place the shift lever in Neutral.

2 Slide the shift lever boot upward on the shift lever.

3 Remove the four shift tower bolts and remove the shift lever and tower.

4 Disassemble the shift lever assembly, clean the parts in solvent, blow everything dry with compressed air, then coat all friction surfaces with clean multi-purpose grease and reassemble.

5 Installation is the reverse of the removal procedure. Be sure to tighten the shift tower bolts to the torque listed in this Chapter's Specifications.

4 Back-up light switch - check and replacement

1   The back-up light switch is located on the side of the transmission case.

CHECK

2   Turn the ignition key to the On position and move the shift lever to the Reverse position; the back-up lights should go on.

3   If the lights don't go on, check the back-up light fuse first (see Chapter 12). If the fuse is blown, trace the back-up light circuit for a short-circuit condition.

4   If the fuse is okay, raise the vehicle and support it securely on jackstands. Place the shifter in Reverse.

5   Working under the vehicle, unplug the back-up light switch electrical connector. Using an ohmmeter, check for continuity across the terminals of the switch. Continuity should exist. If not, replace the switch.

6   If the switch has continuity, check for voltage at the electrical connector; one of the two terminals should have battery voltage present with the ignition key in the On position. If no voltage is present, trace the circuit between the fuse block and the electrical connector for an open circuit condition.

7   If voltage is present, trace the back-up light circuit between the electrical connector and the back-up light bulbs for an open circuit condition.

➡Note: Although not very likely, the back-up light bulbs could both be burned out; don't rule out this possibility.

REPLACEMENT

8   Raise the vehicle and support it securely on jackstands, if not already done.

9   Unplug the back-up light switch electrical connector.

10 Unscrew the back-up light switch from the transmission case.

11 Apply RTV sealant or Teflon tape to the threads of the new switch to prevent leakage. Install the switch in the transmission case and tighten it securely. Plug in the electrical connector.

12 Lower the vehicle and check the operation of the back-up lights.

5 Transmission - removal and installation

REMOVAL

1   Disconnect the negative cable from the battery.

2   Shift the transmission into Neutral.

3   Remove the shift tower and lever assembly (see Section 3).

4   Raise the vehicle sufficiently to provide clearance to easily remove the transmission. Support the vehicle securely on jackstands.

5   Unplug the electrical connector for the crankshaft position sensor and remove the sensor (see Chapter 6). Also disconnect the electrical connector from the back-up light switch. Disengage the wiring harness from the clips on the transmission.

6   Remove the skid plate, if equipped.

7   If the transmission is going to be torn down, drain the lubricant (see Chapter 1).

8   Remove the driveshaft (see Chapter 8). Use a plastic bag to cover the end of the transmission to prevent fluid loss and contamination.

9   Remove exhaust system components as necessary for clearance (see Chapter 4).

10 Remove the starter motor (see Chapter 5).

11 On 4WD models, remove the transfer case shift linkage and the transfer case (see Chapter 7C).

12 Support the engine from above with an engine hoist, or place a jack (with a block of wood as an insulator) under the engine oil pan. The engine must remain supported at all times while the transmission is out of the vehicle.

13 Support the transmission with a jack - preferably a special jack made for this purpose.

➡Note: These jacks can be obtained at most equipment rental yards.

Safety chains will help steady the transmission on the jack.

14 Raise the engine slightly and disconnect the transmission mount from the extension housing and the center crossmember.

15 Raise the transmission slightly and remove the bolts and nuts attaching the crossmember to the frame rails.

16 Lower the jacks supporting the transmission and engine assembly. If you're working on an AX15, detach the shift lever from the transmission (see Section 3) and push it upwards out of the way.

17 Disconnect the clutch hydraulic release cylinder from the clutch housing. Move the cylinder aside for clearance.

18 Remove the nuts and bolts attaching the transmission to the engine.

19 Make a final check for any wiring or hoses connected to the transmission, then move the transmission and its jack toward the rear of the vehicle until the transmission input shaft clears the splined hub in the clutch disc. Keep the transmission level as this is done.

20 Once the input shaft is clear, lower the transmission slightly and remove it from under the vehicle.

21 While the transmission is removed, be sure to remove and inspect all clutch components (see Chapter 8). In most cases, new clutch components should be routinely installed if the transmission is removed.

INSTALLATION

22 Insert a small amount of multi-purpose grease into the pilot bearing in the crankshaft and lubricate the inner surface of the bearing. Also apply a light film of grease on the input shaft splines, input shaft bearing retainer and the release lever/bearing contact points (see Chapter 8).

23 Install the clutch components (see Chapter 8).

24 With the transmission secured to the jack as on removal, raise the transmission into position and carefully slide it forward, engaging the input shaft with the clutch plate hub. Do not use excessive force to install the transmission - if the input shaft does not slide into place, readjust the angle of the transmission so it is level and/or turn the input shaft so the splines engage properly with the clutch.

25 Install the transmission-to-engine bolts and tighten them to the torque listed in this Chapter's Specifications.

> ### ✳✳ CAUTION:
>
> **Don't use the bolts to draw the transmission to the engine. If the transmission doesn't slide forward easily and mate with the engine block, find out why before proceeding.**

26 Raise the transmission into place, install the crossmember and attach it to the frame rails. Install the transmission mount between the extension housing and the crossmember. Carefully lower the transmission extension housing onto the mount and the crossmember. When everything is properly aligned, tighten all nuts and bolts securely.

27 Remove the jacks supporting the transmission and the engine.

28 On 4WD models, install the transfer case and shift linkage (see Chapter 7C).

29 Install the various items removed previously, referring to Chapter 8 for the installation of the driveshaft and clutch release cylinder, Chapter 5 for the starter motor, and Chapter 4 for the exhaust system components.

30 Install the crankshaft position sensor (see Chapter 6). Plug in the electrical connector for the back-up light switch. Connect any other wiring attached to the transmission.

31 Remove the jackstands and lower the vehicle.

32 Install the shift tower, lever and extension (see Section 3).

33 Fill the transmission with the specified lubricant to the proper level (see Chapter 1).

34 Connect the negative battery cable.

35 Road test the vehicle for proper operation and check for leakage.

6 Transmission overhaul - general information

Overhauling a manual transmission is a difficult job for the do-it-yourselfer. It involves the disassembly and reassembly of many small parts. Numerous clearances must be precisely measured and, if necessary, changed with select fit spacers and snap-rings. As a result, if transmission problems arise, it can be removed and installed by a competent do-it-yourselfer, but overhaul should be left to a transmission repair shop. Rebuilt transmissions may be available - check with your dealer parts department and auto parts stores. At any rate, the time and money involved in an overhaul is almost sure to exceed the cost of a rebuilt unit.

Nevertheless, it's not impossible for an inexperienced mechanic to rebuild a transmission if the special tools are available and the job is done in a deliberate step-by-step manner so nothing is overlooked.

The tools necessary for an overhaul include internal and external snap-ring pliers, a bearing puller, a slide hammer, a set of pin punches, a dial indicator and possibly a hydraulic press. In addition, a large, sturdy workbench and a vise or transmission stand will be required.

During disassembly of the transmission, make careful notes of how each piece comes off, where it fits in relation to other pieces and what holds it in place. If you note how each part is installed before removing it, getting the transmission back together again will be much easier.

Before taking the transmission apart for repair, it will help if you have some idea what area of the transmission is malfunctioning. Certain problems can be closely tied to specific areas in the transmission, which can make component examination and replacement easier. Refer to the *Troubleshooting* Section at the front of this manual for information regarding possible sources of trouble.

Specifications

General

Transmission lubricant type	See Chapter 1

Torque specifications

	Ft-lbs (unless otherwise indicated)
Crossmember-to-frame bolts	45 to 55
Shift tower-to-transmission bolts (NV1500, 3500)	75 in-lbs
Transmission mount-to-transmission bolts	24 to 44
Transmission-to-engine bolts	
AX15	28
NV1500, NV3500	80

Section

1　General information
2　Diagnosis - general
3　Shift cable - check, adjustment and replacement
4　Throttle Valve (TV) cable - check, adjustment and replacement
5　Park/Neutral position switch/back-up light switch - check and replacement
6　Shift indicator cable - adjustment
7　Transmission mount - check and replacement
8　Automatic transmission - removal and installation

Reference to other Chapters

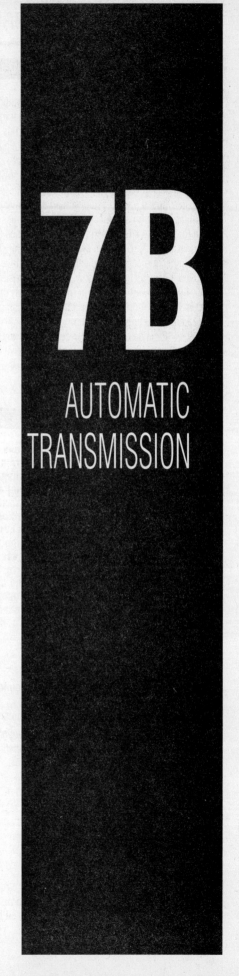

7B

AUTOMATIC
TRANSMISSION

1 General information

All vehicles covered in this manual come equipped with a five-speed manual transmission or a four-speed automatic transmission. Information on the manual transmission is in Part A of this Chapter. You'll also find certain procedures common to both automatic and manual transmissions - such as oil seal replacement - in Part A. Information on the automatic transmission is included in this Part of Chapter 7.

The models covered by this manual use either a 42RE, 46RE or 46RFE four-speed transmission with an electronic governor. They are all similar in design and function. These transmissions are equipped with a torque converter clutch (TCC) that engages in fourth gear, and in third gear when the overdrive switch is turned off. The TCC provides a direct connection between the engine and the drive wheels for improved efficiency and economy. The TCC consists of a solenoid controlled by the Powertrain Control Module (PCM) that locks the converter in third or fourth when the vehicle is cruising on level ground and the engine is fully warmed up.

The 46RFE is an electronically-controlled transmission used with the 4.7L V8 engine. This is a multi-speed automatic which uses an additional planetary gearset that allows the transmission control module to choose between two second gears, resulting in smoother passing gear operation. On 2003 applications, this transmission (with 4.7L V8) does not have a separate transmission control module, but rather a new processor called the NGC1 (New Generation Controller 1) which has all the transmission and engine management functions in one computer.

All of these transmissions feature an overdrive unit consisting of an overdrive clutch, direct clutch, planetary gear set and overrunning clutch. The overdrive clutch is applied only in fourth gear. The direct clutch is applied in all ranges except fourth.

Due to the complexity of the automatic transmissions covered in this manual and the need for specialized equipment to perform most service operations, this Chapter contains only general diagnosis, routine maintenance, adjustment and removal and installation procedures.

If the transmission requires major repair work, it should be left to a dealer service department or an automotive or transmission repair shop. You can, however, remove and install the transmission yourself and save the expense, even if the repair work is done by a transmission shop.

2 Diagnosis - general

➡Note: Automatic transmission malfunctions may be caused by five general conditions: poor engine performance, improper adjustments, hydraulic malfunctions, mechanical malfunctions or malfunctions in the computer or its signal network. Diagnosis of these problems should always begin with a check of the easily repaired items: fluid level and condition (see Chapter 1), shift cable adjustment and Throttle Valve (TV) cable adjustment. Next, perform a road test to determine if the problem has been corrected or if more diagnosis is necessary. If the problem persists after the preliminary tests and corrections are completed, additional diagnosis should be done by a dealer service department or transmission repair shop. Refer to the *Troubleshooting* section at the front of this manual for information on symptoms of transmission problems.

PRELIMINARY CHECKS

1   Drive the vehicle to warm the transmission to normal operating temperature.

2   Check the fluid level as described in Chapter 1:

a) *If the fluid level is unusually low, add enough fluid to bring the level within the designated area of the dipstick, then check for external leaks (see below).*

b) *If the fluid level is abnormally high, drain off the excess, then check the drained fluid for contamination by coolant. The presence of engine coolant in the automatic transmission fluid indicates that a failure has occurred in the internal radiator walls that separate the coolant from the transmission fluid (see Chapter 3).*

c) *If the fluid is foaming, drain it and refill the transmission, then check for coolant in the fluid or a high fluid level.*

3   Check the engine idle speed.

➡Note: If the engine is malfunctioning, do not proceed with the preliminary checks until it has been repaired and runs normally.

4   Inspect the shift cable (see Section 3). Make sure it's properly adjusted and that it operates smoothly.

5   Check the throttle valve cable for freedom of movement. Adjust it if necessary (see Section 4).

➡Note: The Throttle Valve (TV) cable may function properly when the engine is shut off and cold, but it may malfunction once the engine is hot. Check it cold and at normal engine operating temperature.

FLUID LEAK DIAGNOSIS

6   Most fluid leaks are easy to locate visually. Repair usually consists of replacing a seal or gasket. If a leak is difficult to find, the following procedure may help.

7   Identify the fluid. Make sure it's transmission fluid and not engine oil or brake fluid (automatic transmission fluid is a deep red color).

8   Try to pinpoint the source of the leak. Drive the vehicle several miles, then park it over a large sheet of cardboard. After a minute or two, you should be able to locate the leak by determining the source of the fluid dripping onto the cardboard.

9   Make a careful visual inspection of the suspected component and the area immediately around it. Pay particular attention to gasket mating surfaces. A mirror is often helpful for finding leaks in areas that are hard to see.

10 If the leak still cannot be found, clean the suspected area thoroughly with a degreaser or solvent, then dry it.

11 Drive the vehicle for several miles at normal operating temperature and varying speeds. After driving the vehicle, visually inspect the suspected component again.

12 Once the leak has been located, the cause must be determined before it can be properly repaired. If a gasket is replaced but the sealing flange is bent, the new gasket will not stop the leak. The bent

flange must be straightened.

13 Before attempting to repair a leak, check to make sure that the following conditions are corrected or they may cause another leak.

➡Note: Some of the following conditions cannot be fixed without highly specialized tools and expertise. Such problems must be referred to a transmission repair shop or a dealer service department.

Gasket leaks

14 Check the pan periodically. Make sure the bolts are tight, no bolts are missing, the gasket is in good condition and the pan is flat (dents in the pan may indicate damage to the valve body inside).

15 If the pan gasket is leaking, the fluid level or the fluid pressure may be too high, the vent may be plugged, the pan bolts may be too tight, the pan sealing flange may be warped, the sealing surface of the transmission housing may be damaged, the gasket may be damaged or the transmission casting may be cracked or porous. If sealant instead of gasket material has been used to form a seal between the pan and the transmission housing, it may be the wrong type sealant.

Seal leaks

16 If a transmission seal is leaking, the fluid level or pressure may be too high, the vent may be plugged, the seal bore may be damaged, the seal itself may be damaged or improperly installed, the surface of the shaft protruding through the seal may be damaged or a loose bearing may be causing excessive shaft movement.

17 Make sure the dipstick tube seal is in good condition and the tube is properly seated.

Case leaks

18 If the case itself appears to be leaking, the casting is porous and will have to be repaired or replaced.

19 Make sure the oil cooler hose fittings are tight and in good condition.

Fluid comes out vent pipe or fill tube

20 If this condition occurs, the transmission is overfilled, there is coolant in the fluid, the case is porous, the dipstick is incorrect, the vent is plugged or the drain-back holes are plugged.

3   Shift cable - check, adjustment and replacement

CHECK

1   Firmly apply the parking brake and try to momentarily operate the starter in each shift lever position. The starter should operate in Park and Neutral only. If the starter operates in any position other than Park or Neutral, adjust the shift cable (see below). If, after adjustment, the starter still operates in positions other than Park or Neutral, the Park/Neutral position switch is defective (see Section 5).

ADJUSTMENT

▶ Refer to illustrations 3.3a, 3.3b and 3.5

2   Place the shift lever in Park.

3   On 2000 models, locate the shift cable adjuster in the engine compartment, below the master cylinder and next to the steering shaft. Squeeze the two tangs on the adjuster lock and disengage the lock (see illustration). On later models, the shift cable lock is below the steering column. Remove the driver's knee bolster and pull out the lock adjuster tab (see illustration).

4   Raise the vehicle and support it securely on jackstands.

➡Note: The rear of the vehicle must also be raised, so the driveshaft can be turned in Step 7 (to verify that the transmission is completely engaged in Park).

3.3a Squeeze these two tangs (arrows) and disengage the lock on the cable adjuster (2000 models)

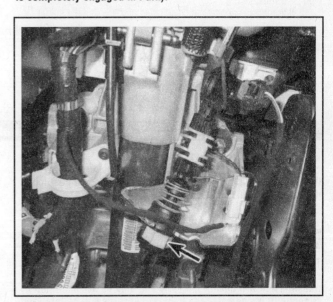

3.3b On 2001 and later models, the shift cable adjuster is just below the steering column - release the locking tab before adjusting the cable

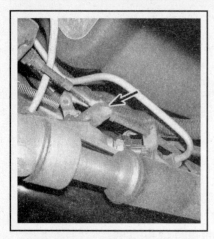

3.5 Use a screwdriver to pry the shift cable off the shift lever at the transmission

3.15 Pry the cable end from the shift lever on the steering column (arrow)

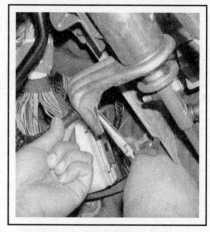

3.16 Squeeze the tangs on the cable retainer and pass the cable and casing through the bracket

5   Working at the transmission end of the cable, pry the cable end off the shift lever (see illustration).

6   Be sure the shift lever on the transmission is all the way to the rear, in the last detent. This is the Park position.

7   Make sure the parking pawl in the transmission is engaged by trying to rotate the driveshaft. The driveshaft will not rotate if the transmission is completely engaged in Park.

8   Connect the shift cable to the shift lever on the transmission. If necessary, adjust the length of the cable casing to allow the cable end to be centered on the lever (the cable casing will move in-or-out, within the adjuster).

9   Lower the vehicle.

10 With the parking brake firmly applied, make sure the engine starts (don't move the shift lever from Park yet).

11 Push the cable adjuster lock back into place until the locking tangs are engaged.

12 If the linkage appears to be adjusted properly, but the starter operates in positions other than Park or Neutral, check the Park/Neutral position switch (see Section 5).

REPLACEMENT

▶ **Refer to illustrations 3.15 and 3.16**

13 Remove the knee bolster and its reinforcement from under the dash (see Chapter 11).

14 Make sure the shift lever is in the Park position.

15 Pry the cable end off the lever on the steering column (see illustration).

16 Squeeze the tangs on the cable retainer to detach the cable casing from the bracket (see illustration).

17 Remove the two nuts securing the cable casing to the firewall (see illustration). Push the cable through the firewall and into the engine compartment.

18 Raise the vehicle and support it securely on jackstands.

19 Squeeze the tangs on the cable retainer and detach the cable casing from the bracket on the transmission. Remove the cable from the vehicle.

20 Installation is the reverse of removal. Adjust the cable as described in Steps 2 through 12.

21 If the indicator doesn't register the selected gear range, the cable will have to be adjusted (see Section 6).

---

4   Throttle Valve (TV) cable - check, adjustment and replacement

➡**Note: The electronic 545-RFE transmission does not have a throttle cable, since the PCM communicates throttle position to the TCM (Transmission Control Module)**

Check

✳✳ CAUTION:

This adjustment is critical; it must be correct for the transmission to function properly. If the cable is adjusted too loose, the transmission will upshift too early and may be accompanied by slippage; if it's adjusted too tight, the upshifts will be late (and downshifts during part-throttle operation will occur too soon).

1   The throttle lever on the transmission is cable-operated. When the throttle valve cable is correctly adjusted, the throttle lever on the

transmission will open and close in accordance with the throttle control lever on the throttle body, from idle all the way to wide-open throttle.

2   Turn the ignition key to the Off position.

3   Remove the air cleaner duct and elbow from the throttle body and air cleaner housing (see Chapter 4).

4   Verify that the lever on the throttle body is resting against its stop. Also verify that the throttle valve lever on the transmission is also resting against its stop.

5   Detach the cable from the control lever stud on the throttle body. To do this, hold the lever still and slide the plastic cable end forward, off its stud. Don't pry it off - use your fingers only.

6   Release the cable and compare the position of the cable end to the attachment stud on the throttle body lever (see illustration 4.11). The end of the cable and the attachment stud on the throttle lever

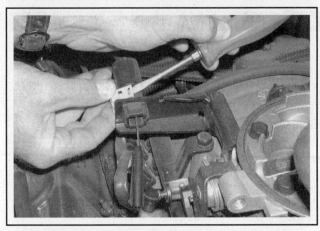

4.10 Disengage the retaining clip with a small screwdriver, then slide it out of the adjuster

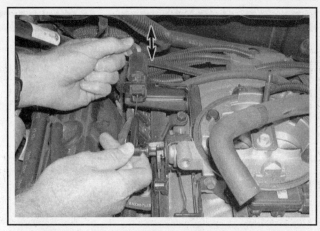

4.11 Move the cable casing in-or-out within the adjuster, as necessary, to center the cable end on the throttle lever stud

should be aligned (or centered on one another) to within 1/32-inch in either direction. If the cable end and the attachment stud are misaligned (off center), the cable must be adjusted as described in the following adjustment procedure.

ADJUSTMENT

▶ **Refer to illustrations 4.10 and 4.11**

7   Turn the ignition switch to the Off position.

8   Detach the end of the cable from the attachment stud on the throttle lever, if not already done (see Step 5).

9   Verify that the throttle valve lever on the transmission is in the fully closed position, then verify that the throttle lever on the throttle body is at the curb idle position.

10   Using a small screwdriver, disengage the retaining clip from the cable adjuster and remove it (see illustration).

11   Move the cable casing in-or-out within the adjuster, as necessary, and center the cable end on the attachment stud to within 1/32-inch (see illustration).

12   While holding the cable casing in this position, reinstall the

retaining clip in the adjuster.

13   Reconnect the cable end to the stud on the throttle lever.

14   Check the cable adjustment.

REPLACEMENT

▶ **Refer to illustrations 4.16 and 4.18**

15   Remove the air cleaner duct and elbow from the throttle body and air cleaner housing, if not already done (see Chapter 4).

16   Detach the end of the TV cable from the lever on the throttle body (see Step 5), then squeeze the tangs on the cable casing retainer and pass the cable through the bracket (see illustration).

17   Raise the vehicle and support it securely on jackstands.

18   Disconnect the cable from the throttle lever on the transmission, then detach the cable casing from its bracket (see illustration).

19   Disengage the cable from any clips which may be supporting it.

20   Note the routing of the old cable, then remove it.

21   Installation is the reverse of removal. Adjust the cable as described in Steps 7 through 14.

22   Reinstall the air cleaner duct and elbow.

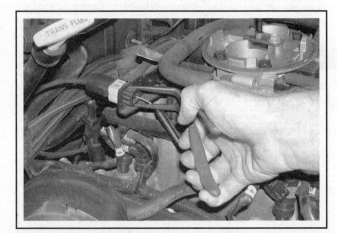

4.16 Squeeze the retaining tangs and push the cable and housing through the bracket

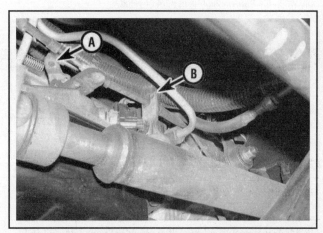

4.18 Pop the TV cable end off the transmission throttle valve lever (A), then detach the cable casing from its bracket (B)

5 Park/Neutral position switch/back-up light switch - check and replacement

5.3 Unplug the electrical connector from the Park/Neutral position switch; the center terminal (arrow) is the ground terminal for the starter solenoid circuit when the transmission is in Neutral or Park

2000 MODELS

1   The Park/Neutral position switch is threaded into the left side of the transmission case. The Neutral start and back-up light switch functions are combined into one unit, with the center terminal of the switch grounding the starter solenoid circuit when the transmission is in Park or Neutral, allowing the engine to start. The outer terminals make up the back-up light switch circuit.

Check

▶ **Refer to illustration 5.3**

2   Prior to checking the switch, make sure the shift cable is properly adjusted (see Section 3). Raise the vehicle and support it securely on jackstands.

3   Unplug the connector and use an ohmmeter or self-powered test light to check for continuity between the center terminal of the switch and the transmission case (see illustration). Continuity should exist only when the transmission is in Park or Neutral.

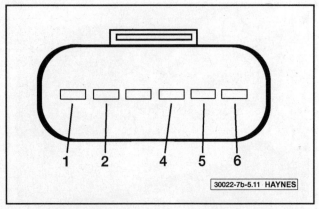

5.11 Transmission range switch electrical connector terminal identification

1	*Ignition voltage*	5 *5V supply*
2	*TRS MUX*	6 *P/NP switch*
4	*Back-up lights*	

4   Check for continuity between the two outer terminals. There should be continuity only when the transmission is in Reverse. There should be no continuity between either of the outer terminals and the transmission case.

Replacement

5   Place a container under the transmission to catch the fluid which will be released, then unscrew the switch from the case.

6   Move the shift lever from Park to Neutral. Make sure that the switch operating fingers are centered in the switch opening in the case. If they aren't, the shift linkage is incorrectly adjusted or there is an internal problem with the transmission.

7   Install the new switch and O-ring (be sure to use a new O-ring, even if installing the original switch), tighten it to the torque listed in this Chapter's Specifications, then recheck the switch before plugging in the connector.

8   Check the fluid level and add some, if necessary, to bring to the appropriate level (see Chapter 1).

2001 AND LATER MODELS

Check

▶ **Refer to illustrations 5.11 and 5.12**

9   Later models have a Transmission Range Sensor (TRS) in place of a Neutral-Safety switch. The TRS is mounted in roughly the same place on the transmission case where the Neutral Safety switch used to be located and combines the functions of the P/NP switch and back-up light switch, plus it transmits the gear positions to the instrument panel display.

➡**Note: On 545RFE transmission, checking or replacing the TRS should only be done at a dealership or qualified specialist.**

10   Prior to checking the switch, make sure the shift cable is properly adjusted (see Section 3). Raise the vehicle and support it securely on jackstands.

11   Place the transmission arm in the Park position. Unplug the electrical connector and check the terminals on the TRS with an ohmmeter (see illustration). The resistance between pin 6 and the transmission case should be 5 ohms or less.

12   Perform the same test as in Step 11 with the transmission in Neutral. If the reading in either test is higher than Specifications, clean the contacts in the switch and connector.

Transmission position	Resistance (ohms) at MUX pin
Park	522.2
Reverse	206.2
Neutral	108.6
Drive	59.9
2nd	31.9
1st	13.7

30022-7b-5.12 **HAYNES**

5.12 TRS resistance in gear positions

13 Resistance should also be 5 ohms or less when testing pin 4 with the transmission in Reverse.

14 Measure the resistance between the TRS MUX pin and the back-up lights pin. Move the shift lever and check the resistance at each shift position and compare it to Specifications (see illustration).

15 If the TRS fails any of the above tests and cleaning the contacts made no improvement, replace the TRS.

Replacement

◆ Refer to illustration 5.17

16 With a drain pan located under the left side of the transmission, put the transmission gear lever in the Low position.

17 Remove the two bolts securing the TRS to the bracket, then twist the TRS out of the bracket (see illustration).

18 Installation is the reverse of the removal procedure. Make sure to use a new O-ring when reinstalling the TRS.

5.17 The TRS bolts to a mounting bracket on the left side of the transmission

6 Shift indicator cable - adjustment

◆ Refer to illustration 6.3

➡Note: The following procedure applies only to 2000 models.

1 The shift indicator on the instrument panel is controlled by a cable attached to a lever on the shifter portion of the steering column. If the indicator doesn't register the correct gear range, the cable will have to be adjusted.

2 Turn the ignition key to the On position and move the shift lever into the Reverse position, then into the Neutral position (two detents from the Park position).

3 Working under the dash, locate the adjuster for the shift indicator cable (see illustration). Turn the thumbscrew on the adjuster one way or the other until the shift indicator needle is in alignment with the N on the instrument cluster.

6.3 To adjust the shift indicator, place the shift lever in the Neutral position, then turn the thumbscrew (arrow) on the cable adjuster until the needle on the indicator is in alignment with the N on the instrument cluster

7 Transmission mount - check and replacement

CHECK

◆ Refer to illustration 7.2

1 Raise the vehicle and support it securely on jackstands.

2 Insert a large screwdriver or prybar into the space between the transmission extension housing and the crossmember and try to pry the transmission up slightly (see illustration).

3 The transmission should not move much at all and the rubber in the center of the mount should fully insulate the center of the mount from the mount bracket around it.

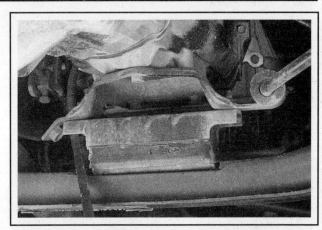

7.2 To check the transmission mount, insert a large screwdriver or prybar between the crossmember and the transmission and try to pry the transmission up - it should move very little (2WD model shown)

REPLACEMENT

4   To replace the mount, remove the bolts or nuts attaching the mount to the crossmember and the bolts attaching the mount to the transmission.

5   Raise the transmission slightly with a jack and remove the mount.

6   Installation is the reverse of the removal procedure. Be sure to tighten all nuts and bolts securely.

8   Automatic transmission - removal and installation

REMOVAL

▶ **Refer to illustrations 8.5, 8.8, 8.10 and 8.21**

✲✲ CAUTION:

The transmission and converter must be removed as a single assembly. If you try to leave the torque converter attached to the driveplate, the converter driveplate, pump bushing and oil seal will be damaged. The driveplate is not designed to support the load, so none of the weight of the transmission should be allowed to rest on the plate during removal.

1   Disconnect the negative cable from the battery.

2   Raise the vehicle and support it securely on jackstands. Remove the skid plate and skid plate crossmember, if equipped.

3   If the transmission is being removed for overhaul, remove the oil pan, drain the transmission fluid and reinstall the pan (see Chapter 1).

4   Remove all exhaust components which interfere with transmission removal (see Chapter 4).

5   Remove the engine-to-transmission struts, if equipped (see illustration).

6   Remove the starter motor (see Chapter 5).

7   Remove the crankshaft position sensor (see Chapter 6).

8   On models with 545RFE transmissions, remove the bolts and the engine-to-transmission brace. Remove the torque converter cover (see Illustration).

9   Mark the relationship of the torque converter to the driveplate so they can be installed in the same position.

10   Remove the torque converter-to-driveplate bolts (see illustration). Turn the crankshaft for access to each bolt. Turn the crankshaft in a clockwise direction only (as viewed from the front).

11   Mark the yokes and remove the driveshaft (see Chapter 8). On 4WD models, remove both driveshafts.

12   Unplug all electrical connectors from the transmission.

13   Disconnect the shift cable from the transmission (see Section 3).

14   On all transmissions except the 545RFE, disconnect the Throttle Valve (TV) cable at the transmission (see Section 4).

15   Remove the fill/dipstick tube bracket bolts and pull the tube out of the transmission. Don't lose the tube O-ring (it can be reused if it's still in good shape). On 4WD models, also remove the bolt which attaches the transfer case vent tube to the converter housing.

16   On 4WD models, remove the transfer case (see Chapter 7C).

➡**Note: If you are not planning to replace the transmission, but are removing it in order to gain access to other components such as the torque converter, it isn't really necessary to remove the transfer case. However, the transmission and transfer case**

8.5   Remove the engine-to-transmission brackets - this view shows the right (passenger's) side bracket typical of V6 and 5.2L/5.9L V8 engines

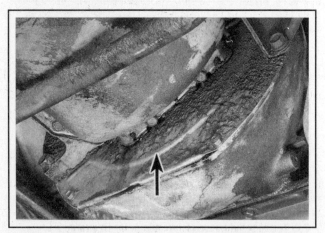

8.8   Unbolt and remove the torque converter cover . . .

8.10   . . . then remove the torque converter-to-driveplate bolts - be sure to mark the relationship of the torque converter to the driveplate for reassembly reference

are awkward and heavy when removed and installed as a single assembly; they're much easier to maneuver off and on as separate units.

If you decide to leave the transfer case attached, disconnect the shift rod from the transfer case shift lever, or remove the shift lever from the transfer case and tie the rod and lever to the chassis (see Chapter 7C).

✳✳ WARNING:

If you decide to leave the transfer case attached to the transmission, be sure to use safety chains to help stabilize the transmission and transfer case assembly and to prevent it from falling off the jack head, which could cause serious damage to the transmission and/or transfer case and serious bodily injury to you.

17 Support the engine with a jack. Use a block of wood under the oil pan to spread the load.

18 Support the transmission with a jack - preferably a jack made for this purpose (available at most tool rental yards). Safety chains will help steady the transmission on the jack.

19 Remove the bolts securing the transmission mount to the transmission and the crossmember, raise the transmission slightly, slide the exhaust hanger arm from the bracket and remove the rear mount. Also remove the crossmember.

20 Remove the bolts securing the transmission to the engine. A long extension and a U-joint socket will greatly simplify this step.

➡Note: The upper bolts are easier to remove after the transmission has been lowered (see the next Step). Also, on some models, you'll have to remove the oil filter (see Chapter 1) before you can remove the lower right (passenger's side) bolt.

21 Lower the engine and transmission slightly and disconnect the transmission cooler lines at the transmission, using a flare-nut wrench (see illustration).

➡Note: You'll need to use a back-up wrench on the transmission cooler line fitting so it doesn't unscrew, causing the line to twist. Plug the ends of the lines to prevent fluid from leaking out after you disconnect them.

22 Clamp a pair of locking pliers onto the lower portion of the transmission case, just in front of the torque converter (but make sure they're not clamped in front of one of the torque converter-to-driveplate bolt locations, or the driveplate will hang up on the pliers). The pliers will prevent the torque converter from falling out while you're removing the transmission. Move the transmission to the rear to disengage it from the engine block dowel pins and make sure the torque converter is detached from the driveplate. Lower the transmission with the jack.

INSTALLATION

23 Prior to installation, make sure the torque converter is securely engaged in the pump. If you've removed the converter, spread transmission fluid on the torque converter rear hub, where the transmission front seal rides. With the front of the transmission facing up, rotate the converter back and forth. It should drop down into the transmission front pump in stages. To make sure the converter is fully engaged, lay a straightedge across the transmission-to-engine mating surface and make sure the converter lugs are at least 1/2-inch below the straightedge. Reinstall the locking pliers to hold the converter in this position.

24 With the transmission secured to the jack, raise it into position. Connect the transmission fluid cooler lines.

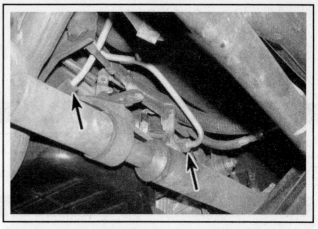

8.21 Transmission fluid cooler line connections (arrows)

25 Turn the torque converter to line up the holes with the holes in the driveplate. The marks on the torque converter and driveplate made in Step 9 must line up.

26 Move the transmission forward carefully until the dowel pins and the torque converter are engaged. Make sure the transmission mates with the engine with no gap. If there's a gap, make sure there are no wires or other objects pinched between the engine and transmission and also make sure the torque converter is completely engaged in the transmission front pump. Try to rotate the converter - if it doesn't rotate easily, it's probably not fully engaged in the pump. If necessary, lower the transmission and install the converter fully.

27 Install the transmission-to-engine bolts and tighten them securely. As you're tightening the bolts, make sure that the engine and transmission mate completely at all points. If not, find out why. Never try to force the engine and transmission together with the bolts or you'll break the transmission case!

28 Install the torque converter-to-driveplate bolts. Tighten them to the torque listed in this Chapter's Specifications.

✳✳ CAUTION:

Using the correct length bolts for bolting the converter to the flywheel is critical. A number of different converters are used on the vehicles covered by this manual. If the bolts are too long, they will damage the converter. If you're planning to use new bolts, make sure you obtain original equipment replacement bolts of the same length.

29 Install the transmission mount and crossmember.

30 Remove the jacks supporting the transmission and the engine.

31 Install the fill/dipstick tube assembly and, if applicable, the vent tube for the transfer case.

32 Install the starter motor (see Chapter 5).

33 Connect the shift cable (see Section 3) and the throttle valve cable (see Section 4).

34 Plug in the transmission electrical connectors.

35 Install the torque converter cover and tighten the bolts securely. On models with the 545RFE transmission, reinstall the engine-to-transmission brace, then tighten the fasteners to the torque listed in this Chapter's Specifications.

36 On 4WD models, install the transfer case, if removed, and the transfer case shift linkage (see Chapter 7C).

37 Install the driveshaft(s) (see Chapter 8).

38 Adjust the shift cable (see Section 3).
39 Adjust the throttle valve cable (see Section 4).
40 Install any exhaust system components that were removed or disconnected (see Chapter 4).

41 Remove the jackstands and lower the vehicle.
42 Fill the transmission with the specified fluid (see Chapter 1), run the engine and check for fluid leaks.

Specifications

General

Transmission fluid type	See Chapter 1

Torque specifications — Ft-lbs (unless otherwise indicated)

Crossmember-to-frame bolts	50
Engine-to-transmission brace	40
Park/Neutral position switch (2000 only)	25
Transmission range sensor-to-bracket bolts	
(2001 and later models)	30 in-lbs
Transmission fluid pan bolts	See Chapter 1
Torque converter-to-driveplate bolts	
2000 models	23
2001 and later models	270 in-lbs

Section

Reference to other Chapters

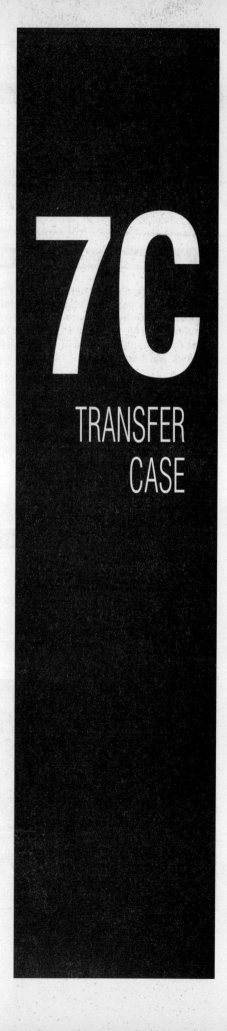

7C

TRANSFER CASE

1 General information

The transfer case is a device that transmits power from the transmission to the front and rear driveshafts. The 2000 models are equipped with either a New Venture (NV) NV231 or NV242 transfer case. The NV231 is a part-time transfer case; the NV242 is a full- and part-time transfer case, and has an internal differential.

The 2001 and later models are equipped with either the NV233 or NV244, the NV233 being a part-time type and the NV244 is a part-time and full-time type. The electronically-controlled transfer cases have an electric shift motor on the case that makes shifts according to input from the shift control switch on the instrument panel.

2 Shift linkage - adjustment (2000 models only)

➡Note: The easiest way to tell what kind of transfer case your vehicle has is to look at the transfer case shift knob. Models equipped with the NV231 transfer case will have three ranges (plus Neutral): 2WD, 4 Hi and 4 Lo. The NV242 case has four ranges (plus Neutral): 2WD, 4 PT (4WD part time), 4 FT (4WD full time), and 4 Lo.

1   If you're working on a vehicle with an NV231 transfer case, place the shift lever in the 4H position. If you're working on a vehicle with an NV242 transfer case, place the shift lever in the 4FT position. Have an assistant hold the lever in the indicated position, or tape it in place.
2   Raise the vehicle and support it securely on jackstands.
3   Loosen the shift rod lock bolt at the trunnion.
4   Check the fit of the shift rod in the trunnion. Make sure it doesn't bind in the trunnion.
5   Verify that the transfer case range lever is in the 4H position (NV231) or the 4FT position (NV242).

➡Note: When the lever is in the 4H position on the NV231 transfer case, it will be positioned in the second detent from the rear (one click from the rearmost position). When the lever is in the 4FT position on the NV242 transfer case, it will be positioned in the third detent from the rear (two clicks from the rearmost position).

6   Tighten the shift rod lock bolt to the torque listed in this Chapter's Specifications.
7   Lower the vehicle and check the operation of the transfer case.

3 Shift lever - removal and installation (2000 models only)

▶ Refer to illustrations 3.1 and 3.2

1   Place the shift lever in the 4L position. Carefully pry the cap out of the shift knob (see illustration).
2   Unscrew the shift knob retaining nut (see illustration).
3   Raise the vehicle and support it securely on jackstands.

4   Loosen the shift rod lock bolt and detach the shift rod from the trunnion.
5   Remove the shift lever mounting bolts and detach the shift lever assembly.
6   Installation is the reverse of removal. Adjust the shift linkage as described in Section 2.

3.1 Pry the cap out of the shift knob . . .

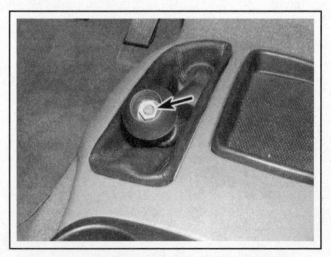

3.2 . . . then unscrew the nut and remove the shift knob

4   Oil seals - replacement

➡**Note: This procedure applies to both the front and rear seals.**

1   Raise the vehicle and support it securely on jackstands.
2   Remove the skid plate, if equipped.
3   Drain the transfer case lubricant (see Chapter 1).

FRONT OUTPUT SHAFT OIL SEAL

▶ **Refer to illustrations 4.7 and 4.10**

4   Remove the front driveshaft (see Chapter 8).
5   Remove the nut from the output shaft yoke or companion flange.
6   Tap the yoke or companion flange off the output shaft with a brass or plastic hammer.
7   Measure how far the seal is recessed in the bore, then carefully pry out the oil seal with a screwdriver or a seal removal tool (see illustration). Make sure you don't scratch or gouge the seal bore.
8   Lubricate the new seal lip with multi-purpose grease.
9   Drive the seal into place with a large socket (see illustration). The outside diameter of the socket should be slightly smaller than the outside diameter of the seal.
10   The remainder of installation is the reverse of removal. Be sure to tighten the flange or yoke mounting nut to the torque listed in this Chapter's Specifications.

EXTENSION HOUSING SEAL

11   This procedure is identical to the extension housing seal replacement procedure for the transmission (see Chapter 7A).

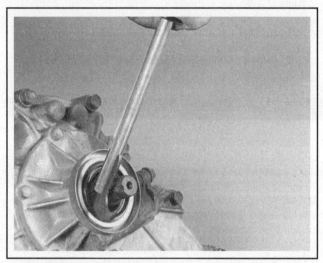

4.7 Use a seal removal tool to pry transfer case seals out (typical)

4.10 The new seal can be driven into place using a seal installer tool or a large socket (typical)

5   Transfer case - removal and installation

▶ **Refer to illustrations 5.5 and 5.12**

REMOVAL

1   Disconnect the cable from the negative terminal of the battery. On 2000 models, place the transfer case shift lever into Neutral. On later models, switch the control switch on the dash to "2WD" for NV233 models, or into "AWD" for NV244 models.
2   Raise the vehicle and support it securely on jackstands.
3   Remove the skid plate, if equipped.
4   Drain the transfer case lubricant (see Chapter 1).
5   Unplug the electrical connector from the range indicator switch (see illustration). On later models, disconnect the electrical connector from the shift motor and mode sensor.
6   Detach the vent hose from the transfer case.
7   On 2000 models, disconnect the shift lever rod from the transfer case shift lever. Press the rod out of the bushing with adjustable pliers.

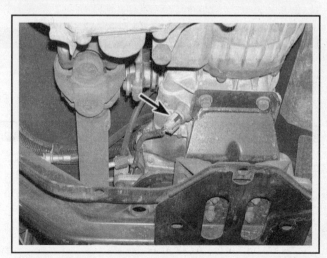

5.5 Unplug the electrical connector from the range indicator switch (arrow)

8   Remove the front and rear driveshafts (see Chapter 8).

9   Support the transmission with a floor jack.

10 Remove the rear crossmember.

11 Support the transfer case with a suitable jack - preferably a transmission jack made for this purpose. Safety chains will help steady the transfer case on the jack.

12 Remove the transfer case-to-transmission nuts.

13 Make a final check that all wires and hoses have been disconnected from the transfer case, then move the transfer case and jack toward the rear of the vehicle until the transfer case is clear of the transmission. Keep the transfer case level as this is done.

14 Once the input shaft is clear, lower the transfer case and remove it from under the vehicle.

INSTALLATION

15 Remove all gasket material from the rear of the transmission and the mating surface of the transfer case. Apply a bead of RTV sealant to the mating surface of the transmission.

16 With the transfer case secured to the jack as on removal, raise it into position behind the transmission and then carefully slide it for-ward, engaging the input shaft with the transmission output shaft. Do not use excessive force to install the transfer case - if the input shaft does not slide into place, readjust the angle so it is level and/or turn the input shaft so the splines engage properly with the transmission.

17 Install the transfer case-to-transmission nuts. Tighten the nuts to the torque listed in this Chapter's Specifications.

18 Detach the safety chains and remove the jack supporting the transfer case.

19 Install the rear crossmember and transmission mount.

20 Remove the jack from under the transmission.

21 Install the driveshafts (see Chapter 8).

22 Reattach the vent hose. Plug in all electrical connectors.

23 On 2000 models, connect the shift rod to the transfer case shift lever.

24 Check the lubricant level in the transfer case and top it off as necessary (see Chapter 1). If the vehicle has a manual transmission, this is also a good time to check the lubricant level for the transmission (see Chapter 1).

25 Install the skid plate, if equipped.

26 Remove the jackstands and lower the vehicle.

27 Connect the negative battery cable.

28 Road test the vehicle for proper operation and check for leakage.

6   Transfer case overhaul - general information

Overhauling a transfer case is a difficult job for the do-it-yourselfer. It involves the disassembly and reassembly of many small parts. Numerous clearances must be precisely measured and, if necessary, changed with select fit spacers and snap-rings. As a result, if transfer case problems arise, it can be removed and installed by a competent do-it-yourselfer, but overhaul should be left to a transmission repair shop. Rebuilt transfer cases may be available - check with your dealer parts department and auto parts stores. At any rate, the time and money involved in an overhaul is almost sure to exceed the cost of a rebuilt unit.

Nevertheless, it's not impossible for an inexperienced mechanic to rebuild a transfer case if the special tools are available and the job is done in a deliberate step-by-step manner so nothing is overlooked.

The tools necessary for an overhaul include internal and external snap-ring pliers, a bearing puller, a slide hammer, a set of pin punches, a dial indicator and possibly a hydraulic press. In addition, a large, sturdy workbench and a vise or transmission stand will be required.

During disassembly of the transfer case, make careful notes of how each piece comes off, where it fits in relation to other pieces and what holds it in place. Note how parts are installed when you remove them; this will make it much easier to get the transfer case back together.

Before taking the transfer case apart for repair, it will help if you have some idea what area of the transfer case is malfunctioning. Certain problems can be closely tied to specific areas in the transfer case, which can make component examination and replacement easier. Refer to the Troubleshooting section at the front of this manual for information regarding possible sources of trouble.

Specifications

General

Transfer case lubricant type	See Chapter 1

Torque specifications	Ft-lbs (unless otherwise indicated)
Shift-rod lock bolt	90 in-lbs
Transfer case-to-transmission nuts	20 to 25
Front output shaft yoke/companion flange nut	90 to 130

Section

Reference to other Chapters

8

CLUTCH AND DRIVELINE

1 General information

The information in this Chapter deals with the components from the rear of the engine to the rear wheels, except for the transmission (and transfer case, if equipped), which is dealt with in the previous Chapter. For the purposes of this Chapter, these components are grouped into three categories: clutch, driveshaft and axles. Separate Sections within this Chapter offer general descriptions and checking procedures for components in each of the three groups.

Since nearly all the procedures covered in this Chapter involve working under the vehicle, make sure it's securely supported on sturdy jackstands or on a hoist where the vehicle can be easily raised and lowered.

2 Clutch - description and check

1 All vehicles with a manual transmission use a single dry plate, diaphragm spring type clutch. The clutch disc has a splined hub which allows it to slide along the splines of the transmission input shaft. The clutch and pressure plate are held in contact by spring pressure exerted by the diaphragm in the pressure plate.

2 The clutch release system is operated by hydraulic pressure. The hydraulic release system consists of the clutch pedal, a master cylinder and fluid reservoir, the hydraulic line, a release (or slave) cylinder which actuates the clutch release lever and the clutch release (or throwout) bearing.

3 When pressure is applied to the clutch pedal to release the clutch, hydraulic pressure is exerted against the outer end of the clutch release lever. As the lever pivots, the shaft fingers push against the release bearing. The bearing pushes against the fingers of the diaphragm spring of the pressure plate assembly, which in turn releases the clutch plate.

4 Terminology can be a problem when discussing the clutch components because common names are in some cases different from those used by the manufacturer. For example, the driven plate is also called the clutch plate or disc, the clutch release bearing is sometimes called a throwout bearing, the release cylinder is sometimes called the operating or slave cylinder.

5 Other than to replace components with obvious damage, some preliminary checks should be performed to diagnose clutch problems.

a) *The first check should be of the fluid level in the clutch master cylinder. If the fluid level is excessively low, add fluid as necessary and inspect the hydraulic system for leaks (fluid level will actually rise as the clutch wears).*

b) *To check "clutch spin down time," run the engine at normal idle speed with the transmission in Neutral (clutch pedal up - engaged). Disengage the clutch (pedal down), wait several seconds and shift the transmission into Reverse. No grinding noise should be heard. A grinding noise would most likely indicate a problem in the pressure plate or the clutch disc.*

c) *To check for complete clutch release, run the engine (with the parking brake applied to prevent movement) and hold the clutch pedal approximately 1/2-inch from the floor. Shift the transmission between First gear and Reverse several times. If the shift is hard or the transmission grinds, component failure is indicated. Check the release cylinder pushrod travel. With the clutch pedal depressed completely, the release cylinder pushrod should extend substantially. If it doesn't, check the fluid level in the clutch master cylinder (see Chapter 1).*

d) *Visually inspect the pivot bushing at the top of the clutch pedal to make sure there is no binding or excessive play.*

e) *Crawl under the vehicle and make sure the clutch release lever is solidly mounted on the ball stud.*

3 Clutch release system - removal and installation

➡**Note: The clutch release system is serviced as a complete unit and has been bled of air at the factory, as individual components or rebuild kits are not available separately. There are no provisions for adjustment of clutch pedal height or freeplay.**

REMOVAL

1 Disconnect the negative cable from the battery.

Master cylinder

2 Remove the clip that attaches the clutch master cylinder pushrod to the clutch pedal.

3 Slide the clutch master cylinder pushrod off the clutch pedal pin.

4 Inspect the condition of the bushing on the pushrod and replace it if it's worn or damaged.

5 Unplug the electrical connector from the clutch pedal position switch.

6 To avoid spillage during removal, verify that the cap on the clutch fluid reservoir is tight.

7 Remove the nuts attaching the clutch fluid reservoir to the engine firewall.

8 Working inside the vehicle, unscrew the clutch master cylinder mounting nuts, then detach the cylinder from the firewall in the engine compartment. Using a piece of wire, secure the cylinder and reservoir to a nearby component while the release cylinder is removed.

Release cylinder

9   Raise the vehicle and support it securely on jackstands.
10 Remove the two release cylinder mounting nuts.
11 Detach the release cylinder from the transmission.
12 If the entire system is being removed or replaced, carefully lift the system from the engine compartment.

Installation

13 Installation is the reverse of removal. If the fluid level is extremely low, fill the clutch master cylinder reservoir with the fluid recommended in the Chapter 1 Specifications Section. Don't add too much, though, because the fluid level actually rises as the clutch components wear.

---

4   Clutch components - removal, inspection and installation

✳✳ WARNING:

Dust produced by clutch wear and deposited on clutch components is hazardous to your health. DO NOT blow it out with compressed air and DO NOT inhale it. DO NOT use gasoline or petroleum-based solvents to remove the dust. Brake system cleaner should be used to flush the dust into a drain pan. After the clutch components are wiped clean with a rag, dispose of the contaminated rags and cleaner in a covered, marked container.

✳✳ CAUTION:

The pickup for the oil pump is very close to the bottom of the oil pan. If the pan is bent or distorted in any way, engine oil starvation could occur.

REMOVAL

♦ **Refer to illustration 4.6**

1   Access to the clutch components is normally accomplished by removing the transmission, leaving the engine in the vehicle. If, of course, the engine is being removed for major overhaul, then check the clutch for wear and replace worn components as necessary. However, the relatively low cost of the clutch components compared to the time and trouble spent gaining access to them warrants their replacement anytime the engine or transmission is removed, unless they are new or in near perfect condition. The following procedures are based on the assumption the engine will stay in place.
2   Unbolt the release cylinder and position it out of the way (see Section 3).
3   Referring to Chapter 7 Part A, remove the transmission from the vehicle. Support the engine while the transmission is out. Preferably, an engine hoist should be used to support it from above. However, if a jack is used underneath the engine, make sure a piece of wood is positioned between the jack and oil pan to spread the load.

4   The clutch fork and release bearing can remain attached to the bellhousing for the time being.
5   To support the clutch disc during removal, install a clutch alignment tool through the clutch disc hub.
6   Carefully inspect the flywheel and pressure plate for indexing marks. The marks are usually an X, an O or a white letter. If they cannot be found, scribe marks yourself so the pressure plate and the flywheel will be in the same alignment during installation (see illustration).
7   Turning each bolt only 1/4-turn at a time, loosen the pressure plate-to-flywheel bolts. Work in a criss-cross pattern until all spring pressure is relieved. Then hold the pressure plate securely and completely remove the bolts, followed by the pressure plate and clutch disc.

INSPECTION

♦ **Refer to illustrations 4.9, 4.11, 4.13a and 4.13b**

8   Ordinarily, when a problem occurs in the clutch, it can be attributed to wear of the clutch driven plate assembly (clutch disc). However, all components should be inspected at this time.
9   Inspect the flywheel for cracks, heat checking, grooves and other obvious defects (see illustration). If the imperfections are slight, a machine shop can machine the surface flat and smooth, which is highly recommended regardless of the surface appearance. Refer to

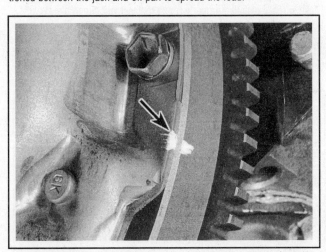

4.6 Be sure to mark the pressure plate and flywheel in order to insure proper alignment during installation (this won't be necessary if a new pressure plate is to be installed)

4.9 Check the flywheel for cracks, hot spots and other obvious defects (slight imperfections can be removed by a machine shop)

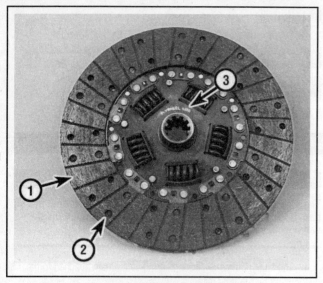

4.11 The clutch plate

1 **Lining** - This will wear down in use
2 **Rivets** - These secure the lining and will damage the flywheel or pressure plate if allowed to contact the surfaces
3 **Markings** - "Flywheel side" or something similar

Chapter 2 for the flywheel removal and installation procedure.

10 Inspect the pilot bearing (see Section 6).

11 Inspect the lining on the clutch disc. There should be at least 1/16-inch of lining above the rivet heads. Check for loose rivets, distortion, cracks, broken springs and other obvious damage (see illustration). As mentioned above, ordinarily the clutch disc is routinely replaced, so if in doubt about the condition, replace it with a new one.

12 The release bearing should also be replaced along with the clutch disc (see Section 5).

13 Check the machined surfaces and the diaphragm spring fingers of the pressure plate (see illustrations). If the surface is grooved or otherwise damaged, replace the pressure plate. Also check for obvious damage, distortion, cracking, etc. Light glazing can be removed with sandpaper or emery cloth. If a new pressure plate is required, new and factory-rebuilt units are available.

4.13b Examine the pressure plate friction surface for score marks, cracks and evidence of overheating

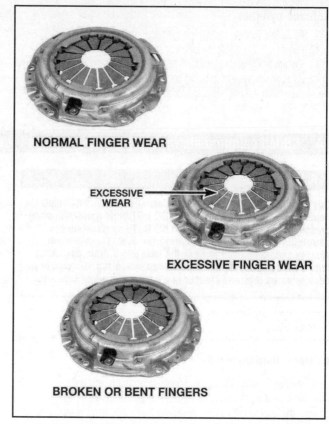

NORMAL FINGER WEAR

EXCESSIVE WEAR

EXCESSIVE FINGER WEAR

BROKEN OR BENT FINGERS

4.13a Replace the pressure plate if excessive wear is noted

INSTALLATION

♦ **Refer to illustration 4.15**

14 Before installation, clean the flywheel and pressure plate machined surfaces with brake system cleaner. It's important that no oil or grease is on these surfaces or the lining of the clutch disc. Handle the parts only with clean hands.

15 Position the clutch disc and pressure plate against the flywheel with the clutch held in place with an alignment tool (see illustration). Make sure it's installed properly (most replacement clutch plates will be marked "flywheel side" or something similar - if not marked, install the clutch disc with the damper springs toward the transmission).

16 Tighten the pressure plate-to-flywheel bolts only finger tight, working around the pressure plate.

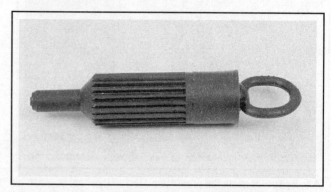

4.15 Center the clutch disc using a clutch alignment tool

17 Center the clutch disc by ensuring the alignment tool extends through the splined hub and into the pilot bearing in the crankshaft. Wiggle the tool up, down or side-to-side as needed to bottom the tool in the pilot bearing. Tighten the pressure plate-to-flywheel bolts a little at a time, working in a criss-cross pattern to prevent distorting the cover. After all of the bolts are snug, tighten them to the torque listed in this Chapter's Specifications. Remove the alignment tool.

18 Using high-temperature grease, lubricate the inner groove of the release bearing. Also place grease on the release lever contact areas and the transmission input shaft bearing retainer.

19 Install the clutch release bearing as described in Section 5.

20 Install the transmission, release cylinder and all components removed previously. Tighten all fasteners to the proper torque specifications.

5 Clutch release bearing - removal, inspection and installation

✳✳ WARNING:

Dust produced by clutch wear and deposited on clutch components is hazardous to your health. DO NOT blow it out with compressed air and DO NOT inhale it. DO NOT use gasoline or petroleum-based solvents to remove the dust. Brake system cleaner should be used to flush the dust into a drain pan. After the clutch components are wiped clean with a rag, dispose of the contaminated rags and cleaner in a covered, marked container.

REMOVAL

▶ **Refer to illustration 5.3**

1 Disconnect the negative cable from the battery.

2 Remove the transmission and bellhousing (see Chapter 7, Part A).

3 Remove the clutch release fork from the pivot stud, then remove the bearing and sleeve from the fork (see illustration).

INSPECTION

▶ **Refer to illustrations 5.4 and 5.5**

4 Hold the center of the bearing and rotate the outer portion while applying pressure (see illustration). If the bearing doesn't turn smoothly or if it's noisy, remove it from the sleeve and replace it with a new one. Wipe the bearing with a clean rag and inspect it for damage, wear and cracks. Don't immerse the bearing in solvent - it's sealed for

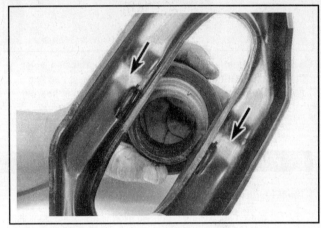

5.3 To detach the release bearing from the release fork, slide the bearing down and disengage the wire retainers from their slots in the fork

life and to do so would ruin it. Also check the release fork for cracks and other damage.

5 Check the wire retainer clip on the release fork to make sure it still fits tightly on the pivot ball; if not, replace it (see illustration).

INSTALLATION

▶ **Refer to illustrations 5.6a and 5.6b**

6 Apply a light coat of high-temperature grease to the release fork

5.4 To check the release bearing, hold the hub in one hand and turn the bearing with the other; if it feels rough or dry, replace it

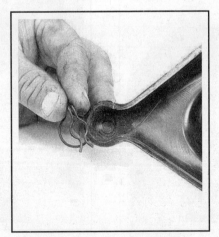

5.5 Remove the wire retainer clip for the pivot ball and check to make sure it still fits tightly; if it's loose, replace it

5.6a Using high-temperature grease, lubricate the inner groove of the release bearing

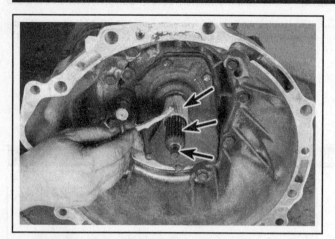

5.6b Lightly lubricate the bearing retainer surface on which the release bearing slides, the input shaft splines and the nose of the input shaft that is supported by the pilot bearing

pivot ball, the contact points of the release fork, the bore of the release bearing, the splines of the transmission input shaft and the release bearing sliding surface on the input shaft bearing retainer (see illustrations).

7   Attach the release bearing and sleeve to the release fork.

8   Apply a light coat of high-temperature grease to the face of the release bearing, where it contacts the pressure plate diaphragm fingers.

9   The remainder of installation is the reverse of the removal procedure.

6   Pilot bearing - inspection and replacement

▶ **Refer to illustrations 6.5 and 6.6**

1   The clutch pilot bearing is pressed into the rear of the crankshaft. It is greased at the factory and does not require additional lubrication. Its primary purpose is to support the front of the transmission input shaft. The pilot bearing should be inspected whenever the clutch components are removed from the engine. Due to its inaccessibility, if you are in doubt as to its condition, replace it with a new one.

➡ **Note: If the engine has been removed from the vehicle, disregard the following steps which do not apply.**

2   Remove the transmission (refer to Chapter 7 Part A).

3   Remove the clutch components (see Section 4).

4   Inspect for any excessive wear, scoring, lack of grease, dryness or obvious damage. If any of these conditions are noted, the bearing should be replaced. A flashlight will be helpful to direct light into the recess.

5   Removal can be accomplished with a slide hammer fitted with a puller attachment (see illustration), which are available at most auto parts stores or equipment rental yards.

6   To install the new bearing, lightly lubricate the outside surface with multi-purpose grease, then drive it into the recess with a hammer and bearing/bushing driver (see illustration). Make sure the bearing seal faces toward the transmission. If you don't have a bearing driver, carefully tap it into place with a hammer and a socket.

✳✳ CAUTION:

Be careful not to let the bearing become cocked in the bore.

7   Install the clutch components, transmission and all other components removed previously, tightening all fasteners properly.

6.5 A small slide-hammer puller is handy for removing the pilot bearing

6.6 If available, use a bearing driver to install the pilot bearing

7   Clutch pedal position switch - check and replacement

CHECK

1   The clutch pedal position switch, which is part of the starter relay circuit, is mounted on the clutch master cylinder pushrod. The switch closes the starter relay circuit only when the clutch pedal is fully depressed.

2   To test the switch, verify that the engine will not crank over when the clutch pedal is in the released position, and that it does crank over with the pedal depressed.

3   If the engine starts without depressing the clutch pedal, replace the switch.

REPLACEMENT

4   The switch is an integral part of the clutch master cylinder pushrod and can't be serviced separately. If the switch must be replaced, so must the clutch hydraulic release system (see Section 3).

8   Driveshaft(s) and universal joints - general information and inspection

GENERAL INFORMATION

▶ **Refer to illustration 8.1a and 8.1b**

1   A driveshaft is a tube, or a pair of tubes, that transmits power between the transmission (or transfer case on 4WD models) and the differential (see illustrations). Universal joints are located at either end of the driveshaft and in the center on two-piece driveshafts.

2   Driveshafts on 2WD models employ a splined yoke at the front, which slips into the extension housing of the transmission. This arrangement allows the driveshaft to slide back-and-forth within the transmission during vehicle operation. An oil seal prevents leakage of fluid at this point and keeps dirt from entering the transmission. If leakage is evident at the front of the driveshaft, replace the oil seal (see Chapter 7, Part B).

3   If a two-piece driveshafts is used, a slip joint is employed on the rear driveshaft section.

4   Two-piece driveshafts also have a center support bearing. The center bearing is a ball-type bearing mounted in a rubber cushion attached to a frame crossmember. The bearing is pre-lubricated and sealed at the factory.

5   On 4WD models, driveshafts have either a splined yoke or companion flange at the transfer case.

6   On all models, the driveshaft assembly requires very little service. The universal joints are lubricated for life and must be replaced if problems develop. The driveshaft must be removed from the vehicle for this procedure.

7   Since the driveshaft is a balanced unit, it's important that no undercoating, mud, etc. be allowed to stay on it. When the vehicle is raised for service it's a good idea to clean the driveshaft and inspect it for any obvious damage. Also, make sure the small weights used to originally balance the driveshaft are in place and securely attached. Whenever the driveshaft is removed it must be reinstalled in the same relative position to preserve the balance.

8   Problems with the driveshaft are usually indicated by a noise or vibration while driving the vehicle. A road test should verify if the problem is the driveshaft or another vehicle component. Refer to the *Troubleshooting* section at the front of this manual. If you suspect trouble, inspect the driveline.

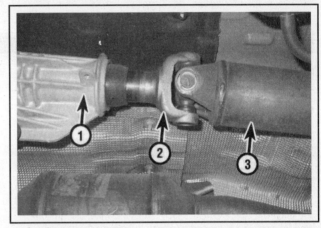

8.1a   Details of the rear driveshaft yoke at the transmission end

1	Transmission extension housing	2	Splined yoke
		3	Rear driveshaft

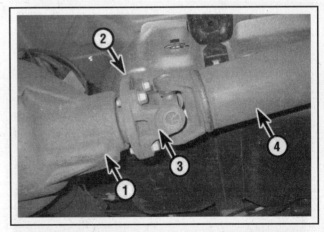

8.1b   Details of the rear driveshaft at the differential pinion

1	Rear axle (differential)	3	Companion yoke
2	Companion flange (pinion flange)	4	Rear driveshaft

INSPECTION

9   Raise the rear of the vehicle and support it securely on jack-stands. Block the front wheels to keep the vehicle from rolling off the stands.

10   Crawl under the vehicle and visually inspect the driveshaft. Look for any dents or cracks in the tubing. If any are found, the driveshaft must be replaced.

11   Check for oil leakage at the front and rear of the driveshaft. Leakage where the driveshaft enters the transmission or transfer case indicates a defective transmission/transfer case seal (see Chapter 7). Leakage where the driveshaft enters the differential indicates a defective pinion seal (see Section 16).

12   While under the vehicle, have an assistant rotate a rear wheel so the driveshaft will rotate. As it does, make sure the universal joints are operating properly without binding, noise or looseness. Listen for any noise from the center bearing (if equipped), indicating it's worn or damaged. Also check the rubber portion of the center bearing for cracking or separation, which will necessitate replacement.

13   The universal joint can also be checked with the driveshaft motionless, by gripping your hands on either side of the joint and attempting to twist the joint. Any movement at all in the joint is a sign of considerable wear. Lifting up on the shaft will also indicate movement in the universal joints.

14   Finally, check the driveshaft mounting bolts at the ends to make sure they're tight.

15   On 4WD models, the above driveshaft checks should be repeated on all driveshafts. In addition, check for grease leakage around the sleeve yoke, indicating failure of the yoke seal.

16   Check for leakage where the driveshafts connect to the transfer case and front differential. Leakage indicates worn oil seals.

17   At the same time, check for looseness in the joints of the front driveaxles. Also check for grease or oil leakage from around the driveaxles by inspecting the rubber boots and both ends of each axle. Oil leakage at the differential junction indicates a defective side oil seal. Grease leakage at the wheel side indicates a defective front hub seal, while leakage at the boots means a damaged rubber boot. For servicing of these components, see the appropriate Sections.

9   Driveshaft(s) - removal and installation

REAR DRIVESHAFT

▶ **Refer to illustrations 9.3 and 9.4**

Removal

1   Disconnect the negative cable from the battery.

2   Raise the vehicle and support it securely on jackstands. Place the transmission in Neutral with the parking brake off.

3   Make reference marks on the driveshaft and the pinion flange in line with each other (see illustration). This is to make sure the driveshaft is reinstalled in the same position to preserve the balance.

4   Remove the bolts securing the driveshaft flange to the differential flange (see illustration).

5   On vehicles with a two-piece driveshaft, unbolt the center support bearing.

6   Lower the rear of the driveshaft. Slide the front of the driveshaft out of the transmission or transfer case.

7   Wrap a plastic bag over the transmission or transfer case housing and hold it in place with a rubber band. This will prevent loss of fluid and protect against contamination while the driveshaft is out.

Installation

8   Remove the plastic bag from the transmission or transfer case and wipe the area clean. Inspect the oil seal carefully. Procedures for replacement of this seal can be found in Chapter 7.

9   Slide the front of the driveshaft into the transmission or transfer case.

10   Raise the rear of the driveshaft into position, checking to be sure the marks are in alignment. If not, turn the rear wheels to match the pinion flange and the driveshaft.

11   Install the bolts and tighten them to the torque listed in this Chapter's Specifications. Lower the vehicle and connect the negative battery cable.

FRONT DRIVESHAFT (4WD MODELS)

Removal

12   Disconnect the cable from the negative terminal of the battery. Raise the vehicle and place it securely on jackstands.

13   Remove the skid plate (if equipped).

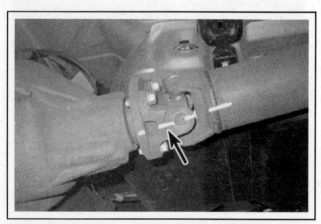

9.3   Mark the relationship of the driveshaft to the pinion flange

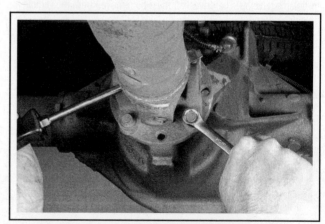

9.4   Insert a screwdriver through the driveshaft yoke to prevent the shaft from turning when you loosen the bolts

14 Mark the relationship of the driveshaft to the front differential flange and the transfer case flange (see illustration 9.3).

15 Remove the bolts from the differential flange and the transfer case flange.

16 Push the rear half of the driveshaft forward far enough to separate it from the transfer case flange, then lower it and separate it at the differential flange.

Installation

17 Attach the front end of the driveshaft to the front differential flange and install the clamps and bolts finger-tight.

18 Extend or compress the driveshaft as necessary, attach the rear end to the transfer case flange, install the clamps and bolts and tighten all bolts to the torque listed in this Chapter's Specifications.

19 Install the skid plate (if equipped).

20 Lower the vehicle and connect the negative battery cable.

10 Driveshaft center support bearing - removal and installation

1 Remove the rear driveshaft (see Section 9).

2 Loosen the boot clamps and slide the boot and clamps to the rear of the driveshaft.

3 Separate the two sections of the driveshaft, then slide the collar and bearing off the front section.

4 Installation is the reverse of removal.

11 Universal joints - replacement

SINGLE-CARDAN U-JOINTS

▶ Refer to illustrations 11.2, 11.4a, 11.4b, 11.6 and 11.8

➡Note: A press or large vise will be required for this procedure. It may be a good idea to take the driveshaft to a repair or machine shop where the universal joints can be replaced for you, normally at a reasonable charge.

1 Remove the driveshaft as outlined in Section 9.

2 Use a pair of pliers to remove the snap-rings from the spider (see illustration).

3 Supporting the driveshaft, place it in position on either an arbor press or on a workbench equipped with a vise.

4 Place a piece of pipe or a large socket with the same inside diameter over one of the bearing caps. Position a socket which is of slightly smaller diameter than the cap on the opposite bearing cap (see illustration) and use the vise or press to force the cap out (inside the pipe or large socket), stopping just before it comes completely out of the yoke. Use the vise or large pliers to work the cap the rest of the way out (see illustration).

5 Transfer the sockets to the other side and press the opposite

11.2 Use pliers to remove or install a snap-ring from the U-joint

bearing cap out in the same manner.

6 Pack the new universal joint bearings with chassis grease. Posi-

11.4a Removing the bearing caps from the yoke with sockets and a large vise

11.4b Pliers can be used to grip the cup to detach it from the yoke after it has been pushed out

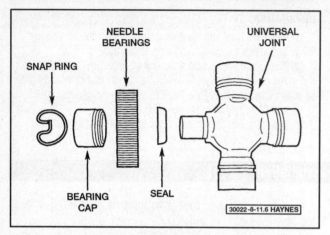

11.6 U-joint repair kit components

SNAP RING
NEEDLE BEARINGS
UNIVERSAL JOINT
BEARING CAP
SEAL

30022-8-11.6 HAYNES

11.8 If the joint feels tight after assembly, strike the yoke with a hammer to relieve the tension in the joint

tion the spider in the yoke and partially install one bearing cap in the yoke (see illustration). If the replacement spider is equipped with a grease fitting, be sure it's offset in the proper direction (toward the driveshaft).

7   Start the spider into the bearing cap and then partially install the other cap. Align the spider and press the bearing caps into position, being careful not to damage the dust seals.

8   Install the snap-rings. If difficulty is encountered in seating the snap-rings, press the bearing cap(s) in a little more. If the joint is stiff after assembly, strike the yoke sharply with a hammer; this will spring the yoke ears slightly and free-up the joint (see illustration).

9   Install the grease fitting (if equipped) and fill the joint with grease. Be careful not to overfill the joint, as this could blow out the grease seals.

10 Install the driveshaft (see Section 9).

DOUBLE-CARDAN U-JOINTS

11 Use the above procedure, but note that it will have to be repeated because the double-Cardan joint is essentially made up of two single Cardan joints.

12 Front and rear axles - description and check

DESCRIPTION

1   The rear axle assembly is a hypoid, semi-floating type (the centerline of the pinion gear is below the centerline of the ring gear). The differential carrier is a casting with a pressed steel cover and the axle tubes are made of steel, pressed and welded into the carrier.

2   An optional locking rear axle is also available. This differential allows for normal operation until one wheel loses traction. The unit utilizes multi-disc clutch packs which lock both axleshafts together, applying equal rotational power to both wheels, when one wheel loses traction.

3   On 4WD models, a fully independent front axle assembly is used. This consists of a differential, two axleshafts (similar to the rear axleshafts) and a pair of driveaxles. Each driveaxle has an inner and outer Constant Velocity (CV) joint. Because the differential - like the transfer case - is offset to the left, the distance between the differential and the right front wheel is greater than the distance from the differential to the left wheel. In order to use two equal-length driveaxles, an extended axleshaft is employed on the right side to make up the difference.

CHECK

4   Many times a problem is suspected in an axle area when, in fact,

it lies elsewhere. For this reason, a thorough check should be performed before assuming an axle problem.

5   The following noises are those commonly associated with axle diagnosis procedures:

a) *Road noise is often mistaken for mechanical faults. Driving the vehicle on different surfaces will show whether the road surface is the cause of the noise. Road noise will remain the same if the vehicle is under power or coasting.*

b) *Tire noise is sometimes mistaken for mechanical problems. Tires which are worn or low on pressure are particularly susceptible to emitting vibrations and noises. Tire noise will remain about the same during varying driving situations, where axle noise will change during coasting, acceleration, etc.*

c) *Engine and transmission noise can be deceiving because it will travel along the driveline. To isolate engine and transmission noises, make a note of the engine speed at which the noise is most pronounced. Stop the vehicle and place the transmission in Neutral and run the engine to the same speed. If the noise is the same, the axle is not at fault.*

6   Overhaul and general repair of the front or rear axle differential is beyond the scope of this manual due to the many special tools and critical measurements required. Thus, the procedures listed here will involve axleshaft removal and installation, axleshaft oil seal replacement, axleshaft bearing replacement and removal of the entire unit for repair or replacement.

13 Axleshaft - removal and installation

◆ **Refer to illustrations 13.4a, 13.4b and 13.5**

➡**Note: This procedure applies to the front and rear axleshafts.**

1   If you're removing a front axleshaft, refer to Section 18 and remove the driveaxle.

2   Loosen the wheel lug nuts, raise the vehicle and support it securely on jackstands. If you're removing a rear axleshaft, remove the wheel and brake drum (refer to Chapter 9).

3   If you're removing the right-front axleshaft, remove the shock absorber (see Chapter 10).

4   Remove the cover from the differential housing and allow the oil to drain into a container (see Chapter 1). If you're removing a rear axle-shaft, remove the lock bolt from the differential pinion shaft (see illustration). Remove the pinion shaft (see illustration).

5   If you're removing a rear axleshaft, push the outer (flanged) end of the axleshaft in and remove the C-lock from the inner end of the shaft (see illustration).

6   If you're removing a front axleshaft, remove the E-clip from the inner end of the shaft.

7   Withdraw the axleshaft, taking care not to damage the oil seal in the end of the axle housing as the splined end of the axleshaft passes through it (unless, of course, you are going to replace the seal anyway).

8   Installation is the reverse of removal. Apply a non-hardening thread-locking compound to the threads of the lock bolt, then tighten the lock bolt to the torque listed in this Chapter's Specifications (rear axle only). When installing the axleshaft, be sure to lubricate the seal lip and the bore in the axle bearing with clean differential lubricant.

9   Clean off all traces of old gasket material from the differential

13.4a Remove the pinion shaft lock bolt . . .

cover and axle housing, then apply a bead of RTV sealant to the cover. Install the cover and bolts, tightening the bolts to the torque listed in this Chapter's Specifications.

10 Refill the axle with the correct quantity and grade of lubricant (see Chapter 1).

11 Tighten the wheel lug nuts to the torque listed in the Chapter 1 Specifications.

13.4b . . . then carefully remove the pinion shaft from the differential case (don't turn the wheels or the case after the shaft has been removed, or the pinion gears may fall out)

13.5 Push the axle flange in, then remove the C-lock from the inner end of the axleshaft

14 Axleshaft oil seal - replacement

▶ **Refer to illustrations 14.2a, 14.2b and 14.3**

1   Remove the axleshaft (see Section 13).

2   Pry the oil seal out of the end of the axle housing with a seal removal tool or the inner end of the axleshaft (see illustrations).

3   Apply high-temperature grease to the oil seal recess and tap the new seal evenly into place with a hammer and seal installation tool (see illustration), large socket or piece of pipe so the lips are facing in and the metal face is visible from the end of the axle housing. When correctly installed, the face of the oil seal should be flush with the end of the axle housing.

4   Install the axleshaft (see Section 13).

14.2a Using a seal removal tool to remove the old seal from the rear axle housing

14.2b You can use the end of the axleshaft to pry out the old seal

14.3 Use a seal driver (shown) or a large socket to install the new seal

15 Axle bearing - replacement

▶ **Refer to illustrations 15.2, 15.3 and 15.4**

1   Remove the axleshaft (see Section 13) and the oil seal (see Section 14).

2   A bearing puller which grips the bearing from behind will be required for this job (see illustration).

3   Attach a slide hammer to the puller and extract the bearing and seal from the axle housing (see illustration).

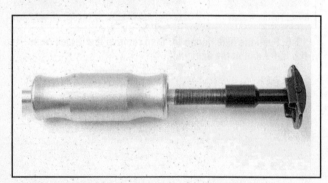

15.2 A typical slide hammer and axleshaft bearing removal attachment

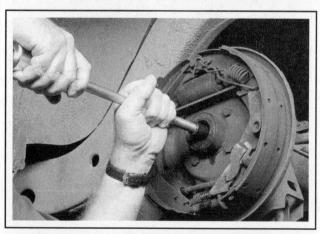

15.3 Using the slide hammer and puller attachment to remove the axleshaft bearing

15.4 Use a special bearing installer tool or a large socket to tap the bearing evenly into the axle housing

4   Clean out the bearing recess and drive in the new bearing with a bearing installer or a large socket positioned against the outer bearing race (see illustration). Make sure the bearing is tapped in to the full depth of the recess and the numbers on the bearing are visible from the outer end of the axle housing.

5   Install a new oil seal (see Section 14), then install the axleshaft (see Section 13).

16 Pinion oil seal - replacement

▶ **Refer to illustrations 16.6, 16.7, 16.10 and 16.11**

1   If you're replacing a rear pinion oil seal, loosen the rear wheel lug nuts. Raise the front (for front differential) or rear (for rear differential) of the vehicle and support it securely on jackstands. Block the opposite set of wheels to keep the vehicle from rolling off the stands.

2   If you're replacing the front pinion seal on a 4WD model, be sure that the transfer case is in 2WD.

3   Disconnect the driveshaft and fasten it out of the way.

4   If you're replacing the front differential pinion seal on a 4WD model, detach the inner CV joints from the axleshafts. Support the driveaxles with lengths of wire so they don't hang by the outer CV joints.

5   If you're replacing a rear pinion oil seal, remove the brake drums (see Chapter 9).

6   Rotate the pinion a few times by hand. Use a beam-type or dial-type inch-pound torque wrench to check the torque required to rotate the pinion (see illustration). Record it for use later.

7   A special tool, available at some auto parts stores, can be used to keep the companion flange from moving while the self-locking pinion nut is loosened. A chain wrench can also be used to immobilize the flange (see illustration).

8   Remove the pinion nut.

9   Withdraw the companion flange. It may be necessary to use a

16.6 Use an inch-pound torque wrench to check the torque necessary to rotate the pinion shaft

two or three-jaw puller engaged behind the flange to draw it off. Do not attempt to pry or hammer behind the flange or hammer on the end of the pinion shaft.

10 Pry out the old seal and discard it (see illustration).

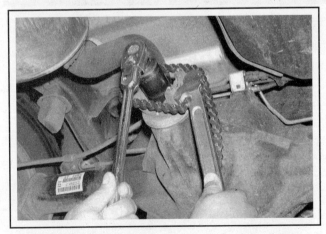

16.7 A chain wrench can be used to hold the pinion flange while the nut is loosened

16.10 Use a seal removal tool or a large screwdriver to remove the pinion seal (be careful not to disturb the pinion while doing this)

16.11 A large socket with a diameter the same as that of the new seal can be used to drive the pinion seal into the differential housing

11 Lubricate the lips of the new seal with high-temperature grease or clean gear oil and tap it evenly into position with a seal installation tool or a large socket (see illustration). Make sure it enters the housing squarely and is tapped in to its full depth.

12 Install the companion flange. If necessary, tighten the pinion nut to draw the flange into place. Do not try to hammer the flange into position.

13 Apply a bead of RTV sealant to the ends of the splines visible in the center of the flange so oil will be sealed in.

14 Install the washer and pinion nut. Tighten the nut to the initial torque listed in this Chapter's Specifications.

15 Measure the torque required to rotate the pinion and tighten the nut in small increments (no more than 5 ft-lbs) until it matches the figure recorded in Step 6. In order to compensate for the drag of the new oil seal, the nut should be tightened more until the rotational torque of the pinion exceeds earlier recording by 5 in-lbs.

16 Reinstall all components removed previously by reversing the removal Steps, tightening all fasteners to their specified torque values.

17 Axle assembly (rear) - removal and installation

REMOVAL

1 Loosen the rear wheel lug nuts, raise the rear of the vehicle and support it securely on jackstands. Block the front wheels to keep the vehicle from rolling off the stands. Remove the rear wheels.

2 Position a jack under the rear axle differential housing.

3 Disconnect the driveshaft from the rear axle companion flange. Fasten the driveshaft out of the way with a piece of wire from the underbody.

4 Disconnect the shock absorbers at their lower mounts (see Chapter 10).

5 Disconnect the vent hose from the fitting on the axle housing and fasten it out of the way.

6 Disconnect the brake hose from the junction block on the axle housing, then plug the hose to prevent fluid leakage.

7 Unplug the electrical connector from the wheel speed sensor at the top of the differential housing.

8 Remove the brake drums.

9 Disconnect the parking brake cables from the actuating levers and the backing plates (see Chapter 9).

10 Disconnect the spring U-bolts. Remove the spacers and spring plates. On all except 4WD Dakota models, unbolt the rear of the springs from the shackles and let them hang down.

11 Lower the jack under the differential, then remove the rear axle assembly from under the vehicle.

INSTALLATION

12 Installation is the reverse of removal. Tighten the U-bolt nuts and the shock absorber fasteners (and the leaf spring-to-shackle bolts/nuts on all except 4WD Dakota models) to the torque values listed in the Chapter 10 Specifications.

13 Bleed the brakes (see Chapter 9).

18 Driveaxle (4WD models) - removal and installation

18.2 Loosen the driveaxle/hub nut while the wheel is still on the ground

▶ **Refer to illustration 18.2**

REMOVAL

1 Pry out the cap from the center of the wheel. Remove the cotter pin, nut lock and spring washer.

2 Loosen the hub nut 1/4-turn (see illustration). Raise the front of the vehicle and support it securely on jackstands.

3   If equipped, disconnect and remove the ABS wheel sensor.

4   Position two large prybars between the axle housing and the end of the inner axle joint and pry to release the axleshaft from the axle housing.

5   Separate the outer end of the axleshaft from the hub by tapping it with a soft-faced hammer. If this doesn't work, the wheel, brake caliper, brake rotor and hub bearing must be removed (see Chapter 9). A two-jaw puller can be used to push the axle out of the hub.

INSTALLATION

6   Installation is the reverse of removal. Be sure to tighten the driveaxle/hub nut to the torque listed in this Chapter's Specifications.

➡Note: Don't fully tighten the driveaxle/hub nut until the vehicle has been lowered to the ground.

If the wheel was removed, tighten the wheel lug nuts to the torque listed in the Chapter 1 Specifications. Install a new cotter pin to secure the hub nut.

19 Driveaxle boot (4WD models) - replacement

➡Note: If the CV joints exhibit wear, indicating the need for an overhaul (usually due to torn boots), explore all options before beginning the job. Complete rebuilt driveaxles may be available on an exchange basis, which eliminates a lot of time and work. Whatever is decided, check on the cost and availability of parts before disassembling the joints.

INNER CV JOINT

▶ Refer to illustrations 19.5a, 19.5b, 19.11, 19.19 and 19.20

Disassembly

1   Remove the driveaxle (see Section 18).

2   Mount the driveaxle in a bench vise with wood blocks to protect it.

✳✳ CAUTION:

Do not overtighten the vise.

3   Remove the boot retaining clamps and slide the inner boot back onto the shaft.

4   Pull the inner CV joint housing off the shaft and tripod.

5   On 2001 and earlier models, expand the inner snap-ring and slide the tripod back toward the center of the driveaxle shaft, then remove the C-clip from the groove at the end of the shaft (see illustrations).

6   On 2002 and later models, use a pair of snap-ring pliers and remove the outer snap-ring.

19.5a Expand the inner snap-ring and slide it back on the splines

7   Remove the tripod and inner snap-ring from the shaft.

8   Remove the boot from the shaft.

9   Clean the housing and the tripod with solvent.

10 Check the tripod components and the housing for excessive wear and/or damage. If any components are worn or damaged, the entire joint must be replaced.

Assembly

11 Wrap the splines of the shaft with tape to prevent damage to the boot, then install the small boot clamp and boot onto the shaft (see illustration).

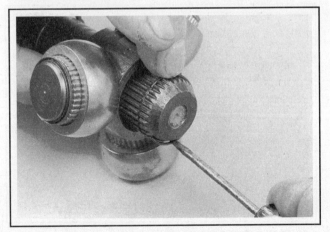

19.5b Remove the C-clip from the end of the shaft

19.11 Wrap the driveshaft splines with electrical tape to prevent damaging the boot as it's slid onto the shaft

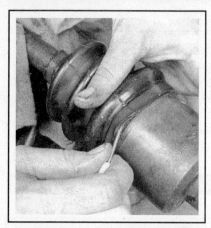

19.19 After positioning the joint mid-way through its travel, equalize the pressure inside the boot by inserting a small, dull screwdriver between the boot and the CV joint housing

19.20 Depending on the type of clamps furnished with the replacement boot, you'll most likely need a special pair of clamp tightening pliers (most auto parts stores carry these)

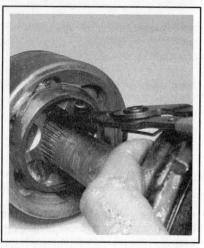

19.23 After expanding the snap-ring, the outer joint assembly can be removed

12 Install the inner snap-ring on the shaft, past the groove in which it seats.

13 Install the tripod onto the end of the shaft, with the chamfered end of the tripod facing the end of the shaft.

14 On 2001 and earlier models, install the outer C-clip into its groove on the shaft, then slide the tripod up against it and seat the inner snap-ring into its groove. On 2002 and later models, tap the tripod onto the shaft with a brass drift until it's seated and install the snap-ring.

15 Apply the grease included with the replacement boot to the tripod and interior of the housing.

➡**Note: If grease was not included with the new boot, obtain some CV joint grease - don't use any other type of grease.**

16 Apply the remainder of the grease into the boot. Position the large-diameter end of the boot over the edge of the housing and seat the lip of the boot into the locating groove at the edge of the housing.

17 Insert the lip of the small-diameter end of the boot into the locating groove on the shaft.

18 Adjust the length of the joint by positioning it mid-way through its travel.

19 Insert a small screwdriver between the boot and the housing to equalize the pressure inside the boot (see illustration)

20 Tighten the boot clamps (see illustration).

OUTER CV JOINT

▶ **Refer to illustrations 19.23, 19.27, 19.28, 19.30, 19.31, 19.33a, 19.33b, 19.34, and 19.40**

Disassembly

21 Mount the axleshaft in a vise with wood blocks to protect it, remove the boot clamps and push the boot back.

22 Wipe the grease from the joint.

23 Using a pair of snap-ring pliers, expand the snap-ring retaining the outer joint to the shaft, then remove the joint (see illustration).

24 Slide the boot off the driveaxle.

25 Clean the axle spline area and inspect for wear, damage, corrosion and broken splines.

26 Clean the outer CV joint bearing assembly with a clean cloth to remove excess grease.

27 Mark the relative position of the bearing cage, inner race and housing (see illustration).

19.27 Mark the bearing cage, inner race and housing relationship after removing the grease

19.28 With the cage and inner race tilted, the balls can be removed one at a time

19.30 Align one of the elongated windows in the cage with one of the lands on the housing (outer race), then rock the cage and inner race out of the housing

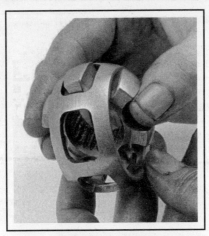

19.31 Tilt the inner race 90-degrees, align the race lands with the windows in the cage, then separate the two components

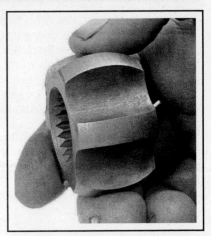

19.33a Check the inner race lands and grooves for pitting and score marks

28 Mount the CV joint in the vise with wood blocks to protect the stub shaft. Push down one side of the cage and remove the ball bearing from the opposite side (see illustration). The balls may have to be pried out.

29 Repeat this procedure until all of the balls are removed. If the joint is tight, tap on the inner race (not the cage) with a hammer and brass drift.

30 Remove the bearing assembly from the housing by tilting it vertically and aligning two opposing cage windows in the area between the ball grooves (see illustration).

31 Turn the inner race 90-degrees to the cage and align one of the spherical lands with an elongated cage window. Raise the land into the window and swivel the inner race out of the cage (see illustration).

32 Clean all of the parts with solvent and dry them with compressed air (if available).

33 Inspect the housing, splines, balls and races for damage, corrosion, wear and cracks. Check the inner race for wear and scoring. If any of the components are not serviceable, the entire CV joint assembly must be replaced with a new one (see illustrations).

34 Check the slinger for damage and distortion. If it is damaged or worn, pry it from the housing (see illustration) and replace it with a new one. A special tool is made for this purpose, but a large section of pipe will work if care is exercised (do not nick or gouge the seal mating surface).

➡**Note: Lubricate the inner diameter of the slinger with grease before installing it.**

Assembly

35 Apply a thin coat of oil to all CV joint components before beginning reassembly.

36 Align the marks and install the inner race in the cage so one of the race lands fits into the elongated window (see illustration 19.31).

37 Rotate the inner race into position in the cage and install the assembly in the CV joint housing, again using the elongated window for clearance (see illustration 19.30).

38 Rotate the inner race into position in the housing. Be sure the large counterbore of the inner race faces out. The marks made during disassembly should face out and be aligned.

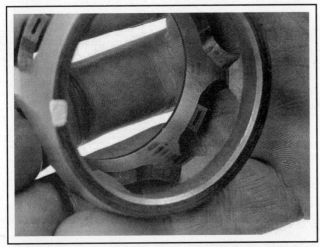

19.33b Check the cage for cracks, pitting and score marks (shiny spots are normal and don't affect operation)

19.34 The slinger can be pried off the housing with a large screwdriver if replacement is necessary

39 Pack the lubricant from the kit into the ball races and grooves.

40 Install the balls into the holes, one at a time, until they are all in position. Fill the joint with grease through the splined hole, then insert a wooden dowel into the splined hole to force the grease into the joint (see illustration).

41 Place the driveaxle in the vise and slide the inner clamp and boot over it (wrap the shaft splines with tape to prevent damaging the boot - see illustration 19.11).

42 Place the CV joint housing in position on the axle, align the splines and push it into place. If necessary, tap it on with a soft-face hammer. Make sure it is seated on the circlip by attempting to pull it from the shaft.

43 Install and tighten the clamps (see illustration 19.20).

19.40 Apply grease through the splined hole, then insert a wooden dowel into the hole and push down - the dowel will force the grease into the joint

20 Axle assembly (front) - removal and installation

1 Raise the front of the vehicle and support it securely on jackstands.

2 If the vehicle is equipped with a skid plate, remove it.

3 Detach the inner CV joints from the axleshafts. Support the driveaxles with lengths of wire so they don't hang by the outer CV joints.

4 Remove the front driveshaft (see Section 9).

5 Disconnect the vent tube from the front differential housing.

6 Place a floor jack under the differential housing, then remove the bolts securing the front axle assembly to the engine-to-transmission brackets and the bolts securing the axle to the engine mounts.

7 Slowly and carefully lower the assembly to the ground.

8 Installation is the reverse of removal. Install all of the mounting bolts before tightening any of them to the torque values listed in this Chapter's Specifications.

Specifications

General

Clutch hydraulic fluid type	See Chapter 1
Clutch disc lining thickness	1/16 inch (above rivet)

Torque specifications   Ft-lbs (unless otherwise indicated)

Clutch

Pressure plate-to-flywheel bolts	
Four-cylinder engine	20
V6 and V8 engines	
5/16-inch diameter bolts	17
3/8-inch diameter bolts	30
Release fork pivot stud	16
Clutch release cylinder mounting nuts	16
Clutch master cylinder mounting nuts	40
Clutch fluid reservoir mounting screws	40 in-lbs
Flywheel bolts	
V6 and 5.2L/5.9L V8	55
4.7L V8	70

Driveshaft

Front driveshaft-to-differential companion flange	80
Front driveshaft-to-transfer case pinion yoke	20
Front driveshaft-to-transfer case companion flange	22
Rear driveshaft-to-differential companion flange	80
Center support bearing bolts	50

Driveaxles (4WD models)

Driveaxle/hub nut	180

Rear axle

Pinion shaft lock bolt	96 in-lbs
Differential cover bolts	30
Pinion nut initial torque	210

Front axle (4WD models)

Differential cover bolts	
2000 models	180 in-lbs
2001 and later models	30
Front axle assembly-to-engine mount fasteners	75
Front axle assembly-to-bracket bolts	40
Pinion nut initial torque	200

Notes

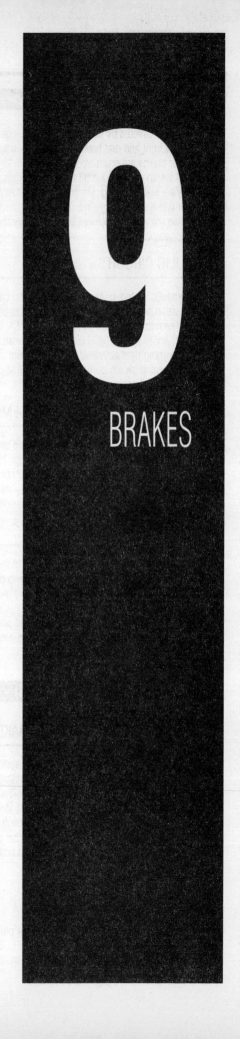

9

BRAKES

Section

Reference to other Chapters

1 General information

The vehicles covered by this manual are equipped with hydraulically operated front and rear brake systems. The front brakes are disc type; the rear brakes are drum type on all models through 2002. Rear disc brakes are an option on 2003 and later models. Both the front and rear brakes are self adjusting. The front disc brakes automatically compensate for pad wear, while the rear drum brakes incorporate an adjustment mechanism which is activated as the brakes are applied when the vehicle is driven in reverse.

HYDRAULIC CIRCUITS

The hydraulic system consists of two separate circuits; if a leak or failure occurs in one hydraulic circuit, the other circuit will remain operative. The master cylinder has separate pistons and reservoirs for each circuit. A visual warning of circuit failure or air in the system is given by a warning light activated by displacement of the piston in the pressure differential switch portion of the combination valve from its normal "in balance" position.

MASTER CYLINDER/RESERVOIR ASSEMBLY

The master cylinder is located under the hood on the driver's side, and can be identified by the fluid reservoir on top. The master cylinder has separate primary and secondary piston assemblies for the front and rear circuits. The master cylinder is not rebuildable; the reservoir and reservoir grommets are the only replaceable components.

COMBINATION VALVE

The combination valve, located on the front of the master cylinder, performs several functions: A metering valve limits pressure to the front brakes until a predetermined front-brake pressure is reached and the rear brakes have been activated.

A fixed-rate proportioning valve meters outlet pressure to the rear brakes once a predetermined rear input pressure has been reached, preventing premature rear-wheel lock-up during heavy braking.

The combination valve is also designed to ensure full pressure to one circuit should the other circuit fail. A brake pressure differential switch continuously compares the front and rear brake pressures. If a failure occurs somewhere in the system, a red warning light on the instrument cluster comes on. Once a failure has occurred, the warning light remains on until the system has been repaired.

POWER BRAKE BOOSTER

A dual-diaphragm, vacuum-operated power brake booster, mounted between the firewall and the master cylinder, utilizes engine manifold vacuum and atmospheric pressure to provide assistance to the hydraulic brake system. The power brake booster is not rebuildable.

PARKING BRAKE SYSTEM

The parking brake system consists of a pedal mounted on the driver's side kick panel, a front cable connecting this pedal to a pair of rear cables, a tensioner for adjusting the cables, and the rear brake shoes.

SERVICE

After completing any operation involving disassembly of any part of the brake system, always test drive the vehicle to check for proper braking performance before resuming normal driving. When testing the brakes, perform the tests on a clean, dry flat surface. Conditions other than these can lead to inaccurate test results.

Test the brakes at various speeds with both light and heavy pedal pressure. The vehicle should stop evenly without pulling to one side or the other. Avoid locking the front brakes on RWAL equipped models because this slides the tires and diminishes braking efficiency and control of the vehicle.

Tires, vehicle load and front-end alignment are factors which also affect braking performance.

2 Anti-lock Brake System (ABS) - general information

REAR WHEEL ANTI-LOCK (RWAL) BRAKE SYSTEM

1   The Rear Wheel Anti-Lock (RWAL) brake system is standard equipment on all models. It is designed to maintain vehicle maneuverability, directional stability and optimum deceleration under severe braking conditions on most road surfaces. RWAL does so by monitoring the rotational speed of the rear wheels and controlling the brake line pressure to the rear wheels while braking. This prevents the rear wheels from locking up prematurely during hard braking, regardless of the payload.

Components

Rear wheel speed sensor

2   A wheel speed sensor mounted in the rear differential housing transmits speed and rate-of-deceleration inputs, in analog form (variable voltage signal), to the electronic control module. The sensor is actuated by an "exciter ring" pressed onto the differential carrier adjacent to the ring gear. The exciter ring is the trigger mechanism: as it rotates, the teeth on the ring interrupt the magnetic field around the sensor pole (the sensor is similar in construction and operation to a pick-up coil in an electronic distributor). The rate of interruption produces a variable voltage signal which is transmitted to the control module.

Controller Anti-lock Brakes (CAB)

▶ **Refer to illustration 2.3**

3   The Controller Anti-lock Brakes (CAB) (see illustration) is mounted in the engine compartment, on the left inner fender panel. The module inputs variable voltage signals from the rear wheel speed sensor, converts this analog signal into digital data, processes this data and controls the isolation and dump valves inside the RWAL valve, which modulates hydraulic line pressure to the rear wheel cylinders to

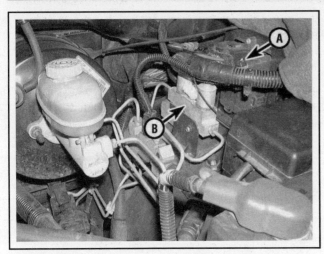

2.3 Location of the RWAL Controller Anti-lock Brake (A) and RWAL valve (B)

2.10 Location of the ABS hydraulic control unit

avoid wheel lock-up. The module also has self-diagnostic capabilities which enable it to continuously monitor the system for malfunctions during vehicle operation.

RWAL valve

4   The RWAL valve (see illustration 2.3) is located next to the master cylinder. It contains a dump valve and an isolation valve. If the module senses that the rate of rear wheel speed deceleration exceeds the rate of vehicle deceleration, it energizes a solenoid which opens the isolation valve to prevent any further increase in driver-induced brake fluid pressure to the rear wheels. If this initial stage fails to prevent rear wheel lock-up, the module momentarily energizes a second solenoid which opens the dump valve to vent a small amount of "isolated" rear brake pressure to the accumulator. The movement of fluid to the accumulator reduces the isolated pressure at the wheel cylinders. This "dump cycle" (or pressure venting) is limited to very short time intervals (milliseconds). The module pulses the dump valve until rear wheel deceleration matches vehicle deceleration. The system switches back to normal operation as soon as the rear wheels are no longer locking up.

Warning light

5   If a problem develops within the system, the ABS warning light will glow on the dashboard. A diagnostic code will also be stored, which, when retrieved by a service technician, will indicate the problem area or component.

Diagnosis and repair

6   If the ABS warning light on the dashboard comes on and stays on, make sure the parking brake is not applied and there's no problem with the standard brake hydraulic system. If neither of these is the cause, the RWAL system is probably malfunctioning. Check the following:

 a) *Make sure the brake shoes, pads, calipers and wheel cylinders are in good condition.*
 b) *Check the electrical connectors at the control module assembly.*
 c) *Check the fuses.*
 d) *Follow the wiring harness to the speed sensor and valve and make sure all connections are secure and the wiring isn't damaged.*

7   If the above preliminary checks don't identify the problem, have

the system diagnosed by a dealer service department or other qualified repair shop. A special breakout box or DRB scan tool is required to retrieve any stored trouble codes.

ANTI-LOCK BRAKE SYSTEM (ABS)

Description

8   The four-wheel Anti-lock Brake System (ABS) prevents wheel lock-up under heavy braking conditions on virtually any road surface. Preventing the wheels from locking up maintains vehicle maneuverability, preserves directional stability, and allows optimal deceleration. It does this by monitoring the rotation speed of the wheels and controlling the brake line pressure to the calipers/wheel cylinders at each wheel during braking.

Components

Wheel speed sensors

9   A wheel speed sensor is mounted at each front wheel. A sensor ring, or "tone wheel," is located on the hub/bearing assembly (2WD models) or in the hub bearing housing (4WD models). As the tone wheel turns, its teeth interrupt the magnetic field around the speed sensor (which is similar to a pick-up coil in an electronic distributor), producing a voltage signal that varies in proportion to the speed of rotation of each wheel. The analog outputs from the two front wheel speed sensors are transmitted to the ABS control module. A third wheel speed sensor, for the rear wheels, is located in the rear differential housing. It's identical in function and operation to the rear wheel speed sensor previously described for RWAL systems.

Controller Anti-lock Brake (CAB)

▶ **Refer to illustration 2.10**

10 The Controller Anti-lock Brake (CAB) (see illustration), which is located on the hydraulic control unit on the left inner fender panel in the engine compartment, monitors wheel speeds and controls the hydraulic control unit to prevent wheel lockup. The module receives three analog voltage signals (one from each front wheel speed sensor and one from the rear wheel speed sensor), converts these signals into digital data, processes this data and adjusts the solenoids inside the hydraulic control unit accordingly.

Hydraulic Control Unit (HCU)

11 The Hydraulic Control Unit (HCU) (see illustration 2.10) is located in the engine compartment, on the left inner fender panel. The HCU contains the anti-lock valves and the pump/motor assembly. The anti-lock valves consist of a solenoid valve body with individual valves to control pressure to each front brake, and one valve to control pressure to the rear brakes.

Diagnosis and repair

12 The ABS system has self-diagnostic capabilities. Each time the ignition key is turned to On, the system runs a self-test. If it finds a problem, the ABS warning lights come on and remain on. If there's no problem with the system, the lights go out after a second or two.

13 If the ABS warning lights come on, and stay on during vehicle operation, there is a problem in the ABS system. Two things now happen: The controller stores a diagnostic trouble code (which can be dis-

played with a DRB scan tool) and the ABS system is shut down. Once the ABS system is disabled, it will remain disabled until the problem is fixed and the trouble code is erased. However, the regular brake system will continue to function normally.

14 Although a DRB scan tool (a special electronic tester) is necessary to properly diagnose the system, you can make a few preliminary checks before taking the vehicle to a repair shop:

 a) *Make sure the brake calipers and wheel cylinders are in good condition.*
 b) *Check the electrical connector at the controller.*
 c) *Check the fuses.*
 d) *Follow the wiring harness to the speed sensors and brake light switch and make sure all connections are secure and the wiring isn't damaged.*

15 If the above preliminary checks don't rectify the problem, the vehicle should be diagnosed by a dealer service department or other qualified repair shop.

3   Disc brake pads - replacement

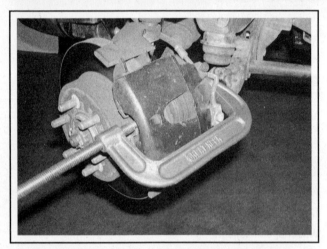

3.5 Using a large C-clamp, push the piston back into the caliper bore - note that one end of the clamp is on the flat area on the backside of the caliper and the other end (screw end) is pressing against the outer brake pad

3.6a Before removing the caliper, wash off all traces of brake dust with brake system cleaner

▶ Refer to illustrations 3.5 and 3.6a through 3.6o

✳ WARNING:

Disc brake pads must be replaced on both front wheels at the same time - never replace the pads on only one wheel. Also, the dust created by the brake system is harmful to your health. Never blow it out with compressed air and don't inhale any of it. An approved filtering mask should be worn when working on the brakes. Do not, under any circumstances, use petroleum-based solvents to clean brake parts. Use brake system cleaner only!

2002 AND EARLIER MODELS

1   Remove the cap from the brake fluid reservoir.

2   Loosen the wheel lug nuts, raise the front of the vehicle and support it securely on jackstands.

3   Remove the front wheels. Work on one brake assembly at a time, using the assembled brake for reference if necessary.

4   Inspect the brake disc carefully as outlined in Section 5. If machining is necessary, follow the information in that Section to

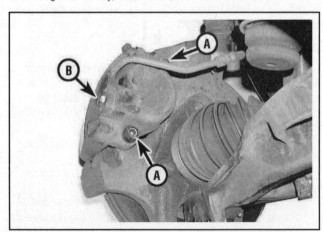

3.6b To remove the caliper, remove these two mounting pins (A); don't remove the brake hose-to-caliper banjo bolt (B) unless you are replacing the caliper

3.6c Remove the caliper from the steering knuckle

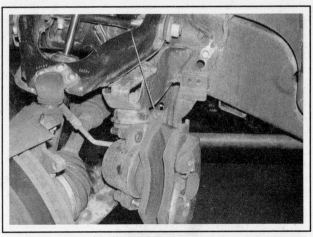

3.6d Whenever you have to let go of the caliper, hang it with a piece of wire - DON'T let it hang by the brake hose!

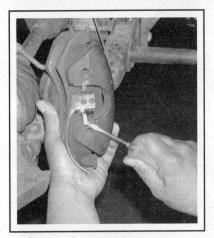

3.6e Pry the ends of the pad retaining spring away from the caliper and remove the outer pad

3.6f Pull the inner pad retaining clips out of the piston

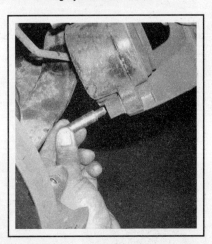

3.6g Pull out both mounting pins and inspect them for corrosion and wear; if either pin is damaged, replace it

remove the disc, at which time the pads can be removed from the caliper as well.

5 Push the piston back into the bore to provide room for the new brake pads. A C-clamp can be used to accomplish this (see illustration). As the piston is depressed to the bottom of the caliper bore, the

fluid in the master cylinder will rise. Make sure it doesn't overflow. If necessary, siphon off some of the fluid.

6 Follow the accompanying illustrations, beginning with 3.6a, for the actual pad replacement procedure. Be sure to stay in order and read the caption under each illustration.

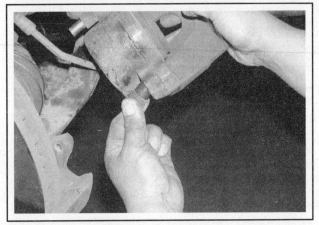

3.6h If either rubber dust boot for the pins is cracked, torn or otherwise deteriorated, replace it

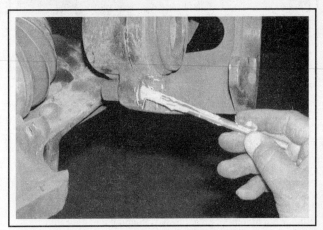

3.6i Coat the bushings with high-temperature grease

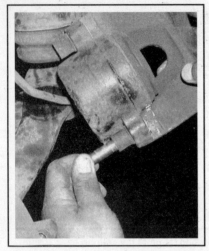

3.6j Install the mounting pins

3.6k Depress the caliper piston all the way into the caliper to make room for the new, thicker pads

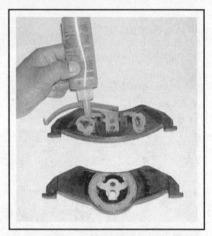

3.6l Apply a film of disc brake anti-squeal compound to the backs of the new pads (follow the directions on the product)

3.6m Install the new inner brake pad by popping the retaining clips into the piston; make sure the clips are fully engaged (the pad should be seated flat against the piston)

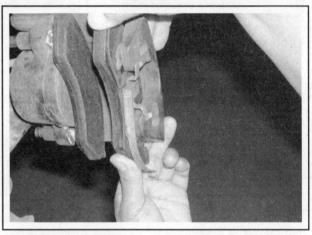

3.6n Install the new outer brake pad in the caliper; make sure the pad is properly seated and the ends of the retaining spring fully engaged

7   When reinstalling the caliper, be sure to tighten the mounting pins to the torque listed in this Chapter's Specifications. After the job has been completed, firmly depress the brake pedal a few times to bring the pads into contact with the disc.

8   Check for fluid leakage and make sure the brakes operate normally before driving in traffic.

2003 AND LATER MODELS

→Note: This procedure applies to both front and rear disc brakes.

9   Remove the cap from the brake fluid reservoir.

10 Loosen the wheel lug nuts, raise the vehicle and support it securely on jackstands.

11 Remove the front or rear wheels. Work on one brake assembly at a time, using the assembled brake for reference if necessary.

12 Inspect the brake disc carefully as outlined in Section 5. If machining is necessary, follow the information in that Section to remove the disc, at which time the pads can be removed from the caliper as well.

3.6o Install the caliper and pads over the disc, starting with the lower end and making sure the long spring is positioned under the mounting boss (arrow). Swing the caliper into place and install the mounting pins, tightening them to the torque listed in this Chapter's Specifications

13 Before removing the caliper, wash off all traces of brake dust with brake system cleaner.

14 Push the piston back into the bore to provide room for the new brake pads. A C-clamp can be used to accomplish this. As the piston is depressed to the bottom of the caliper bore, the fluid in the master cylinder will rise. Make sure it doesn't overflow. If necessary, siphon off some of the fluid.

15 Remove the caliper mounting pins and remove the caliper. Hang the caliper with a coat hanger, don't let it hang by the brake hose.

16 Remove the inner brake pad, then remove the outer brake pad.

17 Remove and inspect the upper and lower anti-rattle springs,

18 Lubricate the anti-rattle springs with brake grease, then install them into their respective grooves in the caliper mounting bracket.

→Note: The anti-rattle springs are not interchangeable.

19 Install the inner pad and the outer pad onto the caliper mounting bracket.

20 Inspect the caliper for brake fluid leaks and torn piston boots, replacing them if necessary. Place the bottom end of the caliper on the brake disc and under the caliper mounting bracket. Push the caliper down onto the bracket and seat the caliper.

21 Before installing the caliper mounting pins, clean them and check them for corrosion and damage. If they're significantly corroded or damaged, replace them. Be sure to tighten the caliper mounting pins to the torque listed in this Chapter's Specifications.

22 Install the brake pads on the opposite wheel, then install the wheels and lower the vehicle. Tighten the lug nuts to the torque listed in the Chapter 1 Specifications.

23 If necessary, add brake fluid to the reservoir until it's full (see Chapter 1). Pump the brakes several times to seat the pads against the disc, then check the fluid level again.

24 Check the operation of the brakes before driving the vehicle in traffic. Try to avoid heavy brake applications until the brakes have been applied lightly several times to seat the pads.

4   Disc brake caliper - removal and installation

☀ WARNING:

Dust created by the brake system is harmful to your health. Never blow it out with compressed air and don't inhale any of it. An approved filtering mask should be worn when working on the brakes. Do not, under any circumstances, use petroleum-based solvents to clean brake parts. Use brake system cleaner only!

→Note 1: Always replace the calipers in pairs - never replace just one of them.

→Note 2: Rear disc brakes became an option on 2003 models. The caliper procedures described here are typical of both front and rear calipers.

REMOVAL

1   Loosen the wheel lug nuts, raise the front of the vehicle and support it securely on jackstands. Remove the front wheels.

2   Using a C-clamp, push the piston back into the caliper bore (see illustration 3.5).

3   To disconnect the brake hose from the caliper, remove the brake hose-to-caliper banjo bolt (see illustration 3.6b).

→Note: Do not disconnect the brake hose from the caliper if you are only removing the caliper. Have a rag handy to catch spilled fluid and immediately plug the hose fitting to prevent fluid loss and contamination.

4   Unscrew the two caliper mounting pins and detach the caliper (see Section 3). If you're just removing the caliper for access to other components, hang it with a piece of wire - DON'T let it hang by the brake hose.

INSTALLATION

5   Inspect the caliper mounting pins for wear or corrosion, replacing them if necessary.

6   Clean, inspect and lubricate the caliper mounting pin and bushings.

7   Install the caliper (see Section 3), tightening the mounting pins to the torque listed in this Chapter's Specifications.

8   Install the brake hose and banjo bolt, using new sealing washers. Tighten the bolt to the torque listed in this Chapter's Specifications.

9   Bleed the brakes (see Section 11).

10 Install the wheels and lower the vehicle. Tighten the wheel lug nuts to the torque listed in the Chapter 1 Specifications.

11 After the job has been completed, firmly depress the brake pedal a few times to bring the pads into contact with the disc.

12 Check brake operation before driving the vehicle in traffic.

5   Brake disc - inspection, removal and installation

→Note: This procedure applies to both front and rear brake discs.

INSPECTION

▶ Refer to illustrations 5.3, 5.4a, 5.4b, 5.5a and 5.5b

1   Loosen the wheel lug nuts, raise the vehicle and support it securely on jackstands. Remove the wheel and reinstall the lug nuts to hold the disc in place (washers may be required). If the rear brake disc is being worked on, release the parking brake.

2   Remove the brake caliper and pads (see Section 3) but don't disconnect the brake hose from the caliper, or you'll have to bleed the brakes when everything is reassembled. After removing the caliper bolts, suspend the caliper out of the way with a piece of wire (see illustration 3.6d).

5.3 The brake pads on this vehicle were obviously neglected, as they wore down completely and cut deep grooves into the disc - wear this severe means the disc must be replaced

5.4a Use a dial indicator to check disc runout - if the reading exceeds the specified allowable runout limit, the disc will have to be machined or replaced

3   Visually inspect the disc surface for score marks and other damage. Light scratches and shallow grooves are normal after use and may not always be detrimental to brake operation, but deep scoring requires disc removal and refinishing by an automotive machine shop. Be sure to check both sides of the disc (see illustration). If pulsating has been noticed during application of the brakes, suspect disc runout.

4   To check disc runout, place a dial indicator at a point about 1/2-inch from the outer edge of the disc (see illustration). Set the indicator to zero and turn the disc. The indicator reading should not exceed the specified allowable runout limit. If it does, the disc should be refinished by an automotive machine shop.

➡Note: The discs should be resurfaced regardless of the dial indicator reading, as this will impart a smooth finish and ensure a perfectly flat surface, eliminating any brake pedal pulsation or other undesirable symptoms related to questionable discs. At the very least, if you elect not to have the discs resurfaced, remove the glaze from the surface with emery cloth using a swirling motion (see illustration).

5   It's absolutely critical that the disc not be machined to a thickness under the specified minimum allowable thickness. The minimum thickness is cast into the inside of the disc (see illustration). The disc thickness can be checked with a micrometer (see illustration).

REMOVAL

▶ **Refer to illustration 5.6**

6   Remove the caliper mounting bracket, on models so equipped. Remove the lug nuts which were put on to hold the disc in place and remove the disc from the hub. If the disc is held in place by pressed metal washers, cut them off with diagonal cutters (see illustration) and discard them.

INSTALLATION

7   Place the disc in position over the wheel studs. Install the

5.4b Using a swirling motion, remove the glaze from the disc surface with sandpaper or emery cloth

5.5a The minimum thickness is cast into the inside of the disc

5.5b Use a micrometer to measure disc thickness at several points

mounting bracket (if equipped), tightening the bolts to the torque listed in this Chapter's Specifications.

8   Install the brake pads and caliper (see Section 3). Tighten the caliper mounting pins to the torque listed in this Chapter's Specifications.

9   Install the wheel, lower the vehicle and tighten the lug nuts. Tighten the lug nuts to the torque listed in the Chapter 1 Specifications.

10 Pump the brake pedal a few times to bring the brake pads into contact with the disc. Bleeding won't be necessary unless the brake hose was disconnected from the caliper. Check the operation of the brakes carefully before driving the vehicle.

5.6 If the disc is retained by pressed-metal washers, cut them off and discard them (there is no need to reinstall them)

6   Drum brake shoes - replacement

▶ Refer to illustrations 6.3, 6.4a through 6.4ff and 6.5

✳ WARNING:

Drum brake shoes must be replaced on both wheels at the same time - never replace the shoes on only one wheel. Also, the dust created by the brake system is harmful to your health. Never blow it out with compressed air and don't inhale any of it. An approved filtering mask should be worn when working on the brakes. Do not, under any circumstances, use petroleum-based solvents to clean brake parts. Use brake system cleaner only!

✳ CAUTION:

Whenever the brake shoes are replaced, the retracting and hold-down springs should also be replaced. Due to the continuous heating/cooling cycle that the springs are subjected to, they lose their tension over a period of time and may allow the shoes to drag on the drum and wear at a much faster rate than normal.

1   Loosen the wheel lug nuts, raise the rear of the vehicle and support it securely on jackstands. Block the front wheels to keep the vehicle from rolling.

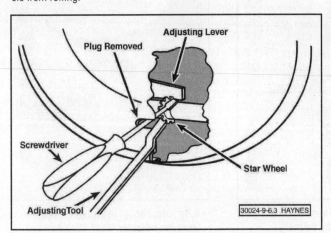

6.3 Use a thin screwdriver to push the lever away, then use an adjusting tool or another screwdriver to back off the star wheel

2   Release the parking brake.
3   Remove the wheel and brake drum.

➡Note: If the brake drum cannot be easily pulled off the axle, make sure that the parking brake is completely released, then apply some penetrating oil at the hub-to-drum joint. Allow the oil to soak in and try to pull the drum off. If the drum still cannot be pulled off, the brake shoes will have to be retracted.

This is accomplished by first removing the plug from the backing plate. With the plug removed, push the lever off the adjusting star wheel with one narrow screwdriver while turning the adjusting wheel with another narrow screwdriver (or a brake adjusting tool), moving the shoes away from the drum (see illustration). The drum should now come off.

4   Follow the accompanying illustrations (6.4a through 6.ff) for the replacement of the brake shoes. Be sure to stay in order and read the caption under each illustration.

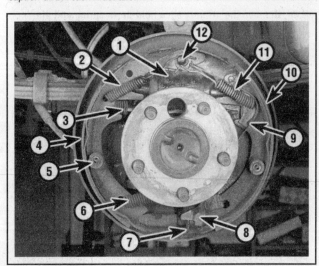

6.4a Rear drum brake components

1	Wheel cylinder	7	Adjuster wheel
2	Return spring	8	Adjuster lever
3	Parking brake strut and spring	9	Adjuster cable and guide
4	Primary shoe	10	Secondary shoe
5	Hold-down spring and pin	11	Return spring
6	Shoe spring	12	Anchor pin

6.4b Before removing any internal drum brake components, wash them off with brake cleaner and allow them to dry - position a drain pan under the brake to catch the residue - DO NOT USE COMPRESSED AIR TO BLOW THE BRAKE DUST FROM THE PARTS!

6.4c Remove the primary shoe return spring from the anchor plate pin

➡Note: All four rear brake shoes must be replaced at the same time, but to avoid mixing up parts, work on only one brake assembly at a time.

5   Before reinstalling the drum it should be checked for cracks, score marks, deep scratches and hard spots, which will appear as small discolored areas. If the hard spots cannot be removed with fine emery cloth or if any of the other conditions listed above exist, the drum must be taken to an automotive machine shop to have it turned.

➡Note: Professionals recommend resurfacing the drums whenever a brake job is done. Resurfacing will eliminate the possibility of out-of-round drums. If the drums are worn so much that they can't be resurfaced without exceeding the maximum allowable diameter (stamped into the drum) (see illustration), then new ones will be required. At the very least, if you elect not to have the drums resurfaced, remove the glazing from the surface with medium-grit emery cloth using a swirling motion.

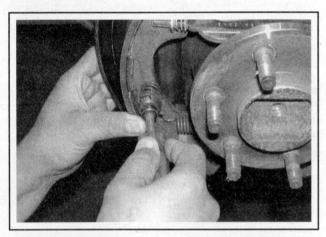

6.4d Remove the primary shoe hold-down spring and pin (push the retainer in and turn it 90-degrees to release it from the pin)

6.4e Spread the bottoms of the shoes apart and remove the adjuster screw assembly

6.4f Disconnect the shoe-to-shoe spring and remove the primary brake shoe

6.4g Disconnect the adjuster cable from the adjuster lever, then remove the adjuster lever and lever spring

6.4h Remove the parking brake strut and spring

6.4i Remove the secondary shoe return spring and cable guide . . .

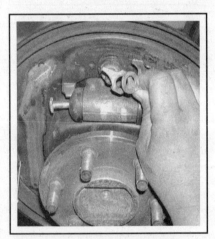

6.4j . . . followed by the adjuster cable and anchor plate

6.4k Remove the secondary shoe hold down spring and retainer

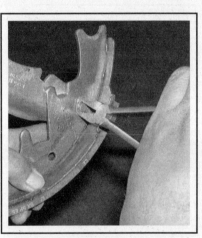

6.4l Remove the clip from the pin on the parking brake lever and detach the lever from the old shoe . . .

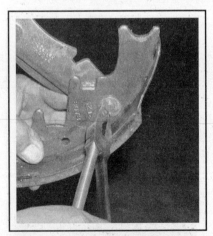

6.4m . . . transfer the parking brake lever to the new secondary shoe and secure it with a new clip

6.4n Lubricate the brake shoe contact areas (arrows) with high-temperature grease. Now is a good time to check the wheel cylinder for fluid leakage

6.4o Position the secondary shoe on the backing plate, making sure the wheel cylinder pushrod seats properly in its notch, insert the hold-down pin through the backing plate and brake shoe . . .

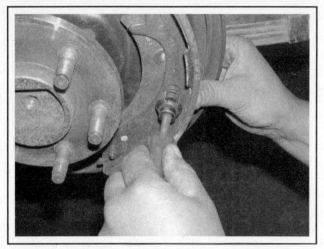

6.4p ... then install the hold-down spring and retainer

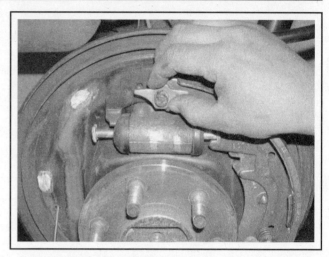

6.4q Install the anchor plate

6.4r Place the end of the adjuster cable over the anchor pin ...

6.4s ... install the cable guide ...

6.4t ... insert the shoe return spring through the guide and stretch the spring over the anchor pin

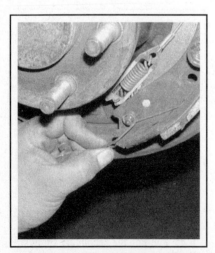

6.4u Install the adjuster lever spring ...

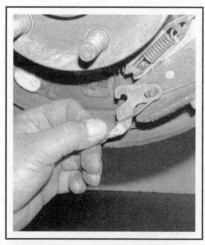

6.4v ... followed by the adjuster lever ...

6.4w ... then connect the adjuster cable to the adjuster lever

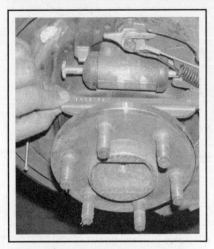

6.4x Install the parking brake strut, making sure it properly engages the secondary shoe and parking brake lever

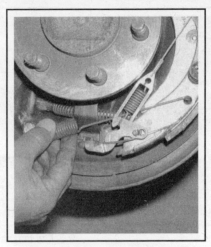

6.4y Connect the shoe-to-shoe spring to the secondary shoe

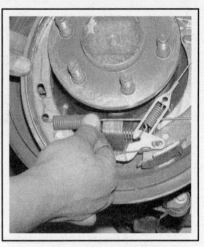

6.4z Place the primary shoe in position and connect the shoe-to-shoe spring to it

6.4aa Make sure the parking brake strut and wheel cylinder pushrod properly engage the primary shoe

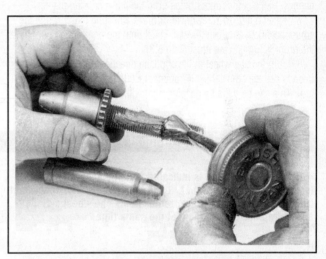

6.4bb Disassemble the adjuster screw, clean it, then lubricate the threads and button with high-temperature grease

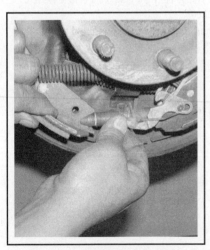

6.4cc Spread the shoes apart and install the adjuster screw

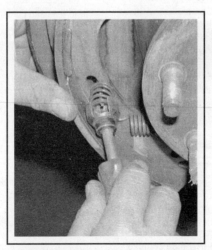

6.4dd Secure the primary shoe with the hold-down spring and retainer

6.4ee Install the return spring into the hole in the primary shoe . . .

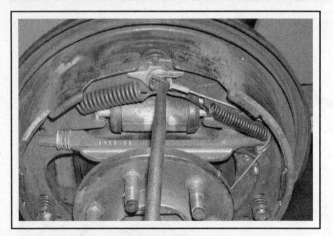

6.4ff . . . and stretch it over the anchor pin

6.5 The maximum allowable inside diameter is cast into the drum

6   Once the new shoes are in place, install the drums on the axle flanges. Remove the rubber plugs from the brake backing plates.

7   Insert a narrow screwdriver or brake adjusting tool through the adjustment hole and turn the star wheel until the brakes drag slightly as the drum is turned (see illustration 6.3).

8   Turn the star wheel in the opposite direction until the drum turns freely. Keep the adjuster lever from contacting the star wheel or it won't turn. This can be done by pushing on it with a narrow screwdriver.

9   Repeat the adjustment on the opposite wheel and install the backing plate plugs.

10 Mount the wheel, install the lug nuts, then lower the vehicle. Tighten the lug nuts to the torque listed in the Chapter 1 Specifications.

11 Make a number of forward and reverse stops to allow the brakes to further adjust themselves.

12 Check brake operation before driving the vehicle in traffic.

7   Wheel cylinder - removal and installation

➡Note: If replacement is indicated (usually because of fluid leakage or sticky operation), it is recommended that new wheel cylinders be installed. Never replace only one wheel cylinder - always replace both of them at the same time.

REMOVAL

▶ Refer to illustration 7.4

1   Raise the rear of the vehicle and support it securely on jack-

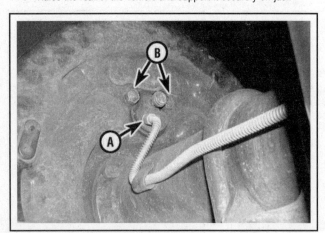

7.4 Completely loosen the brake line fitting (A), then remove the two wheel cylinder mounting bolts (B)

stands. Block the front wheels to keep the vehicle from rolling.

2   Remove the brake shoes (see Section 6).

3   Remove all dirt and foreign material from around the wheel cylinder.

4   Completely loosen the brake line fitting (see illustration). Don't pull the brake line away from the wheel cylinder, as the line might become kinked.

5   Remove the wheel cylinder mounting bolts (see illustration 7.4).

6   Detach the wheel cylinder from the brake backing plate and place it on a clean workbench. Immediately plug the brake line to prevent fluid loss and contamination.

➡Note: If the brake shoe linings are contaminated with brake fluid, install new brake shoes.

INSTALLATION

7   Place the wheel cylinder in position and, while it's still loose, connect the brake line to it being careful not to cross-thread the fitting.

8   Install the bolts and tighten them to the torque listed in this Chapter's Specifications. Tighten the brake line fitting securely. Install the brake shoes.

9   Bleed the brakes (see Section 11).

10 Check brake operation before driving the vehicle in traffic.

8 Combination valve - removal and installation

✳✳ WARNING:

This is a procedure that should not be attempted on a model equipped with four-wheel ABS. To properly bleed the air from the hydraulic control unit on models with four-wheel ABS, the manufacturer states that the system must be bled using the conventional method (as described in Section 11), then with the use of a DRB scan tool to purge any air from the HCU. After that has been done the system must be bled using the conventional method once again. This tool is very expensive and generally available only to dealership service departments. If your vehicle is equipped with four-wheel ABS and develops a problem with the combination valve, have it towed to a dealer service department or other repair shop equipped with the necessary tools for bleeding the system.

CHECK

8.1 Location of the combination valve on a model with RWAL brakes

Metering valve

♦ **Refer to illustration 8.1**

1 To check the metering valve, have an assistant apply and release the brake pedal while you watch the valve stem (the small black button on the front of the combination valve) (see illustration). If the valve is operating correctly, the stem will extend slightly when the brakes are applied and retract when the brakes are released. If the valve does not protrude slightly each time the brake pedal is applied, replace the combination valve.

Pressure differential switch

2 Raise the vehicle and place it securely on jackstands.
3 Connect a bleeder hose to a rear wheel cylinder and immerse the other end of the hose in a container partially filled with brake fluid. Loosen the bleeder screw slightly.
4 To check the pressure differential switch, have your helper sit inside the vehicle, apply the brake pedal, and watch the red brake warning light.
5 If the warning light comes on, the switch is operating correctly. Bleed the rear wheel cylinder to ensure no air was let into the system.
6 If the warning light doesn't come on, check the circuit fuse, the bulb and the wiring (see Chapter 12). (One quick way to eliminate the

fuse and bulb as the problem is to apply the parking brake; if the parking brake switch turns on the light, the fuse and bulb are okay). Repair the circuit or replace parts as necessary and retest the warning light switch. Don't forget to bleed the rear wheel cylinder to ensure no air was let into the system.
7 If, after making the necessary repairs and/or part replacements, the warning light still doesn't come on, the switch is faulty. Replace the combination valve.

REPLACEMENT

8 Unplug the electrical connector from the combination valve (see illustration 8.1).
9 Disconnect the brake lines from the combination valve, using a flare nut wrench if available. Plug the ends of the lines to prevent loss of brake fluid and the entry of dirt.
10 Remove the combination valve mounting bolt and detach the valve.
11 Installation is the reverse of removal. Be sure to tighten the brake line fitting nuts securely.
12 Bleed the system (see Section 11) when you're done.

9 Master cylinder - removal and installation

♦ **Refer to illustrations 9.3 and 9.6**

✳✳ WARNING:

This is a procedure that should not be attempted on a model equipped with four-wheel ABS. To properly bleed the air from the hydraulic control unit on models with four-wheel ABS, the manufacturer states that the system must be bled using the conventional method (as described in Section 11), then with the use of a DRB scan tool to purge any air from the HCU. After that has been done the system must be bled using the conventional method once again. This tool is very expensive and generally

available only to dealership service departments. If your vehicle is equipped with four-wheel ABS and develops a problem with the master cylinder, have it towed to a dealer service department or other repair shop equipped with the necessary tools for bleeding the system.

REMOVAL

1 Place rags under the brake line fittings and prepare caps or plastic bags to cover the ends of the lines once they're disconnected.

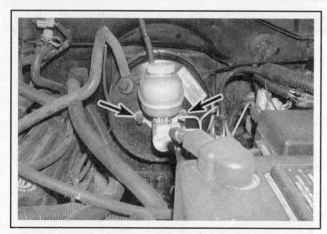

9.3 The master cylinder is retained to the power brake booster with two nuts

Brake fluid will damage paint. Cover all painted surfaces and avoid spilling fluid during this procedure. Brake fluid can be siphoned out of the reservoir using a squeeze bulb, but wear safety goggles.

2   Loosen the tube nuts at the ends of the brake lines where they enter the master cylinder. To prevent rounding off the flats on these nuts, a flare-nut wrench, which wraps around the nut, should be used. Pull the brake lines away from the master cylinder slightly and plug the ends to prevent contamination.

3   Remove the two master cylinder mounting nuts (see illustration). Remove the master cylinder from the booster, taking care not to kink the hydraulic lines.

4   Remove the reservoir cap, then discard any fluid remaining in the reservoir.

INSTALLATION

5   Bench bleed the new master cylinder before installing it. Mount the master cylinder in a vise, with the jaws of the vise clamping on the mounting flange.

6   Attach a pair of master cylinder bleeder tubes to the outlet ports of the master cylinder (see illustration).

7   Fill the reservoir with brake fluid of the recommended type (see Chapter 1).

8   Slowly push the pistons into the master cylinder (a large Phillips screwdriver can be used for this) - air will be expelled from the pressure chambers and into the reservoir. Because the tubes are submerged in fluid, air can't be drawn back into the master cylinder when you release the pistons.

9   Repeat the procedure until no more air bubbles are present.

9.6 The best way to bleed air from the master cylinder before installing it on the vehicle is with a pair of bleeder tubes that direct brake fluid into the reservoir during bleeding

10 Remove the bleed tubes, one at a time, and install plugs in the open ports to prevent fluid leakage and air from entering. Install the reservoir cap.

11 Install the master cylinder over the studs on the power brake booster and tighten the attaching nuts only finger tight at this time.

12 Thread the brake line fittings into the master cylinder. Since the master cylinder is still a bit loose, it can be moved slightly in order for the fittings to thread in easily. Do not strip the threads as the fittings are tightened.

13 Tighten the mounting nuts to the torque listed in this Chapter's Specifications, then the brake line fittings.

14 Fill the master cylinder reservoir with fluid, then bleed the master cylinder and the rest of the brake system as described in Section 11. To bleed the cylinder on the vehicle, have an assistant depress the brake pedal and hold the pedal to the floor. Loosen the fitting nut to allow air and fluid to escape. Repeat this procedure on both fittings at the master cylinder until the fluid is clear of air bubbles.

Have plenty of rags on hand to catch the fluid - brake fluid will ruin painted surfaces. After the bleeding procedure is completed, rinse the area under the master cylinder with clean water.

15 Test the operation of the brake system carefully before placing the vehicle into normal service.

Do not operate the vehicle if you are in doubt about the effectiveness of the brake system.

10 Brake hoses and lines - inspection and replacement

INSPECTION

1   About every six months, with the vehicle raised and supported securely on jackstands, the rubber hoses which connect the steel brake lines with the front and rear brake assemblies should be inspected for cracks, chafing of the outer cover, leaks, blisters and other damage. These are important and vulnerable parts of the brake system and inspection should be complete. A light and mirror will be helpful for a thorough check. If a hose exhibits any of the above conditions, replace it with a new one.

REPLACEMENT

Front brake hose

2 Disconnect the brake line from the hose fitting, being careful not to bend the frame bracket or brake line. Use a flare nut wrench, if available.

3 Remove the U-clip from the hose fitting with a pair of pliers. Unbolt the hose bracket from the frame.

4 Remove the banjo bolt from the brake caliper (see illustration 3.6b) and separate the hose from the caliper. Discard the sealing washers.

5 To install the hose, first attach it to the caliper, using new sealing washers on both sides of the fitting. Tighten the inlet fitting bolt to the torque listed in this Chapter's Specifications.

6 Without twisting the hose, connect the brake line to the hose fitting, but don't tighten it yet. Install the U-clip.

7 Install the bolt retaining the hose bracket to the frame, tightening it securely.

8 Tighten the brake line-to-hose fitting securely.

9 When the brake hose installation is complete, there should be no kinks in the hose. Make sure the hose doesn't contact any part of the suspension. Check this by turning the wheels to the extreme left and right positions. If the hose makes contact, remove it and correct the installation as necessary. Bleed the system (see Section 11).

Rear brake hose

10 Using a back-up wrench, disconnect the hose at the frame bracket, being careful not to bend the bracket or steel lines. Use a flare-nut wrench, if available.

11 Remove the U-clip with a pair of pliers and separate the female fitting from the bracket.

12 Disconnect the two hydraulic lines at the junction block, then unbolt and remove the hose. Use a flare-nut wrench on the line fittings, if available.

13 Bolt the junction block to the axle housing and connect the lines, tightening them securely. Without twisting the hose, install the female end of the hose in the frame bracket.

14 Install the U-clip retaining the female end to the bracket.

15 Using a back-up wrench, attach the steel line fittings to the female fittings. Again, be careful not to bend the bracket or steel line.

16 Make sure the hose installation did not loosen the frame bracket. Tighten the bracket if necessary.

17 Fill the master cylinder reservoir and bleed the system (see Section 11).

Metal brake lines

18 When replacing brake lines be sure to use the correct parts. Don't use copper tubing for any brake system components. Purchase steel brake lines from a dealer or auto parts store.

19 Prefabricated brake line, with the tube ends already flared and fittings installed, is available at auto parts stores and dealers. These lines can be bent to the proper shapes using a tubing bender.

20 When installing the new line, make sure it's securely supported in the brackets and has plenty of clearance between moving or hot components.

21 After installation, check the master cylinder fluid level and add fluid as necessary. Bleed the brake system as outlined in the next Section and test the brakes carefully before driving the vehicle in traffic.

11 Brake system bleeding

▶ **Refer to illustrations 11.7 and 11.10**

❋❋ WARNING 1:

The following procedure is a manual bleeding procedure. This is the only bleeding procedure which can be performed at home without special tools. However, if air has found its way into the hydraulic control unit on a model with four-wheel ABS, they must be bled manually, then with a DRB scan tool, then manually a second time. If the brake pedal feels "spongy" even after bleeding the brakes, have the vehicle towed to a dealer service department and have the brake system bled. Driving the vehicle without doing so could be dangerous because there may be air trapped in the hydraulic control unit (HCU).

❋❋ WARNING 2:

Wear eye protection when bleeding the brake system. If the fluid comes in contact with your eyes, immediately rinse them with water and seek medical attention.

➡Note: Bleeding the hydraulic system is necessary to remove any air that manages to find its way into the system after it has been opened during removal and installation of a hydraulic system component.

1 It will probably be necessary to bleed the system at all four brakes if air has entered the system due to low fluid level, or if the brake lines have been disconnected at the master cylinder. If this is the case, and your vehicle is equipped with four-wheel ABS, have the vehicle towed to a dealer service department or other repair shop equipped with a DRB scan tool.

2 If a brake line was disconnected only at a wheel, then only that caliper or wheel cylinder must be bled.

3 If a brake line is disconnected at a fitting located between the master cylinder and any of the brakes, that part of the system served by the disconnected line must be bled.

4 Remove any residual vacuum from the brake power booster by applying the brake several times with the engine off.

5 Remove the master cylinder reservoir cap and fill the reservoir with brake fluid. Reinstall the cap.

➡Note: Check the fluid level often during the bleeding operation and add fluid as necessary to prevent the fluid level from falling low enough to allow air bubbles into the master cylinder.

6 Have an assistant on hand, as well as a supply of new brake fluid, a clear container partially filled with clean brake fluid, a length of hose to fit over the bleeder valve and a wrench to open and close the bleeder valve.

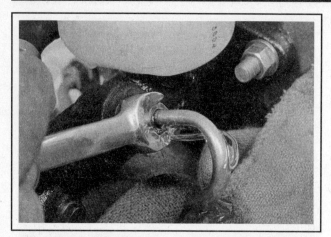

11.7 Have an assistant depress the brake pedal and hold it down, then loosen the fitting nut, allowing air and fluid to escape; repeat this procedure on both fittings until the fluid is clear of air bubbles

11.10 When bleeding the brakes, a hose is connected to the bleeder valve at the caliper or wheel cylinder and then submerged in brake fluid. Air will be seen as bubbles in the tube and container. All air must be expelled before moving to the next wheel.

MODELS WITH REAR WHEEL ANTI-LOCK (RWAL) BRAKES

7   To bleed the entire system, begin by bleeding the master cylinder, starting with the rear fitting. Place rags under the master cylinder to absorb brake fluid. Have your assistant depress the brake pedal slowly and hold it down, then loosen the fitting and allow the fluid and air to escape. Repeat this until bubble-free fluid flows from the fitting (see illustration).

8   Use the technique described in the previous Step to bleed the combination valve (the fittings on the underside of the valve), then the RWAL valve (the rear fitting).

9   Moving on to the left rear wheel, loosen the bleeder valve slightly, then tighten it to a point where it is snug but can still be loosened quickly and easily.

10 Place one end of the hose over the bleeder valve and submerge the other end in brake fluid in the container (see illustration).

11 Have the assistant push the brake pedal slowly to the floor, then hold the pedal firmly depressed.

12 While the pedal is held depressed, open the bleeder valve just enough to allow a flow of fluid to leave the valve. Watch for air bubbles to exit the submerged end of the tube. When the fluid flow slows after a couple of seconds, close the valve and have your assistant release the pedal.

13 Repeat Steps 11 and 12 until no more air is seen leaving the tube, then tighten the bleeder valve and proceed to the right rear wheel,

the right front wheel and the left front wheel, in that order, and perform the same procedure. Be sure to check the fluid in the master cylinder reservoir frequently.

14 Never use old brake fluid. It contains moisture which can boil, rendering the brakes useless.

15 Refill the master cylinder with fluid at the end of the operation.

16 Check the operation of the brakes. The pedal should feel solid when depressed, with no sponginess. If necessary, repeat the entire process.

✳✳ WARNING:

Do not operate the vehicle if you are in doubt about the effectiveness of the brake system.

17 As soon as you have completed this procedure, test drive the vehicle and verify that the brake system is in good working order.

MODELS WITH FOUR-WHEEL ANTI-LOCK BRAKES (ABS)

18 Bleeding the brake system on these models should be limited to components "downstream" of the Hydraulic Control Unit (HCU), since a special DRB scan tool is required to bleed the HCU (see **Warning 1** at the beginning of this Section). The basic brake system, however, can be bled by following Steps 9 through 17.

12 Power brake booster - check, removal and installation

OPERATING CHECK

1   Depress the pedal and start the engine. If the pedal goes down slightly, operation is normal.

2   Depress the brake pedal several times with the engine running and make sure that there is no change in the pedal reserve distance.

AIRTIGHTNESS CHECK

3   Start the engine and turn it off after one or two minutes. Depress the brake pedal several times slowly. If the pedal goes down farther the first time but gradually rises after the second or third depression, the booster is airtight.

4   Depress the brake pedal while the engine is running, then stop the engine with the pedal depressed. If there is no change in the pedal reserve travel after holding the pedal for 30 seconds, the booster is air-tight.

REMOVAL

▶ **Refer to illustration 12.7**

5   On models with Rear Wheel Anti-Lock brakes, unbolt the RWAL valve and the combination valve from their brackets. On models with four-wheel Anti-lock Brakes, unbolt the Hydraulic Actuator Unit bracket from the inner fender panel. Unbolt the brake master cylinder from the booster (see Section 9) and carefully pull it forward, leaving the lines attached.

✳✳ **CAUTION:**

Be careful not to kink any of the lines.

6   Detach the vacuum hose from the booster.
7   Working inside the vehicle, remove the pushrod retaining clip (see illustration) and slip the pushrod off the pin.
8   Peel the insulation on the firewall back to gain access to the booster mounting nuts. Remove the four nuts holding the brake booster to the firewall (see illustration 12.7).
9   Slide the booster straight out from the firewall until the studs clear the holes and pull the booster, spacer and gaskets from the engine compartment.

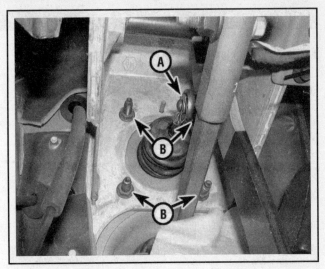

12.7 Remove the retaining clip (A) and detach the pushrod from the brake pedal, then remove the brake booster mounting nuts (B)

INSTALLATION

10 Installation is the reverse of removal. Be sure to tighten the booster mounting nuts and the master cylinder mounting nuts to the torque values listed in this Chapter's Specifications.

13 Brake light switch - check, replacement and adjustment

▶ **Refer to illustration 13.1**

1   The brake light switch is mounted on a flange on the pedal support bracket. The switch is secured in the bracket by means of an integral retainer on the switch body (see illustration).

CHECK

2   If the brake lights do not come on when the pedal is depressed, check the fuse first.
3   If the fuse is good, check for voltage to the switch on terminal no. 1 (the Pink/Dark Blue wire). If no voltage is present, trace and repair the circuit between the switch and the fuse block.
4   If the switch is getting voltage, verify that there is voltage at terminal no. 2 when the brake pedal is depressed. With an ohmmeter, check for continuity between terminals 1 and 2. There should be continuity only when the switch is depressed.
5   If there is no voltage at terminal no. 2 when the pedal is depressed, replace the switch. If the switch is operating properly but the brake lights are inoperative, trace and repair the circuit between the switch and the brake lights.
➡**Note: Also check the brake light bulbs, although it is not very probable that they would all fail at the same time.**

REPLACEMENT

6   Depress the brake pedal and hold it down.
7   Rotate the switch about 30-degrees in a counterclockwise direction to unlock the switch retainer, then pull the switch out of its bracket.

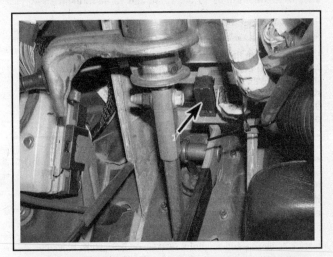

13.1 The brake light switch (arrow) is attached to a bracket near the top of the brake pedal

8   Unplug the switch electrical connector and remove the switch.
9   Plug in the electrical connector to the new switch.
10 Press and hold the brake pedal in its fully-applied position.
11 Align the tab on the switch with the notch in the switch bracket, then insert the switch in the bracket and turn it clockwise about 30-degrees to lock it into place.
12 Move the lever on the switch towards the support bracket (this will connect the contacts inside the switch).
13 Try the brakes and verify that the switch is operating properly.

14 Parking brake - adjustment

▶ **Refer to illustration 14.2**

1   Raise the rear of the vehicle and support it securely on jackstands. Block the front wheels to prevent the vehicle from rolling.

2   Adjust the rear brakes as described in Section 6. Loosen the adjusting nut at the equalizer enough to create slack in the cables (see illustration).

3   Verify that the drums rotate freely without drag, then fully apply the parking brake.

4   Mark the tensioner rod about 1/4-inch from the tensioner bracket.

5   Tighten the adjusting nut at the equalizer until the mark on the tensioner rod moves into alignment with the tensioner bracket.

❊❊ CAUTION:

Do NOT loosen or tighten the tensioner adjusting nut for any reason after completing this adjustment.

6   Release the parking brake pedal and verify that the rear wheels rotate freely without any drag.

7   Remove the jackstands and lower the vehicle.

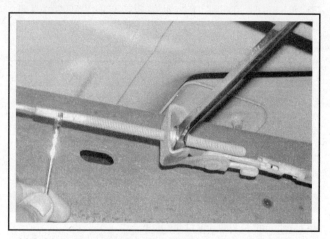

14.2 Loosen the adjuster nut and detach the front cable from the connector (prevent the threaded rod from turning by holding it with a wrench or pliers)

8   Test the operation of the parking brake on an incline (be sure to remain in the vehicle for this check!).

15 Parking brake shoes (models with rear disc brakes) - removal and installation

▶ **Refer to illustrations 15.3a, 15.3b and 15.4a through 15.4o**

❊❊ WARNING:

Dust created by the brake system is harmful to your health. Never blow it out with compressed air and don't inhale any of it. An approved filtering mask should be worn when working on the brakes. Do not, under any circumstances, use petroleum-based solvents to clean brake parts. Use brake system cleaner only!

➡Note: Although the typical procedure illustrated here is shown with the axle still in place, it takes some dexterity to work behind the axle flange while replacing the parking brake shoes. If this proves difficult, you can remove the axle for better access (see Chapter 8).

1   Loosen the wheel lug nuts, release the parking brake, raise the rear of the vehicle and support it securely on jackstands. Block the front wheels to keep the vehicle from rolling. Remove the rear wheels.

2   Remove the rear brake caliper (see Section 4) and hang it with a length of wire, then remove the caliper mounting bracket, on models so equipped (see Section 5).

3   Remove the brake disc (see Section 5).

➡Note: If the brake disc cannot be easily pulled off the axle and shoe assembly, make sure that the parking brake is completely released, then apply some penetrating oil at the hub-to-disc joint. Allow the oil to soak in and try to pull the disc off. If the disc still cannot be pulled off, the parking brake shoes will have to be retracted. This is accomplished by first removing the

plug from the backing plate. With the plug removed, turn the adjusting wheel with a narrow screwdriver or brake adjusting tool, moving the shoes away from the braking surface (see illustrations). The disc should now come off.

4   Clean the parking brake shoe assembly with brake system cleaner, then follow the accompanying illustrations (15.4a through 15.4o) for the parking brake shoe replacement procedure. Be sure to stay in order and read the caption under each illustration.

➡Note: All four parking brake shoes must be replaced at the same time, but to avoid mixing up parts, work on only one brake assembly at a time.

15.3a Remove the plug from the hole in the brake backing plate, insert a brake adjuster tool through the hole . . .

15.3b . . . position the tool at the top of the adjuster star wheel and rotate the wheel down (clockwise, as viewed from the rear of the vehicle, facing forward), moving the parking brake shoes away from the disc hub (which is already removed in this photo for the sake of clarity)

15.4a Pushing on the pin from the backing plate side with your finger, pry the front hold-down clip loose, then pull the pin out

15.4b Remove the rear hold-down clip and pin the same way

15.4c Disengage the lower spring from the parking brake shoes

15.4d Remove the adjuster

15.4e Disengage the upper spring from the rear parking brake shoe

15.4f Remove both parking brake shoes

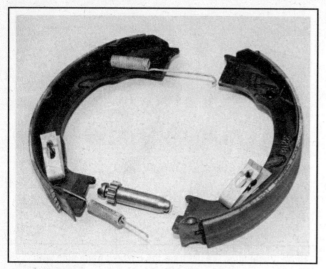

15.4g Here's how the shoes, springs and adjuster go together

15.4h Holding them together with the upper spring, install the new shoes

15.4i Spread the upper ends of the shoes apart and engage them with the anchor as shown

15.4j Install the adjuster

15.4k Make sure the adjuster is engaged with the shoes as shown

15.4l Install the lower spring

15.4m Make sure the coils of the lower spring are facing down, away from the adjuster, as shown

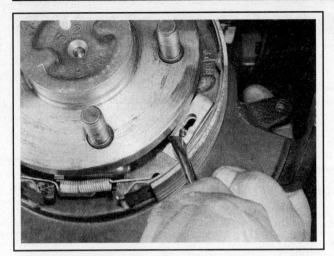

15.4n Install the rear pin and hold-down clip as shown, with the head of the pin firmly seated into the lower, smaller part of the hole in the clip

15.4o Install the front pin and hold-down clip the same way

5   Before reinstalling the disc, check the parking brake surfaces of the disc hub for cracks, score marks, deep scratches and hard spots, which will appear as small discolored areas. If hard spots or any of the other conditions listed above cannot be removed with sandpaper or emery cloth, the disc must be replaced.

6   Once all of the new parking brake shoes are in place, install the brake discs (see Section 5) and the brake calipers (see Section 4).

7   Remove the rubber plugs from the brake backing plates, insert a narrow screwdriver or brake adjusting tool through the adjustment hole and turn the star wheel until the shoes drag slightly as the disc is turned (see illustrations 15.3a and 15.3b). Turn the star wheel in the opposite direction until the disc turns freely. Install the backing plate plugs.

8   Install the rear wheels and lug nuts, lower the vehicle and tighten the lug nuts to the torque listed in the Chapter 1 Specifications.

9   Operate the parking brake lever several times to release the lock-out spring and adjust the cables.

10 Carefully check the operation of the brakes before placing the vehicle in normal service.

Specifications

General

Brake fluid type	See Chapter 1

Disc brakes

Disc minimum thickness	Stamped or cast into disc
Maximum allowable disc thickness variation	0.0005 inch
Disc runout (maximum)	0.004 inch
Brake pad minimum thickness	See Chapter 1

Drum brakes

Drum maximum diameter	Stamped or cast into drum
Minimum brake lining thickness	See Chapter 1

Torque specifications — Ft-lbs (unless otherwise indicated)

Power brake booster mounting nuts	250 in-lbs
Master cylinder mounting nuts	160 in-lbs
Caliper mounting pins	22
Brake hose-to-caliper banjo bolt	20
Caliper mounting bracket bolts (2003 and later models)	
Dakota (front)	148
Durango (front and rear)	130
Wheel cylinder mounting bolts	
Dakota	
1/4-20	132 in-lbs
5/16-18	16
Durango	15

Section

Reference to other Chapters

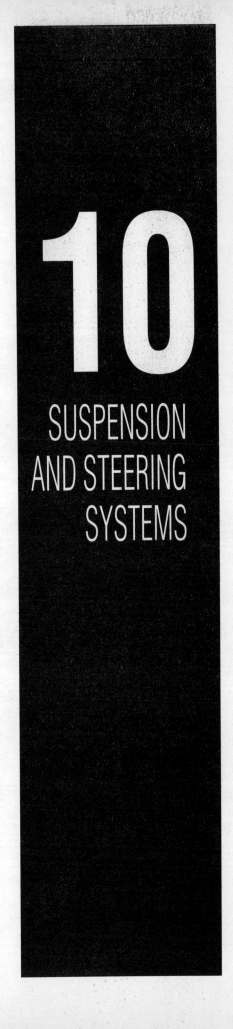

10

SUSPENSION AND STEERING SYSTEMS

♦ **Refer to illustrations 1.1 and 1.3**

The front suspension (see illustration) is fully independent. Each wheel is connected to the frame by a steering knuckle, upper and lower balljoints and upper and lower control arms. Coil springs and shock absorbers are used on 2WD models; 4WD models use shocks and torsion bars. A stabilizer bar, connected to the frame and to the two lower control arms, reduces body roll during cornering.

The steering system on all models consists of a rack-and-pinion steering gear and two adjustable tie-rods.

The rear suspension (see illustration) consists of a pair of multi-leaf springs, two shock absorbers and a stabilizer bar. The rear axle assembly is attached to the leaf springs by U-bolts. The front ends of the springs are attached to the frame at the front hangers, through rubber bushings. The rear ends of the springs are attached to the frame by shackles which allow the springs to alter their length as they compress and rebound.

Frequently, when working on the suspension or steering system components, you may come across fasteners which seem impossible to loosen. These fasteners on the underside of the vehicle are continually subjected to water, road grime, mud, etc., and can become rusted or "frozen," making them extremely difficult to remove. In order to unscrew these stubborn fasteners without damaging them (or other

1.1 Front suspension and steering components (2WD models)

1	Stabilizer bar	3	Tie-rod end	5	Coil spring	7	Steering gear
2	Lower control arm	4	Shock absorber	6	Lower balljoint		

components), be sure to use lots of penetrating oil and allow it to soak in for a while. Using a wire brush to clean exposed threads will also ease removal of the nut or bolt and prevent damage to the threads. Sometimes a sharp blow with a hammer and punch is effective in breaking the bond between a nut and bolt threads, but care must be taken to prevent the punch from slipping off the fastener and ruining the threads. Heating the stuck fastener and surrounding area with a torch sometimes helps too, but isn't recommended because of the obvious dangers associated with fire. Long breaker bars and extension, or "cheater," pipes will increase leverage, but never use an extension pipe on a ratchet - the ratcheting mechanism could be damaged. Sometimes, turning the nut or bolt in the tightening (clockwise) direction first will help to break it loose. Fasteners that require drastic measures to unscrew should always be replaced with new ones.

Since most of the procedures that are dealt with in this Chapter involve jacking up the vehicle and working underneath it, a good pair of jackstands will be needed. A hydraulic floor jack is the preferred type of jack to lift the vehicle, and it can also be used to support certain components during various operations.

✳✳ WARNING:

Never, under any circumstances, rely on a jack to support the vehicle while working on it. Also, whenever any of the suspension or steering fasteners are loosened or removed they must be inspected and, if necessary, replaced with new ones of the same part number or of original equipment quality and design. Torque specifications must be followed for proper reassembly and component retention. Never attempt to heat or straighten suspension or steering components. Instead, replace bent or damaged parts with new ones.

1.3 Rear suspension components

| 1 | Rear axle | 3 | Stabilizer bar link | 5 | Leaf springs |
| 2 | Stabilizer bar | 4 | Shock absorber | 6 | Spring plate |

2 Shock absorber (front) - removal and installation

♦ **Refer to illustrations 2.2 and 2.3**

1   Loosen the front wheel lug nuts, raise the front of the vehicle and support it securely on jackstands. Apply the parking brake. Remove the wheels.

2   Using an open-end wrench or a pair of locking pliers on the flats of the shock rod to prevent the shock from turning, remove the upper mounting nut (see illustration). Remove the retainer and bushing.

3   Working from underneath the vehicle, remove the two lower mounting bolts (2WD models) or bolt (4WD models) and pull the shock out from below (see illustration).

4   To install the shock absorber, install the lower retainer and bushing onto the shock rod.

➡**Note: The lower retainer is marked with an "L;" the upper retainer is marked with a "U."**

Guide the shock up into position in the frame bracket, then install the upper bushing, retainer and nut.

➡**Note: Apply a non-hardening thread locking compound to the threads of the nut.**

5   Install the lower mounting bolts (2WD models) or bolt (4WD models). Tighten the mounting fasteners to the torque listed in this Chapter's Specifications.

6   Install the wheel and lug nuts. Lower the vehicle and tighten the lug nuts to the torque listed in the Chapter 1 Specifications.

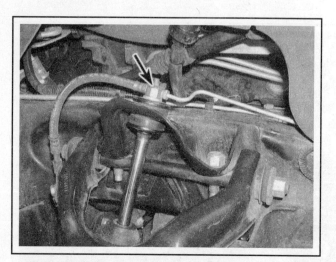

2.2 Remove the shock absorber upper mounting nut

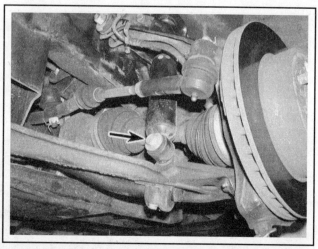

2.3 To detach the lower end of the shock absorber from the lower control arm on a 4WD model, remove this bolt

3 Stabilizer bar (front) - removal and installation

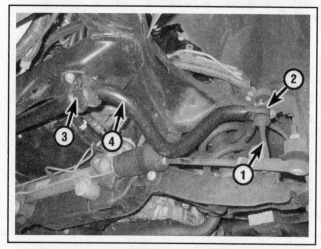

3.2 Stabilizer bar mounting details - 2WD models

1	Stabilizer bar link	3	Stabilizer bar clamp
2	Rubber bushing	4	Stabilizer bar

2WD MODELS

♦ **Refer to illustration 3.2**

1   Raise the vehicle and support it securely on jackstands.

2   Remove the upper nuts and bushings from the links, then detach the links from the lower control arms (see illustration). Keep the rubber bushings and washers in order.

3   Remove the stabilizer bar clamp bolts and remove the clamps.

4   Remove the stabilizer bar. Remove the rubber bushings from the stabilizer bar.

5   Inspect all rubber bushings for wear and damage. If any of the rubber parts are cracked, torn or generally deteriorated, replace them.

6   Installation is the reverse of removal. Be sure to tighten all fasteners to the torque listed in this Chapter's Specifications.

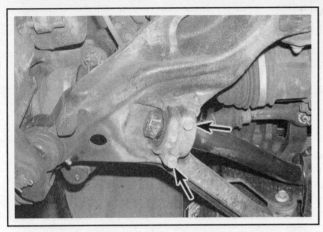

3.8 Remove the bolts from the stabilizer bar retainers (4WD models)

3.9 On 4WD models, the stabilizer bar clamps are secured to the frame with a bolt and nut

4WD MODELS

▶ Refer to illustrations 3.8 and 3.9

➡Note: The vehicle must be at normal ride height (not raised) during this procedure.

7 Remove the skid plate, if equipped.
8 Unbolt the stabilizer bar retainers from the lower control arms

(see illustration).

9 Unbolt the stabilizer bar clamps from the frame (see illustration).
10 Remove the stabilizer bar. Remove the rubber bushings from the stabilizer bar.
11 Inspect all rubber bushings for wear and damage. If any of the rubber parts are cracked, torn or generally deteriorated, replace them.
12 Installation is the reverse of removal. Be sure to tighten all fasteners to the torque listed in this Chapter's Specifications.

4 Torsion bar (4WD models) - removal, installation and adjustment

▶ Refer to illustrations 4.2a, 4.2b, 4.3 and 4.5

➡Note: The torsion bars are marked L for left and R for right; they aren't interchangeable.

REMOVAL

1 Loosen the front wheel lugs nuts, raise the vehicle and support it securely on jackstands placed under the frame rails. Remove the wheel.
2 Mark the relationship of the torsion bar to the lower control arm and to the torsion bar anchor (see illustrations).

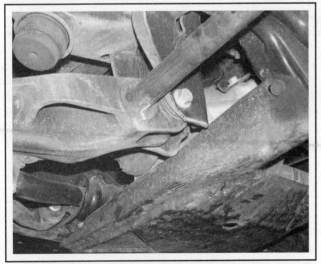

4.2a Mark the relationship of the torsion bar to the lower control arm . . .

4.2b . . . and to the torsion bar anchor

4.3 Count the number of threads between the anchor and the crossmember, or make a mark on the adjustment bolt were it passes through the crossmember (this will ease the adjustment process after the torsion bar has been installed)

3   Make a mark on the adjustment bolt where it goes through the crossmember (see illustration), or count the number of threads showing between the crossmember and the anchor.

4   Unscrew the adjustment bolt from the swivel. Remove the swivel.

5   Remove the anchor from the torsion bar (see illustration).

6   Pull the torsion bar out of the lower control arm.

INSTALLATION

7   Installation is the reverse of removal. Be sure to clean out the hexagonal hole in the lower control arm and lube it with multi-purpose grease before inserting the torsion bar into the arm. Also apply some grease to the hex ends of the torsion bar, to the top of the anchor and to the adjustment bolt. Make sure that the marks you made on the rear end of the torsion bar and the crossmember and on the front end of the torsion bar and the control arm line up. And make sure that the torsion

4.5 Remove the anchor from the torsion bar

bar adjustment bolt is tightened until the same number of threads are showing between the crossmember and anchor that were showing before removal.

8   Install the wheel, remove the jackstands and lower the vehicle.

9   Tighten the wheel lug nuts to the torque listed in the Chapter 1 Specifications.

ADJUSTMENT

10   Drive the vehicle back-and-forth a few times to settle the suspension.

11   Make sure the tires are properly inflated and the vehicle is unloaded. Measure the vehicle's ride height on each side, from equal points on the frame to the ground. If the side that has been worked on is higher or lower than the other side, turn the torsion bar adjustment bolt accordingly until the vehicle sits level. This may take a few tries, and it's important to roll the vehicle back and forth between adjustments, to settle the suspension and get an accurate reading.

12   Have the front end alignment checked, and if necessary, adjusted.

5   Coil spring (2WD models) - removal and installation

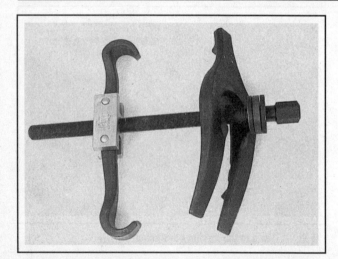

5.4 A typical aftermarket internal spring compressor tool: the hooked arms grip the upper coils of the spring, the plate is inserted below the lower coil, and when the nut on the threaded rod is turned, the spring is compressed

▶ **Refer to illustration 5.4**

REMOVAL

1   Loosen the wheel lug nuts, raise the vehicle and support it securely on jackstands. Remove the wheel.

2   Detach the stabilizer bar link from the lower control arm (see Section 3).

3   Remove the shock absorber (see Section 2).

4   Install a suitable internal type spring compressor in accordance with the tool manufacturer's instructions (see illustration). Compress the spring enough to relieve all pressure from the spring seats (but don't compress it any more than necessary, or it could be ruined). When you can wiggle the spring, it's compressed enough. (You can buy a suitable spring compressor at most auto parts stores or rent one from a tool rental yard.)

5   Separate the lower control arm balljoint from the steering

knuckle (see Section 7).

6   Pull down on the lower control arm and remove the compressed spring.

7   If the spring is to be replaced, slowly loosen the spring compressor until the spring is fully extended, then install it on the new spring.

INSTALLATION

8   Place the insulator on top of the coil spring (the upper end of the spring is the more closed end).

9   Install the top of the spring into the spring pocket and the bottom in the lower control arm.

10 Connect the lower control arm to the steering knuckle (see Section 7). Remove the spring compressor.

11 The remainder of installation is the reverse of removal. Tighten all fasteners to the proper torque values. Tighten the wheel lug nuts to the torque listed in the Chapter 1 Specifications.

12 Have the front end alignment checked, and if necessary, adjusted.

6   Upper control arm - removal and installation

▶ **Refer to illustrations 6.2, 6.3, 6.5 and 6.6**

REMOVAL

1   Loosen the wheel lug nuts, raise the front of the vehicle and support it securely on jackstands. Remove the wheel. Position a floor jack under the lower control arm in the area underneath the balljoint. Raise the jack slightly to take the spring pressure off the upper control arm.

❊❊ WARNING:

The jack must remain in this position throughout the entire procedure.

2   If you're working on a 2WD model, mark the relationship of the pivot shaft mounting nuts to the pivot shaft. If you're working on a 4WD model, mark the position of the pivot shaft mounting bolts to the frame bracket (see illustration).

3   Unbolt the brake hose bracket from the upper control arm (see illustration). On 2WD models, unbolt the brake caliper and suspend it on a wire out of the way (see Chapter 9). Do not let the caliper hang by the brake hose!

4   If you're working on a 4WD model, remove the shock absorber (see Section 2).

5   To disconnect the upper control arm from the steering knuckle, remove the cotter pin from the balljoint castle nut, loosen the nut a few

6.2 Mark around the heads of the pivot shaft bolts to preserve alignment (4WD shown)

turns (don't remove it), install a balljoint remover and break the balljoint loose from the knuckle. Now remove the nut.

➡**Note: If you don't have the proper balljoint removal tool, a "picklefork" type balljoint separator can be used, but keep in mind that this type of tool will probably damage the balljoint boot (see illustration).**

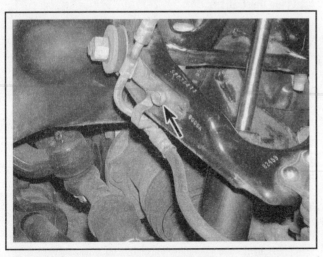

6.3 Remove the bolt and detach the brake hose bracket from the upper control arm

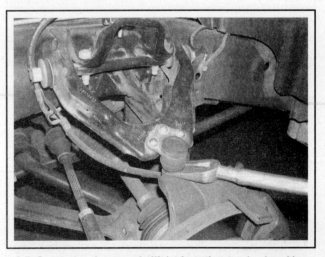

6.5 Separating the upper balljoint from the steering knuckle

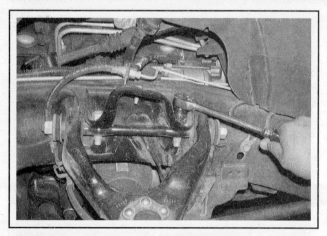

6.6 Remove the pivot shaft bolts (4WD models)

6   Remove the upper control arm pivot bolts (4WD models) or nuts (2WD models) (see illustration). Remove the control arm.

INSTALLATION

7   Position the arm on the frame bracket and install the bolts or nuts. Make sure the marks you made prior to disassembly are aligned, then tighten the bolts or nuts to the torque listed in this Chapter's Specifications.

8   Attach the balljoint to the steering knuckle and tighten the ball-stud nut to the torque listed in this Chapter's Specifications.

9   The remainder of installation is the reverse of removal. Tighten the wheel lug nuts to the torque listed in the Chapter 1 Specifications.

10 Have the front end alignment checked and, if necessary, adjusted.

7   Lower control arm - removal and installation

◆ Refer to illustrations 7.8 and 7.9

REMOVAL

1   If you're working on a 4WD model, loosen the driveaxle/hub nut

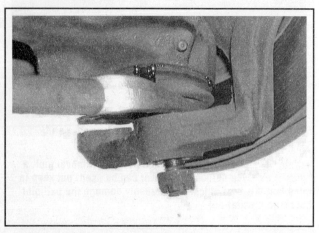

7.8 Separating the lower balljoint from the steering knuckle

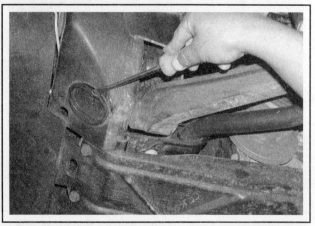

7.9 Pry out the pugs in the frame to gain access to the lower control arm front pivot bolts

(see Chapter 8). Also remove the stabilizer bar (see Section 3).

2   Loosen the wheel lug nuts, raise the vehicle and support it securely on jackstands placed under the frame rails. Remove the wheel.

3   If you're working on a 4WD model, remove the driveaxle (see Chapter 8).

4   Remove the shock absorber (see Section 2).

➡**Note: On 4WD models it is only necessary to remove the lower mounting bolt.**

5   Detach the stabilizer bar link from the lower control arm (2WD models) (see Section 3).

6   If you're working on a 2WD model, compress the coil spring as described in Section 5.

7   If you're working on a 4WD model, remove the torsion bar.

8   To disconnect the lower control arm from the steering knuckle, remove the cotter pin from the balljoint castle nut, loosen the nut a few turns (don't remove it), install a balljoint remover and break the balljoint loose from the knuckle. Now remove the nut.

➡**Note: If you don't have the proper balljoint removal tool, a "picklefork" type balljoint separator can be used, but keep in mind that this type of tool will probably damage the balljoint boot (see illustration).**

9   If present, pry out the plugs in the frame for access to the lower control arm front pivot bolts (see illustration). Remove the lower control arm pivot bolts and pull the lower arm from its frame brackets.

INSTALLATION

10 Installation is the reverse of removal. Don't tighten the pivot bolt nuts until the vehicle is back on the ground, at normal ride height, then tighten all fasteners to the torque listed in this Chapter's Specifications.

➡**Note: You can also raise the lower control arm with a floor jack to simulate normal ride height, then tighten the nuts/bolts.**

11 Install the wheel and lug nuts. Lower the vehicle and tighten the lug nuts to the torque listed in the Chapter 1 Specifications.

12 If you're working on a 4WD model, be sure to check and adjust the ride height (see Section 4).

13 Have the front end alignment checked and, if necessary, adjusted.

8 Balljoints - check and replacement

1   Inspect the control arm balljoints for looseness anytime either of them is separated from the steering knuckle. See if you can turn the ballstud in its socket with your fingers. If the balljoint is loose, or if the ballstud can be turned, replace the balljoint. You can also check the balljoints with the suspension assembled as follows.

UPPER BALLJOINTS

2   Raise the lower control arm with a floor jack until the tire just barely touches the ground.

3   Attach a dial indicator to the upper suspension arm, with the plunger of the indicator touching the steering knuckle, in line with the axle.

4   Grasp the top of the tire and "rock" the tire in-and-out. The dial indicator should indicate no more than 0.060-inch deflection. If the indicated reading exceeds this figure, replace the upper control arm (see Section 6); the balljoint cannot be replaced separately.

LOWER BALLJOINTS

5   Loosen the wheel lug nuts, raise the vehicle and support it securely on jackstands. Remove the wheels.

6   Place a floor jack under the lower control arm, near the outer end, and raise it until the upper control arm lifts off its rebound bumper. Attach a dial indicator to the lower control arm and position the indicator plunger against the balljoint boss on the underside of the steering knuckle (the machined surface through which the balljoint stud protrudes). Using a large prybar inserted under the upper control arm pivot shaft, pry down on the upper control arm, then zero the dial indicator.

7   Now, insert the prybar under the upper control arm and pry up. The needle should not deflect more than 0.060-inch. If it does, the balljoint is worn out. The lower control arm must be replaced.

9 Hub and bearing assembly - replacement

➡**Note: The hub and bearing assembly is a sealed unit and isn't serviceable. If it's defective, it must be replaced.**

2WD MODELS

▶ **Refer to illustration 9.4**

Removal

1   Loosen the front wheel lug nuts, raise the front of the vehicle and support it securely on jackstands. Remove the wheel.

9.4 It may be necessary to lightly tap the hub assembly off the steering knuckle

2   Remove the brake caliper and support it out of the way with a piece of wire. Also remove the brake disc (see Chapter 9).

3   If equipped with four-wheel ABS, remove the wheel speed sensor so as not to damage it.

4   Remove the spindle nut and slide the hub and bearing assembly off the spindle (see illustration).

Installation

5   Clean the spindle and apply a light coat of high-temperature grease to it.

6   Slide the hub and bearing assembly onto the spindle and install a new nut, tightening it to the torque listed in this Chapter's Specifications.

7   The remainder of installation is the reverse of the removal procedure. Be sure to tighten the caliper mounting pins to the torque listed in the Chapter 9 Specifications, and the wheel lug nuts to the torque listed in the Chapter 1 Specifications.

4WD MODELS

▶ **Refer to illustrations 9.10 and 9.12**

Removal

8   Remove the wheel hub cover, remove the cotter pin, nut lock and wave washer, then break loose the driveaxle/hub nut with a socket and large breaker bar (see Chapter 8).

9   Loosen the wheel lug nuts, raise the vehicle and support it securely on jackstands. Remove the wheel. Remove the driveaxle/hub nut.

9.10 Remove these bolts and detach the splash shield

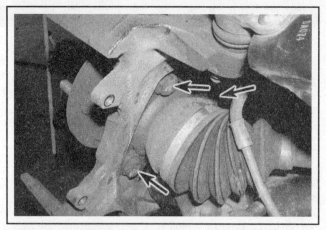

9.12 The hub and bearing assembly is retained by three bolts (4WD models)

10 Remove the brake caliper and hang it out of the way with a piece of wire, then remove the brake disc (see Chapter 9). Also remove the splash shield (see illustration).

11 On models with 4-wheel ABS, remove the wheel speed sensor retaining bolt, remove the sensor from the knuckle and set the sensor and wire harness safely aside.

12 Remove the hub assembly-to-steering knuckle bolts (see illustration).

13 Tap the hub assembly from side-to-side to break it loose from the steering knuckle. Pull the hub assembly off the end of the driveaxle. Wrap the end of the driveaxle with a rag to prevent damaging it. If the hub is stuck on the splines on the end of the driveaxle, use a jaw-type puller to free it.

✳✳ CAUTION:

Be careful not to overextend the inner CV joint.

Installation

14 Installation is the reverse of the removal procedure. Be sure to lubricate the driveaxle splines with multi-purpose grease. Tighten the caliper mounting pins to the torque listed in the Chapter 9 Specifications, the hub-to-knuckle bolts to the torque listed in this Chapter's Specifications and the wheel lug nuts to the torque listed in the Chapter 1 Specifications.

10 Wheel studs - replacement

♦ **Refer to illustrations 10.3 and 10.4**

➡**Note: This procedure applies to both the front and rear wheel studs.**

1 Loosen the wheel lug nuts, raise the vehicle and support it securely on jackstands. Remove the wheel.

2 Remove the brake disc or drum (see Chapter 9).

3 Install a lug nut part way onto the stud being replaced. Push the stud out of the hub flange with a press tool (see illustration).

4 Insert the new stud into the hub flange from the back side and

10.3 Use a press tool to push the stud out of the flange

1 *Hub flange*   2 *Lug nut on stud*   3 *Press tool*

10.4 Install a spacer and a lug nut on the stud, then tighten the nut to draw the stud into place

1 *Hub flange*   2 *Spacer*

install a spacer or several flat washers and a lug nut on the stud (see illustration).

5   Tighten the lug nut until the stud is seated in the flange.

6   Reinstall the brake drum or disc. Install the wheel and lug nuts. Lower the vehicle and tighten the lug nuts to the torque listed in this Chapter's Specifications.

11 Steering knuckle - removal and installation

1   If you're working on a 4WD model, remove the hub cover and loosen the driveaxle/hub nut (see Chapter 8). Loosen the wheel lug nuts, raise the vehicle and support it securely on jackstands. Remove the wheel.

2   Support the lower control arm with a floor jack. Raise the jack slightly.

⁂ WARNING:

The jack must remain in this position throughout the entire procedure.

3   Remove the wheel.

4   Remove the brake caliper and brake disc (see Chapter 9). Hang the caliper out of the way on a piece of wire (don't disconnect the brake hose). If equipped with four-wheel ABS, unbolt the wheel speed sensor from the steering knuckle.

5   Remove the disc splash shield from the steering knuckle.

6   Remove the stabilizer link (see Section 3). Remove the hub and bearing assembly (see Section 9). If you're working on a 4WD model, refer to Chapter 8 and remove the driveaxle.

7   Disconnect the tie-rod end from the knuckle (see Section 17).

8   Disconnect the balljoints from the steering knuckle (see Sections 6 and 7).

9   Remove the steering knuckle.

10   Installation is the reverse of removal. Be sure to tighten all fasteners to the torque values listed in this Chapter's Specifications. Tighten the wheel lug nuts to the torque listed in the Chapter 1 Specifications. Tighten the driveaxle/hub nut to the torque listed in the Chapter 8 Specifications (4WD models).

12 Shock absorber (rear) - removal and installation

▸ **Refer to illustrations 12.3a and 12.3b**

1   Raise the rear of the vehicle and support it securely on jackstands. Block the front wheels so the vehicle doesn't roll off the stands.

➡**Note: It isn't necessary to remove the rear wheels, but doing so will improve access to the shock absorbers.**

2   Support the rear axle with a floor jack placed under the axle tube closest to the shock absorber being removed.

3   Remove the shock absorber upper and lower mounting fasteners (see illustrations).

4   Remove the shock absorber.

5   Installation is the reverse of removal. Tighten all fasteners to the torque values listed in this Chapter's Specifications.

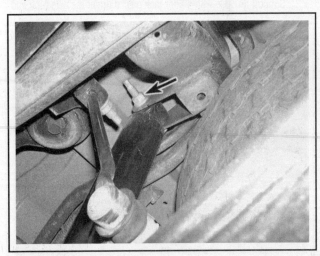

12.3a Rear shock absorber lower mounting nut/bolt

12.3b Rear shock absorber upper mounting nut/bolt

13 Stabilizer bar (rear) - removal and installation

▶ **Refer to illustrations 13.2 and 13.4**

1   Loosen the rear wheel lug nuts, raise the rear of the vehicle and support it securely on jackstands. Block the front wheels to keep the vehicle from rolling off the stands. Remove the rear wheels.

2   Remove the stabilizer bar link-to-frame nuts/bolts (see illustration).

3   Remove the cotter pins and nuts from the lower ends of the links,

then separate the link from the bar with a small puller.

4   Remove the stabilizer bar clamp bolts (see illustration) and remove the stabilizer bar assembly.

5   Inspect the stabilizer bar bushings and link bushings for cracks, tears and other signs of deterioration. Replace as necessary.

6   Installation is the reverse of removal. Be sure to tighten all fasteners to the torque listed in this Chapter's Specifications.

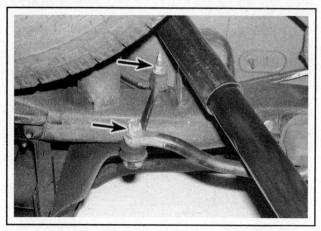

13.2 The rear stabilizer bar links are secured to the frame with a nut and bolt; the lower ends must be separated with a puller or balljoint separator after the nut has been removed

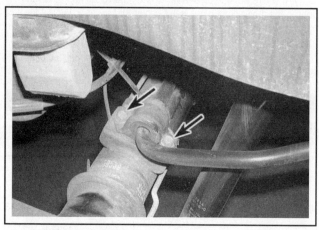

13.4 Remove the stabilizer bar clamp bolts from the axle housing

14 Leaf spring - removal and installation

▶ **Refer to illustrations 14.3, 14.4 and 14.5**

1   Loosen the rear wheel lug nuts, raise the rear of the vehicle and support it securely on jackstands. Block the front wheels to keep the vehicle from rolling off the stands. Remove the rear wheels.

2   Support the axle with a floor jack placed under the axle tube and

raise it slightly to take the weight of the axle. Detach the lower end of the shock absorber from the spring plate (see illustration 12.3a)

3   Remove the four U-bolt nuts (see illustration), the spring plate and the two U-bolts.

4   At the front end of the spring, remove the nut and bolt from the spring-to-front bracket (see illustration).

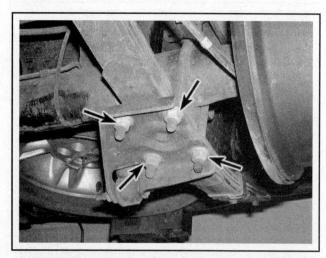

14.3 Remove the four U-bolt nuts (arrows), then remove the spring plate and the two U-bolts

14.4 At the front end of the leaf spring, remove the nut and bolt (arrow) that attach the spring to the frame bracket

5   At the rear end of the spring, remove the lower spring-to-shackle nut and bolt (see illustration).

6   Remove the spring assembly.

7   If the bushings at the ends of the spring are worn or deteriorated, an automotive machine shop or dealer service department can press the old ones out and press new ones in.

8   Installation is the reverse of removal. Gradually tighten the U-bolt nuts in a criss-cross pattern to the torque listed in this Chapter's Specifications. Don't tighten the spring-to-front bracket bolt/nut or the spring-to-shackle bolt/nut until the vehicle has been lowered.

9   Install the wheel and lug nuts. Lower the vehicle and tighten the lug nuts to the torque listed in the Chapter 1 Specifications.

10   Tighten the spring-to-front bracket bolt/nut and the spring-to-shackle bolt/nut to the torque listed in this Chapter's Specifications.

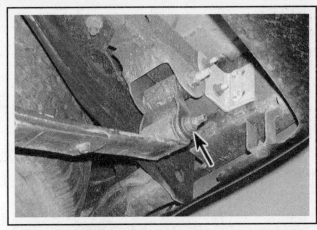

14.5 At the rear end of the spring, remove the lower spring-to-shackle nut and bolt (arrow)

15 Steering wheel - removal and installation

▶ Refer to illustrations 15.2, 15.3a, 15.3b, 15.4, 15.5, 15.6 and 15.8

※ WARNING:

The models covered by this manual are equipped with airbags. Always disable the airbag system when working in the vicinity of airbag system components (see Chapter 12).

REMOVAL

1   Park the vehicle with the wheels pointing straight ahead. Disconnect the cable from the negative terminal of the battery. Wait at least two minutes before proceeding (to allow the backup power supply for the airbag system to become depleted).

2   Remove the two airbag module retaining screws (see illustration) and lift off the airbag module.

3   Unplug the electrical connectors for the horn and airbag (see illustrations), then remove the airbag module.

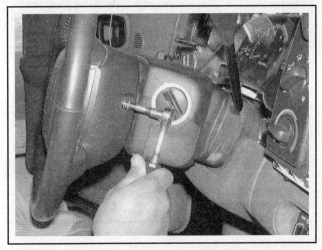

15.2 To detach the airbag module from the steering wheel, remove the airbag module retaining screws

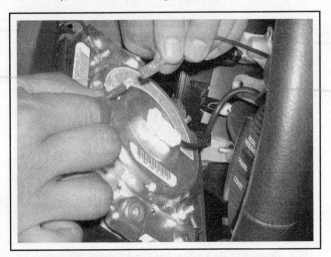

15.3a Unplug the electrical connector for the horn . . .

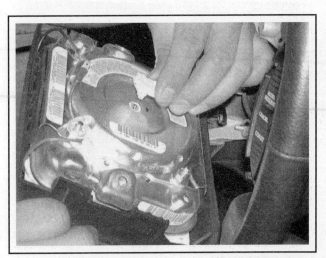

15.3b . . . then unplug the electrical connector for the airbag module

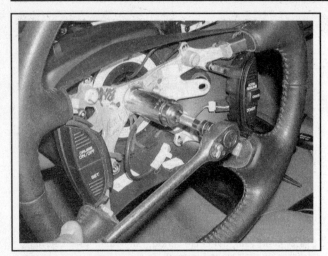

15.4 Remove the steering wheel retaining nut

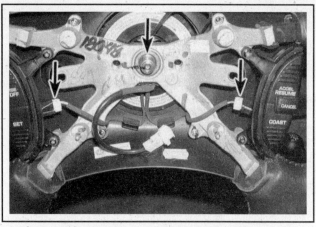

15.5 Mark the relationship of the steering wheel to the steering shaft before removing the wheel, and unplug these two electrical connectors (arrows)

❊❊ WARNING:

Carry the airbag module with the trim cover facing away from you, and set the airbag module in a safe, isolated location with the trim cover facing up.

4   Remove the steering wheel nut (see illustration).
5   Mark the relationship of the steering wheel to the steering shaft and unplug the electrical connectors from the switches on the steering wheel (see illustration).
6   Remove the steering wheel with a steering wheel puller (see illustration).

❊❊ CAUTION:

Any attempt to remove the steering wheel without using a puller can damage the column.

INSTALLATION

7   The airbag clockspring has a locking mechanism which prevents it from rotating after the steering wheel has been removed. Before

installing the steering wheel, however, make sure the clockspring is properly centered. If it is, the wiring harness for the horn will be at the top, while the wiring harness for the airbag and cruise control (if equipped) and remote-mounted radio controls (if equipped) will be at the bottom. Take note of any other alignment marks or instructions which may be present on the clockspring.
8   If the clockspring is not aligned properly, remove it from the steering column to recenter it. Remove the steering column shroud (see Chapter 11), unplug the electrical connectors at the clockspring (see illustration) and also the clockspring harness connector at the base of the steering column. Unlatch the clockspring and detach it from the steering column.
9   Depress the locking tabs and rotate the hub of the clockspring clockwise until it stops (don't apply too much force). Then, turn the hub 2-1/2 turns in the other direction and release the locking tabs.
10   Reinstall the clockspring by reversing the removal procedure.
11   To install the wheel, align the mark on the steering wheel hub with the mark on the shaft, then slip the wheel onto the shaft, guiding the various wires into their proper positions. Install the nut and tighten it to the torque listed in this Chapter's Specifications.
12   Install the airbag module, tightening the screws to the torque listed in this Chapter's Specifications.
13   Reconnect the negative battery cable.

15.6 Remove the steering wheel with a puller that bolts to the hub of the wheel - do not try to hammer the steering wheel off or you will damage the column bearings

15.8 The airbag clockspring has two electrical connectors plugged into it, plus another one in the wiring harness near the base of the steering column

16 Steering column - removal and installation

✳✳ WARNING:

The models covered by this manual are equipped with airbags. Always disable the airbag system when working in the vicinity of airbag system components (see Chapter 12).

REMOVAL

▶ **Refer to illustration 16.7**

1 Park the vehicle with the wheels pointing straight ahead. Disconnect the cable from the negative terminal of the battery. Wait at least two minutes before proceeding (to allow the backup power supply for the airbag system to become depleted).

2 Remove the steering wheel (see Section 15), then turn the ignition key to the LOCK position to prevent the steering shaft from turning.

✳✳ CAUTION:

If this is not done, the airbag clockspring could be damaged.

3 Remove the knee bolster and the reinforcement behind it (see Chapter 11). On models with a column-mounted shifter, detach the shift cable from the shift lever on the column. Also detach the shift indicator cable, or the electrical connector on 2002 and later models (see Chapter 7B).

4 If the vehicle is equipped with a tilt column, unscrew the tilt lever.

5 Remove the steering column shrouds (see Chapter 11).

6 Remove the screw and detach the electrical connector from the multi-function switch (see Chapter 12). Unplug any other electrical connectors that would interfere with column removal.

7 Remove the shaft coupler nut and bolt (securing the steering shaft to the upper intermediate shaft) (see illustration). Separate the intermediate shaft from the steering shaft.

8 Remove the steering column mounting nuts, lower the column and pull it to the rear, making sure nothing is still connected.

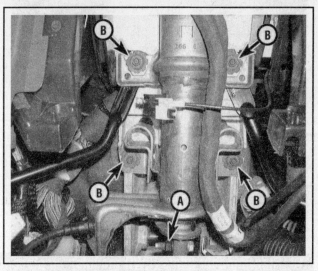

16.7 Typical steering column mounting details

   A   Shaft coupler bolt/nut
   B   Steering column mounting nuts

INSTALLATION

➡**Note: If a new column is being installed, check to see if a shipping lock pin is present. If so, remove it.**

9 Guide the steering column into position and install the mounting nuts, but don't tighten them yet.

10 Connect the intermediate shaft to the steering column. Install a new coupler bolt and nut, then tighten the nut to the torque listed in this Chapter's Specifications.

11 Tighten the column mounting nuts to the torque listed in this Chapter's Specifications.

12 The remainder of installation is the reverse of removal. Adjust the shift cable and the shift indicator cable following the procedures described in Chapter 7B.

17 Tie-rod ends - removal and installation

▶ **Refer to illustrations 17.2 and 17.3**

➡**Note: This procedure applies to 2WD and 4WD models.**

REMOVAL

1 Loosen the wheel lug nuts, raise the front of the vehicle and support it securely on jackstands. Apply the parking brake and block the rear wheels to keep the vehicle from rolling off the jackstands. Remove the wheel.

2 Break loose the tie-rod end jam nut (see illustration). Don't back the nut off; Once it has just been loosened, it will serve as the point to which the tie-rod end will be threaded. If you are removing the tie-rod end to replace the steering gear boot, mark the threads of the tie-rod on the inner side of the nut.

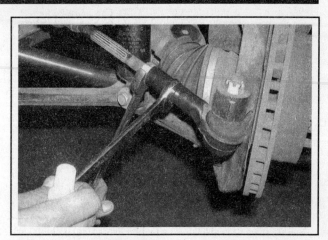

17.2 Hold the tie-rod still with a wrench, then break loose the jam nut

17.3 Back-off the castle nut a few turns, then separate the tie-rod end from the steering knuckle (leaving the nut on the ballstud will prevent the tie-rod end from separating violently)

3   Remove the cotter pin, loosen the castle nut and disconnect the tie-rod end from the steering knuckle arm with a puller (see illustration).
4   Remove the castle nut and unscrew the tie-rod end from the tie-rod.

INSTALLATION

5   If the jam nut was removed, thread it onto the tie-rod until it meets the mark applied in Step 2. Thread the tie-rod end onto the tie-rod until it contacts the jam nut, then connect the tie-rod end to the steering arm. Install the castle nut and tighten it to the torque listed in this Chapter's Specifications. Install a new cotter pin.
6   Tighten the jam nut securely and install the wheel. Lower the vehicle and tighten the lug nuts to the torque listed in the Chapter 1 Specifications.
7   Have the front end alignment checked and, if necessary, adjusted.

18 Steering gear boots (2WD models) - replacement

1   Remove the steering gear from the vehicle (see Section 20).
2   Remove the tie-rod ends from the tie-rods (see Section 17).
3   Remove the jam nuts and outer boot clamps.
4   Cut off both inner boot clamps and discard them.
5   Mark the location of the breather tube (if used) in relation to the rack assembly, then remove the boots and the tube.
6   Install a new clamp on the inner end of the boot.
7   Apply multi-purpose grease to the groove on the tie-rod (where the outer end of the boot will ride) and the mounting grooves on the steering gear (where the inner boot end will be clamped).
8   Line up the breather tube with the marks made during removal and slide the new boot onto the steering gear housing.
9   Make sure the boot isn't twisted, then tighten the new inner clamp.
10 Install the outer clamps and tie-rod end jam nuts.
11 Install the tie-rod ends (see Section 17).
12 Install the steering gear assembly.
13 Have the front end alignment checked and, if necessary, adjusted.

19 Steering gear - removal and installation

▶ Refer to illustration 19.6

✳✳ WARNING:

DO NOT allow the steering column shaft to rotate with the steering gear removed or damage to the airbag system could occur. As a method of preventing the shaft from turning, wrap the seat belt around the rim of the steering wheel and buckle the belt in place.

1   Loosen the front wheel lug nuts, raise the front of the vehicle and support it securely on jackstands. Apply the parking brake. Remove the wheels.
2   Remove the skid plate bolts and remove the skid plate, if equipped.
3   Mark the relationship of the intermediate shaft coupler to the steering gear input shaft and remove the pinch bolt (see illustration 19.6).
4   Detach the tie-rod ends from the steering knuckles (see Section 17).
5   Position a drain pan under the steering gear. Using a flare-nut wrench, if available, unscrew the power steering pressure and return lines from the steering gear. Cap the lines to prevent leakage.
6   Unscrew the mounting bolts and lower the steering gear from the vehicle (see illustration). On 4WD models, tilt the driver's side of the gear and remove the steering gear out the right side of the vehicle.

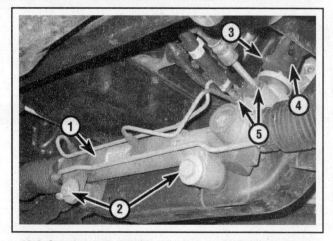

19.6 Steering gear details

1 Steering gear	3 Pinch bolt
2 Steering gear mounting	4 Coupler
bolts	5 Power steering line fittings

7   Installation is the reverse of removal. Be sure to tighten all fasteners to the torque values listed in this Chapter's Specifications. Tighten the wheel lug nuts to the torque listed in the Chapter 1 Specifications. Check the power steering fluid level and add some, if necessary (see Chapter 1), then bleed the system as described in Section 21.

20 Power steering pump - removal and installation

FOUR-CYLINDER MODELS

1 Remove the drivebelt (see Chapter 1).

2 Position a drain pan under the power steering pump, then disconnect the hoses from the pump. Plug the hoses to prevent excessive fluid loss and the entry of contaminants.

3 Remove the pump mounting bolts, then loosen the bracket bolts and lift the pump from the engine compartment, being careful not to let any power steering fluid drip on the vehicle's paint.

4 If pulley replacement is required (or if you are installing a new pump and it didn't come with a pulley installed), special tools are required to draw the pulley off and to install it on the shaft (see illustrations 20.10 and 20.13).

5 Installation is the reverse of removal. Tighten the pump mounting bolts and mounting bracket bolts to the torque listed in this Chapter's Specifications. Fill the power steering reservoir with the recommended fluid (see Chapter 1) and bleed the system following the procedure described in the next Section.

V6 AND V8 MODELS

▸ **Refer to illustrations 20.8, 20.9, 20.10, 20.11 and 20.13**

6 Remove the drivebelt (see Chapter 1).

7 Place a drain pan under the power steering pump.

8 Detach the pressure and return lines from the back of the power steering pump (see illustration). Plug the lines to prevent excessive fluid loss and the entry of contaminants.

9 If you're working on a 4.7L model, remove the three bolts that attach the power steering pump to the cylinder head. The bolts can be accessed through the holes in the power steering pump pulley. All other models, remove the nut securing the battery ground cable to the mounting bracket, and the bolts securing the pump mounting bracket to the engine block (see illustration). Remove the pump and mounting bracket.

10 If you're replacing the pump, use a pulley removal tool, available at most auto parts stores, to draw the pulley off the shaft (see illustration).

11 Remove the bolts securing the pump to the mounting bracket (see illustration).

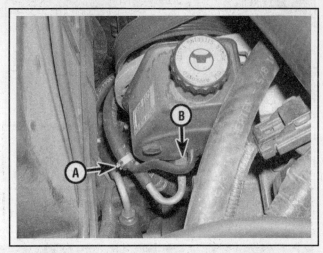

20.8 Loosen the clamp and disconnect the return line (A) from the power steering pump, then unscrew the pressure line fitting (B)

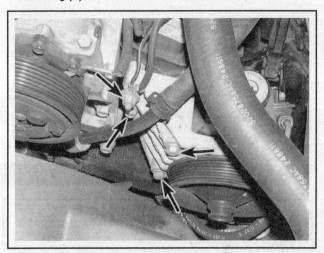

20.9 Power steering pump mounting bracket bolts (V6 and V8 models) - also remove the nut that secures the battery ground cable

20.10 Remove the pulley from the power steering pump with a pulley removal tool . . .

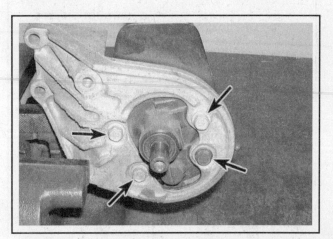

20.11 . . . then remove the mounting bolts and separate the pump from the bracket (5.9L model shown)

20.13 Press the pulley onto the shaft with a pulley installation tool

12 Assemble the pump to the mounting bracket and tighten the bolts to the torque listed in this Chapter's Specifications.

13 Install the pulley to the pump, using a pulley installation tool (available at most auto parts stores) (see illustration). Press the pulley onto the shaft until the hub of the pulley is flush with the end of the shaft.

14 Install the pump/mounting bracket assembly and tighten the bolts to the torque listed in this Chapter's Specifications.

15 Fill the power steering reservoir with the recommended fluid (see Chapter 1) and bleed the system following the procedure described in the next Section.

21 Power steering system - bleeding

1 Following any operation in which the power steering fluid lines have been disconnected, the power steering system must be bled to remove all air and obtain proper steering performance.

2 With the front wheels in the straight ahead position, check the power steering fluid level and, if low, add fluid until it reaches the Cold mark on the dipstick.

3 Start the engine and allow it to run at fast idle. Recheck the fluid level and add more if necessary to reach the Cold mark on the dipstick.

4 Bleed the system by turning the wheels from side-to-side, without hitting the stops. This will work the air out of the system. Keep the reservoir full of fluid as this is done.

5 When the air is worked out of the system, return the wheels to the straight ahead position and leave the vehicle running for several more minutes before shutting it off.

6 Road test the vehicle to be sure the steering system is functioning normally and noise free.

7 Recheck the fluid level to be sure it's up to the Hot mark on the dipstick while the engine is at normal operating temperature. Add fluid if necessary (see Chapter 1).

22 Wheels and tires - general information

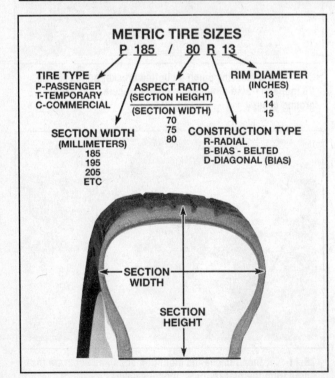

22.1 Metric tire size code

▶ Refer to illustration 22.1

Most vehicles covered by this manual are equipped with metric-size fiberglass or steel belted radial tires (see illustration), or inch-pattern light truck tires. Use of other size or type of tires may affect the ride and handling of the vehicle. Don't mix different types of tires, such as radials and bias belted, on the same vehicle as handling may be seriously affected. It's recommended that tires be replaced in pairs on the same axle, but if only one tire is being replaced, be sure it's the same size, structure and tread design as the other.

Because tire pressure has a substantial effect on handling and wear, the pressure on all tires should be checked at least once a month or before any extended trips (see Chapter 1).

Wheels must be replaced if they're bent, dented, leak air, have elongated bolt holes, are heavily rusted, out of vertical symmetry or if the lug nuts won't stay tight. Wheel repairs that use welding or peening are not recommended.

Tire and wheel balance is important to the overall handling, braking and performance of the vehicle. Unbalanced wheels can adversely affect handling and ride characteristics as well as tire life. Whenever a tire is installed on a wheel, the tire and wheel should be balanced by a shop with the proper equipment.

23 Front end alignment - general information

▶ **Refer to illustration 23.1**

A front end alignment (see illustration) refers to the adjustments made to the front wheels so they're in proper angular relationship to the suspension and the ground. Front wheels that are out of proper alignment not only affect steering control, but also increase tire wear.

Getting the proper front wheel alignment is a very exacting process, one in which complicated and expensive machines are necessary to perform the job properly. Because of this, you should have a technician with the proper equipment perform these tasks. We will, however, use this space to give you a basic idea of what is involved with front end alignment so you can better understand the process and deal intelligently with the shop that does the work.

Toe-in is the turning in of the front wheels. The purpose of a toe specification is to ensure parallel rolling of the front wheels. In a vehicle with zero toe-in, the distance between the front edges of the wheels will be the same as the distance between the rear edges of the wheels. The actual amount of toe-in is normally only a fraction of an inch. Toe-in is adjusted by turning the tie-rod in the tie-rod end to lengthen or shorten the tie-rod. Incorrect toe-in will cause the tires to wear improperly by making them scrub against the road surface.

Camber is the tilting of the front wheels from the vertical when viewed from the front of the vehicle. When the wheels tilt out at the top, the camber is said to be positive (+). When the wheels tilt in at the top the camber is negative (-). The amount of tilt is measured in degrees from the vertical and this measurement is called the camber angle. This angle affects the amount of tire tread which contacts the road and compensates for changes in the suspension geometry when the vehicle is cornering or traveling over an undulating surface. Camber is adjusted by moving the upper control arm in-or-out in relation to its mount.

Caster is the tilting of the top of the front steering axis from the vertical. A tilt toward the rear is positive caster and a tilt toward the front is negative caster. Caster is adjusted by moving the rear of the upper control arm in-or-out in relation to its mount.

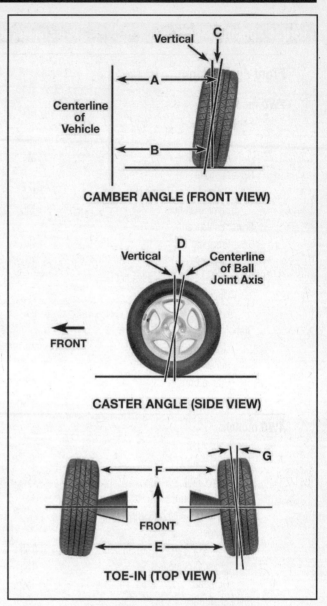

CAMBER ANGLE (FRONT VIEW)

CASTER ANGLE (SIDE VIEW)

TOE-IN (TOP VIEW)

23.1 Front end alignment details

A minus B = C (degrees camber)
D = degrees caster
E minus F = toe-in (measured in inches)
G = toe-in (expressed in degrees)

Specifications

Torque specifications	Ft-lbs (unless otherwise indicated)

Front suspension

2WD models

Shock absorber	
Upper nut	19
Lower bolts	21
Upper control arm	
Pivot shaft-to-frame nuts	155
Pivot shaft nuts	130
Lower control arm	
Front nut	130
Rear nut	80
Balljoint-to-steering knuckle nut	
Upper	60
Lower	94
Stabilizer bar	
Upper link nut	27
Ballstud nut	35
Clamp bolts	45
Hub/bearing assembly spindle nut	185

4WD models

Shock absorber	
Upper nut	19
Lower bolt	80
Upper control arm	
Pivot shaft-to-frame bolts/nuts	
Dakota	
2002 and earlier models	165
2003 models	155
Durango	150
Pivot shaft nuts	95
Lower control arm	
Front bolt	80
Rear bolt	140
Balljoint-to-steering knuckle nut	
Upper	60
Lower	135
Stabilizer bar	
Bracket-to-fame bolt/nut	
Bolt	80
Nut	140
Bracket-to-control arm	25
Hub/bearing assembly-to steering knuckle nuts	123

Torque specifications	Ft-lbs (unless otherwise indicated)

Rear suspension

Shock absorber	
Upper nut	70
Lower nut	70
Stabilizer bar	
Link nut	
Upper	
Dakota	40
Durango	70
Lower	
Dakota	40
Durango	50
Clamp bolts	40
Leaf spring	
U-bolt nuts	
Dakota	110
Durango	90
Front spring-to-frame bolt/nut	
Dakota	120
Durango	85
Rear shackle bolts/nuts	
Dakota	120
Durango	85

Steering

Steering gear-to-frame bolts	
2001 and earlier models	190
2002 and later models	200
Intermediate shaft pinch bolt	
2001 and earlier models	36
2002 and later models	42
Tie-rod end nut	
2001 and earlier models	80
2002 and later models	60

Steering column

Airbag module-to-steering wheel screws	90 in-lbs
Steering wheel nut	
2000 models	35
2001 and later models	45
Steering column bracket nuts	
2000 models	105 in-lbs
2001 and later models	250 in-lbs

Power steering pump

Four-cylinder models	
Pump mounting bolts	21
Mounting bracket bolts	21

Torque specifications	Ft-lbs (unless otherwise indicated)

Power steering pump (continued)
    V6 and 5.2L/5.9L V8 models
        2002 and earlier models

Pump-to-bracket bolts	30
Mounting bracket-to-engine bolts	30

        2003 models

Pump-to-bracket bolts	30
Mounting bracket-to-engine bolts	40

    4.7L V8

Pump mounting bolts	21

Section

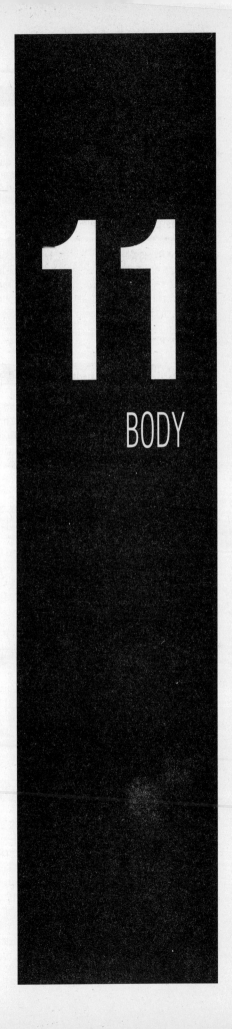

11

BODY

General information

✳ WARNING:

The models covered by this manual are equipped with Supplemental Restraint Systems (SRS), more commonly known as airbags. Always disable the airbag system before working in the vicinity of any airbag system components to avoid the possibility of accidental deployment of the airbags, which could cause personal injury (see Chapter 12).

The vehicles covered by this manual are built with body-on-frame construction. The frame is a ladder-type, consisting of two C-sectioned steel side rails joined by crossmembers. The front 1/3 portion of the frame is boxed for extra rigidity in powertrain and suspension mounting. A number of lateral crossmembers are used, with some being welded or riveted to the side rails. Crossmembers designed for removal (such as the transmission crossmember) are bolted to the side rails. The Durango frame is of three sections formed to fit together and then welded.

The Dakota body is in two separate sections, the cab and the bed, while the Durango body incorporates the cab, back-seat area and cargo compartment in one unitized structure.

Certain components are particularly vulnerable to accident damage and can be unbolted and repaired or replaced. Among these parts are the hood, doors, seats, tailgate, liftgate, bumpers and front fenders.

Only general body maintenance practices and body panel repair procedures within the scope of the do-it-yourselfer are included in this Chapter.

2 Body - maintenance

1   The condition of your vehicle's body is very important, because the resale value depends a great deal on it. It's much more difficult to repair a neglected or damaged body than it is to repair mechanical components. The hidden areas of the body, such as the wheel wells, the frame and the engine compartment, are equally important, although they don't require as frequent attention as the rest of the body.

2   Once a year, or every 12,000 miles, it's a good idea to have the underside of the body steam cleaned. All traces of dirt and oil will be removed and the area can then be inspected carefully for rust, damaged brake lines, frayed electrical wires, damaged cables and other problems. The front suspension components should be greased after completion of this job.

3   At the same time, clean the engine and the engine compartment with a steam cleaner or water-soluble degreaser.

4   The wheel wells should be given close attention, since undercoating can peel away and stones and dirt thrown up by the tires can cause the paint to chip and flake, allowing rust to set in. If rust is found, clean down to the bare metal and apply an anti-rust paint.

5   The body should be washed about once a week. Wet the vehicle thoroughly to soften the dirt, then wash it down with a soft sponge and plenty of clean, soapy water. If the surplus dirt is not washed off very carefully, it can wear down the paint.

6   Spots of tar or asphalt thrown up from the road should be removed with a cloth soaked in tar remover or kerosene lamp oil.

7   Once every six months, wax the body and chrome trim. If a chrome cleaner is used to remove rust from any of the vehicle's plated parts, remember that the cleaner also removes part of the chrome, so use it sparingly.

3 Vinyl trim - maintenance

Don't clean vinyl trim with detergents, caustic soap or petroleum-based cleaners. Plain soap and water works just fine, with a soft brush to clean dirt that may be ingrained. Wash the vinyl as frequently as the rest of the vehicle. After cleaning, application of a high-quality rubber and vinyl protectant will help prevent oxidation and cracks. The protectant can also be applied to weather-stripping, vacuum lines and rubber hoses, which often fail as a result of chemical degradation, and to the tires.

4 Upholstery and carpets - maintenance

1   Every three months remove the floormats and clean the interior of the vehicle (more frequently if necessary). Use a stiff whiskbroom to brush the carpeting and loosen dirt and dust, then vacuum the upholstery and carpets thoroughly, especially along seams and crevices.

2   Dirt and stains can be removed from carpeting with basic household or automotive carpet shampoos available in spray cans. Follow the directions and vacuum again, then use a stiff brush to bring back the "nap" of the carpet.

3   Most interiors have cloth or vinyl upholstery, either of which can be cleaned and maintained with a number of material-specific cleaners or shampoos available in auto supply stores. Follow the directions on the product for usage, and always spot-test any upholstery cleaner on an inconspicuous area (bottom edge of a backseat cushion) to ensure that it doesn't cause a color shift in the material.

4   After cleaning, vinyl upholstery should be treated with a protectant.

➡ **Note: Make sure the protectant container indicates the product can be used on seats - some products may make a seat too slippery.**

5   Leather upholstery requires special care. It should be cleaned regularly with saddlesoap or leather cleaner. Never use alcohol, gaso-

line, nail polish remover or thinner to clean leather upholstery.

6   After cleaning, regularly treat leather upholstery with a leather conditioner, rubbed in with a soft cotton cloth. Never use car wax on leather upholstery.

7   In areas where the interior of the vehicle is subject to bright sunlight, cover leather seating areas of the seats with a sheet if the vehicle is to be left out for any length of time.

5   Body repair - minor damage

PLASTIC BODY PANELS

The following repair procedures are for minor scratches and gouges. Repair of more serious damage should be left to a dealer service department or qualified auto body shop. Below is a list of the equipment and materials necessary to perform the following repair procedures on plastic body panels. Although a specific brand of material may be mentioned, it should be noted that equivalent products from other manufacturers may be used instead.

Wax, grease and silicone removing solvent
Cloth-backed body tape
Sanding discs
Drill motor with three-inch disc holder
Hand sanding block
Rubber squeegees
Sandpaper
Non-porous mixing palette
Wood paddle or putty knife
Curved-tooth body file
Flexible parts repair material

Flexible panels (front and rear bumper fascia)

1   Remove the damaged panel, if necessary or desirable. In most cases, repairs can be carried out with the panel installed.

2   Clean the area(s) to be repaired with a wax, grease and silicone removing solvent applied with a water-dampened cloth.

3   If the damage is structural, that is, if it extends through the panel, clean the backside of the panel area to be repaired as well. Wipe dry.

4   Sand the rear surface about 1-1/2 inches beyond the break.

5   Cut two pieces of fiberglass cloth large enough to overlap the break by about 1-1/2 inches. Cut only to the required length.

6   Mix the adhesive from the repair kit according to the instructions included with the kit, and apply a layer of the mixture approximately 1/8-inch thick on the backside of the panel. Overlap the break by at least 1-1/2 inches.

7   Apply one piece of fiberglass cloth to the adhesive and cover the cloth with additional adhesive. Apply a second piece of fiberglass cloth to the adhesive and immediately cover the cloth with additional adhesive in sufficient quantity to fill the weave.

8   Allow the repair to cure for 20 to 30 minutes at 60-degrees to 80-degrees F.

9   If necessary, trim the excess repair material at the edge.

10 Remove all of the paint film over and around the area(s) to be repaired. The repair material should not overlap the painted surface.

11 With a drill motor and a sanding disc (or a rotary file), cut a "V" along the break line approximately 1/2-inch wide. Remove all dust and loose particles from the repair area.

12 Mix and apply the repair material. Apply a light coat first over the damaged area; then continue applying material until it reaches a level slightly higher than the surrounding finish.

13 Cure the mixture for 20 to 30 minutes at 60-degrees to 80-degrees F.

14 Roughly establish the contour of the area being repaired with a body file. If low areas or pits remain, mix and apply additional adhesive.

15 Block sand the damaged area with sandpaper to establish the actual contour of the surrounding surface.

16 If desired, the repaired area can be temporarily protected with several light coats of primer. Because of the special paints and techniques required for flexible body panels, it is recommended that the vehicle be taken to a paint shop for completion of the body repair.

STEEL BODY PANELS

◆ **See photo sequence**

Repair of minor scratches

17 If the scratch is superficial and does not penetrate to the metal of the body, repair is very simple. Lightly rub the scratched area with a fine rubbing compound to remove loose paint and built up wax. Rinse the area with clean water.

18 Apply touch-up paint to the scratch, using a small brush. Continue to apply thin layers of paint until the surface of the paint in the scratch is level with the surrounding paint. Allow the new paint at least two weeks to harden, then blend it into the surrounding paint by rubbing with a very fine rubbing compound. Finally, apply a coat of wax to the scratch area.

19 If the scratch has penetrated the paint and exposed the metal of the body, causing the metal to rust, a different repair technique is required. Remove all loose rust from the bottom of the scratch with a pocketknife, then apply rust inhibiting paint to prevent the formation of rust in the future. Using a rubber or nylon applicator, coat the scratched area with glaze-type filler. If required, the filler can be mixed with thinner to provide a very thin paste, which is ideal for filling narrow scratches. Before the glaze filler in the scratch hardens, wrap a piece of smooth cotton cloth around the tip of a finger. Dip the cloth in thinner and then quickly wipe it along the surface of the scratch. This will ensure that the surface of the filler is slightly hollow. The scratch can now be painted over as described earlier in this Section.

These photos illustrate a method of repairing simple dents. They are intended to supplement Body repair - minor damage in this Chapter and should not be used as the sole instructions for body repair on these vehicles.

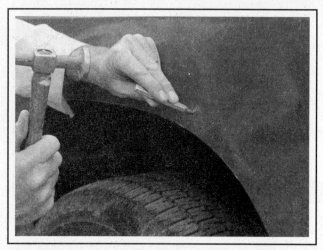

1   If you can't access the backside of the body panel to hammer out the dent, pull it out with a slide-hammer-type dent puller. In the deepest portion of the dent or along the crease line, drill or punch hole(s) at least one inch apart . . .

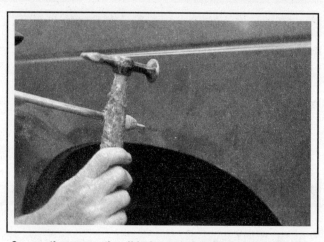

2   . . . then screw the slide-hammer into the hole and operate it. Tap with a hammer near the edge of the dent to help 'pop' the metal back to its original shape. When you're finished, the dent area should be close to its original contour and about 1/8-inch below the surface of the surrounding metal

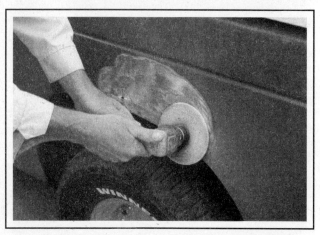

3   Using coarse-grit sandpaper, remove the paint down to the bare metal. Hand sanding works fine, but the disc sander shown here makes the job faster. Use finer (about 320-grit) sandpaper to feather-edge the paint at least one inch around the dent area

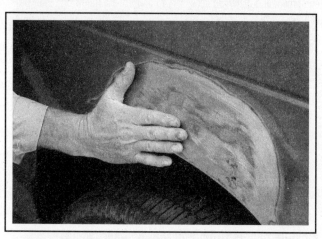

4   When the paint is removed, touch will probably be more helpful than sight for telling if the metal is straight. Hammer down the high spots or raise the low spots as necessary. Clean the repair area with wax/silicone remover

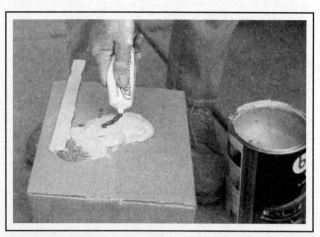

5   Following label instructions, mix up a batch of plastic filler and hardener. The ratio of filler to hardener is critical, and, if you mix it incorrectly, it will either not cure properly or cure too quickly (you won't have time to file and sand it into shape)

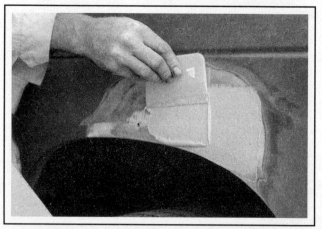

6   Working quickly so the filler doesn't harden, use a plastic applicator to press the body filler firmly into the metal, assuring it bonds completely. Work the filler until it matches the original contour and is slightly above the surrounding metal

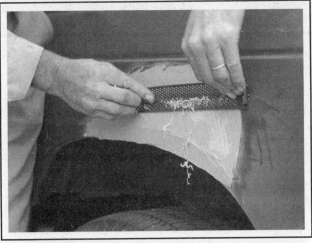

7   Let the filler harden until you can just dent it with your fingernail. Use a body file or Surform tool (shown here) to rough-shape the filler

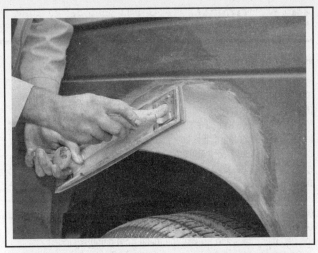

8   Use coarse-grit sandpaper and a sanding board or block to work the filler down until it's smooth and even. Work down to finer grits of sandpaper - always using a board or block - ending up with 360 or 400 grit

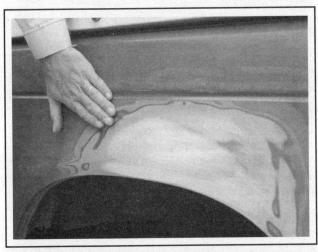

9   You shouldn't be able to feel any ridge at the transition from the filler to the bare metal or from the bare metal to the old paint. As soon as the repair is flat and uniform, remove the dust and mask off the adjacent panels or trim pieces

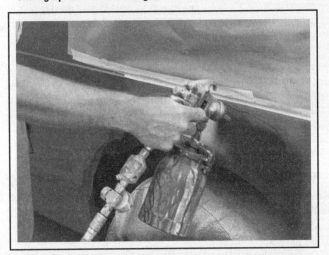

10   Apply several layers of primer to the area. Don't spray the primer on too heavy, so it sags or runs, and make sure each coat is dry before you spray on the next one. A professional-type spray gun is being used here, but aerosol spray primer is available inexpensively from auto parts stores

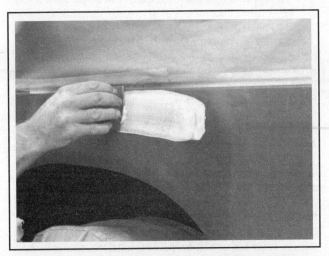

11   The primer will help reveal imperfections or scratches. Fill these with glazing compound. Follow the label instructions and sand it with 360 or 400-grit sandpaper until it's smooth. Repeat the glazing, sanding and respraying until the primer reveals a perfectly smooth surface

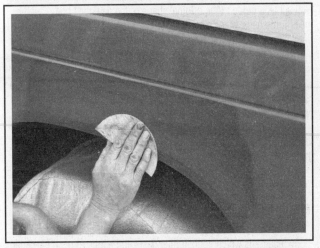

12   Finish sand the primer with very fine sandpaper (400 or 600-grit) to remove the primer overspray. Clean the area with water and allow it to dry. Use a tack rag to remove any dust, then apply the finish coat. Don't attempt to rub out or wax the repair area until the paint has dried completely (at least two weeks)

Repair of dents

20 When repairing dents, the first job is to pull the dent out until the affected area is as close as possible to its original shape. There is no point in trying to restore the original shape completely as the metal in the damaged area will have stretched on impact and cannot be restored to its original contours. It is better to bring the level of the dent up to a point that is about 1/8-inch below the level of the surrounding metal. In cases where the dent is very shallow, it is not worth trying to pull it out at all.

21 If the backside of the dent is accessible, it can be hammered out gently from behind using a soft-face hammer. While doing this, hold a block of wood firmly against the opposite side of the metal to absorb the hammer blows and prevent the metal from being stretched.

22 If the dent is in a section of the body which has double layers, or some other factor makes it inaccessible from behind, a different technique is required. Drill several small holes through the metal inside the damaged area, particularly in the deeper sections. Screw long, self-tapping screws into the holes just enough for them to get a good grip in the metal. Now pulling on the protruding heads of the screws with locking pliers can pull out the dent.

23 The next stage of repair is the removal of paint from the damaged area and from an inch or so of the surrounding metal. This is easily done with a wire brush or sanding disk in a drill motor, although it can be done just as effectively by hand with sandpaper. To complete the preparation for filling, score the surface of the bare metal with a screwdriver or the tang of a file or drill small holes in the affected area. This will provide a good grip for the filler material. To complete the repair, see the Section on filling and painting.

Repair of rust holes or gashes

24 Remove all paint from the affected area and from an inch or so of the surrounding metal using a sanding disk or wire brush mounted in a drill motor. If these are not available, a few sheets of sandpaper will do the job just as effectively.

25 With the paint removed, you will be able to determine the severity of the corrosion and decide whether to replace the whole panel, if possible, or repair the affected area. New body panels are not as expensive as most people think and it is often quicker to install a new panel than to repair large areas of rust.

26 Remove all trim pieces from the affected area except those which will act as a guide to the original shape of the damaged body, such as headlight shells, etc. Using metal snips or a hacksaw blade, remove all loose metal and any other metal that is badly affected by rust. Hammer the edges of the hole in to create a slight depression for the filler material.

27 Wire-brush the affected area to remove the powdery rust from the surface of the metal. If the back of the rusted area is accessible, treat it with rust inhibiting paint.

28 Before filling is done, block the hole in some way. This can be done with sheet metal riveted or screwed into place, or by stuffing the hole with wire mesh.

29 Once the hole is blocked off, the affected area can be filled and painted. See the following subsection on filling and painting.

Filling and painting

30 Many types of body fillers are available, but generally speaking, body repair kits which contain filler paste and a tube of resin hardener are best for this type of repair work. A wide, flexible plastic or nylon applicator will be necessary for imparting a smooth and contoured finish to the surface of the filler material. Mix up a small amount of filler on a clean piece of wood or cardboard (use the hardener sparingly). Follow the manufacturer's instructions on the package, otherwise the filler will set incorrectly.

31 Using the applicator, apply the filler paste to the prepared area. Draw the applicator across the surface of the filler to achieve the desired contour and to level the filler surface. As soon as a contour that approximates the original one is achieved, stop working the paste. If you continue, the paste will begin to stick to the applicator. Continue to add thin layers of paste at 20-minute intervals until the level of the filler is just above the surrounding metal.

32 Once the filler has hardened, the excess can be removed with a body file. From then on, progressively finer grades of sandpaper should be used, starting with a 180-grit paper and finishing with 600-grit wet-or-dry paper. Always wrap the sandpaper around a flat rubber or wooden block, otherwise the surface of the filler will not be completely flat. During the sanding of the filler surface, the wet-or-dry paper should be periodically rinsed in water. This will ensure that a very smooth finish is produced in the final stage.

33 At this point, the repair area should be surrounded by a ring of bare metal, which in turn should be encircled by the finely feathered edge of good paint. Rinse the repair area with clean water until all of the dust produced by the sanding operation is gone.

34 Spray the entire area with a light coat of primer. This will reveal any imperfections in the surface of the filler. Repair the imperfections with fresh filler paste or glaze filler and once more smooth the surface with sandpaper. Repeat this spray-and-repair procedure until you are satisfied that the surface of the filler and the feathered edge of the paint are perfect. Rinse the area with clean water and allow it to dry completely.

35 The repair area is now ready for painting. Spray painting must be carried out in a warm, dry, windless and dust free atmosphere. These conditions can be created if you have access to a large indoor work area, but if you are forced to work in the open, you will have to pick the day very carefully. If you are working indoors, dousing the floor in the work area with water will help settle the dust that would otherwise be in the air. If the repair area is confined to one body panel, mask off the surrounding panels. This will help minimize the effects of a slight mismatch in paint color. Trim pieces such as chrome strips, door handles, etc., will also need to be masked off or removed. Use masking tape and several thickness of newspaper for the masking operations.

36 Before spraying, shake the paint can thoroughly, then spray a test area until the spray painting technique is mastered. Cover the repair area with a thick coat of primer. The thickness should be built up using several thin layers of primer rather than one thick one. Using 600-grit wet-or-dry sandpaper, rub down the surface of the primer until it is very smooth. While doing this, the work area should be thoroughly rinsed with water and the wet-or-dry sandpaper periodically rinsed as well. Allow the primer to dry before spraying additional coats.

37 Spray on the top coat, again building up the thickness by using several thin layers of paint. Begin spraying in the center of the repair area and then, using a circular motion, work out until the whole repair area and about two inches of the surrounding original paint is covered. Remove all masking material 10 to 15 minutes after spraying on the final coat of paint. Allow the new paint at least two weeks to harden, then use a very fine rubbing compound to blend the edges of the new paint into the existing paint. Finally, apply a coat of wax.

6   Body repair - major damage

1   Major damage must be repaired by an auto body shop specifically equipped to perform body and frame repairs. These shops have the specialized equipment required to do the job properly.
2   If the damage is extensive, the body must be checked for proper alignment or the vehicle's handling characteristics may be adversely affected and other components may wear at an accelerated rate.

3   Due to the fact that all of the major body components (hood, fenders, etc.) are separate and replaceable units, any seriously damaged components should be replaced rather than repaired. Sometimes the components can be found in a wrecking yard that specializes in used vehicle components, often at considerable savings over the cost of new parts.

7   Hinges and locks - maintenance

Once every 3000 miles, or every three months, the hinges and latch assemblies on the doors, hood and trunk should be given a few drops of light oil or lock lubricant. The door latch strikers should also be

lubricated with a thin coat of grease to reduce wear and ensure free movement. Lubricate the door and trunk locks with spray-on graphite lubricant.

8   Windshield and fixed glass - replacement

Replacement of the windshield and fixed glass requires the use of special fast-setting adhesive/caulk materials and some specialized tools and techniques. These operations should be left to a dealer ser-

vice department or a shop specializing in glasswork. On Durango models, the fixed glass also includes the quarter windows and liftgate glass.

9   Radiator grille - removal and installation

▶ Refer to illustration 9.2

1   Open the hood.
2   Remove the mounting screws and nuts, then detach the grille assembly from the assembly bracket (see illustration).
3   Remove the screws attaching the assembly bracket to the hood and lower it from the hood.
4   Installation is the reverse of removal.

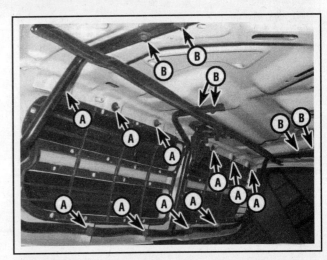

9.2 Remove the grille mounting fasteners and detach the grille (A), then remove the fasteners attaching the assembly bracket and remove the bracket (B)

10   Hood - removal, installation and adjustment

▶ Refer to illustrations 10.2, 10.10 and 10.11

➡Note: The hood is heavy and somewhat awkward to remove and install - at least two people should perform this procedure.

REMOVAL AND INSTALLATION

1   Use blankets or pads to cover the cowl area of the body and the fenders. This will protect the body and paint as the hood is lifted off.

2 Scribe alignment marks around the hinge flanges to insure proper alignment during installation (paint or a permanent-type felt-tip marker also will work for this) (see illustration).

3 Disconnect the electrical connector at the underhood light.

4 Have an assistant support the weight of the hood. Remove the hinge-to-hood nuts.

5 Lift off the hood.

6 Installation is the reverse of removal.

➡**Note: If the grille is still attached when the hood is removed, take care when setting it down to avoid damage to the grille. It can be easily misaligned by rough handling.**

ADJUSTMENT

7 Fore-and-aft and side-to-side adjustment of the hood is done by moving the hood in relation to the hinge flanges after loosening the nuts.

8 Scribe or trace a line around the entire hinge plate so you can judge the amount of movement.

9 Loosen the nuts and move the hood into correct alignment. Move it only a little at a time. Tighten the hinge nuts and carefully lower the hood to check the alignment.

10 Adjust the hood latch so the hood closes securely (see illustration).

11 Adjust the hood bumpers on the radiator support so the hood is

10.2 Use paint or a marking pen to draw a line (white lines in photo) where the hood hinges meet the hood then support the hood and remove the nuts (arrows)

flush with the fenders when closed (see illustration).

12 The safety catch assembly on the hood itself can also be adjusted fore-and-aft and side-to-side after loosening the bolts.

13 The hood latch assembly, as well as the hinges, should be periodically lubricated with white lithium-base grease to prevent sticking and wear.

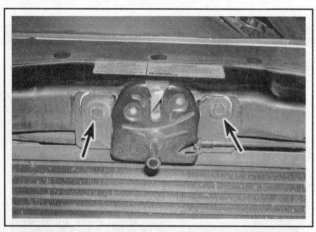

10.10 Loosen the hood latch bolts (arrows), then move the latch as necessary to adjust the hood-closed position

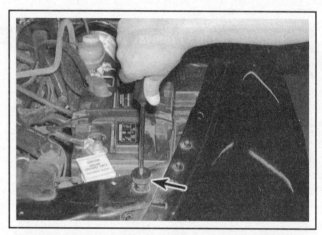

10.11 Use a Phillips-head screwdriver to thread the rubber bumper (arrow) in-or-out to make fine adjustments to the hood closed height

11 Hood latch and release cable - removal and installation

♦ Refer to illustrations 11.1 and 11.4

※※ WARNING:

The models covered by this manual are equipped with Supplemental Restraint Systems (SRS), more commonly known as airbags. Always disable the airbag system before working in the vicinity of any airbag system components to avoid the possibility of accidental deployment of the airbags, which could cause personal injury (see Chapter 12).

LATCH

1 Remove the bolts and detach the latch assembly. Unhook the spring and use a screwdriver to detach the cable end from the latch (see illustration).

2 Installation is the reverse of removal.

CABLE

3 Disconnect the cable from the latch (see illustration 11.1). Detach the cable from the fasteners along the left inner fender.

11.1 Disconnect the hood latch release cable (arrow) from the latch

11.4 Remove the two screws (arrows) and detach the hood release cable/handle from under the instrument panel

4   Refer to Section 26 and remove the driver's knee bolster. Working in the passenger compartment, remove the screws and detach the hood-release cable and handle assembly from the instrument panel (see illustration).

5   Pull the cable through the firewall grommet into the passen-ger compartment.

6   Insert the end of the new cable through the firewall grommet into the engine compartment.

7   Pull the cable through from the engine compartment side.

8   The remainder of installation is the reverse of removal.

12 Bumpers - removal and installation

▶ **Refer to illustrations 12.3 and 12.9**

❊❊ **WARNING:**

The models covered by this manual are equipped with Supplemental Restraint Systems (SRS), more commonly known as airbags. Always disable the airbag system before working in the vicinity of any airbag system components to avoid the possibility of accidental deployment of the airbags, which could cause personal injury (see Chapter 12).

1   Front bumpers on all models are composed of a plastic fascia, or exterior skin, and a structural beam. Rear bumpers on Durango models also have a fascia.

FRONT BUMPER

2   Support the bumper with a jack or jackstand.

3   With an assistant supporting the bumper, remove the bolts/nuts retaining the bumper to the frame (see illustration).

4   Remove the inner bumper bracket mounting bolts and the push-in fasteners securing the air deflector to the bottom of the bumper fascia.

5   Disconnect any wiring harnesses that would interfere with bumper removal and detach the bumper.

6   Installation is the reverse of removal.

REAR BUMPER

7   Support the bumper with a jack or jackstand.

8   Disconnect the license plate light.

9   With an assistant supporting the bumper, remove the bolts, nuts and stud plates retaining the bumper to the frame (see illustration).

12.3 Front bumper-to-frame mounting bolts

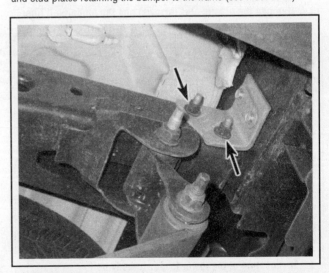

12.9 Remove the bumper bracket mounting nuts

10 On Durango models, if only the rear bumper fascia is to be removed, the bumper can remain attached to the frame. Pry up the rubber step pad, remove the rivets at the rear of the fenderwell and the pushpins, then pull off the fascia.

➡Note: If the step pad is to be removed, some of the projecting pins on the bottom of the pad may be damaged. A new step pad may have to be installed.

11 Installation is the reverse of removal.

13 Front fender - removal and installation

➤ Refer to illustrations 13.4, 13.8a, 13.8b and 13.8c

❋❋ WARNING:

The models covered by this manual are equipped with Supplemental Restraint Systems (SRS), more commonly known as airbags. Always disable the airbag system before working in the vicinity of any airbag system components to avoid the possibility of accidental deployment of the airbags, which could cause personal injury (see Chapter 12).

1 Disconnect the negative cable from the battery (see Chapter 1). Loosen the wheel lug nuts, raise the vehicle, support it securely on jackstands and remove the front wheel.

2 Remove the composite headlight assembly, side marker and turn signal lamps (see Chapter 12).

3 If removing the left fender, remove the battery and battery tray (see Chapter 5), and remove the bolts securing the Power Distribution Center (PDC). Set the PDC aside without disconnecting the electrical cables.

4 Pry out the plastic rivets, remove the screws and remove the inner fenderwell liner (see illustration).

5 If removing the right fender, unbolt and set aside the Powertrain Control Module, the air filter housing and the windshield washer tank.

6 Disconnect the antenna (see Chapter 12) and all lighting system electrical connectors and other components that would interfere with fender removal. Detach the electrical harnesses that are clipped to each fender, and the hood-release cable (left fender).

7 At the left fender, remove the bolts securing the ABS hydraulic control unit to the fender (see Chapter 9). Without disconnecting the hydraulic lines, move the unit just enough to clear the studs so the fender can be removed.

8 Remove the upper and lower fender mounting bolts (see illustrations). Remove the fender-to-cowl mounting bolts and fender-to-lower radiator closure panel. If you're working on the left front fender, remove

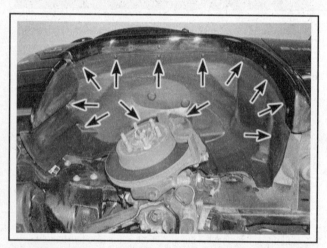

13.4 Remove the plastic pins (arrows) and the fenderwell liner

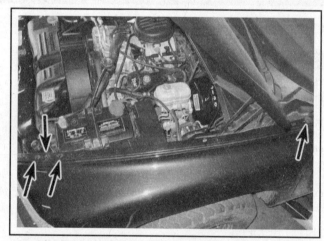

13.8a Front fender upper mounting bolts

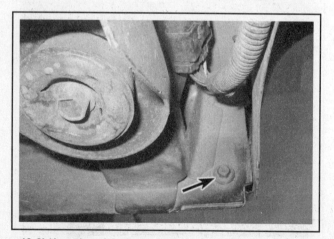

13.8b Location of the lower fender-to-body bolt

13.8c Remove the fender-to-battery support bracket mounting bolts

the bolts securing the fender to the battery support bracket (see illustration).

9   Detach the fender. It's a good idea to have an assistant support the fender while it's being moved away from the vehicle to prevent damage to the surrounding body panels.

10 Installation is the reverse of removal. If a new fender is being installed, transfer the plastic fenderwell lip to the new fender.

11 Tighten all nuts, bolts and screws securely.

14 Cowl cover - removal and installation

▶ **Refer to illustrations 14.3a and 14.3b**

1   Mark the position of the windshield wiper blades on the windshield with a wax marking pencil.

2   Remove the wiper arms (see Chapter 12).

3   Remove the plastic cowl grille retainers, disconnect the windshield washer hoses and detach the cowl grille from the vehicle (see illustrations).

4   Installation is the reverse of removal. Make sure to align the wiper blades with the marks made during removal.

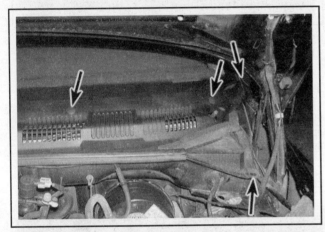

14.3a Remove the plastic nuts and rivets (arrows, left side of cowl shown) and pull up the cowl cover

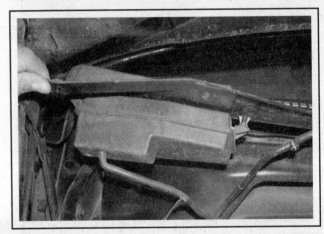

14.3b Once the cowl cover is raised, disconnect and plug the hose from the windshield washer reservoir (attached to bottom of cowl cover)

15 Door trim panels - removal and installation

▶ **Refer to illustrations 15.2, 15.3, 15.5 and 15.6**

1   Disconnect the negative cable from the battery (see Chapter 1).

2   Remove all door trim panel retaining screws and door pull/arm-rest assemblies (see illustration).

3   On manual window models, remove the window crank (see illustration).

4   Pull upward and outward at the same time to release the door panel from the clips on the door.

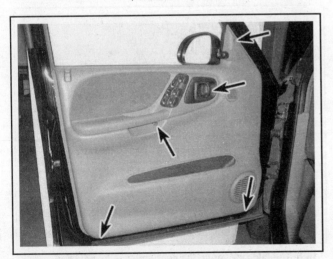

15.2 Use a Phillips screwdriver to remove the screws (arrows) in the door panel - don't overlook the one in the door pull

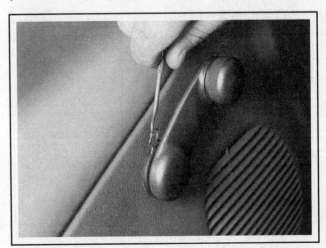

15.3 Use a hooked tool to remove the retaining clip, then detach the window crank handle (manual windows)

15.5 Pull the panel away from the door and unplug the electrical connectors

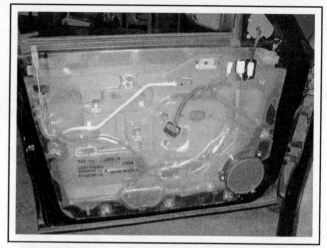

15.6 Peel the water deflector carefully away from the door, taking care not to tear it

5 Once all of the clips are disengaged, raise the trim panel up and off the door. Disconnect any wiring harness connectors and remove the trim panel from the vehicle (see illustration).

6 For access to the inner door, carefully peel back the plastic watershield (see illustration).

7 Prior to installation of the door panel, be sure to reinstall any clips in the panel which may have come out during the removal proce-

dure and remain in the door itself.

8 Connect the wiring harness connectors and place the panel in position on the door. Press the trim panel straight against the door until the clips on the trim panel align with all the holes in the door, then push down on the panel until the clips are seated.

9 Install the armrest/door pulls and the window crank. Connect the negative battery cable.

16 Door - removal, installation and adjustment

♦ **Refer to illustrations 16.3 and 16.5**

1 Remove the door trim panel (see Section 15). Disconnect any electrical connectors and push them through the door opening so they won't interfere with door removal. Leave the wiring harness boot attached to the door but disconnected from the body.

2 Place a jack under the door or have an assistant on hand to support it when the hinge bolts are removed.

➡ **Note: If a jack is used, place a rag between it and the door to protect the door's painted surfaces.**

3 Scribe around the mounting bolt/nut heads with a marking pen, remove the fasteners and carefully lift off the door (see illustration).

4 Installation is the reverse of removal, making sure to align the hinge with the marks made during removal before tightening the bolts.

5 Following installation of the door, check the alignment and

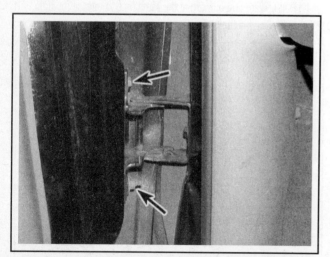

16.3 Mark their locations, then remove the door retaining bolt (upper arrow) and nut (lower arrow) at each hinge

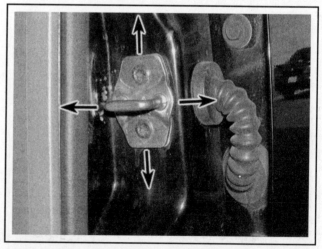

16.5 The latch striker on the doorjamb can be adjusted slightly up/down or in/out

adjust the hinges, if necessary. Adjust the door lock striker, centering it in the door latch (see illustration).

6   Rear doors on Durango models are removed and installed as described above for front doors, except that the door is attached to the body "B" pillar and the pillar trim must be removed before removing the door.

17 Door latch, lock cylinder and handles - removal and installation

▶ **Refer to illustrations 17.2, 17.4 and 17.8**

LATCH

1   Raise the window completely and remove the door trim panel and watershield (see Section 15).

2   Loosen the bolts at the rear glass run channel, move the channel away from the latch, and secure the channel (see illustration). This provides a little extra working room in the latch area inside the door.

3   Rotate the plastic retaining clips off the rods, then detach the latch links.

4   Remove the three Torx-head mounting screws (it may be necessary to use an impact-type screwdriver to loosen them), then remove the latch from the door (see illustration).

5   Place the latch in position and install the screws. Tighten the screws securely.

6   Connect the link rods to the latch.

7   Check the door to make sure it closes properly. If adjustment is necessary, see Section 16.

LOCK CYLINDER

8   Remove the outside door handle (see below). Disconnect the link, use a pair of pliers to pull the key lock cylinder retainer off and withdraw the lock cylinder from the door handle (see illustration).

9   Installation is the reverse of removal.

OUTSIDE HANDLE

10   Remove the access plug at the top rear of the inner doorskin,

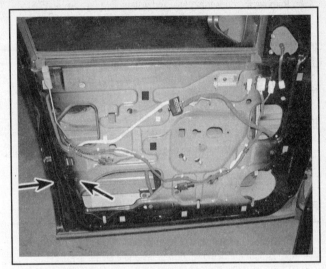

17.2 Remove the two bolts at the rear glass run channel, then move the channel for more working room at the latch

then disconnect the outside handle link from the latch, remove the mounting nuts and detach the handle from the door.

11   Place the handle in position, attach the link and install the nuts. Tighten the nuts securely.

INSIDE HANDLE

12   The inside door handle is permanently bonded to the door trim panel. If the handle is broken, a new door panel must be installed.

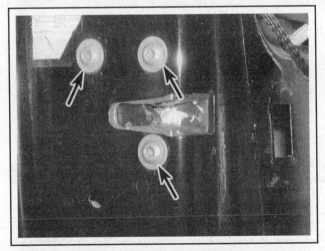

17.4 Remove the Torx bolts (arrows) securing the latch to the door

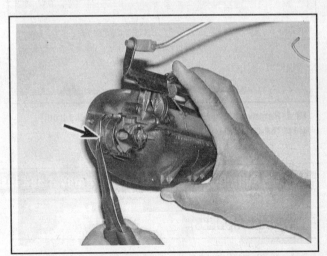

17.8 Remove the lock cylinder retainer clip (handle removed for clarity)

18 Door window glass - removal and installation

FRONT

▶ **Refer to illustrations 18.3, 18.4 and 18.5**

1 Remove the door trim panel and watershield (see Section 15).
2 Lower the glass.
3 Pry the inner weather seal out of the door glass opening (see illustration). Remove the outer door weatherstrip by prying up the strip at the rear of the door and sliding the strip to the rear.
4 Remove the two bolts and the front glass run channel (see illustration).
5 Remove the two nuts retaining the glass to the window regulator track (see illustration).
6 Lift the glass up and out of the door through the glass opening.
7 To install, lower the glass into the door, slide it into position and install the nuts.
8 The remainder of installation is the reverse of removal.

REAR

9 The rear doors are serviced similarly to the front doors, except that there is both a moving window glass and a stationary glass.

➥**Note: On Quad-Cab Dakota models, the rear door quarter glass is difficult to remove from the door without damage to the trim panel. It's recommended that these windows should be removed/installed only at a professional auto glass shop.**

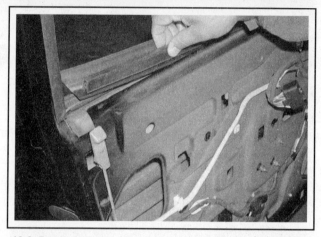

18.3 Pry the inner weather seal out of the door glass opening

10 Follow Steps 1 through 4 as above for the front door glass.
11 Pull the glass run weatherstrip from around the opening of the moving glass. This is the upper weatherstrip the glass seats against when it is fully raised.
12 Remove the nuts securing the glass to the regulator.
13 Remove the glass run channel bolts and pull out the glass. The stationary glass will come out, with the rear run channel, after the moving glass is removed.
14 Installation is the reverse of the removal procedure.

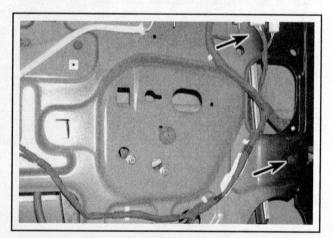

18.4 Remove these bolts (arrows) and remove the front glass run channel

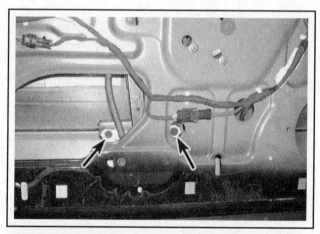

18.5 Align the window so that the nuts (arrows) can be removed from the glass track

19 Door window glass regulator - removal and installation

FRONT (ALL MODELS)

▶ **Refer to illustration 19.3**

WARNING:

Do not remove the electric motor from the regulator assembly.

The lift arm is under tension from the counterbalance spring and could cause personal injury if allowed to retract.

1 Remove the door trim panel and watershield.
2 Remove the door window glass (see Section 18).
3 Remove the window regulator-to-door and track attaching bolts (see illustration).

4   On power window equipped models, unplug the electrical connector.
5   Remove the regulator from the door.
6   Installation is the reverse of removal.

REAR

7   The rear door regulator on these models is removed in much the same manner as for the front door regulator. Follow Steps 1 through 3 as above, but note the mounting bolts are at the top and bottom of the vertical regulator frame.

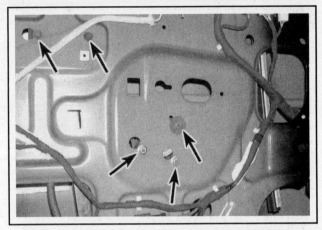

19.3 Door window regulator mounting bolt locations (arrows)

20 Mirrors - removal and installation

♦ **Refer to illustration 20.4**

OUTSIDE MIRRORS

1   Remove the door trim panel (see Section 15).
2   On power mirrors, unplug the electrical connector.
3   Remove the triangular watershield over the mirror mounting.
4   Remove the nuts and detach the mirror from the door (see illustration).
5   Installation is the reverse of removal.

INSIDE MIRROR

6   Remove the setscrew, then slide the mirror up off the support base on the windshield. On models with optional automatic day/night mirror, disconnect the electrical connector.

➡**Note: On some models the setscrew is a Torx and on others a Phillips-head.**

7   Installation is the reverse of removal.
8   If the support base for the mirror has come off the windshield, it can be reattached with a special mirror-adhesive kit available at auto

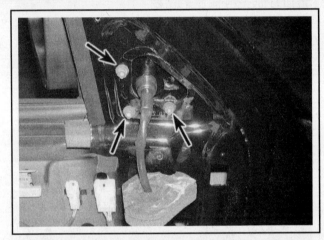

20.4 Remove the three outside mirror mounting nuts (arrows)

parts stores. Clean the glass and support base thoroughly and follow the directions on the adhesive package, allowing the base to bond overnight before attaching the mirror.

21 Tailgate (Dakota models) - removal and installation

♦ **Refer to illustrations 21.1 and 21.2**

1   Open the tailgate and detach the retaining cables (see illustration).

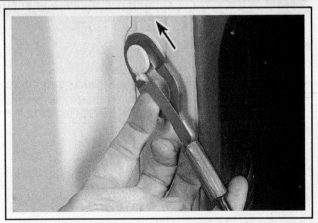

21.1 Lift the spring retainer up and slide the cable end off the pin

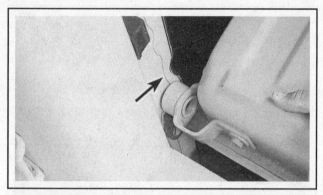

21.2 Align the flat on the right side hinge pin with the slot in the hinge pocket and lift the tailgate off the vehicle

2   Lower the tailgate until the flat on the right side hinge-pin aligns with the slot in the hinge pocket. Lift the tailgate out of the pocket (see illustration). With the help of an assistant to support the weight, withdraw the left hinge pin from the body and remove the tailgate from the vehicle.

3   Installation is the reverse of removal.

22 Tailgate latch and handle (Dakota models) - removal and installation

▶ **Refer to illustrations 22.2 and 22.4**

1   Use a small screwdriver or trim tool to pry off the handle bezel. Once the bottom is pried out, pull the bezel down and away from the tailgate. If a screwdriver is used, cover the tip with electrical tape to prevent scratching the paint.

2   Rotate the plastic retaining clips off the control rods and detach the rods from the handle (see illustration).

3   Remove the retaining screws and detach the handle from the tailgate.

4   Remove the screws and withdraw the latch assembly from the end of the tailgate (see illustration).

5   Installation is the reverse of removal. Tighten all fasteners securely.

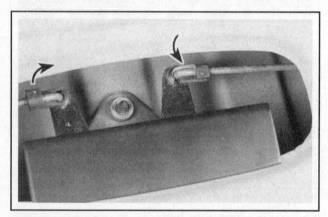

22.2 Rotate the plastic retaining clips off the control rods and detach the rods from the handle

22.4 Latch-to-tailgate mounting screws

23 Liftgate (Durango models) - removal and installation

▶ **Refer to illustration 23.5**

1   Open the liftgate and cover the upper body area around the opening with pads or cloths to protect the painted surfaces when the liftgate is removed.

2   Remove the liftgate upper trim panel, then disconnect the body-to-liftgate electrical connectors (see Section 24).

3   Paint or scribe alignment marks around the liftgate hinge flanges.

4   While an assistant supports the liftgate, detach the support struts (see Section 24).

5   Remove the hinge bolts and detach the liftgate from the vehicle

23.5 Remove the liftgate hinge-to-body mounting bolts

(see illustration).

6   Installation is the reverse of removal. Be extremely careful with the wire harness when threading it back into the liftgate or you could cut it on a metal edge.

7   After installation, close the liftgate and make sure it's in proper

alignment with the surrounding body panels.

8   If the liftgate needs to be adjusted, loosen the hinge bolts slightly, gently close the liftgate and verify that it's centered (the striker should center it). Then carefully open the liftgate and retighten the hinge bolts.

24 Liftgate panels, lock cylinder, latch and support struts (Durango models) - removal and installation

INTERIOR TRIM PANELS

▶ Refer to illustrations 24.1, 24.2 and 24.3

1   Remove the upper trim panel by pulling it outward carefully to free it from the spring clips (see illustration).

2   The upper trim panel must be removed for access to the two upper mounting screws of the lower (larger) liftgate trim panel. Remove the screws at the top and the bottom edge of the lower panel (see illustration).

3   With the lower panel pulled away from the liftgate, disconnect the electrical connectors at the courtesy lights (see illustration).

4   Installation is the reverse of the removal procedure.

LOCK CYLINDER

5   Remove the trim panels from the liftgate.

6   Through the large access hole, disconnect the electrical connector, the linkage rod and pull the retaining clip. Push the lock cylinder out of the liftgate handle assembly.

7   Installation is the reverse of the removal procedure.

OUTSIDE HANDLE

▶ Refer to illustration 24.10

8   Remove the trim panels.

9   Remove the lock cylinder.

10 Remove the handle-to-latch rod, then the mounting nuts (see illustration).

11 Installation is the reverse of the removal procedure.

24.1 Pull the upper liftgate trim panel from the liftgate

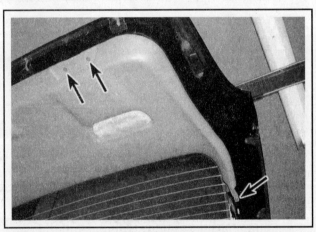

24.2 Remove the upper and lower screws (arrows) from the lower trim panel (right side shown, left side similar)

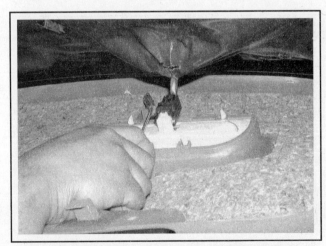

24.3 Disconnect the electrical connectors to the courtesy lights (one is shown, there are two)

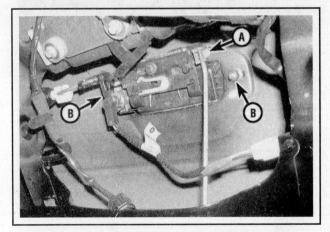

24.10 Disconnect the handle-to-latch rod (A), then remove the handle mounting nuts (B)

LATCH

▶ **Refer to illustrations 24.13 and 24.14**

12 Remove the interior liftgate panels.
13 From inside, disconnect the electrical connector and handle-to-latch rod (see illustration).
14 From below, remove the two latch mounting bolts (see illustration).
15 Installation is the reverse of the removal procedure.

SUPPORT STRUTS

▶ **Refer to illustrations 24.17a and 24.17b**

16 Open the liftgate and prop it securely in the full open position.
17 Remove the support strut mounting screws at each end (see illustrations).
18 Installation is the reverse of the removal procedure.

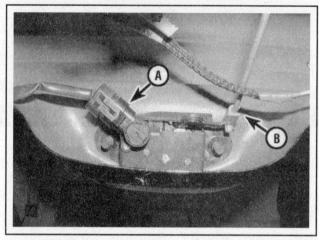

24.13 Disconnect the electrical connector (A) at the latch, then the handle-to-latch rod (B)

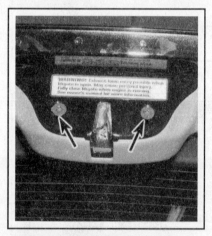

24.14 Remove the two bolts from below (arrows) to remove the latch

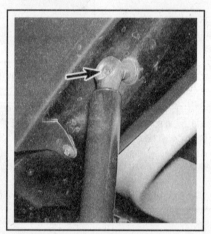

24.17a Detach the upper end of the support struts from the liftgate by removing the screw (arrow)

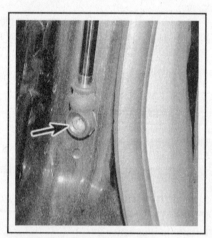

24.17b Detach the lower end of the support struts from the body by removing the screw (arrow)

25 Center console - removal and installation

❊❊ WARNING:

The models covered by this manual are equipped with Supplemental Restraint Systems (SRS), more commonly known as airbags. Always disable the airbag system before working in the vicinity of any airbag system components to avoid the possibility of accidental deployment of the airbags, which could cause personal injury (see Chapter 12).

CENTER FLOOR CONSOLE

▶ **Refer to illustrations 25.1a and 25.1b**

1 On all models, open the console lid and remove the bolts securing the console to the floorpan (see illustrations).
2 Remove the inserts from the cup holders (on Dakota models, there is only the front cup holder, while Durango models have a front and a rear) and remove the front and rear console mounting bolts.

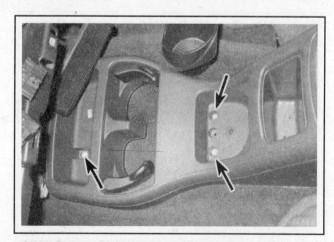

25.1a Remove the center console mounting screws at the front . . .

3   On Durango models with rear heat/air, disconnect the electrical connector for the rear blower.

4   Unplug any electrical connectors and remove the console from the vehicle.

5   Installation is the reverse of removal.

OVERHEAD CONSOLE

6   Disconnect the negative battery cable.

7   Remove the retaining screws at the front, pull the front of the console down and toward the rear to detach the clips. Unplug the electrical connector and lower the console.

➡**Note: When pulling down the console, try to get your fingertips under each side of the console, in the area between the glasses storage bin and the garage door opener storage.**

8   Installation is the reverse of removal.

25.1b . . . and rear of the console

---

26 Dashboard trim panels - removal and installation

✳✳ WARNING:

The models covered by this manual are equipped with Supplemental Restraint Systems (SRS), more commonly known as airbags. Always disable the airbag system before working in the vicinity of any airbag system components to avoid the possibility of accidental deployment of the airbags, which could cause personal injury (see Chapter 12).

INSTRUMENT CLUSTER BEZEL

◆ **Refer to illustrations 26.1 and 26.2**

1   On models with automatic transmission and column shift, apply the parking brake and put the shift lever in the Low position. If equipped with a tilt steering column, lower the column. Remove the screws above the instrument cluster (see illustration).

2   Use a trim removal tool or a flat-blade screwdriver with the tip taped to pry around the complete edge of the instrument cluster bezel (see illustration).

3   Grasp the bezel securely and pull out sharply to detach the retaining clips from the instrument panel.

4   Pull the panel out far enough to disconnect all electrical connectors.

5   Installation is the reverse of removal

26.1 Remove the two screws above the instrument cluster

KNEE BOLSTER

◆ **Refer to illustrations 26.6, 26.7 and 26.8**

6   Remove the screws at the bottom of the driver's knee bolster, then use a dull, flat-bladed tool around the top of the panel to release it from the clips at the top (see illustration).

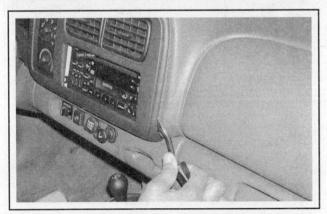

26.2 Pry with a dull trim tool, then grasp the cluster bezel securely and pull out sharply to detach the clips

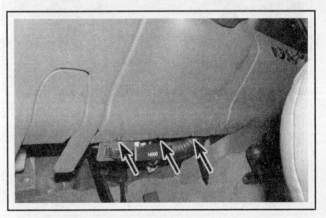

26.6 The knee bolster is held in place by three screws (arrows) at the bottom, and clips at the top

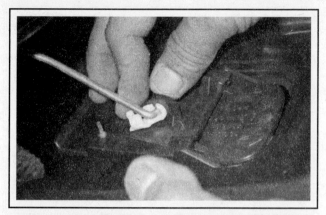

26.7 Under the left side of the dashboard, release the clip securing the parking brake release lever rod and disengage the rod

7 Disconnect the linkage clip on the parking brake release handle and release the rod from the handle (see illustration).

8 If the knee bolster reinforcement panel needs to be removed for any reason, disconnect the electrical harness clips, hood release lever and diagnostic connector from the brace, then remove the bolts (see illustration).

9 Installation is the reverse of removal.

CENTER INSTRUMENT PANEL LOWER BEZEL

▶ **Refer to illustration 26.11**

10 Remove the instrument cluster bezel and open the glove box.

11 Remove the screws at the bottom, side and top of the lower bezel (see illustration).

12 Pull the panel away from the instrument panel enough to disconnect the electrical connectors behind it.

13 Installation is the reverse of removal.

GLOVE BOX

2000 models

14 Open the glove box door.

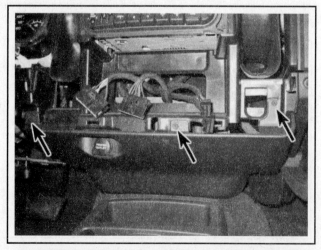

26.11 Remove the top, side and bottom screws securing the lower panel

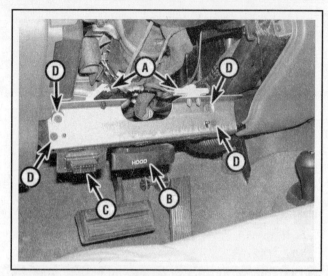

26.8 Pull the two electrical harness clips (A) from the reinforcement bar, remove the two bolts at the hood release handle (B), depress the two side tabs on the diagnostic connector (C) to remove it, then remove the mounting bolts (D)

15 There are three screws in the bottom of the glove compartment. Remove the center screw.

16 Squeeze the two sides of the glove compartment bin together and pull the door down until the bumpers on the bin have cleared the stops.

17 Pull the glove box door away from the instrument panel until the three hinge clips on the glove box door clear the pins in the instrument panel.

18 Installation is the reverse of removal.

2001 and later models

▶ **Refer to illustrations 26.21, 26.22 and 26.23**

19 Remove the instrument cluster bezel and center instrument panel lower bezel.

20 Remove the right side instrument panel end cap (see Section 28).

21 Remove the one glove box mounting screw at the far left (see illustration).

22 Where the instrument panel end cap had been removed, take out

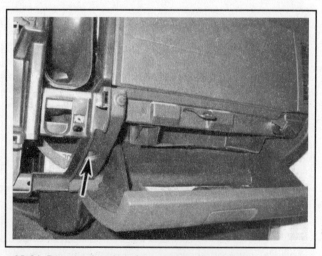

26.21 Remove the glove box screw at the far left

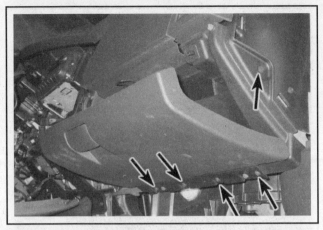

26.22 Remove the one screw under the right-side instrument panel end cap and the screws along the bottom

the one screw and four at the bottom (see illustration).

23 Remove the four glove box screws at the top of the glovebox opening (see illustration).

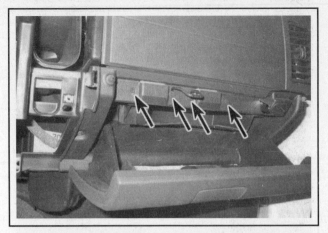

26.23 While supporting the glove box assembly, remove the upper mounting screws

24 Pull the glove box out and disconnect the electrical connector at the glove box light.

25 Installation is the reverse of the removal procedure.

27 Steering column covers - removal and installation

▶ **Refer to illustration 27.2**

1   Refer to Section 26 and remove the driver's knee bolster.

2   Remove the screws securing the upper cover to the lower cover (see illustration).

3   Pull the upper cover up until the snaps are released, then remove the cover.

4   Remove the one lower cover screw at the column lock housing, and remove the lower cover.

5   Installation is the reverse of the removal procedure.

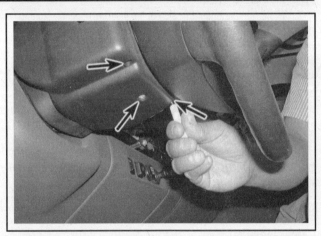

27.2 Remove the screws (arrows) at the lower column shroud

28 Instrument panel - removal and installation

▶ **Refer to illustrations 28.13a and 28.13b**

✳✳ WARNING:

The models covered by this manual are equipped with Supplemental Restraint Systems (SRS), more commonly known as airbags. Always disable the airbag system before working in the vicinity of any airbag system components to avoid the possibility of accidental deployment of the airbags, which could cause personal injury (see Chapter 12).

➡Note: This is a difficult procedure for the home mechanic. There are many hidden fasteners, difficult angles to work in and many electrical connectors to tag and disconnect/connect. We recommend that this procedure be done at a dealership or qualified shop.

1   Turn the front wheels to the straight-ahead position and lock the steering column, disconnect the negative battery cable and disable the airbag system (see Chapter 12).

2   Remove the right and left side cowl trim ("kick") panels. To access the rear screw on each kick panel, pry up the front end of the door sill plates with a trim tool. Remove the instrument panel end caps. On the driver's side, the end cap has a finger pull, but use a trim tool to remove the passenger side end cap.

3   Refer to Section 26 and remove the glove box, instrument cluster bezel, lower center instrument panel lower bezel, knee bolster, and knee bolster reinforcement. Remove the instrument cluster (see Chapter 12).

4   Remove steering column covers (see Section 27).

5   Refer to Chapter 10 and lower the steering column.

➡Note: There will be more working room if the front seats are moved back as far as possible, and even more room if the driver's seat is removed (see Section 29).

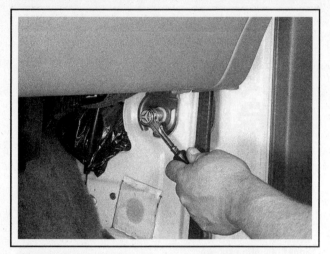

28.13a Remove the screws securing the center support bracket, then loosen the hinge bolts at each end of the instrument panel

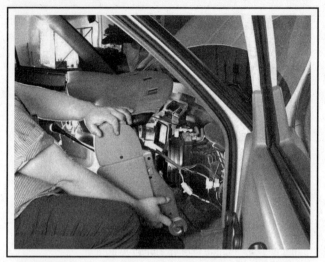

28.13b Rotate the instrument panel back and lift it off the hinge bolts

6   Under the driver's side of the instrument panel, disconnect the large electrical bulkhead connector (by removing the screw in the center), and the two large connectors (without screws) on either side of the main bulkhead connector.

7   While working under that side of the instrument panel, tag and disconnect all other electrical connectors connected to the instrument panel.

➡**Note: Watch for ground straps bolted to the cowl or the area behind the kick panels.**

8   Refer to Chapter 9 and release the parking brake rod from the release lever, which is part of the instrument panel.

9   Under the center of the instrument panel, disconnect the ground strap and dash harness connector from the airbag control module.

10   Remove the screws attaching the instrument panel center support bracket to the airbag control module and the instrument panel. Remove the bracket.

11   Working through the glovebox opening and below the passenger-side of the instrument panel, tag and disconnect any electrical connectors coming from the instrument panel, including the radio, heating/air conditioning system and passenger airbag.

➡**Note: Watch for ground straps bolted to the cowl or the area behind the kick panels.**

12   Use a trim tool to remove the two inside windshield pillar trim panels. Use the tool to go all around the perimeter of the defroster grille, prying up until the grille can be removed.

13   Loosen the pivot bolts at each end, then rotate the instrument panel back (see illustrations). Attach a chain, strap or rod between the top of the instrument panel and the cowl to hold the instrument panel in the "rolled-back" position.

14   Disconnect any remaining electrical connectors. Disconnect the heater/air conditioning vacuum harness from the control panel and disconnect the temperature control cable from the heater core housing.

15   Remove the instrument panel from the vehicle.

16   Installation is the reverse of removal.

29   Seats - removal and installation

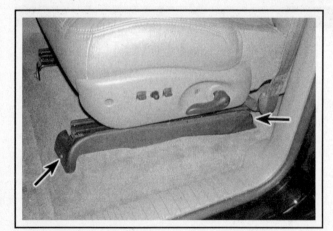

29.2 Remove the front and rear screws (arrows), then remove the front seat track cover

FRONT SEAT (ALL MODELS)

▶ **Refer to illustrations 29.2, 29.3a and 29.3b**

1   In the Dakota pickup models, there are three styles of front seats: bench, split-bench and bucket seats. Durango models have bucket seats with either a console or center seat cushion between the buckets. All are removed in a similar fashion.

2   Remove the screws and the plastic covers over the outer tracks (see illustration).

3   Remove the seat track-to-floor bolts and remove the front seat assembly (see illustrations).

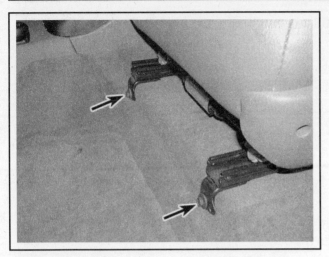

29.3a Remove the front bolt (arrows) from the front seat . . .

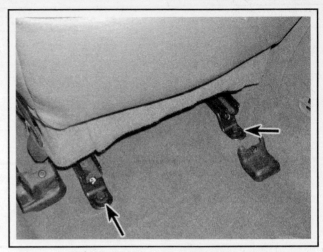

29.3b . . . then remove the plastic caps and the two rear bolts (arrows) per seat

➡Note: This is a job for two people.

4   If the bucket seats need to be separated from each other for repair, turn the assembly over, preferably onto a blanket for protection of the upholstery. Remove the four bolts securing the center seat cushion to the two inside tracks of the bucket seats.

5   Installation is the reverse of removal. When reassembling the two bucket seats to the center cushion, make sure the alignment is as it was, or the seat track-to-floor bolts may not line up properly.

2ND SEAT (DURANGO MODELS)

▶ Refer to illustration 29.7

6   Fold the left and right seat backs forward, then release the catch behind each unit and flip the seat and bottom forward.

7   On each side, remove the two bolts holding the tube-and-bracket to the floor, and the one seat belt bolt on each side of the center cushion (see illustration).

8   Remove the seat assembly as a unit.

➡Note: This is a job for two people.

9   Installation is the reverse of removal.

3RD SEAT (DURANGO MODELS)

▶ Refer to illustration 29.11

10   Flip the 3rd seat bottom cushion up and forward, so that it lies flat, exposing the 3rd seat bracket.

11   Remove the two bolts on each side of the floor bracket (see illustration). Flip the seat bottom back into place and have an assistant help you remove the whole 3rd seat.

12   Installation is the reverse of removal.

REAR SEAT (QUAD-CAB DAKOTA MODELS)

13   Each section of the 60/40 split-bench seat is removable separately.

14   Pull up the seat cushion and fold it forward for access to the seat fasteners.

15   Remove the nuts on the floor studs and lift the seat to release the clips at the back of the cab. Work the seatbelts through and remove the seats.

16   Installation is the reverse of the removal procedure.

29.7 Remove the bolts (arrows) at each 2nd seat bracket and the seat belt mounting bolt - remove these same three bolts on the other side, too (left side shown, right side similar)

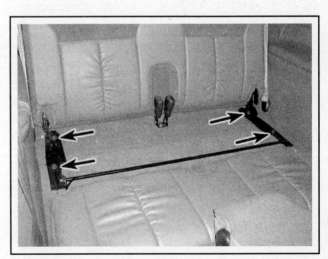

29.11 Remove the two bolts (arrows) on each side of the 3rd seat floor bracket frame

Notes

Section

12

CHASSIS ELECTRICAL SYSTEM

1 General information

The electrical system is a 12-volt, negative ground type. Power for the lights and all electrical accessories is supplied by a lead/acid-type battery that is charged by the alternator.

This Chapter covers repair and service procedures for the various electrical components not associated with the engine. Information on the battery, alternator, distributor and starter motor can be found in Chapter 5.

It should be noted that when portions of the electrical system are serviced, the negative cable should be disconnected from the battery to prevent electrical shorts and/or fires.

2 Electrical troubleshooting - general information

▶ **Refer to illustrations 2.5a, 2.5b, 2.6, 2.9 and 2.15**

A typical electrical circuit consists of an electrical component, any switches, relays, motors, fuses, fusible links or circuit breakers related to that component and the wiring and connectors that link the component to both the battery and the chassis. To help you pinpoint an electrical circuit problem, wiring diagrams are included at the end of this Chapter.

Before tackling any troublesome electrical circuit, first study the appropriate wiring diagrams to get a complete understanding of what makes up that individual circuit. Trouble spots, for instance, can often be narrowed down by noting if other components related to the circuit are operating properly. If several components or circuits fail at one time, chances are the problem is in a fuse or ground connection, because several circuits are often routed through the same fuse and ground connections.

Electrical problems usually stem from simple causes, such as loose or corroded connections, a blown fuse, a melted fusible link or a failed relay. Visually inspect the condition of all fuses, wires and connections in a problem circuit before troubleshooting the circuit.

If test equipment and instruments are going to be utilized, use the diagrams to plan ahead of time where you will make the necessary connections in order to accurately pinpoint the trouble spot.

The basic tools needed for electrical troubleshooting include a circuit tester or voltmeter (a 12-volt bulb with a set of test leads can also be used), a continuity tester, which includes a bulb, battery and set of test leads, and a jumper wire, preferably with a circuit breaker incorporated, which can be used to bypass electrical components (see illustrations). Before attempting to locate a problem with test instruments, use the wiring diagram(s) to decide where to make the connections.

VOLTAGE CHECKS

Voltage checks should be performed if a circuit is not functioning properly. Connect one lead of a circuit tester to either the negative battery terminal or a known good ground. Connect the other lead to a connector in the circuit being tested, preferably nearest to the battery or fuse (see illustration). If the bulb of the tester lights, voltage is present, which means that the part of the circuit between the connector and the battery is problem free. Continue checking the rest of the circuit in the same fashion. When you reach a point at which no voltage is present,

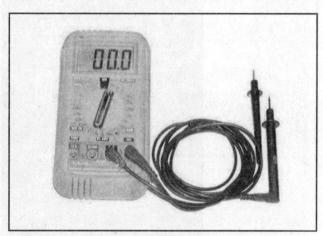

2.5a The most useful tool for electrical troubleshooting is a digital multimeter that can check volts, amps, and test continuity

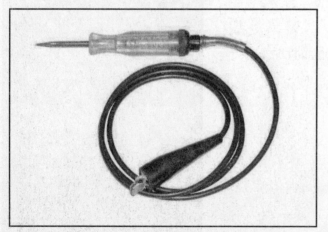

2.5b A simple test light is very handy, especially when testing for voltage

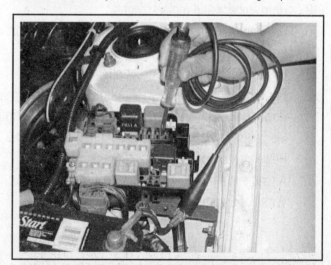

2.6 In use, a basic test light's lead is clipped to a known good ground, then the pointed probe can test connectors, wires or electrical sockets - if the bulb lights, the part being tested has battery voltage

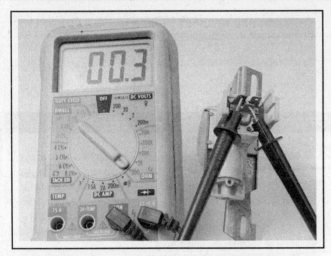

2.9 With a multimeter set to the ohms scale, resistance can
be checked across two terminals - when checking for
continuity, a low reading indicates continuity, a high reading
indicates lack of continuity

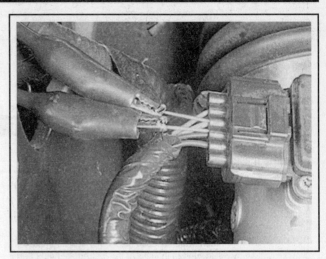

2.15 To backprobe a connector, insert a small, sharp probe
(such as a straight-pin) into the back of the connector
alongside the desired wire until it contacts the metal
terminal inside; connect your meter leads to the probes - this
allows you to test a functioning circuit

the problem lies between that point and the last test point with voltage.
Most of the time the problem can be traced to a loose connection.

➡Note: Keep in mind that some circuits receive voltage only
when the ignition key is in the Accessory or Run position.

FINDING A SHORT

One method of finding shorts in a circuit is to remove the fuse and
connect a test light or voltmeter in place of the fuse terminals. There
should be no voltage present in the circuit. Move the wiring harness
from side-to-side while watching the test light. If the bulb goes on,
there is a short to ground somewhere in that area, probably where the
insulation has rubbed through. The same test can be performed on
each component in the circuit, even a switch.

GROUND CHECK

Perform a ground test to check whether a component is properly
grounded. Disconnect the battery and connect one lead of a continuity
tester or multimeter (set to the ohms scale), to a known good ground.
Connect the other lead to the wire or ground connection being tested. If
the resistance is low (less than 5 ohms), the ground is good. If the
bulb on a self-powered test light does not go on, the ground is not
good.

CONTINUITY CHECK

A continuity check is done to determine if there are any breaks in a
circuit - if it is passing electricity properly. With the circuit off (no
power in the circuit), a self-powered continuity tester or multimeter can
be used to check the circuit. Connect the test leads to both ends of the
circuit (or to the "power" end and a good ground), and if the test light
comes on the circuit is passing current properly (see illustration). If the
resistance is low (less than 5 ohms), there is continuity; if the reading
is 10,000 ohms or higher, there is a break somewhere in the circuit.
The same procedure can be used to test a switch, by connecting the
continuity tester to the switch terminals. With the switch turned On, the
test light should come on (or low resistance should be indicated on a
meter).

FINDING AN OPEN CIRCUIT

When diagnosing for possible open circuits, it is often difficult to
locate them by sight because the connectors hide oxidation or terminal
misalignment. Merely wiggling a connector on a sensor or in the
wiring harness may correct the open circuit condition. Remember this
when an open circuit is indicated when troubleshooting a circuit. Intermittent problems may also be caused by oxidized or loose connections.

Electrical troubleshooting is simple if you keep in mind that all
electrical circuits are basically electricity running from the battery,
through the wires, switches, relays, fuses and fusible links to each
electrical component (light bulb, motor, etc.) and to ground, from
which it is passed back to the battery. Any electrical problem is an
interruption in the flow of electricity to and from the battery.

CONNECTORS

Most electrical connections on these vehicles are made with multi-
wire plastic connectors. The mating halves of many connectors are
secured with locking clips molded into the plastic connector shells.
The mating halves of large connectors, such as some of those under
the instrument panel, are held together by a bolt through the center of
the connector.

To separate a connector with locking clips, use a small screwdriver
to pry the clips apart carefully, then separate the connector halves. Pull
only on the shell, never pull on the wiring harness as you may damage
the individual wires and terminals inside the connectors. Look at the
connector closely before trying to separate the halves. Often the locking clips are engaged in a way that is not immediately clear. Addition-
ally, many connectors have more than one set of clips.

Each pair of connector terminals has a male half and a female half.
When you look at the end view of a connector in a diagram, be sure to
understand whether the view shows the harness side or the component
side of the connector. Connector halves are mirror images of each
other, and a terminal shown on the right side end-view of one half will
be on the left side end view of the other half.

It is often necessary to take circuit voltage measurements with a connector connected. Whenever possible, carefully insert a small straight pin (not your meter probe) into the rear of the connector shell to contact the terminal inside, then clip your meter lead to the pin. This kind of connection is called "backprobing" (see illustration). When

inserting a test probe into a male terminal, be careful not to distort the terminal opening. Doing so can lead to a poor connection and corrosion at that terminal later. Using the small straight pin instead of a meter probe results in less chance of deforming the terminal connector.

3   Fuses and fusible link - general information

▶ **Refer to illustrations 3.1a, 3.1b and 3.3**

The electrical circuits of the vehicle are protected by a combination of fuses, circuit breakers and a fusible link. The main fuse and relay block, called the power distribution center, is located on the left side of the engine compartment, just behind the battery (see illustration). There is also a fuse block, which houses the flasher unit and headlight relay as well as fuses, located in the end of the instrument panel under a cover (see illustration).

Each of the fuses is designed to protect a specific circuit, and the various circuits are identified on the fuse panel itself.

Miniaturized fuses are employed in the fuse block. These compact fuses, with blade terminal design, allow fingertip removal and replacement. If an electrical component fails, always check the fuse first. A blown fuse is easily detected with a test light - if voltage is available on one side of the fuse but not the other, it's blown (the circuit must be energized for this check). You can also visually inspect the element for evidence of damage (see illustration).

Be sure to replace blown fuses with the correct type. Fuses of different ratings are physically interchangeable, but only fuses of the proper rating should be used. Replacing a fuse with one of a higher or lower value than specified is not recommended. Each electrical circuit needs a specific amount of protection. The amperage value of each fuse is molded into the fuse body.

If the replacement fuse immediately fails, don't replace it again until the cause of the problem is isolated and corrected. In most cases, the cause will be a short circuit in the wiring caused by a broken or deteriorated wire.

Fuses should be replaced when the ignition key is in the Off position only.

FUSIBLE LINK

The fusible link is located in the power distribution center in the engine compartment. This 140-amp link looks like a very large fuse, and through the plastic cover you can see if it is blown or not.

To replace the fusible link, first disconnect the negative cable from the battery. Disconnect the burned-out link and replace it with a new one (available from your dealer or auto parts store). Always determine the cause for the overload that melted the fusible link before installing a new one.

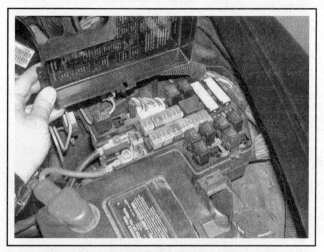

3.1a The power distribution center in the engine compartment contains fuses and relays

3.1b The fuse block is located in the left end of the instrument panel under a cover - it also contains several relays and circuit breakers (arrow indicates the IOD fuse)

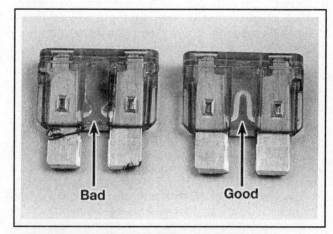

3.3 When a fuse blows, the element between the terminals melts - the fuse on the left is blown, the one on the right is good

4   Circuit breakers - general information

Circuit breakers protect components such as power windows, power door locks and headlights. Some circuit breakers are located in the fuse box.

Some circuit breakers reset automatically, so an electrical overload in a circuit breaker-protected system will cause the circuit to fail momentarily, then come back on. If the circuit does not come back on, check it immediately. Once the condition is corrected, the circuit breaker will resume its normal function.

5   Relays - general information and testing

GENERAL INFORMATION

1   Several electrical accessories in the vehicle, such as the fuel injection system, horns, starter, and fog lamps use relays to transmit the electrical signal to the component. Relays use a low-current circuit (the control circuit) to open and close a high-current circuit (the power circuit). If the relay is defective, that component will not operate properly. Most relays are mounted in the engine compartment and interior fuse/relay boxes (see illustrations 3.1a and 3.1b). If a faulty relay is suspected, it can be removed and tested using the procedure below or by a dealer service department or a repair shop. Defective relays must be replaced as a unit.

TESTING

▶ **Refer to illustration 5.5**

2   Most of the relays used in these vehicles are often called "ISO" relays, which refers to the International Standards Organization. The terminals of ISO relays are numbered to indicate their usual circuit connections and functions.

3   Refer to the wiring diagram for the circuit to determine the proper connections for the relay you're testing. If you can't determine the correct connection from the wiring diagrams, however, you may be able to determine the test connections from the information that follows.

4   Two of the terminals are the relay control circuit and connect to the relay coil. The other relay terminals are the power circuit. When the relay is energized, the coil creates a magnetic field that closes the larger contacts of the power circuit to provide power to the circuit loads.

5   Terminals 85 and 86 are normally the control circuit (see illustration). If the relay contains a diode, terminal 86 must be connected to battery positive (B+) voltage and terminal 85 to ground. If the relay contains a resistor, terminals 85 and 86 can be connected in either direction with respect to B+ and ground.

6   Terminal 30 is normally connected to the battery voltage (B+) source for the circuit loads. Terminal 87 is connected to the ground side of the circuit, either directly or through a load. If the relay has sev-

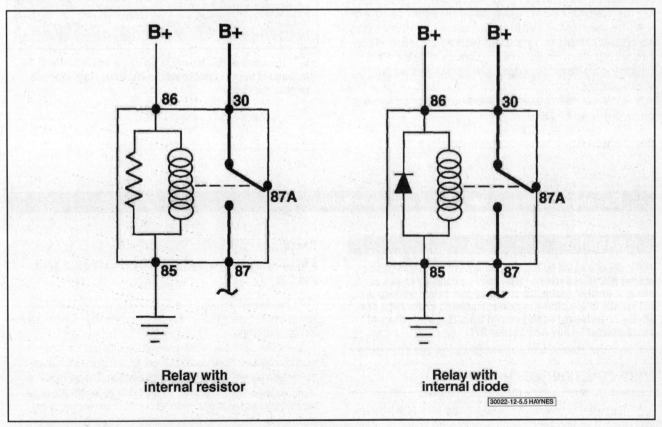

Relay with internal resistor

Relay with internal diode

30022-12-5.5 HAYNES

5.5 Typical ISO relay designs, terminal numbering and circuit connections

eral alternate terminals for load or ground connections, they usually are numbered 87A, 87B, 87C, and so on.

7   Use an ohmmeter to check continuity through the relay control coil.

   a) Connect the meter according to the polarity shown in illustration 55 for one check; then reverse the ohmmeter leads and check continuity in the other direction.

   b) If the relay contains a resistor, resistance should be the specified value with the ohmmeter in either direction.

   c) If the relay contains a diode, resistance should be the specified coil resistance value with the ohmmeter in the forward polarity direction. With the meter leads reversed, resistance should be lower.

   d) If the ohmmeter shows infinite resistance in both directions, replace the relay.

8   Remove the relay from the vehicle and use the ohmmeter to check for continuity between the relay power circuit terminals. There should be no continuity between terminal 30 and 87 with the relay de-energized.

9   Connect a fused jumper wire to terminal 86 and the positive battery terminal. Connect another jumper wire between terminal 85 and ground. When the connections are made, the relay should click.

10   With the jumper wires connected, check for continuity between the power circuit terminals. Now, there should be continuity between terminals 30 and 87.

11   If the relay fails any of the above tests, replace it.

6   Turn signal and hazard flashers - check and replacement

▶ **Refer to illustration 6.1**

1   When the emergency flasher switch on top of the steering column is On, the "combination" flasher flashes the turn signals and all four signals. On 2000 models, the flasher is in the fuse box and on 2001 and later models, it is located behind the instrument panel, just above the Data Link connector (see illustration).

2   When the flasher unit is functioning properly, an audible click can be heard during its operation. If the turn signals fail on one side or the other and the flasher unit does not make its characteristic clicking sound, a faulty turn signal bulb is indicated.

3   If both turn signals fail to blink, the problem may be due to a blown fuse, a faulty flasher unit, a broken switch or a loose or open connection. If a quick check of the fuse box indicates that the turn signal fuse has blown, check the wiring for a short before installing a new fuse.

4   The type of combination flasher unit used on the covered models has complex internal circuitry, and can't be tested using standard electrical test equipment. Refer to the wiring diagrams at the end of this Chapter and test the circuitry before replacing the flasher with a known-good unit.

5   To remove the flasher, simply disconnect the electrical harness connector and pull the flasher out.

6   Make sure that the replacement unit is identical to the original. Compare the old one to the new one before installing it.

6.1 The combination flasher is under the driver's side of the instrument panel - disconnect the electrical connector and remove the flasher

7   Installation is the reverse of removal.

8   If the flasher unit is not the problem, refer to Section 7 and test the turn signal/hazard portion of the multi-function switch.

7   Steering column switches - check and replacement

✳✳ WARNING:

The models covered by this manual are equipped with Supplemental Restraint Systems (SRS), more commonly known as airbags. Always disable the airbag system before working in the vicinity of any airbag system components to avoid the possibility of accidental deployment of the airbags, which could cause personal injury (see Section 27).

MULTI-FUNCTION SWITCH

1   The multi-function switch is located on the left side of the steering column. It incorporates the turn signal, four-way flasher, headlight dimmer and windshield wiper/washer functions into one switch.

Check

▶ **Refer to illustrations 7.2, 7.3a, 7.3b, 7.3c, 7.3d, 7.3e and 7.3f**

2   Remove the steering column covers and the knee bolster for access (see Chapter 11). Disconnect the multi-function switch connector (see illustration).

3   Use an ohmmeter or self-powered test light and the accompanying diagrams (see illustrations) to check for continuity between the switch terminals with the switch in each position. The pin locations shown in illustrations 7.3a and 7.3d are the same for the turn signal, wiper/washer and headlight dimming checks. If any portion of the multi-function switch fails the tests, the switch must be replaced as a unit.

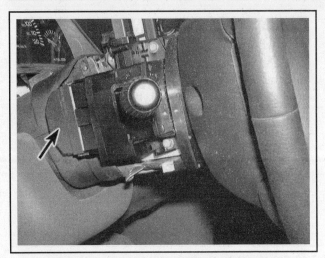

7.2 Remove the plastic cover (arrow) and disconnect the multi-function switch connector beneath it

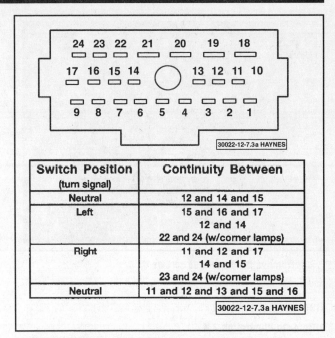

7.3a Turn signal and hazard flasher terminal guide and continuity chart - 2000 models

Switch Position (turn signal)	Continuity Between
Neutral	12 and 14 and 15
Left	15 and 16 and 17
	12 and 14
	22 and 24 (w/corner lamps)
Right	11 and 12 and 17
	14 and 15
	23 and 24 (w/corner lamps)
Neutral	11 and 12 and 13 and 15 and 16

Switch Position (wiper)	Continuity Between
Off	6 and 7
Delay	8 and 9
	2 and 4
	1 and 2
	1 and 4
Low	4 and 6
High	4 and 5
Wash	3 and 4

7.3b Windshield wiper/washer continuity chart - 2000 models

Switch Position (headlight dimmer)	Continuity Between
Low beam	18 and 19
High beam	19 and 20
Flash	20 and 21

7.3c Headlight dimmer continuity chart - 2000 models

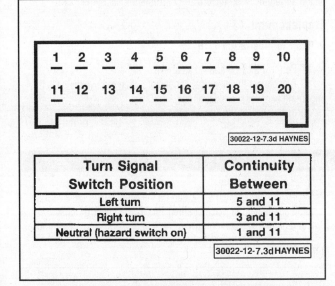

Turn Signal Switch Position	Continuity Between
Left turn	5 and 11
Right turn	3 and 11
Neutral (hazard switch on)	1 and 11

7.3d Multi-function switch terminal guide and continuity chart for turn/hazard functions - 2001 and later models

Wipe/Wash Switch Position	Continuity Between
Off	14 and 15
Delay	4 and 8, 14 and 15
Low	15 and 17
High	15 and 16
Wash	18 and 19

7.3e Continuity chart for multi-function switch, wiper/washer functions - 2001 and later models

Headlight Switch Position (dimmer)	Continuity Between
Low beam	6 and 9
High beam	8 and 9
Flash	7 and 8

7.3f Headlight dimmer continuity chart -2001 and later models

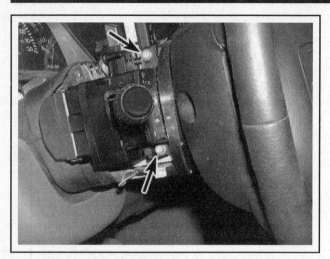

7.4 Remove the Torx-head screws

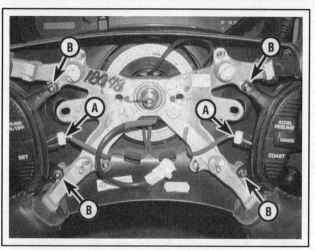

7.18 Disconnect the electrical connectors (A) at the two cruise-control switches, then remove the mounting screws (B)

Replacement

▶ **Refer to illustration 7.4**

4   Remove the multi-function switch bolts (on 2000 models, this will require a special anti-tamper Torx head tool), then detach the switch from the steering column (see illustration).
5   Installation is the reverse of removal.

REMOTE RADIO SWITCHES

Check

6   Some models with optional high-line stereo systems have remote radio-operation switches mounted on the backside of the steering wheel (facing the instrument panel).
7   The two switches control volume and seek functions without the driver having to take his hands off the wheel.
8   The switches are wired to the Central Timer Module under the left side of the instrument panel, and can only be checked with a factory-type scan tool. If the switches malfunction, have them tested at a dealer or other repair facility.

Replacement

9   Refer to Section 27 and disable the airbag system.
10   Refer to Chapter 10 and remove the driver's side airbag.
11   Remove the cruise-control switches (see below) and disconnect

the electrical connector at the radio switch to be replaced.
12   Squeeze the four clips securing the switch to the steering wheel back cover and push the switch out.
13   Installation is the reverse of removal.

CRUISE CONTROL SWITCHES

Check

14   The two cruise-control switch modules on the steering wheel perform the On/Off and Set/Resume/Accel/Cancel/Coast functions. The switches on the steering wheel can't be tested by themselves, because all cruise-control functions are controlled by the PCM.
15   Diagnostic Trouble Codes (DTCs) will be stored in the PCM memory if there is a malfunction in any part of the cruise-control system. Refer to Chapter 6 for a list of DTCs.
16   Refer to Section 22 for tests of the switches that can be made using a multimeter on the cruise-control terminals of the PCM.

Replacement

▶ **Refer to illustration 7.18**

17   Perform Steps 9 and 10 as above.
18   Disconnect the electrical connectors, then remove the switch mounting screws (see illustration).
19   Installation is the reverse of removal.

---

8   Ignition switch and key lock cylinder - check and replacement

▶ **Refer to illustrations 8.3a and 8.3b**

✳✳ WARNING:

The models covered by this manual are equipped with Supplemental Restraint Systems (SRS), more commonly known as airbags. Always disable the airbag system before working in the vicinity of any airbag system components to avoid the possibility of accidental deployment of the airbags, which could cause personal injury (see Section 27).

1   The ignition switch is located on the right side of the steering column and is held in place by three Torx T-20 tamper-proof screws which require a special tool (available at auto parts stores) for removal.

CHECK

2   Remove the switch (see Steps 5 and 6).
3   Use an ohmmeter or self-powered test light and check for continuity between the indicated switch terminals in each switch position (see illustrations).
4   If the switch does not have the correct continuity, replace it.

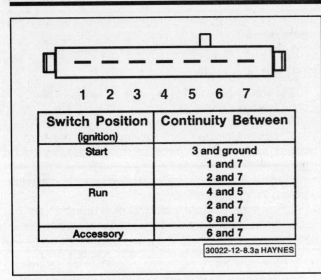

Switch Position (ignition)	Continuity Between
Start	3 and ground 1 and 7 2 and 7
Run	4 and 5 2 and 7 6 and 7
Accessory	6 and 7

30022-12-8.3a HAYNES

8.3a Ignition switch terminal guide and continuity chart - 2000 models

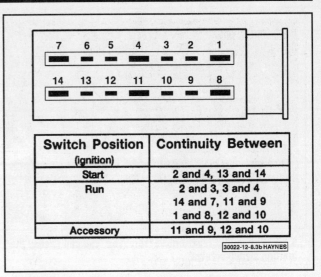

Switch Position (ignition)	Continuity Between
Start	2 and 4, 13 and 14
Run	2 and 3, 3 and 4 14 and 7, 11 and 9 1 and 8, 12 and 10
Accessory	11 and 9, 12 and 10

30022-12-8.3b HAYNES

8.3b Ignition switch terminal guide and continuity chart - 2001 and later models

8.7a The ignition switch is held in place by three Torx-head tamper-proof screws (arrows)

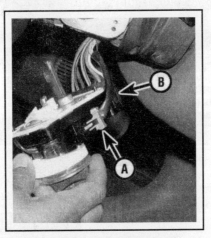

8.7b With the switch pulled away from the column, disconnect the key-in-lock connector (A) and the main connector (B)

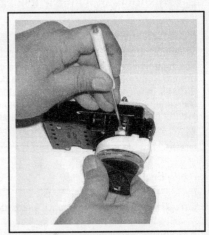

8.8 Push the retaining pin in to unseat the lock cylinder, then withdraw the key and cylinder

REPLACEMENT

♦ Refer to illustrations 8.7a, 8.7b, 8.8, 8.10 and 8.15

2000 models

5   Disconnect the negative battery cable.

6   Remove the steering column covers (see Chapter 11).

7   Remove the tamper-proof screws and detach the switch from the steering column (see illustration). Disconnect the electrical connectors and remove the switch (see illustration).

8   Place the key in the lock and rotate clockwise until the retainer pin is exposed. Push in the pin and pull the key and lock cylinder from the ignition switch (see illustration).

9   Installation is the reverse of removal. Align the retainer with the retainer slot in the switch, then rotate the key to the Lock position.

10   On models with automatic transmissions, the shift linkage must be in Park before installing the ignition switch on the column. As the switch is engaged to the column park-slider linkage, make sure the

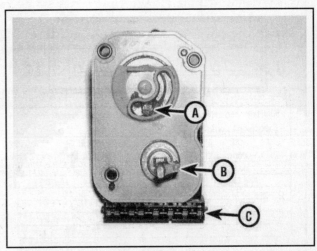

8.10 Make sure the park lock dowel pin (A) is in this position and the switch column lock flag (B) is parallel with the electrical connector (C) before installation

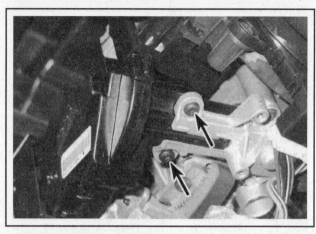

8.15 With the tilt lever bracket removed, you can access the ignition switch screws

column lock flag on the switch is parallel with the electrical connectors (see illustration).

11 The remainder of installation is the reverse of removal.

2001 and later models

12 Disconnect the negative battery cable and remove the steering column covers (see Chapter 11).

13 Insert the key and turn the ignition switch to the Run position.

14 To access the ignition switch screws, disconnect the two connectors to the clockspring, then move the wiring harness away from the steering column tilt lever bracket.

15 Remove the screws and the bracket to access the ignition switch mounting screws (see illustration).

16 Remove the screws and release the locking tab with a screwdriver. Remove the ignition switch and disconnect its electrical connector.

17 Installation is the reverse of the removal procedure.

9 Instrument panel switches - check and replacement

✳✳ WARNING:

The models covered by this manual are equipped with Supplemental Restraint Systems (SRS), more commonly known as airbags. Always disable the airbag system before working in the vicinity of any airbag system components to avoid the possibility of accidental deployment of the airbags, which could cause personal injury (see Section 27).

HEADLIGHT SWITCH

▶ **Refer to illustrations 9.2, 9.5a and 9.5b**

Check

1   The headlight switch must be removed from the instrument panel for testing. See text below for removal.

2   Using an ohmmeter or self-powered continuity tester, check the switch for proper continuity between the terminals (see illustration). Refer to the wiring diagrams at the end of this Chapter for the wire colors and circuits. If the switch fails any of the tests, replace the switch.

Replacement

3   Disconnect the negative cable at the battery.

4   Remove the instrument cluster bezel (see Chapter 11).

5   Disconnect the electrical connector, then remove the retaining screws (see illustrations).

✳✳ WARNING:

If the switch had been On for some time, allow it to cool before removing it.

6   Installation is the reverse of removal.

Switch Position (headlight switch)	Continuity Between
Off	2 and 4, 1 and 14
Park	3 and 4
Head	4 and 6
Fog Lamp	12 and 9,1 and 14, 1 and 8
Interior Lamp Dimmer	1 and 14, 12 and 9
Parade	1 and 14, 12 and 9
Dome	1 and 8, 1 and 14, 10 and 9
Cargo	1 and 14, 1 and 8, 10 and 9, 11 and 5

30022-12-9.2 HAYNES

9.2 Headlight switch terminal identification - 1999 models

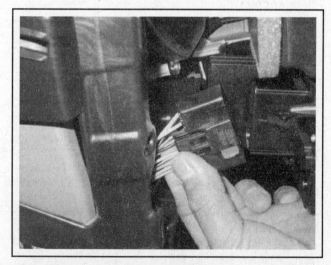

9.5a Disconnect the electrical connectors

FOG LIGHT SWITCH

Check

7   The fog light switch function is part of the multi-function switch. Refer to Section 7 for testing and replacement

REAR WINDOW DEFOGGER SWITCH (DURANGO AND QUAD-CAB)

Replacement

➡Note: On 2001 and later models, if the switch is bad, the whole heating/air conditioning control panel must be replaced. Refer to Chapter 3 for removal.

8   Disconnect the cable from the negative battery terminal.
9   The switch is located in the lower center instrument panel bezel. Remove the panel bezel (see Chapter 11).
10   Disconnect the electrical connector, then remove the screws

securing the switch to the bezel.
11   Installation is the reverse of removal.

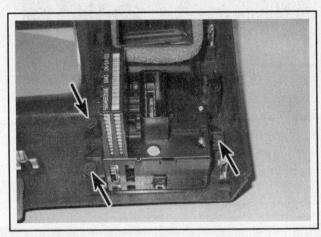

9.5b Remove the headlight switch retaining screws

---

10 Fuel and temperature gauges - check

▶ **Refer to illustration 10.6**

1   Gauges on these models are part of an integrated electronic instrument cluster, which receives its input in the form of messages from the PCM.
2   Although the fuel and temperature gauges cannot be tested by themselves, the sending units can be tested. Refer to Chapter 3 for the ECT sensor testing and Chapter 4 for the fuel level sending unit testing.
3   The integrated instrument cluster can perform a self-diagnosis test that will give you some basic information. Have a pen and note-book handy for the following Steps.

4   With the ignition key Off, push in on the odometer reset button and hold it in.
5   While holding the button in, turn the key to the On position (do NOT start the vehicle!).
6   When "CHEC" is shown in the odometer display, let the button out. Take notes of any 3-digit codes that might appear in the odometer display. Refer to the chart (see illustration) for a description.
7   Any diagnosis beyond this point must be done with a factory-type scan tool. Individual components of the instrument cluster cannot be replaced separately. If defective the entire cluster must be replaced.

Code (in odometer display)	Description
110	Failure in cluster RAM, CPU or EEPROM
900	PCI data bus not working
920	No vehicle speed message from PCM
921	No distance pulse message from PCM
940	No airbag lamp-on message from ACM
950	No airbag lamp-on message from CAB
960	No shift indicator message from TCM
999	Error

10.6 Instrument cluster diagnostic codes

30022-12-10.6 HAYNES

---

11 Instrument cluster - removal and installation

▶ **Refer to illustration 11.3**

❄❄❄ WARNING:

The models covered by this manual are equipped with Supplemental Restraint Systems (SRS), more commonly known as airbags. Always disable the airbag system before working in

the vicinity of any airbag system components to avoid the possibility of accidental deployment of the airbags, which could cause personal injury (see Section 27).

1   Disconnect the negative cable from the battery.
2   Remove the instrument cluster bezel (see Chapter 11).

11.3 Instrument cluster mounting screws (typical)

3   Remove the four screws securing the cluster to the instrument panel (see illustration).

4   Pull the cluster forward enough to disengage the two electrical connectors at the back. The connectors are fixed to the instrument panel and will disconnect when the cluster is pulled straight out from the dash.

5   On 2000 models equipped with an automatic transmission, pull the cluster out enough to disconnect the shift indicator.

6   Installation is the reverse of removal. Attach the shift indicator first, then push the cluster straight into place, making sure the two electrical connectors engage.

12   Radio and speakers - removal and installation

✳✳ WARNING:

The models covered by this manual are equipped with Supplemental Restraint Systems (SRS), more commonly known as airbags. Always disable the airbag system before working in the vicinity of any airbag system components to avoid the possibility of accidental deployment of the airbags, which could cause personal injury (see Section 27).

✳✳ CAUTION:

When disconnecting the antenna cable from the radio, pull out the locking sleeve around the cable first, or the cable or radio may be damaged.

3   Installation is the reverse of removal.

DOOR SPEAKERS

RADIO

▶ **Refer to illustrations 12.2a and 12.2b**

1   Disconnect the negative battery cable, then remove the instrument cluster bezel (see Chapter 11).

2   Remove the mounting bolts, pull the radio out of the instrument panel, disconnect the connectors, then remove it from the vehicle (see illustrations).

▶ **Refer to illustration 12.5**

4   Remove the door trim panel (see Chapter 11).

➡ Note: Durango and Dakota Quad Cab models have six door speakers, two in each front door, and one in each rear door. Dakota single cab and Club Cab models have one speaker in each door and one rear speaker on each side mounted in the rear corner trim panel except premium models, which have an extra tweeter in each front door panel. All are mounted in a similar fashion.

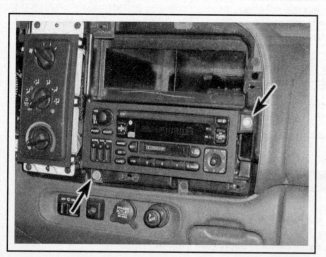

12.2a Remove the bolts and pull the radio out (early model shown, late model similar

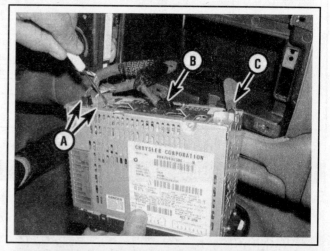

12.2b Disconnect the connectors (A) from the back of the radio, then disconnect the ground wire (B) and the antenna cable (C)

5   Remove the screws and detach the speaker (see illustration). Pull the speaker out of the door, disconnect the electrical connector and remove the speaker from the vehicle.

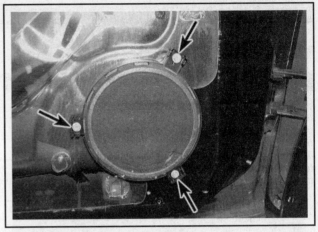

12.5 Door speaker mounting screws (arrows)

13 Antenna - removal and installation

▶ **Refer to illustrations 13.2a and 13.2b**

1   Disconnect the negative battery cable.

2   Use a small open-end wrench to unscrew the antenna mast, then remove the cap nut and lift off the upper adapter and gasket (see illustrations). Be very careful - the tools could slip and scratch the fender. It's a good idea to surround the base of the antenna with masking tape to prevent scratching.

3   Working with the right door open, disconnect the twist-lock antenna cable connector and withdraw the cable end with the antenna, through the door opening.

4   If the entire cable is to be replaced, attach a wire or cord to the end of the cable (at the connection) in the door opening, then remove the kick panel (see Chapter 11) and pull the cable into the passenger compartment. Disconnect any clips or ties securing the cable to the back of the instrument panel or the top of the heating/air conditioning unit.

5   Refer to Section 12 and disconnect the cable from the radio.

6   Push the new cable into the radio, then route the cable as originally installed.

7   Connect the string or wire to the antenna end of the new cable and pull it through. Connect it to the antenna at the twist-lock connection.

8   Installation of the antenna base and mast is the reverse of the removal procedure.

9   Install the right side kick panel/sill cover and connect the battery negative cable.

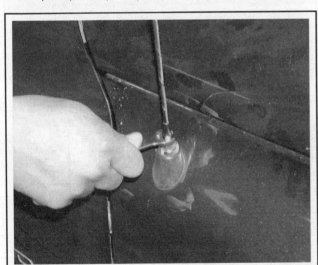

13.2a Use a small wrench to remove the mast . . .

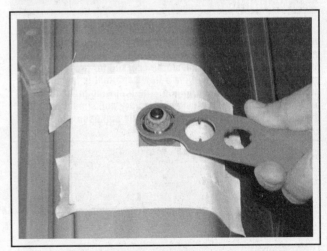

13.2b . . . then remove the base bezel nut with snap-ring pliers or an antenna removal tool (shown, available at auto parts stores)

14 Headlight bulb - replacement

▶ Refer to illustrations 14.4a and 14.4b

☼☼ WARNING:

Halogen bulbs are gas-filled and under pressure and may shatter if the surface is scratched or the bulb is dropped. Wear eye protection and handle the bulbs carefully, grasping only the base whenever possible. Don't touch the surface of the bulb with your fingers because the oil from your skin could cause it to overheat and fail prematurely. If you do touch the bulb surface, clean it with rubbing alcohol.

1 Disconnect the negative cable from the battery.
2 Open the hood.
3 Remove the headlight housing (see Section 16).
4 Disconnect the electrical connector, unscrew the headlight bulb-retaining ring and withdraw the bulb (see illustrations).
5 Installation is the reverse of the removal procedure, but handle the new bulb only with gloves or a clean rag.

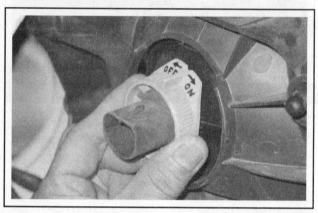

14.4a Unscrew the headlight bulb retaining ring . . .

14.4b . . . then withdraw the headlight bulb from the housing

15 Headlights - adjustment

▶ Refer to illustrations 15.1 and 15.3

☼☼ WARNING:

The headlights must be aimed correctly. If adjusted incorrectly, they could temporarily blind the driver of an oncoming vehicle and cause an accident or seriously reduce your ability to see the road. The headlights should be checked for proper aim every 12 months and any time a new headlight is installed or front-end bodywork is performed. The following procedure is only an interim step to provide temporary adjustment until the headlights can be adjusted by a properly equipped shop.

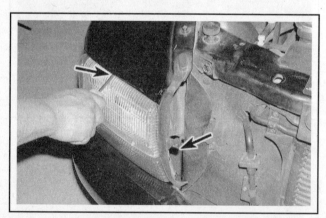

15.1 Open the hood and adjust the headlight up/down alignment with the top screw, and horizontal aiming with the screw in the grille area (arrows)

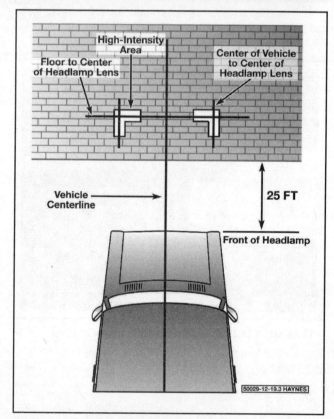

15.3 Headlight adjustment details

1   Headlights have two spring-loaded adjusting screws (see illustration).

2   This procedure requires a blank wall, masking tape and a level floor.

3   Position masking tape vertically on the wall in reference to the vehicle centerline and the centerlines of both headlights (see illustration).

4   Position a horizontal tape line in reference to the centerline of all the headlights.

➡**Note: It may be easier to position the tape on the wall with the vehicle parked only a few inches away.**

5   Adjustment should be made with the vehicle parked 25 feet from the wall, sitting level, the gas tank full and no unusually heavy load in the vehicle.

6   Starting with the low beam adjustment, position the high intensity zone so it's two inches below the horizontal line and two inches to the side of the headlight vertical line away from oncoming traffic. Adjustment is made by turning the top adjusting screw clockwise to raise the beam and counterclockwise to lower the beam. The adjusting screw on the side should be used in the same manner to move the beam left or right.

7   With the high beams on, the high-intensity zone should be vertically centered with the exact center just below the horizontal line.

➡**Note: It may not be possible to position the headlight aim exactly for both high and low beams. If a compromise must be made, keep in mind that the low beams are the most used and have the greatest effect on driver safety.**

8   Have the headlights adjusted by a dealer service department or service station at the earliest opportunity.

16 Headlight housing - replacement

▶ **Refer to illustration 16.2**

❊❊ **WARNING:**

The models covered by this manual are equipped with Supplemental Restraint Systems (SRS), more commonly known as airbags. Always disable the airbag system before working in the vicinity of any airbag system components to avoid the possibility of accidental deployment of the airbags, which could cause personal injury (see Section 27).

1   Open the hood.

2   Remove the headlight housing mounting bolts (see illustration).

3   Remove the bolts and pull the headlight housing straight out to disengage it from clips in the fender opening.

4   Installation is the reverse of removal. After you're done, check the headlight adjustment (see Section 15).

16.2 Headlight housing bolts (shown with park/turn signal lights removed)

17 Bulb replacement

❊❊ **WARNING:**

Bulbs can remain hot for up to twenty minutes after they're turned off. Be sure bulbs are off and cool before you touch them.

TURN SIGNAL/PARKING/SIDE MARKER LIGHTS

▶ **Refer to illustrations 17.1 and 17.2**

1   Remove the small screw that secures the turn signal/parking light housing, then pull the housing out for access to the bulb holders (see illustration).

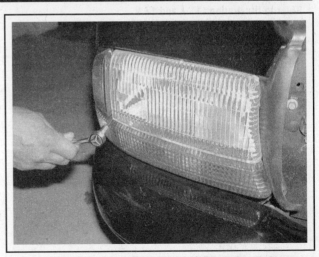

17.1 Remove the small Torx head screw and detach the park/turn signal light housing

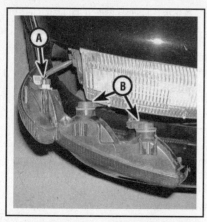

17.2 Rotate the bulb holder and lift it out to change the bulbs for the side marker lamp (A) and the Park/Turn signal (B)

17.4 Lower the tailgate to gain access to the taillight housing mounting screws (Dakota models)

17.5 Remove the taillight housing screws (Durango models)

2 Turn the bulb holder counterclockwise to remove it and pull the bulb straight out (see illustration).

3 Installation is the reverse of removal.

TAIL/STOP/TURN/BACKUP LIGHT

▶ **Refer to illustrations 17.4, 17.5 and 17.6**

4 On all models, these rear lights are all in one housing. On Dakota models, lower the tailgate and remove the two screws (see illustration). Rotate the housing out to disengage the hooks from in the body.

5 On Durango models, open the liftgate and remove the two screws, then rotate the housing so the hooks will clear the holes in the body (see illustration).

6 On all models, rotate the bulb holders 1/4-turn counterclockwise and pull from the housing. Replace the bulb, then insert the holder into the housing and rotate 1/4-turn clockwise to lock (see illustration).

7 Installation is the reverse of removal.

CENTER HIGH-MOUNTED STOP LIGHT (CHMSL)/CARGO LAMP

▶ **Refer to illustrations 17.8 and 17.9**

8 Standing in the truck bed on Dakota models, remove the two

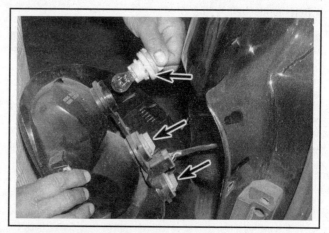

17.6 Rotate the bulb holder and pull it out to remove it (arrows, Durango shown)

Phillips-head screws and withdraw the CHMSL/cargo lamp housing from the cab (see illustration).

9 On Durango models, raise the liftgate and remove the liftgate upper trim panel (see Chapter 11). The bulb holders are now accessible (see illustration).

10 On all models, rotate the bulb holder 1/4-turn clockwise and

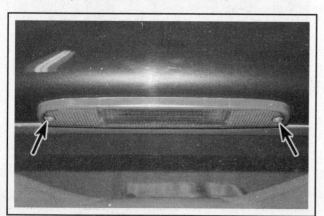

17.8 Remove the screws and pull the CHMSL/cargo light housing out (Dakota models)

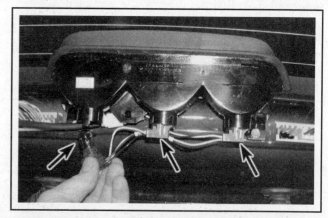

17.9 On Durango models, the CHMSL bulbs (arrows) are accessible once the upper liftgate trim panel is removed

17.12 Reach up behind the bumper to rotate and remove the bulb holder (arrow)

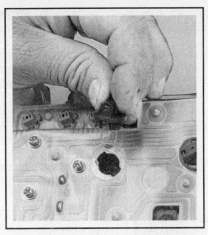

17.15 Rotate the instrument cluster bulb housing and lift it out

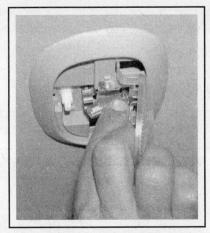

17.19 Pull the dome light bulb straight down, out of its two sockets

withdraw it, then replace the bulb by pulling it straight from the holder.

11 Installation is the reverse of removal.

LICENSE PLATE BULB

▶ **Refer to illustration 17.12**

12 The license plate lamp is attached to the rear bumper with two screws, but the bulb holder can be removed by reaching up behind the bumper (see illustration).

13 Installation is the reverse of removal.

INSTRUMENT CLUSTER LIGHTS

▶ **Refer to illustration 17.15**

14 To gain access to the instrument cluster illumination lights, the instrument cluster will have to be removed (see Section 11). The bulbs can then be removed and replaced from the rear of the cluster.

15 Rotate the bulb counterclockwise to remove it (see illustration).

16 Installation is the reverse of removal.

INTERIOR LIGHTS

Overhead console lights

17 Remove the two screws securing the overhead console, then pull downward on the side of the console to release it .

18 Seat the new bulb in the holder, and the holder in the cage. Hold the lens level and press it into place.

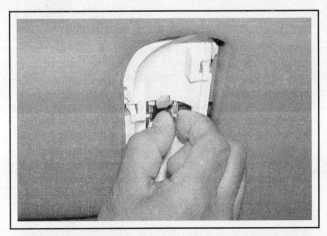

17.21 Pull the liftgate cargo lamp bulb-holder out to replace the bulb

Dome light

▶ **Refer to illustration 17.19**

19 Pry the left side of the dome light lens down, then let it hang there. Replace the bulb by pulling it straight out (see illustration).

Liftgate cargo lights (Durango)

▶ **Refer to illustration 17.21**

20 Pry the lenses off the two liftgate cargo lamps with a small screwdriver.

21 Remove the bulb holder from the light body, replace the bulb and insert it back into the light body (see illustration). Replace the lens.

18 Wiper motor - check and replacement

FRONT

▶ **Refer to illustrations 18.2 and 18.4**

1   Disconnect the negative cable from the battery.
2   Mark the positions of the wiper arms on the windshield, then

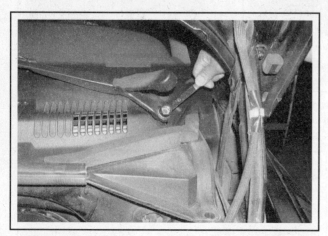

18.2 Lift the cover, then use a wrench to remove the nut on the wiper shaft, then grasp the wiper arm and use a rocking motion to detach it from the shaft

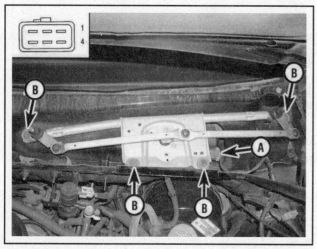

18.4 Remove the electrical connector (A), and the mounting fasteners (B)

remove the wiper arms (see illustration).
3   Remove the cowl grille (see Chapter 11).
4   Remove the wiper motor/linkage mounting bolts (see illustration).
5   Remove the assembly and unbolt the motor from the linkage.
6   Installation is the reverse of removal.

REAR (DURANGO MODELS)

▶ **Refer to illustration 18.10**

7   Disconnect the negative cable from the battery.
8   Mark the positions of the wiper arm on the liftgate glass, then remove the wiper arm cover and nut at the outside of the liftgate, then the bezel. Be careful not to scratch the paint on the liftgate.
9   Refer to Chapter 11 and remove the upper and lower liftgate interior trim panels.
10 Disconnect the electrical connector at the rear wiper motor, then remove the two mounting bolts (see illustration).

> ✳✳ **CAUTION:**
>
> **Support the motor while removing the bolts.**

11 Installation is the reverse of removal.

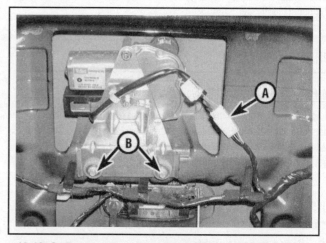

18.10 On Durango models, disconnect the electrical connector (A) at the rear wiper motor, then remove the two mounting bolts (B)

19 Horn - check and replacement

CHECK

▶ **Refer to illustration 19.2**

1   Remove the cover from the power distribution center (see illustration 3.1a) and check the horn fuse and relay, replacing any faulty components.

2   Disconnect the electrical connectors from the horns (see illustration).
3   Have an assistant press the horn button and use a voltmeter to make sure there is battery voltage at the dark green/red wire of the connector. If the relay is good and there's no voltage at the horn, the wire (which leads to the relay) has a fault.
4   Use an ohmmeter to measure the resistance between the wiring

connector black wire and a good ground. There should be zero ohms.

5   If there's voltage at the horn and the wiring circuits are good, the horn is faulty and must be replaced.

REPLACEMENT

6   Disconnect the electrical connectors, remove the mounting bolts and detach the horns (see illustration 19.2).

7   Installation is the reverse of removal.

19.2 Disconnect the horn connectors (A) and remove the mounting bolts (B) at the radiator support

20 Daytime running lights (DRL) - general information

The Daytime Running Lights (DRL) system used illuminates the headlights whenever the engine is running. The only exception is with the engine running and the parking brake engaged. Once the parking brake is released, the lights will remain on as long as the ignition switch is on, even if the parking brake is later applied. The DRL system is used on Canadian models of all covered years, and on 2003 US models.

The DRL system supplies reduced power to the headlights so they won't be too bright for daytime use, while prolonging headlight life.

21 Rear window defogger - check and repair

1   The rear window defogger consists of a number of horizontal heating elements baked onto the inside surface of the glass. Power is supplied through a large fuse from the power distribution box in the engine compartment. The heater is controlled by the instrument panel switch.

2   Small breaks in the element can be repaired without removing the rear window.

CHECK

▶ Refer to illustrations 21.5, 21.6 and 21.8

3   Turn the ignition switch and defogger switch to the ON position.

4   Using a voltmeter, place the positive probe against the defogger grid positive terminal and the negative probe against the ground terminal. If battery voltage is not indicated, check the fuse, defogger switch and related wiring. If voltage is indicated, but all or part of the defogger doesn't heat, proceed with the following tests.

5   When measuring voltage during the next two tests, wrap a piece of aluminum foil around the tip of the voltmeter positive probe and press the foil against the heating element with your finger (see illustration). Place the negative probe on the defogger grid ground terminal.

6   Check the voltage at the center of each heating element (see illustration). If the voltage is 5 to 6 volts, the element is okay (there is

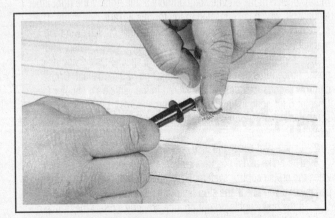

21.5 When measuring the voltage at the rear window defogger grid, wrap a piece of aluminum foil around the positive probe of the voltmeter and press the foil against the wire with your finger

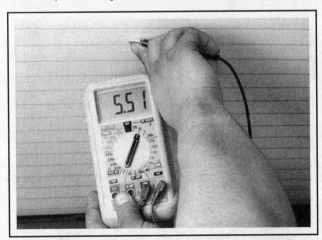

21.6 To determine if a wire has broken, check the voltage at the center of each wire. If the voltage is 5 to 6 volts, the wire is unbroken; if the voltage is 10 to 12 volts, the wire is broken between the center of the wire and the ground side; if the voltage is 0 volts, the wire is broken between the center of the wire and the power side

21.8 To find the break, place the voltmeter negative lead against the defogger ground terminal, place the voltmeter positive lead with the foil strip against the heat wire at the positive terminal end and slide it toward the negative terminal end - the point at which the voltmeter deflects from several volts to zero volts is the point at which the wire is broken

no break). If the voltage is 0 volts, the element is broken between the center of the element and the positive end. If the voltage is 10 to 12 volts, the element is broken between the center of the element and the ground side. Check each heating element.

7   If none of the elements are broken, connect the negative probe to a good chassis ground. The voltage reading should stay the same, if it doesn't the ground connection is bad.

8   To find the break, place the voltmeter negative probe against the defogger ground terminal. Place the voltmeter positive probe with the foil strip against the heating element at the positive side and slide it toward the negative side. The point at which the voltmeter deflects from several volts to zero is the point where the heating element is broken (see illustration).

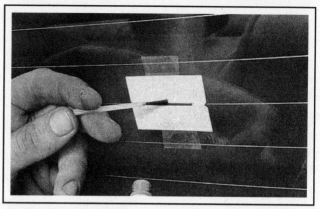

21.14 To use a defogger repair kit, apply masking tape to the inside of the window at the damaged area, then brush on the special conductive coating

REPAIR

▶ **Refer to illustration 21.14**

9   Repair the break in the element using a repair kit specifically for this purpose, such as Dupont paste No. 4817 (or equivalent). The kit includes conductive plastic epoxy.

10 Before repairing a break, turn off the system and allow it to cool for a few minutes.

11 Lightly buff the element area with fine steel wool; then clean it thoroughly with rubbing alcohol.

12 Use masking tape to mask off the area being repaired.

13 Thoroughly mix the epoxy, following the kit instructions.

14 Apply the epoxy material to the slit in the masking tape, overlapping the undamaged area about 3/4-inch on either end (see illustration).

15 Allow the repair to cure for 24 hours before removing the tape and using the system.

22 Cruise control system - description and check

22.5a Typical cruise control system component layout - A is the servo, B is the cable, C is the connection at the throttle linkage

▶ **Refer to illustrations 22.5a and 22.5b**

1   The cruise control system maintains vehicle speed with a servo motor located in the engine compartment at the front of the right inner fenderwell, which is connected to the throttle linkage by a cable. The system consists of the servo motor, brake switch (clutch switch on manual transmission models), control switches, speed sensor and relays. Some features of the system require special testers and diagnostic procedures that are beyond the scope of this manual. Cruise control diagnostic codes will be stored in the vehicle's computer (see Chapter 6 for code list and extraction procedures). Listed below are some general procedures that may be used to locate common problems.

2   Locate and check the fuse (see Section 3).

3   The brake pedal position switch (or stop-lamp switch) deactivates the cruise control system. Have an assistant press the brake pedal while you check the stop lamp operation.

4   If the brake lights do not operate properly, correct the problem and retest the cruise control.

5   Check the control cable between the cruise control servo/ampli-

fier and the throttle linkage and replace as necessary (see illustrations).

6   The cruise control system use input from the vehicle speed sensor. To test the speed sensor, see Chapter 6.

7   Test-drive the vehicle to determine if the cruise control is now working. If it isn't, take it to a dealer service department or an automotive electrical specialist for further diagnosis.

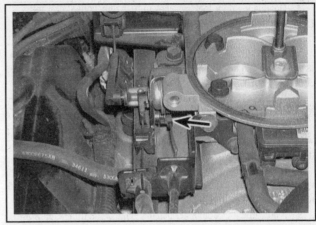

22.5b The cruise control cable connector (arrow) at the throttle linkage is a delicate part - do not try to pry it off the linkage - hold the throttle arm and push the cable end toward the firewall to detach it

23 Power window system - description and check

1   The power window system operates electric motors, mounted in the doors, which lower and raise the windows. The system consists of the control switches, the motors, regulators, glass mechanisms and associated wiring.

2   The power windows can be lowered and raised from the master control switch by the driver or by remote switches located at the individual windows. Each window has a separate motor that is reversible. The position of the control switch determines the polarity and therefore the direction of operation.

3   The circuit is protected by a fuse and a circuit breaker. Each motor is also equipped with an internal circuit breaker; this prevents one stuck window from disabling the whole system.

4   The power window system will only operate when the ignition switch is ON. In addition, many models have a window lockout switch at the master control switch which, when activated, disables the switches at the rear windows and, sometimes, the switch at the passenger's window also. Always check these items before troubleshooting a window problem.

5   These procedures are general in nature, so if you can't find the problem using them, take the vehicle to a dealer service department or other properly equipped repair facility.

6   If the power windows won't operate, always check the fuse and circuit breaker first.

7   If only the rear windows are inoperative (Durango), or if the windows only operate from the master control switch, check the rear window lockout switch for continuity in the unlocked position. Replace it if

it doesn't have continuity.

8   Check the wiring between the switches and fuse panel for continuity. Repair the wiring, if necessary.

9   If only one window is inoperative from the master control switch, try the other control switch at the window.

➡️ **Note: This doesn't apply to the drivers door window.**

10 If the same window works from one switch, but not the other, check the switch for continuity.

11 If the switch tests OK, check for a short or open in the circuit between the affected switch and the window motor.

12 If one window is inoperative from both switches, remove the door panel of the affected door and check for voltage at the switch and at the motor while the switch is operated.

13 If voltage is reaching the motor, disconnect the glass from the regulator (see Chapter 11). Move the window up and down by hand while checking for binding and damage. Also check for binding and damage to the regulator. If the regulator is not damaged and the window moves up and down smoothly, replace the motor. If there's binding or damage, lubricate, repair or replace parts, as necessary.

14 If voltage isn't reaching the motor, check the wiring in the circuit for continuity between the switches and motors. You'll need to consult the wiring diagram for the vehicle. If the circuit is equipped with a relay, check that the relay is grounded properly and receiving voltage.

15 Test the windows after you are done to confirm proper repairs.

24 Power door lock and keyless entry system - description and check

1   The power door lock system operates the door lock actuators mounted in each door. The system consists of the switches, actuators, relays and associated wiring. Diagnosis can usually be limited to simple checks of the wiring connections and actuators for minor faults that can be easily repaired. Part of the door lock system is routed through the Central Timer Module, which controls and communicates with the door lock system, anti-theft system and other convenience systems. Testing of the CTM is best done by a technician with a scan tool and

diagnostic readout box.

2   Power door lock systems are operated by bi-directional solenoids located in the doors. The lock switches have two operating positions: Lock and Unlock. These switches activate a relay, which in turn connects voltage to the door lock solenoids. Depending on which way the relay is activated, it reverses polarity, allowing the two sides of the circuit to be used alternately as the feed (positive) and ground side.

3   Always check the fuse first (see Section 3).

4   Operate the door lock switches in both directions (Lock and Unlock) with the engine off. Listen for the faint click of the relay operating.

5   If there's no click, check for voltage at the switches. If no voltage is present, check the wiring between the fuse block and the switches for shorts and opens.

6   If voltage is present but no click is heard, test the switch for continuity. Replace it if there's no continuity in both switch positions.

7   If the switch has continuity but the relay doesn't click, check the wiring between the switch and relay for continuity. Repair the wiring if there's no continuity.

8   If the relay is receiving voltage from the switch but is not sending voltage to the solenoids, check for a bad ground at the relay case. If the relay case is grounding properly, replace the relay.

9   If only one lock solenoid operates, remove the trim panel from the affected door (see Chapter 11) and check for voltage at the solenoid while the lock switch is operated. One of the wires should have voltage in the Lock position; the other should have voltage in the Unlock position.

10   If the inoperative solenoid is receiving voltage, replace the solenoid.

11   If the inoperative solenoid isn't receiving voltage, check for an open or short in the wire between the lock solenoid and the relay.

➡**Note: It's common for wires to break in the portion of the harness between the body and door (opening and closing the door fatigues and eventually breaks the wires).**

KEYLESS ENTRY SYSTEM

12   The keyless entry system consists of a remote control transmitter that sends a coded infrared signal to a receiver, which then operates the door lock system.

13   Replace the batteries when the transmitter doesn't operate the locks at a distance of 10 feet. Normal range should be about 23 feet.

14   Use a small screwdriver to carefully separate the case halves.

15   Replace the two CR2016 lithium batteries.

16   Snap the case halves together.

25 Electric side view mirrors - description and check

SIDE MIRROR

▶ **Refer to illustrations 25.6a and 25.6b**

1   The electric rear view mirrors use two motors to move the glass; one for up and down adjustments and one for left-right adjustments.

2   The control switch has a selector portion which sends voltage to the left or right side mirror. With the ignition ACC position and the engine OFF, roll down the windows and operate the mirror control switch through all functions (left-right and up-down) for both the left and right side mirrors.

3   Listen carefully for the sound of the electric motors running in the mirrors.

4   If the motors can be heard but the mirror glass doesn't move, there's probably a problem with the drive mechanism inside the mirror. Power mirrors have no user-serviceable parts inside, a defective mirror must be replaced as a unit.

5   If the mirrors don't operate and no sound comes from the mirrors, check fuse 12 in the fuse block located in the left side of the dash (all

models) and fuse 4 in the PDC on Durango models (see Section 3).

6   If the fuse is OK, remove the switch bezel for access to the back of the mirror control switch without disconnecting the wires attached to it (see illustrations). Turn the ignition ON and check for voltage at the switch. There should be voltage at one terminal. If there's no voltage at the switch, check for an open or short in the wiring between the fuse panel and the switch.

7   If there's voltage at the switch, disconnect it. Check the switch for continuity in all its operating positions. If the switch does not have continuity, replace it.

8   Re-connect the switch. Locate the wire going from the switch to ground. Leaving the switch connected, connect a jumper wire between this wire and ground. If the mirror works normally with this wire in place, repair the faulty ground connection.

9   If the mirror still doesn't work, remove the mirror and check the wires at the mirror for voltage. Check with ignition ON and the mirror selector switch on the appropriate side. Operate the mirror switch in all its positions. There should be voltage at one of the switch-to-mirror wires in each switch position (except the neutral "off" position).

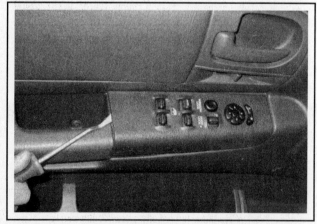

25.6a The power mirror switch is a component of the driver's door switch panel, pry up the switch panel with a trim tool . . .

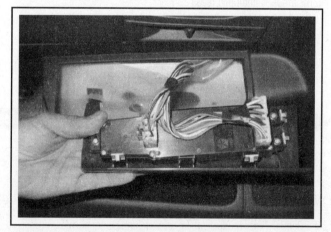

25.6b . . . to access the wires behind it

10 If voltage is absent in each switch position, check the wiring between the mirror and control switch for opens and shorts.

11 If there's voltage, remove the mirror and test it off the vehicle with jumper wires. Replace the mirror if it fails this test.

AUTOMATIC/DAY NIGHT MIRROR

12 To reduce glare, the automatic day/night mirror adjusts the amount of light reflected according to conditions. This is achieved with two photocell sensors, one facing forward and one facing rearward, that darken or lighten the thin layer of electrochromic material incorporated into the mirror glass.

13 If the mirror is not operating, check the fuse in the interior fuse panel (see Section 3).

14 Disconnect the electrical connector from the mirror. With the ignition On, the connector cavity with the dark brown/white wire should have battery voltage.

15 With the ignition Off, the cavity with the black wire should have continuity to ground. If not, there is a loose ground connection in the circuit.

16 With the shift selector in Reverse and the ignition switch On, place the mirror switch in the On position. The connector cavity with the violet/black wire should have battery voltage. If not there is a fault in the backup lights circuit.

17 With the shift selector in Neutral and the ignition switch On, place the mirror switch in the On position.

18 Cover the forward facing sensor, shine a light into the rear facing sensor, make sure the glass darkens, then shift the transmission into reverse and make sure it lightens. If it doesn't, replace the mirror (see Chapter 11).

26 Power seats - description and check

1   Power seats allow you to adjust the position of the seat with little effort. These models feature a six-way seat that goes forward and backward, up and down and tilts forward and backward. The seats are powered by three reversible motors, mounted in one housing, that are controlled by switches on the side of the seat. Each switch changes the direction of seat travel by reversing polarity to the drive motor.

2   Diagnosis is a simple matter, using the following procedures.

3   Look under the seat for any object which may be preventing the seat from moving.

4   If the seat won't work at all, check the fuse in the PDC.

5   With the engine off to reduce the noise level, operate the seat controls in all directions and listen for sound coming from the seat motors.

6   If the motor doesn't work or make noise, check for voltage at the motor while an assistant operates the switch. With the door open, try the seat switch again. If the dome light dims while trying to operate the seat, this indicates something may be jammed in the seat tracks.

7   If the motor is getting voltage but doesn't run, test it off the vehicle with jumper wires. If it still doesn't work, replace it.

8   If the motor isn't getting voltage, remove the switch and check for voltage. If there's no voltage at the switch (black/pink wire), check the wiring between the fuse block and the switch. If there's battery voltage at the switch, check the other terminals for voltage while moving the switch around. If the switch is OK, check for a short or open in the wiring between the switch and motor.

9   Test the completed repairs.

27 Airbag system - general information

▶ **Refer to illustration 27.1**

These models are equipped with a Supplemental Restraint System (SRS), more commonly called an airbag system. This system is designed to protect the driver and front-seat passenger from serious injury in the event of head-on or frontal collision. It consists of an airbag module in the center of the steering wheel, a second airbag module above the glovebox area of the instrument panel, and an Airbag Control Module (ACM) which contains a microprocessor, energy-storage capacitor, safing sensor and an impact sensor. The ACM is located on the floorpan, under the center area of the instrument panel (see illustration).

AIRBAG MODULE

The airbag module contains a housing incorporating the cushion (airbag) and inflator unit. The inflator assembly is mounted on the back of the housing over a hole through which gas is expelled, inflating the bag almost instantaneously when an electrical signal is sent from the

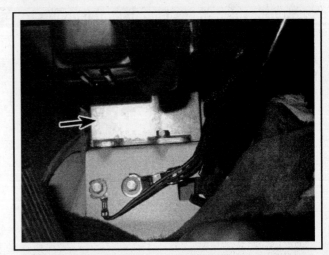

27.1 The airbag control module is located under the center of the instrument panel - do not tamper with the yellow connectors attached to it

system. The specially wound wire that carries this signal to the module is called a clockspring. The clockspring is a flat, ribbon-like electrically conductive tape, which is wound so it can transmit an electrical signal regardless of steering wheel position.

SIDE-IMPACT AIRBAGS

Some 2002 and later Durango models have optional "window" (side-impact) airbags. These airbags are mounted in a long tube secured to the upper roof rail, and provide side-impact protection to the driver and front and rear-seat passengers.

SENSORS

The system has an impact sensor and a safing sensor in the Airbag Control Module (ACM).

The crash sensor is basically a "decelerometer" switch that completes an electrical circuit during an impact of sufficient G force. The safing sensor detects collisions of lesser impact. Both sensors must signal the ACM in order for the airbag system to deploy.

AIRBAG CONTROL MODULE (ACM)

The ACM contains the sensors, a capacitor that maintains electrical system power if the battery is damaged and an on-board microprocessor which monitors the operation of the system. It checks this system every time the vehicle is started, causing the AIRBAG light to go on for seven seconds, then off, if the system is operating properly. If there is a fault in the system, the light will go on and stay on and the ACM will store fault codes indicating the nature of the fault. If the AIRBAG light does go on and stay on, the vehicle should be taken to your dealer immediately for service. On models equipped with side-impact airbags, side-impact control modules are located near the bottom of the B-pillars in the body.

DISABLING THE AIRBAG SYSTEM

Whenever working in the vicinity of the steering wheel, steering column or near other components of the airbag system, the system should be disarmed. To disarm the system perform the following steps:
a) Turn the ignition switch to the Off position.
b) Disconnect the cable from the negative battery terminal and isolate the cable.
c) Wait at least two minutes for the backup power supply to be depleted before beginning work.

ENABLING THE SYSTEM

To enable the airbag system, perform the following steps:
a) Turn the ignition switch to the Off position.
b) Connect the cable to the negative battery terminal.
c) Turn the ignition switch to the On position. Confirm that the airbag warning light glows for 6 to 8 seconds, then goes out, indicating the system is functioning properly.

PASSENGER AIRBAG ON/OFF SWITCH

All pickup models except the Quad-Cab are equipped with a switch on the instrument panel that disarms the passenger-side airbag, if the driver wishes, when certain child seats are used in the right front seat of the vehicle. The switch is operated with a key, and can only be switched with the vehicle's ignition key.

When the driver inserts the ignition key in the airbag On/Off switch and turns it clockwise, the passenger airbag will be disabled, and an LED "OFF" light on the switch will light. If the key is inserted again and turned counterclockwise, the passenger airbag is armed again.

⁂ WARNING:

The key should never be left in the switch.

28 Wiring diagrams - general information

Since it isn't possible to include all wiring diagrams for every year and model covered by this manual, the following diagrams are those that are typical and most commonly needed.

Prior to troubleshooting any circuits, check the fuse and circuit breakers (if equipped) to make sure they're in good condition. Make sure the battery is properly charged and check the cable connections (see Chapter 1).

When checking a circuit, make sure that all connectors are clean, with no broken or loose terminals. When disconnecting a connector, do not pull on the wires. Pull only on the connector housings themselves.

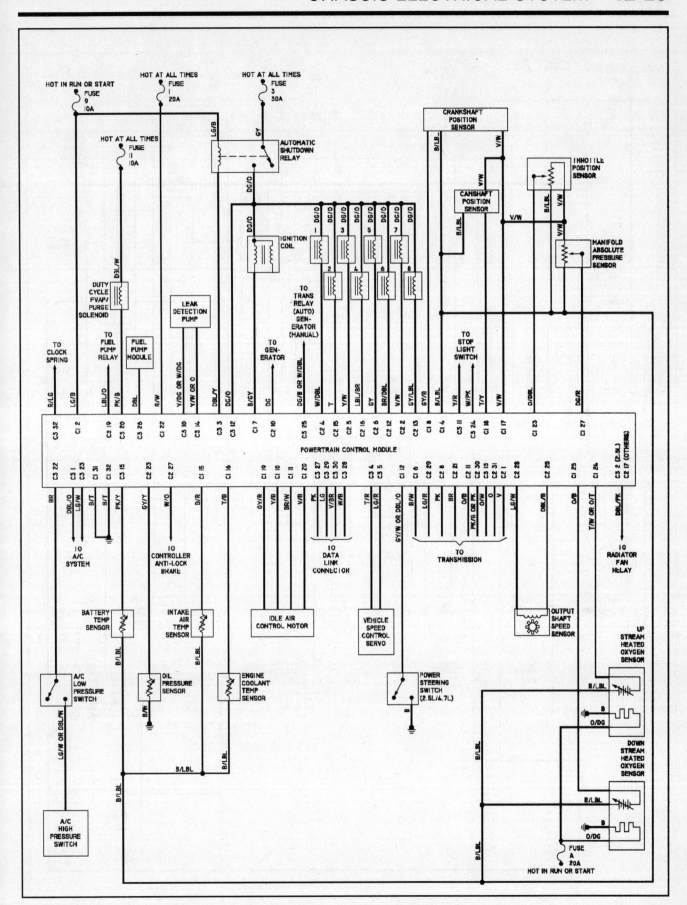

Engine control system (four-cylinder, V6, 5.2L/5.9L V8 engines) - 2000 Dakota models

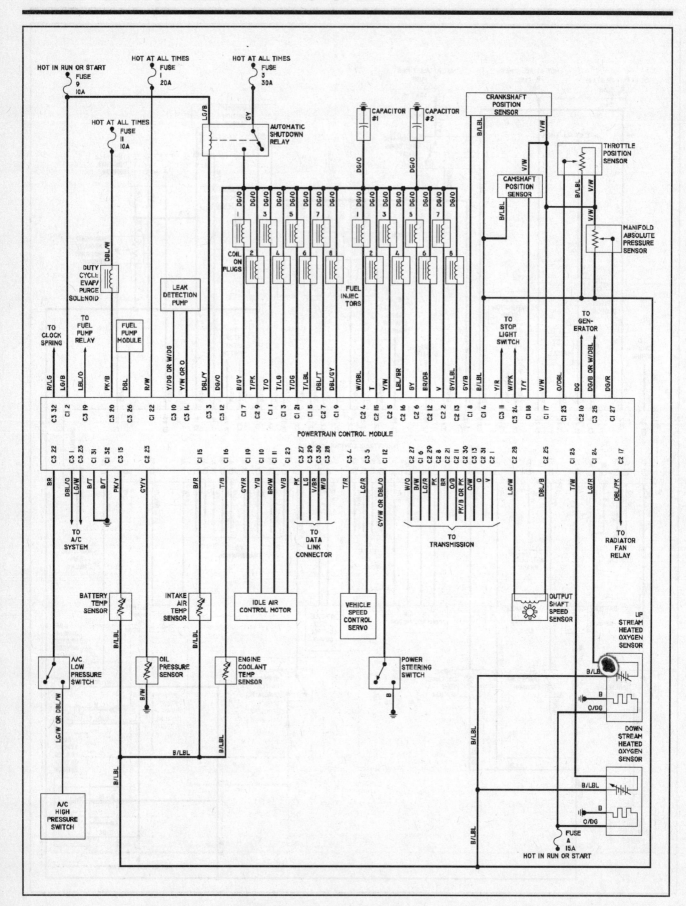

Engine control system (4.7L V8 engine) - 2000 Dakota models (except California)

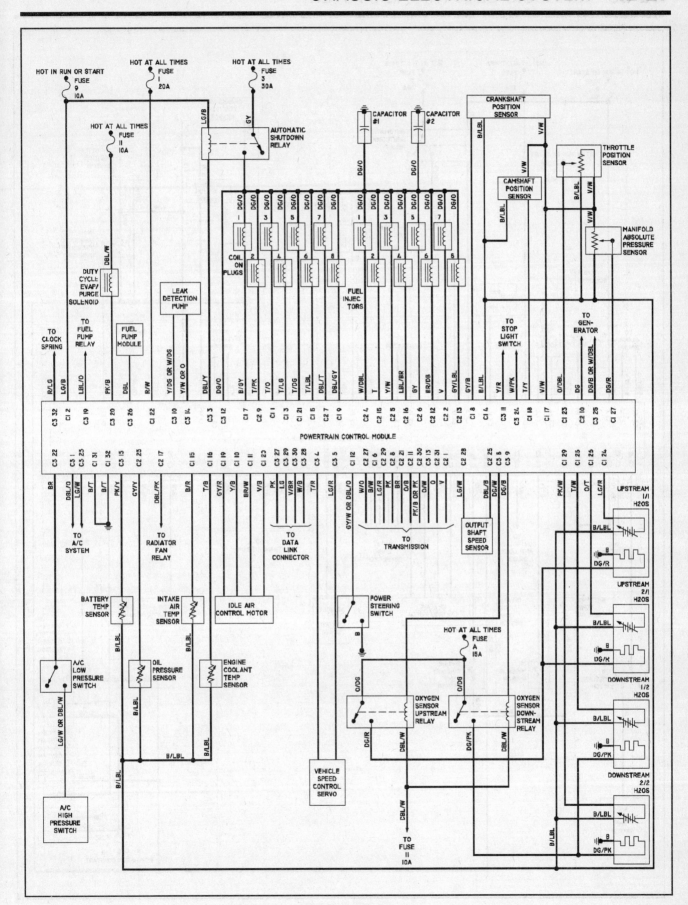

Engine control system (4.7L V8 engine) - 2000 Dakota models (California)

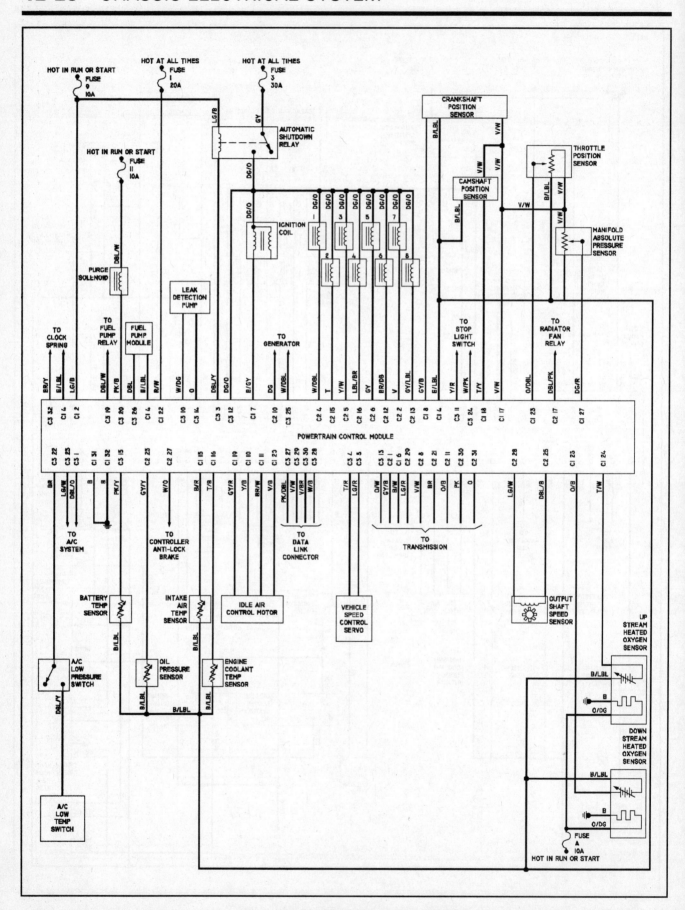

Engine control system (V6, 5.2L/5.9L V8 engines) - 2000 Durango models (except California)

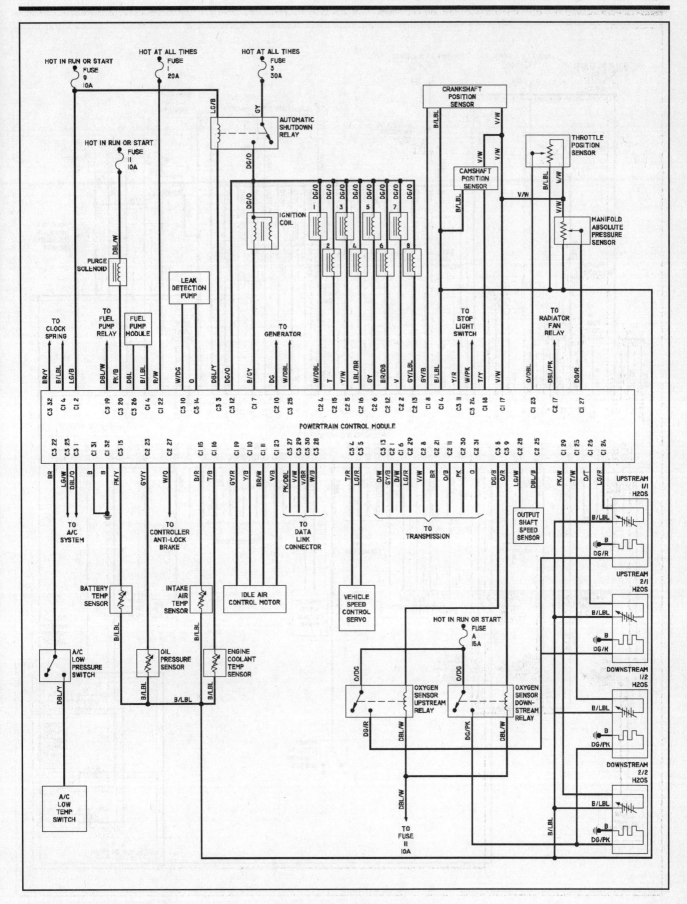

Engine control system (V6, 5.2L/5.9L V8 engines) - 2000 Durango models (California)

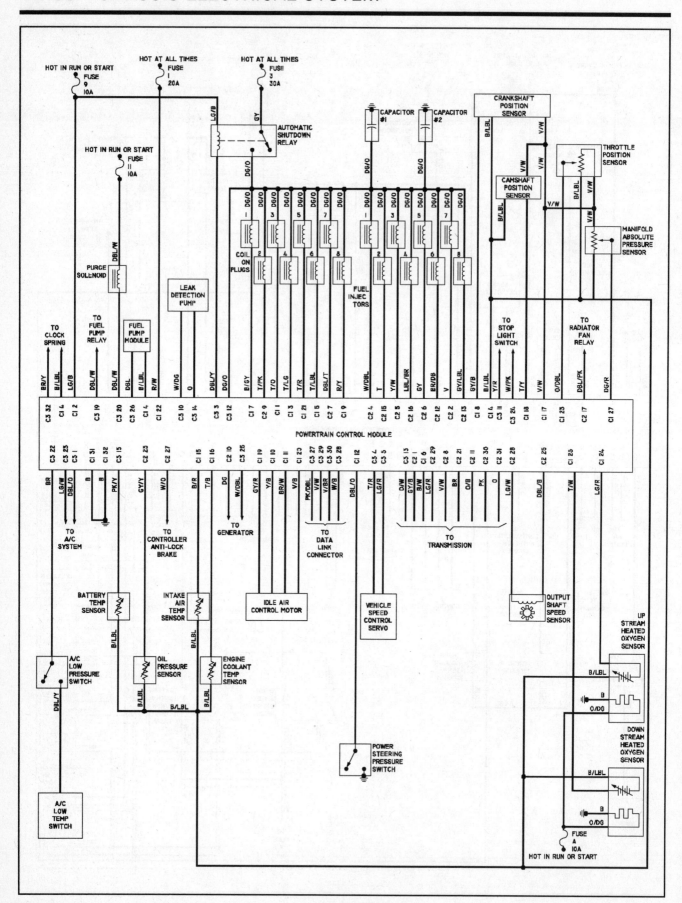

Engine control system (4.7L V8 engine) - 2000 Durango models (except California)

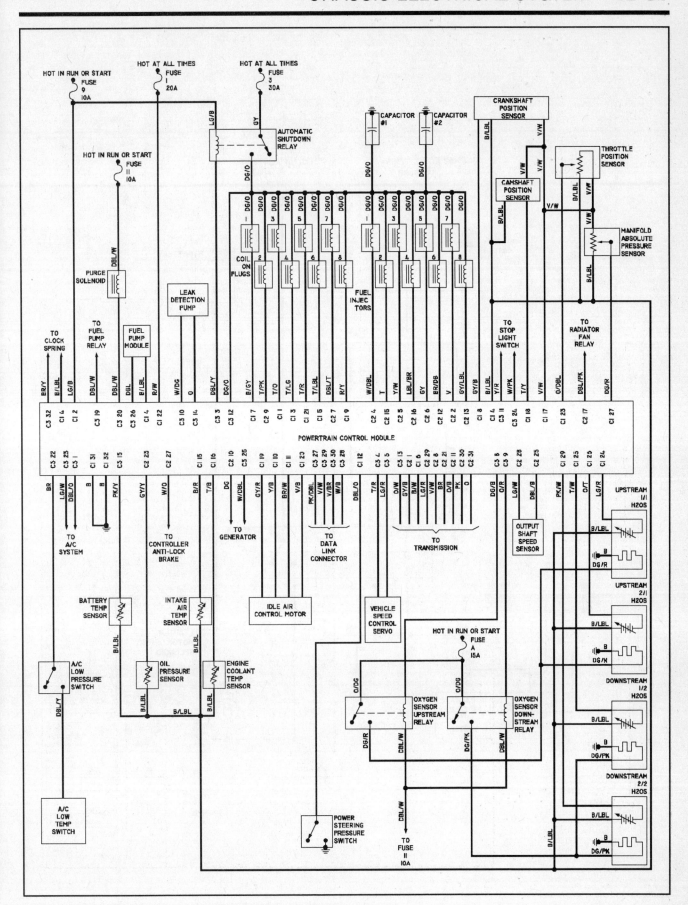

Engine control system (4.7L V8 engine) - 2000 Durango models (California)

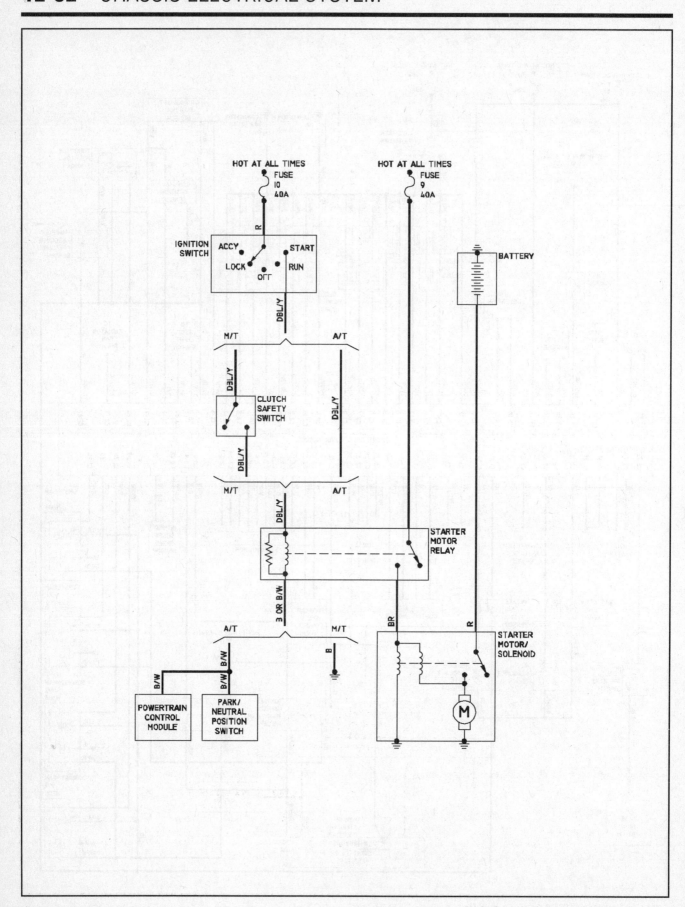

Starting system - 2000 Dakota models

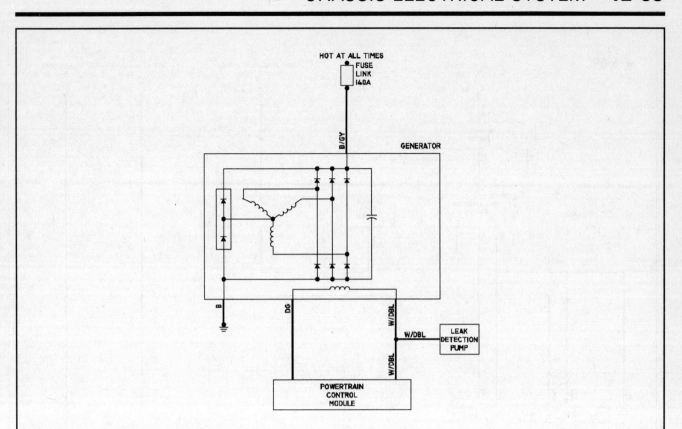

Charging system - 2000 Dakota models

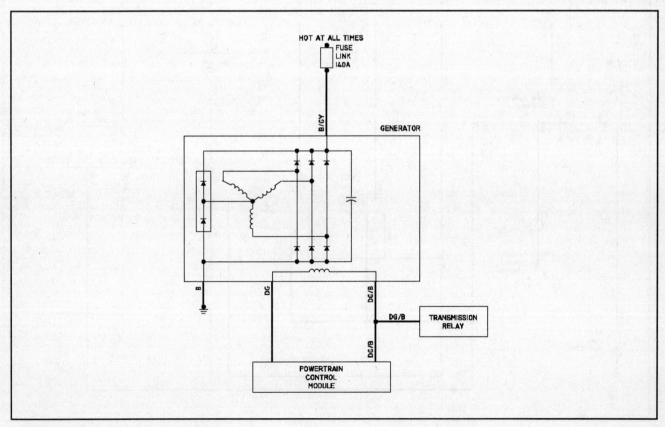

Charging system - 2000 Durango models

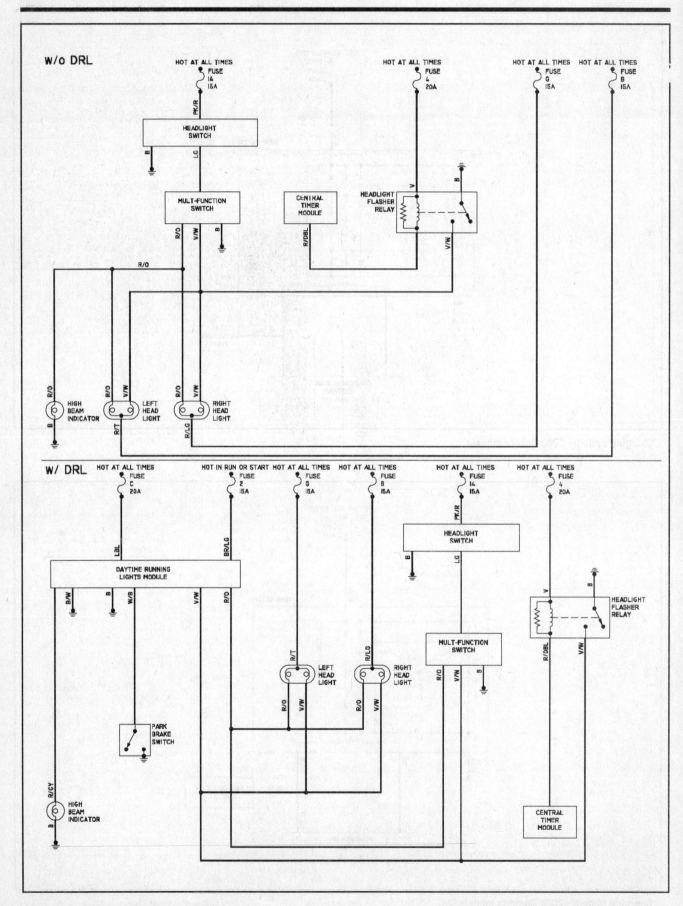

Headlight system - 2000 Dakota models

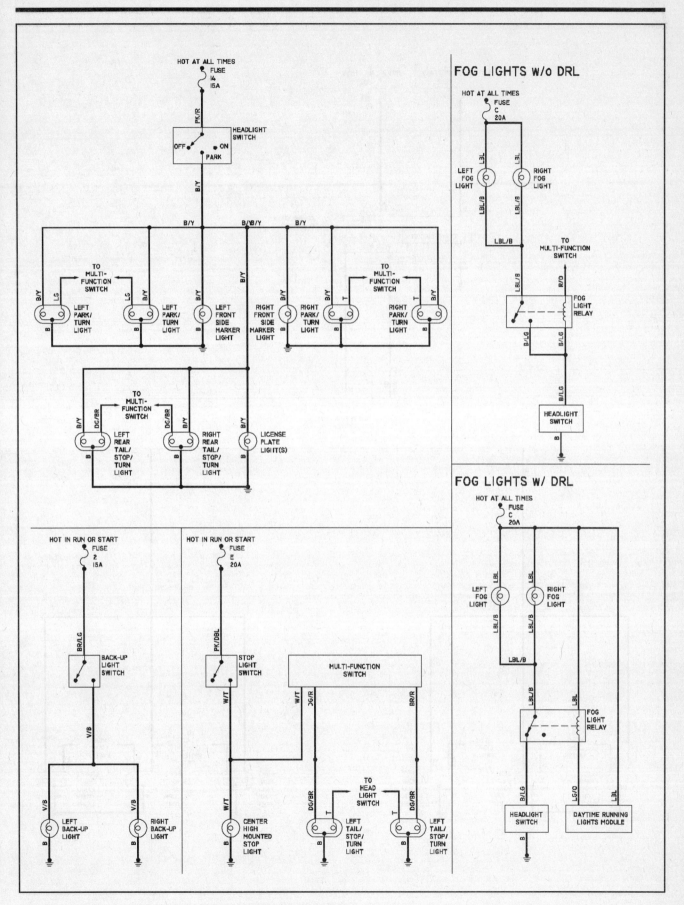

Exterior lighting system (except headlights) - 2000 Dakota models

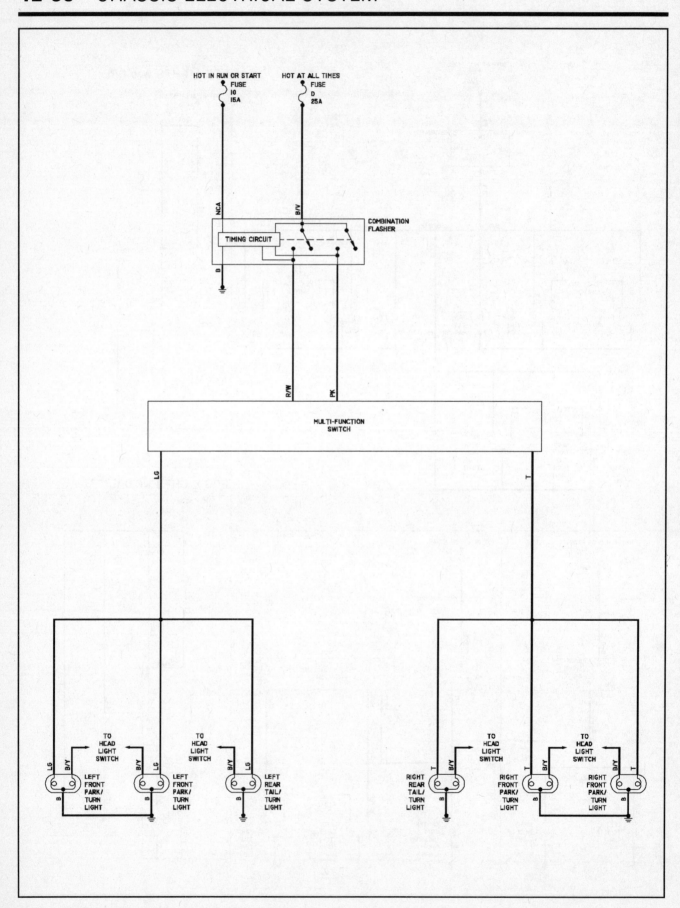

Turn signal/hazard flasher system - 2000 Dakota models

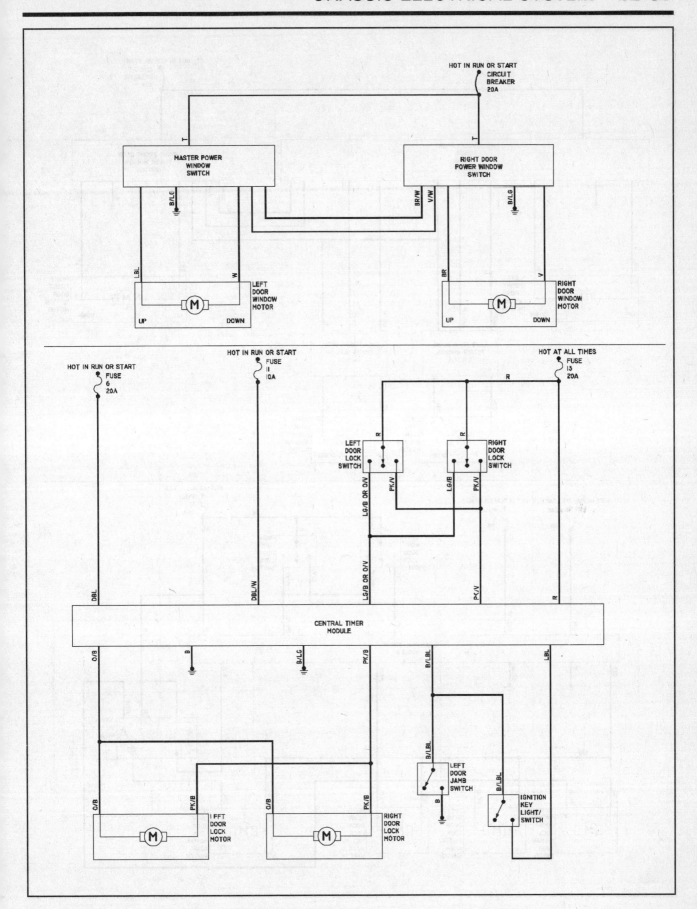

Power window and door lock systems - 2000 Dakota two-door models

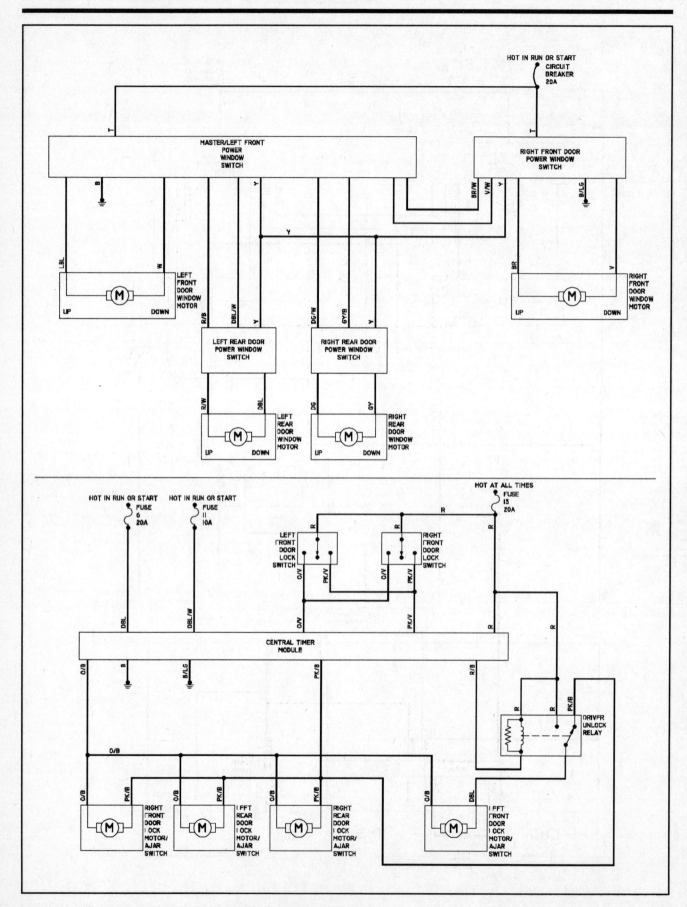

Power window and door lock systems - 2000 Dakota four-door models

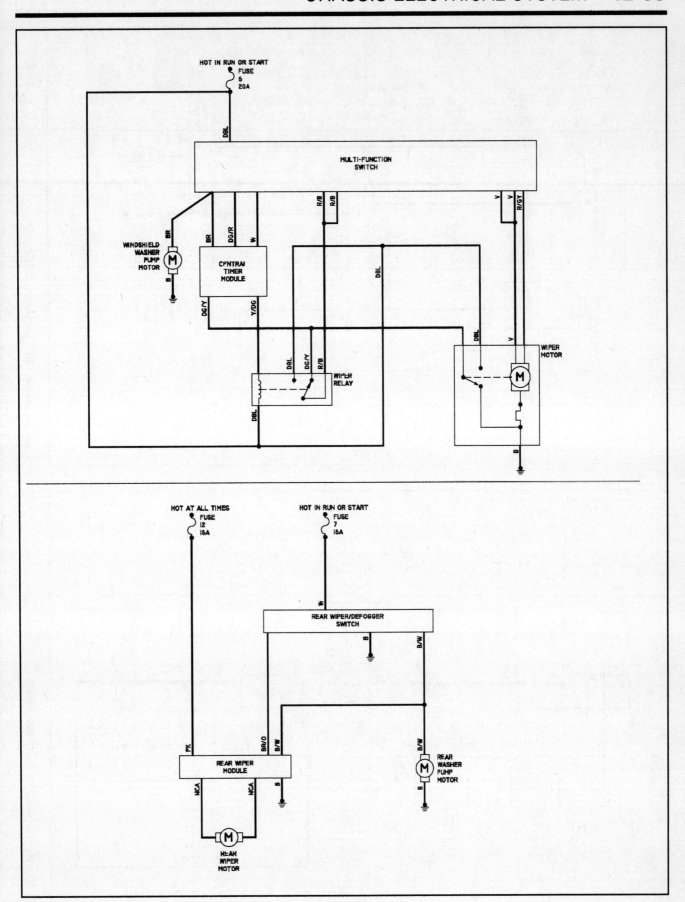

Windshield and rear wiper systems - 2000 Dakota and Durango models

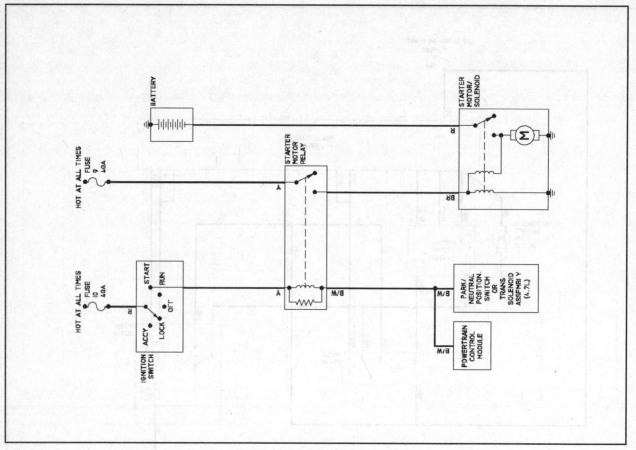

Starting system - 2000 Durango models

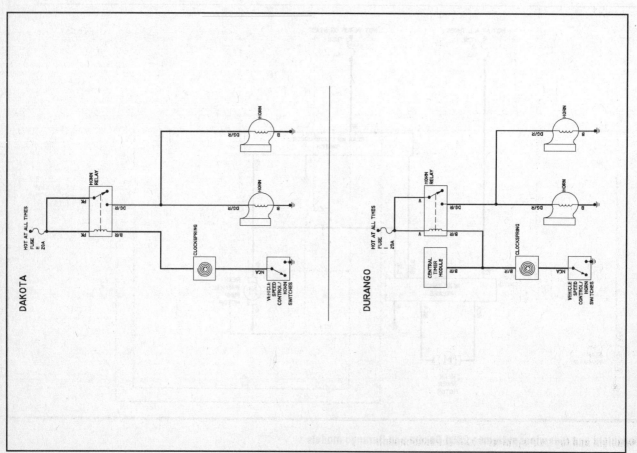

Horn system - 2000 Dakota and Durango models

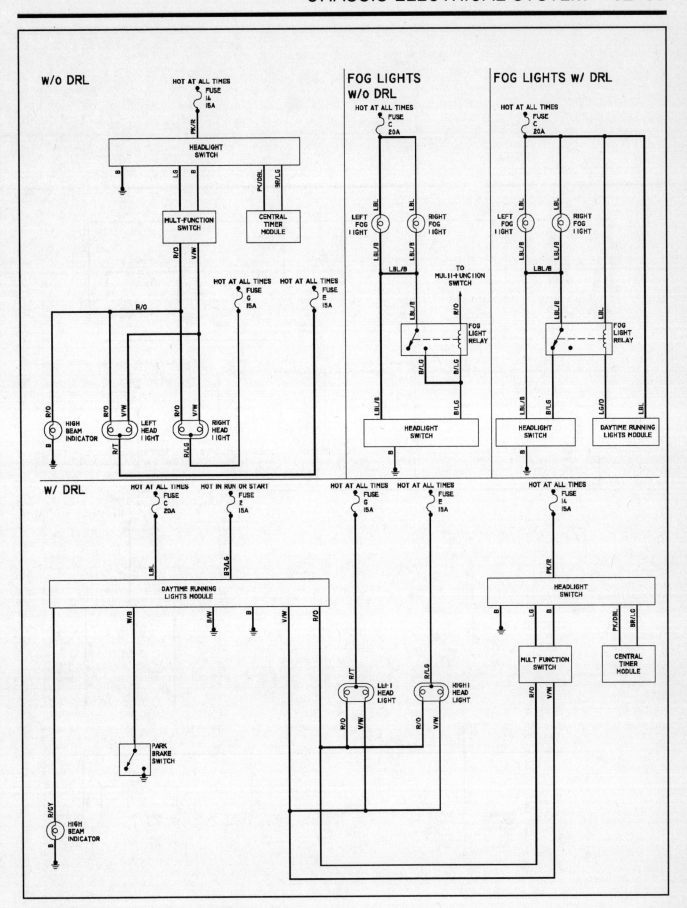

Headlight and fog light systems - 2000 Durango models

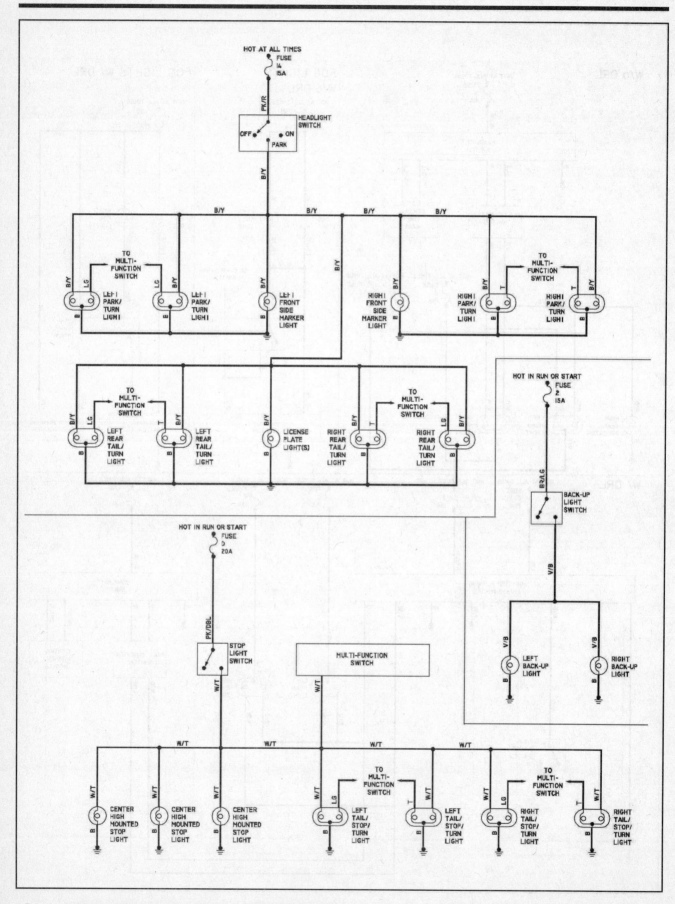

Exterior lighting system (except headlights) - 2000 Durango models

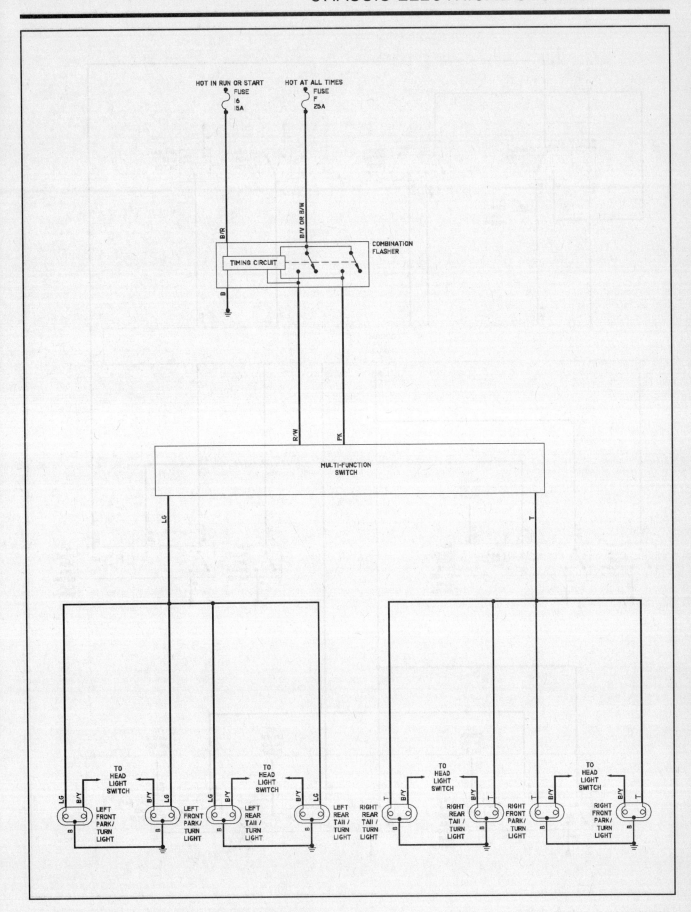

Turn signal/hazard flasher system - 2000 Durango models

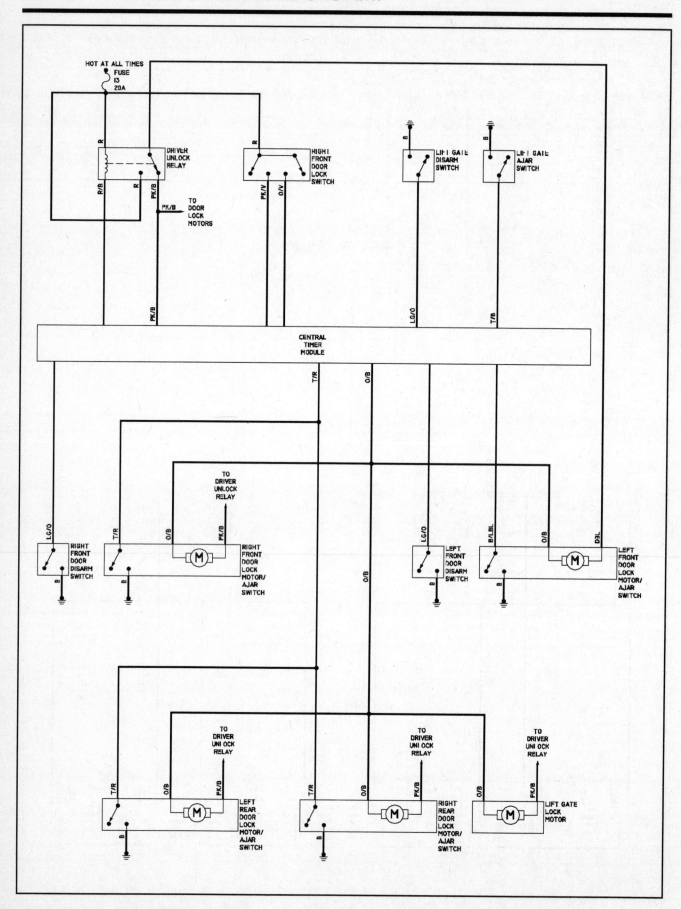

Power door lock system - 2000 Durango models

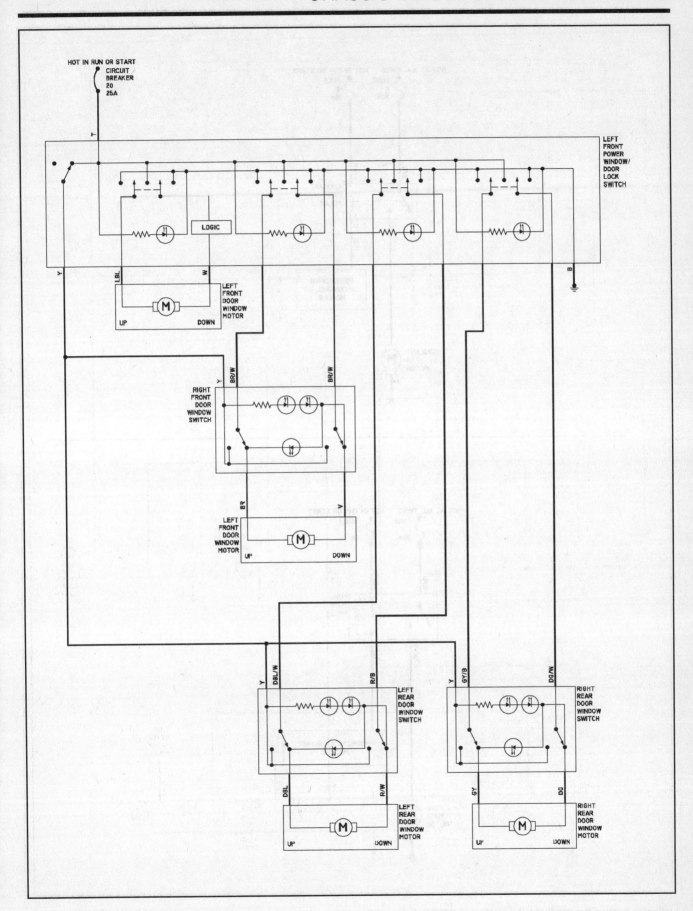

Power window system - 2000 Durango models

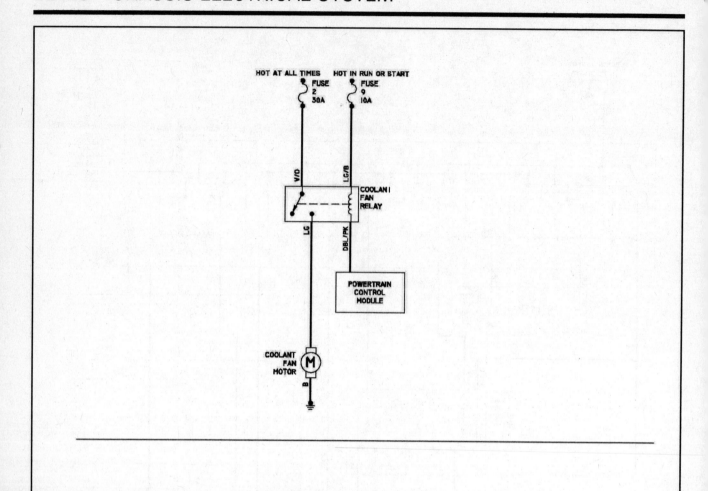

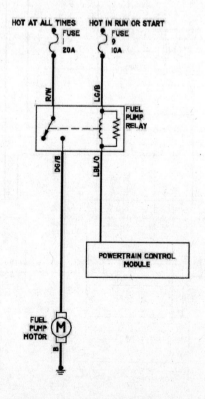

Engine cooling fan and fuel pump systems - 2000 Dakota and Durango models

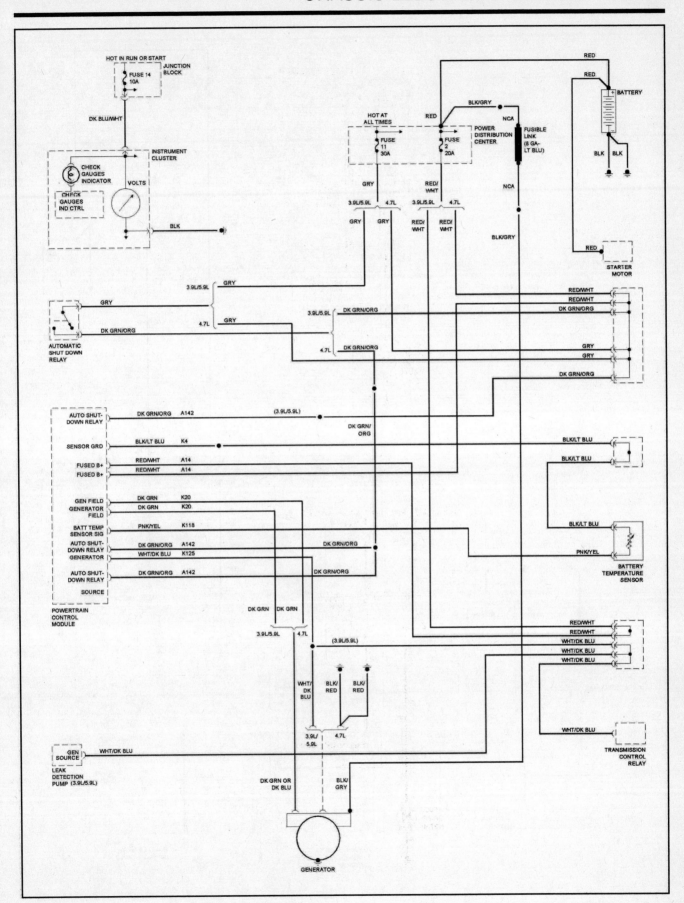

Charging system - 2001 and later Dakota and Durango models

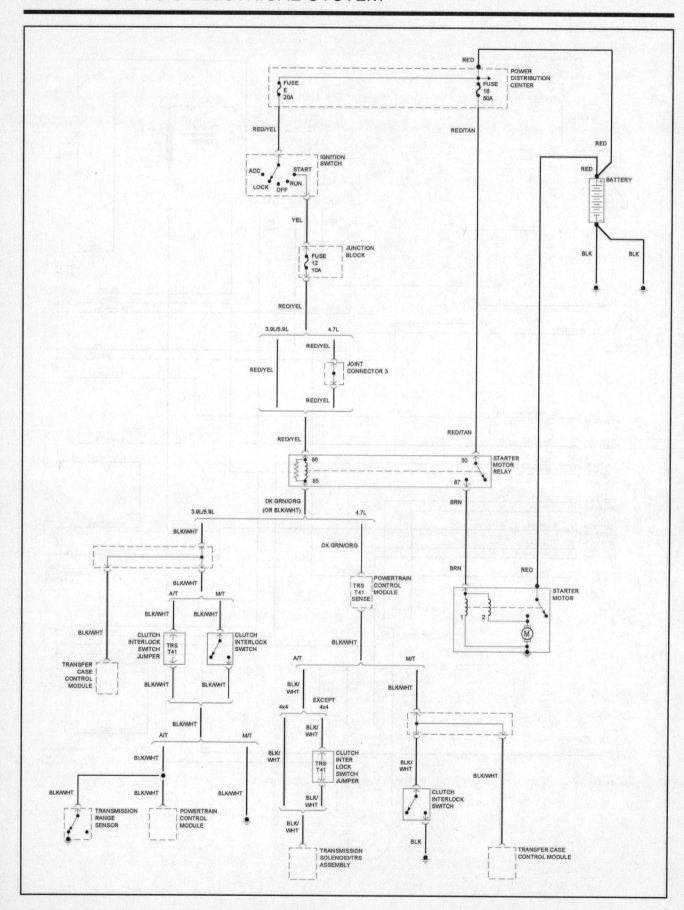

Starting system - 2001 and later Dakota and Durango models

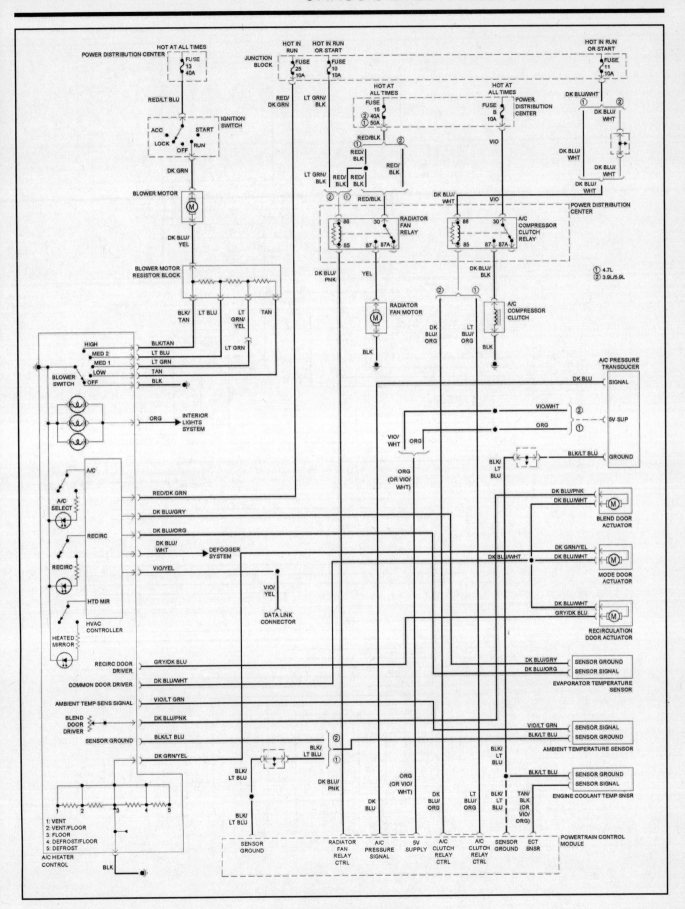

Air conditioning and engine cooling fan systems - 2001 and later Dakota models

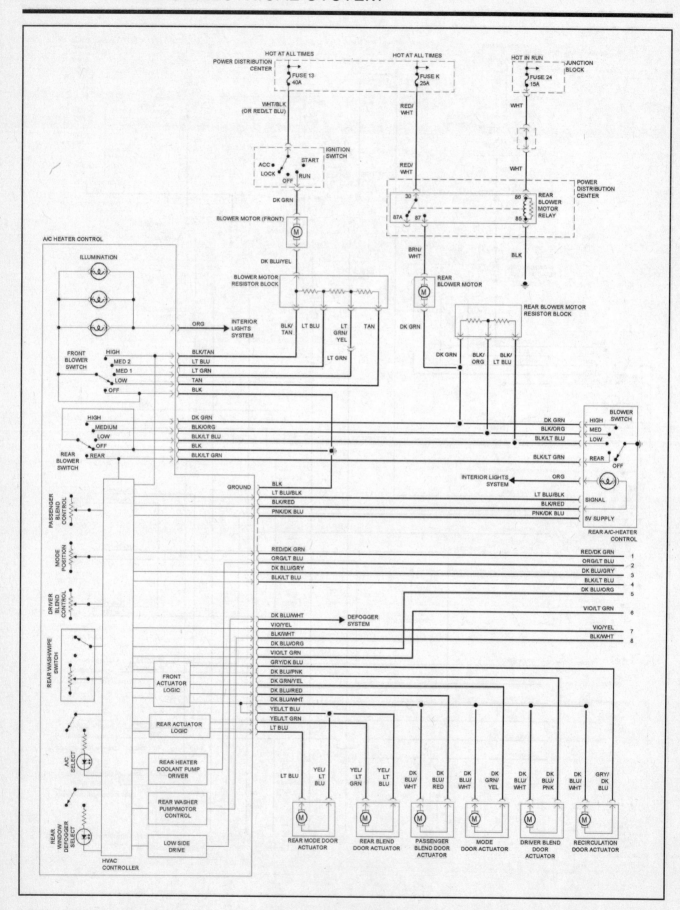

Air conditioning and engine cooling fan systems - 2001 and later Durango models (1 of 2)

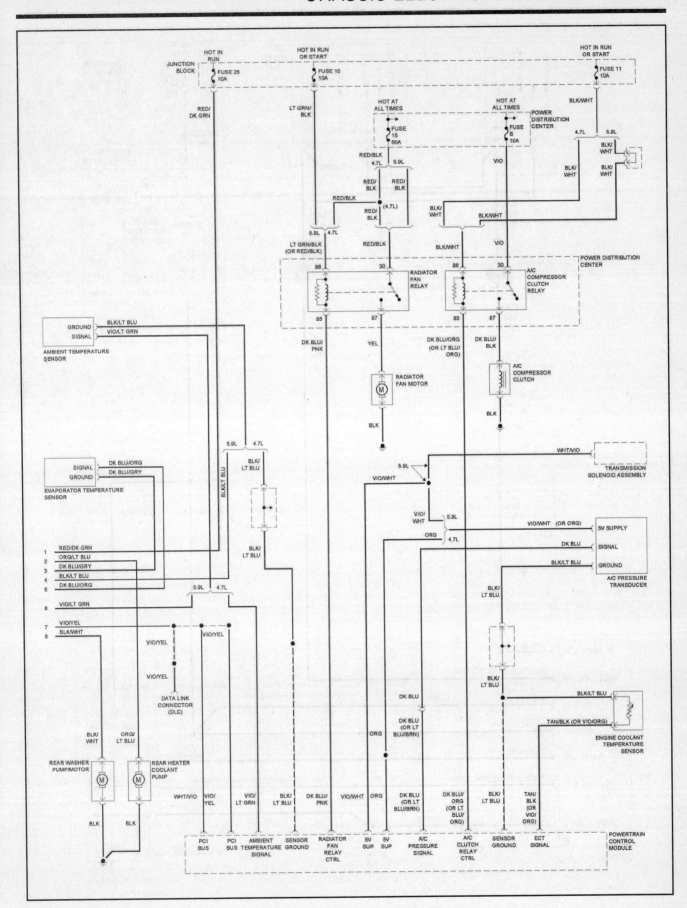

Air conditioning and engine cooling fan systems - 2001 and later Durango models (2 of 2)

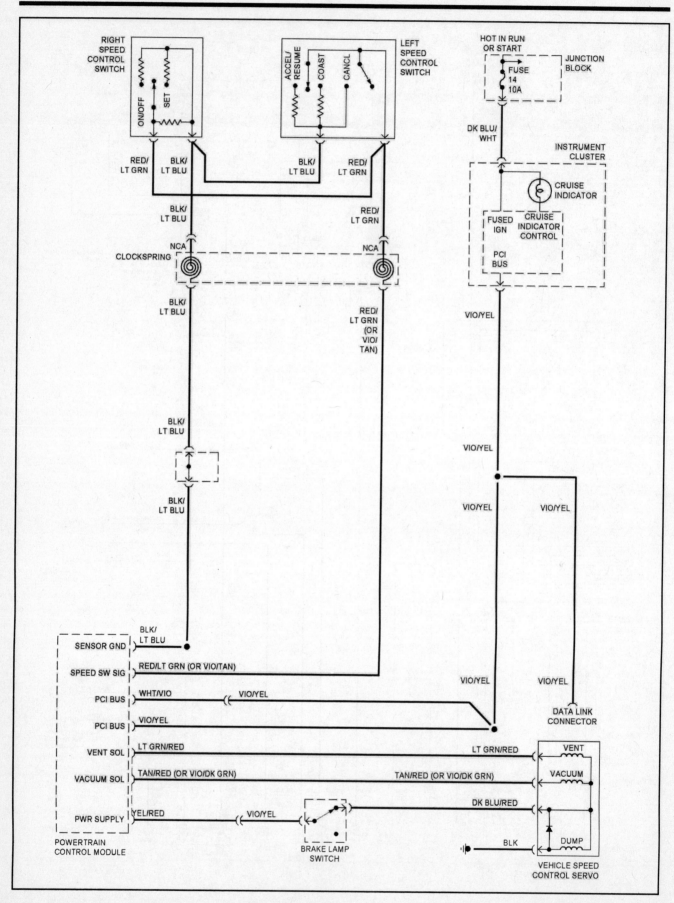

Cruise control system - 2001 and later Dakota and Durango models

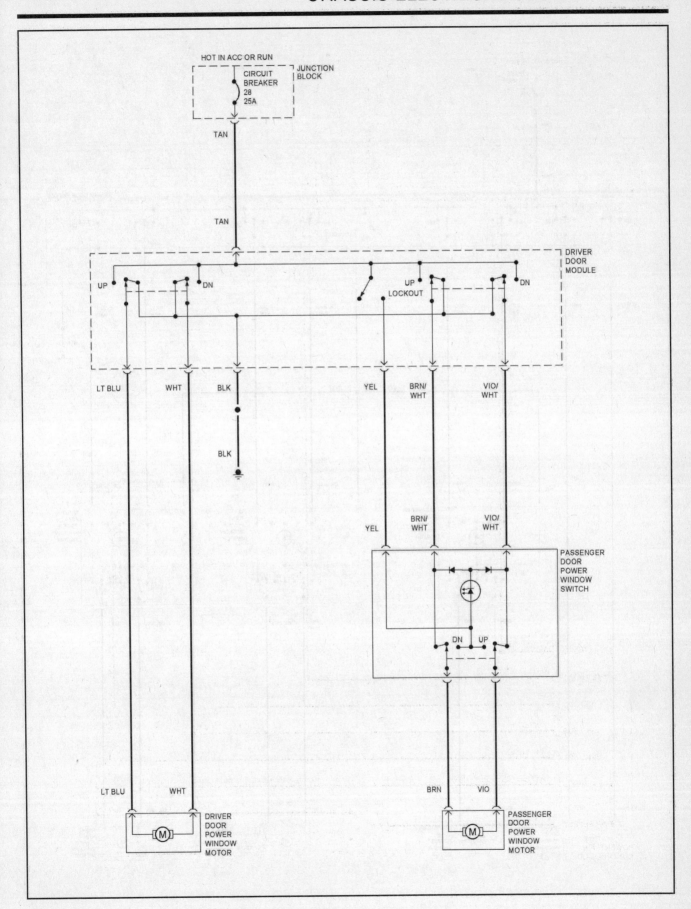

Power window system - 2001 and later Dakota two-door models

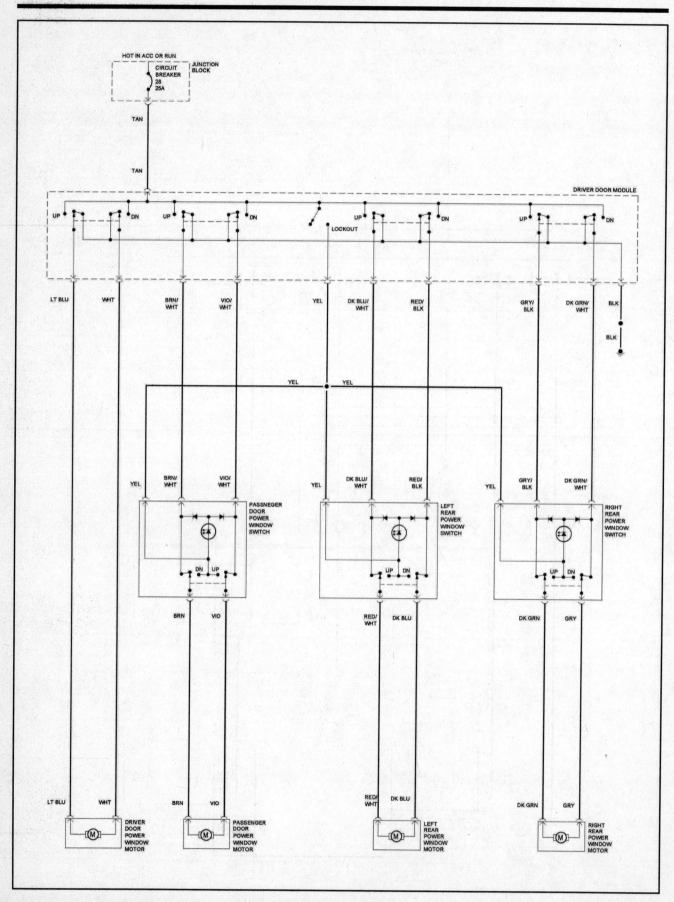

Power window system - 2001 and later Durango and Dakota four-door models

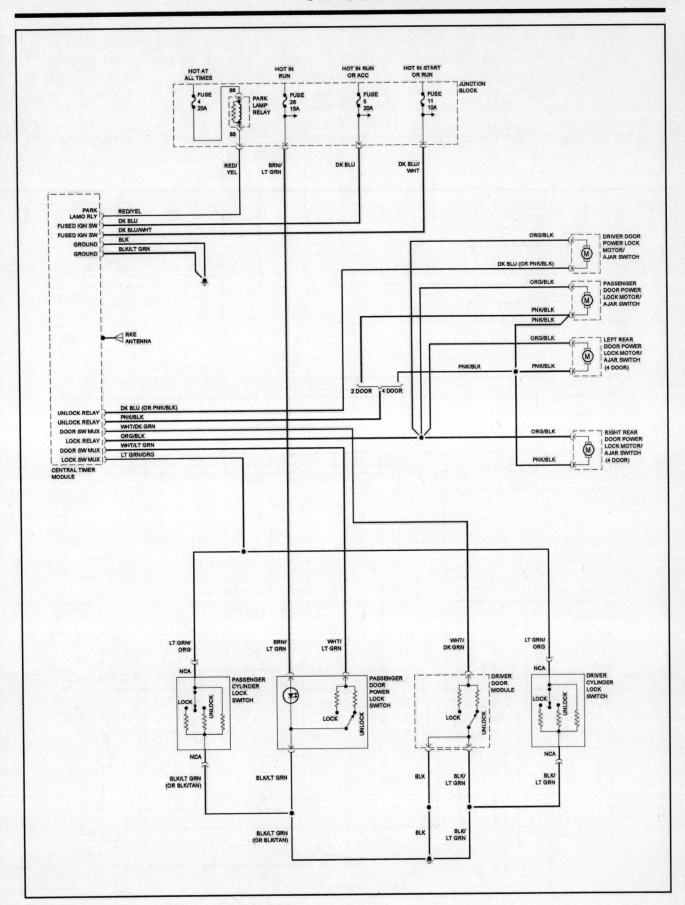

Power door lock system - 2001 and later Dakota models

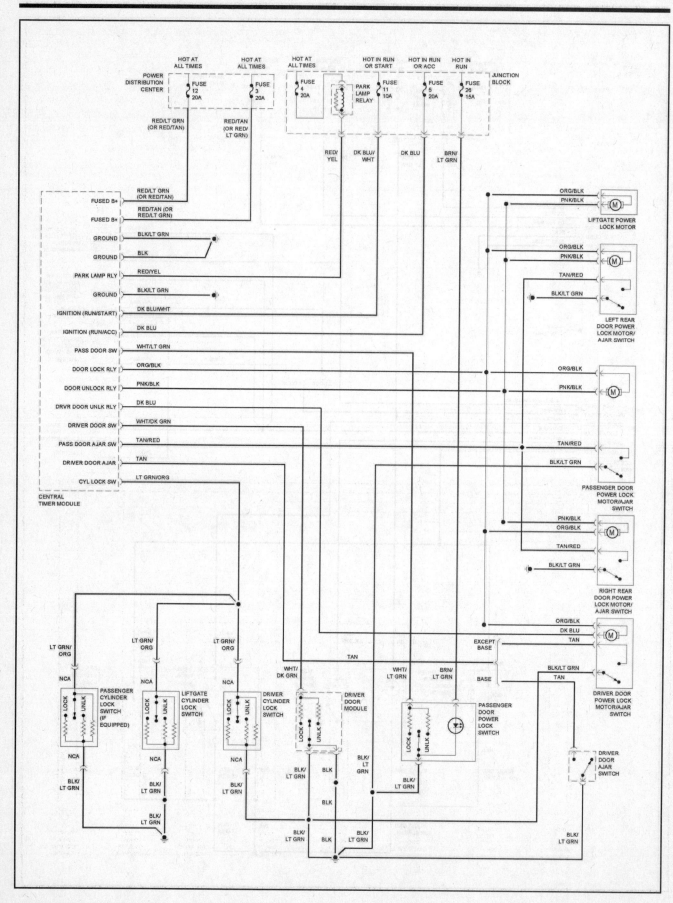

Power door lock system - 2001 and later Durango models

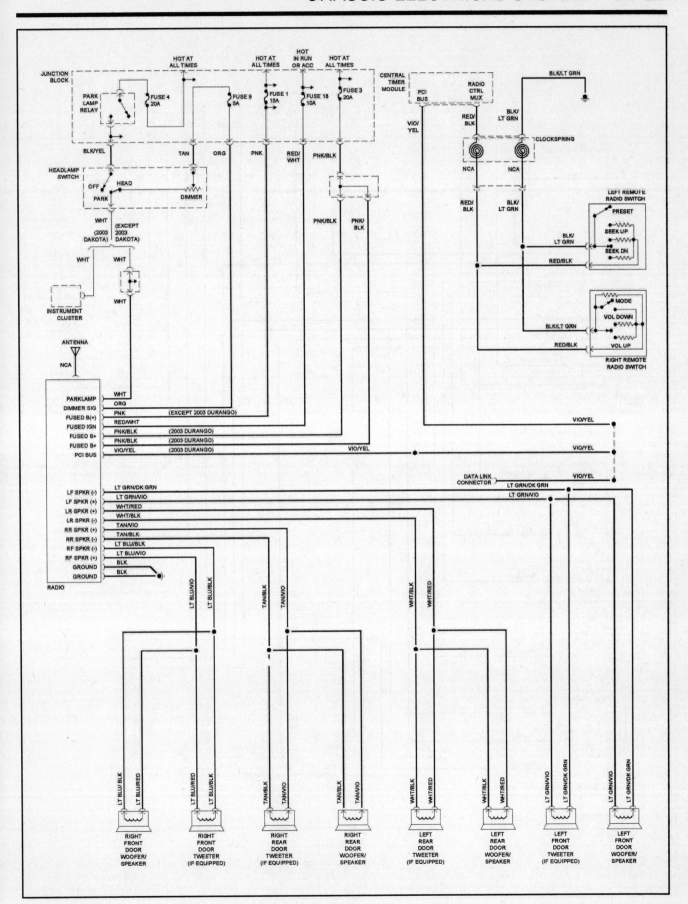

Audio system (base) - 2001 and later Dakota and Durango models

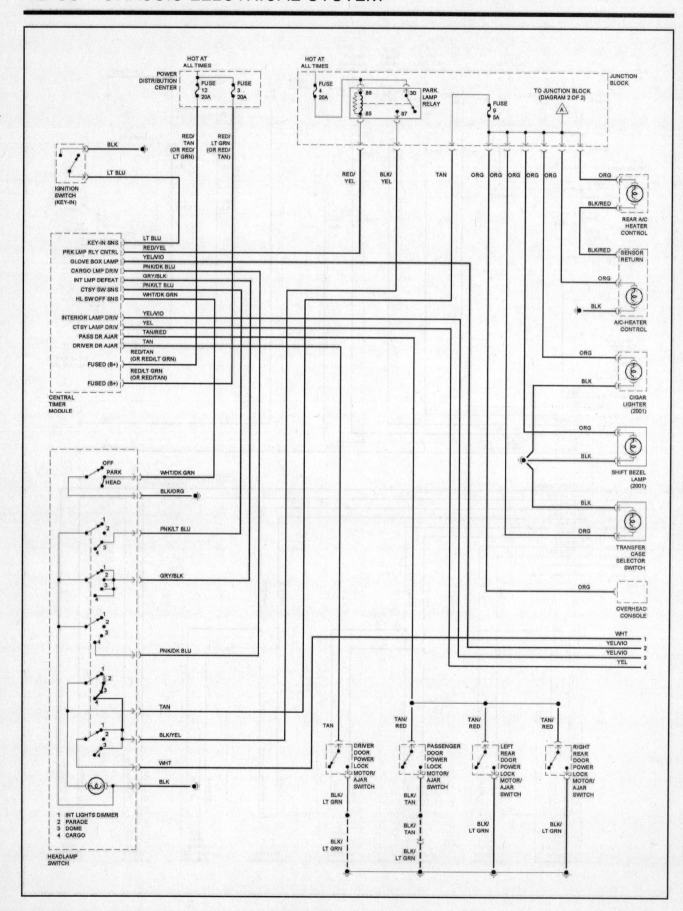

Interior lighting system - 2001 and later Durango models (1 of 2)

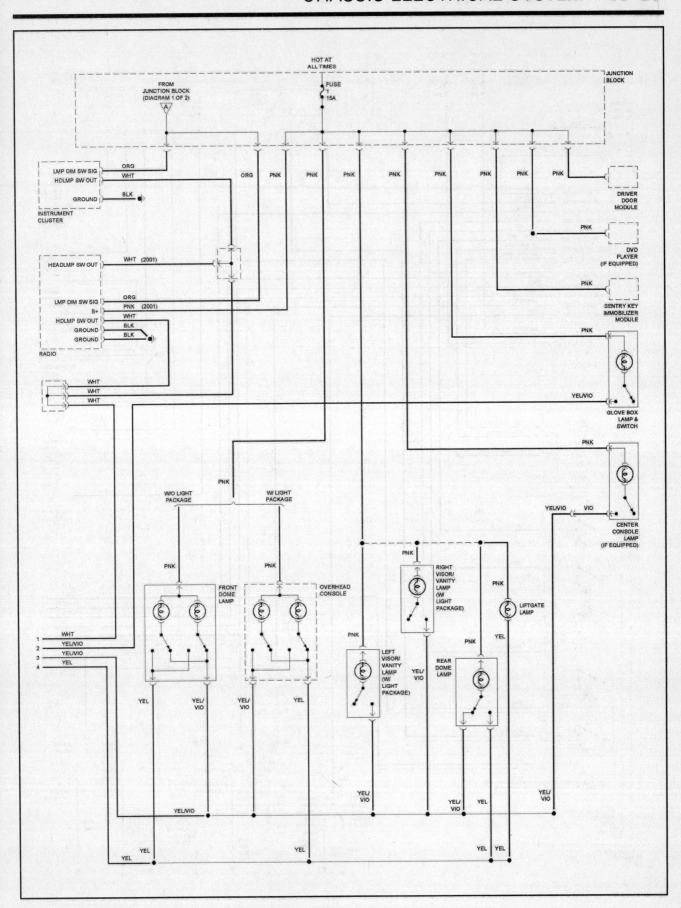

Interior lighting system - 2001 and later Durango models (2 of 2)

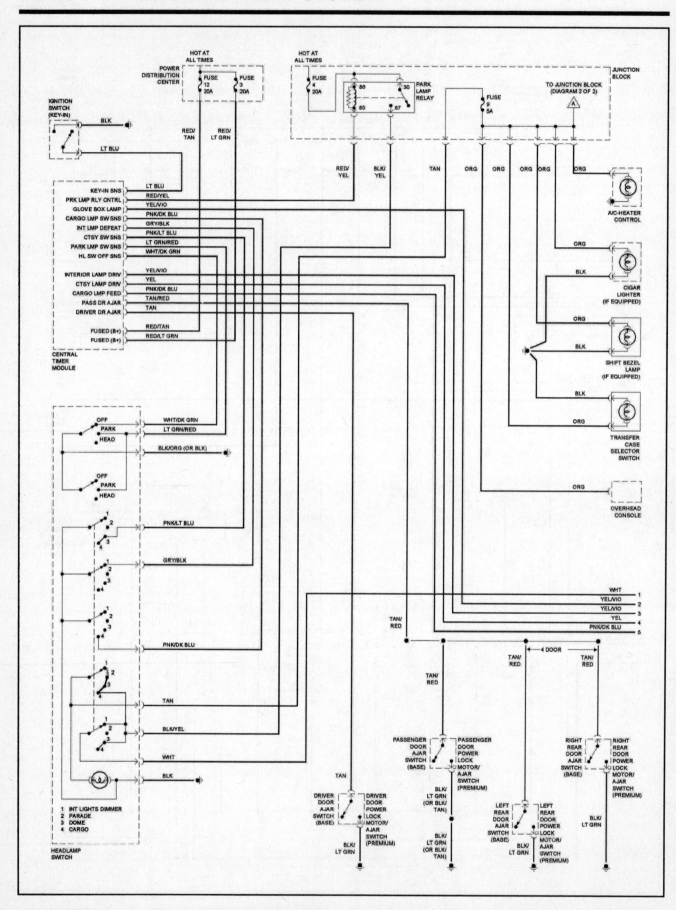

Interior lighting system - 2001 and later Dakota models (1 of 2)

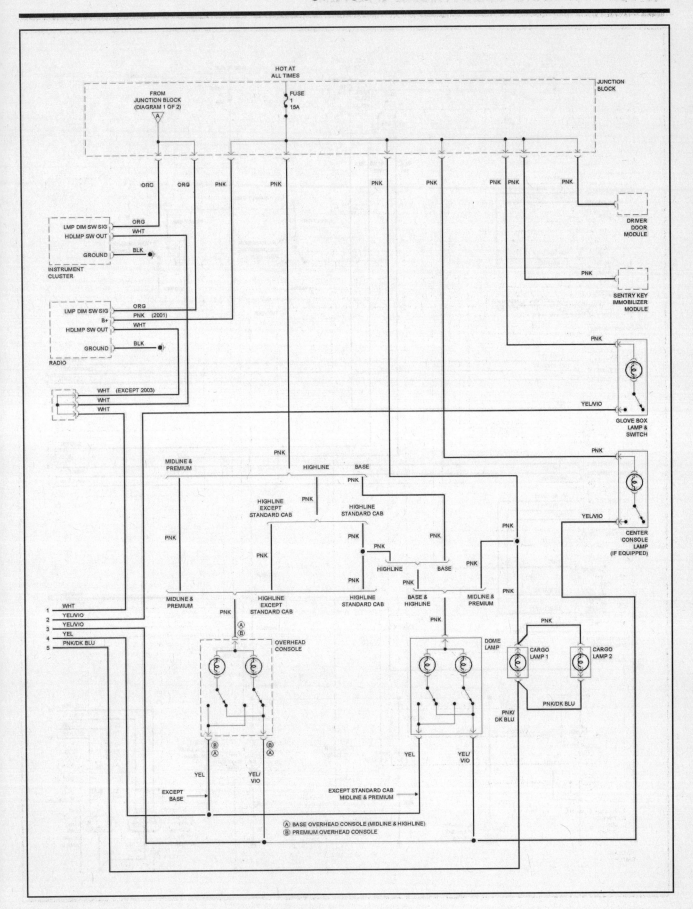

Interior lighting system - 2001 and later Dakota models (2 of 2)

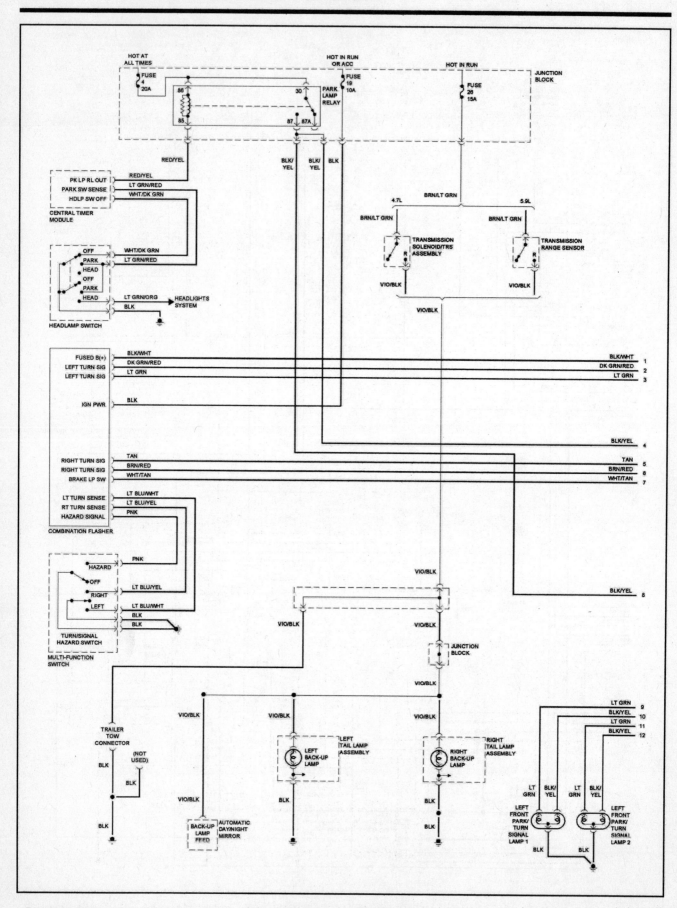

Exterior lighting system (except headlights) - 2001 and later Durango models (1 of 2)

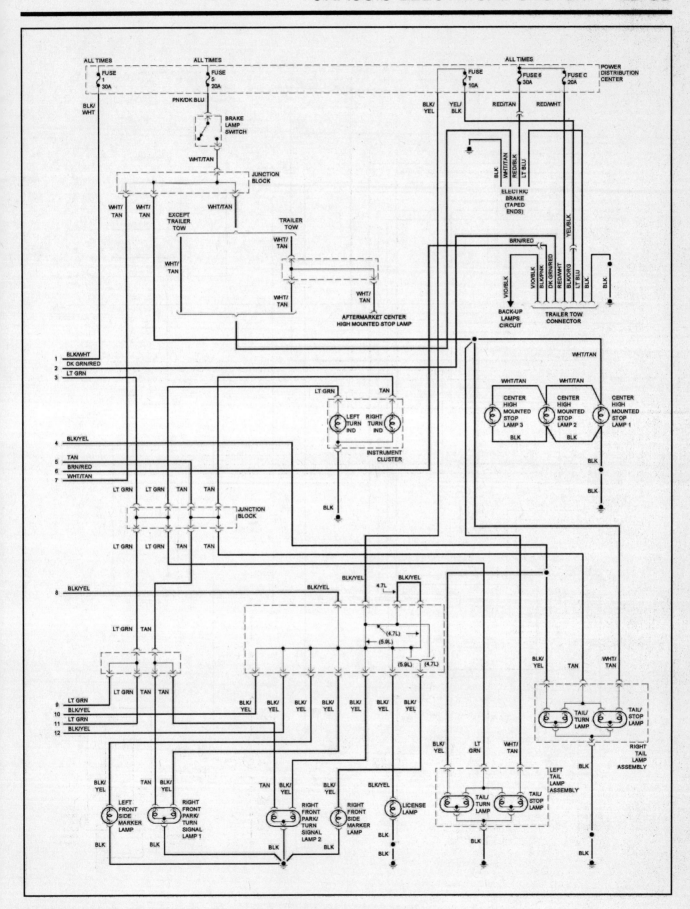

Exterior lighting system (except headlights) - 2001 and later Durango models (2 of 2)

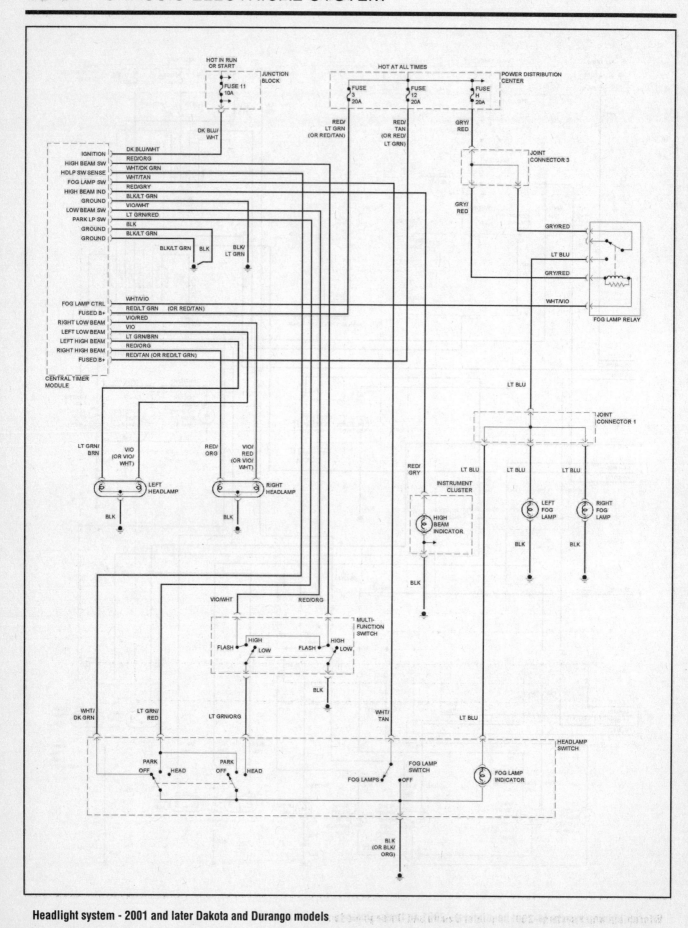

Headlight system - 2001 and later Dakota and Durango models

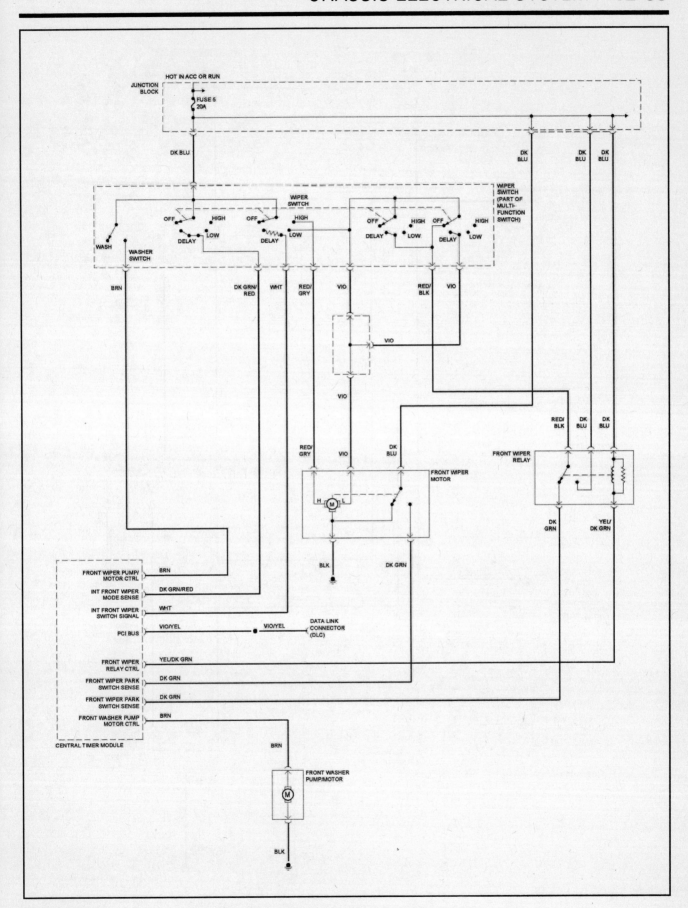

Windshield wiper system - 2001 and later Dakota and Durango models

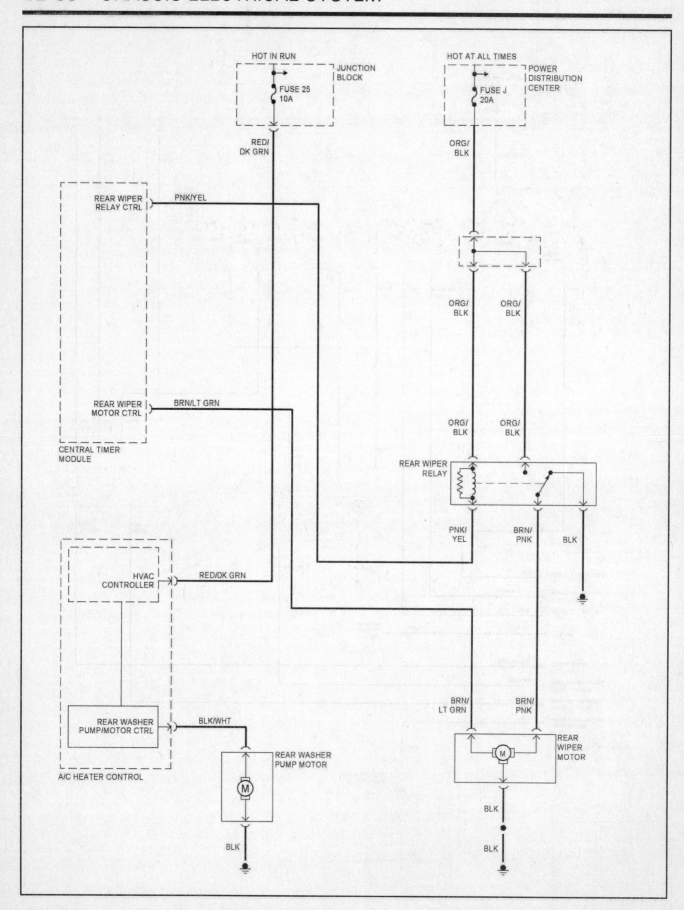

Rear window wiper system - 2001 and later Durango models

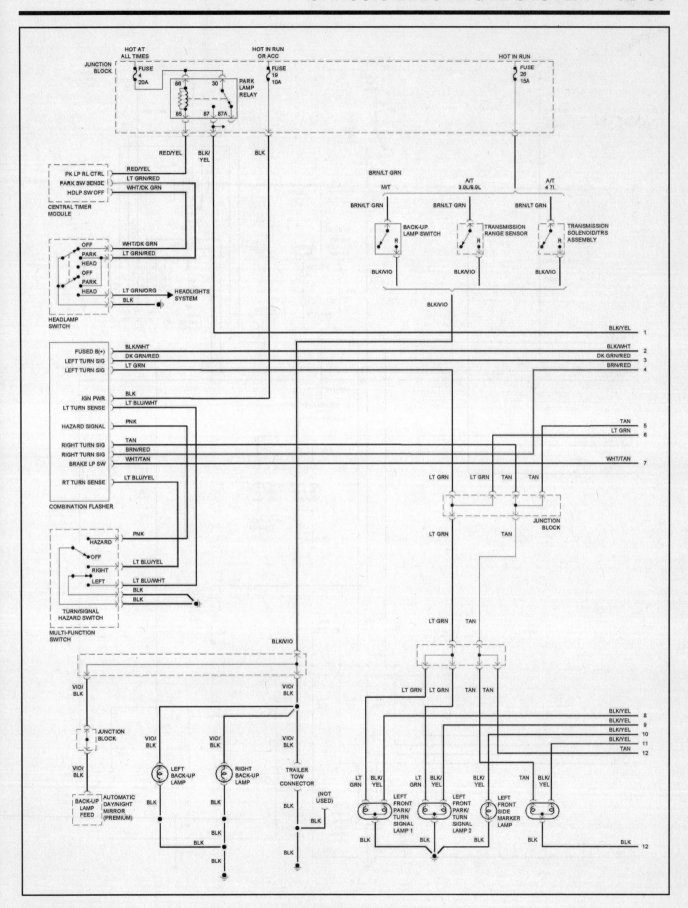

Exterior lighting system (except headlights) - 2001 and later Dakota models (1 of 2)

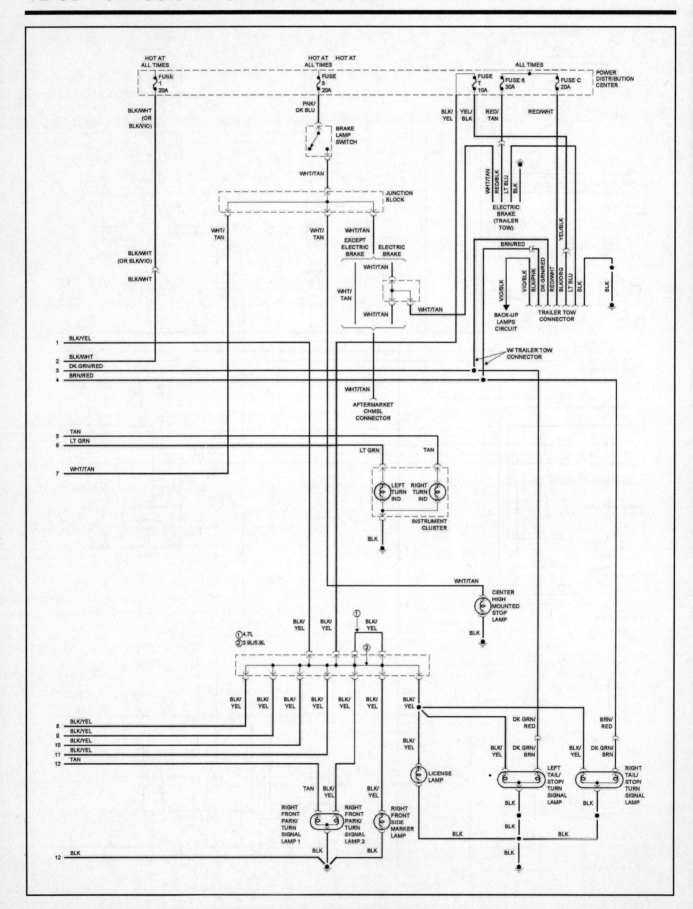

Exterior lighting system (except headlights) - 2001 and later Dakota models (2 of 2)

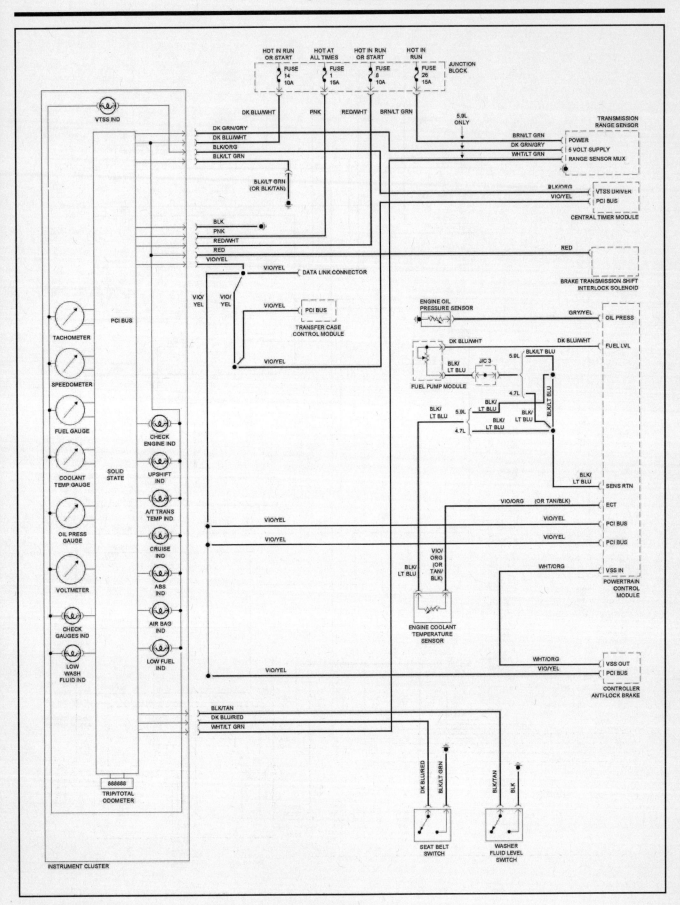

Warning lights and gauges systems - 2001 and later Durango models

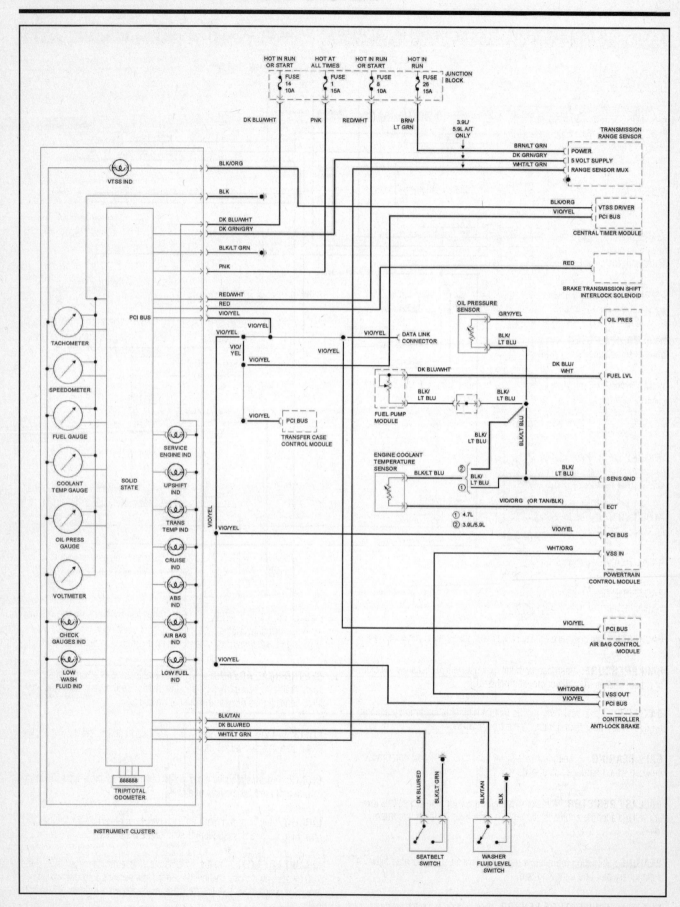

Warning lights and gauges systems - 2001 and later Dakota models

GLOSSARY

AIR/FUEL RATIO: The ratio of air-to-gasoline by weight in the fuel mixture drawn into the engine.

AIR INJECTION: One method of reducing harmful exhaust emissions by injecting air into each of the exhaust ports of an engine. The fresh air entering the hot exhaust manifold causes any remaining fuel to be burned before it can exit the tailpipe.

ALTERNATOR: A device used for converting mechanical energy into electrical energy.

AMMETER: An instrument, calibrated in amperes, used to measure the flow of an electrical current in a circuit. Ammeters are always connected in series with the circuit being tested.

AMPERE: The rate of flow of electrical current present when one volt of electrical pressure is applied against one ohm of electrical resistance.

ANALOG COMPUTER: Any microprocessor that uses similar (analogous) electrical signals to make its calculations.

ARMATURE: A laminated, soft iron core wrapped by a wire that converts electrical energy to mechanical energy as in a motor or relay. When rotated in a magnetic field, it changes mechanical energy into electrical energy as in a generator.

ATMOSPHERIC PRESSURE: The pressure on the Earth's surface caused by the weight of the air in the atmosphere. At sea level, this pressure is 14.7 psi at 32°F (101 kPa at 0°C).

ATOMIZATION: The breaking down of a liquid into a fine mist that can be suspended in air.

AXIAL PLAY: Movement parallel to a shaft or bearing bore.

BACKFIRE: The sudden combustion of gases in the intake or exhaust system that results in a loud explosion.

BACKLASH: The clearance or play between two parts, such as meshed gears.

BACKPRESSURE: Restrictions in the exhaust system that slow the exit of exhaust gases from the combustion chamber.

BAKELITE: A heat resistant, plastic insulator material commonly used in printed circuit boards and transistorized components.

BALL BEARING: A bearing made up of hardened inner and outer races between which hardened steel balls roll.

BALLAST RESISTOR: A resistor in the primary ignition circuit that lowers voltage after the engine is started to reduce wear on ignition components.

BEARING: A friction reducing, supportive device usually located between a stationary part and a moving part.

BIMETAL TEMPERATURE SENSOR: Any sensor or switch made of two dissimilar types of metal that bend when heated or cooled due to the different expansion rates of the alloys. These types of sensors usually function as an on/off switch.

BLOWBY: Combustion gases, composed of water vapor and unburned fuel, that leak past the piston rings into the crankcase during normal engine operation. These gases are removed by the PCV system to prevent the buildup of harmful acids in the crankcase.

BRAKE PAD: A brake shoe and lining assembly used with disc brakes.

BRAKE SHOE: The backing for the brake lining. The term is, however, usually applied to the assembly of the brake backing and lining.

BUSHING: A liner, usually removable, for a bearing; an anti-friction liner used in place of a bearing.

CALIPER: A hydraulically activated device in a disc brake system, which is mounted straddling the brake rotor (disc). The caliper contains at least one piston and two brake pads. Hydraulic pressure on the piston(s) forces the pads against the rotor.

CAMSHAFT: A shaft in the engine on which are the lobes (cams) which operate the valves. The camshaft is driven by the crankshaft, via a belt, chain or gears, at one half the crankshaft speed.

CAPACITOR: A device which stores an electrical charge.

CARBON MONOXIDE (CO): A colorless, odorless gas given off as a normal byproduct of combustion. It is poisonous and extremely dangerous in confined areas, building up slowly to toxic levels without warning if adequate ventilation is not available.

CARBURETOR: A device, usually mounted on the intake manifold of an engine, which mixes the air and fuel in the proper proportion to allow even combustion.

CATALYTIC CONVERTER: A device installed in the exhaust system, like a muffler, that converts harmful byproducts of combustion into carbon dioxide and water vapor by means of a heat-producing chemical reaction.

CENTRIFUGAL ADVANCE: A mechanical method of advancing the spark timing by using flyweights in the distributor that react to centrifugal force generated by the distributor shaft rotation.

CHECK VALVE: Any one-way valve installed to permit the flow of air, fuel or vacuum in one direction only.

CHOKE: A device, usually a moveable valve, placed in the intake path of a carburetor to restrict the flow of air.

CIRCUIT: Any unbroken path through which an electrical current can flow. Also used to describe fuel flow in some instances.

CIRCUIT BREAKER: A switch which protects an electrical circuit from overload by opening the circuit when the current flow exceeds a predetermined level. Some circuit breakers must be reset manually, while most reset automatically.

COIL (IGNITION): A transformer in the ignition circuit which steps up the voltage provided to the spark plugs.

COMBINATION MANIFOLD: An assembly which includes both the intake and exhaust manifolds in one casting.

COMBINATION VALVE: A device used in some fuel systems that routes fuel vapors to a charcoal storage canister instead of venting them into the atmosphere. The valve relieves fuel tank pressure and allows fresh air into the tank as the fuel level drops to prevent a vapor lock situation.

COMPRESSION RATIO: The comparison of the total volume of the cylinder and combustion chamber with the piston at BDC and the piston at TDC.

CONDENSER: 1. An electrical device which acts to store an electrical charge, preventing voltage surges. 2. A radiator-like device in the air conditioning system in which refrigerant gas condenses into a liquid, giving off heat.

CONDUCTOR: Any material through which an electrical current can be transmitted easily.

CONTINUITY: Continuous or complete circuit. Can be checked with an ohmmeter.

COUNTERSHAFT: An intermediate shaft which is rotated by a mainshaft and transmits, in turn, that rotation to a working part.

CRANKCASE: The lower part of an engine in which the crankshaft and related parts operate.

CRANKSHAFT: The main driving shaft of an engine which receives reciprocating motion from the pistons and converts it to rotary motion.

CYLINDER: In an engine, the round hole in the engine block in which the piston(s) ride.

CYLINDER BLOCK: The main structural member of an engine in which is found the cylinders, crankshaft and other principal parts.

CYLINDER HEAD: The detachable portion of the engine, usually fastened to the top of the cylinder block and containing all or most of the combustion chambers. On overhead valve engines, it contains the valves and their operating parts. On overhead cam engines, it contains the camshaft as well.

DEAD CENTER: The extreme top or bottom of the piston stroke.

DETONATION: An unwanted explosion of the air/fuel mixture in the combustion chamber caused by excess heat and compression, advanced timing, or an overly lean mixture. Also referred to as "ping".

DIAPHRAGM: A thin, flexible wall separating two cavities, such as in a vacuum advance unit.

DIESELING: A condition in which hot spots in the combustion chamber cause the engine to run on after the key is turned off.

DIFFERENTIAL: A geared assembly which allows the transmission of motion between drive axles, giving one axle the ability to turn faster than the other.

DIODE: An electrical device that will allow current to flow in one direction only.

DISC BRAKE: A hydraulic braking assembly consisting of a brake disc, or rotor, mounted on an axle, and a caliper assembly containing, usually two brake pads which are activated by hydraulic pressure. The pads are forced against the sides of the disc, creating friction which slows the vehicle.

DISTRIBUTOR: A mechanically driven device on an engine which is responsible for electrically firing the spark plug at a predetermined point of the piston stroke.

DOWEL PIN: A pin, inserted in mating holes in two different parts allowing those parts to maintain a fixed relationship.

DRUM BRAKE: A braking system which consists of two brake shoes and one or two wheel cylinders, mounted on a fixed backing plate, and a brake drum, mounted on an axle, which revolves around the assembly.

DWELL: The rate, measured in degrees of shaft rotation, at which an electrical circuit cycles on and off.

ELECTRONIC CONTROL UNIT (ECU): Ignition module, module, amplifier or igniter. See Module for definition.

ELECTRONIC IGNITION: A system in which the timing and firing of the spark plugs is controlled by an electronic control unit, usually called a module. These systems have no points or condenser.

END-PLAY: The measured amount of axial movement in a shaft.

ENGINE: A device that converts heat into mechanical energy.

EXHAUST MANIFOLD: A set of cast passages or pipes which conduct exhaust gases from the engine.

FEELER GAUGE: A blade, usually metal, of precisely predetermined thickness, used to measure the clearance between two parts.

FIRING ORDER: The order in which combustion occurs in the cylinders of an engine. Also the order in which spark is distributed to the plugs by the distributor.

FLOODING: The presence of too much fuel in the intake manifold and combustion chamber which prevents the air/fuel mixture from firing, thereby causing a no-start situation.

FLYWHEEL: A disc shaped part bolted to the rear end of the crankshaft. Around the outer perimeter is affixed the ring gear. The starter drive engages the ring gear, turning the flywheel, which rotates the crankshaft, imparting the initial starting motion to the engine.

FOOT POUND (ft. lbs. or sometimes, ft.lb.): The amount of energy or work needed to raise an item weighing one pound, a distance of one foot.

FUSE: A protective device in a circuit which prevents circuit overload by breaking the circuit when a specific amperage is present. The device is constructed around a strip or wire of a lower amperage rating than the circuit it is designed to protect. When an amperage higher than that stamped on the fuse is present in the circuit, the strip or wire melts, opening the circuit.

GEAR RATIO: The ratio between the number of teeth on meshing gears.

GENERATOR: A device which converts mechanical energy into electrical energy.

HEAT RANGE: The measure of a spark plug's ability to dissipate heat from its firing end. The higher the heat range, the hotter the plug fires.

HUB: The center part of a wheel or gear.

HYDROCARBON (HC): Any chemical compound made up of hydrogen and carbon. A major pollutant formed by the engine as a byproduct of combustion.

HYDROMETER: An instrument used to measure the specific gravity of a solution.

INCH POUND (inch lbs.; sometimes in.lb. or in. lbs.): One twelfth of a foot pound.

INDUCTION: A means of transferring electrical energy in the form of a magnetic field. Principle used in the ignition coil to increase voltage.

INJECTOR: A device which receives metered fuel under relatively low pressure and is activated to inject the fuel into the engine under relatively high pressure at a predetermined time.

INPUT SHAFT: The shaft to which torque is applied, usually carrying the driving gear or gears.

INTAKE MANIFOLD: A casting of passages or pipes used to conduct air or a fuel/air mixture to the cylinders.

JOURNAL: The bearing surface within which a shaft operates.

KEY: A small block usually fitted in a notch between a shaft and a hub to prevent slippage of the two parts.

MANIFOLD: A casting of passages or set of pipes which connect the cylinders to an inlet or outlet source.

MANIFOLD VACUUM: Low pressure in an engine intake manifold formed just below the throttle plates. Manifold vacuum is highest at idle and drops under acceleration.

MASTER CYLINDER: The primary fluid pressurizing device in a hydraulic system. In automotive use, it is found in brake and hydraulic clutch systems and is pedal activated, either directly or, in a power brake system, through the power booster.

MODULE: Electronic control unit, amplifier or igniter of solid state or integrated design which controls the current flow in the ignition primary circuit based on input from the pick-up coil. When the module opens the primary circuit, high secondary voltage is induced in the coil.

NEEDLE BEARING: A bearing which consists of a number (usually a large number) of long, thin rollers.

OHM: (Ω) The unit used to measure the resistance of conductor-to-electrical flow. One ohm is the amount of resistance that limits current flow to one ampere in a circuit with one volt of pressure.

OHMMETER: An instrument used for measuring the resistance, in ohms, in an electrical circuit.

OUTPUT SHAFT: The shaft which transmits torque from a device, such as a transmission.

OVERDRIVE: A gear assembly which produces more shaft revolutions than that transmitted to it.

OVERHEAD CAMSHAFT (OHC): An engine configuration in which the camshaft is mounted on top of the cylinder head and operates the valve either directly or by means of rocker arms.

OVERHEAD VALVE (OHV): An engine configuration in which all of the valves are located in the cylinder head and the camshaft is located in the cylinder block. The camshaft operates the valves via lifters and pushrods.

OXIDES OF NITROGEN (NOx): Chemical compounds of nitrogen produced as a byproduct of combustion. They combine with hydrocarbons to produce smog.

OXYGEN SENSOR: Use with the feedback system to sense the presence of oxygen in the exhaust gas and signal the computer which can reference the voltage signal to an air/fuel ratio.

PINION: The smaller of two meshing gears.

PISTON RING: An open-ended ring with fits into a groove on the outer diameter of the piston. Its chief function is to form a seal between the piston and cylinder wall. Most automotive pistons have three rings: two for compression sealing; one for oil sealing.

PRELOAD: A predetermined load placed on a bearing during assembly or by adjustment.

PRIMARY CIRCUIT: the low voltage side of the ignition system which consists of the ignition switch, ballast resistor or resistance wire, bypass, coil, electronic control unit and pick-up coil as well as the connecting wires and harnesses.

PRESS FIT: The mating of two parts under pressure, due to the inner diameter of one being smaller than the outer diameter of the other, or vice versa; an interference fit.

RACE: The surface on the inner or outer ring of a bearing on which the balls, needles or rollers move.

REGULATOR: A device which maintains the amperage and/or voltage levels of a circuit at predetermined values.

RELAY: A switch which automatically opens and/or closes a circuit.

RESISTANCE: The opposition to the flow of current through a circuit or electrical device, and is measured in ohms. Resistance is equal to the voltage divided by the amperage.

RESISTOR: A device, usually made of wire, which offers a preset amount of resistance in an electrical circuit.

RING GEAR: The name given to a ring-shaped gear attached to a differential case, or affixed to a flywheel or as part of a planetary gear set.

ROLLER BEARING: A bearing made up of hardened inner and outer races between which hardened steel rollers move.

ROTOR: 1. The disc-shaped part of a disc brake assembly, upon which the brake pads bear; also called, brake disc. 2. The device mounted atop the distributor shaft, which passes current to the distributor cap tower contacts.

SECONDARY CIRCUIT: The high voltage side of the ignition system, usually above 20,000 volts. The secondary includes the ignition coil, coil wire, distributor cap and rotor, spark plug wires and spark plugs.

SENDING UNIT: A mechanical, electrical, hydraulic or electro-magnetic device which transmits information to a gauge.

SENSOR: Any device designed to measure engine operating conditions or ambient pressures and temperatures. Usually electronic in nature and designed to send a voltage signal to an on-board computer, some sensors may operate as a simple on/off switch or they may provide a variable voltage signal (like a potentiometer) as conditions or measured parameters change.

SHIM: Spacers of precise, predetermined thickness used between parts to establish a proper working relationship.

SLAVE CYLINDER: In automotive use, a device in the hydraulic clutch system which is activated by hydraulic force, disengaging the clutch.

SOLENOID: A coil used to produce a magnetic field, the effect of which is to produce work.

SPARK PLUG: A device screwed into the combustion chamber of a spark ignition engine. The basic construction is a conductive core inside of a ceramic insulator, mounted in an outer conductive base. An electrical charge from the spark plug wire travels along the conductive core and jumps a preset air gap to a grounding point or points at the end of the conductive base. The resultant spark ignites the fuel/air mixture in the combustion chamber.

SPLINES: Ridges machined or cast onto the outer diameter of a shaft or inner diameter of a bore to enable parts to mate without rotation.

TACHOMETER: A device used to measure the rotary speed of an engine, shaft, gear, etc., usually in rotations per minute.

THERMOSTAT: A valve, located in the cooling system of an engine, which is closed when cold and opens gradually in response to engine heating, controlling the temperature of the coolant and rate of coolant flow.

TOP DEAD CENTER (TDC): The point at which the piston reaches the top of its travel on the compression stroke.

TORQUE: The twisting force applied to an object.

TORQUE CONVERTER: A turbine used to transmit power from a driving member to a driven member via hydraulic action, providing changes in drive ratio and torque. In automotive use, it links the driveplate at the rear of the engine to the automatic transmission.

TRANSDUCER: A device used to change a force into an electrical signal.

TRANSISTOR: A semi-conductor component which can be actuated by a small voltage to perform an electrical switching function.

TUNE-UP: A regular maintenance function, usually associated with the replacement and adjustment of parts and components in the electrical and fuel systems of a vehicle for the purpose of attaining optimum performance.

TURBOCHARGER: An exhaust driven pump which compresses intake air and forces it into the combustion chambers at higher than atmospheric pressures. The increased air pressure allows more fuel to be burned and results in increased horsepower being produced.

VACUUM ADVANCE: A device which advances the ignition timing in response to increased engine vacuum.

VACUUM GAUGE: An instrument used to measure the presence of vacuum in a chamber.

VALVE: A device which control the pressure, direction of flow or rate of flow of a liquid or gas.

VALVE CLEARANCE: The measured gap between the end of the valve stem and the rocker arm, cam lobe or follower that activates the valve.

VISCOSITY: The rating of a liquid's internal resistance to flow.

VOLTMETER: An instrument used for measuring electrical force in units called volts. Voltmeters are always connected parallel with the circuit being tested.

WHEEL CYLINDER: Found in the automotive drum brake assembly, it is a device, actuated by hydraulic pressure, which, through internal pistons, pushes the brake shoes outward against the drums.

A

B